SUMERIAN ADMINISTRATIVE AND LEGAL DOCUMENTS
CA. 2900–2200 BC IN THE SCHØYEN COLLECTION

The publication of
CORNELL UNIVERSITY STUDIES IN ASSYRIOLOGY AND SUMEROLOGY
Volume 35
was made possible thanks to generous subventions from anonymous donors

Cornell University Studies in
Assyriology and Sumerology
(CUSAS)

Volume 35

MANUSCRIPTS IN THE SCHØYEN COLLECTION

CUNEIFORM TEXTS X

Sumerian Administrative and Legal Documents *ca.* 2900–2200 BC in the Schøyen Collection

by

Vitali Bartash

CDL Press
Bethesda, Maryland
2017

Library of Congress Cataloging-in-Publication

Names: Bartash, Vitali, author.
Title: Sumerian administrative and legal documents ca. 2900-2200 BC in the Schøyen Collection / by Vitali Bartash.
Other titles: Cornell University studies in Assyriology and Sumerology ; volume 35.
Description: Bethesda, Maryland : CDL Press, 2017. | Series: Cornell University studies in Assyriology and Sumerology (CUSAS) ; volume 35
Identifiers: LCCN 2017019383 | ISBN 9781934309735 (alk. paper)
Subjects: LCSH: Cuneiform inscriptions, Sumerian. | Legal documents—Iraq—History. | Law, Sumerian.
Classification: LCC KL708 .B37 2017 | DDC 340.5/355—dc23
LC record available at https://lccn.loc.gov/2017019383

ISBN 9781934309735

Table of Contents

Statement of Provenance

THE NEAR EASTERN PICTOGRAPHIC TABLETS, CUNEIFORM TABLETS AND SEALS

A. *Ownership History*

The holdings of pictographic tablets, cuneiform tablets and seals in The Schøyen Collection were collected mainly in the late 1980s, with further items in the 1990s. They derive from a great variety of former collections and sources. It would not have been possible to collect so many items, of such major textual importance, if it had not been based on the endeavour of some of the greatest collectors in earlier times. Collections that once held tablets and seals now in The Schøyen Collection are:

- Institute of Antiquity and Christianity, Claremont Graduate School, Claremont, California (1970–94)
- Erlenmeyer Collection and Foundation, Basel (ca. 1935–88)
- Cumberland Clark Collection, Bournemouth, UK (1920s–1941)
- Lord Amherst of Hackney, UK (1894–1909)
- Crouse Collection, Hong Kong and New England (1920s–80s)
- Dring Collection, Surrey, UK (1911–90)
- Rihani Collection, Irbid (ca. 1935) and Amman, Jordan (before 1965–88) and London (1988–)
- Lindgren Collection, San Francisco, California (1965–85)
- Rosenthal Collection, San Francisco, California (1953–88)
- Kevorkian Collection, New York (ca. 1930–59) and Fund (1960–77)
- Kohanim Collection, Tehran, Paris and London (1959–85)
- Simmonds Collection, UK (1944–87)
- Schaeffer Collection, Collège de France, Zürich (1950s)
- Henderson Collection, Boston, Massachusetts (1930s–50s)
- Pottesman Collection, London (1904–78)
- Geuthner Collection, France (1960s–80s)
- Harding Smith Collection, UK (1893–1922)
- Rev. Dr. W. F. Williams, Mosul (ca. 1850–60)
- Frida Hahn Collection, Berlin (1925–73)

These collections are the source of almost all the tablets and seals. Other items were acquired through Christie's and Sotheby's, where in a few cases the names of their former owners were not revealed.

The sources of the oldest collections, such as Amherst, Harding Smith and Cumberland Clark, were antiquities' dealers who acquired tablets and seals in the Near East in the 1890s–1930s. During this period many tens of thousands of tablets came on the market: in the summers of 1893–94 alone some 30,000 tablets. While most of these were bought by museums, others were acquired by private collectors. In this way some of the older of these collections were the source of some of the later collections. For instance, a large number of the tablets in the Crouse Collection came from the Cumberland Clark, Kohanim, Amherst and Simmonds collections. The Claremont tablets came from the Schaeffer Collection, and the Dring tablets came from the Harding Smith Collection.

B. *Archaeological Provenance, Findspots*

In most cases the original findspots of tablets that came on the market in the 1890s–1930s and later are unknown. Therefore great parts of the holdings of most major museums in Europe and the United States are without archaeological provenance. This also applies to The Schøyen Collection. Based on the texts of the tablets themselves the following provenances can nevertheless be identified:

About 90% of the Old Babylonian tablets come from Larsa.

About 70% of the Early Dynastic and Old Akkadian tablets come from palace and temple archives in Adab and Umma.

The Old Assyrian tablets all come from Kanesh (Kültepe) excavation level II.

From Lagash and its vicinity there are tablets from E–Ninnu temple, Ninkar temple in Nimin, Ningishzida temple, Nindara and Ningirsu temples in Girsu, Ur–Bau temple in Uru-kug, and Inanna and Emush temples in Bad-Tibira.

From Nineveh: The Royal Library of Ashurbanipal, and the Ezida temple of Nabu.

From Nimrud: North-west palace of Ashurnasirpal II, the library of Nabû–zuqup–kena, and the palace of Sargon II.

In addition to further major sites like Ur, Uruk, Eridu, Isin, Babylon, Nippur, Susa, Persepolis, there are tablets and seals from at least thirty further sites.

Martin Schøyen

MANUSCRIPTS IN THE SCHØYEN COLLECTION

CUNEIFORM TEXTS

Vol. I. Jöran Friberg, *A Remarkable Collection of Babylonian Mathematical Texts*
Sources and Studies in the History of Mathematics and Physical Sciences
New York: Springer, 2007

Vol. II. Bendt Alster, *Sumerian Proverbs in the Schøyen Collection*
Cornell University Studies in Assyriology and Sumerology 2
Bethesda, Md.: CDL Press, 2007

Vol. III. Stephanie Dalley, *Babylonian Tablets from the First Sealand Dynasty in the Schøyen Collection*
Cornell University Studies in Assyriology and Sumerology 9
Bethesda, Md.: CDL Press, 2009

Vol. IV. A. R. George, *Babylonian Literary Texts in the Schøyen Collection*
Cornell University Studies in Assyriology and Sumerology 10
Bethesda, Md.: CDL Press, 2009

Vol. V. Miguel Civil, *The Lexical Texts in the Schøyen Collection*
Cornell University Studies in Assyriology and Sumerology 12
Bethesda, Md.: CDL Press, 2010

Vol. VI. A. R. George, *Cuneiform Royal Inscriptions and Related Texts in the Schøyen Collection*
with contributions by M. Civil, G. Frame, P. Steinkeller, F. Vallat, M.Weeden, and C. Wilcke
Cornell University Studies in Assyriology and Sumerology 17
Bethesda, Md.: CDL Press, 2011

Vol. VII. A. R. George, *Babylonian Divinatory Texts Chiefly in the Schøyen Collection*
with an appendix of materials from the papers of W. G. Lambert
Cornell University Studies in Assyriology and Sumerology 18
Bethesda, Md.: CDL Press, 2013

Vol. VIII. A. R. George, *Mesopotamian Incantations and Related Texts in the Schøyen Collection*
Cornell University Studies in Assyriology and Sumerology 32
Bethesda, Md.: CDL Press, 2016

Vol. IX. A. R. George, T. Hertel, J. Llop-Raduà, K. Radner and W. H. van Soldt, *Assyrian Archival Texts in the Schøyen Collection and Other Documents from North Mesopotamia and Syria*
Cornell University Studies in Assyriology and Sumerology 34
Bethesda, Md.: CDL Press, 2017

Vol. X. V. Bartash, *Sumerian Administrative and Legal Documents ca. 2900–2200 BC in the Schøyen Collection*
Cornell University Studies in Assyriology and Sumerology 35
Bethesda, Md.: CDL Press, 2017

Other volumes in preparation

Series Editor's Preface

CUSAS 35 by Vitali Bartash completes the publication of nearly all remaining tablets from the Early Dynastic through Sargonic periods in the Schøyen Collection. The majority (451) of the 521 tablets included below is identified as coming from Adab and Umma while the rest (70) is attributed to four identified and unknown sites. The tablets reflect the range of texts known previously from these periods and sites and are associated often with texts and archival groups known from earlier publications. They add substantial new data to the history, socio-economic issues, agricultural and legal practices, religion and cult, and metrology and lexicography of these periods. Indeed, the publications in CUSAS have provided an extraordinary addition and contribution to our knowledge of the formative periods in Mesopotamian history and should encourage additional research to incorporate these new data.

Given the long hiatus of excavations in Iraq and the lack of controlled excavation of texts from the third millennium, these publications are providing scholars and students with a means to continue to develop a more detailed understanding of Sumerian and Akkadian culture and history until and beyond the moment when excavation and discovery resume. The lack of excavated context of these tablets, lamentable as it might be, cannot, nor should it, deter scholars from utilizing the data from these texts to further our knowledge of Mesopotamian civilization any more so today than the study and publication of unprovenanced texts have been in the past.

We must be grateful to Vitali Bartash for undertaking this comprehensive study and publication, to Andrew George, the editor of the Schøyen Collection series, for organizing and supervising its publication, and to Martin Schøyen for facilitating its rapid appearance.

David I. Owen
Curator of Tablet Collections
Jonathan and Jeannette Rosen
Ancient Near Eastern Studies Seminar
Cornell University, Ithaca, New York
April 2017

Acknowledgments

I express my deep gratitude to Martin Schøyen for permission to edit and publish these manuscripts. Through his hospitality and cooperation, my work in the Collection was an enjoyable task.

David I. Owen kindly accepted the manuscript for the publication in the series *Cornell Studies in Assyriology and Sumerology*. Aage Westenholz shared with me his preliminary transliterations of the majority of the documents edited here, which facilitated the work on the project. His remarks on the interpretation of a number of personal names in the manuscript are greatly appreciated. The Department of the Ancient Near Eastern Archaeology, Jan-Waalke Meyer, Thomas Richter, and the research training group "Value and Equivalence" of the University of Frankfurt/Main provided financial support for the first two trips to the Collection in 2013 and 2014. A third visit took place in 2015.

Walther Sallaberger read portions of the manuscript and provided a number of significant corrections. Andrew George offered manifold support, which included logistical advice, making final collations of several tablets, and taking required photographs. He also identified three additional tablets that are included in this book and helped with copy-editing. Manuel Molina provided the transliterations of the Sargonic Adab texts in the Real Academia de Historia in Madrid prior to their publication, read this manuscript, and supplied me with a number of sharp-eyed corrections. Palmiro Notizia offered a number of corrections and remarks on the edition of ED IIIb documents from the Umma region. Jorge Hernández shared his knowledge of the early texts from Isin. Camille Lecompte gave corrections and suggestions on the three ED I–II texts. Robert Middeke-Conlin clarified calculations in three Sargonic texts about fields. Armando Bramanti assisted with vector graphic software and offered several useful remarks concerning the Umma texts. Bram Jagersma gave me his skillful feedback concerning verbal forms in one text.

My dear wife Volha and our son Dominic I thank for constant encouragement and happy times during the work on this project that followed us all over the world, in Frankfurt, Washington D.C., Helsinki, Vienna, Jena, and Munich.

Vitali Bartash
Munich, April 2017

Abbreviations

Lexical lists are cited according to DCCLT, unless otherwise specified.

AAICAB 1/1 J.-P. Grégoire, *Archives administratives et inscriptions cunéiformes de l'Ashmolean Museum et de la Bodleian Collection d'Oxford* 1. Paris, 1996.

ARET 13 P. Fronzaroli, *Testi di cancelleria: I rapporti con le città (Archivio L. 2769).* Archivi Reali di Ebla, Testi, XIII. Rome, 2003.

BdI 1 F. Pomponio, G. Visicato and A. Westenholz, *Le tavolette cuneiformi delle collezioni della Banca d'Italia. I. Tavolette cuneiformi di Adab delle collezioni della Banca d'Italia.* Rome, 2006.

BdI 2 F. Pomponio, M. Stol and A. Westenholz, *Le tavolette cuneiformi delle collezioni della Banca d'Italia. II. Tavolette cuneiformi di varia provenienza delle collezioni della Banca d'Italia.* Rome, 2006.

BIN 8 G. G. Hackman, *Sumerian and Akkadian Administrative Texts from Predynastic Times to the End of the Akkad Dynasty.* Babylonian Inscriptions in the Collection of B. J. Nies 8. New Haven, Conn., 1958.

BPOA 1 T. Ozaki and M. Sigrist, *Ur III Administrative Tablets from the British Museum. Part One.* Biblioteca del Próximo Oriente Antiguo 1. Madrid, 2006.

CAD *The Assyrian Dictionary of the Oriental Institute of the University of Chicago.* Chicago, 1956–2010.

CDLI R. K. Englund, Cuneiform Digital Library Initiative. http://cdli.ucla.edu. Los Angeles.

CHEU G. Contenau, *Contribution à l'histoire économique d'Umma.* BEHE, Sciences philologiques et historiques 219. Paris, 1915.

CST T. Fish, *Catalogue of Sumerian Tablets in the John Rylands Library.* Manchester, 1932.

CUSAS 3 D. I. Owen and R. Mayr, *The Garšana Archives.* Cornell University Studies in Assyriology and Sumerology 3. Bethesda, Md., 2007.

CUSAS 4 A. Kleinerman and D. I. Owen, *Analytical Concordance to the Garšana Archives.* Cornell University Studies in Assyriology and Sumerology 4. Bethesda, Md., 2009.

CUSAS 11 G. Visicato and A. Westenholz, *Early Dynastic and Early Sargonic Tablets from Adab in the Cornell University Collections.* Cornell University Studies in Assyriology and Sumerology 11. Bethesda, Md., 2010.

CUSAS 12 M. Civil, *The Lexical Texts in the Schøyen Collection.* Cornell University Studies in Assyriology and Sumerology 12. Bethesda, Md., 2010.

CUSAS 13 M. Maiocchi, *Classical Sargonic Tablets Chiefly from Adab in the*

Cornell University Collections. Cornell University Studies in Assyriology and Sumerology 13. Bethesda, Md., 2009.

CUSAS 14 S. F. Monaco, *Early Dynastic mu-iti Cereal Texts in the Cornell University Cuneiform Collections*. Cornell University Studies in Assyriology and Sumerology 14. Bethesda, Md., 2011.

CUSAS 17 A. R. George (ed.), *Cuneiform Royal Inscriptions and Related Texts in the Schøyen Collection*. Cornell University Studies in Assyriology and Sumerology 17. Bethesda, Md., 2011.

CUSAS 19 M. Maiocchi and G. Visicato, *Classical Sargonic Tablets Chiefly from Adab in the Cornell University Collections, Part II*. Cornell University Studies in Assyriology and Sumerology 19. Bethesda, Md., 2012.

CUSAS 20 F. Pomponio and G. Visicato, *Middle Sargonic Tablets Chiefly from Adab in the Cornell University Collections*. Cornell University Studies in Assyriology and Sumerology 20. Bethesda, Md., 2015.

CUSAS 23 V. Bartash, *Miscellaneous Early Dynastic and Sargonic Texts in the Cornell University Collections*. Cornell University Studies in Assyriology and Sumerology 23. Bethesda, Md., 2013.

CUSAS 24 J. Zarins, *The Domestication of Equidae in Third-Millennium BCE Mesopotamia*. Cornell University Studies in Assyriology and Sumerology 24. Bethesda, Md., 2014.

CUSAS 26 A. Westenholz, *A Third-Millennium Miscellany of Cuneiform Texts*. Cornell University Studies in Assyriology and Sumerology 26. Bethesda, Md., 2014.

CUSAS 27 L. Milano and A. Westenholz, *The "Šuilišu Archive" and Other Sargonic Texts in Akkadian*. Cornell University Studies in Assyriology and Sumerology 27. Bethesda Md., 2015.

CUSAS 33 P. Notizia and G. Visicato, *Early Dynastic and Early Sargonic Administrative Texts Mainly from the Umma Region in the Cornell University Cuneiform Collections*. Cornell University Studies in Assyriology and Sumerology 33. Bethesda, Md., 2016.

DCCLT N. Veldhuis, Digital Corpus of Cuneiform Lexical Texts. http://oracc.museum.upenn.edu/dcclt/corpus.

DP F.-M. Allotte de la Fuÿe, *Documents présargoniques*. Paris, 1908–1920.

ECTJ A. Westenholz, *Early Cuneiform Texts in Jena*. Copenhagen, 1975.

EDATŠ F. Pomponio and G. Visicato, *Early Dynastic Administrative Tablets of Šuruppak*. IUON Series Maior VI. Naples, 1994.

EDPV A M. Civil, *The Early Dynastic Practical Vocabulary A (Archaic HAR-ra A)*. Archivi Reali di Ebla, Studi 4. Rome, 2008.

ELTS I. J. Gelb, P. Steinkeller and R. M. Whiting, *Earliest Land Tenure Systems in the Near East. Ancient Kudurrus*. 2 vols. University of Chicago Oriental Institute Publications 104. Chicago, 1991.

ePSD The Pennsylvania Sumerian Dictionary, http://psd.museum.upenn.edu

FAOS 6 H. Behrens and H. Steible, *Glossar zu den altsumerischen Bau- und Weihinschriften*. Freiburger

Altorientalische Studien 6. Wiesbaden, 1983.

FAOS 15/1 G. J. Selz, *Altsumerische Verwaltungstexte aus Lagaš. Teil 1. Die altsumerischen Wirtschaftsurkunden der Eremitage zu Leningrad.* Freiburger Altorientalische Studien 15/1. Stuttgart, 1989.

FAOS 15/2 G. J. Selz, *Altsumerische Verwaltungstexte aus Lagaš. Teil 2. Die altsumerischen Wirtschaftsurkunden aus amerikanischen Sammlungen.* Freiburger Altorientalische Studien 15/2. Stuttgart, 1993.

FAOS 17 P. Steinkeller, *Sale Documents of the Ur-III-Period.* Freiburger Altorientalische Studien 17. Stuttgart, 1989.

FAOS 19 B. Kienast and K. Volk, *Die sumerischen und akkadischen Briefe des III. Jahrtausends aus der Zeit vor der III. Dynastie von Ur.* Freiburger Altorientalische Studien 19. Stuttgart, 1995.

HSS 10 T. J. Meek, *Excavations at Nuzi conducted by the Semitic Museum and the Fogg Art Museum of Harvard University.* Harvard Semitic Series 10. Cambridge Mass., 1935.

ITT 1 F. Thureau-Dangin, *Inventaire des tablettes de Tello, conservées au Musée Impérial Ottoman* 1. Paris, 1910.

LAK A. Deimel, *Liste der archaischen Keilschriftzeichen.* Leipzig, 1922.

MAD 3 I. J. Gelb, *Glossary of Old Akkadian.* Materials for the Assyrian Dictionary 3. Chicago, 1957.

MAD 4 I. J. Gelb, *Sargonic Texts in the Louvre Museum.* Materials for the Assyrian Dictionary 4. Chicago, 1970.

MC 4 P. Steinkeller, *Third Millennium Legal and Administrative Texts in the Iraq Museum, Baghdad.* With Hand Copies by J. N. Postgate. Mesopotamian Civilizations 4. Winona Lake, Ind., 1992.

MC 5 A. R. George, *House Most High. The Temples of Ancient Mesopotamia.* Mesopotamian Civilizations 5. Winona Lake, Ind., 1993.

MEE 3 G. Pettinato, *Testi lessicali monolingui della biblioteca L. 2769.* Materiali Epigrafici di Ebla 3. Napoli, 1981.

MEE 4 G. Pettinato, *Testi lessicali bilingui della biblioteca L. 2769.* Materiali Epigrafici di Ebla 4. Napoli, 1982.

MEE 15 S. A. Picchioni, *Testi lessicali monolingui „EŠ.BAR.KIN$_x$“.* Materiali Epigrafici di Ebla 15. Roma, 1997.

MSL 5 B. Landsberger, *The Series ḪAR-ra = ḫubullu, Tablets I–IV.* Materials for the Sumerian Lexicon 5. Rome, 1957.

MSL 6 B. Landsberger, *The Series ḪAR-ra = ḫubullu, Tablets V–VII.* Materials for the Sumerian Lexicon 6. Rome, 1958.

MSL 9 B. Landsberger and M. Civil, *The Series ḪAR-ra = ḫubullu, Tablet XV and Related Texts.* Materials for the Sumerian Lexicon 9. Rome, 1967.

MSL 11 E. Reiner, *The Series ḪAR-ra = ḫubullu Tablets XX–XXIV.* Materials for the Sumerian Lexicon 11. Rome, 1974.

MSL 12 M. Civil, *The Series lú = ša and Related Texts.* Materials for the Sumerian Lexicon 12. Rome, 1969.

MSL 13 M. Civil, *Izi = išātu, Ká-gal = abullu and Níg-ga = makkūru.* Materials for the Sumerian Lexicon 13. Rome, 1971.

MSL 16 I. L. Finkel, *The Series SIG$_7$.ALAN = Nabnītu.* Materials for the Sumerian Lexicon 16. Rome, 1982.

MVN 3 — D. I. Owen, *The John Frederick Lewis Collection*. Materiali per il Vocabolario Neosumerico 3. Rome, 1975.

MVN 10 — J. P. Grégoire, *Inscriptions et archives administratives cunéiformes, 1e Partie*. Materiali per il Vocabolario Neosumerico 10. Rome, 1981.

MZL — R. Borger, *Mesopotamiches Zeichenlexikon*. Alter Orient und Altes Testament 305. Münster, 2004.

NATN — D. I. Owen, *Neo-Sumerian Archival Texts Primarily from Nippur in the University Museum, the Oriental Institute and the Iraq Museum*. Winona Lake, Ind., 1982.

NG — A. Falkenstein, *Die neusumerischen Gerichtsurkunden* 1–3. Abhandlungen der Bayerischen Akademie der Wissenschaften, phil.-hist. Kl., N.F. 39, 40 and 44. Munich, 1956–57.

Nik 2 — M.V. Nikol'skij, *Dokumenty chozjajstvennoj otčetnosti drevnej epochi Chaldei iz sobranija N.P. Lichačeva. Drevnosti Vostočnyja. Epocha dinastii Agade i epocha dinastii Ura*. Trudy Vostočnoj Komisii Imperatorskago Moskovskago Archeologiceskago Obščestva 5. Moscow, 1915.

NISABA 9 — M. Molina and M. Such-Gutiérrez, *Neo-Sumerian Administrative Texts in the British Museum BM 107926–108315*. Nisaba: Studi Assiriologici Messinesi 9. Messina, 2005.

NTSŠ — R. Jestin, *Nouvelles tablettes sumériennes de Šuruppak au Musée d'Istanbul*. Paris, 1957.

OAIC — I. J. Gelb, Old Akkadian Inscriptions in Chicago Natural History Museum: Texts of Legal and Business Interest. *Fieldiana Anthropology* 44/2 (1955) 161–338.

OIP 14 — D. D. Luckenbill, *Inscriptions from Adab*. University of Chicago Oriental Institute Publications 14. Chicago, 1930.

OIP 99 — R. D. Biggs, *Inscriptions from Tell Abū Ṣalābīkh*. University of Chicago Oriental Institute Publications 99. Chicago, 1974.

OSP 1 — A. Westenholz, *Literary and Lexical Texts and the Earliest Administrative Documents from Nippur*. Bibliotheca Mesopotamica 1. Malibu, Calif., 1975.

OSP 2 — A. Westenholz, *Old Sumerian and Old Akkadian Texts in Philadelphia Chiefly from Nippur. Part Two: The 'Akkadian' Texts, the Enlilemaba Texts, and the Onion Archive*. Carsten Niebuhr Institute of Ancient Near Eastern Studies. Copenhagen, 1987.

PPAC 1 — Zh. Yang, *Sargonic Inscriptions from Adab*. Periodic Publications on Ancient Civilizations 1. Changchun, China, 1989.

PSD — Å. K. Sjöberg *et al.*, *The Sumerian Dictionary of the University Museum of the University of Pennsylvania*. Philadelphia, 1984–.

RGTC 2 — D. O. Edzard and G. Farber, *Die Orts- und Gewässernamen der Zeit der 3. Dynastie von Ur*. Répertoire Géographique des Textes Cunéiformes 2. Beihefte zum Tübinger Atlas des Vorderen Orients. Wiesbaden, 1974.

RIME 1 — D. R. Frayne, *Presargonic Period (2700–2350 BC)*. Royal Inscriptions of Mesopotamia. Early Periods 1. Toronto, 2008.

RIME 2	D. R. Frayne, *Sargonic and Gutian Periods (2334–2113 BC)*. Royal Inscriptions of Mesopotamia. Early Periods 2. Toronto, 1993.
RIME 3/2	D. R. Frayne, *Ur III Period (2112–2004 BC)*. Royal Inscriptions of Mesopotamia. Early Periods 3/2. Toronto, 1997.
RTC	F. Thureau-Dangin, *Recueil de tablettes chaldéennes*. Paris, 1903.
SCTRAH	M. Molina, *Sargonic Cuneiform Tablets in the Real Academia de la Historia: The Carl L. Lippmann Collection*. Madrid, 2014.
SF	A. Deimel, *Schultexte aus Fara*. Inschriften von Fara 2. Leipzig, 1923.
STTI	V. Donbaz and B. R. Foster, *Sargonic Texts from Telloh in the Istanbul Archaeological Museums*. Occ. Publ. Babyl. Fund 5. American Research Institute in Turkey Monographs 2. Philadelphia, 1982.
Subartu 12	L. Milano, W. Sallaberger, Ph. Talon and K. Van Lerberghe, *Third Millennium Cuneiform Texts from Tell Beydar (Seasons 1996–2002)*. Subartu 12. Brepols, 2004.
TCTI 2	B. Lafont and F. Yildiz, *Tablettes cunéiformes de Tello au Musée d'Istanbul datant de l'époque de la IIIe Dynastie d'Ur* 2. Leiden, 1996.
TSŠ	R. R. Jestin, *Tablettes sumériennes de Šuruppak conservées au Musée de Stamboul*. Paris, 1937.
UET 2	E. Burrows, *Archaic Texts*. Ur Excavation Texts II. London, 1935.
UET 9	D. Loding, *Economic Texts from the Third Dynasty*. Ur Excavations Texts IX. London, 1976.
USP	B. R. Foster, *Umma in the Sargonic Period*. Memoirs of the Connecticut Academy of Art and Sciences 20. Hamden, Conn., 1982.
VS 25	J. Marzahn, *Altsumerische Verwaltungstexte aus Girsu/Lagaš*. Vorderasiatische Schriftdenkmäler der Staatlichen Museen zu Berlin 25. Berlin, 1991.
VS 27	J. Marzahn, *Altsumerische Verwaltungstexte und ein Brief aus Girsu /Lagas*. Vorderasiatische Schriftdenkmäler der Staatlichen Museen zu Berlin 27. Berlin, 1996.
WF	A. Deimel, *Wirtschaftstexte aus Fara*. Inschriften von Fara 3. Leipzig, 1924.
ZATU	M. W. Green and H. J. Nissen, *Zeichenliste der archaischen Texte aus Uruk*. Archaische Texte aus Uruk 2. Berlin, 1987.

Introduction

General Remarks

The 521 texts edited in this volume are mostly administrative and legal documents that can be dated by paleographic criteria to about 2900–2200 BC. The earliest texts are roughly contemporaneous with the Early Dynastic I–II ("archaic") texts from the city of Ur. Several very late documents immediately precede the Ur III period and may belong to the so-called Late Sargonic or Gutian period.

Other major editions of the Early Dynastic and Sargonic texts in the Schøyen Collection include CUSAS 12 and CUSAS 17, lexical texts and monumental/royal inscriptions respectively. Mathematical texts were published in Friberg 2007. Twenty-five texts written in Akkadian that belong to the "Šuilišu archive" of Sargonic date from the town *Maškan-ili-Akkade* appeared recently in CUSAS 27.[1] A single Sargonic text was included in CUSAS 26.[2] Several documents kept in the Schøyen Collection were excluded from the corpus by the present author for different reasons.[3] Finally, the collection houses three Early Dynastic incantation tablets, published in 2016,[4] and a further four Early Dynastic tablets that are inscribed with unidentified Old Sumerian literary compositions and await publication.

Since the documents edited here are devoid of excavation context, their dates and provenances are based mostly on external and internal characteristics. To the former belong measurements, format, and color of the clay. The latter include scribal conventions particular to a certain location, language, and specific phraseology. Finally, onomastics are helpful in many cases. Thus, in most cases the provenance and date of a document can be established with a high degree of certainty. In the course of work on this project the author tried to determine the provenance of as many texts as possible, but some remain without identifiable provenance. Further work is necessary to place these in their respective chronologies and locations.

The high number of texts, alongside the fact that they come from at least half a dozen sites in Iraq and Syria, makes it unfeasible here to sum-

1 CUSAS 27: MS 1952/8 (no. 226), MS 2191/22 (no. 237), MS 2246 (no. 25), MS 2248 (no. 88), MS 2254 (no. 179), MS 2872/1 (no. 58), MS 2872/2 (no. 73), MS 2872/3 (no. 60), MS 2872/4 (no. 71), MS 2872/5 (no. 62), MS 3550 (no. 104), MS 4191 (no. 196), MS 4198a (no. 160), MS 4198b (no. 43), MS 4215 (no. 153), MS 4227a (no. 149), MS 4227b (no. 211), MS 4236 (no. 35), MS 4251 (no. 176), MS 4254 (no. 161), MS 4263 (no. 137), MS 4267a (no. 78), MS 4267b (no. 212), MS 5005 (no. 228), MS 5006 (no. 72).

2 CUSAS 26: MS 3186 (no. 270).

3 MS 1952/38 is a school tablet of a later date, probably Ur III. MS 5048/11 and MS 5044/14 contain only seal impressions. MS 2666 of allegedly Sargonic date was not located. Finally, MS 2191/20 is an unsuccessful attempt to copy a multicolumn document of a date somewhere between the Early Dynastic IIIa and Middle Sargonic periods (= fake).

4 CUSAS 32: MS 4549/1–2 and MS 4550 (nos. 1–3).

marize the particulars of their physical and textual formats, paleography, contents, distinctive features of grammar and syntax, and all other new data relevant to the field of cuneiform studies and the history of the ancient Near East. Short introductions to the larger groups of texts are provided in the editions below, but since most of the texts edited here belong to "archives" and "files" previously known and discussed at length elsewhere, only general remarks as to the structure and contents of these texts are offered.

Of the 521 texts, 484 are of administrative content. They deal with matters related to the economy and administration of palace and temple organizations of the Early Dynastic and Sargonic periods: management of land, labor, animals, animal husbandry, agriculture, remuneration, taxation, etc. There are seven letters among these texts, but they do not make up a separate group, since individuals that appear in them are mentioned in other documents that are administrative in the strict sense ("accounts").

A much smaller group of 25 texts are legal documents. They add significantly to our understanding of legal procedures and social relations in early Mesopotamia. Finally, the book includes school tablets and exercises that, in their format, resemble administrative documents.

The language of the majority of texts is Sumerian. Only twelve texts are Semitic. One document (No. 467) derives from Ebla and likely is to be read in the Eblaite language but, since the text is purely logographic, no Semitic forms appear. The other eleven Semitic texts are in Akkadian. However, in most cases this fact is determined only by the syntax of the measures (i.e. "measure + accounted goods" instead of the Sumerian word order "accounted goods + measure"), by the sporadic appearance of lexemes such as u_3 "and," and by other manifestations of the Akkadian language that are typical of logographically written texts of the period.

The Temporal and Geographical Distribution of the Texts

The majority of the documents belongs to the Early Dynastic IIIb and Early Sargonic periods. Only a small number are of earlier date. There are three Early Dynastic I–II (*ca.* 2900–2700 BC) documents of unclear provenance (Nos. 471–73) and eleven documents of Early Dynastic IIIa or "Fara" date (*ca.* 2600–2500 BC). Two of the latter are from Šuruppak (Fara) itself. The provenance of the rest is uncertain but the region of Umma is a likely candidate for at least some of them. The exact date of one school document is difficult to establish more precisely than simply as "Sargonic" (No. 520). The distribution of all other texts according to date is the following:

Early Dynastic IIIb (*ca.* 2500–2350 BC)	61
Early Dynastic to Early Sargonic (*ca.* 2350–2300 BC)	214
Early Sargonic (*ca.* 2300–2270 BC)	78
Middle Sargonic (*ca.* 2270–2230 BC)	68
Classical Sargonic (*ca.* 2230–2180 BC)	74
Late Sargonic (*ca.* 2180–2110 BC)	11

The supposed provenance of all documents in the volume is as follows:

Adab	348
Adab?	15
Umma region	85
Umma region?	3
Isin	13
Isin?	2
Šuruppak (Fara)	2
Ebla	1
Sagub	1
unclear	51

PART 1: *Texts from Adab.* Together the two charts show that the majority of the documents in this book are Early Dynastic to Early Sargonic texts from Adab. The term "Meskigala texts" was coined in the cuneiform studies for these documents because they date to the governorship of Meskigala (Mes-ki-gal-la). He was installed as governor ($ensi_2$) of Adab by Lugalzagesi after his conquest of that city during the late Early Dynastic IIIb period. The long career of

Meskigala in a time of drastic political and social change suggests that he was a shrewd and unusual character. He switched his support from Lugalzagesi to Sargon after the latter had begun his successful conquest of Sumer. Meskigala's evidently brilliant political career marked a period of a semi-independence for the province of Adab within the Akkad state, but must have ended ingloriously after the suppression of a revolt of the Sumerian aristocracy against Rimuš, the son of Sargon.[1] His governorship can be considered a distinct period in the history of Adab, and the term "Early Dynastic to Early Sargonic" in most cases refers more precisely to documents composed during his time in office.

The majority of Adab texts of this date record the administration of goods, animals, and personnel within several central households. The most important of them, besides the palace (e_2-gal), were e_2-TUR (or e_2-dumu) and e_2-AḪ. A certain Silim-Utu, who appears in a large number of Early Dynastic/Early Sargonic texts from Adab, was apparently the supervisor (nu-$banda_3$) of the e_2-TUR. For major publications of "Meskigala texts," see primarily BdI 1 and CUSAS 11.

This volume also includes a considerable number of later texts from Adab. Middle Sargonic texts are treated in detail in SCTRAH and CUSAS 20, whereas OIP 14, PPAC 1, BdI 1, CUSAS 13 and CUSAS 19 are the major publications of Classical Sargonic texts from this city. CUSAS 23 offers a substantial number of Middle and Classical Sargonic texts from Adab.

The term "Middle Sargonic" is of doubtful value in the description of Adab tablets. In the almost complete absence of year date formulae in administrative records, it is hard to link specific documents to particular rulers. Onomastics often prove ineffective here, since the same persons may appear in both Early Sargonic and Middle Sargonic tablets. For example, these are the texts that mention a group of individuals including Niĝir-abzu, IM-ki-du_{10}, E'amaš, etc. Therefore, the term "Middle Sargonic" in the present work does not specifically denote the reign of Maništusu and the early reign of Naram-Suen, but is a rather impressionistic statement that the text in question is younger than the Meskigala texts but older than the distinctive right-angular texts of Classical Sargonic date.

In the case of a number of texts a provenance in Adab is possible but not certain. They may come from other cities (Isin, Kiš, Ĝirsu) or archives ("Lugal-ra archive," "Mesag archive").

PART 2: *Texts from Isin.* For an overview of the early Isin texts, see MC 4 pp. 5–8. The majority of Isin texts in the volume belongs to a private archive, for which see CUSAS 26 nos. 45–59. In these texts several temples function as courts of justice. These are Egalmaḫ, the temple of the goddess Ninisina, and a temple dedicated to her consort, Pabilsaĝ. The content of these documents is typical of legal texts of this period and city. The matters include purchases of immobilia, contesting these purchases, slave purchases, contesting slave status, etc. Most of the texts from the archive are of Classical Sargonic date. One text is certainly of an earlier date but belongs to this group nevertheless. This shows that the archive was formed over a certain period of time.

PART 3: *Texts from the Umma region.* There are two major group of texts in this section. The first and larger group comprises Early Dynastic IIIb documents that record the administration of Inana's temple household at Zabala. These texts most likely originate in that city. The second group includes documents from Early Sargonic Umma that date to the office of *Šuruskēn* (*Su_4-ru-us_2*-GI), the governor of the province of Umma during the reign of Sargon. Finally, there are some texts from Umma of later date.

Recent major publications of Early Dynastic texts from the Umma region are BdI 2,

1 For an overview of ED/ES Meskigala texts, see Schrakamp 2013: 201 fn. 3 with additional references. For a recent concise up-to-date summary of the political history of the Akkad Empire, see Schrakamp 2016: 1–10. For Meskigala in historical context, see Sallaberger and Schrakamp 2015: 43, 88, 93–95 and Marchesi 2015: 143, 152.

CUSAS 14, CUSAS 23 and CUSAS 33. For a detailed list of principal and minor publications of this textual corpus, see Schrakamp 2013: 202 fn. 9. On the "Umma debate," the question of which archaeological site was Umma in which historical period, see Bartash 2015c.

A substantial number of the Early Dynastic IIIb documents from Umma region in this volume may be attributed to the time of the governor Me'anedu (Me-an-ne$_2$-du$_{10}$ ensi$_2$), who had a long reign of at least thirty-two years. His contemporaries were Enme'ana of Adab and Enanatum of Lagaš. For the chronology of these rulers, see Marchesi 2015: 142 f. and Monaco 2015: 162 f.

PART 4: *Texts from other locations.* These include two Fara sale contracts, a document from the Mesag archive from Sagub, and a record of textiles from Early Dynastic Ebla.

PART 5: *Texts with uncertain provenance.* Finally, there are fifty-one texts of various dates whose provenance is hard to establish, although in some cases there are clues that may allow an identification. Because of their contents the documents in this part are among the most fascinating in the volume. Notable is the presence of a considerable number of ED IIIa ("Fara") documents with numerous lexemes that are taken directly from lexical lists, the so-called "practical vocabularies."

Contents: Highlights

The contents of specific groups of texts are summarized in their editions. Here it will suffice to draw attention to a number of texts that yield unique or noteworthy information.

Historical information. A remarkable document is text No. 107, which records an allocation of beer. The event for which the beer is distributed is the reception of two high-ranking guests from Kiš and Ĝirsu. One of them is the *kuš$_7$*-official of the "king of Kiš." Sargon is probably meant here. The text originates from his early career. It is known that Sargon became king long before he began the conquest of Sumer. Ebla evidence mentions an anonymous "king of Kiš" who was most likely Sargon. Literary compositions suggest that Sargon was the successor of Ur-Zababa, a king of Kiš whom he eliminated by a coup. Text No. 107 offers further information on Sargon's rise to power. The text suggests that negotiations occurred between representatives of Adab, the "king of Kiš," represented by his animal manager, and the chief cook of Ĝirsu. These high-ranking officials must have assembled because of some important matter. The present document may hint at an unsuccessful attempt to draw the Lagaš state over to Sargon's side. Note that the document records beer for a second banquet that lasted several days. This shows that there were at least two meetings.

Society. Numerous texts contribute to our better understanding of urban society in southern Mesopotamia during the Early Dynastic and Sargonic periods. An example is No. 360, which records a great number of high and middle-level officials in Adab during the reign of Naram-Suen. Another text, No. 363, provides a vivid picture of high priests, officials, and professionals in three major households in Classical Sargonic Adab. These organizations are the e$_2$-maḫ, e$_2$-GANA$_2$.IŠ, and the temple of the god Ašgi, e$_2$ ^{d}Aš$_7$-gi$_4$. A number of *sila* of an unknown commodity distributed to the list of persons doubtlessly relates to their respective status. Saĝĝa, the chief temple-administrator, lu$_2$-maḫ, the high priest, and the chief scribe are at the top of the hierarchy. By contrast, the priests šu-luḫ-ḫa and brewers are referred to not individually but as a group, and receive the least amount.

Bread and grain products. A considerable number of the Adab texts of the Late Early Dynastic IIIb and Early Sargonic periods in this volume records allocations of bread, beer, and other grain products to a multitude of individuals, workers, temples, and gods. These goods were issued by several organizations, the most prominent of which were the e$_2$-AḪ and the e$_2$-dumu. Like many Early Dynastic/Early Sargonic Adab tablets, most tablets that mention the e_2-AḪ are pierced in the middle with a hole of about 3.5 mm.

Another related group of texts from Adab records the allocation of bread and beer to a fixed number of deities, households, and individuals. The deities are Inana, Iškur, Ninmug, Enki, ENEsi and Bara-Enlilĝar. The households include the e_2-dam, e_2-dumu and e_2-AḪ. The individuals are recorded without their titles. However, they were most likely high officials. They are PUŠA-Ašgi, Ma'U, Ur-Šerda, Urnu, Numuna, and Ilala. These texts together with the "E'AḪ file" constitute a single archive that must have recorded transactions during a relatively short period of time.

Section 1.4.5 (texts Nos. 275–88) is a Middle Sargonic dossier of bread allocations. It records a great variety of professional titles and gives a vivid impression of the social structures within the central households in Adab. A notable detail is the high frequency of references to officials and other persons directly connected to the king. The king's son is also mentioned.

An interesting text is No. 399, an ED IIIb tablet from the Umma region. It is a list of various grain products, some of which represent rare ingredients for beer.

Legal procedures. Text No. 7 is a unique legal document that was incised on a stone tablet. A list of luxury items, including jewelry, precious metals, garments and other luxuries, occupies the major part of the document. These goods were in the possession of a certain stone-cutter and his wife. Several individuals are proclaimed to be thieves. The final section of the document calculates the sum of the pecuniary injury done by the theft. The appearance of governor Enme'ana of Adab and the quotation of his words at the end of the document suggest that it must have been a capital case.

Chariots. Two Early Dynastic/Early Sargonic texts from Adab (Nos. 198–99) record parts of chariots or wagons. Text No. 196 is a unique document, which, despite its poor state of preservation, seems to record the blueprint of an Ešnunna-type chariot.

Women and children. Text No. 283 is a document that records the allocation of bread to a number of individuals who belonged to a central organization, probably the palace of the governor of Adab. Notably, the two first individuals are nin $ensi_2$ "governor's sister" and $geme_2$ $ensi_2$ "governor's maid." As might be expected, the sister receives twice as much bread as the maid.

A number of texts in the volume (Nos. 264–65, 299, 301, 303–5) form an addition to a Middle Sargonic dossier that records the administration of a wool and textile workshop: the so-called "Mama-ummi's file." For a discussion of this dossier and additional texts, see SCTRAH and CUSAS 20. The workshop was staffed by women and their supervisors were also female.

Text No. 446 records the allocation of a garment to a woman who bears the title *karkid*. The term *karkid* is usually associated with prostitutes.

Text No. 23 is a record of Subareans. Only women, boys, and girls are mentioned. The children are recorded as branded or not branded. Three supervisors are in charge of them. The reference to a building e_2-kešda-a, interpreted as a textile workshop, indicates that these women and children were employed as foreign labor in the governor's domain. The absence of men suggests that these people were forcibly abducted from their homeland and the men executed or employed elsewhere.

Numerical tablets. Two (mostly) numerical texts, Nos. 315–16, record deliveries of wood to a warehouse. These texts, among other partly or fully numerical tablets of Early Dynastic and Sargonic date, explicitly show that administrative records were part of daily management in central households in early Mesopotamia, and were often made simultaneously with the transactions they recorded. In the present case, the scribe noted by tens the loads of wood that were brought into a warehouse.

Metrology. A number of texts offer new information about metrology and measurement practices during the Early Dynastic and Sargonic periods. For example, No. 171 obv. i 5 offers a notation that resembles the writing for 2 *ban* in capacity in connection to oil. The writing must denote a fraction of the unit umbin, however. Several texts show that a single sign N_8 ("bariga") played multiple metrological roles depending on period and context (see the index of discussed signs and lexemes).

Priests and cult. Numerous texts in the volume add significantly to the reconstruction of the religious cults of Adab and Umma, and illustrate the role of priests in these cults and in society. Text No. 354 records the allocation of sheep heads and hearts to priests and deities in Adab. The cultic functionaries include the high priests of the goddess Diĝirmaḫ and the high priestess of the gods Ašgi and Ninšubur. The text does not explicitly state the purpose of the allocation. Do these heads and hearts represent the ingredients for some *cordon bleu* meals for the priests or were they used in religious practices?

A considerable number of texts from Adab are lists that record the distribution or offering of food to gods and temples. They create a clear image of the Adab "pantheon" and the sequence of temples and deities gives an indication of their respective importance. For instance, text No. 361 places the temple e_2-maḫ, the abode of the goddess Diĝirmah/Ninḫursaĝa, the titular deity of Adab, at the top of the text. She is followed by Enlil, the chief "national" Sumerian god, and Ašgi, the main male deity at Adab. These are followed by other major Sumerian deities of that period: Inana, Iškur, Ninšubur, Ašnan, Enki, Utu and Su'en. Other offering lists, such as Nos. 356 and 340, are further sources for the study of the deities who were worshipped in Adab during the Classical Sargonic period. Text No. 362 records valuable gifts by a number of individuals to Lala, a priestess who at Adab embodied the wife of the god Ašgi (dam ^{d}Aš$_8$-gi$_4$).

Transliterations

With rare exceptions, transliterations follow Rykle Borger's MZL. In some cases, when the syllabic or logographic reading is rare, the "name" of the sign is given in brackets. Some other explanations also appear in brackets. For instance, since the "northern" scribal tradition differentiates between the signs ARAD and UŠ/ĜEŠ$_3$ (see Sommerfeld 2012: 199), one finds gala(ARAD.KU) instead of the usual writing gala = UŠ.KU.

Following the practice already employed in CUSAS 23, numbers are transliterated in full as they appear on the tablet. For example, 1(gur) 1(bariga) 1(ban$_2$) 1 sila$_3$ is set down, instead of 1.1.1.1 sila$_3$. Although the latter notation is a handy way to economize on space, the former style is especially useful if the numbers are written unusually, as is the case in many texts in this book. Similarly, the numbers for fractions of weight measures are transliterated in such a way as to exactly render the writing. Therefore, instead of the usual ⅔ ma-na, one will find ^{šu_2}2N_8 ma-na and ^{šu_2}|1N_8.1N_8| ma-na for the same fraction "two-thirds mina." The N-numbers (N_8, etc.) refer to the list of conventions employed in ZATU p. 166.

Following the practice adopted in CUSAS 23 from CDLI, all damaged signs are marked with half square brackets instead of full square brackets: ⸢DA⸣ instead of [D]A or D[A].

Translations

All texts are provided with translations. Needless to say in some cases, for instance when manuscripts are damaged or employ hitherto unknown terminology, the translation is a preliminary interpretation. Nevertheless, the aim is to provide specialists and scholars from other disciplines with a tool that will give easy access to these texts and facilitate their further study.

All proper nouns are translated with initial capital letter. Akkadian names often appear in a reconstructed form in the translation. In cases where the author is unsure of the meaning and phonemic structure of a name, it is simply put in italics to denote that it may be Semitic.

Photographs of the Tablets

This volume includes 144 images of tablets and bullae. Photographs of all documents edited in the book may be viewed and downloaded at the site of the *Cuneiform Library at Cornell University* (http://cuneiform.library.cornell.edu/publications) or the *Cuneiform Digital Library Initiative* website search interface, by inputting the collection number of the desired tablet into the respective field (cdli.ucla.edu/search/). Photographs of the tablets in the present book were made by agents of the Schøyen Collection, mostly in the early 2000s.

Catalogue

Text no.	MS no.	Period	Ruler / Archive	Year	Month	Day	Provenance	Contents	L×W×T mm
1	1952/33	ED IIIb	–	–	–	–	Adab	Sale of a house.	130×121×13
2	2464	ED IIIb	Ur-saĝ-Keš$_3$ ensi$_2$:ĜAR	–	–	–	Adab	Sale of a house.	115×118×32
3	3792	ED IIIb	En×me-na$_2$ ensi$_2$:ĜAR Adab^{ki}	–	–	–	Adab	Sale of a house.	163×174×25
4	3795	ED IIIb	Ur-saĝ-Keš$_3$ [ensi$_2$:ĜAR]	–	–	–	Adab	Sale of a house.	76★×51★×22
5	3798	ED IIIb	[...] ensi$_2$:ĜAR Adab^{ki}	–	–	–	Adab	Legal document concerning silver. A governor of Adab acts as judge and hands over the silver to the temple of Nini-sina.	77★×78×27
6	3811	ED/ES	–	–	–	–	Adab	Sale of a house(?).	83★×82★×14
7	3029	ED IIIb	En×me-na$_2$ ensi$_2$:ĜAR Adab^{ki}	–	–	–	Adab	Stone tablet recording legal case concerning theft.	92×92×12
8	4745	ED IIIb	Ur-saĝ-Keš$_3$ ensi$_2$ Adab^{ki}	–	–	–	Adab	Legal document concerning property.	60×60×25
9	2191/32	ES	–	–	–	–	Adab	Silver for various purposes.	60×56×24
10	2191/33	ED IIIb		–	–	–	Adab	Receipt of barley as price of various commodities.	41×40×24
11	2463	ED/ES	–	–	–	–	Adab?	Barley for various purposes.	56×58×22

12	3789/7	ED/ES	-	-	-	-	Adab	Financial document concerning barley and silver.	39×39×19
13	3790/17	ED/ES	-	-	-	-	Adab	Financial document concerning barley and silver.	34×34×20
14	3804	ED/ES	-	-	-	-	Adab	Financial document concerning transactions with barley and silver.	63×63*×26
15	3806	ED/ES	-	-	-	-	Adab?	Expenditure of grain for various purposes.	33×35×23
16	3807	ED/ES	-	-	-	-	Adab	Financial document about barley as means of payment for bitumen and for other purposes.	48×46×20*
17	3836	ED/ES	-	-	-	-	Adab	Account of barley for various purposes.	54×53×22
18	5048/13	ED IIIb	-	-	-	-	Adab	Account of barley in connection to two fields.	53×55×19
19	4250	ED/ES	-	-	-	-	Adab	Account of barley.	77×62×27
20	1952/41	ED/ES	-	-	-	-	Adab	Account of personnel.	45×45×25
21	2362	ED/ES	-	-	-	-	Adab	Account of personnel.	27×29×14
22	3790/40	ED/ES	Silim-[d]Utu nu-banda$_3$	-	-	u$_4$ 1	Adab	Assignment of personnel to named individuals in connection to agricultural work.	57×52*×24*
23	3813	ES/MS	-	-	-	-	Adab	Account of Subarean slaves: women, boys and girls, branded and non-branded.	51*×52×23
24	3830	ED/ES	-	-	-	-	Adab	Account of cattle, sheep, hides and adult and child slaves sent from Irisaĝrig to Uruk.	47×45×20

25	3844	ED/ES	–	–	–	–	Adab	Account of soldiers, on the morning watch and sick.	46×43×21
26	4225	ED/ES	–	–	–	–	Adab	Letter-order concerning a worker.	32×32×17
27	4728	ED/ES	–	–	–	–	Adab?	Account of personnel.	62×50×22
28	5002	ED/ES	–	–	–	–	Adab	Letter-order concerning personnel.	47×40×17*
29	1952/34	ED IIIb					Adab	Account of land.	61×62×26
30	1952/40	ED/ES	–	–	–	–	Adab	Account of land.	45×47×23
31	1952/45	ED IIIb	–	–	–	–	Adab	Account of land.	38×38×18
32	1952/42	ED IIIb	–	–	–	–	Adab	Account of land.	42×41×21
33	3789/22	ED/ES	–	–	–	u_4 2	Adab	Account of land.	40×39×18
34	3790/61	ED/ES	–	–	–	–	Adab	Account of land.	60×59×25
35	3833	ED/ES	–	–	–	–	Adab	Account of land.	82×80×28
36	2181/1	ED/ES	–	–	iti ab-e_3-zi-ga	–	Adab	Issue of bread and beer to palace soldiers.	23×25×10
37	2181/2	ED/ES	–	–	iti še-gur_x (|ŠE.ŠE|.KIN)-am_3	–	Adab	Issue of bread and beer to personnel at a canal.	28×30×10
38	2181/3	ED/ES	–	–	iti a_2-ki-ti	–	Adab	Issue of bread and beer to palace soldiers.	22×25×10
39	2181/4	ED/ES	–	–	iti še-gur_x-am_3	–	Adab	Issue of bread and beer to personnel at a canal	26×27×9
40	2181/5	ED/ES	–	–	iti a_2-ki-ti	–	Adab	Issue of bread and beer to palace soldiers.	24×27×8
41	2181/6	ED/ES	–	–	iti šu-ĝar	–	Adab	Issue of bread and beer to personnel at a field.	21×24×7
42	2181/7	ED/ES	–	–	iti šu-ĝar	–	Adab	Issue of bread and beer to a "Silver (and) lapis-lazuli boat."	21×24×8

43	2181/8	ED/ES	-	-	iti a_2-ki-ti	-	Adab	Issue of bread and beer to palace soldiers.	21×25×9
44	2181/9	ED/ES	-	-	iti ^{d}Šuba$_3$-nun	-	Adab	Issue of bread and beer to personnel in the "garden of Urdu-Ašgi."	22×25×8
45	2181/10	ED/ES	-	-	iti šu-ĝar	-	Adab	Issue of bread and beer to boatmen.	22×25×7
46	2181/11	ED/ES	-	-	iti še-gur$_x$ (|ŠE.ŠE|.KIN)-am$_3$	-	Adab	Issue of bread and beer to an individual.	23×26×8
47	2181/12	ED/ES	-	-	iti ab-e$_3$-zi-ga	-	Adab	Issue of bread and beer to menial laborers connected to the "New Palace."	21×24×8
48	2181/13	ED/ES	-	-	iti še-gur$_x$ (|ŠE.ŠE|.KIN)-am$_3$	-	Adab	Issue of bread and beer to a "Silver (and) lapis-lazuli boat."	25×27×9
49	2181/14	ED/ES	-	-	iti a_2-ki-ti	-	Adab	Issue of bread and beer to palace soldiers.	21×24×8
50	2181/15	ED/ES	-	-	iti še-gur$_x$ (|ŠE.ŠE|.KIN)-am$_3$	-	Adab	Issue of bread and beer to (personnel at) the "New Canal."	21×24×7
51	2181/16	ED/ES	-	-	iti ni$_3$-kiri$_6$	-	Adab	Issue of bread and beer to palace soldiers.	23×25×8
52	2181/17	ED/ES	-	-	iti aša$_5$-il$_2$-šu-ĝar	-	Adab	Issue of bread and beer to palace soldiers.	25×26×11
53	2181/18	ED/ES	-	-	iti ni$_3$-kiri$_6$	-	Adab	Issue of bread and beer to boatmen.	21×24×8
54	2181/19	ED/ES	-	-	iti a_2-ki-ti	-	Adab	Issue of bread and beer to palace soldiers.	22×25×10
55	2181/20	ED/ES	-	-	iti a_2-ki-ti	-	Adab	Issue of bread and beer to palace soldiers.	22×25×10
56	2181/21	ED/ES	-	-	iti ab-e$_3$-zi-ga	-	Adab	Issue of bread and beer to personnel at a canal.	23×25×10

57	2181/22	ED/ES	-	-	iti du$_6$-ku$_3$	-	Adab	Issue of bread and beer to (personnel in) the palace.	22×28×8
58	2181/23	ED/ES	-	-	iti aša$_5$-il$_2$-šu-ĝar	-	Adab	Issue of bread and beer to palace soldiers.	26×27×12
59	2181/24	ED/ES	-	-	iti ni$_3$-kiri$_6$	-	Adab	Issue of bread and beer to palace soldiers.	21×23×7
60	2181/25	ED/ES	-	-	iti aša$_5$-il$_2$-šu-ĝar	u$_4$ 13	Adab	Issue of bread and beer to palace soldiers.	24×26×12
61	2181/26	ED/ES	-	-	iti ni$_3$-kiri$_6$	-	Adab	Issue of bread and beer to palace soldiers.	22×25×8
62	2181/27	ED/ES	-	-	iti aša$_5$-il$_2$-šu-ĝar	-	Adab	Issue of bread and beer to palace soldiers.	21×27×12
63	2181/28	ED/ES	-	-	iti a$_2$-ki-ti	-	Adab	Issue of bread and beer to palace soldiers.	22×25×9
64	2181/29	ED/ES	-	-	iti še-gur$_x$ (|ŠE.ŠE|.KIN)-am$_3$	-	Adab	Issue of bread and beer to the governors of Ĝeša (Umma) and Lagaš.	26×29×9*
65	2181/30	ED/ES	-	-	iti ^{d}Šuba$_3$-nun	-	Adab	Issue of bread and beer to personnel in the garden of Ašgi-pa'e.	20×22×7
66	2181/31	ED/ES	-	-	iti du$_6$-ku$_3$	-	Adab	Issue of bread and beer to an individual.	21×24×8
67	2181/32	ED/ES	-	-	iti ni$_3$-kiri$_6$	-	Adab	Issue of bread and beer to palace soldiers.	20×23×7
68	2181/33	ED/ES	-	-	iti ^{d}Šuba$_3$-nun	-	Adab	Issue of bread and beer to palace soldiers.	21×24×8
69	2181/34	ED/ES	-	-	iti aša$_5$-il$_2$-šu-ĝar	-	Adab	Issue of bread and beer to (personnel in) the "garden of Urdu-Ašgi."	23×25×8
70	2181/35	ED/ES	-	-	iti ab-e$_3$-zi-ga	-	Adab	Issue of bread and beer to (personnel in) the palace.	21×24×7

71	2181/36	ED/ES	–	–	iti ni$_{3}$-kiri$_{6}$	–	Adab	Issue of bread and beer to palace soldiers.	19×23×7
72	2181/37	ED/ES	–	–	iti du$_{6}$-ku$_{3}$	–	Adab	Issue of bread and beer to (personnel in) the palace.	22×25×7
73	2181/38	ED/ES	–	–	iti aša$_{5}$-il$_{2}$-šu-ĝar	–	Adab	Issue of bread and beer to palace soldiers.	26×27×11
74	2181/39	ED/ES	–	–	–	–	Adab	Issue of bread and beer to palace soldiers.	23×25×9
75	2181/40	ED/ES	–	–	iti še-saĝ-sig$_{15}$-ga	–	Adab	Issue of bread and beer.	22×23×7
76	2181/41	ED/ES	–	–	iti še-saĝ-sig$_{15}$-ga	–	Adab	Issue of bread and beer to (personnel in) the palace.	20×23×7
77	2181/42	ED/ES	–	–	iti ni$_{3}$-kiri$_{6}$	–	Adab	Issue of bread and beer.	22×25×8
78	2181/43	ED/ES	–	–	iti še-saĝ-sig$_{15}$-ga	–	Adab	Issue of bread and beer to (personnel in) the palace.	18×24×8
79	2181/44	ED/ES	–	–	iti aša$_{5}$-il$_{2}$-šu-ĝar	–	Adab	Issue of bread and beer to palace soldiers.	22×24×10
80	2181/45	ED/ES	–	–	iti ab-e$_{3}$-zi-ga	–	Adab	Issue of bread and beer to palace soldiers.	22×24×9
81	2181/46	ED/ES	–	–	iti še-gur$_{x}$ (|ŠE.ŠE|.KIN)-am$_{3}$	–	Adab	Expenditure of groats and malt to an individual.	21×24×8
82	2181/47	ED/ES	–	–	iti ni$_{3}$-kiri$_{6}$	–	Adab	Expenditure of barley flour to a bodyguard of the king.	25×27×10
83	2467	ES	–	–	–	–	Adab	Account of barley distributed to a household, gods (obv.) and personnel (rev.).	61×59×20
84	3789/1	ED/ES	–	–	iti ^{d}Šuba$_{3}$-nun	u$_{4}$ 20	Adab	Daily allocation of bread and beer to deities, households and individuals.	57×57×22

85	3789/2	ED/ES	-	-	iti še-gur$_x$ (ŠE.KIN)-am$_3$	u$_4$ 23	Adab	Daily allocation of bread and beer to deities, households and individuals.	71×71×23
86	3789/3	ED/ES	-	-	[...]	[...]	Adab	Daily allocation of bread and beer to deities, households and individuals.	62×60×15*
87	3789/4	ED/ES	-	-	iti aša$_5$-il$_2$-šu-ĝar	u$_4$ 20 ab-ta-zal	Adab	Daily allocation of bread and beer to deities, households and individuals.	61×62×20
88	3789/8	ED/ES	-	-	iti a$_2$-ki-ti	u$_4$ 3	Adab	Daily allocation of bread and beer to deities, households and individuals.	47×46×20
89	3789/18	ED/ES	-	-	iti ^{d}Šuba$_3$-nun	u$_4$ 25	Adab	Daily allocation of bread and beer to deities, households and individuals.	66×68×21
90	3789/26	ED/ES	-	-	iti ni$_3$-kiri$_6$	u$_4$ 14	Adab	Daily allocation of bread and beer to deities, households and individuals.	64×65×24
91	3789/27	ED/ES	-	-	iti še-kin-ku$_5$	u$_4$ 1	Adab	Daily allocation of bread and beer to e$_2$-dumu.	27×27×14
92	3789/28	ED/ES	-	-	iti du$_6$-ku$_3$	u$_4$ 3 mu-ĝal$_2$	Adab	Daily allocation of bread and beer to individuals.	46×46×22
93	3789/29	ED/ES	-	-	iti aša$_5$-il$_2$-šu-ĝar	u$_4$ 1	Adab	Daily allocation of bread and beer to individuals and households.	40×40×20
94	3789/31	ED/ES	-	-	iti du$_6$-ku$_3$	u$_4$ 23	Adab	Daily allocation of bread and beer to deities, households and individuals.	65×67×28
95	3789/33	ED/ES	-	-	iti ^{d}MUŠ$_3$×KUR.ZA	u$_4$ 7	Adab	Daily allocation of bread and beer to deities, households and individuals.	69*×72×26

96	3789/35	ED/ES	-	-	[…]	[…]	Adab	Daily allocation of bread and beer to deities, households and individuals.	55*×60×13*
97	3789/39	ED/ES	-	-	iti ab-e_3-zi-ga	u_4 27	Adab	Daily allocation of bread and beer to individuals.	50×51×23
98	3789/40	ED/ES	-	-	iti še-kin-ku_5-kam	u_4 21+n	Adab	Daily allocation of bread and beer to households and individuals.	46×47×23
99	3789/41	ED/ES	-	-	-	-	Adab	Expenditure of bread for (labor in) orchard(s), metalworkers and households.	66×64×22
100	3789/44	ED/ES	-	-	iti $aša_5$-il_2-šu-ĝar	u_4 23	Adab	Daily allocation of bread and beer to households and individuals.	51×49×25
101	3790/34	ED/ES	-	-	iti ab-e_3-zi-ga	u_4 21	Adab	Daily allocation of bread and beer to deities, households and individuals.	61*×61×21
102	3790/62	ED/ES	u_4-ba $ensi_2$ A-ga-de_3^{ki} u_3-mu-ti-la-a	-	-	-	Adab	Account of bread, beer and broth during the governor's stay in Agade.	33×33×17
103	3832	ES	-	-	-	-	Adab	Account of bread.	36×38×21
104	3789/23	ED/ES	-	-	-	-	Adab	Allocation of beer to individuals from various locations.	35×37×22
105	3790/56	ED/ES	-	-	-	-	Adab	Allocation of beer.	43*×43×26
106	3790/70	ED/ES	-	-	iti ni_3-$kiri_6$	u_4 30-$še_3$	Adab	Account of beer.	28×27×14
107	4999	ED/ES	lugal Kiš^{ki}	-	iti še-gur_x (|ŠE.ŠE|.KIN)-a	u_4 1	Adab	Record of beer for the reception of high-profile guests. A "king of Kiš" is mentioned.	52×41×19
108	2191/2	ED/ES	Silim-^{d}Utu nu-$banda_3$	-	-	-	Adab	Account of flour, beer and wooden objects.	49×49×20

109	2191/8	ED/ES	Silim-^{d}Utu nu-banda$_{3}$	–	–	–	Adab	Expenditure of a large amount of barley.	43×43×17
110	2191/16	ED/ES	(Silim-^{d}Utu nu-banda$_{3}$)	–	–	–	Adab	Allocation of grain and grain flour.	66×68×20
111	3789/9	ED/ES	–	–	iti a$_{2}$-ki-ti-kam	–	Adab	Account of barley for groats.	37×38×17
112	3789/10	ED/ES	–	–	iti šu-ĝar-kam	–	Adab	Account of barley for groats.	36×37×18
113	3789/11	ED/ES	–	–	iti a$_{2}$-ki-ti-kam	–	Adab	Account of barley for groats.	38×38×18
114	3789/15	ED/ES	–	–	–	–	Adab	Account of barley flour.	30×30×15
115	3789/17	ED/ES	–	–	iti šu-ĝar-kam	–	Adab	Account of barley and barley groats.	33×33×15
116	3789/19	ED/ES	–	–	iti še-saĝ-sig$_{15}$-ga	–	Adab	Account of barley.	$30^{\star}$×32×16
117	3789/24	ED/ES	Silim-^{d}Utu nu-banda$_{3}$	–	–	–	Adab	Account of barley measured.	30×28×17
118	3789/25	ED/ES	Silim-^{d}Utu nu-banda$_{3}$	–	iti ^{d}Šuba$_{3}$-nun	–	Adab	Allocation of emmer to temple households.	31×31×17
119	3789/32	ED/ES	–	–	–	–	Adab	Allocation of malt.	52×49×20
120	3789/34	ED/ES	–	–	–	–	Adab	Issue of grain in a granary.	42×37×22
121	3789/36	ED/ES	–	–	iti ĝa$_{2}$-udu-ur$_{4}$-kam	–	Adab	Monthly allocation of barley to two female workers and a child.	$34^{\star}$×35×16
122	3789/38	ED/ES	–	–	iti aša$_{5}$-il$_{2}$-šu-ĝar	–	Adab	Account of barley flour.	36×36×15
123	3789/45	ED/ES	Silim-^{d}Utu nu-banda$_{3}$	–	–	–	Adab	Account of barley.	35×36×16
124	3789/46	ED/ES	[Silim-^{d}Utu] nu-banda$_{3}$	–	–	–	Adab	Account of barley.	$45^{\star}$×$42^{\star}$×23
125	3790/1	ED/ES	–	–	iti ab-e$_{3}$-zi-ga	–	Adab	Account of barley flour.	47×47×22

126	3790/2	ED/ES	-	-	iti mu-tir	-	Adab	Account of barley flour.	35×35×18
127	3790/3	ED/ES	Silim-^{d}Utu nu-banda$_3$	-	iti a$_2$-ki-ti-kam	-	Adab	Account of wheat and emmer.	40×40×23
128	3790/6	ED/ES	(Silim-^{d}Utu nu-banda$_3$)	-	iti še-kin-ku$_5$	-	Adab	Account of barley flour mentioning a maid of the supervisor.	36×36×20
129	3790/7	ED/ES	-	-	iti ni$_3$-kiri$_6$	-	Adab	Delivery of premium flour to the "New Palace."	38*×40×19
130	3790/10	ED/ES	-	-	iti mu-tir	-	Adab	Account of barley.	33×33×17
131	3790/11	ED/ES	-	-	iti šu-ĝar	-	Adab	Account of grain products.	34*×36×16
132	3790/13	ED/ES	-	-	[...]	-	Adab	Account of barley.	35*×40×15*
133	3790/16	ED/ES	Silim-^{d}Utu nu-banda$_3$	-	iti a$_2$-ki-ti	-	Adab	Account of flour and grain products.	37×38×18
134	3790/20	ED/ES	(Silim-^{d}Utu nu-banda$_3$)	-	-	-	Adab	Account of barley bread.	35×35×18
135	3790/21	ED/ES	(Silim-^{d}Utu nu-banda$_3$)	-	-	-	Adab	Account of emmer.	36×36×20
136	3790/23	ED/ES	-	-	iti še-gur$_x$ (|ŠE.ŠE|.KIN)-a	-	Adab	Account of premium barley.	32×34×19
137	3790/25	ED/ES	ensi$_2$ (Meskigala)	-	iti še-kin-ku$_5$	-	Adab	Account of grain products.	45×45×22
138	3790/29	ED/ES	-	-	iti mu-tir	-	Adab	Account of barley flour.	31×31×16
139	3790/30	ED/ES	-	-	iti a$_2$-ki-ti	-	Adab	Account of GU.LUL seeds.	38×38×18
140	3790/36	ED/ES	-	-	-	-	Adab	Allocation of grain to personnel.	77×78×25
141	3790/38	ED/ES	-	-	iti ĝa$_2$-udu-ur$_4$	-	Adab	Account of barley flour.	33×32×29

142	3790/41	ED/ES	–	–	iti še-kin-ku$_5$-kam	–	Adab	Account of barley flour, barley and flour for bread.	43×41×17
143	3790/42	ED/ES	–	–	iti du$_6$-ku$_3$	–	Adab	Account of grain products.	48★×48×22
144	3790/44	ED/ES	(Silim-^{d}Utu nu-banda$_3$)	–	iti še-saĝ-sig$_{15}$-ga	–	Adab	Account of grain products.	43×42×21★
145	3790/45	ED/ES	–	–	iti ni$_3$-kiri$_6$	–	Adab	Account of barley flour.	37×37×18
146	3790/50	ED/ES	–	–	–	–	Adab	Account of emmer.	42×43×22
147	3790/51	ED/ES		[...]	[...]	[...]	Adab	Account of large amounts of barley.	65×65×28
148	3790/52	ED/ES	(Silim-^{d}Utu nu-banda$_3$)	–	še-gur$_x$ (|ŠE.ŠE|.KIN)-a	–	Adab	Account of barley flour.	37×37×14★
149	3790/53	ED/ES	–	–	iti šu-ĝar	u$_4$ 2-kam	Adab	Account of barley flour.	35×34×22
150	3790/54	ED/ES	–	–	iti ĝa$_2$-udu-ur$_4$	–	Adab	Account of barley, emmer and grain products.	43×44×20
151	3790/55	ED/ES	Silim-^{d}Utu nu-banda$_3$	–	iti mu-tir	–	Adab	Account of barley allocation to individuals.	51×54×24
152	3790/57	ED/ES	–	–	iti aša$_5$-il$_2$-šu-ĝar	–	Adab	Account of barley flour.	42×42×19
153	3790/58	ED/ES	–	–	iti du$_6$-ku$_3$	–	Adab	Account of emmer-wheat flour.	44×44×20
154	3790/59	ED/ES	–	–	–	–	Adab	Unfinished account of barley.	32★×32×18
155	3790/60	ED/ES	–	–	iti ab-e$_3$-zi-ga	–	Adab	Account of barley flour.	43×42×2
156	3790/66	ED/ES	–	–	iti ĝa$_2$-udu-ur$_4$	–	Adab	Account of emmer-wheat flour.	35×34★×13
157	3790/68	ED/ES	–	–	iti ĝa$_2$-udu-ur$_4$	–	Adab	Account of grain and grain flour.	42×42×20

158	3790/71	ED/ES	–	–	iti ĝa$_2$-udu-ur$_4$	–	Adab	Account of flour and bread.	40*×41*×24
159	3799	ED/ES	–	–	–	–	Adab	Account of barley in connection to officials and households.	66×66×31
160	3809	ED/ES	–	–	iti ni$_3$-kiri$_6$	–	Adab	Account of emmer-wheat flour.	51×51×21
161	3815	ED/ES	–	–	iti du$_6$-ku$_3$	–	Adab	Account of barley flour.	39×39×19
162	3817	ED/ES	–	–	–	–	Adab?	Account of barley.	45×45×21
163	3819	ED/ES	–	–	–	–	Adab	Account of an outstanding expenditure of barley.	39×38×17
164	3820	ED/ES	–	–	iti il$_2$-aša$_5$-šu-ĝar	–	Adab	Account of barley flour and premium flour.	42×42×22
165	3826	ES	–	–	–	–	Adab	Account of grain products, beer, cheese and butter.	46×38×21
166	3831	ED/ES	–	–	–	–	Adab?	Expenditure of grain from two fields.	31×32×20
167	3835	ED/ES	–	–	–	–	Adab	Delivery of grain.	29×31×14
168	3840	ED/ES	–	–	iti ^{d}Šuba$_3$-nun; iti še-kin-ku$_5$; iti še-gur$_x$ (|ŠE.ŠE|.KIN)-gur$_x$ (|ŠE.ŠE|.KIN)	–	Adab	Account of barley of several months.	40×42×24
169	3841	ED/ES	–	–	iti ab-e$_3$-zi-ga	–	Adab	Account of barley flour.	29×30×17
170	5033	ED/ES	–	–	iti ab-e$_3$-zi-ga	–	Adab	Account of emmer-wheat flour.	26×25×16
171	3827	ED/ES	–	–	–	–	Adab	Account of various foodstuffs.	44×48×24
172	3828	ES/MS	–	–	–	–	Adab	Provisions for a journey.	45×39×19

173	3789/14	ED/ES	Silim-^{d}Utu nu-banda$_3$	–	iti še-sag-sig$_{15}$-ga	–	Adab	Account of sheep.	42×42×18
174	3789/16	ED/ES	–	–	–	–	Adab	Account of a goat for Inana.	28×28×15
175	3790/14	ED/ES	–	–	iti mu-tir	–	Adab	Account of sheep.	29×30×15
176	3790/18	ED/ES	–	–	iti ĝa$_2$-udu-ur$_4$-kam	–	Adab	Account of sheep.	30×32×16
177	3790/19	ED/ES	Silim-^{d}Utu nu-banda$_3$	–	iti še-kin-ku$_5$	–	Adab	Account of sheep.	34×32×19
178	3790/26	ED/ES	Silim-^{d}Utu nu-banda$_3$	–	iti še-kin-ku$_5$-kam	–	Adab	Account of sheep(?) on the occasion of a journey.	41×41×20
179	3790/31	ED/ES	Silim-^{d}Utu nu-banda$_3$	–	iti mu-tir	–	Adab	Account of sheep on the occasion of a journey.	45★×45×17★
180	3790/35	ED/ES	Silim-^{d}Utu nu-banda$_3$	–	iti Šuba$_3$-nun	–	Adab	Account of sheep.	72×72×23
181	3790/37	ED/ES	Silim-^{d}Utu nu-banda$_3$	–	iti še-kin-ku$_5$-kam	–	Adab	Account of sheep.	42★×43★×15★
182	3790/39	ED/ES	Silim-^{d}Utu nu-banda$_3$	–	iti ab-e$_3$-zi-ga	–	Adab	Account of sheep for a journey.	42×42×22★
183	3790/69	ED/ES	–	–	iti a$_2$-ki-ti	–	Adab	Account of sheep.	27×27×16
184	3801	ED/ES	Silim-^{d}Utu nu-banda$_3$	–	[...]	–	Adab	Account of sheep.	34×35×16
185	3816	ED/ES	–	–	[...]	–	Adab	Account of sheep.	50★×55×20
186	3834	ED/ES	–	–	iti a$_2$-ki-ti	–	Adab	Account of goats.	23×23×12
187	3789/12	ED/ES	–	–	iti še-saĝ-sig$_{15}$-ga	–	Adab	Account of ewe hides.	32★×34×14
188	3789/20	ED/ES	–	–	iti ni$_3$-kiri$_6$	–	Adab	Account of pig hides.	37×37×18
189	3790/4	ED/ES	Silim-^{d}Utu nu-banda$_3$	–	iti du$_6$-ku$_3$	–	Adab	Account of a ewe hide and dried meat.	40×40×18
190	3790/5	ED/ES	–	–	iti še-saĝ-sig$_{15}$-ga	–	Adab	Account of a lamb hide and dried meat.	35×37×17

191	3790/8	ED/ES	–	–	iti a$_2$-ki-ti-kam	–	Adab	Account of ewe hides and dried meat.	34×35×15
192	3790/46	ED/ES	Silim-^{d}Utu nu-banda$_3$	–	iti še-saĝ-sig$_{15}$-ga	–	Adab	Account of sheep hides.	49×49×19
193	3790/49	ED/ES	–	–	iti ni$_3$-kiri$_6$	–	Adab	Account of goat hides and dried meat.	36×37×28
194	3802	ED/ES	Silim-^{d}Utu nu-banda$_3$	–	iti še-saĝ-sig$_{15}$-ga	–	Adab	Account of waterskins and goat hides.	32×33×18
195	3805	ED/ES	–	–	–	–	Adab	Delivery and receipt of animal horns.	35×36×21
196	1952/36	ES	–	–	–	–	Adab	Design of an Ešnunna-type chariot.	58×54★×21
197	1952/43	ED/ES	–	–	–	–	Adab	Account of wooden implements.	42×42×22
198	2365/15	ED/ES	–	–	–	–	Adab	Wooden implements for chariots.	35×35×14
199	3789/6	ED/ES	–	–	saĝ iti ni$_3$-kiri$_6$	–	Adab	Account of wooden parts of a chariot.	50×51×24
200	3789/42	ED/ES	–	–	–	–	Adab	Account of wooden beams (exercise?).	34×35×18
201	3790/47	ED/ES	–	–	iti šu-ĝar	–	Adab	Account of wooden implements ḫar-an.	48×48×22★
202	3790/48	ED/ES	–	–	iti ĝa$_2$-udu-ur$_4$-kam	–	Adab	Account of wooden implements.	52×52×23
203	3790/64	ED/ES	–	–	–	–	Adab	Account of weapons.	36×35×18
204	3803	ED/ES	–	–	–	–	Adab	Account of metal objects.	33×34×20
205	3821	ES	–	–	–	–	Adab	Account of saws.	43×40×16
206	3822	ES	–	–	–	–	Adab	Account of saws.	35×31×17
207	3837	ED/ES	Az nu-banda$_3$	–	–	–	Adab	Account of a variety of copper (MUŠ$_3$-uruda).	53×53×20

208	3789/5	ED/ES	–	–	iti aša$_5$-il$_2$-šu-ĝar	–	Adab	Issue of oil to a sailor.	30×28×17
209	3790/43	ED/ES	Silim-^{d}Utu nu-banda$_3$	–	iti a$_2$-ki-ti	–	Adab	Account of dates.	46×46*×20
210	3789/13	ED/ES	–	–	–	–	Adab	Account of rushes.	40×40×20
211	3790/9	ED/ES	–	–	iti aša$_5$-il$_2$-šu-ĝar	–	Adab	Account of reed mats.	30×29×17
212	3790/27	ED/ES	–	–	iti a$_2$-ki-ti	–	Adab	Account of reed baskets.	28×27×15
213	3790/32	ED/ES	–	–	iti šu-ĝar	–	Adab	Account of reed baskets.	33×34×19
214	3790/63	ED/ES	–	–	–	–	Adab	Unfinished account of reed baskets and wooden implements.	40×38×19
215	3823	ES		–	–	–	Adab	Account of reed *gur*-containers.	55×49×20
216	3790/15	ED/ES	Silim-^{d}Utu nu-banda$_3$	–	iti ab-e$_3$-zi-ga	–	Adab	Account of onions.	35×37×17
217	3790/22	ED/ES	–	–	–	–	Adab	Transfer of onions to a merchant from Ĝeša.	36×37×14
218	3790/65	ED/ES	–	–	iti ^{d}Šuba$_3$ (MUŠ$_3$×ZA)-nun	–	Adab	Account of flax in bundles.	30×30×17
219	3800	ED IIIb	–	–	–	–	Adab?	Account of flax in bundles.	40×40×16
220	3789/21	ED/ES	–	–	iti ab-e$_3$-zi-ga	–	Adab	Account of bitumen.	33×34×20
221	3789/43	ED/ES	–	–	[...]	–	Adab	Account of bitumen.	38×42×18
222	3790/24	ED/ES	–	–	iti aša$_5$-il$_2$-šu-ĝar	–	Adab	Account of bitumen.	30×30×17
223	3789/37	ED/ES	–	–	iti a$_2$-ki-ti	–	Adab	Account of buckets	42×43×23
224	3790/12	ED/ES	–	–	iti šu-ĝar	–	Adab	Account of buckets.	32×32×17

225	3790/28	ED/ES	–	–	iti še-<<še>>-kin-ku$_5$	–	Adab	Account of fish.	42×42×22
226	3838	ES	–	–	–	–	Adab	Account of fish.	36×32×16
227	3842	ES	–	–	–	–	Adab	Account of aromatics.	34×28×15
228	3843	ES	–	–	–	–	Adab	Account of garments.	51×56×24
229	3812	ED/ES	–	–	–	–	Adab	Account of miscellaneous goods.	51×54×20
230	3789/30	ED/ES	–	–	iti ni$_3$-kiri$_6$	–	Adab	Account of uncertain items (MA$_2$×EŠE$_2$…).	36×37★×21
231	3829	ES	–	–	–	–	Adab	Account of an uncertain item (MA$_2$×EŠE$_2$-gid$_2$).	39×35×18
232	3790/67	ES	–	mu šeg$_{12}$ Karkara (IM)^{ki} ^{ĝeš}šub-ba ĝar	iti ĝa$_2$-udu-ur$_4$	–	Adab	Account of uncertain goods dated by the "year when the brick of Karkara was placed in the mould."	38★×41×20
233	3181	ED/ES	–	–	–	–	Adab?	Bulla-shaped letter-order	38×31×12
234	5018	ED/ES	–	–	–	u$_4$ 12	Adab	Bulla recording bread and beer.	26×21×-
235	5019	ED/ES	–	–	–	u$_4$ 2	Adab	Bulla recording expenditure of reeds.	25×17×-
236	5020	ED/ES	–	–	iti ab-e$_3$-zi-ga	–	Adab	Bulla recording barley.	25×18×-
237	5021	ED/ES	–	–	–	–	Adab	Bulla recording barley.	34×24×-
238	5047/2	ED/ES	–	–	iti še-kin-ku$_5$	–	Adab	Bulla that was attached to a tablet box.	46★×30×22 ½-diameter
239	5047/3	ED/ES		–	–	–	Adab	Bulla that was attached to a tablet box.	42×35×16 ½-diameter
240	2724/6	ES/MS	–	–	–	–	Adab	Account of junior shepherds in service of individuals.	77×62×20

241	2724/10	ES/MS	–	–	–	–	Adab	Account of labor in service of individuals.	62×43×21
242	2724/11	ES/MS	–	–	–	–	Adab	Account of personnel.	66×55×22
243	1952/35	ES	–	–	–	–	Adab	Allocation of land.	57×56×22
244	2724/1	ES	–	–	–	–	Adab	Account of goats.	54×46×21
245	2724/7	ES/MS	–	–	–	–	Adab	Account of sheep and goats.	54×43×18
246	2724/9	ES/MS	–	–	–	–	Adab	Expenditure of sheep.	45×35×17
247	2724/13	ES	–	–	–	–	Adab	Account of sheep in connection to Lagaš (obv.); allocation of barley from the temple E-SAR (rev.).	61×57×21
248	3818	ES	–	–	–	–	Adab	Account of sheep.	43×37×18
249	4193	ES/MS	–	–	–	–	Adab	Account of sheep and pigs.	57×42×18
250	2724/2	ES	–	–	–	–	Adab	Account of sheep and wool.	55×48×24
251	2724/4	ES	–	–	–	–	Adab	Account of sheep and wool.	47×41×17
252	3814	ES	–	–	–	–	Adab?	Account of wool.	36×33×18
253	2724/12	ES/MS	–	–	–	–	Adab	Account of cattle of varying age.	54×40×18
254	4202	ES/MS	–	–	–	–	Adab	Account of hides.	52×40×23
255	4235	ES/MS	–	–	–	–	Adab	Account of cheese.	45×33×17
256	4271	MS	–	–	–	–	Adab	Turning over of cheese.	66×47×20
257	2724/5	ES	–	–	–	–	Adab	Account of grain.	40×38×20
258	2724/14	ES	–	–	–	–	Adab	Account of barley arrears of shepherds.	60×64×21
259	2724/3	ES	–	–	–	–	Adab	Account of silver and barley.	58×45×24

260	3839	ES	–	–	–	–	Adab	Account of silver.	62×62×24
261	3808	ES	–	–	–	–	Adab	Record of copper.	68×56×28
262	2724/8	ES/MS	–	–	–	–	Adab	Expenditure of miscellaneous goods.	63×47×19
263	2465	MS	–	–	–	–	Adab	Cumulative account briefly recording various transactions concerning people, animals and a house.	82×83×25
264	4208	MS	Mama-ummi's file	–	–	–	Adab	Account of female workers with their supervisors, in service and "living in the field."	58×36×18
265	4233	MS	Lugal-aja$_2$-ĝu$_{10}$ ensi$_2$; Mama-ummi's file	–	–	–	Adab	Account of female workers in service with their supervisors.	64×35×17
266	4261	MS	–	–	–	–	Adab	Account of personnel living in "reed thicket."	40×31×16
267	4327	MS	–	[...]	[...]	[...]	Adab	Account of workers (*ĝuruš*) together with their overseers.	59★×43×17
268	4761	MS	–	–	–	–	Adab	Transfer of personnel.	38×29×15
269	5001	MS	–	–	–	–	Adab	Assignment of personnel.	49×42×22
270	5003	MS	–	–	–	–	Adab	Transfer of personnel.	49×51×27
271	5004	MS	–	–	–	–	Adab	Record concerning the residence of two women and a girl.	50×41×21
272	2191/27	MS/CS	–	–	–	–	Adab	A note concerning a field.	31×26×14
273	2191/17	MS	–	–	iti še-saĝ-sig$_{15}$-ga-am$_3$	–	Adab	Expenditure of barley flour and *zidgu*-flour.	22×23×15

274	2191/24	MS/CS	–	–	–	–	Adab	Barley.	32×28×16
275	2109/1	ES/MS	–	–	[...]	[...]	Adab	Allocation of bread.	72×68×18
276	2109/2	ES/MS	–	–	iti Šuba$_{3}$-nun	u$_{4}$ 4	Adab	Allocation of bread.	67×65×20
277	2109/3	ES/MS	–	–	–	–	Adab	Allocation of bread.	76×77×27
278	2109/4	ES/MS	–	–	iti a$_{2}$-ki-ti	u$_{4}$ 25	Adab	Allocation of bread.	81×80×17
279	2191/19	MS	–	–	iti eše$_{2}$-gar$_{3}$-ra-šu-ĝar-am$_{3}$	–	Adab	Account of bread and beer.	45×32×18
280	2191/21	MS	–	–	iti mu-tir	–	Adab	Bread.	67×47×18
281	2250	MS	–	–	iti Šuba$_{2}$-nun	–	Adab	Allocation of bread to a sick worker.	24×21×14
282	4189	MS	–	–	ĝa$_{2}$-udu-ur$_{4}$	u$_{4}$ 14-kam	Adab	Allocation of bread.	60×51×17*
283	4277/1	MS	–	–	iti Šuba$_{3}$-nun	u$_{4}$ 20 la$_{2}$ 2	Adab	Allocation of bread.	80×60×18
284	4277/2	MS	–	–	iti Šuba$_{3}$-nun	u$_{4}$ 11	Adab	Allocation of bread.	80×60×20
285	4277/3	MS	–	–	–	–	Adab	Allocation of bread.	59×42×21
286	4277/4	MS	–	–	–	–	Adab	Allocation of bread.	54×40×19
287	4277/5	MS	–	–	–	–	Adab	Allocation of bread.	53×36×17
288	4199	MS/CS	–	[...]	[...]	[...]	Adab	Allocation of bread.	68×64×19
289	2191/26	MS/CS	–	–	–	–	Adab	Account of goats.	42×37×17
290	2227/2	ES/MS	–	–	–	–	Adab	Account of sheep.	30*×25*×16
291	4224	MS	–	mu ^{geš}inda al-du$_{3}$-am$_{3}$	iti a$_{2}$-ki-ti	–	Adab	Inventory of cattle.	60×45×20
292	4243	MS	–	–	–	–	Adab	Account of cattle.	78×65×22

293	4272	MS	–	–	–	–	Adab	Account of "mountain" cattle.	62×42×20
294	4275	MS	–	–	–	–	Adab	Expenditure of sheep.	37×30×15
295	4209	MS	–	–		–	Adab	Expenditure of hides.	42×30×14
296	4214	MS	–	–	–	–	Adab	Delivery of hides.	81×63×20
297	4232	MS	–	–	–	–	Adab	Account of wool.	43×30×16
298	4237	MS	–	–	–	–	Adab	Account of wool in connection to shepherds.	50×33×14
299	4049	MS	Mama-ummi's file	–	[iti] še-saĝ-sig$_{15}$-ga-a	–	Adab	Account of wool.	68×37×17
300	4195	MS	–	–	–	–	Adab	Allocation of textiles.	85★×83★×28
301	4204	MS	Mama-ummi's file	–	–	–	Adab	Account of produced garments with weight indicated.	66×36×17
302	4207	MS	–	–	–	–	Adab	Turning over and delivery of textiles.	55×34×19
303	4229	MS	Mama-ummi's file	–	–	–	Adab	Account of textiles.	55×35×18
304	4276		Mama-ummi's file	–	–	–	Adab	Account of produced garments with weight indicated.	63★×63×18
305	4450	MS	Mama-ummi's file	–	–	–	Adab	Account of textiles with weight indicated.	77×41×19
306	2191/23	MS	–	–	iti ĝa$_2$-udu-ur$_4$	–	Adab	Account of bitumen.	62★×48×17
307	4210	MS/CS	–	–	–	–	Adab	Tally of baskets.	35×32×15
308	4211	MS/CS	–	–	–	–	Adab?	Account of neck spines of sacrificial bulls.	44×30×14
309	4262	MS	–	–	iti ĝa$_2$-udu-ur$_4$	–	Adab	Delivery and expenditure of flax in bundles.	38×30×15

310	4754	MS	–	–	–	–	Adab	Arrears of flax.	38×28×16
311	4212	MS/CS	–	–	–	–	Adab?	Calculations of onions associated with two plots of land and recorded with persons in charge.	53×37×20
312	4216	MS/CS	–	–	–	–	Adab?	Receipt of the price of onions.	33×27×13
313	4244	MS	–	–	iti Šuba$_3$-nun	–	Adab	Receipt and expenditure of oil.	40×29×15
314	4221	MS	–	–	iti du$_6$-ku$_3$	–	Adab	Turning over of salt.	42×29×16
315	2425/1	MS/CS	–	–	–	–	Adab	Numerical tablet. Delivery of wood.	55×35×19
316	2425/2	MS/CS	–	–	–	–	Adab	(Almost) numerical tablet. Delivery of wood.	54×32×19
317	2191/25	MS	–	–	–	–	Adab	Account of gypsum, potash and aromatic substances.	57×38×16
318	4194	MS	–	–	–	–	Adab	Account of miscellaneous goods.	53×33×17
319	4238	MS/CS	–	–	iti še-kin-ku$_5$	–	Adab	Expenditure of food: barley flour, oil, fish and sheep for meat.	42×33×16
320	1952/21	CS	–	[...]	[...]	[...]	Adab	Allocation of barley.	26×25×11
321	2191/35	CS	–	–	–	–	Adab?	Account of barley.	22×20×14
322	2365/1	CS	–	–	–	–	Adab	Barley.	40×35×15
323	2365/2	CS	–	–	iti mu-tir	–	Adab	Barley for bread and beer.	43×38×16
324	2365/3	CS	–	–	iti a$_2$-ki-ti	–	Adab	Barley for bread and beer.	37×34×17
325	2365/4	CS	–	–	iti šu-ĝar	–	Adab	Account of barley flour.	35×32×14
326	2365/5	CS	–	–	–	–	Adab	Receipt of barley.	32×29×13

327	2365/6	CS	–	–	iti eše$_2$-gar$_3$-šu-ĝar	–	Adab	Account of barley flour.	27×25×12
328	2365/7	CS	–	–	–	–	Adab	Barley, processed emmer, groats.	37×29×15
329	2365/8	CS	–	–	iti ezen ^{d}Nin-mug	u$_4$ 12 al-zal	Adab	Barley, emmer flour and peas.	44×40×17
330	2365/9	CS	–	–	–	–	Adab	Processed emmer and peas.	38×34×16
331	2365/10	CS	–	–	–	–	Adab	Barley in connection to a merchant.	32×28×13
332	2365/11	CS	–	–	–	–	Adab	Issue of barley.	33×31×14
333	2365/12	CS	–	–	–	–	Adab	Account of malt.	29×26×11
334	2365/13	CS/LS	–	–	–	–	Adab	Allocation of barley flour and groats.	75×43×18
335	2642	CS	–	–	–	–	Adab?	Allocation of barley.	42×35×15
336	4190	CS	–	–	–	–	Adab?	Account of barley measured by the large *gur*.	46×40×17
337	4201	CS	–	–	–	–	Adab?	Inventory of barley and emmer available in a field and a storehouse.	49×38×21
338	4222	CS/LS	–	–	–	–	Adab	Receipt of groats.	62×42×24
339	4240a	CS	–	–	–	–	Adab	Account of barley and emmer.	40*×46×20*
340	4240b	CS	–	–	–	–	Adab	Offering of grain to gods.	58*×46×22
341	4249	CS/LS	–	–	iti še-gur$_x$ (|ŠE.ŠE|.KIN)-am$_3$	–	Adab	Receipt and arrears of barley.	64×41×17
342	4258	CS	–	–	–	–	Adab?	Account of grain and grain products with price relations in barley and silver.	64*×44×18
343	4192	CS	–	–	iti ĝa$_2$-udu-ur$_4$	–	Adab	Expenditure of beer.	67×40×18

344	4196	CS	–	–	–	u_4 7	Adab?	Allocation of bread and beer.	56★×47×21
345	4197	CS		–	–	u_4 2-kam	Adab?	Allocation of bread and beer.	67★×45×23
346	4248	CS	–	–	–	–	Adab	Allocation of bread and beer.	92×47×21
347	4252	CS	–	–	–	u_4 3-kam	Adab	Account of bread and beer.	70×46×20
348	4256	CS	–	–	–	–	Adab	Account of bread and beer.	80×44×21
349	2191/28	CS	–	–	–	–	Adab	Inventory of dead cattle.	30×27×12
350	2191/29	MS/CS	–	–	–	–	Adab	Account of sheep and goats.	48×36×17
351	2301	CS/LS	–	–	–	–	Adab	Delivery of a goat.	26×25×11
352	2365/14	CS	–	–	–	–	Adab	Account of sheep.	37×27×13
353	4076	CS	–	–	iti šu-ĝar	–	Adab	Sheep.	20×19×10
354	4203	CS	–	–	iti ni_3-$^{ĝeš}kiri_6$	–	Adab	Allocation of sheep's heads and hearts to high priests and priestesses.	66×46×20
355	4257	CS	–	–	–	–	Adab?	Account of sheep and meat.	65★×44×20
356	4748	CS	–	–	–	–	Adab	Offering of sheep to gods and temples.	106×76×32
357	4268	MS/CS	–	–	iti mu-tir	–	Adab	Allocation of sandals.	62×34×16
358	4228	CS	–	–	–	–	Adab?	Account of lard and oil.	35×30×14
359	4264	CS	–	–	–	–	Adab?	Expenditure of agricultural implements.	40×27×14
360	4206	CS	Naram-Suen	*in* 1 mu *A-zu-ḫi-nim*^{ki}	–	–	Adab	Account of gold and silver in connection to high dignitaries.	103★×105×26
361	4223	CS/LS		–	–	–	Adab	Offering of sheep and bread.	75×44★×21

362	4255	CS	–	–	–	–	Adab	Account of metals, textiles and wool as presents.	77×39×19
363	4213	CS	–	–	–	–	Adab	Allocation of unidentified goods to temple personnel.	100×75×25
364	4273	ES	–	–	–	–	Isin	Receipt of miscellaneous goods.	52×55×21
365	4274	ES/MS	–	–	–	–	Isin?	Witnessed document concerning silver.	59×49×25
366	4200	CS	"Private archive"	–	–	–	Isin	Weighing out of silver to a number of individuals.	75*×38×19
367	4205	CS	"Private archive"	–	–	–	Isin	Purchase of land.	91×67×23
368	4217	CS/LS	"Private archive"(?)	–	–	–	Isin? (or Adab?)	Inventory of the treasure of a person.	73×41×20
369	4234	CS	"Private archive"	–	–	–	Isin	Legal document of uncertain nature concerning silver.	70*×40×20
370	4239	CS	"Private archive"	–	–	–	Isin	Witnessed document. Contents uncertain.	67×42×19
371	4242	CS	"Private archive"	–	–	–	Isin	Purchase of a field	57*×60×22
372	4245	CS	"Private archive"	–	–	–	Isin	Self-sale into slavery.	92×50×21
373	4246	CS	"Private archive"	–	–	–	Isin	Purchase of miscellaneous goods.	44*×42×17
374	4247	CS	"Private archive"	–	–	–	Isin	Witnessed document recording a purchase(?) of mostly metal objects.	58*×40×21
375	4260	CS	"Private archive"	–	–	–	Isin	Contesting the purchase of a garden resolved by the chief temple-administrator of Isin in the temple in Ninisina.	50*×48×22

376	4265	CS	"Private archive"	–	–	–	Isin	Purchase of immovable property.	100×72×24
377	4266	MS	"Private archive"	–	–	–	Isin	Witnessed receipt of barley and silver.	50×35×14
378	4270	CS	"Private archive"	–	–	–	Isin	Purchase of a house.	74×42×20
379	2466	ED IIIb	–	–	–	–	Umma region	Account of workers (*ĝuruš*) recorded in groups.	61×62×20
380	3791/3	ED IIIb	–	–	–	–	Umma region?	Account of personnel.	42×45×15
381	3791/8	ED IIIb	–	–	–	–	Umma region	Craftsmen of the palace in teams with their supervisors.	42*×43×20
382	2191/31	ED IIIb	–	–	–	–	Umma region	Inventory of land in possession of elders.	46×52×15
383	2661/1	ED IIIb	–	–	–	–	Umma region	Account of land.	60×65×17
384	2661/2	ED IIIb	–	–	–	–	Umma region	Account of land.	66×72×21
385	2824	ED IIIb	Me-an-ne$_2$-du$_{10}$ ensi$_2$	[...]	[...]	[...]	Umma region	Account of land.	165×185×33
386	3791/11	ED IIIb	–	–	–	–	Umma region	Account of land.	42×45×15
387	3791/14	ED IIIb	(Me-an-ne$_2$-du$_{10}$ ensi$_2$)	30 la$_2$ 3 mu	iti 8	–	Umma region	Account of land.	68×73×23
388	3791/15	ED IIIb	–	–	–	–	Umma region	Account of land.	84×83×24
389	3791/18	ED IIIb	(Me-an-ne$_2$-du$_{10}$ ensi$_2$)	30 la$_2$ 3 mu	iti 8	–	Umma region	Account of land.	41×44×16
390	3791/19	ED IIIb	–	... mu	iti ...	–	Umma region	Account of land.	69×56×23
391	3791/23	ED IIIb	–	–	–	–	Umma region	Account of land.	42×37×17

392	3791/27	ED IIIb	-	… mu	iti …	-	Umma region	Account of land.	64×70×19
393	3791/28	ED IIIb	Silim-^{d}Utu saĝĝa	26 mu	iti 13	-	Umma region	Account of land.	110×117×38
394	3791/31	ED IIIb	Šubur ensi$_2$	30$^?$ la$_2$ 2 mu	-	-	Umma region	Account of land.	53×59×20
395	3824	ED IIIb	-	-	-	-	Umma region	Account of land in connection to silver issued.	34×34×22
396	1952/6	ED/ES	-	-	-	-	Umma region	Allocation of barley flour.	57*×60×16
397	2191/7	ED IIIb	-	16 mu	13 iti	-	Umma region	Delivery of bread to the palace.	30×33×18
398	3791/1	ED IIIb	(Me-an-ne$_2$-du$_{10}$ ensi$_2$)	30 la$_2$ 2 mu	iti 4	-	Umma region	Allocation of barley.	57*×47×17
399	3791/9	ED IIIb	-	-	-	-	Umma region	Account of bread, beer and beer ingredients.	49×43×14
400	3791/13	ED IIIb	-	-	-	-	Umma region	Account of barley.	49×57×18
401	3791/21	ED IIIb	-	-	-	-	Umma region	Account of barley.	45×50×16
402	3791/4	ED IIIb	-	[n+?] 3 mu	-	-	Umma region	Contribution of sheep.	38×31×12
403	3791/5	ED IIIb	(Me-an-ne$_2$-du$_{10}$ ensi$_2$)	30 la$_2$ 3 mu	iti 7	-	Umma region	Account of sheared sheep.	53×60×22
404	3791/7	ED IIIb	-	25 mu	iti 11	-	Umma region	Account of sheep.	34×35×17
405	3791/10	ED IIIb	-	…mu	iti …	-	Umma region	Account of sheep.	48×40×20
406	3791/12	ED IIIb	Nagar-ša$_3$ (saĝĝa; Me-an-ne$_2$-du$_{10}$ ensi$_2$)	30 la$_2$ 2 mu	4 iti	-	Umma region	Account of sheep and goats.	39×41×18
407	3791/16	ED IIIb	Me-an-ne$_2$-du$_{10}$ (ensi$_2$)	30 la$_2$ 1 mu	iti 4	-	Umma region	Account of sheep and goats.	67×57×27
408	3791/17	ED IIIb	-	-	-	-	Umma region	Account of plow oxen.	58×51×17

409	3791/22	ED IIIb	Nagar-ša$_3$ saĝĝa (Me-an-ne$_2$-du$_{10}$ ensi$_2$)	30 la$_2$ 2 mu	11 iti	-	Umma region	Delivery of dead sheep to the palace.	43*×49×15
410	3791/24	ED IIIb	(Me-an-ne$_2$-du$_{10}$ ensi$_2$)	30 la$_2$ 2 mu	iti 11	-	Umma region	Account of sheep, ready for plucking or dead, and of hides.	86*×69×22
411	3791/25	ED IIIb	(Me-an-ne$_2$-du$_{10}$ ensi$_2$)	30 la$_2$ 2 mu	iti 6	-	Umma region	Account of sheep.	72×62×16
412	3791/29	ED IIIb	-	-	-	-	Umma region	Account of sheep(?).	60×45×20*
413	3791/30	ED IIIb	(Me-an-ne$_2$-du$_{10}$ ensi$_2$)	30 la$_2$ 3 mu	7 iti	-	Umma region	Account of sheep.	50×56×21
414	3791/32	ED IIIb	(Me-an-ne$_2$-du$_{10}$ ensi$_2$)	30 la$_2$ 3 mu	-	-	Umma region	Account of sheep and hides.	73×65×22
415	3791/33	ED IIIb	(Me-an-ne$_2$-du$_{10}$ ensi$_2$)	[10+] 16 mu	iti 12	-	Umma region	Account of sheep and hides.	85×79×27
416	4929	ED IIIb	-	-	-	-	Umma region	Account of sheep.	67×45×23
417	3791/6	ED IIIb	-	20 la$_2$ 3 mu	-	-	Umma region	Account of loans in barley.	92×94×29
418	3791/26	ED IIIb	-	30 la$_2$ 1 mu	-	-	Umma region	Loan of barley and metal.	62×65×22
419	3794	ED IIIb	-	-	-	-	Umma region	Account of silver and sheep.	67×71×23
420	3796	ED IIIb	-	-	-	-	Umma region	Inventory of property and goods.	73*×81×22
421	3810	ED IIIb	-	-	-	-	Umma region	Inventory of property and goods.	73×79×21
422	3797	ED IIIb	-	[...]	[...]	-	Umma region	Account of silver, sheep and goats.	66×67×28
423	2247	ED IIIb	(Me-an-ne$_2$-du$_{10}$ ensi$_2$)	30 la$_2$ 2 mu	iti 12	-	Umma region	Delivery of ropes and a net.	22×24×12

424	2249	ED IIIb	(Me-an-ne$_2$-du$_{10}$ ensi$_2$)	30 la$_2$ 3 mu	iti 6	–	Umma region	Account of covers and a plow for ox teams.	57×60×22
425	4259	ED IIIb	–	–	–	–	Umma region	Account of some unnamed goods.	57×48×20
426	1952/2	ES	*Su$_4$-ru-us$_2$*-GI ensi$_2$	[n+] 3 mu	–	–	Umma region	Sale of a house.	73★×73★×22
427	1952/3	ES	(*Su$_4$-ru-us$_2$*-GI ensi$_2$)	10 mu	3 iti	–	Umma region	Sale of a house.	71×78×22
428	1952/12	MS	–	–	–	–	Umma region?	Record contesting a slave purchase.	50×37×20
429	1952/13	ES/MS	–	1 mu	10 la$_2$ 1 iti	–	Umma region	Contesting slave status.	44×36×17
430	1952/1	ES/MS	–	4 mu	10 iti	–	Umma region	Withdrawal of workers (saĝ-dub, šeš-sur$_x$-ra).	83×83★×27
431	1952/4	ES	–	–	–	–	Umma region	Withdrawal of people who "went to the city."	57★×55★×21
432	1952/5	MS/CS	–	3 mu	11 iti	–	Umma region	Transfer of craftsmen.	51★×64×22
433	2191/13	ES/MS	–	–	8 iti	–	Umma region	Record of two persons residing with another.	34×26×15
434	2191/38	ES/MS	–	–	–	–	Umma region?	Account of eren$_2$-people.	42×30×17
435	1952/7	MS	–	[...]	[...]	–	Umma region	Expenditure of emmer to a number of individuals.	58×57×20
436	1952/9	ES/MS	–	4 mu	13 iti	–	Umma region	Allocation of barley flour to individuals native to Zabala.	47×50×18
437	1952/10	ES/MS	–	[...]	[...]	–	Umma region	Account of large amounts of barley.	47×51×19
438	1952/28	ES	–	5 mu	7 iti	–	Umma region	Receipt of barley.	29×24×12
439	1952/31	ES	–	[...] mu	iti 7	–	Umma region	Delivery and receipt of beer and bread.	34×29×12

440	1952/16a	MS	–	[...]	[...]	–	Umma region	Record of oxen living with a herdsman.	17*×37×15
441	1952/17	ES/MS	–	3 mu	iti 7	–	Umma region	Account of sheep and wool.	46×40×20
442	1952/20	MS	–	6 mu	10 iti	–	Umma region	Expenditure of hides.	33×27×13
443	1952/15	ES	*Su$_4$-ru-us$_2$*-GI	6 mu	1? iti	–	Umma region	Allocation of textiles to high-ranking persons from Nippur and Irisaĝrig by the governor *Šurus-kēn* in the temple Eĝidru.	44×31×15
444	1952/25	ES	–	5 mu	iti 10	–	Umma region	Account of textiles belonging to a scribe available with a fuller.	26*×23×15
445	1952/27	ES	–	[...]	[...]	–	Umma region	Account of a *maš-dari'a*-contribution in textiles.	26*×23×14
446	1952/29	ES	–	6 mu	iti [...]	–	Umma region	Allocation of a garment to a *karkid*-woman.	27×22×11
447	1952/30	ES	–	4 mu	iti 5+n	–	Umma region	Receipt of garments by Subareans at the outlet of Zabum.	24×21×10
448	1952/47	ES	–	5 mu	2 iti	–	Umma region	Account of textiles mentioning a king's wife.	25*×28×13
449	2191/14	ES/MS	–	5 mu	10 la$_2$ 1 iti	–	Umma region	Allocation of textiles.	30×24×12
450	1952/16b	ES/MS	–	[...]	[...]	–	Umma region	Arrears of metal objects.	22*×37×15
451	1952/26	ES	–	5 mu	iti 2	–	Umma region	Weighing of copper.	24×24×11
452	1952/32	ES	–	5 mu	[...]	–	Umma region	Receipt of silver.	30×24×11
453	2191/15	ES	–	5 mu	10 iti	–	Umma region	Account of arrows.	27×22×12
454	2227/1	ES	–	7 mu	iti 12	–	Umma region	Delivery of weapons.	30*×29×15

455	1952/48	ES	–	6 mu	3 iti	–	Umma region	Delivery of beams to the palace.	27×24×11
456	2191/10	ES	–	6 mu	6 iti	–	Umma region	Delivery of timber from the house of the governor in Agade with its subsequent receipt in a workshop.	31×26×11
457	2191/30	ES	–	[…] mu	6 iti	–	Umma region	Account of bricks.	52*×55×17
458	1952/11	ES/MS	–	[…]	8 iti	–	Umma region	Expenditure of rings and textiles in connection to a high-profile mission at various localities.	58×53×20
459	2191/9	ES	–	2[+n] mu	11 iti	–	Umma region	List of luxurious goods sent by a governor of Subir.	41×34×16
460	2191/34	ES	–	[...]	[...]	–	Umma region	Expenditure of miscellaneous commodities.	57×48×21
461	5048/17	MS/CS	–	mu 3?	7 iti	–	Umma region	Receipt of baskets(?).	24×28×12
462	2191/4	ES/MS	–	[10] la_2 1 mu	2 iti	–	Umma region	Inspection of uncertain goods ($AŠ_2$-SA).	41×36×17
463	2191/12	ES	–	1 mu	iti 7	–	Umma region	Arrears of some material measured by weight.	27×23×16
464	2044	CS	–	–	–	–	Umma region	Letter concerning the transfer of barley and allocation of land.	96×48×20
465	1952/18	CS	–	–	5 [iti]	–	Umma region	Adding two persons to a list.	44×39×18
466	1952/19	CS/LS	–	7 mu	5 iti	–	Umma region	Account of baked bricks.	25×23×10
467	5091	ED IIIb	–	–	–	–	Ebla	Account of garments.	45*×50×13*
468	4544	CS	"Mesag archive"	–	–	–	Sagub	List of women not present at work.	62×34×18

469	1718	ED IIIa	–	–	–	–	Šuruppak (Fara)	Purchase of a field.	90×93×20
470	2725	ED IIIa	–	–	–	–	Šuruppak (Fara)	Purchase of a house.	100×103×18
471	2522	ED I–II	–	–	–	–	unclear	Contents uncertain.	60×56×25
472	2523	ED I–II	–	–	–	–	unclear	Account of personnel.	73*×75×32
473	4928	ED I–II	–	–	–	–	unclear (Ur?)	Account of sheep.	60×57×26
474	1384	ED IIIa	–	–	–	–	unclear	Account of sown and wet land.	60×60×25
475	2076	ED IIIa	–	–	–	–	unclear (Abu Ṣālabīkh?)	Assignation of workers (*ĝuruš*) to a number of professionals.	58×57×17
476	2190	ED IIIa/b	–	–	–	–	unclear	Account of miscellaneous commodities.	67×70×26
477	2899	ED IIIa	–	–	–	–	unclear (Lagaš region?)	Stone tablet recording an allocation of fleece and copper.	85×82×25
478	3790/33	ED IIIa	–	–	–	–	unclear	List of brewers.	61×62×26
479	4746	ED IIIa	–	–	–	–	unclear (Umma region?)	List of personnel.	72×73×28
480	3791/20	ED IIIa	–	–	–	–	unclear (Umma region?)	Account of textiles and other goods.	60×59×18
481	4735	ED IIIa	–	–	–	–	unclear (Umma region?)	Delivery of silver to the palace.	52×53*×26
482	5008	ED IIIa	–	–	–	–	unclear	List of personnel.	74×76×29
483	3825	ED/ES	–	–	–	–	unclear	Expenditure of barley as fodder for animals and allocations to workers and childen.	39×40×18
484	1952/51	ES	–	–	–	–	unclear	Account of reeds.	48×45×26

485	1952/23	MS/CS	"Northern Deliveries" file	–	–	–	unclear	Delivery of food to Gasur.	46×38×17
486	1952/44	MS/CS	"Northern Deliveries" file	–	–	–	unclear	Delivery and receipt of grain at Keš(?).	44×38×17
487	1952/24	MS	–	–	–	–	unclear	Account of butter, oil, lard and wine.	28×22×14
488	2191/36	MS	–	–	–	–	unclear	Cumulative record of various transactions with silver.	66×60×19
489	2191/37	MS	–	–	–	–	unclear	Weighing of wool.	20×21×12
490	1952/49	CS	"ANIza"	–	iti za-lul	–	unclear	Receipt of barley.	22×20×11
491	1952/50	CS	"ANIza"	–	iti ba-ḫi-ir-EGIR	–	unclear	Expenditure of barley.	23×22×10
492	4269/1	CS	"Qa'u"	–	–	–	unclear	Barley as interest on a loan.	34×30×13
493	4269/3	CS	"Qa'u"	–	–	–	unclear	Account of barley flour.	42×37×16
494	4269/2	CS	"Qa'u"	–	–	–	unclear	Assignation of female workers.	31×30×15
495	4269/4	CS	"Qa'u"	–	–	u$_4$ 2-kam	unclear	Allocation of barley to female workers mentioning their overseers.	40×32×14
496	4219	CS/LS		–	–	–	unclear	Account of fields.	91×67×23
497	4226	CS/LS	–	–	–	–	unclear	Account of fields.	83×64×26
498	4253	CS/LS	–	–	–	–	unclear	Account of fields.	88×48×21
499	4241	CS	–	–	–	–	unclear	Assignation of workers (*ĝuruš*) to a number of individuals.	79×44×19
500	1893	CS	–	–	–	–	unclear	Account of silver as i$_3$-bi$_2$-za.	66×62×20
501	1952/14	CS	–	–	–	–	unclear (Umma region?)	Account of beads (jewelry).	45★×43×17

502	2191/11	CS	–	–	–	–	unclear	Grain as payment for various purposes.	34×32×12
503	2251	CS	–	–	–	–	unclear	Expenditure of emmer on the occasion of the festival of Dumuzi.	24×21×10
504	2252	CS	–	–	–	–	unclear	Account of regular food delivery.	24×22×10
505	2253	CS	–	–	–	–	unclear (Umma region?)	Account of beer.	20×18×9
506	4218	CS	–	–	–	–	unclear	Expenditure of barley.	65×46×17
507	4230	CS	–	–	–	–	unclear (Ĝirsu or Umma?)	Calculation of unnamed commodity, probably grain, in connection to a temple.	49×37×17
508	4231	CS	–	–	–	–	unclear	Allocation of bread.	59×39×17
509	4427	CS	–	–	–	–	unclear	Expenditure of beer.	70×46×22
510	1952/22	CS	–	–	–	–	unclear	Expenditure of wool.	29×27×11
511	2045	CS	–	–	–	–	unclear	Account of animals classified as males, females and sucklings.	75×46×19
512	2191/5	CS		–	–	–	unclear	Account of the yield of an onion plot.	31×26×10
513	2191/6	CS		–	–	–	unclear	Account of the yield of an onion plot.	33×29×13
514	2191/3	CS	–	–	–	–	unclear (Umma region?)	Account of the ingredients for five jars of aromatic oil.	56×38×15
515	4220a	LS	–	–	–	–	unclear (Umma region?)	Expenditure of ropes for yokes measured by weight.	93×50×20
516	4220b	ES	–	–	–	–	unclear	Account of goats.	–×–×–

517	2191/1	CS	–	–	–	–	unclear	Letter-order concerning a boat.	35×32×15
518	3793	ED IIIb	–	–	–	–	unclear	Exercise.	54×55×24
519	1902	ED/ES	–	–	–	–	unclear	School tablet recording fruit trees and sweets.	45×48×10
520	1952/46	Sargonic	–	–	–	–	unclear	School exercise concerning cattle.	38×37×21
521	2191/18	ES	–	–	–		unclear (Adab?)	Exercise. Personal names and syllabic values.	65×59×25

Concordance of Tablet Numbers

MS no.	Text no.	MS no.	Text no.	MS no.	Text no.
1384	474	1952/40	30	2181/22	57
1718	469	1952/41	20	2181/23	58
1893	500	1952/42	32	2181/24	59
1902	519	1952/43	197	2181/25	60
1952/1	430	1952/44	486	2181/26	61
1952/2	426	1952/45	31	2181/27	62
1952/3	427	1952/46	520	2181/28	63
1952/4	431	1952/47	448	2181/29	64
1952/5	432	1952/48	455	2181/30	65
1952/6	396	1952/49	490	2181/31	66
1952/7	435	1952/50	491	2181/32	67
1952/9	436	1952/51	484	2181/33	68
1952/10	437	2044	464	2181/34	69
1952/11	458	2045	511	2181/35	70
1952/12	428	2076	475	2181/36	71
1952/13	429	2109/1	275	2181/37	72
1952/14	501	2109/2	276	2181/38	73
1952/15	443	2109/3	277	2181/39	74
1952/16a	440	2109/4	278	2181/40	75
1952/16b	450	2181/1	36	2181/41	76
1952/17	441	2181/2	37	2181/42	77
1952/18	465	2181/3	38	2181/43	78
1952/19	466	2181/4	39	2181/44	79
1952/20	442	2181/5	40	2181/45	80
1952/21	320	2181/6	41	2181/46	81
1952/22	510	2181/7	42	2181/47	82
1952/23	485	2181/8	43	2190	476
1952/24	487	2181/9	44	2191/1	517
1952/25	444	2181/10	45	2191/2	108
1952/26	451	2181/11	46	2191/3	514
1952/27	445	2181/12	47	2191/4	462
1952/28	438	2181/13	48	2191/5	512
1952/29	446	2181/14	49	2191/6	513
1952/30	447	2181/15	50	2191/7	397
1952/31	439	2181/16	51	2191/8	109
1952/32	452	2181/17	52	2191/9	459
1952/33	1	2181/18	53	2191/10	456
1952/34	29	2181/19	54	2191/11	502
1952/35	243	2181/20	55	2191/12	463
1952/36	196	2181/21	56	2191/13	433

MS no.	Text no.	MS no.	Text no.	MS no.	Text no.
4208	264	4243	292	4277/2	284
4209	295	4244	313	4277/3	285
4210	307	4245	372	4277/4	286
4211	308	4246	373	4277/5	287
4212	311	4247	374	4327	267
4213	363	4248	346	4427	509
4214	296	4249	341	4450	305
4216	312	4250	19	4544	468
4217	368	4252	347	4728	27
4218	506	4253	498	4735	481
4219	496	4255	362	4745	8
4220a	515	4256	348	4746	479
4220b	516	4257	355	4748	356
4221	314	4258	342	4754	310
4222	338	4259	425	4761	268
4223	361	4260	375	4928	473
4224	291	4261	266	4929	416
4225	26	4262	309	4999	107
4226	497	4264	359	5001	269
4228	358	4265	376	5002	28
4229	303	4266	377	5003	270
4230	507	4268	357	5004	271
4231	508	4269/1	492	5008	482
4232	297	4269/2	494	5018	234
4233	265	4269/3	493	5019	235
4234	369	4269/4	495	5020	236
4235	255	4270	378	5021	237
4237	298	4271	256	5033	170
4238	319	4272	293	5047/2	238
4239	370	4273	364	5047/3	239
4240a	339	4274	365	5048/13	18
4240b	340	4275	294	5048/17	461
4241	499	4276	304	5091	467
4242	371	4277/1	283		

Part 1 – Documents from Adab

1.1 – Early Dynastic IIIb and Early Sargonic Tablets

1.1.1 – Legal

No. 1 – MS 1952/33

Sale of a house, Early Dynastic IIIb, Adab.

obv. i	[n e$_2$ sar …]	[house of x space]
	[PN$_1$=še$_3$]	[from PN]
	[PN$_2$=e]	[PN]
	[e-še$_3$-sa$_{10}$]	[has purchased].
	⸢ni$_3$⸣-[…]	…
	x […]	…

	e$_2$ [...]	the house ...
	ni$_3$-⸢sa$_{10}^{?}$⸣-[bi$^{?}$]	[its?] price
	[break]	...
ii	[break]	...
	[...] ⸢x⸣	...
	[n] ⸢še⸣-gunu$_3$ ⸢sila$_3$⸣	... *sila* of speckled barley;
	[10] ⸢i$_3$⸣ sila$_3$	[10] *sila* of oil;
	[n] ⸢x⸣ [...]	...
iii	[break]	...
	10 ⸢ninda⸣ ma-na	10 minas of bread;
	10 i$_3$ sila$_3$	10 *sila* of oil;
	10 ti udu	10 sheep's ribs;
	10 sa nisig	10 bundles of greens:
	Da-ti-na	(for) Datina;
	10 ninda ma-na	10 mina of bread;
iv	[break]	...
	10 ⸢ninda ma-na⸣	10 mina of bread;
	10 i$_3$ ⸢sila$_3$⸣	10 *sila* of oil;
	10 ur$_2$ ⸢udu⸣	10 sheep's legs;
	10 sa ⸢nisig⸣	10 bundles of greens:
	A-ḫa-⸢tum⸣	(for) *'Aḫatum*.
	10 ninda ma-na	10 mina of bread;
	1 i$_3$ sila$_3$	1 *sila* of oil;
	1 ti udu	1 sheep's rib;
v	[break]	...
	20 ninda	20 breads:
	Ur-gu	(for) Urgu,
	nu-eš$_3$	the *nu'eš*-priest
	^{d}Iškur	of (the god) Iškur.
vi	[break]	...
	⸢20 ninda⸣	20 breads:
	[...]	[for PN]
	simug	the smith.
	20 ninda	20 breads:
	Pu$_3$-su-GI	(for) *Pūšu-kēn*;
	20 ninda	20 breads:
	NE-NE	(for) NENE;
	20 ninda	20 breads;
	1 i$_3$ [sila$_3$]	1 [*sila*] of oil;
vii	[mostly destroyed]	...
viii	[break]	...
	2 ⸢še-gunu$_3$ sila$_3$⸣	2 *sila* of speckled barley;
	1 sa [nisig]	1 bundle of [greens]:
	Ur$_5$-⸢du$_2$⸣	(for) Urdu,
	SIG$_7$	*the SIG-official/priest*;

	[break]	…
	[n] ⸢ninda⸣	x breads:
	[2 lines broken]	…
rev. i	[…]-⸢x⸣	…
	60 ninda	60 breads;
	1 dug	1 jar (of beer):
	An-da-ti-le	(for) Andatile,
	ugula-e$_2$	the overseer of the household;
	60 ninda	60 breads;
	1 i$_3$ umbin×LU	1 *umbin*-measure of oil;
	1 dug	1 jar (of beer):
	Teš$_2$-teš$_2$ sukkal	(for) Tešteš, the secretary;
	60 ninda	60 breads;
	1 i$_3$ umbin×LU	1 *umbin*-measure of oil;
	1 dug	1 jar (of beer):
	niĝir-gal	(for) the chief herald;
	60 ninda	60 breads;
	1 dug	1 jar (of beer);
	1 eštub^{ku6}	1 carp;
	4 še-gunu$_3$ sila$_3$	4 *sila* of speckled barley:
	Ba-za	(for) Baza,
	pisaĝ-dub	the archivist;
	40 ninda	40 breads;
	½ i$_3$ umbin×LU	½ *umbin*-measure of oil;
	2 še-gunu$_3$ sila$_3$	2 *sila* of speckled barley;
	1 ku$_6$	1 fish:
ii	Il$_2$	(for) Il(a),
	dub-sar	the scribe;
	10 ninda	10 breads:
	Lugal-agrig-zi	(for) Lugal-agrigzi,
	dumu Pu$_3$-lu$_5$	son of Pulu,
	engar-maḫ	the chief agricultural manager;
	30 ninda	30 breads;
	1 i$_3$ sila$_3$	1 *sila* of oil;
	1 dug	1 jar (of beer):
	Ma-ma-ḫir-su	(for) *Ma(n)-māḫiršu*,
	niĝir-sila	the street herald.
	(blank)	
iii	Ša$_3$-lu$_2$-na-ba	Šalunaba,
	kinda-gal	the chief barber;
	Igi-zi-bar-ra	Igizibara,
	saĝĝa e$_2$-SAR	the chief temple-administrator of the E-SAR (temple);
	An-da-ti-le	Andatile,
	ugula-e$_2$	the overseer of the household;
	Teš$_2$-teš$_2$	Tešteš,

	sukkal ni$_3$-kas$_4$	the secretary of ...;
	En-za-ra-nu-gi$_4$	Enzara-nugi,
	niĝir-gal	the chief herald;
	Ba-za	Baza,
	pisaĝ-dub	the archivist;
	Šudu$_3$-Utu niĝir e$_2$-gal	Šudu-Utu, the herald of the palace;
	Lugal-ša$_3$-su$_{13}$ SIG$_7$	Lugal-šasu, *the SIG-official/priest*;
	Ur-gu	Urgu,
	nu-eš$_3$	the *nu'eš*-priest;
	⌜Ur-e$_2$-igi⌝-nim	Ur-E'iginim,
iv	simug-gal	the chief smith;
	Ma-ma-ḫir-su	*Ma(n)-māḫiršu*,
	niĝir	the herald:
	lu$_2$-ki-inim-ma-bi-me	they are its witnesses.
	(blank)	
v	Na-na	Nana,
	Zadim$^?$-nun-ne$_2$	(to) ...nune
	in-na-sa$_{10}$	has paid to him (for the house).
	gag-bi eĝar$_x$(SIG$_4$)-ra ab-du$_3$	Its nail has been driven into the wall.
	i$_3$-bi za$_3$-ge	Its oil on the side
	ab-ak	has been spread.
	inim-bi al-til	This matter is settled.
	(blank)	
vi	(blank)	

This sale contract is remarkable in many ways. It mentions three different categories of heralds. The "chief herald" (niĝir-gal) appears without a name, apparently because there was no need to mention it, since there was only one chief herald in the city. The other two heralds are the "street herald" (niĝir-sila) and the "herald of the palace" (niĝir e$_2$-gal). Another feature is that the text uses verbal forms with the prefix chain a=b(i$_2$)-. Lastly, the senior officials of the well-known Adab temple e$_2$-SAR. The reading of the last sign in the temple name that appears in later texts as E$_2$-maḫ "Lofty house" is uncertain. See remark in Such-Gutiérrez 2005–2006: 10 fn. 95. Besides the reading E$_2$-sar, another possibility is E$_2$-sig$_x$ "The Green House." For SAR = sig$_x$, see Schrakamp 2015b.

obv. i 6: 1 sila$_3$ is unlikely here since a commodity should be placed between the numeral and the measure.

obv. iv 3': See CUSAS 12 p. 150 l. 32.

obv. v 3': See SCTRAH, p. 78 with further references for this priestly title.

obv. vi 5': See CUSAS 11 no. 50 obv. i 4 for probably the same individual.

obv. viii 4', rev. iii 14: For SIG$_7$ = si$_{12}$-(a) "blind (worker)," see SCTRAH p. 209 with further references. The presence of such a laborer in the present context is suspicious. Alternatively, SIG$_7$ may refer to some variety of priest or official.

rev. i 7: UMBIN×LU is the Adab variant of the sign UMBIN(LAK289). Umbin was a capacity measure used for oil. See SCTRAH p. 112 and ELTS p. 54a bottom. The latter publication equates one *umbin* with two *sila*. Due to the presence of 1 *sila* of oil (rev. ii 8) instead of "½ *umbin* of oil," and ½ *umbin* of oil (rev. i 21) instead of "1 *sila* oil," this metrological interpretation seems unlikely in the present text.

rev. ii 10: The name is Akkadian: *Ma(n)-māḫir-šu* "Who is his rival?." The same individual appears in two other legal documents below, Nos. 2 and 4.

rev. iii 8: The interpretation of ni$_3$-kas$_4$ is uncertain. See the commentary to text No. 283 rev. i 6.

rev. iii 13: The interpretation of PU$_3$.UD as Šudu$_3$-Utu is tentative. Another possibility would be to interpret the name as Akkadian **Pū-Šamšim*(UTU) "(By) the mouth (= word) of the Sun-god."

rev. v 2: Cf. BIN 8 nos. 67 obv. iv 6, 68 obv. v 1, recording the same name. There, the sign in question is probably ZADIM, although a personal name *Zadim-nun-ne$_2$ makes little sense. In our case, the sign in question looks like a ZADIM with an extra vertical wedge at the end:

It might be a narrowly written nita$_2$(ARAD). Cf. also Ĝiri$_2$-nun-ne$_2$-si in No. 6 obv. v' 12'.

rev. v 4–5: Cf. Wilcke 2007: 87–88 for the same formula in Early Dynastic IIIb Ĝirsu with minor differences in the choice of verbal prefixes (bi$_2$-du$_3$ and bi$_2$-ak). See ELTS pp. 23, 44, 240, on the peg driven into the wall of a sold house, a ceremony performed by the main seller or by a herald. Cf. ib. p. 241 for i$_3$...ak "spreading of oil." The usual writing for "wall" is e$_2$-ĝar$_8$(SIG$_4$). However, this and the following documents suggest that the sign SIG$_4$ alone had the meaning "wall" in ED IIIb Adab, thus requiring a reading eĝar$_x$.

No. 2 – MS 2464

Sale of a house, Early Dynastic IIIb (governor Ursaĝ-Keš), Adab.

obv. i	10 ninda	10 breads;
	1 tu$_7$ sila$_3$	1 *sila* of stew:
	Adab^{ki}-ki-gal-la	(for) Adabkigala;
	15 ninda	15 breads;
	1 i$_3$ sila$_3$	1 *sila* of oil;
	1 tu$_7$ sila$_3$	1 *sila* of stew:
	Ama-a-zu$_5$(NINDA$_2$×ME)	Ama'azu;
	10 ninda 1 i$_3$ sila$_3$	10 breads, 1 *sila* of oil:
	Ur-tur	Urtur;
	10 ninda	10 breads;
ii	1 i$_3$ sila$_3$	1 *sila* of oil:
	Nin-ig-gal	Niniggal,
	gala	the cult-singer;
	10 ninda 1 tu$_7$ sila$_3$	10 breads, 1 *sila* of stew:
	E$_2$-da-ḫul$_2$	Edaḫul;
	10 ninda	10 breads;
	1 tu$_7$ sila$_3$	1 *sila* of stew:
	Muš-tur	Muštur;
	10 ninda	10 breads;
	1 tu$_7$ sila$_3$	1 *sila* of stew;
	1 i$_3$ sila$_3$	1 *sila* of oil:
	Lugal-uš-su$_x$(MUŠ)	Lugal-uššu,
	nu-kiri$_6$	the gardener;
iii	10 ninda 1 i$_3$ sila$_3$	10 breads, 1 *sila* of oil;
	1 tu$_7$ sila$_3$	1 *sila* of stew:
	Iš-me-i$_3$-lum	*Yišme-'ilum*;
	15 ninda	15 breads;
	1 i$_3$ sila$_3$ 1 ⸢tu$_7$⸣ sila$_3$	1 *sila* of oil; 1 *sila* of stew:
	Šu-ni-diĝir	Šunidiĝir;
	10 ninda 1 tu$_7$ sila$_3$	10 breads, 1 *sila* of stew:
	Ra-bi$_2$-i$_3$-lum	*Rabi-'ilum*;
	10 ninda	10 breads;
	1 i$_3$ sila$_3$	1 *sila* of oil;
	1 tu$_7$ sila$_3$	1 *sila* of stew:
	Nin-a-zu$_5$(NINDA$_2$×ME)	Ninazu;
iv	10 Mu-aja$_2$	10 (breads): Mu'aja;
	10 Im-aja$_2$	10: Imaja;
	10 *La-ma-Aš+tar$_2$*	10: *Lama-'Aštar*;
	10 Lugal-en-nun	10: Lugal-ennun;
	10 Lu$_2$-⸢lil⸣-la	10: Lulila,
	baḫar$_2$	the potter;
	10 Lugal-ĝeštu$_3$-gal	10: Lugalĝeštugal;
	20 ninda	20 breads;
	½ i$_3$ sila$_3$	½ *sila* of oil:

	Nin-du$_6$-a	Nindu'a;
v	10 Dur$_2$-dub$_2$	10 (breads): Durdub.
	(blank space) / lu$_2$-ki-inim-ma-me	They are the witnesses.
	1 ninda	1 bread;
	1 i$_3$ umbin×LU	1 *umbin*-measure of oil;
	2 tu$_7$ sila$_3$	2 *sila* of stew;
	½ ku$_3$ giĝ$_4$	½ shekel of silver;
	1 dug	1 jar (of beer):
	Niĝar(ŠU$_2$.UD.KID$^{!}$)-mud	Niĝarmud,
vi	dub-sar	the scribe;
	20 ninda	20 breads;
	1 i$_3$ sila$_3$	1 *sila* of oil;
	1 tu$_7$ sila$_3$	1 *sila* of stew:
	Lugal-kalam(LAK729)-tu$^{!}$	Lugalkalamtu;
	10 ninda	10 breads;
	1 i$_3$ sila$_3$	1 *sila* of oil:
	Ama-si	Ama(barage)si;
	[...]-⸢x⸣	...
rev. i	60 ninda	60 breads;
	1 udu	1 sheep;
	1 i$_3$ umbin×LU	1 *umbin*-measure of oil;
	1 dug	1 jar (of beer);
	1 uzu(LAK350)-ur$_2$	1 dry-cured leg:
	niĝir-gal	the chief herald;
	60 ninda	60 breads;
	1 <<sila$_3$>> udu	1 (*sila*, erased) sheep;
	1 i$_3$ umbin×LU	1 *umbin*-measure of oil;
	1 dug	1 jar (of beer);
	1 uzu(LAK350)-ur$_2$	1 dry-cured leg:
ii	⸢x⸣-da	...da;
	40 ninda	40 breads;
	1 i$_3$ sila$_3$	1 *sila* of oil;
	1 tu$_7$ sila$_3$	1 *sila* of stew:
	⸢Šeš$^{?}$-x-gal⸣	Šeš...gal(?);
	40 ninda	40 breads;
	1 i$_3$ sila$_3$	1 *sila* oil:
	Ma-ma-ḫir-su	*Ma(n)-māḫiršu*;
	40 ninda	40 breads;
	1 i$_3$ sila$_3$	1 *sila* of oil:
	Šeš-ni$_3$-lu$_5$-le	Šešnilule;
iii	40 ninda	40 breads;
	1 i$_3$ sila$_3$	1 *sila* of oil:
	Ur-Saman$_x$(ŠE$^{!}$.BU.NUN)	Ur-Saman;
	20 ninda	20 breads:
	dumu Ur-GUL-PA$_5^{?}$	the son of Ur...;

	20 (ras.) ninda	20 (erasure) breads;
	1 i$_{3}$ sila$_{3}$	1 *sila* of oil:
	Šudu$_{3}$-Utu	Šudu-Utu;
	20 ninda 1 i$_{3}$ sila$_{3}$	20 breads, 1 *sila* of oil:
	E$_{2}$-DU	EDU:
	niĝir-me	they are heralds;
iv	10 ninda 1 tu$_{7}$ sila$_{3}$	10 breads, 1 *sila* of stew:
	Ur-^{d}Zu:en	Ur-Zu'en;
	10 ninda 1 tu$_{7}$	10 breads, 1 (*sila* of) stew:
	Ur-^{d}Dumu-zi-⸢da⸣	Ur-Dumuzida;
	(blank space)	
	u$_{4}$ e$_{2}$ sa$_{10}$	When the house was sold,
	ni$_{3}$-sa$_{10}$ *10* e$_{2}$ giĝ$_{4}$	(it was) the purchase of a house of 10 shekels area (= $^{1}/_{6}$ *sar*),
	Ur-saĝ-Keš$_{3}$	Ursaĝ-Keš,
	ensi$_{2}$:ĜAR	the governor.
v	Ĝeš-ša$_{3}$-ki-du$_{10}$	Ĝeššakidu
	lu$_{2}$ ni$_{3}$-sa$_{10}$ gu$_{7}$	is the person who accepted the price (= seller);
	AB-KISAL	ABKISAL
	ni$_{3}$-sa$_{10}$ ak	is (the person) who made the price (= buyer).
	gag-bi eĝar$_{x}$(SIG$_{4}$) ⸢a⸣-du$_{3}$	Its nail has been driven into the wall.
	i$_{3}$-bi	Its oil has been spread on the side.
	za$_{3}$ a-ak / inim al$_{6}$-til	The matter is settled.

A striking detail is the unusual format of the text. It omits the entry formula that records the names of the parties. The text begins with the list of witnesses. The notation of the house's area comes only at the end. There is no mention of the price that was paid. Also notable are the verbal forms that describe the ceremonies following the transaction, where the prefix a= is found instead of a=b= of text No. 1.

obv. ii 12: For this personal name, see Andersson 2012: 400, with further references to ED IIIa documents from Adab and Šuruppak.

obv. vi 5: The sign TU does not have the initial wedges "ŠE."

rev. i 5: See CUSAS 23 no. 179, with references to the previous literature, for uzu(LAK350) "flesh" that also may designate cured meat (*prosciutto*, flitch).

rev. i 8: Apparently, a slip of the pen by the scribe.

rev. iii 8: This individual appears as the "herald of the palace" in text No. 1 rev. iii 13.

rev. iii 10: The name appears as E$_{2}$-DU-DU in numerous ED and later documents. Its interpretation remains uncertain.

No. 3 – MS 3792

Sale of a house, Early Dynastic IIIb (governor Enme'ana), Adab.

obv. i	1 e$_{2}$ sar 7 giĝ$_{4}$	A house of 1 "garden plot" and 7 shekels:
	ni$_{3}$-sa$_{10}$-bi	its price:
	$^{\text{šu2}}$1N$_{8}$ *2* ⸢ku$_{3}$ giĝ$_{4}$⸣	⅓ mina 2 shekels silver;
	1 še gur	1 *gur* of barley;
	4 siki ma-na	4 minas of wool:
	iš-[gana$_{2}$-bi]	its additional payment.
	[break of *ca.* 5 lines]	…
	2 […]	2 …
	1 ⸢še⸣ [gur]	1 *gur* barley;
	1 […]	…
	Za$_{3}$-[mu$^{?}$]	Za[mu](?)
	60 […]	60 …
	1 […]	1 …
	1 […]	1 …
	1 […]	1 …

	[...]	...
	[Za$_3$]-⸢mu⸣	[Za]mu,
	lu$_2$ ni$_3$-sa$_{10}$ gu$_7$-a-am$_6$	the person who accepted the price (= seller).
ii	30 ninda	30 breads;
	½ i$_3$ sila$_3$	½ *sila* of oil;
	2 tu$_7$ sila$_3$	2 *sila* of stew;
	1 nisig sa	1 bundle of greens;
	1 ti	1 rib:
	[x]-⸢LAL$_3$?⸣	...;
	30 ⸢ninda⸣	30 breads;
	[1] i$_3$ [sila$_3$]	[1 *sila*] of oil;
	[break]	...
	[1] ⸢ti⸣	[1] rib;
	1 nisig sa	1 bundle of greens:
	Lugal-usar$_3$(LAL$_2$.LAGAB)-ĝu$_{10}$	Lugal-usarĝu;
iii	30 ninda	30 breads;
	1 i$_3$ sila$_3$	1 *sila* of oil;
	1 tu$_7$ sila$_3$	1 *sila* of stew:
	Geme$_2$-u$_4$-su$_{13}$	Geme'usu;
	30 ninda	30 breads;
	1 i$_3$ sila$_3$	1 *sila* of oil;
	[1 tu$_7$] ⸢sila$_3$⸣	[1] *sila* of [stew];
	[break]	...
	20 ninda 1 i$_3$ sila$_3$	20 breads, 1 *sila* of oil;
	1 tu$_7$ sila$_3$	1 *sila* of stew;
	1 ti	1 rib
iv	1 nisig sa	1 bundle of greens:
	Um-mi-mi	Ummimi,
	dam	wife
	Ur-^{d}Aš$_8$-gi$_4$	of Ur-Ašgi;
	20 ninda 1 i$_3$ sila$_3$	20 breads, 1 *sila* of oil;
	1 tu$_7$ sila$_3$	1 *sila* of stew;
	[break]	...
	1 i$_3$ sila$_3$	1 *sila* of oil:
	Ur-ab-ba	Ur-abba;
	10 ninda	10 breads;
	1 i$_3$ sila$_3$	1 *sila* of oil;
	1 tu$_7$ sila$_3$	1 *sila* of stew:
	Gan-^{d}En-lil$_2$	Gan-Enlil;
v	10 ninda 1 i$_3$ sila$_3$	10 breads, 1 *sila* of oil;
	1 tu$_7$ sila$_3$	1 *sila* of stew:
	Aja$_2$-ne-da	Ajaneda;
	10 ninda 1 sila$_3$	10 breads, 1 *sila* of oil;
	1 tu$_7$ sila$_3$	1 *sila* of stew:
	AN-ne$_2$	ANne:

	lu$_2$ E$_2$-zu-me	they are people of Ezu;
	⸢10⸣ ninda	10 breads;
	[1] i$_3$ ⸢sila$_3$⸣	[1] *sila* of oil;
	[1 tu$_7$] ⸢sila$_3$⸣	[1] *sila* of [stew];
	[break]	. . .
	10 ninda	10 breads;
	1 i$_3$ sila$_3$	1 *sila* of oil;
	1 tu$_7$ sila$_3$	1 *sila* of stew:
	Ne-saĝ	Nesaĝ,
vi	ki-SAR-SAR	the *plot manager*(?);
	10 ninda	10 breads;
	1 i$_3$ sila$_3$	1 *sila* of oil;
	1 tu$_7$ sila$_3$	1 *sila* of stew:
	A$_2$-diĝir-ĝu$_{10}$-ta	Adiĝirĝuta
	Šuruppak$_2$(LAM.KUR.RU)^{ki}	(from) Šuruppak;
	10 ninda	10 breads;
	1 i$_3$ sila$_3$	1 *sila* of oil;
	1 tu$_7$ sila$_3$	1 *sila* of stew:
	Ur-Šubur	Ur-Šubur,
	dumu Ur-^{d}Tu	son of Ur-Tu(da);
	10 ninda	10 breads;
	[1] tu$_7$ sila$_3$	[1] *sila* of stew:
	[x]-⸢u$_4$⸣-su$_{13}$-⸢še$_3$⸣	. . .usuše;
	[...] ⸢x⸣	. . .
	[10] ninda	[10] breads;
	[1 i$_3$] sila$_3$	[1] *sila* of [oil];
	1 tu$_7$ sila$_3$	1 *sila* of stew:
	Inim-ku$_3$-ga-ni	Inimkugani;
	10 ninda	10 breads;
	1 i$_3$ sila$_3$	1 *sila* of oil;
	1 tu$_7$ sila$_3$	1 *sila* of stew:
	E$_2$-⸢pi$^?$⸣-pi$^?$	E. . .;
vii	10 ninda	10 breads;
	1 i$_3$ sila$_3$	1 *sila* of oil;
	1 tu$_7$ sila$_3$	1 *sila* of stew:
	E$_2$-NE-NE	ENENE,
	gala	the cult-singer;
	10 ninda	10 breads;
	1 i$_3$ sila$_3$	1 *sila* of oil;
	1 tu$_7$ sila$_3$	1 *sila* of stew;
	La-mu	Lamu,
	agrig$^!$(IGI.UM)	the steward
	Bara$_2$-^{d}En-lil$_2$-ĝar	(of) Bara-Enlilĝar(a) (deified dais of Enlil);
	10 ninda	10 breads;
	1 i$_3$ sila$_3$	1 *sila* of oil;

Column	Transliteration	Translation
	1 tu$_7$ sila$_3$	1 *sila* of stew:
	Igi-e$_2$-maḫ-še$_3$	Igi-Emaḫše,
	igi-du	the *legal official*
	e$_2$-SAR	of the E-SAR (temple);
	10 ninda	10 breads;
	[1 i$_3$] sila$_3$	[1] *sila* of [oil;]
	[1 tu$_7$ sila$_3$]	[1 *sila* of stew:]
	[break]	. . .
viii	10 ninda	10 breads;
	1 i$_3$ sila$_3$	1 *sila* of oil;
	1 tu$_7$ sila$_3$	1 *sila* of stew:
	E$_2$-dam-si	Edamsi;
	10 ninda	10 breads;
	1 i$_3$ sila$_3$	1 *sila* of oil;
	1 tu$_7$ sila$_3$	1 *sila* of stew:
	Ur-nu	Urnu;
	10 ninda	10 breads;
	1 tu$_7$ sila$_3$	1 *sila* of stew:
	KUM-DUR$_2$-ŠE$_3$	KUMDURŠE;
	10 ninda	10 breads;
	1 i$_3$ sila$_3$	1 *sila* of oil;
	1 tu$_7$ sila$_3$	1 *sila* of stew:
	Niĝir-Ab-zu	Niĝir-Abzu;
	10 ninda	10 breads;
	1 i$_3$ sila$_3$	1 *sila* of oil;
	1 tu$_7$ sila$_3$	1 *sila* of stew:
	Qur$_x$(GUR$_8$)*-da-il*	*Qurda-'il*;
	10 ninda	10 breads;
	1 i$_3$ sila$_3$	1 *sila* of oil;
	1 tu$_7$ sila$_3$	1 *sila* of stew:
	DUB$^?$-DUG	. . .;
	[10] ninda	[10 breads];
	[1] tu$_7$ sila$_3$	[1] *sila* of stew:
ix	Ur-ZA$_7$	UrZA;
	10 ninda	10 breads;
	1 tu$_7$ sila$_3$	1 *sila* of stew:
	E$_2$-DU	EDU,
	niĝir	the herald,
	arad$_2$ ensi$_2$:ĜAR	slave of the governor.
	lu$_2$-ki-inim-ma-me	They are the witnesses.
	gag-bi eĝar$_x$(SIG$_4$) ab-du$_3$	Its nail has been driven into the wall.
	i$_3$-bi za$_3$-ge	Its oil on the side
	ab-ak	has been spread.
	inim-bi al-til	Its matter is settled.
	Za$_3$-mu	Zamu,

	e$_2$ ni$_3$-<sa$_{10}$>-bi nu-⸢til⸣	the price of the house is not paid in full,
	lu$_2$ ni$_3$-sa$_{10}$ gu$_7$-a	(is) the person who accepted the price (= seller).
	Lugal-usar$_3$(LAL$_2$.LAGAB)-ĝu$_{10}$	Lugal-usarĝu,
x	ĝeš-šu-ri-ri	the *timber-worker*,
	lu$_2$ ni$_3$-sa$_{10}$ ak-am$_6$	is the person who offered the price (= buyer).
	(blank space)	
	60 ninda	60 breads;
	1 i$_3$ umbin×LU	1 *umbin*-measure of oil;
	1 dug	1 jar (of beer);
	1 ti	1 rib;
	2 tu$_7$ sila$_3$	2 *sila* of stew;
	1 nisig sa	1 bundle of greens;
	1 ku$_3$ giĝ$_4$	1 shekel of silver:
	Šeš-šeš	(for) Šeššeš,
	niĝir-gal	the chief herald;
	60 ninda	60 breads;
	1 i$_3$ umbin×LU	1 *umbin*-measure of oil;
	1 dug	1 jar (of beer);
	< > ti	< > rib;
	< > nisig sa	< > bundle of greens;
	½ ku$_3$ giĝ$_4$	½ shekel of silver:
rev. i	40 ninda	40 breads;
	½ i$_3$ sila$_3$	½ *sila* of oil;
	2 tu$_7$ sila$_3$	2 *sila* of stew:
	E$_2$-sa$_6$-ga	Esaga;
	40 ninda ½ i$_3$ sila$_3$	40 breads, ½ *sila* of oil;
	2 tu$_7$ sila$_3$	2 *sila* of stew:
	Ad-da	Adda;
	40 ninda ½ i$_3$ sila$_3$	40 breads, ½ *sila* of oil;
	2 tu$_7$ sila$_3$	2 *sila* of stew:
	E$_2$-šudu$_3$	Ešudu:
	niĝir-me	they are heralds.
	u$_4$-ba	When
	En×me-na$_2$	Enme(a)na (was)
	ensi$_2$:ĜAR	the governor
	Adab^{ki}	of Adab.
	Lu$_2$-UN-tu	LuUNtu
	dub-sar-bi	(was) its (the contract's) scribe.

obv. i 1: A plot of *ca.* 40 m^2.

obv. i 4–6: These lines are absent on the photograph. They are owed to a transliteration made by A. Westenholz before the conservation and photographing of the tablet.

obv. i 6: For iš-gana$_2$ as an additional payment in sale contract, see ELTS p. 221 and OSP 2 p. 71 no. 55.

obv. vi 1: This is probably a professional title unattested alsewhere. See MSL 16 p. 218 l. 223 (*Nabnītu*

XXIII) for ki-SAR-SAR-ak = MIN = *še-ru* = *šer'u*, "furrow, cultivated field" (CAD Š[2] 327). It might be rendered as ki-mu_2-mu_2...ak, literally "to perform planting of soil." Consequently, ki-mu_2-mu_2 may be a person in charge of this activity.

obv. vi 6: The usual writing for Fara-Šuruppak is SU.KUR.RU.

obv. vii 9–11: The temple of the deified dais of Enlil $^{(d)}$Bara$_2$-^{d}En-lil$_2$-ĝar appears in numerous Early Dynastic and Sargonic texts from Adab, which points to the importance of its cult there. See CUSAS 11 nos. 142, 208–9, 212–13, 216; CUSAS 13 nos. 84, 106, 111+112, 141, 152; CUSAS 19 no. 85; CUSAS 23 no. 167 and Such-Gutiérrez 2005–6: 14.

obv. vii 16: For igi-du (igištu) as a court official, see OSP 2 p. 66 no. 49, with further references. Another igi-du appears in a legal context in CUSAS 26 no. 46 obv. 12. In the present text, igi-du is an official in E-SAR (a legal representative?), the temple of Diĝirmaḫ in Adab and economically one of the most prominent households.

obv. viii 11: The reading of the name is uncertain. See the commentary to CUSAS 23 no. 38.

obv. viii 19: The name is Semitic and means "The god is strong." See MAD 3 pp. 226–27, stem *QRD*.

obv. ix 4–6: See text No. 2 rev. iii 10 for the same individual. Here he is stated to be the "slave," i.e., servant, of the governor.

obv. ix 13: The sign ŠAM$_2$ is omitted for some reason. See NG no. 104 l. 8 for this construction.

obv. x 1: See SCTRAH p. 37 for this professional title, probably meaning "joiner." The term appears in a number of Early Dynastic and Sargonic texts: see BdI 1 no. 61 obv. ii 8, OSP 1 no. 46 iii 15, OSP 2 no. 58 l. 13.

obv. x 17: The absence of a recipient for these goods is probably an omission of the scribe, for the obverse ends here. Note also the absence of numerals before the greens and the rib.

rev. i 14: See Marchesi 2015: 152 for this ED IIIb ruler of Adab. The full writing of the name is En-me-a-na$_2$. Another possible reference to the ruler appears in CUSAS 26 no. 70 rev. ii 4' where En×me-na$_2$ is the recipient of a plot of land.

rev. i 16: Cf. Lugal-kalam(LAK729)-tu in text No. 2 obv. vi 5.

No. 4 – MS 3795

Sale of a house, Early Dynastic IIIb (governor Ursaĝ-Keš), Adab. Half of a large tablet.

obv. i–ii	[broken]	…
iii	Ur-^{d}⌜Saman$_3$⌝	Ur-Saman,
	dumu	son
	Lu$_2$-ti-ti	of Lutiti,
	[n+] ⌜10⌝ ninda 1 i$_3$ sila$_3$	x+10 breads, 1 *sila* of oil:
	Lugal-⌜inim⌝-še$_3$-ĝal$_2$	Lugalinimšeĝal;
	[n ninda] 1 i$_3$ sila$_3$	[x breads], 1 *sila* of oil:
	⌜Lugal⌝-[x]-NE	Lugal…NE;
	[n ninda 1] i$_3$ ⌜sila$_3$⌝	[x breads, 1] *sila* of oil:
	[...]-⌜x⌝	…
	[break]	…
iv	IB	the IB-official;
	40 ninda 1 i$_3$ sila$_3$	40 breads, 1 *sila* of oil:
	Lugal-nita-zi	Lugalnitazi,
	dumu Lugal-uš-su$_x$(MUŠ)	son of Lugalušsu;
	60 ninda	60 breads;
	1 ku$_3$ giĝ$_4$	1 shekel of silver;
	1 i$_3$ umbin	1 *umbin*-measure of oil;
	1 dug	1 jar (of beer):
	niĝir-gal	the chief herald;
	60 ninda	60 breads;

	1 i$_{3}$ umbin×LU	1 *umbin*-measure of oil;
	1 ku$_{3}$ giĝ$_{4}$	1 shekel of silver;
	[break]	...
v	Šeš-ni$_{3}$-lu$_{5}$-le	Šešnilule;
	40 ninda 1 i$_{3}$ sila$_{3}$	40 breads, 1 *sila* of oil:
	Šeš-ad$_{2}$-gal	Šešadgal;
	40 ninda 1 i$_{3}$ sila$_{3}$	40 breads, 1 *sila* of oil:
	Ma-ma-ḫir-su	*Ma(n)-māḫiršu*;
	40 ninda 1 i$_{3}$ sila$_{3}$	40 breads, 1 *sila* of oil:
	Ur-⸢Saman$_{3}$⸣	Ur-Saman;
	10 ninda ⸢x⸣-[...]	10 breads: ...;
	10 [...]	10 [...];
rev. i	[break]	...
	10 E$_{2}$-[...]	10: E...;
	10 ⸢x⸣-[...]	10: ...;
	10 [...]	10 ...;
	⸢x⸣ [...] SAĜ/KA [...]	...
	20 ninda 1 i$_{3}$ [sila$_{3}$]	20 breads, 1 [*sila* of] oil:
	Ama-nu-nu	Amanunu.
	gag-bi	Its nail
	(blank space)	(blank space)
ii	[eĝar$_{x}$(SIG$_{4}$) ab-du$_{3}$]	[has been driven into the wall.]
	[i$_{3}$-bi za$_{3}$-ge]	[Its oil on the side]
	[ab-ak]	[has been spread.]
	[inim-bi al-til]	[Its matter is settled.]
	[Lugal-uš]-⸢su$_{x}$(MUŠ)-x⸣	[to Lugal]ušsu(?),
	me-⸢x⸣	...
	lu$_{2}$ ni$_{3}$-sa$_{10}$ ak	(is) the person who offered the price (= buyer);
	Lugal-uš-su$_{x}$(MUŠ)	Lugalušsu,
	šu-i$_{\text{-tenû}}$	the barber,
	lu$_{2}$ ni$_{3}$-sa$_{10}$ gu$_{7}$	(is) the person who accepted the price (= seller).
	u$_{4}$-ba	When
	Ur-saĝ-Keš$_{3}$	Ursaĝ-Keš
iii	[ensi$_{2}$:ĜAR Adab[ki] ...]	[was the governor of Adab ...]
	(blank)	

obv. iv 1: See Molina 1991: 144 for other references to this unclear professional title.

obv. iv 4: The same name appears in text No. 2 obv. ii 12, where it belongs to a gardener. The individual who sells the house in the present document (see rev. ii 8) is a barber and most likely a different person.

obv. v 5: See Nos. 1 and 2 for the same individual.

rev. ii 12: See Marchesi 2015: 142, 152, for this governor of Adab, who ruled during the ED IIIb period.

No. 5 – MS 3798

Legal document concerning silver, Early Dynastic IIIb, Adab.

A governor of Adab acts as judge and hands over a sum of silver to the temple of Ninisina. Though Ninisina was the titular goddess of Isin, the prosopography of the text suggests Adab as its provenance.

obv. i	[…] ⌜ku$_3$⌝ $^{\text{šu2}}$IN$_8$ [ma]-⌜na$^?$⌝	x + ⅓ mina silver:
	Ur-⌜zikum⌝-ra	to Urzikum,
	Ur-bara$_2$-saĝ-ke$_4$	Urbarasaĝ
	in-la$_2$	has weighed out.
	Ur-^{d}En-lil$_2$	Ur-Enlil,
	šeš Ur-zikum	brother of Urzikum,
ii	[2 lines destroyed]	…
	ensi$_2$:ĜAR	the governor
	Adab^{ki}	of Adab
	di-bi in-ku$_5$	judged this case.

	Lugal-agrig-zi	Lugal-agrigzi
	Lu$_5$-lu$_5$	(and) Lulu
iii	⸢lu$_2$⸣-ki-inim-ma-me	were the witnesses.
	⸢ensi$_2$⸣:ĜAR-⸢ke$_4$⸣	The governor
	e$_2$ ^{d}⸢Nin⸣-Isin$_2$-še$_3$	to the temple of (the goddess) Ninisin(a)
	šu in-ne-us$_2$	has sent it over to them.
	Ur-du$_6$-ke$_4$	Urdu,
	Igi-mu-NE	IgimuNE,
iv	i$_3$-du$_8$-gal	the chief doorman,
	Ur-^{še3}Šer$_7$-da	Ur-Šerda,
	lu$_2$-ma$_2$-kas$_4$	the ...,
	E$_2$-šudu$_3$	E-šudu,
	lu$_2$-ma$_2$-kas$_4$	the ...,
rev. i	Im-ta	Imta,
	ugula	the overseer,
	Mu-ni-zal	Munizal,
	ugula-e$_2$	the overseer of the household,
	Lu$_2$-šu-dim$_2$	Lušudim,
	ugula geme$_2$	the overseer of female workers,
	lu$_2$-ki-inim-ma-me	are the witnesses.
	(rest blank)	

obv. ii 3 f.: The governor of Adab, whose name is unfortunately lost in the break (it was probably Ursaĝ-Keš), acts as the judge in this case. He hands over the silver in question to the temple household of Ninisina for several individuals, probably for Urzikum and his brother. It is not certain, however, whether this is the temple situated in Isin itself or a temple of Ninisina in Adab.

obv. ii 4: Note the curious form of "NUN" in the writing of Adab.

obv. iv 3, 5: lu$_2$-ma$_2$-kas$_4$ is literally a "person (of) the messenger boat." The term is otherwise unattested as far as the author knows. Other interpretations are possible. Note that the herald Ešudu of Nos. 3 rev. i 10 and 6 obv. iv' 2' may be identical to the Ešudu who has the title lu$_2$-ma$_2$-kas$_4$ in the present text.

rev. i 5: Contra CUSAS 11 no. 154 obv. i 6 (lu$_2$-šu šitim). Cf. CUSAS 11 no. 275 obv. i 4 for likely the same individual.

No. 6 – MS 3811

Sale of a house(?), Early Dynastic IIIb, Adab. Fragment of a clay tablet imitating a stone one.

obv. i'	[break]	…
	[n] ninda	x breads;
	[n] ⸢tu$_7$⸣ sila$_3$	x *sila* of stew;
	[n] ⸢ku$_6$⸣ gurdub$_2$	x *gurdub*-baskets of fish
	IM-ki	IMki;
	[n] ninda	x breads;
	[n] tu$_7$ sila$_3$	x *sila* of stew:
	Im-ta	Imta;
	[…] 15	15 …
	[break]	…
ii'	[break]	…
	20 ninda	20 breads;
	1 tu$_7$ sila$_3$	1 *sila* of stew:
	Saḫar-ra-ni	Saḫarani;
	20 ninda	20 breads;
	1 tu$_7$ sila$_3$	1 *sila* of stew:
	Lugal-a-ĝi$_6$	Lugalaĝi,
	dumu	son
	En-DU-DU	(of) EnDUDU,
	baḫar$_2$-me	they (both) are potters;

	20 ninda	20 breads;
	1 tu$_7$ sila$_3$	1 *sila* of stew:
	Ur-gu	Urgu,
	⸢lu$_2$-EDIN⸣.GUR	the …
iii'	[break]	…
	[…]-⸢Nanna⸣	…-Nanna.
	(blank space)	(blank space)
	lu$_2$-ki-inim-ma-me	They are the witnesses.
	120 ninda	120 breads;
	1 ur$_2$	1 leg;
	1 i$_3$ umbin×LU	1 *umbin*-measure of oil;
	2 tu$_7$ sila$_3$	2 *sila* of stew;
	2 sum sa	2 bundles of onions;
	1 dug	1 jar (of beer);
	1 ku$_3$ giĝ$_4$	1 shekel of silver:
	Šeš-šeš	Šeššeš,
	niĝir-gal	the chief herald;
	120 ninda	120 breads;
	1 ur$_2$	1 leg;
	1 i$_3$ umbin×LU	1 *umbin*-measure of oil;
	[break]	…
iv'	[…] ⸢x x⸣	…:
	E$_2$-šudu$_3$	Ešudu;
	40 ninda	40 breads;
	1 i$_3$ sila$_3$	1 *sila* of oil;
	1 tu$_7$ sila$_3$	1 *sila* of stew:
	Ur-^{d}Tu	Ur-Tu(da);
	40 ninda	40 breads;
	1 i$_3$ sila$_3$	1 *sila* of oil;
	1 tu$_7$ sila$_3$	1 *sila* of stew:
	Ad-da	Adda.
	(blank space)	(blank space)
	niĝir-me	They are heralds.
	20 ninda	20 breads;
	1 tu$_7$ sila$_3$	1 *sila* of stew;
	[break]	…
v'	[…]-⸢x⸣	…,
	niĝir	the herald;
	10 ninda	10 breads;
	1 tu$_7$ sila$_3$	1 *sila* of stew:
	A-ba-^{d}En-lil$_2$	Aba-Enlil;
	10 ninda	10 breads;
	1 tu$_7$ sila$_3$	1 *sila* of stew:
	E$_2$-MUŠ-DUG-AN	EMUŠDUGAN,
	dumu	they (both) are sons

10'	Ur-^{d}Tu-me	of Ur-Tu(da).
	20 ninda 1 tu$_{7}$ sila$_{3}$	20 breads, 1 *sila* of stew:
	Ĝiri$_{2}$-nun-ne$_{2}$-si	Ĝirinunesi;
	20 ninda 1 tu$_{7}$ sila$_{3}$	20 breads, 1 *sila* of stew:
	U$_{2}$-da-ur$_{4}$-ra	Uda'ura;
rev.	[destroyed/blank]	…

obv. i' 4': This is probably an abbreviation of the personal name Karkara(IM)-ki-du$_{10}$; cf. e.g. CUSAS 23 no. 196 rev. 4.

obv. v' 8': The interpretation of the name is uncertain.

No. 7 – MS 3029

Stone tablet recording legal proceedings in a case of theft, Early Dynastic IIIb (governor Enme(a)na), Adab.

obv. i	[n] tu-dur aga$_3$	x jewelry pearl of a tiara:
	U$_3$-mu-NI-NI	UmuNINI,
	dumu Ur-mu-da-	son of Urmuda,
	-ka-ke$_4$	
	Ur-^{d}En-lil$_2$ ⸢zadim⸣-ra	to Ur-Enlil, the stonecutter,
	bur$_3$-re$_2$-de$_3$	for perforating
	mu-na-šum$_2$	he has given to him.
	e$_2$-de$_5$-de$_5$-ga	In(?) *Ededega*
	ba-de$_6$	he has taken it away.
	10 5 ku$_3$-bi giĝ$_4$	Its 15 shekels silver,
	U$_3$-mu-NI-NI	UmuNINI,
ii	dumu Ur-mu-da-	son of Urmuda,
	-ka-ke$_4$	
	ba-ši-de$_6$	he has taken it there.

	1 zabar-dilim$_2$-da^{uruda}	1 bronze mirror with handle:
	ki-la$_2$-bi 1 ma-na	its weight: 1 mina,
	Unug^{ki}-ga	in Uruk,
	3 ku$_3$ giĝ$_4$	(its value is) 3 shekels of silver,
	im-ma-de$_6$	it is brought.
	1 zabar-KU-LAGAB×ḪAL^{uruda}	1 bronze … mirror:
	ki-la$_2$-bi ^{šu2}1N$_8$ giĝ$_4$	its weight: ⅓ (mina as 20) shekels.
	[…]	…
iii	ba-de$_6$	has taken away.
	2N$_8$ lagab za:gin$_3$ giĝ$_4$	a plaque of lapis-lazuli of ⅔ (mina as 40) shekels (in weight)
	10 ku$_3$ giĝ$_4$	(for) 10 shekels silver,
	Unug^{ki}-ta$^{!}$	in Uruk
	am$_3$-sa$_{10}$	he has bought.
	2 kišib$_3$(DUB)-za:gin$_3$	2 lapis-lazuli seals:
	ki-la$_2$-bi *3* giĝ$_4$	their weight: 3 shekels,
	3 ku$_3$ giĝ$_4$	(of) 3 shekels of silver (value):
	Lugal-men	Lugalmen,
	zabar-dab$_6$(URUDA) šu-du$_8$-e	the *zabardab*-official, the guarantee(?),
	ba-ši-de$_6$ 1 bur	has taken it away there. 1 (stone) bowl
	[(blank?)]	[(blank?)]
iv	*2* ku$_3$ igi-*3*-ĝal$_2$ giĝ$_4$	(of) 2⅓ shekels of silver (value)
	ba-de$_6$	he has taken it away.
	1 za:gin$_3$-tur$_5$(TU)	1 translucent lapis lazuli (stone)
	dur ad-tab$_x$(*2*)	(for) the knot of a decorative collar;
	ki-la$_2$-bi 5 giĝ$_4$	its weight: 5 shekels;
	1 za:gin$_3$-tur$_5$ dur ad-tab$_x$(*2*)	1 translucent lapis lazuli (stone for) the knot of a decorative collar:
	ki-la$_2$-bi 10 giĝ$_4$	its weight: 10 shekels;
	2 gug$_x$(GUL.ZA)-tur-tur ad-tab$_x$(*2*)	2 small carnelians (for) a decorative collar:
	ki-la$_2$-bi *2* giĝ$_4$	their weight: 2 shekels;
	5 NE-ussu(*8*)-ku$_3$	5 silver …;
	⸢x-x⸣	…
v	1 za ku$_3$-sig$_{17}$ gu$_2$ am$_3$-e$_3$	1 stone bead covered with gold;
	1 kišib$_3$ za:gin$_3$	1 lapis-lazuli seal:
	ki-la$_2$-bi ½ [giĝ$_4$]	its weight: ½ [shekel];
	1 ku$_3$ giĝ$_4$	(value:) 1 shekel of silver:
	Me-an-en-da	Me'anenda,
	dub-sar-⸢e⸣	the scribe,
	ba-ši-de$_6$	has taken it there;
	1 kišib$_3$ za:gin$_3$	1 lapis-lazuli seal:
	ki-la$_2$-bi ½ [giĝ$_4$]	its weight: ½ [shekel]:
	ĜIŠ-RI	ĜIŠRI,
	dumu ĜIŠ-LUM	son of ĜIŠLUM,
	nu-banda$_3$-ke$_4$	the supervisor,

	½ ku$_3$ giĝ$_4$	½ shekel of silver
rev. i	ba-ši-de$_6$	has taken there.
	1 kišib$_3$ ⸢za⸣:gin$_3$ ⸢saĝ⸣-ĝa$_2$	1 lapis-lazuli seal of premium quality;
	ki-la$_2$-bi [*n* giĝ$_4$]	its weight: [x shekel];
	UD-re$_2$ [(x)]	...re (personal name),
	½ ku$_3$ giĝ$_4$	½ shekel silver (is its value)
	ba-⸢ši⸣-de$_6$	has brought there.
	⸢1⸣ ni$_3$-⸢sur⸣$^{[\text{tug2}]}$	1 ... garment;
	1 aktum(A.⸢SU⸣)$^{[\text{tug2}]}$	1 heavy garment;
	6 ⸢siki⸣ [(x)] ma-[na]	6 minas of ... wool;
	[n ...] ⸢x⸣ [ma]-⸢na⸣	x minas of ...;
	[n ni$_3$]-NU×U-a bar-dul$_5$ sal-la-kam	x fine thread(s) for *bardul*-garments;
	[n] ni$_3$-NU×U-a ni$_3$-SAL-saĝ-keš$_2$	x thread(s) for *headbands*(?);
ii	šu:za:gin$_3$(KUR.ZA.ŠU) ki-la$_2$-bi *2* ⸢giĝ$_4$⸣	(one) lapis-lazuli "hand": its weight: 2 shekels;
	NU$_{11}$-⸢GU⸣-BI-NA 2 ma-na	... (of) 2 minas:
	⸢Ur⸣-^{d}En-lil$_2$	Ur-Enlil,
	zadim-e	the stonecutter,
	Unug^{ki}-ta	from Uruk
	mu-de$_6$	he has brought.
	1 giĝ$_4$-⸢zabar⸣^{uruda}	1 bronze axe:
	ki-la$_2$-bi ½ ma-na	its weight: ½ mina;
	⸢x-zi$^{?}$-x⸣ [...]	...
	[...]	...
	[n ...]-⸢x⸣ ki-la$_2$-bi 5 giĝ$_4$	x ... its weight: 5 shekels;
iii	⸢za⸣:gin$_3$-⸢tur$_5$⸣ 10 giĝ$_4$	(one) translucent lapis lazuli (stone weighing) 10 shekels;
	1 kišib$_3$ za:gin$_3$	1 lapis-lazuli seal:
	ki-la$_2$-⸢bi⸣ 5 giĝ$_4$	its weight: 5 shekels;
	1 saĝ ⸢za⸣:gin$_3$-tur$_5$ BU-⸢x⸣	1 head of ... of translucent lapis lazuli:
	ki-la$_2$-bi 5 giĝ$_4$	its weight: 5 shekels;
	Aja$_2$-diĝir-ĝu$_{10}$	Ajadiĝirĝu,
	dub-sar-maḫ-e	the chief scribe,
	$^{\text{šu2}}$1N$_8$ ku$_3$ giĝ$_4$	(as) ⅓ (mina as 20) shekels silver
	in-sar	has written down.
	(blank line)	(blank line)
	⸢ni$_3$-gur$_{11}$⸣	The property
	Ur-⸢^{d}⸣En-lil$_2$	(of) Ur-Enlil,
	zadim	the stonecutter,
	⸢e$_2$⸣-de$_5$-de$_5$-[ga]	in the *Ededega*
	[ba]-⸢de$_6$⸣	he has taken it away.
iv	[...]	...
	⸢x-na/ki⸣	... (and)
	⸢Šu⸣-ni-diĝir	Šunidiĝir:
	nu-zuḫ-me	they are the thieves.
	En×me-na$_2$	Enme(a)na,

	ensi$_{2}$	the governor
	Adab^{ki}-ke$_{4}$	of Adab,
	Geme$_{2}$-e$_{2}$-maḫ	(of) Geme-Emaḫ,
	dam Ur-^{d}En-lil$_{2}$ zadim	wife of Ur-Enlil, the stonecutter,
	ni$_{3}$-gur$_{11}$-ra-ni	her property
	ki ⸢na$_{4}$⸣-ka	in the place of stone weights
	⸢ib$_{2}$⸣-[la$_{2}^{?}$]	*has weighed*(?)
	⸢SAĜ NE?⸣	…
	[3 lines broken]	…
v	ba-de$_{6}$	he has taken it away.
	ziz$_{2}$-da-bi 5 ku$_{3}$ ma-na	Its compensation: 5 minas of silver;
	na-ba-de$_{6}$	he has taken away indeed.
	⸢En⸣×[me]-na$_{2}$	Enme(a)na,
	ensi$_{2}$	the governor
	Adab^{ki}-ke$_{4}$	of Adab,
	SAL.⸢DI$^{?}$⸣-zu nu-til	"Your … is not yet completed/finished,"
	ma-du$_{11}$	he told me.
	Aja$_{2}$-⸢diĝir⸣-ĝu$_{10}$	Ajadiĝirĝu,
	dub-sar-maḫ	the chief scribe,
	⸢ni$_{3}^{?}$-x-bi$^{?}$⸣	*this matter*(?)
	igi-⸢ni-ta⸣ in-⸢sar⸣	in front of him/her has written down.
	Šeš-⸢šeš⸣	Šeššeš,
	[…]	…
	[…] ⸢za:gin$_{3}$⸣	lapis lazuli …
l. e.	[…] ⸢x x⸣ / inim-bi / maškim-bi	…, this matter, its commissioner.
r. e.	[…]-⸢x⸣	

This remarkable legal document is incised on a stone tablet. It seems to record legal proceedings concerning a theft. A list of luxury items, including objects from gems, precious metals, garments, etc. occupies the major part of the document. These goods are the possession of a stonecutter and his wife. Several individuals are proclaimed thieves. The final section of the document calculates the sum of the pecuniary injury done by the theft. The presence of the governor Enme'ana of Adab and the quotation of his(?) speech at the end of the document suggest that the case must have been capital. An interesting detail is the reference to some transactions with Uruk.

The lower edge of the tablet continues the columns of the obverse, while the top edge continues the text of the reverse. The end of the text was inscribed on the left and right edges of the tablet.

Walther Sallaberger suggested to the author that inconsistencies in grammar and writing, such as suffix -ra before zadim in obv. i 5, the writing of two entries in one entry as in obv. iii 11, and the writing of TA in obv. iii 4, indicate that the tablet is either an ancient copy of an original document or a modern fake based on an original document.

obv. i 1: For a pearl used in jewelry tu-dur, see Molina 1989: 85, 92; Paoletti 2012: 144. The presence of a stone-worker and the reference to perforating the stones (bur(u)$_{3}$) implies that the work to be done involved boring holes in stones or gems.

obv. i 3: Ur-mu-da appears in a context with fields and canals in CUSAS 23 no. 36 obv. i 2 and rev. 3. That text's provenance should be corrected to "Adab."

obv. i 5: Written Ur-^{d}En-lil$_2$-ra ⸢zadim⸣, which violates the rules of Sumerian grammar.

obv. i 6: See CAD P 58–59 for bur(u)$_3$ = *palāšu* "to pierce, bore."

obv. i 8, rev. iii 14: The same term appears in a Sargonic document from Ĝirsu, STTI no. 82 rev. 3: ni$_3$-gur$_{11}$ e$_2$-de$_5$-de$_5$-ga-kam "it is the property of the 'collected' house." Cf. also ni$_3$-de$_5$-de$_5$-ga designating metal scraps in Foster 1982, *USP* p. 37. The term e$_2$-de$_5$-de$_5$-ga may refer not to a locus but instead may designate personal estate, all the movable property in a household (suggestion courtesy W. Sallaberger).

obv. i 10–ii 3: The interpretation of this clause depends on the understanding of the transaction. The terminative marker in the verbal form refers to the e$_2$-de$_5$-de$_5$-ga if we assume that the silver is either payment for the work to be done or is the materials for the work.

obv. ii 4: For the interpretation of zabar as "mirror," see Steinkeller 1987a: 347–49. See CUSAS 12 p. 205 7:11 for dilim$_2$-da^{zabar} in a copy of the "Early Dynastic Practical Vocabulary B" (MS 2340+). The same item appears in CUSAS 23 no. 158 obv. 4 and STTI no. 8 obv. 5 in context with other copper and bronze objects. Based on the term zabar$_3$ dilim$_2$ ma$_2$-Dilmun-da, which often appears in ED IIIb texts from Ĝirsu and means "mirror with a handle in the form of a Dilmunite ship," the term in question may designate a mirror with a handle.

obv. ii 9: This seems to be another type of mirror. See EDPV A p. 71 no. 72 for a similar designation of stone bowl, bur-KU-LAGAB×AN, where LAGAB×AN is a variant of LAGAB×ḪAL = esir$_2$ "bitumen." Civil's interpretation of the term as "bowl of fire(?)" is unconvincing. Bitumen was a material used to fix parts of an object together; cf. KU = ku "to place" and tuš "to sit."

obv. ii 10, iii 2: See CUSAS 33, 222 commentary to rev. ii 3 for these notations of the shekel's and the mina's fractions "one-third" and "two-thirds" in the local scribal tradition at Early Dynastic Umma. However, the reference to igi-*3*-ĝal$_2$ giĝ$_4$ in obv. iv 1 shows that the passages in question designate the fractions "one-third" and "two-thirds" of the mina and not of the shekel. Nevertheless, it is unusual that this text uses the Umma writing $^{(\text{šu}_2)}$N$_8$ giĝ$_4$ instead of the Adab notations $^{\text{šu}_2}$N$_8^{(\text{ša-na})}$ for "⅓" and 2N$_8$ ša-na-pi for "⅔" of the mina.

obv. iii 2: See EDPV A p. 54 no. 5 for lagab as "a flat, solid piece (as a raw material, or as a decorative artifact)."

obv. iii 4: The sign TA is written without the final vertical wedge.

obv. iii 6–7: See EDPV A p. 61 no. 29. The weight 1.5 shekels for each object fits well with the weights of seals that occur in cuneiform documents.

obv. iii 10: zabar-dab$_6$(URUDA) may be another writing for zabar-dab$_5$(KU). This was the highest cultic official during the Ur III period. His principal role was chief cupbearer; see Sallaberger 1999: 186–88. The term for "guarantee" is šu-du$_8$-a. For DU$_8$.ŠU as šu-du$_8$ in an Adab(?) text dated to the reign of the Lagashite governor Akurgal, see CUSAS 26 no. 69 rev. ii 4. Westenholz interprets this term as "prisoner of war," based on a context where a certain Ur-ĝirdu is described as DU$_8$.ŠU but also labeled lu$_2$ ni$_3$-mul-an "the person (who brought) news." Although this interpretation seems logical, šu-du$_8$ may be a professional title in both cases. At any rate, the interpretation "prisoner of war" seems unsuited to Lugalmen in the present line.

obv. iv 3, 6: tur$_5$(TU) for duru$_5$ (suggestion courtesy A. R. George).

obv. iv 4, 6, 8: Cf. EDPV A p. 114 no. 254 for ad-tab$_x$(DIŠ-*tenû*×2; simply "*2*" in the present edition) as "headstall of a harness," and probably for another meaning of the term when it appears in the context of jewelry. Line 124 of EDPV A provides a clue to the meaning: here ad of ad-DU^{uruda} is a "metal collar to reinforce the attachment of a shaft to a tool." Westenholz comes close to the correct interpretation in OSP 2 p. 66, commentary to no. 49 i 4, where he suggests that za ad-tab is a "kind of necklace." Steinkeller has suggested that ad-tab za-gin$_3$ in ELTS no. 32 (p. 296) is a "decorative collar." Therefore, za:gin$_3$-tur$_5$ dur ad-tab$_x$ refers to a lapis-lazuli stone as part of a decorative collar.

obv. iv 8: GUL.ZA is another writing for "carnelian," gug(ZA.GUL) = *sāmtu*.

obv. iv 10: The objects are unidentified. Another possibility would be to read ussu as the number 8.

obv. v 1: gu$_2$ … e$_3$ = *ḫalāpu* "to cover (with something)"; see CAD Ḫ 35.

rev. i 7: See EDPV A p. 95 no. 181 for a term sur^{tug_2}.

rev. i 11–12: See Van de Mieroop 1987: 35–36 for ni$_3$-NU×U-a as a string for closing a waterskin. The same NU×U appears in a similar term for threads, si-NU×U; see e.g. EDPV A p. 131 no. 312.

rev. i 12: See EDPV A no. 194 for ni$_3$-saĝ-keš$_2$, "belt" or "sash." Apparently, this term is expanded by the sign SAL. Cf. also ni$_3$-SAL-la$_2$-saĝ "headband" in Nos. 420–21.

rev. ii 1: See EDPV A no. 27 for "probably a hand-shaped amulet, rather than a, not impossible, 'handle'." The low weight of the object, at *ca.* 17 grams, makes the former suggestion more plausible.

rev. ii 2: The term remains unidentified. It could be a stone; cf. NU$_{11}$ = ĝešnu "alabaster."

rev. iii 4: The interpretation of SAĜ at the beginning and apparently of BU at the end is tentative. Cf. BU+BU = unu$_{12}$ = *udugu* "pin"(?) in EDPV A no. 3. The weight of this object is too great for it to be a garment pin.

rev. iii 9: The interpretation presumes that the scribe estimated the value and recorded the goods that belonged to the stonecutter.

rev. iv 3: The same Šu-ni-diĝir may appear in another legal text, No. 2 obv. iii 6.

rev. iv 4: See Wilcke 2007: 119 fn. 386 for nu-zuḫ(KA) "thief." The term appears in ED Lu$_2$ B 46 (MSL 12 p. 13).

rev. iv 11: ki NI.⌜UD⌝-ka: see EDPV A p. 52 for this writing for "stone."

rev. v 2: See Wilcke 2007: 59 fn. 180 for ziz$_2$-da = Akk. *kiššātum* as "compensation, indemnity." According to this, the document calculates the value of the stolen goods and records that this compensation has been delivered. It is possible that the goods listed in the main part of this document are not stolen but goods that represent the compensation.

rev. v 3: See Thomsen 1984: 196, Edzard 2003: 119–20 for the prefix /na=/ as "affirmative (2)," and Jagersma 2010: 579–81 f. for the "non-negative {na}." Since in our case the form is perfective, it is probably unrelated to the negative modal prefix na(n)- that is used almost exclusively with *marû*-forms (see ibid. pp. 565 f.). Nevertheless, the presence of the negated form nu-til "not completed" below makes the interpretation of na-ši-de$_6$ as "he does not need to take it away there," or similar, attractive.

rev. v 7–8: The broken sign has a diamond shape. It may be DI, ḪAR, KI or similar. See MC 4 no. 52 l. 11 for another occurrence of the verbal form ma-du$_{11}$ in a legal context.

rev. v 12: See FAOS 15/2 p. 394 for this expression.

No. 8 – MS 4745

Legal document concerning property, Early Dynastic IIIb (governor Ursaĝ-Keš), Adab.

obv. i	⸢1⸣ [+n] ⸢e$_2$ sar⸣	A house of 1+x … units of area;
	480 še gur	480 *gur* of barley;
	300 udu-ḫi-a	300 various sheep;
	Diĝir-ur-saĝ	Diĝirursaĝ;
	Diĝir-lu-maḫ	Diĝirlumaḫ:
	nita-me	they are males.
	A-na-i$_3$-ak	Ana'i'ak;
ii	Ni$_3$-ki-šu$_4$-a	Nikišu'a;
	Me-|A.DU/A.DU|-e	Me…e:
	saĝ-munus-me	they are female slaves.
	Ne-saĝ	Nesaĝ;
	Ur-e$_2$-maḫ	Ur-Emaḫ:
	saĝ-nita-me	they are male slaves,
	ama-tu-me	they are house-born slaves;
	$^{\text{šu2}}$1N$_8$ ku$_3$ gîg$_4$	⅓ (mina as 20) shekels of silver:
	ni$_3$-gur$_{11}$	this is the property
iii	Ur-^{d}Inana-kam	of Ur-Inana.
	Ama-a-zu$_5$	Ama'azu,
	dam Ur-^{d}Inana-ke$_4$	wife of Ur-Inana,
	e$_2$ Si-um-ka	in the house of Si'um
	i$_3$-de$_6$	she has brought it.
	(blank space)	
rev. i	Ur-saĝ-⸢Keš$_3$⸣	Ursaĝ-Keš,
	ensi$_2$	the governor
	Adab^{ki}-ke$_4$	of Adab,
	di-bi si bi$_2$-sa$_2$	has regulated this lawsuit.
	Gaba-šu	Gabašu
	inim-bi	(of) its matter,
ii	maškim-bi	(he is) its commissioner.
	ni$_3$-gur$_{11}$-bi	Its property
	teš$_2$-teš$_2$ a-ne-šum$_2$	it has been given to them together.
	(blank)	
iii	(blank)	

The document records the possessions (ni$_3$-gur$_{11}$) of a certain Ur-Inana: a house, a large quantity of grain, a considerable number of sheep, and seven slaves in total: two males, three females and two house-born male slaves (for ama-tu "house-born slave," see Wilcke 2007: 54). Finally, an amount of silver rounds up this impressive accumulation of possessions.

obv. i 2–3: The number of sheep and the quantity of barley in possession of Ur-Inana are strikingly high. Nevertheless, the writing of the numerals does not allow confusion between the signs for 60 and 1.

obv. ii 2: The interpretation of the name is uncertain.

obv. iii 2–5: These lines state the matter of the lawsuit. Since the name Si-um-(me) is well attested in the Early Dynastic/Sargonic corpus, it seems that the house of a certain Si'um is concerned in the matter.

rev. i 5: A personal name gaba-šu "rival" is otherwise unknown to me. Perhaps it is not a personal name here either, but signifies that the matter should not be contested by a "rival" (i.e. contesting party).

rev. ii 3: The expression teš$_{2}$-teš$_{2}$-a … ĝar "to combine (amounts)" appears in numerous ED IIIb documents from Ĝirsu, e.g. in DP 280 rev. ii 3. See also ĝeš teš$_{2}$-teš$_{2}$-e e-da-la$_{2}$ "they fought each other" on the Stele of Vultures l. 153', RIME 1 p. 131, ix 1. Cf. also UR = teš$_{2}$ = *ištēniš* "together, jointly, as one group, in one act, etc." (CAD I/J 279; MSL 9 p. 133 l. 471). Based on the latter meaning, teš$_{2}$-teš$_{2}$ may refer to the fact that the property has been given to both Ur-Inana and his wife without a division.

1.1.2 – Financial Documents

The documents in this section are labeled "financial" because they feature the use of silver and barley as means of payment and record transactions in them as monies. This sets them apart from other barley and silver documents.

No. 9 – MS 2191/32

Silver for various purposes, Early Sargonic, Adab.

obv. i	*4* ku$_{3}$ giĝ$_{4}$	4 shekels silver:
	Bad$_{3}$-^{d}En-lil$_{2}$-tuku	(for) Bad-Enliltuku;
	4 ku$_{3}$ giĝ$_{4}$	4 shekels silver
	5 še gur	(and) 5 *gur* of barley:
	Du$_{11}$-ga-ni	(for) Dugani;
	mu Lugal-abba$_{2}$	the year (when) Lugalabba
	A-za-bum-a	in Azabum
	mu-ti-a-am$_{6}$	lived.
ii	*8* ku$_{3}$ giĝ$_{4}$	8 shekels silver:
	Lugal-ki-gal-si	Lugalkigalsi
	ba-de$_{6}$	has taken it away
	A-ga-de$_{3}^{ki}$	(for) Agade.
	3 Lugal-du$_{8}$	3 (shekels silver): Lugaldu.
	Ti-bi$_{2}$-<ra>^{ki}	(of) Tibi(ra);
	2$^{?}$ Im-ta	2$^{?}$: Imta,
	aga$_{3}$-us$_{2}$ nu-banda$_{3}$	the soldier of the supervisor;
	8 E$_{3}$-a	8: E'a,
	sagi	the cupbearer
	nu-banda$_{3}$	of the supervisor;
rev. i	10 *6* Inim-ma-ni-zi	16: Inimanizi,
	ĝiri$_{3}$-ĝen-na-a	it is for the journey
	En-sila-kam	of Ensila.

	Kur-⸢x⸣-TAR	(To the locality?) Kur…
	⸢*2* ku$_{3}$⸣ giĝ$_{4}$	2 shekels silver:
	[…]-LAGAB×⸢x⸣	…:
	⸢Lugal⸣-ma$_{2}$-gur$_{8}$	Lugalmagur;
	3 ku$_{3}$ NINDA$_{2}$×1N$_{1}$+ŠE giĝ$_{4}$ ma-na	3 shekels 1 little mina silver:
ii	Lugal-sila	Lugalsila.
	(blank space)	(blank space)
	ku$_{3}$ A-za-⸢bum⸣-kam	It is the silver of (the locality) Azabum.
	Lugal-ezen	Lugalezen
	⸢i$_{3}$-de$_{6}$⸣ (erased?)	<<has brought it(?)>>,
	i$_{3}$-la$_{2}$	he has weighed it.

obv. i 6–7: Individual(s) by name Lugal-abba$_{2}$-(ĝu$_{10}$) appear in several ED/ES Adab texts. They have the titles sipa "shepherd" in CUSAS 11 no. 142 and maškim "commissioner" in CUSAS 11 no. 203. Lugal-abba$_{2}$ of the present text must have been an important official, since the transaction is dated by the time he stayed at a certain locality. For a similar document and expression, see CUSAS 11 no. 108, where the supervisor Silim-Utu lives in Azabum. This locality was situated in northern Babylonia; see Schrakamp 2013: 214, id. 2015a: 199.

rev. i 2: For ĝiri$_{3}$-ĝen-na "expedition, journey," see SCTRAH no. 44 commentary, with further references.

rev. ii 4: The line was probably erased by the scribe.

No. 10 – MS 2191/33

Receipt of barley as the price of various commodities, Early Dynastic IIIb, Adab.

obv. i	*2* ku$_{3}$ giĝ$_{4}$	2 shekels silver,
	ni$_{3}$-sa$_{10}$-bi	its price:
	1(gur) 2(bariga) še	1 *gur* 2 *bariga* barley.
	Ab-zu-ir-nun	Abzu'irnun
	šu ba-ti	has received it.
	1 bar-si-tug$_{2}$	1 *barsi(g)*-garment:
ii	(ras.) E$_{2}$:pu$_{2}$(LAGAB×U)	(of) Epu(?);
	ni$_{3}$-sa$_{10}$-bi	its price (is)
	1(gur) la$_{2}$ 4(ban$_{2}$) še	1 *gur* minus 4 *ban* barley.
	Za-ŠIM×ḪI	Za…
	šu ba-ti	received.
rev.	(blank)	

The document records the receipt of barley by two individuals as the price for a quantity of silver and a garment.

obv. ii 1: The line is written over erasure. Although the name E$_{2}$-pu$_{2}$ (or -tul$_{2}$) is well attested, the occurrence of a person here is unexpected.

obv. ii 4: The reading of the sign ŠIM×ḪI is unknown to me.

No. 11 – MS 2463

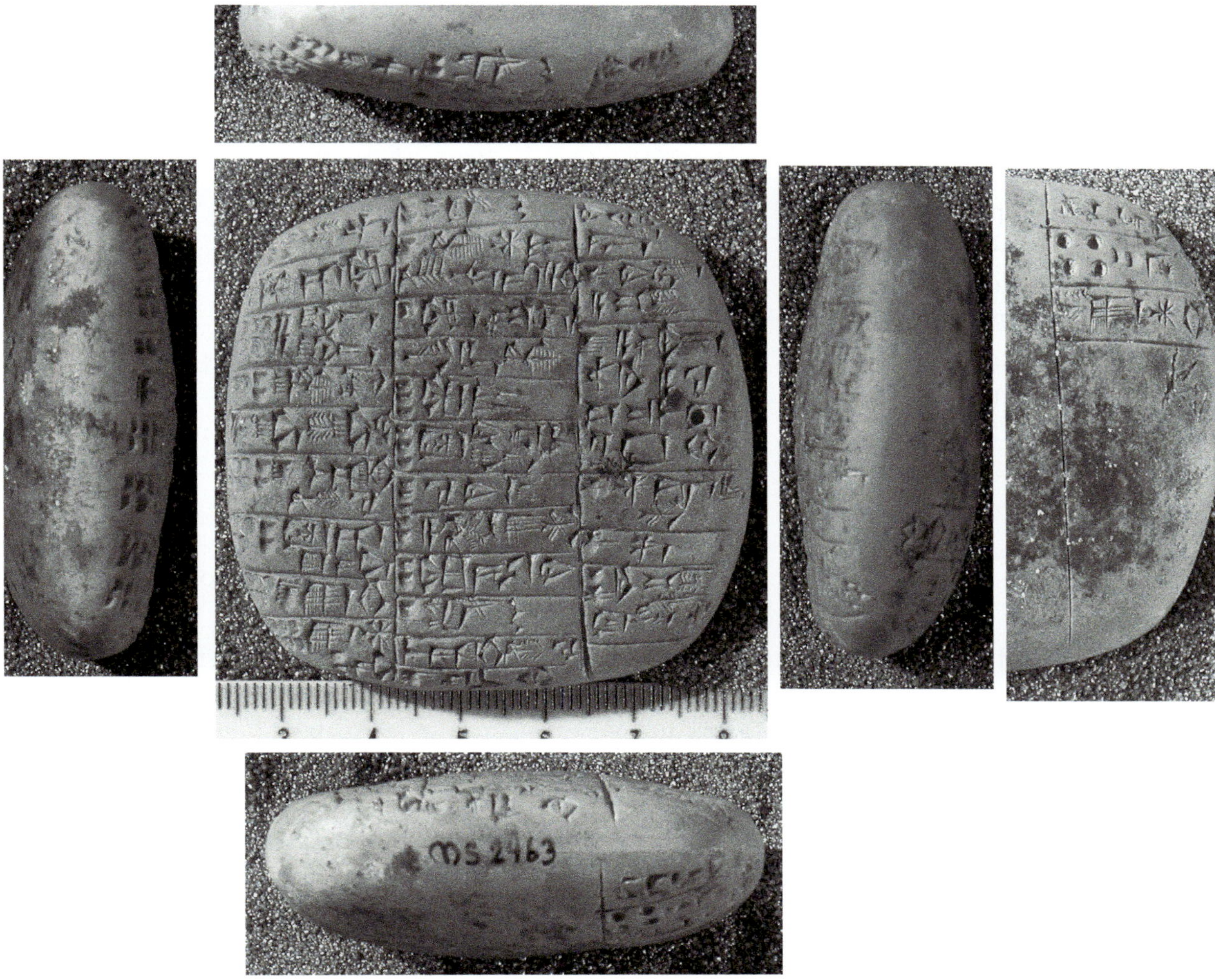

Account of barley for various purposes, Early Dynastic/Early Sargonic, Adab?

obv. i	5 še gur	5 *gur* barley:
	Lugal-eš$_3$-dam	Lugal-ešdam;
	5 Aja$_2$-ne-ne	5: Ajanene;
	2(gur) 2(bariga) Lugal-a$_2$	2 *gur* 2 *bariga*: Lugal-a.
	A-li-li-kam	It is of *'Al-'ilī*;
	6(gur) 2(bariga) 4(ban$_2$) Me-Unug^{ki}-ge-si	6 *gur* 2 *bariga* 4 *ban*: Me-Unugesi;
	5(gur) 2(bariga) Ama-eš$_3$-lil$_2$-ta	5 *gur* 2 *bariga*: Ama'ešlilta;
	5(gur) 5(ban$_2$) E$_2$-ki	5 *gur* 5 *ban*: Eki;
	8(gur) 3(bariga) E$_2$-an-ta	8 *gur* 3 *bariga*: E'anta;
ii	2(bariga) ĜIR$_3$-ERIN$_2$	2 *bariga*: …;
	3(ban$_2$) lu$_2$ ^{d}Dumu-zi-Ma-URU.A^{ki}	3 *ban*: the man of Dumuzi-Maru.
	1(gur) dam Ad-da	1 *gur*: the spouse of Adda
	šeš Ur-lu$_2$	(and) the brother of Urlu.
	3(bariga) Nin-tur	3 *bariga*: Nintur;

	3(bariga) Ama-ni-al-sa$_6$	3 *bariga*: Amani'alsa;
	3(bariga) Si-ni-sa	3 *bariga*: Sinisa;
	2(bariga) Aja$_2$-gil-sa-ĝu$_{10}$	2 *bariga*: Ajagilsaĝu;
	2(bariga) Nin-ur$_2$-ni	2 *bariga*: Ninurni;
	1(bariga) ĜIR$_3$-ERIN$_2$	1 *bariga*: ...
	Me-Unug^{ki}-ge-si	(of) Me-Unugesi.
	4(ban$_2$) al-kam	4 *ban*: it is of *the hoe (work)*(?):
iii	i$_3$-gu$_7$ šidim	*consumed; the builder*(?)
	2(ban$_2$) i$_3$-šah$_2$ a-sa$_{10}$	2 *ban*: the lard was bought.
	5(ban$_2$) addir$_x$(A.ĜIŠGAL×A. / GADA.ĜAR.A.SI) / ^{ĝeš}mar gigir$_2$ / huĝ-ĝa$_2$-kam	5 *ban*: it is the hire of the *margigir*-wagon(s);
	1(ban$_2$) ^{d}Inana-teš$_2$-ĝu$_{10}$	1 *ban*: Inanatešĝu;
	1(ban$_2$) NIM	1 *ban*: NIM;
	1(bariga) 2(ban$_2$) ni$_3$-sa$_{10}$ tug$_2$ PEŠ2 ak	1 *bariga* 2 *ban*: the price of ... textiles.
rev. i	šu+niĝin$_2$-bi	Its total:
	42(gur) la$_2$ 2(ban$_2$)	42 *gur* minus 2 *ban*.
	še e$_2$ AN^{ki}-kam	It is the barley of the house(hold of) Ki'AN(?).
	(blank)	

obv. i 6: This and the following text mention the individual Me-Unug^{ki}-ge-si, a person recorded in other ED/ES texts that deal with financial matters. He appears as the official IB in CUSAS 33 no. 281 obv. ii 6, which Notizia and Visicato attribute to Adab and connect to CUSAS 23 no. 82, itself attributed to Adab by the present author. Note, however, that reference to the household of the city of Ki'AN alongside the personal name Dumuzi-Maru occurs in ED IIIb Umma texts. This may indicate that all texts mentioning Me-Unugesi are from somewhere else. Either at Adab or at Umma the absence of date formulae is unusual.

obv. ii 1: The term appears several times in this volume but its interpretation remains challenging. On the one hand, it may be anše-sur$_x$ "yoked donkeys." However, an additional NI in text No. 15 obv. ii 2 implies anše-erin$_2$-ne$_2$. The interpretation of this is difficult but can hardly be "his/her yoked donkeys." On the other hand, the term may be ĝiri$_3$ erin$_2$ "(grain for) the journey of troops." Note that in all cases the term is mentioned in connection to grain, fodder, or journey provisions.

obv. ii 2: For the geographical name that is written Ma-ru$_{14}$(URU×A) in ED sources from Umma, see CUSAS 33 p. 41 commentary to no. 14 obv. ii 1, with further references.

obv. ii 3: The name of this woman appears in CUSAS 11 no. 150 obv. ii 1–2: Iri-zi dam Ad-da "Irizi, the spouse of Adda."

obv. ii 8: The name means "Father is my treasure."

obv. ii 12–iii 1: Both entries remain problematic.

obv. iii 2: The interpretation implies that two *ban* of barley were used as money to buy an unspecified quantity of lard.

obv. iii 3: For ^{ĝeš}mar-gigir, see Civil 1968: 8 *sub* e$_2$-su-lum-ma. It is possible that the passage has to be understood as ^{ĝeš}mar gigir$_2$ "(hire for) wagons and chariots."

obv. iii 6: A textile tug$_2$-PEŠ$_2$-ak is unattested to my knowledge.

rev. i 3: There are several possibilities for the sign sequence E$_2$-AN-KI. First, E$_2$-an-ki "the House Heaven and Earth" may be a temple name; see MC 5 p. 67 nos. 68–70 (72). Second, it may be e$_2$ AN^{ki} "the house(hold of) Ki'AN," a town in the Umma region. Third, the writing may refer to a personal name, še E$_2$-an-ki-kam "it is the barley of E'anki." The latter could be an abbreviation of the personal name E$_2$-dur$_x$-an-ki recorded in CUSAS 11 no. 77 rev. i 5.

No. 12 – MS 3789/7

Financial document concerning silver and barley, Early Dynastic/Early Sargonic, Adab. Pierced tablet.

obv. i	*4* ½ ku$_3$ giĝ$_4$	4½ shekels silver:
	saĝ ku$_3$-kam	it is the capital amount.
	1 še gur *1* ku$_3$ giĝ$_4$-⸢kam⸣	It is 1 *gur* barley of 1 shekel silver.
	3(bariga) še 1 ku$_3$ giĝ$_4$-kam	It is 3 *bariga* barley of 1 shekel silver.
	ku$_3$ igi-*4*-ĝal$_2$	¼ (shekel) silver.
	⸢4(ban$_2$) še⸣ ku$_3$ igi-*4*-ĝal$_2$	4 *ban* barley: ¼ (shekel) silver.
ii	*1* ku$_3$ giĝ$_4$	1 shekel silver:
	ni$_3$-sa$_{10}$	these are the means of payment.
	Lugal-sila-kam	of Lugalsila.
	ni$_3$-ĝa$_2$ bar-ba	The extra amount
	ba-de$_6$	he has taken away.
	(blank space)	
rev.	(blank)	

obv. ii 2: For the different meanings of ni$_3$-sa$_{10}$-(ma), "purchase price" and "merchandise, means of payment," see Selz 1993: 454–56, with further literature.

obv. ii 4–5: The interpretation is provisional. Its literal meaning is "of the thing (= amount?), its outside": /niĝ$_2$=a(k) bar=bi=a/.

No. 13 – MS 3790/17

Financial document concerning silver and barley, Early Dynastic/Early Sargonic, Adab.

obv. i	30 še gur	30 *gur* barley:
	ni$_3$-sa$_{10}$-⸢bi⸣	its price:
	10 5 ku$_3$ giĝ$_4$	15 shekels silver,
	Ad-da	Adda,
	tibira	the metalworker,
ii	mu-[x]-⸢x⸣	has ...ed it.
	[break]	
	⸢Lugal⸣-abba$_2$-ĝu$_{10}$	Lugalabbaĝu
	mu-ni-sa$_{10}$	has purchased.
rev. i	e$_2$-dumu-še$_3$	For the "House of the son."
ii	(blank)	
rev.	(blank)	

rev. i 1: For the interpretation of e$_2$-TUR as e$_2$-dumu-(saĝ), see the commentary to text No. 127 obv. i 3.

No. 14 – MS 3804

Financial document concerning transactions with barley and silver, Early Dynastic/Early Sargonic, Adab. Pierced tablet.

obv. i	[n+] 2 še gur	x+2 *gur* barley:
	Ir$_x$(UŠ)-*mi-il*-⸢kam$^?$⸣	*Yirmi-'Il.*
	1 Ur-niĝir	1 (*gur*): Urniĝir;
	Silim-^{d}Utu	Silim-Utu (is in charge).
	⸢2⸣ še gur	2 *gur* barley:
	[...]-su$_3$-[...]-⸢x⸣	...su...;
	[...]	...
ii	Aja$_2$-zu-zu	Ajazuzu.
	E$_2$-šudu$_3$-ke$_4$	Ešudu
	Silim-^{d}Utu	(to) Silim-Utu,
	i$_3$-na-šum$_2$	has given.
	2 ku$_3$ giĝ$_4$	2 shekels silver;
	⸢x UMBIN$^?$ DUR$^?$⸣	...,
	Silim-^{d}Utu-ra	to Silim-Utu,
	E$_2$-dam-si	Edamsi,
	[x] i$_3$-na-šum$_2$	has given to him ...
iii	⸢*8*⸣ [ku$_3$ giĝ$_4$]	8 [shekels silver]:
	Ka$_5$-⸢a$^?$⸣	(For) Ka'a(?),
	unu$_3$	the cowherd,
	Silim-^{d}Utu-ke$_4$	Silim-Utu
	im-ma-ta-⸢e$_3$⸣	let it out.
	2 ku$_3$ ⸢giĝ$_4$⸣	2 shekels silver:
	Silim-^{d}Utu	Silim-Utu
	aša$_5$ ambar [(x)]	(for) the field "Swamp"
rev. i	im-ma-e$_3$	he let it out.
	⸢x⸣ [...] ⸢Unug⸣^{ki}	... (the city of) Uruk;
	[break]	...
	10 ⸢x⸣ [...]	10 ...
	Ur-nun-zi-⸢da⸣	Urnunzida,
ii	dumu UD-⸢x⸣-ke$_4$	son of UD...
	Silim-^{d}Utu-ra	to Silim-Utu,
	⸢i$_3$-na-šum$_2$⸣	he has given it.

obv. i 2: See BdI 1 no. 30 obv. i 3 for this individual. The same text mentions a certain Edamsi, who also occurs below. For the Semitic interpretation of the name as *Ir*$_3$(ARAD)-*mi-il*, see Sommerfeld 2010: 86 and *passim* there.

obv. i 4: See Steinkeller 2015 for the reading of the personal name DI-$^{(d)}$Utu.

obv. iii 7–rev. i 1: The presence of a field instead of an individual is puzzling. Cf. this field in text No. 18 obv. iii 1.

No. 15 – MS 3806

Expenditure of grain for various purposes, Early Dynastic/Early Sargonic, Adab?

obv. i	2(bariga) še dam Ad-da	2 *bariga* barley: the wife of Adda;
	2(bariga) ^{d}Imma$_x$(ĜA$_2$×SIG$_7$.ME)-bad$_3$ Ur-^{d}Lum-ma	2 *bariga*: Immabad (and) Ur-Lumma;
	1(bariga) simug	1 *bariga*: the smith;
	3(bariga) U$_2$-u$_2$	3 *bariga*: U'u;
	1(gur) 1(bariga) Me-Unug^{ki}-ge-si	1 *gur* 1 *bariga*: Me-Unugesi;
	4(ban$_2$) ni$_3$-sa$_{10}$	4 *ban*: it is the price
	eše$_2$-dal-la-kam	of … ropes;
ii	1(bariga) 2(ban$_2$) ni$_3$-sa$_{10}$ mušen	1 *bariga* 2 *ban*: the price of bird(s);
	2(bariga) ĜIR$_3$-ERIN$_2$-NI	2 *bariga*: …;
	4(ban$_2$) anše-DUN.GI	4 *ban*: (for) horses;
	2(ban$_2$) ⸢dam⸣ $^{[d]}$Imma$_x$-⸢bad$_3$⸣	2 *ban*: the wife of Immabad;
rev. i	2(bariga) ziz$_2$ ⸢SAL$^?$⸣-tur	2 *bariga* emmer: SALtur(?);
	[...]	…
	1(bariga) dam Ad-da	1 *bariga*: the wife of Adda;
	2(ban$_2$) ^{d}Imma$_x$-bad$_3$	2 *ban*: Immabad;
	3(ban$_2$) *Im$_x$*(DU)-*ta$_2$-lik*	3 *ban*: *Yimtalik*;
ii	1(bariga) 1(ban$_2$) Me-Unug^{ki}-ge-si	1 *bariga* 1 *ban*: Me-Unugesi.
	še ziz$_2$	Barley (and) emmer:
	Me-Unug^{ki}-ge-si	Me-Unugesi
	i$_3$-zi	has expended.

obv. i 7: The interpretation of this type of rope is uncertain.

obv. ii 3: For the identification of anše-DUN.GI as a "true horse," see CUSAS 24 pp. 178–80.

No. 16 – MS 3807

Financial document featuring barley as means of payment for bitumen and for other purposes, Early Dynastic/Early Sargonic, Adab.

obv. i	3 še gur	3 *gur* barley:
	[ni$_3$]-sa$_{10}$	it is the price
	esir$_2$-ḫad$_2$-kam	of dry bitumen.
	10 Ur-⸢tur⸣	10 *gur*: Urtur.
	1(gur) 2(bariga) še gur	1 *gur* 2 (*bariga*) barley:
	ni$_3$-sa$_{10}$	it is the price
ii	esir$_2$-ḫad$_2$-kam	of dry bitumen:
	Ur-lu$_2$	Urlu.
	(blank space)	
	[n] še-numun	x (measures of) seed grain;
	1(bariga) še anše gu$_7$	1 *bariga* barley: for donkeys to eat.
	aša$_5$ 1-kam	It is of the first(?) field.
rev. i	1(bariga) 3(ban$_2$) še anše gu$_7$	1 *bariga* 3 *ban* barley: for donkeys to eat.

	Amar-GUL-kam	It is of AmarGUL.
	aša$_5$-ḪI$^?$-APIN-kam	It is of the field …
ii	(blank)	

The nature of the document is only partly "financial," due to the presence of the barley as money for the bitumen.

obv. i 3: For dry bitumen, see EDPV A p. 134 no. 320 and Stol 2012: 49.

No. 17 – MS 3836

Account of barley for various purposes, Early Dynastic/Early Sargonic, Adab.

obv. i	10 še gur	10 *gur* barley:
	addir$_x$(ĜISAL×A.GADA.ĜAR. / A.DIRI) ma$_2$-kam	it is (for) the hire of boat(s).
	5(gur) 2(bariga) še gur	5 *gur* 2 *bariga* barley:
	Me-me	Meme;
	4(bariga) še ^{d}Nin-sumun$_2$	4 *bariga* barley: (for the temple of the goddess) Nin-sumun;
	1(bariga) 1(ban$_2$) ĝiri$_3$ ma$_2$-gid$_2$	1 *bariga*: (for) the journey of the boat-hauler;
	1(ban$_2$) ĝiri$_3$ Ur-EN×KU$_3^?$	1 *ban*: (for) the journey (of) Ur…;
ii	1(bariga) ni$_3$-sa$_{10}$ ku$_6$-kam	1 *bariga*: the purchase of fish;
	1(bariga) ni$_3$-sa$_{10}$ ⸢mun⸣-kam	1 *bariga*: the purchase of salt;
	2(bariga) 4(ban$_2$) še kaš$_x$(DUG)	2 *bariga* 4 *ban*: barley (for) beer;
	4(ban$_2$) Lu$_2$-igi	4 *ban*: Lu'igi;
	1(ban$_2$) Ur-eš$_3$	1 *ban*: Ur-eš;
	4(ban$_2$) Ni$_3$-na-ga	4 *ban*: Ninaga;
	2(bariga) 1$^?$(ban$_2$) še gur	2 *bariga* 1$^?$ *ban gur* barley:
	maš$_2$ bar-du$_8$-a	(for) long-haired kid goats.
rev. i	(the column is erased)	

obv. ii 4: See the commentary to lu$_2$-igi in CUSAS 23 no. 13, which comes from Adab and not Umma. As in that text, here lu$_2$-igi receives several times more barley than does the individual in the next line. This may support the view that lu$_2$-igi is a category of individuals. Nevertheless, Lu$_2$-igi is also a personal name: see e.g. the "descendents of Lu'igi" in the Maništusu Obelisk (ELTS no. 40 B vii' 6). Here it is probably also a personal name.

obv. ii 6: For the personal name Ni$_3$-na-ga-ma, see CUSAS 11 no. 193 obv. i 11. CUSAS 20 no. 18 obv. i 12 offers lu$_2$-ni$_3$-na-ga, probably also a personal name. In OSP 1 no. 23 obv. v 23 ni$_3$-na-ga is certainly a personal name.

obv. ii 8: For further references to the term bar-du$_8$-a meaning "long-haired goats," see SCTRAH no. 148 pp. 136–37.

No. 18 – MS 5048/13

Account of barley in connection to two fields, Early Dynastic IIIb, Adab. Read from photographs.

obv. i	20 la$_2$ 2 še gur	20 minus 2 *gur* barley:
	UD-re$_2$	UDre;
	15 Lugal-iri	15 *gur*: Lugal-iri;
	16 2(bariga) 4(ban$_2$) Lugal-ni$_3$-U.TA	16 *gur* 2 *bariga* 4 *ban*: LugalniUTA;
	8 Diĝir-teš$_2$-ĝu$_{10}$	8 *gur*: Diĝirtešĝu;
ii	8 la$_2$ 3(ban$_2$) Al-mu	8 *gur* minus 3 *ban*: Almu;
	30 la$_2$ 2 Ur-Ab-zu	30 *gur* minus 2: Ur-Abzu;
	13 1(bariga) Ĝiri$_3$-ni	13 *gur* 1 *bariga*: Ĝirini,
	azlag$_7$	the fuller;
	15 la$_2$ 1(bariga) ⸢Kilim(PEŠ$_2$)⸣ zadim	15 *gur* minus 1 *bariga*: Kilim, the stonecutter;
	15 Šu-ni-diĝir ašgab	15 *gur*: Šunidiĝir, the leather-worker;
iii	(blank space)	
	aša$_5$ ambar	the field "Swamp."
	7 2(bariga) ĜAR-⸢x⸣	7 *gur* 2 *bariga*: GAR…;
	15 ⸢x⸣-NE	15 *gur*: …NE;
	4 2(bariga) *Ra*-[(x)]-⸢NI⸣	4 *gur* 2 *bariga*: *Ra*…;
	2 Ur-⸢x-x-x⸣	2 *gur*: Ur…;

	3 I_3-li_2-⌜x⌝	3 *'Ilī-...;*
rev. i	aša$_5$ e$_2$-DUN-gu-la	the field "Big ... House."
	(rest blank)	

The individuals Al-mu, Ur-Ab-zu and Ĝiri$_3$-ni also occur in text No. 19 below.

obv. i 4: For this name, see Andersson 2012: 84 and 372–73.

obv. iii 1: For the same field, see text No. 14 obv. iii 8.

rev. i 1: Cf. the canal i$_7$ e$_2$-DUN in Adab texts Nos. 37 obv. i 3, 291 rev. 3.

No. 19 – MS 4250

Account of barley, Early Dynastic/Early Sargonic, Adab.

obv. i	1 še gur	1 *gur* barley:
	Šu-i$^{!}$(*6*)	Šu'i ("Barber");
	1 Lu$_2$-UN-tu	1: LuUNtu;
	1 Ur-SAL.UŠ	1: UrSALUŠ;
	1 Ur-tur	1: Urtur;
	1 E$_2$-aša$_5$	1: E'aša;
	1 Ur-^{d}Lamma	1: Ur-Lamma;
	1 A-rin$_2$	1: Arina;
	1 Ad-da	1: Adda;
	1 E$_2$-zi	1: Ezi;
ii	1 Lugal-al-sa$_6$	1: Lugal-alsa;
	1 Ur-Šubur	1: Ur-Šubur;
	1 Ur$_2$-ni	1: Urni,
	gala	the cult-singer;
	1 E$_2$-da	1: Eda;
	1 Ur-Ba-ba	1: Ur-Baba;
	1 Ur-Šubur	1: Ur-Šubur;
	1 Za$_3$-mu	1: Zamu;
	2(bariga) Aja$_2$-ni-diĝir	2 *bariga*: Ajanidiĝir;
	2(bariga) Ur-^{d}En-da-ga-ra	2 *bariga*: Ur-Endagara;
rev. i	2(gur) Lu$_5$-lu$_5$	2 *gur*: Lulu;
	2(gur) la$_2$ 4(ban$_2$) Šubur kas$_4$	2 *gur* minus 4 *ban*: Šubur, the runner;
	3(ban$_2$) Ur-^{d}MUŠ	3 *ban*: Ur-MUŠ;

1(gur) Ur-^{d}Ku$_3$-su$_{13}$	1 *gur*: Ur-Kusu;
2(bariga) Al-mu	2 *bariga*: Almu;
3(gur) Lugal-e	3 *gur*: Lugale;
1(gur) Ur-Ab-zu	1 *gur*: Ur-Abzu;
2(bariga) Ĝiri$_3$-ni	2 *bariga*: Ĝirini
I$_3$-lum-kalag	(and) *'Ilum-dān*;
1(gur) Lu$_2$-šu-la	1 *gur*: Lušula;
ii 2(gur) 2(bariga) ĜIR$_3$-ERIN$_2$	2 *gur* 2 *bariga*: …;
1(gur) Lu$_2$-gid$_2$	1 *gur*: Lugid;
1(bariga) 4(ban$_2$) šaḫ$_2$-niga	1 *bariga* 4 *ban*: (for) fattened pigs;
1(bariga) 2(ban$_2$) nu-kiri$_6$	1 *bariga* 2 *ban*: the gardener;
1 *Su-mu-lum*	1 (gur): *Šumu(m)-'ilum*;
1 Ur-^{d}Nin-urta	1: Ur-Ninurta;
1 Ur-nu	1: Urnu;
1 Nin-PA-PI$_{\textit{-nutillû}}$.PI	1: Nin…
1 Im-ta	1: Imta.

Note the rich selection of personal names compounded with deities rarely recorded in Adab documents: Baba, Endagara, Kusu, Lamma and Ninurta.

obv. i 4: SAL.UŠ = mussa(SAL.UŠ$^{\text{sa}_2}$) is "son-in-law": see MC 4 pp. 37–38, SAL.UŠ in ED Lu$_2$ E = MSL 12 p. 19 l. 155 in context with kinship terms, and MSL 14 p. 395 (*Ea* V) for SAL.UŠ = gidlam$_4$, nitalam$_4$, etc. (< nita "man" + dam "spouse") = *ḫīrtu* "spouse." ED IIIa administrative documents from Fara show that this sign combination was used also as a professional title related to musicians (nar) and female personnel geme$_2$-kar-kid$_2$; see EDATŠ p. 41.

rev. i 2: Note that this would be the only name with a professional title. A writing lu$_2$-kas$_4$ is expected for such a title, so perhaps this is a personal name Šubur-kas$_4$.

rev. i 4: ^{d}Ku$_3$-su$_{13}$ is written ^{d}Ku$_3$-su$_{3/20}$ during Ur III. For this deity, see commentary to no. 297 obv. 5.

rev. ii 8: The unfinished PI is probably a mistake for Nin-PA-pi-pi. Cf. Nin-pi-pi in BdI 1 no. 13 obv. i 3.

1.1.3 – Personnel

No. 20 – MS 1952/41

Account of personnel, Early Dynastic/Early Sargonic, Adab.

obv. i	1 Ur-uš-bar	1 Ur-ušbar;
	1 Eš$_3$-iri-si	1 Eš-irisi;
	1 ⸢Niĝir⸣-Ab-zu	1 Niĝir-Abzu.
ii	(blank)	
rev.	(blank)	

No. 21 – MS 2362

Account of personnel, Early Dynastic/Early Sargonic, Adab. The document is sealed on the reverse.

obv. i	7 lu$_2$ nu-banda$_3$	7 persons: the supervisor;
	3 Lugal-abba$_2$-ĝu$_{10}$	3: Lugalabbaĝu.
ii	(blank)	
rev.	(indistinct seal impression depicting a bull-man)	

obv. i 2: For the same individual in ED/ES Adab texts published in CUSAS 11, see references in Andersson 2012: 304.

No. 22 – MS 3790/40

Assignment of personnel to named individuals in connection with agricultural work, Early Dynastic/Early Sargonic, Adab.

obv. i	[10] la$_2$ 1 lu$_2$	10 minus 1 persons:
	[Lugal]-usar$_3$(LAL$_2$.LAGAB)-ĝu$_{10}$	Lugalusarĝu;
	[n] ⸢Lugal$^?$-sa$_6$-ga⸣	x Lugalsaga;
	[break]	...
	[n] Eden-⸢x-(x)⸣	x Eden...;
	[n] Na-ba-lu$_5$	x Nabalu;
	[break]	...
ii	15 Šu-ku$_6$	15: Šuku;
	8 Ur-saĝ	8: Ursaĝ;
	7 Maḫ-diĝir	7: Maḫdiĝir;
	8 Lu$_2$-bara$_2$-ge	8: Lubarage;
	10 Lugal-ša$_3$	10: Lugalša;
	13 Lugal-Dulum$_2$	13. Lugal-Dulum.
	aša$_5$ ki-saĝ	The field Kisaĝ
	u$_4$ *1*	Day 1.
	Silim-^{d}⸢Utu⸣	Silim-[Utu],
	nu-banda$_3$	the supervisor.
rev.	(blank)	

obv. i 4': Two personal names that occur in ED/ES Adab texts include the sign EDIN: Eden-bi-še$_3$ (e.g., CUSAS 11 no. 90 obv. ii 5) and En-eden-na (e.g., CUSAS 11 no. 77 obv. ii 8).

obv. ii 3: In CUSAS 11 no. rev. i 2, this individual is a person bringing in an amount of silver.
obv. ii 7: See Civil 1994: 57 for ki-saĝ as "width."

No. 23 – MS 3813

Account of Subarean slaves: women, boys and girls, the children specified as branded or not branded. Early/Middle Sargonic, Adab.

obv. i	[n+] 2 ⸢geme$_2$ su⸣-bir$_x$(BAPPIR)-a	x+2 Subarean women;
	1 dumu-nita za$_3$ nu-šu$_2$	1 boy not branded;
	13 dumu-munus za$_3$-šu$_2$	13 girls branded;
	[n] ⸢dumu⸣-munus [za$_3$] nu-šu$_2$	x girls not branded:
	⸢Keš$_3$⸣-men	Kešmen (is the overseer).
ii	4 geme$_2$	4 women;
	1 dumu-nita za$_3$ nu-šu$_2$	1 boy not branded;
	14 dumu-munus	14 girls (not branded?);
	Nin-i$_3$-kuš$_2$	Nin-ikuš (is the overseer).
	4 geme$_2$	4 women;
	1 dumu-munus za$_3$ nu-šu$_2$	1 girl not branded;

rev. i	1 dumu-nita za$_3$ nu-šu$_2$	1 boy not branded;
	14 dumu-munus	14 girls (branded?);
	Šu-im-du$_{11}$-ga	Šu'imduga (is the overseer).
	2 geme$_2$	2 women;
	1 dumu-munus za$_3$-šu$_2$	1 girl branded;
	1 dumu-nita za$_3$-šu$_2$	1 boy branded;
ii	[1] dumu-nita za$_3$ nu-šu$_2$	1 boy not branded;
	[x]-ma	...ma (is the overseer).
	e$_2$-kešda-a	"The house where it is spun."

The document is discussed by Bartash 2015a.

rev. ii 3: For the same building, see CUSAS 11 no. 175 obv. i 4, where it follows a line that mentions e$_2$-gal "palace." Selz interprets e$_2$-keš$_2$-da of ED IIIb Ĝirsu texts as "Rüstkammer(?)"; FAOS 15/2 no. 114 obv. ii 4. However, the interpretation of e$_2$-KEŠ$_2$-a is quite lucid here. KEŠ$_2$ should be compared to the Ur III term gu-kešda which designates "yarn, spun thread." The verb kešda refers to the twisting, spinning of threads from wool. Hence, e$_2$-kešda-a is literally "the house (where it is) spun," i.e., a (part of a) textile workshop. The document records the import of foreign slaves, adults and minors, for the purpose of exploiting their labor in the mass-production textile industry run by the crown.

No. 24 – MS 3830

Account of cattle, sheep, hides, and adult and child slaves sent from Irisagrig to Uruk, Early Dynastic/Early Sargonic, Adab.

obv. i	[n+] 20 la$_2$ 3 gu$_4$ (ras.)	x+20 minus 3: oxen (erasure);
	2 ab$_2$ amar du$_3$-a	2 cows that have already calved;
	2 kuš gu$_4$	2 oxhides;
	10 la$_2$ 1 anše	9 donkeys;
	180 udu-ḫi-a	180 sheep of all sorts;
	1 saĝ ĝuruš	1 slave, male worker;
	šaĝa(LU$_2$×EŠE$_2$) dab$_5$-ba-am$_3$	he is a captive who has been seized;
ii	1 munus	1 woman;
	4 dumu-ni	her 4 children:
	geme$_2$ PU$_3$.ŠA-Aš-tar$_2$-me	they are the female workers of PUŠA-'Aštar.
	1 geme$_2$ Diĝir-maḫ	1 female worker: Diĝirmaḫ;
	1 geme$_2$ Maš dumu saĝĝa	1 female worker: Maš, son of the chief temple-administrator;
	1 geme$_2$ Me-^{sa2}sag$_7$-nu-di	1 female worker: Mesagnudi.
	ni$_3$ Iri-saĝ-rig$_x$(SAL.ḪUB$_2$.DU)^{ki}-kam	There are the things of Irisaĝrig.
rev. i	Unug^{ki}-še$_3$	To Uruk
	šu ab-us$_2$	they have been sent.
	U$_3$-mu-NI-NI	To UmuNINI
	an-na-šum$_2$	they have been given.
ii	(blank)	

The text is placed in this section because, while mentioning cattle, it mainly deals with human beings. The previous text listing branded Subarean children and the context of this text with the vivid phrase "the things that have been sent ..." show a darker side of Mesopotamian civilization.

obv. i 2: See PSD A^{2} 158a for ab$_{2}$ amar du$_{3}$-a.

obv. i 7: See Steinkeller 2013a: 132 ff. for šaga$^{(sic)}$ "captive." As argued by Krecher 1978: 57, the middle consonant in this lexeme is /ĝ/.

obv. ii 7: The use of ni$_{3}$ "thing" here is a clear indication that captives, female laborers and their children were regarded as commodities. The reference to the sending of these persons to Uruk into the hands of a certain UmuNINI shows that they would be employed in the public sector.

No. 25 – MS 3844

Account of soldiers, on the morning watch and sick, Early Dynastic/Early Sargonic, Adab.

obv. i	5 aga$_{3}$-us$_{2}$	5 soldiers:
	⸢Du$_{11}$⸣-ga-ni	with Dugani,
	dumu Za$_{3}$-mu-da	son of Zamu,
	ba-da-ĝen	they went;
	10 Ur-Šubur	10 Ur-Šubur;
	10 Amar-^{d}Ašnan$_{x}$(TIR)	10 Amar-Ašnan;
	10 Adab-ki-bi$_{x}$(DUG)	10 Adabkibi:
ii	u$_{4}$-zal-la-me	they are on the morning (watch).
	1 Inim-ma-ni-zi	1 Inimanizi;
	1 Ur-saĝ	1 Ursaĝ;
	1 Ur-^{d}Tu	1 Ur-Tu(da);
	(blank)	
	1 Ur-gu	1 Urgu;
	1 Lugal-ra	1 Lugalra:
	tu-ra-me / Ur-ki-saĝ	they are sick. Urkisaĝ (is in charge).
rev.	(blank)	

obv. i 7: For this individual, see CUSAS 11 nos. 63 rev. 1, 84 rev. i 2, 151 obv. ii 1 and CUSAS 26 no. 67 obv. i 3. For the use of DUG instead of BI in ED/ES Adab, see the commentary to text No. 116 obv. ii 1.

obv. ii 1: u$_{4}$-zal-la also signifies the third watch of the night, referring to early morning: see u$_{4}$-zal-la = *namārītu* "dawn" in CAD N^{I} p. 208 s.v., lexical section.

No. 26 – MS 4225

Letter-order concerning a worker, Early Dynastic/Early Sargonic, Adab.

obv. i	1N$_8$ Aja$_2$-⸢ne-ne⸣	1 Ajanene,
	lu$_2$-DUN-a	the subordinate of
	Aja$_2$-zu-zu	Ajazuzu,
	ugula	the supervisor,
ii	⸢ba⸣-zah$_3$	went missing.
	šu ḫa-mu-us$_2$-e	He should send him.
rev.	(blank)	

obv. i 1: The sign N$_8$ is used instead of N$_1$ in order to show that the person has fled.

obv. i 2: For lu$_2$-DUN-a "subordinate, dependents," see the commentary to SCTRAH no. 156 obv. 3.

No. 27 – MS 4728

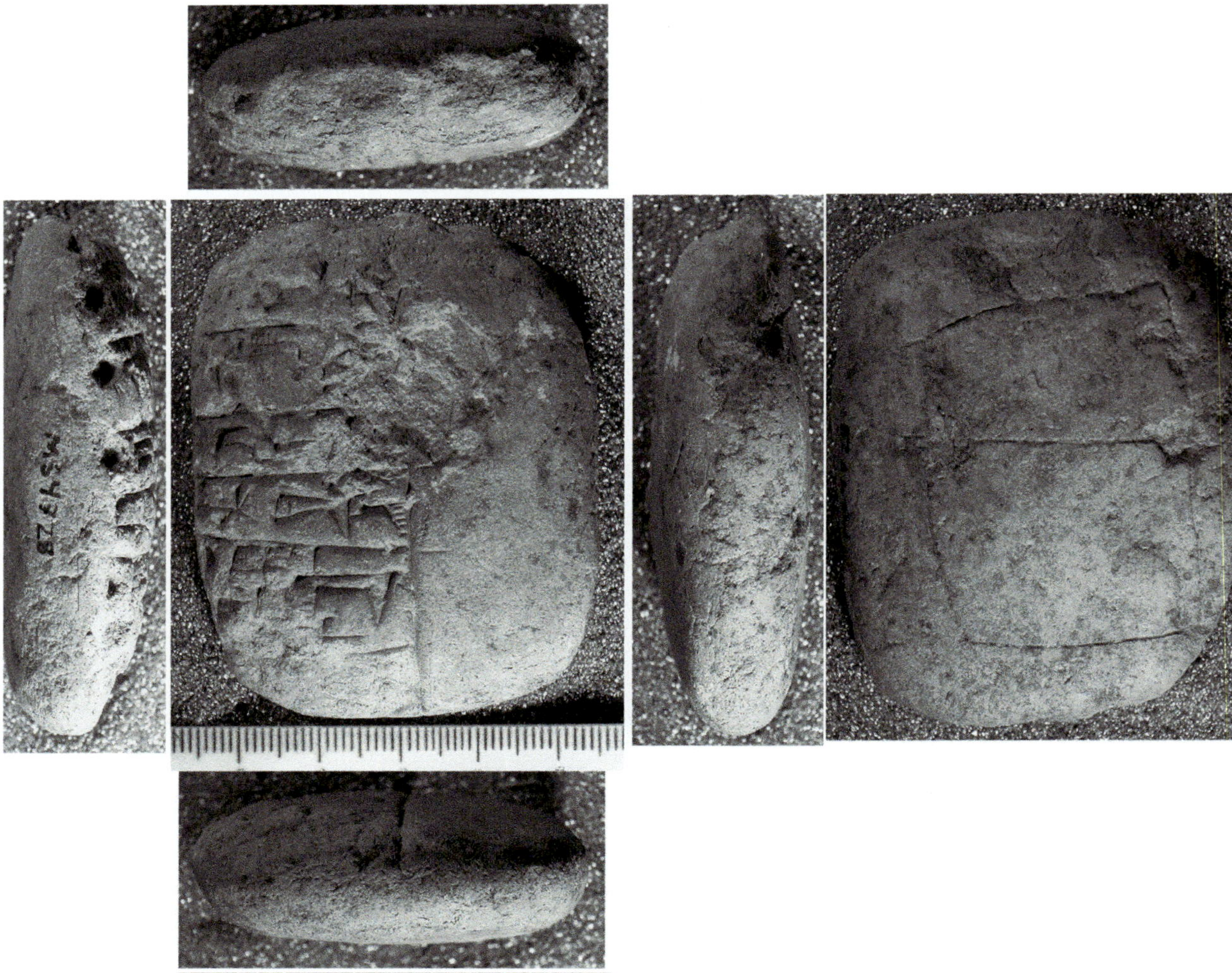

Account of personnel, Early Dynastic/Early Sargonic, Adab?

obv. i	⸢1⸣ […]	1 …
	1 ⸢DIM$_2$-mud⸣	1 DIMmud;
	1 Šubur-⸢tur⸣	1 Šuburtur;
	1 Ur$_2$-[ni]	1 Ur[ni]:
	Me-^{d}X-DAR-⸢x⸣	Me-…
	1 E$_2$-⸢*iš*?⸣-*ta$_2$-kal$_2$*	*Bītiš$^?$-takal*
	[1 …]-⸢li⸣	[1] …li
ii	(blank)	
rev.	(drawing)	

obv. i 5: See no. 75 obv. i 3 for the same unidentified sign. The sign here is: 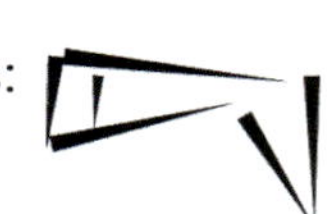

The absence of the number is suspicious although not impossible. Alternatively, Ur$_2$-ni / išib ^{d}… "Urni, the *išib*-priest of the god …."

obv. i 6: The name is probably of the type god/king/etc.-*iš*(terminative-adverbialis)+*takal* "trust!," so "Believe in the temple!"(?). However, E$_2$-*iš-ta$_2$-kal$_2$* does not appear elsewhere to my knowledge. There is *E-li-iš-ta$_2$-kal$_2$* in text No. 288 rev. i 3, but it would be difficult to explain the alternation E/E$_2$ and there is no room for a sign LI.

rev.: The drawing is noteworthy. It is a rectangle with rounded sides divided into two unequal parts by a horizontal line. It may be a field plan or a sketch of some other object.

No. 28 – MS 5002

Letter-order concerning personnel, Early Dynastic/Early Sargonic, Adab.

obv.	1 Ur-^{d}Nin-mug	1 Ur-Ninmug (and)
	1 Ur-$^{d.še_3}$Šer$_7$-da	1 Ur-Šerda
	Adab^{ki}	(in) Adab
	i$_3$-durun$_x$(⸢DUR$_2$⸣.DUR$_2$)-ne$_2$-eš$_2$	they dwell.
	ḫe$_2$-su-be$_2$-a	They should come (here)!
	Aš$_{11}$-lum	*Ašlum*;
	I-ri$_2$-tum	*Y/'iritum*;
rev.	*Šu-x(-x)*-MES	...
	(blank)	

obv. 1–2: Both personal names are well attested in ED/ES Adab texts.

obv. 5: The form ḫe$_2$-su-be$_2$-eš$_2$ "they should come" is expected, instead of one with a seemingly meaningless -a at the end.

obv. 6: This is a Semitic name, attested e.g. at ED IIIb Nabada (Tell Beydar): see Subartu 12 no. 148 obv. ii 3.

obv. 7: Also a Semitic name. The same woman appears in CUSAS 11 no. 151 obv. i 3.

1.1.4 – Land

No. 29 – MS 1952/34

Account of land, Early Dynastic IIIb, Adab.

obv. i	1(eše$_3$) aša$_5$ ⸢x⸣-mu	1 *eše* land: ...;
	1(eše$_3$) Ur -gu	1 *eše*: Urgu
	Ur-^{d}Zu:en	(and) Ur-Zu'en;
	1(eše$_3$) [x]-e$_2^{?}$	1 *eše*: ...;
	1(eše$_3$) Da-da	1 *eše*: Dada;
	1(eše$_3$) ⸢Ku$_3^{?}$⸣-du$_6$	1 *eše*: ...;
	1(eše$_3$) Niĝar-mud	1 *eše*: Niĝarmud.
	Ur-gu maškim	Urgu, the commissioner.
ii-iii	(blank)	
rev.	(blank)	

No. 30 – MS 1952/40

Account of land, Early Dynastic/Early Sargonic, Adab.

obv. i	1(eše$_3$) aša$_5$	1 *eše* land:
	Ma-NI-NI	MaNINI;
	1(eše$_3$) Sig-MU	1 *eše*: SigMU;
	1(eše$_3$) Ur-gu kurušda	1 *eše*: Urgu, the fattener;
	1(eše$_3$) Ur-^{d}Peš$_3$-tur	1 *eše*: Ur-Peštur;
	1(eše$_3$) *Šu-Ma-ma*	1 *eše*: *Šu-Mama*;
	1(iku) PA-⸢x⸣-x-bal	1 *iku*: ...;
ii	Ur-Tu	Ur-Tu(da);
	A-⸢ga$^{?}$⸣-le	... (personal name?)
rev.	(blank)	

No. 31 – MS 1952/45

Account of land, Early Dynastic IIIb, Adab.

obv. i	1(eše$_3$) 3(iku) aša$_5$	1 *eše* 3 *iku* land:
	Lugal-kisal-le-si	Lugalkisalesi;
	1(eše$_3$) A-ta-nu-il$_2$	Atanu'il;
	1(eše$_3$) 3(iku) Lugal-iri-ra	1 *eše* 3 *iku*: for Lugaliri;
ii	ša$_3$-bi 4(iku) aša$_5$ Lugal-a$_2$-zi-da	out of it 4 *iku* land (for) Lugalazida;
	1(eše$_3$) Utu-mu-kuš$_2$	1 *eše*: Utu-mukuš;
	2(eše$_3$) [...]-⸢x⸣	2 *eše*: ...;
rev. i	4(iku) Ur-saĝ-Utu	4 iku: Ursaĝ-Utu.
	aša$_5$ Šu-ku$_6$	The field of Šuku.

obv. i 4: See Andersson 2012: 400 for personal names beginning with Lugal-iri. The name Lugal-iri-ra is otherwise unattested. The sign in question is certainly RA and cannot be saĝĝa(ŠID), GIŠGAL or UKKIN.

rev. i 2: Alternatively, the "field 'Fisherman'."

No. 32 – MS 1952/42

Account of land, Early Dynastic IIIb, Adab.

obv. i	[n] ⸢aša$_5$⸣-mu$_2$ ⸢^{d}⸣Aš$_8$-gi$_4$-ur-saĝ	... of land (with crops) growing: Ašgi-ursaĝ;
	4(iku) Lugal-NE-nu-si	4 *iku*: LugalNEnusi ;
	4(iku) Ur-^{d}Iškur(LAK377)	4 *iku*: Ur-Iškur;
	2(bur$_3$) 3(iku) aša$_5$-mu$_2$ *Su-mu-lum*	2 *bur* 3 *iku* of land (with crops) growing: *Šumu(m)-'ilum*.
ii	(blank)	
rev.	(blank)	

obv. i 4: Su-mu-LUM appears in the Maništusu obelisk, ELTS no. 40 surface A, v' 3. However, the present *Su-mu-lum* is most likely a different person. I interpret the name as Akkadian, constructed of the two parts *šumu(m)* "name, progeny" and *'ilum* "god." For names beginning with the first element, see MAD 3 p. 274.

No. 33 – MS 3789/22

Account of land, Early Dynastic/Early Sargonic, Adab. Pierced tablet.

obv. i	1 ½(iku) aša$_5$	1 ½ *iku* land:
	Ur-Šubur	Ur-Šubur;
	1 ½ A-ba-^{d}En-lil$_2$	1 ½: Aba-Enlil;
	1 ½ Ad-da	1 ½: Adda;
	1 ½ A-ba-mu-na	1 ½: Abamuna;
	1 Mu-ni-uri$_3$	1: Muni'uri(n);
ii	1(bur$_3$) Lu$_2$-pa$_3$-da	1 *bur*: Lupada;
	4(iku) Zur-zur	4 *iku*: Zurzur;
	2(iku) aša$_5$-bi la$_2$×20 sar	2 *iku* its land minus 20 *sar*.
	aša$_5$ UŠ-gal	UŠgal-Field.
	u$_4$ *2*	Day 2.
rev.	(blank)	

obv. ii 4: The term aša$_5$ UŠ-gal appears in a number of ED IIIb Ĝirsu texts: BIN 8 no. 389 obv. ii 1, DP 377 obv. ii 4, DP 400 obv. i 2, etc. Selz in FAOS 15/1 no. 51 pp. 228–29 interprets this as part of a field name. However, since the present text is from Adab, that cannot be the same field.

No. 34 – MS 3790/61

Account of land, Early Dynastic/Early Sargonic, Adab.

obv. i	1 *2* ⸢sar⸣ [(x)]	1 *iku* 2 *sar* (land):
	E$_2$-⸢zi⸣	Ezi;
	3 Lugal-kala	3 *iku*: Lugalkala;
	⸢3⸣ Ur-nu	3 *iku*: Urnu;
	⸢3 x⸣-ad$_2$-gal	3 *iku*: ...adgal;
	< > U$_3$-mu-NI-NI	< > *iku*: UmuNINI;
ii	[break]	...
	1 [+n ...]	1+x *iku* ...;
	2 [...]	2 *iku* ...;
	2 *1* Lugal-Dulum$_2$	2 *iku* 1 *sar*: Lugal-Dulum.
rev.	(blank)	

obv. ii 3': For the same individual in another Adab text, see text No. 22 obv. ii 6.

No. 35 – MS 3833

Account of land, Early Dynastic/Early Sargonic, Adab.

obv. i	[aša$_5$ n+] 4(šar$_2$)	x+4 šar (= x+240 *bur*) [land]:
	[x]-KA	(for) ...KA;
	[break: 2 lines]	...
	4(bur$_3$×u) aša$_5$	40 *bur* land:
	Zur-zur	Zurzur;
	4(bur$_3$×u) aša$_5$	40 *bur* land:
	^{d}Aš$_8$-gi$_4$	Ašgi;
	1(bur$_3$×u) aša$_5$	10 *bur* land:
	[...]	...
ii	2(bur$_3$×u) aša$_5$	20 *bur* land:
	⸢*A*?⸣-*qar-su*	*Aqarsu*(?);
	2(bur$_3$×u) aša$_5$	20 *bur* land:
	i$_3$-du$_8$-gal	the chief door-man;
	2(bur$_3$×u) aša$_5$	20 *bur* land:
	Ma-U$_2$	MaU;
	2(bur$_3$×u) aša$_5$	20 *bur* land:
	Aja$_2$-ni$_3$-du$_{10}$	Ajanidu;
	2(bur$_3$×u) aša$_5$	20 *bur* land:
	Ur-nu	Urnu;
	1(bur$_3$×u) aša$_5$	10 *bur* land:
iii	⸢x⸣-[...]	...;
	2(bur$_3$×u) aša$_5$	20 *bur* land:
	Ur-^{d}En-lil$_2$	Ur-Enlil;
	2(bur$_3$×u) aša$_5$	20 *bur* land:
	Ur-pisaĝ	Urpisaĝ;
	1(bur$_3$×u) aša$_5$	10 *bur* land:
	Lugal-a-⸢ĝi$_6$⸣	Lugalaĝe;
	1(bur$_3$×u) aša$_5$	10 *bur* land:
	Ba-za	Baza;
	1(bur$_3$×u) aša$_5$	10 *bur* land:
	Lugal-^{d}En-lil$_2$	Lugal'Enlil;
iv	1(bur$_3$×u) aša$_5$	10 *bur* land:
	Ra-bi$_2$*-i*$_3$*-lum*	*Rabi-'ilum*;
	1(bur$_3$×u) aša$_5$	10 *bur* land:
	Lugal-aja$_2$-ĝu$_{10}$	Lugalajaĝu;
	1(bur$_3$×u) aša$_5$	10 *bur* land:
	Šu-ni-diĝir	Šunidiĝir;
	3(bur$_3$×u) aša$_5$	30 *bur* land:
	ĜAR-⸢NE/GIBIL⸣	...;
	3(bur$_3$×u) aša$_5$	30 *bur* land:
	Aja$_2$-ti-e	Ajati(l)e
rev. i	3(bur$_3$×u) aša$_5$	30 *bur* land:
	Lugal-bad$_3$	Lugalbad;
	1(bur$_3$×u) aša$_5$	10 *bur* land:
	Ad-da	Adda.

obv. i 8: This is probably an abbreviated personal name.

obv. iv 10: Interpreting TI as til$_3$ "to (let) live." Alternatively, TI stands for teĝ$_4$ "to (let) approach," and the name is Ajateĝe.

1.1.5 – Bread and Beer Texts Mentioning E'AḪ

A number of the Adab texts of the Late Early Dynastic IIIb and Early Sargonic periods in the present volume mentions an organization or building e_2-AḪ. The interpretation of the last sign is uncertain. These texts record allocations of beer and bread and, much rarer, other cereal products to various groups of people associated with the palace. Judging by the contents of the texts, e_2-AḪ may have been the place where these products were produced and/or stored. This "house" also appears in other texts in this volume, as a recipient of goods in context with other buildings, households, temples, gods and individuals. The administrative interpretation of these and similar texts requires a separate study.

Like a large number of other ED/ES Adab tablets, most documents that mention e_2-AḪ have a hole pierced in the middle, of diameter *ca.* 3,5 mm. These holes were probably made with the same stylus that was used to write the number ten. Piercing tablets at Adab is in the corpus of Early Dynastic and Sargonic texts. It might arise from a practice of keeping together tablets of the same time-span or some other administrative characteristic by stringing them on a thread.

No. 36 – MS 2181/1

Issue of bread and beer to palace soldiers, Early Dynastic/Early Sargonic, Adab. Pierced tablet.

obv. i	180 ninda	180 breads;
	2 dug	2 jars (of beer):
	aga_3-us_2	(for) the soldiers
	e_2-gal	(of) the palace.
ii	e_2-AḪ	The E'AḪ.
	iti ab-e_3-zi-ga	Month Ab-eziga.
rev.	(blank)	

No. 37 – MS 2181/2

Issue of bread and beer to personnel at a canal, Early Dynastic/Early Sargonic, Adab. Pierced tablet.

obv. i	3000 la$_2$ 60 ninda	2940 breads;
	40 la$_2$ 2 dug	38 jars (of beer):
	ka i$_7$ e$_2$-DUN	the inlet of the canal at E-DUN.
ii	e$_2$-AḪ	The E'AḪ.
	iti še-gur$_x$(|ŠE.ŠE|.KIN)-am$_3$	Month Šeguram.
rev.	(blank)	

obv. i 3: See RGTC 2 p. 262 for this canal. It also occurs in text No. 291 rev. 3. For a locality E$_2$-DUN^{ki}, see an Ur III text from Nippur, NATN no. 782 obv. 1. The place may have been near Nippur. Its appearance in texts from nearby Adab should not be surprising.

No. 38 – MS 2181/3

Issue of bread and beer to palace soldiers, Early Dynastic/Early Sargonic, Adab. Pierced tablet.

obv. i	180 ninda	180 breads;
	2 dug	2 jars (of beer):
	aga$_3$-us$_2$	(for) the soldiers
	e$_2$-gal$^!$	(of) the palace.
ii	e$_2$-AḪ	The E'AḪ.
	⸢iti⸣ a$_2$-ki-ti	Month Akiti.
	(blank)	
rev.	(blank)	

obv. i 4: GAL is written without the final horizontal wedge.

No. 39 – MS 2181/4

Issue of bread and beer to personnel at a canal, Early Dynastic/Early Sargonic, Adab. Pierced tablet.

obv. i	240 ninda	240 breads;
	12 dug	12 jars (of beer):
	ka ⸢i$_7$⸣-tur-kam	the inlet of the "Small canal."
ii	e$_2$-AḪ	The E'AḪ.
	iti še-gur$_x$(|ŠE.ŠE|.KIN)-am$_3$	Month Šeguram.
rev.	(blank)	

obv. i 3: This canal appears also in SCTRAH no. 1 obv. ii 1.

No. 40 – MS 2181/5

Issue of bread and beer to palace soldiers, Early Dynastic/Early Sargonic, Adab. Pierced tablet.

obv. i	⸢480⸣ ninda	480 breads:
	1(ban$_2$) 10 du$_8$	from 1 *ban* (flour) 10 (loaves) baked;
	5 dug	5 jars (of beer):
	aga$_3$-us$_2$	(for) the soldiers
ii	e$_2$-gal	(of) the palace.
	e$_2$-AḪ	The E'AḪ.
	(blank)	
	⸢iti⸣ a$_2$-ki-ti	Month Akiti.
	(blank)	

No. 41 – MS 2181/6

Issue of bread and beer to personnel at a field, Early Dynastic/Early Sargonic, Adab. Pierced tablet.

obv. i	180 ninda	180 breads,
	⸢3⸣ dug	3 jars (of beer):
	ENGUR-TUM	(for) … personnel,
	aša$_5$ ^{d}Dam-gal-nun	(at) the field of Damgalnun.
ii	e$_2$-AḪ	The E'AḪ.
	iti šu-ĝar	Month Šuĝar.
rev.	(blank)	

obv. i 3: For ID$_2$(A.ENGUR)-TUM, see CUSAS 23 no. 57 (the text is from ED/ES Adab, not from Umma as stated in the edition) rev. ii 1. The appearance of several ENGUR-TUM$_{\textit{-gunû}}$ in CUSAS 11 no. 96 of the same date (Meskigala) among professional titles suggests that the term may refer to a category of workers.

No. 42 – MS 2181/7

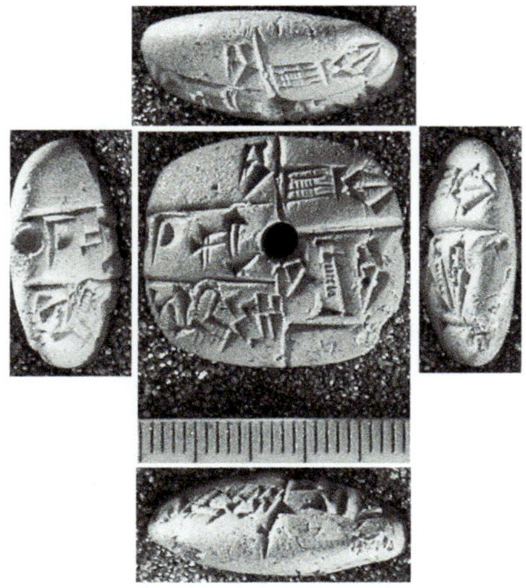

Issue of bread and beer to a "Silver (and) lapis-lazuli boat," Early Dynastic/Early Sargonic, Adab. Pierced tablet.

obv. i	< > ninda	< > breads;
	10 la$_2$ 1 dug	9 jars (of beer):
	ma$_2$-ku$_3$-za:gin$_3$	(for) the "Silver (and) lapis-lazuli boat."
ii	e$_2$-AḪ	The E'AḪ.
	iti šu-ĝar	Month Šuĝar.
rev.	(blank)	

obv. i 3: The identity of this "boat" is uncertain: if indeed a boat, it may be a reference to a ceremonial vessel and the allocation of bread and beer to its crew.

No. 43 – MS 2181/8

Issue of bread and beer to palace soldiers, Early Dynastic/Early Sargonic, Adab. Pierced tablet.

obv. i	180 ninda	180 breads;
	3 dug	3 jars (of beer):
	aga$_3$-us$_2$	(for) the soldiers
	e$_2$-gal	(of) the palace.
ii	e$_2$-AḪ	The E'AḪ.
	iti a$_2$-ki-ti	Month Akiti.
rev.	(blank)	

No. 44 – MS 2181/9

Issue of bread and beer to personnel in the "Garden of Urdu-Ašgi," Early Dynastic/Early Sargonic, Adab. Pierced tablet.

obv. i	180 ⸢ninda⸣	180 breads;
	3 dug	3 jars (of beer):
	kiri$_6$ Ur$_5$-du$_2$-^{d}Aš$_8$-gi$_4$	(for) the (personnel at) the Garden of Urdu'Ašgi.
ii	e$_2$-AḪ	The E'AḪ
	iti ^{d}Šuba$_3$(MUŠ$_3$×ZA)-nun	Month Šubanun.
rev.	(blank)	

obv. i 3: Urdu-Ašgi was a governor (ensi$_2$:ĜAR) of Adab during the ED IIIb period. See CUSAS 11, 67 rev. ii 1–2 and Schrakamp 2013: 202. The "Garden of Urdu-Ašgi" is a geographical name in the present text and does not necessarily mean that this governor was still alive. For the same garden in a much later text (MS/CS Adab), see CUSAS 23 no. 112 rev. 5.

No. 45 – MS 2181/10

Issue of bread and beer to boatmen, Early Dynastic/Early Sargonic, Adab. Pierced tablet.

obv. i	< > ninda	< > breads;
	1 dug	1 jar (of beer):
	lu$_2$-ma$_2$-gur$_8$-me	these are the boatmen.
ii	e$_2$-AḪ	The E'AḪ.
	iti šu-ĝar	Month Šuĝar.
	(blank)	
rev.	(blank)	

No. 46 – MS 2181/11

Issue of bread and beer to an individual, Early Dynastic/Early Sargonic, Adab. Pierced tablet.

u.e.	1(ban$_2$) ⸢5⸣	(From) 1 *ban* (flour) 5$^?$ (breads).
obv. i	300 ⸢ninda⸣-sig$_{15}$	300 premium breads;
	5 dug	5 jars (of beer):
	A-hu$^!$(RI)-*ṭāb*(DU$_{10}$)	(for) *Ahu(m)-ṭāb*.
ii	e$_2$-AḪ	The E'AḪ.
	iti še-gur$_x$(|ŠE.ŠE|.KIN)-am$_3$	Month *Šeguram*.
rev.	(blank)	

upper edge: This was written after the first line of obv. i had been completed. As in other texts, this line refers to a quantity of breads produced from an amount of flour.

No. 47 – MS 2181/12

Issue of bread and beer to menial laborers connected to the "New Palace," Early Dynastic/Early Sargonic, Adab. Pierced tablet.

obv. i	240 ninda	240 breads;
	4 dug	4 jars (of beer):
	UN-il$_2$	(to) menial laborers
	⸢e$_2$⸣-gal-gibil	(of the) new palace.
ii	e$_2$-AḪ	The E'AḪ.
	iti ab-e$_3$-zi-ga	Month Ab-eziga.
rev.	(blank)	

obv. i 3–4: The "New Palace" in Adab appears in later Sargonic texts: see SCTRAH no. 72 rev. 3 commentary with further attestations. These texts show that there were at least two palaces in Sargonic Adab.

No. 48 – MS 2181/13

Issue of bread and beer to a "Silver (and) lapis-lazuli boat," Early Dynastic/Early Sargonic, Adab. Pierced tablet.

obv. i	< > ninda	< > breads;
	10 dug	10 jars (of beer):
	ma$_2$-gin$_3$-ku$_3^!$-za$^!$	(for) the "Silver (and) lapis-lazuli boat."
	e$_2$-AḪ	The E'AḪ.
ii 1	iti še-gur$_x$(|ŠE.ŠE|.KIN)-am$_3$	Month Šeguram.
rev.	(blank)	

obv. i 3: This must be a corrupt writing for ma$_2$-ku$_3$-za:gin$_3$ "Silver (and) lapis lazuli boat" mentioned in text No. 42 above.

No. 49 – MS 2181/14

Issue of bread and beer to palace soldiers, Early Dynastic/Early Sargonic, Adab. Pierced tablet.

obv. i	< > ninda	< > breads;
	2 dug	2 jars (of beer):
	aga$_3$-us$_2$	(for) the soldiers
	e$_2$-gal	(of) the palace.
ii	e$_2$-AḪ	The E'AḪ.
	⸢iti⸣ a$_2$-ki-ti	Month Akiti.
rev.	(blank)	

No. 50 – MS 2181/15

Issue of bread and beer to (personnel at) the "New Canal," Early Dynastic/Early Sargonic, Adab. Pierced tablet.

obv. i	180 ninda	180 breads;
	6 dug	6 jars (of beer):
	i$_7$-gibil	(for the personnel at) the "New Canal."
ii	e$_2$-AḪ	The E'AḪ.
	iti še-gur$_x$(|ŠE.ŠE|.KIN)-am$_3$	Month Šeguram.
rev.	(blank)	

No. 51 – MS 2181/16

Issue of bread and beer to palace soldiers, Early Dynastic/Early Sargonic, Adab. Pierced tablet.

obv. i	180 ninda	180 breads;
	3 dug	3 jars (of beer):
	aga$_3$-us$_2$	(for) the soldiers
	⸢e$_2$⸣-gal	(of) the palace.
ii	e$_2$-AḪ	The E'AḪ.
	iti ni$_3$-kiri$_6$	Month Nikiri.
rev.	(blank)	

No. 52 – MS 2181/17

Issue of bread and beer to palace soldiers, Early Dynastic/Early Sargonic, Adab. Pierced tablet.

obv. i	180 ninda	180 breads;
	2 dug	2 jars (of beer):
	aga$_3$-us$_2$	(for) the soldiers
	e$_2$-gal	(of) the palace.
ii	e$_2$-AḪ	The E'AḪ.
	iti aša$_5$-il$_2$-šu-ĝar	Month Aša'ilšugar.
rev.	(blank)	

No. 53 – MS 2181/18

Issue of bread and beer to boatmen, Early Dynastic/Early Sargonic, Adab. Pierced tablet.

obv. i	180 ninda	180 breads;
	2 dug	2 jars (of beer):
	lu$_2$-ma$_2$-gur$_8$-me	they are the boatmen.
ii	e$_2$-AḪ	The E'AḪ.
	(blank)	
	iti ni$_3$-kiri$_6$	Month Nikiri.
rev.	(blank)	

No. 54 – MS 2181/19

Issue of bread and beer to palace soldiers, Early Dynastic/Early Sargonic, Adab. Pierced tablet.

obv. i	180 ninda	180 breads;
	2 dug	2 jars (of beer):
	aga$_3$-us$_2$	(for) the soldiers
	e$_2$-gal	(of) the palace.
ii	e$_2$-AḪ	The E'AḪ.
	iti a$_2$-ki-ti	Month Akiti.
	(blank)	
rev.	(blank)	

No. 55 – MS 2181/20

Issue of bread and beer to palace soldiers, Early Dynastic/Early Sargonic, Adab. Pierced tablet.

obv. i	180 ⸢ninda⸣	180 breads;
	3 dug	3 jars (of beer):
	aga$_3$-⸢us$_2$⸣	(for) the soldiers
	e$_2$-gal	(of) the palace.
ii	e$_2$-AḪ	The E'AḪ.
	iti a$_2$-ki-ti	Month Akiti.
rev.	(blank)	

No. 56 – MS 2181/21

Issue of bread and beer to the personnel at a canal, Early Dynastic/Early Sargonic, Adab. Pierced tablet.

obv. i	300 ninda	300 breads;
	5 dug	5 jars (of beer):
	ka i$_7$-ensi$_2$	(to personnel at) the inlet of the "Canal of the Governor."
ii	e$_2$-AḪ	The E'AḪ.
	iti ab-e$_3$-zi-ga	Month Ab-eziga.
	(blank)	
rev.	(blank)	

obv. i 3: For other references to this canal in Adab texts, see SCTRAH no. 109, commentary.

No. 57 – MS 2181/22

Issue of bread and beer to (personnel in) the palace, Early Dynastic/Early Sargonic, Adab. Pierced tablet.

obv. i	[n] ninda	... breads;
	3 dug	3 jars (of beer):
	e$_{2}$-gal	(to personnel/soldiers in) the palace.
ii	e$_{2}$-AḪ	The E'AḪ.
	(blank)	
	⸢iti⸣ du$_{6}$-⸢ku$_{3}$⸣	Month Duku.
rev.	(blank)	

No. 58 – MS 2181/23

Issue of bread and beer to palace soldiers, Early Dynastic/Early Sargonic, Adab. Pierced tablet.

obv. i	[n] ninda	... breads;
	[n] dug	... jars (of beer):
	aga$_{3}$-us$_{2}$	(for) the soldiers
	e$_{2}$-gal	(of) the palace.
ii	e$_{2}$-AḪ	The E'AḪ.
	iti aša$_{5}$-il$_{2}$-šu-ĝar	Month Aša'ilšuĝar.
	(blank)	
rev.	(blank)	

No. 59 – MS 2181/24

Issue of bread and beer to palace soldiers, Early Dynastic/Early Sargonic, Adab. Pierced tablet.

obv. i	⸢10⸣ ninda	10 breads;
	⸢1(ban$_{2}$)⸣ [n] ⸢du$_{8}$-am$_{6}$⸣	... (loaves) are baked (from) 1 *ban* (flour).
	⸢n⸣ dug	... (jars of) beer:
	aga$_{3}$-us$_{2}$	(for) the soldiers
	e$_{2}$-gal	(of) the palace.
ii	e$_{2}$-AḪ	The E'AḪ.
	⸢iti⸣ ni$_{3}$-kiri$_{6}$	Month Nikiri.
	(blank)	
rev.	(blank)	

No. 60 – MS 2181/25

Issue of bread and beer to palace soldiers dated by day, Early Dynastic/Early Sargonic, Adab. Pierced tablet.

obv. i	180 ninda	180 breads;
	2 dug	2 jars (of beer):
	aga$_3$-us$_2$	(for) the soldiers
	e$_2$-gal	(of) the palace.
ii	e$_2$-AḪ	The E'AḪ.
	iti aša$_5$-⸢il$_2$⸣-šu-ĝar	Month Aša'ilšuĝar.
	u$_4$ 13	Day 13.
rev.	(blank)	

No. 61 – MS 2181/26

Issue of bread and beer to palace soldiers, Early Dynastic/Early Sargonic, Adab. Pierced tablet.

obv. i	180 ninda	180 breads;
	2 dug	2 jars (of beer):
	aga$_3$-us$_2$	(for) the soldiers
	e$_2$-gal	(of) the palace.
ii	e$_2$-AḪ	The E'AḪ.
	iti ni$_3$-kiri$_6$	Month Nikiri.
	(blank)	
rev.	(blank)	

No. 62 – MS 2181/27

Issue of bread and beer to palace soldiers, Early Dynastic/Early Sargonic, Adab. Pierced tablet.

obv. i	[60 ninda]	[60 breads];
	1 dug	1 jar (of beer):
	aga$_3$-us$_2$	(for) the soldiers
	⸢e$_2$-gal⸣	(of) the palace.
ii	[e$_2$]-⸢AḪ⸣	The E'AḪ.
	iti aša$_5$-il$_2$-šu-⸢ĝar⸣	Month Aša'ilšuĝar.
	(blank)	
rev.	(blank)	

No. 63 – MS 2181/28

Issue of bread and beer to palace soldiers, Early Dynastic/Early Sargonic, Adab. Pierced tablet.

obv. i	<ras.> ninda	<erased> breads;
	2 dug	2 jars (of beer):
	aga$_3$-us$_2$	(for) the soldiers
	e$_2$-gal	(of) the palace.
ii	e$_2$-AḪ	The E'AḪ.
	iti a$_2$-ki-ti	Month Akiti.
	(blank)	
rev.	(blank)	

No. 64 – MS 2181/29

Issue of bread and beer to the governors of Ĝeša (Umma) and Lagaš, Early Dynastic/Early Sargonic, Adab. Pierced tablet.

obv. i	⌜180⌝ ninda	180 breads;
	10 ⌜la$_2$⌝ [n] ⌜dug⌝	7 (to 9) jars (of beer):
	ensi$_2$	(to) the governor
	^{ĝeš}Ĝeša$_x$(UḪ$_3$×KASKAL)^{ki}	(of) Ĝeša ("Umma"),
ii	ensi$_2$	(and to) the governor
	Lagaš$_x$(BUR.ŠIR×AŠ.LA^{mušen})^{ki}	(of) Lagaš.
	e$_2$-AḪ	The E'AḪ.
	iti še-gur$_x$(|ŠE.ŠE|.KIN)-am$_3$	Month Šeguram.
rev.	(blank)	

obv. i 4: See Almamori 2014: 5–12 for variant writings of the city Ĝeša with the sign UḪ$_3$ as the base element. The variant with KASKAL inscribed into UḪ$_3$ is a characteristic of texts from Adab: see CUSAS 33 no. 281 commentary with further references.

obv. ii 2: Note the unusual writing of Lagaš. The usual grapheme is NU$_{11}$(ŠIR×"KAR$_2$").BUR.LA.

No. 65 – MS 2181/30

Issue of bread and beer to personnel in the garden of a certain Ašgi-pa'e. Early Dynastic/Early Sargonic, Adab. Pierced tablet.

obv. i	180 ninda	180 breads;
	3 dug	3 jars (of beer):
	kiri$_6$ ^{d}Aš$_8$-gi$_4$-pa-e$_3$	(to the personnel in) the garden of Ašgi-pa'e.
ii	e$_2$-AḪ	The E'AḪ.
	⸢iti⸣ ^{d}Šuba$_3$(MUŠ$_3$×ZA)-nun	Month Šubanun.
rev.	(blank)	

No. 66 – MS 2181/31

Issue of bread and beer to an individual, Early Dynastic/Early Sargonic, Adab. Pierced tablet.

obv. i	60 ninda	60 breads;
	< > dug	< > jar (of beer):
	Lugal-diĝir-ĝu$_{10}$	(to) Lugaldiĝirĝu.
ii	e$_2$-AḪ	The E'AḪ.
	iti du$_6$-ku$_3$	Month Duku.
	(blank)	
rev.	(blank)	

No. 67 – MS 2181/32

Issue of bread and beer to palace soldiers, Early Dynastic/Early Sargonic, Adab. Pierced tablet.

obv. i	120 ninda	120 breads;
	2 dug	2 jars (of beer):
	aga$_3$-us$_2$	(to) the soldiers
	e$_2$-gal	(of) the palace.
ii	e$_2$-AḪ	The E'AḪ.
	iti ni$_3$-kiri$_6$	Month Nikiri.
rev.	(blank)	

No. 68 – MS 2181/33

Issue of bread and beer to palace soldiers, Early Dynastic/Early Sargonic, Adab. Pierced tablet.

obv. i	180 ninda	180 breads;
	⸢3$^?$⸣ dug	3$^?$ jars (of beer):
	aga$_3$-us$_2$	(to) the soldiers
	e$_2$-gal	(of) the palace.
ii	e$_2$-AḪ	The E'AḪ.
	iti ^{d}Šuba$_3$(MUŠ$_3$×ZA)-nun	Month Šubanun.
rev.	(blank)	

No. 69 – MS 2181/34

Issue of bread and beer to (personnel in) the "Garden of Urdu-Ašgi," Early Dynastic/Early Sargonic, Adab. Pierced tablet.

obv. i	120 ninda	120 breads;
	1 dug	1 jar (of beer):
	kiri$_6$ Ur$_5^!$(AŠ$_8$)-du$_2^!$-[^{d}Aš$_8$]-gi$_4$	(to the personnel in) the "Garden of Urdu-Ašgi."
ii	e$_2$-AḪ	The E'AḪ.
	iti aša$_5$-⸢il$_2$⸣-šu-ĝar	Month Aša'ilšuĝar.
rev.	(blank)	

No. 70 – MS 2181/35

Issue of bread and beer to (personnel in) the palace, Early Dynastic/Early Sargonic, Adab. Pierced tablet.

obv. i	120 ninda	120 breads;
	< > dug	< > jars (of beer):
	e$_2$-gal	(to personnel in) the palace.
ii	e$_2$-AḪ	The E'AḪ.
	iti ab-⸢e$_3$-zi-ga⸣	Month Ab-eziga.
	[(blank)]	
rev.	(blank)	

No. 71 – MS 2181/36

Issue of bread and beer to palace soldiers, Early Dynastic/Early Sargonic, Adab. Pierced tablet.

obv. i	120 ninda	120 breads;
	2 dug	2 jars (of beer):
	aga$_3$-us$_2$	(to) the soldiers
	e$_2$-gal	(of) the palace.
ii	e$_2$-AḪ	The E'AḪ.
	iti ni$_3$-kiri$_6$	Month Nikiri.
rev.	(blank)	

No. 72 – MS 2181/37

Issue of bread and beer to (personnel in) the palace, Early Dynastic/Early Sargonic, Adab. Pierced tablet.

obv. i	180 ninda	180 breads;
	3 dug	3 jars (of beer):
	e$_2$-gal	(to personnel/soldiers in) the palace.
	(blank)	
ii	e$_2$-AḪ	The E'AḪ.

	(blank)	
	iti du$_6$-ku$_3$	Month Duku.
rev.	(blank)	

No. 73 – MS 2181/38

Issue of bread and beer to palace soldiers, Early Dynastic/Early Sargonic, Adab. Pierced tablet.

obv. i	180 ninda	180 breads;
	2 ⸢dug⸣	2 jars (of beer):
	aga$_3$-[us$_2$]	(to) the soldiers
	⸢e$_2$⸣-[gal]	(of) the palace.
ii	e$_2$-AḪ	The E'AḪ.
	⸢iti⸣ aša$_5$-il$_2$-⸢šu⸣-ĝar	Month Aša'ilšuĝar.
	[(blank)]	
rev.	(blank)	

No. 74 – MS 2181/39

Issue of bread and beer to palace soldiers, Early Dynastic/Early Sargonic, Adab. Pierced tablet.

obv. i	240 ninda	240 breads;
	[n] ⸢dug⸣	... jars (of beer):
	[aga$_3$-us$_2$]	[(to) the soldiers]
ii	e$_2$-gal	(of) the palace.
	e$_2$-AḪ	The E'AḪ.
rev.	(blank)	

The document is undated.

No. 75 – MS 2181/40

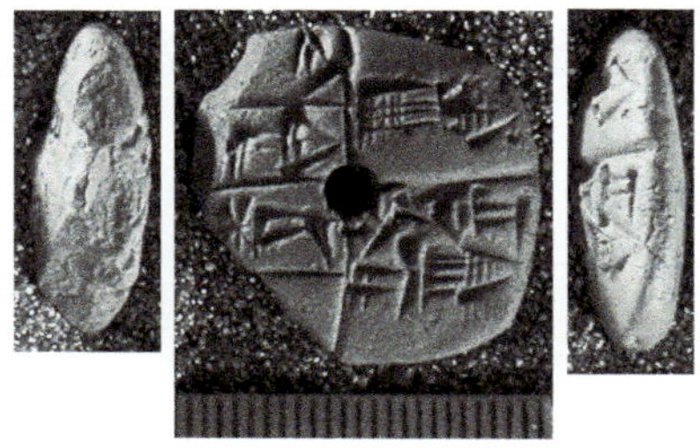

Issue of bread and beer, Early Dynastic/Early Sargonic, Adab. Pierced tablet.

obv. i	[n] ninda	... breads;
	[n] dug	... jars (of beer):
	[Me$^?$]-^{d}X	(for) [Me]... (PN?).
	(blank)	
ii	e$_2$-AḪ	The E'AḪ.
	iti še-saĝ-sig$_{15}$-ga	Month Šesaĝsiga.
rev.	(blank)	

obv. i 3: For the same sign and the personal name(?), see text No. 27 obv. i 5. The sign X here is:

It looks like a NITA$_2$ without the initial horizontal wedge.

No. 76 – MS 2181/41

Issue of bread and beer to (personnel in) the palace, Early Dynastic/Early Sargonic, Adab. Pierced tablet.

obv. i	[n] ninda	... breads;
	1 dug	1 jar (of beer):
	e$_2$-gal	to (personnel/soldiers in) the palace.
ii	e$_2$-AḪ	The E'AḪ.
	iti še-saĝ-sig$_{15}$-ga	Month Šesaĝsiga.
rev.	(blank)	

No. 77 – MS 2181/42

Issue of bread and beer, Early Dynastic/Early Sargonic, Adab. Pierced tablet.

obv. i	120 ninda	120 breads;
	2 dug	2 jars (of beer):
	⌜x x x⌝	...
	(blank)	
ii	e$_2$-AḪ	The E'AḪ
	⌜x x⌝	...
	⌜iti⌝ ni$_3$-kiri$_6$	Month Nikiri.
rev.	(blank)	

No. 78 – MS 2181/43

Issue of bread and beer to (personnel in) the palace, Early Dynastic/Early Sargonic, Adab. Pierced tablet.

obv. i	120 ninda	120 breads;
	2 dug	2 jars (of beer):
	e$_2$-gal	to (personnel in) the palace.
	[(blank)]	
ii	e$_2$-AḪ	The E'AḪ.
	iti še-saĝ-⸢sig$_{15}$⸣-ga	Month Šesaĝsiga.
rev.	(blank)	

No. 79 – MS 2181/44

Issue of bread and beer to palace soldiers, Early Dynastic/Early Sargonic, Adab. Pierced tablet.

obv. i	[n ninda]	[... breads;]
	[n] ⸢dug⸣	... jars (of beer):
	⸢aga$_3$⸣-us$_2$	(to) the soldiers
	⸢e$_2$-gal⸣	(of) the palace.
ii	e$_2$-AḪ	The E'AḪ.
	iti aša$_5$-il$_2$-šu-ĝar	Month Aša'ilšuĝar.
rev.	(blank)	

No. 80 – MS 2181/45

Issue of bread and beer to palace soldiers, Early Dynastic/Early Sargonic, Adab. Pierced tablet.

obv. i	180 ninda	180 breads;
	[n] dug	... jars (of beer):
	[aga$_3$]-us$_2$	(to) the soldiers
	⸢e$_2$⸣-gal	(of) the palace.
ii	e$_2$-AḪ	The E'AḪ.
	⸢iti⸣ ab-⸢e$_3$⸣-zi-ga	Month Ab-eziga.
rev.	(blank)	

No. 81 – MS 2181/46

Expenditure of groats and malt to an individual, Early Dynastic/Early Sargonic, Adab.

obv. i	2(bariga) ni$_3$-ar$_3$-ra gur	2 *bariga* groats;
	2(bariga) munu$_4$	2 *bariga* malt:
	Iš-me-i$_3$-lum	to *Yišme-'ilum*
	an-na-šum$_2$	it has been given.
ii	ni$_3$ zi-ga	Goods expended.
	e$_2$-AḪ	The E'AḪ.
	iti še-gur$_x$(|ŠE.ŠE|.KIN)-am$_3$	Month Šeguram.
rev.	(blank)	

obv. i 4–ii 1: This passage proves that the E'AḪ is the organization that issues the goods. Note that this and the following document, which also has the phrase ni$_3$ zi-ga, are not pierced.

No. 82 – MS 2181/47

Expenditure of barley flour to a bodyguard of the king, Early Dynastic/Early Sargonic, Adab.

obv. i	1(bariga) dabin	1 *bariga* barley flour:
	ni$_3$ zi-ga	the goods expended.
	e$_2$-AḪ	The E'AḪ.
	⌜lu$_2$⌝-tukul	It is the *bodyguard*
ii	lugal-kam	of the king.
	an-na-šum$_2$	It has been given to him.
	(blank)	
	iti ni$_3$-kiri$_6$	Month Nikiri.
rev.	(blank)	

obv. i 4 – ii 1: For a similar text, see CUSAS 11 no. 174, where mar-tu lugal-kam is mentioned instead of the lu$_2$-tukul. See USP pp. 15–16, 112, 119 for lu$_2$-tukul as "gendarme." In the present context and in CUSAS 11 no. 174, the term may refer to the king's bodyguard.

1.1.6 – Other Bread and Beer Texts

Most of the texts in this section have the same format and contents, and doubtlessly originate from the same dossier as the E'AḪ texts. These documents record allocation of bread, beer and grain products to a strictly defined number of entities, including households, temples and deities. The interesting detail is that these are not only individuals of high rank but first and foremost deities and households.

No. 83 – MS 2467

Account of barley distributed to a household, gods and personnel, Early Sargonic, Adab.

obv. i	50 še gur	50 *gur* barley:
	e$_{2}$-saĝ-*1*	Esaĝ...;
	41 ^{d}Pa-bil$_{2}$-saĝ	41: Pabilsaĝ;
	41 Ama-ĝeštin-an	41: Amaĝeštinan(a);
	40 ^{d}Nin-šubur 1(gur)	40: Ninšubur: 1 (*gur*);
	40 ^{d}Nin-imma$_{3}$(SIG$_{7}$) 3(ban$_{2}$)	40: Ninimma: 3 *ban*;
	40 ⸢e$_{2}$-dam⸣	40: the "House of the spouse";
ii	40 ^{d}⸢Ša⸣-ma-gan 2	40: Šamagan: 2 (*gur*);
	20 ^{d}Inana	20: Inana;
	20 Bara$_{2}$-^{d}En-lil$_{2}$-ĝar	20: Bara-Enlilĝar;
	35 ^{d}En-ki	35: Enki.
	(blank)	
rev. i	2(bariga) Igi-du$_{3}$	2 *bariga*: Igidu;
	2(bariga) 3(ban$_{2}$) Ur-^{d}Nin-piriĝ	2 *bariga* 3 *ban*: Ur-Ninpiriĝ;
	4 Nin-du$_{6}$-a	4 *gur*: Nindu'a;
	4 Me-^{d}Ša-ma-gan	4 *gur*: Me-Šamagan;
	5 Ur-[...]	5 *gur*: Ur...;
	Eden-ba [(x)]	Edenba (is responsible).
ii	(blank)	

obv. i 2.: e$_{2}$-saĝ-*1* may be identical to e$_{2}$-saĝ-šu$_{4}$ of text No. 356 obv. ii 13. A similar term appears in the ED IIIa Fara document TSŠ 933. It records the construction/restoration (du$_{3}$) of a building e$_{2}$-1(AŠ)-saĝ by 82 workmen.

obv. i 7: For e$_{2}$-dam, literally "House (of) the Spouse," see Such-Gutiérrez 2005–6: 42–43.

No. 84 – MS 3789/1

Daily allocation of bread and beer to deities, households and individuals, Early Dynastic/Early Sargonic, Adab. Pierced tablet.

obv. i	240 ninda 2 dug	240 breads, 2 jars (of beer):
	^{d}Bara$_2$-En-lil$_2$-ĝar	Bara-Enlilĝar;
	600 la$_2$ 60 ninda 10	540 breads, 10 (jars of beer):
	e$_2$-dumu	the "House of the son";
	440 ninda	440 breads:
	e$_2$-AḪ	the E'AḪ;
	300 ninda	300 breads:
	Ma-U$_2$	MaU;
	240 ninda 4	240 breads, 4 (jars of beer):
ii	Ur-$^{d.še3}$Šer$_7$-da	Ur-Šerda;
	480 ninda 4	480 breads, 4 (jars of beer):
	Ur-nu	Urnu;
	600 ninda	600 breads:
	Nu-mu-na	Numuna;
	160 ninda	160 breads:
	I$_3$-la-la	Ilala.
	u$_4$ 20	Day 20.
	iti ^{d}Šuba$_3$(MUŠ$_3$×ZA)-nun	Month Šubanun.

rev. i	2(ban$_2$) dabin e$_2$-AḪ	2 *ban* barley flour: the E'AḪ;
	2(ban$_2$) Ma-U$_2$	2 *ban*: MaU;
	1(bariga) Ur-nu	1 *bariga*: Urnu;
	2(ban$_2$) Nu-mu-na	2 *ban*: Numuna
	Lugal-lu-ḪAR	(and) LugalluḪAR;
	3(ban$_2$) e$_2$-dumu	3 *ban*: the "House of the son."
	Ur-e$_2$-maḫ ugula	Ur-Emaḫ, the overseer.
ii	(blank space)	
	a$_2$-mi$_2$-a / an-de$_6$	It has been brought in the "Women's House."
	Lugal-diĝir	To Lugaldiĝir
	an-na-šum$_2$	it has been given.
	(blank)	

The tablet records two different transactions. The obverse is a daily allocation of bread and beer. The reverse is the delivery and expenditure of barley flour. The reason why these two transactions were recorded on the same tablet must be that they both happened on the same day.

obv. i 2: Note the writing En-lil$_2$ without a determinative, in contrast to text No. 83 obv. ii 3.

rev. ii 1: A$_2$-mi$_2$ is an unorthographic writing of e$_2$-mi$_2$, "women's house," part of a palace or other building complex that was reserved for female personnel. For a recent discussion of the term, see Bartash 2014. For another possible reference to this abode in a different spelling, see text No. 94 rev. i 4–5: ⸢e$_2$⸣-mi$_2$-še$_3$ an-de$_6$. For the same verbal for with e$_2$-gal "(into) the palace," see text No. 87 rev. i 2.

No. 85 – MS 3789/2

Daily allocation of bread and beer to deities, households and individuals, Early Dynastic/Early Sargonic, Adab. Pierced tablet.

obv. i	< > ninda < > dug	< > breads, < > jars (of beer):
	^{d}Inana	(goddess) Inana;
	120 ninda 1	120 breads, 1 (jar of beer):
	^{d}Iškur(LAK377)	(god) Iškur;
	60 ninda 1	60 breads, 1 (jar of beer):
	^{d}Nin-mug	(goddess) Ninmug;
	60 ninda 2	60 breads, 2 (jars of beer):
	^{d}En-ki	(god) Enki;
	60 ninda 1	60 breads, 1 (jar of beer):
	e$_2$-dam	the "House of the spouse";
	60 ninda	60 breads:
ii	^{d}EN$_2$(ŠU$_2$+ḪAL).E$_2$-si	(deity) ENEsi;
	60 ninda 1	60 breads, 1 (jar of beer):
	^{d}Bara$_2$-En-lil$_2$-ĝar	Bara-Enlilĝar;
	< > ninda < >	< > breads, < > (jars of beer):
	e$_2$-dumu	the "House of the son";
	180 ninda 3	180 breads, 3 (jars of beer):
	e$_2$-AḪ	the E'AḪ;

	60 ninda 1	60 breads, 1 (jar of beer):
	PU$_3$.ŠA-^{d}Aš$_8$-gi$_4$	PUŠA-Ašgi;
	120 ninda 1	120 breads, 1 (jar of beer):
	Ma-U$_2$	MaU;
iii	120 ninda 2	120 breads, 2 (jars of beer):
	Ur-$^{d.še3}$Šer$_7$-da	Ur-Šerda;
	120 ninda 2	120 breads, 2 (jars of beer):
	Ur-nu	Urnu;
	60 ninda	60 breads:
	Nu-mu-na	Numuna;
	120 ninda 2	120 breads, 2 (jars of beer):
	I$_3$-la-la	Ilala.
	u$_4$ 20 *3*	Day 23.
	iti še-gur$_x$(ŠE.KIN)-⌜am$_3$⌝	Month Šeguram.
rev.	(blank)	

obv. ii 1: For a complex sign with unknown reading EN$_2$+E$_2$ = LAK358 in ED IIIa, see Krebernik 1998a: 283. Unlike the ED IIIa sign EN$_2$(ŠU$_2$×AN), here it is ŠU$_2$+ḪAL.

No. 86 – MS 3789/3

Daily allocation of bread and beer to deities, households and individuals, Early Dynastic/Early Sargonic, Adab. Pierced tablet.

obv. i	60 ninda 1 dug	60 breads, 1 jar (of beer):
	^{d}Inana	(goddess) Inana;
	< > ninda < >	< > breads, < > (jars of beer):
	^{d}Iškur(LAK377)	(god) Iškur;
	60 ninda 2 dug	60 breads, 2 jars (of beer):
	^{d}Nin-mug	(goddess) Ninmug;
	< > ninda < >	< > breads, < > (jars of beer):
	^{d}En-ki	(god) Enki;
	60 ninda 2 dug	60 breads, 2 jars (of beer):
	e$_2$-dam	the "House of the spouse";
ii	60 ninda	60 breads:
	^{d}EN$_2$(ŠU$_2$+ḪAL).E$_2$-si	(deity) ENEsi;
	60 ninda 2 dug	60 breads, 2 jars (of beer):
	Bara$_2$-^{d}En-lil$_2$-ĝar	Bara-Enliĝar;
	240 ninda 5 dug	240 breads, 5 jars (of beer):
	e$_2$-dumu	the "House of the son";
	180 ninda	180 breads:
	e$_2$-AḪ	the E'AḪ;
	60 ninda 2 dug	60 breads, 2 jars (of beer):
	PU$_3$.ŠA-^{d}Aš$_8$-gi$_4$	PUŠA-Ašgi;
iii	120 ninda 2 dug	120 breads, 2 jars (of beer):
	Ma-U$_2$	MaU;
	120 ninda 4 dug	120 breads, 4 jars (of beer):

	Ur-$^{d.še3}$Šer$_7$-da	Ur-Šerda;
	120 ninda 3 dug	120 breads, 3 jars (of beer):
	Ur-nu	Urnu;
	60 ninda	60 breads:
	Nu-mu-⸢na⸣	Numuna;
	120 ninda ⸢2⸣ [(+n) dug]	120 breads, 2[(+n) jars (of beer)]:
	I$_3$-la-[la]	Ilala;
	240 ninda	240 breads:
rev. i	Ur-^{d}Nin-mug	Ur-Ninmug
	[n] ninda 1 dug	... breads, 1 jar (of beer):
	[2 lines destroyed]	...
	[iti-ta u$_4$ n ab-ta]-⸢zal$^{?}$⸣	[The *n*th day of the month passed(?)]
ii	⸢20 [+n] ninda-sig$_{15}$⸣	20 [+n] premium breads.
	[break]	...

rev. i 6: For another example of this formula, see the next document.

No. 87 – MS 3789/4

Daily allocation of bread and beer to deities, households and individuals, Early Dynastic/Early Sargonic, Adab. Pierced tablet.

obv. i	60 ninda	60 breads,
	1 dug	1 jar (of beer):
	^{d}Inana	(goddess) Inana;
	60 ninda	60 breads:
	^{d}Iškur(LAK377)	(god) Iškur;
	60 ninda 1	60 breads, 1 (jar of beer):
	^{d}En-ki	(god) Enki;
	60 ninda 1	60 breads, 1 (jar of beer):
	e$_2$-dam	the "House of the spouse";
	60 ninda 1	60 breads, 1 (jar of beer):
	^{d}Bara$_2$-^{d}En-lil$_2$-ĝar	Bara-Enlilĝar;
ii	60 ⸢^{d}EN$_2$(ŠU$_2$+ḪAL)⸣.E$_2$-si	60: (deity) ENEsi;
	120 ninda	120 breads:
	e$_2$-dumu	the "House of the son";
	180 ninda 3	180 breads, 3 (jars of beer):
	e$_2$-AḪ	the E'AḪ;
	60 ninda 2	60 breads, 2 (jars of beer):
	PU$_3$.ŠA-^{d}Aš$_8$-gi$_4$	PUŠA-Ašgi;
	120 ninda 2	120 breads, 2 (jars of beer):
	Ma-U$_2$	MaU;
	120 ninda 2	120 breads, 2 (jars of beer):
	Ur-$^{d.še3}$Šer$_7$-da	Ur-Šerda;
iii	120 ninda 2	120 breads, 2 (jars of beer):
	Ur-⸢nu⸣	Urnu;

	60 ⸢ninda⸣	60 breads:
	Nu-mu-na	Numuna;
	120 ninda 2	120 breads, 2 (jars of beer):
	I$_3$-la-la	Ilala;
	iti-ta u$_4$ 20 ab-ta-zal	The 20th day of the month has passed.
rev. i	ninda e$_2$-gal	The bread has been brought (into) the palace.
	an-de$_6$	
	(blank)	
	iti aša$_5$-il$_2$-šu-ĝar	Month Aša'ilšuĝar.

No. 88 – MS 3789/8

Daily allocation of bread and beer to deities, households and individuals, Early Dynastic/Early Sargonic, Adab. Pierced tablet.

obv. i	60 ninda 1 dug	60 breads, 1 jar (of beer):
	^{d}Inana	(goddess) Inana;
	60 ninda 1 ^{d}Iškur(LAK377)	60 breads, 1 (jar of beer): (god) Iškur;
	60 1 ninda ^{d}Nin-mug	60 breads, 1 (jar of beer): (goddess) Ninmug;
	60 ninda e$_2$-dam	60 breads: the "House of the spouse";
	< > ninda 2 e$_2$-AḪ	< > breads, 2 (jars of beer): the E'AḪ;
	< > ninda 1 PU$_3$.ŠA-^{d}Aš$_8$-gi$_4$	< > breads, 1 (jar of beer): PUŠA-Ašgi;
	60 ninda 2 Ma-U$_2$	60 breads, 2 (jars of beer): MaU;
	60 ninda 2 Ur-$^{d.še3}$Šer$_7$-da	60 breads, 2 (jars of beer): Ur-Šerda;
ii	60 ninda 2 Ur-nu	60 breads, 2 (jars of beer): Urnu;
	60 ninda 2 I$_3$-la-la	60 breads, 2 (jars of beer): Ilala.
	(blank)	
	u$_4$ *3*	Day 3.
	iti a$_2$-ki-ti	Month Akiti.
	e$_2$ nu-banda$_3$	The house of the supervisor.
rev.	(blank)	

rev. i 5: In the texts above a subscript an-de$_6$ records delivery to the palace and a$_2$-mi$_2$ "women's quarters." No verbal form appears here. The administrative role of the "private" house of the supervisor in the transaction may be the same.

No. 89 – MS 3789/18

Daily allocation of bread and beer to deities, households and individuals, Early Dynastic/Early Sargonic, Adab. Pierced tablet.

obv. i	< > ninda < > dug	< > breads, < > jars (of beer):
	^{d}Inana	(goddess) Inana;
	60 ninda	60 breads:
	^{d}Iškur(LAK377)	(god) Iškur;
	60 ninda 1	60 breads, 1 (jar of beer):
	^{d}Nin-mug	(goddess) Ninmug;
	60 ninda	60 breads:
	^{d}En-ki	(god) Enki;
	⌜60⌝ ninda 1	60 breads, 1 (jar of beer):
	e$_2$-dam	the "House of the spouse";
	[60] ninda	[60] breads:
	$^{[d]}$⌜EN$_2$⌝(⌜ŠU$_2$⌝+ḪAL).E$_2$-si	(deity) ENEsi;
ii	<> ninda [<n>]	< > breads:
	⌜^{d}Bara$_2$-En-lil$_2$-ĝar⌝	Bara-Enlilĝar;
	< > ninda 3	< > breads, 3 (jars of beer):
	e$_2$-dumu	the "House of the son";
	180 ninda 3	180 breads, 3 (jars of beer):
	e$_2$-AḪ	the E'AḪ;
	< > ninda < >	< > breads < > (jars of beer):
	PU$_3$.ŠA-^{d}Aš$_8$-gi$_4$	PUŠA-Ašgi;
	120 ninda	120 breads:
	Ur-$^{d.še3}$Šer$_7$-da	Ur-Šerda;
iii	< > ninda < >	< > breads < > (jars of beer):
	⌜Ur⌝-nu	Urnu;
	⌜60 ninda⌝	60 breads:
	Nu-mu-na	Numuna;
	120 ninda 2	120 breads, 2 (jars of beer):
	I$_3$-la-[la]	Ilala.
	(blank)	
	u$_4$ 20 5	Day 25.
	iti ^{d}Šuba$_3$(MUŠ$_3$×ZA)-nun	Month Šubanun.

No. 90 – MS 3789/26

Daily allocation of bread and beer to deities, households and individuals, Early Dynastic/Early Sargonic, Adab. Pierced tablet.

obv. i	[n ninda n] ⸢dug⸣	[1 *bariga* 3 *ban* bread, n] jars (of beer):
	$^{[d]}$⸢Inana⸣	(goddess) Inana;
	⸢1(bariga)+3(ban$_2$)⸣ ninda	1 *bariga* 3 *ban* bread:
	^{d}Iškur(LAK377)	(god) Iškur;
	1(bariga)+3(ban$_2$) ninda	1 *bariga* 3 *ban* bread:
	^{d}Nin-mug	(goddess) Ninmug;
	1(bariga)+3(ban$_2$) ninda	1 *bariga* 3 *ban* bread:
	^{d}En-ki	(god) Enki;
	1(bariga)+3(ban$_2$) ninda	1 *bariga* 3 *ban* bread:
	e$_2$-dam	the "House of the spouse";
	⸢1(bariga)+3(ban$_2$)⸣ ninda	1 *bariga* 3 *ban* bread:
	^{d}EN$_2$(ŠU$_2$+ḪAL).E$_2$-si	(deity) ENEsi;
ii	1(bariga)+3(ban$_2$) ninda	1 *bariga* 3 *ban* bread:
	^{d}Bara$_2$-En-lil$_2$-ĝar	Bara-Enlilĝar;
	<> ninda 4	< > (*gur*) bread, 4 (jars of beer):
	e$_2$-dumu	the "House of the son";
	1(gur) ninda 2	1 (*gur*) breads, 4 (jars of beer):
	e$_2$-AḪ	the E'AḪ;
	< > ninda < >	< > bread, < > (jars of beer):
	PU$_3$.ŠA-^{d}Aš$_8$-gi$_4$	PUŠA-Ašgi;
	2(bariga) ninda	2 *bariga* bread:
	Ma-U$_2$	MaU;
	2(bariga) ninda	2 *bariga* bread:
	Ur-$^{d.še3}$Šer$_7$-da	Ur-Šerda;
iii	< > ninda < >	< > bread, < > (jars of beer):
	Ur-nu	Urnu;
	< > ninda < >	< > bread, < > (jars of beer):
	Nu-mu-na	Numuna;
	< > ninda < >	< > bread, < > (jars of beer):
	I$_3$-la-la	Ilala.
	(blank)	
	u$_4$ 10 *4*	Day 14.
	iti ni$_3$-kiri$_6$	Month Nikiri.
rev.	(blank)	
	2 dug	2 jars (of beer):
	Ur-diĝir	Urdiĝir;
	2 Ma$_2$-laḫ$_4$	2: Malaḫ,
	nu-banda$_3$	the supervisor;
	2 Ne-saĝ nu-banda$_3$	2: Nesaĝ, the supervisor.
	(blank)	

No. 91 – MS 3789/27

Daily allocation of bread and beer to e$_{2}$-dumu, Early Dynastic/Early Sargonic, Adab. Pierced tablet.

obv. i	240 ninda	240 breads,
	< > dug	< > jars (of beer):
	e$_{2}$-dumu	the "House of the son."
ii	(blank)	
	u$_{4}$ *1*	Day 1,
	iti še-kin-ku$_{5}$	month Šekinku.
rev.	(blank)	

The text is of the same format as the texts from the "E'AḪ file." This shows that all these bread and barley texts constituted a single archive which must have recorded transactions during a short period of time.

No. 92 – MS 3789/28

Daily allocation of bread and beer to individuals, Early Dynastic/Early Sargonic, Adab. Pierced tablet.

obv. i	60 ninda 2	60 breads 2 (jars of beer):
	Ma-U$_{2}$	MaU.
	Ur-^{d}Imma$_{x}$(ĜA$_{2}$×SIG$_{7}$.ME)	To Ur-Imma,
	sipa	the shepherd,
	an-na-šum$_{2}$	it has been given.
	Lugal-ni$_{3}$-bara$_{4}$-du$_{10}$	Lugalnibaradu
ii	maškim-bi$_{x}$(DUG)	(is) its commissioner.
	(blank)	
	iti du$_{6}$-ku$_{3}$	Month Duku,
	u$_{4}$ 3 mu-ĝal$_{2}$	There was day 3.
rev.	(blank)	

No. 93 – MS 3789/29

Daily allocation of bread and beer to individuals and households, Early Dynastic/Early Sargonic, Adab. Pierced tablet.

obv. i	120 ninda 2	120 breads 2 (jars of beer):
	I$_{3}$-la-la	(for) Ilala;
	60 ninda	60 breads:
	e$_{2}$-AḪ	(for) the E'AḪ.
	nu-banda$_{3}$	Together with the supervisor
	aša$_{5}$ ^{d}Dam-gal-nun-še$_{3}$	to the Field (of) Damgalnun(a)
ii	an-da-ĝen	it went.
	iti aša$_{5}$-il$_{2}$-šu-ĝar	Month Aša'ilšuĝar,
	u$_{4}$ *1*	day 1.
rev.	(blank)	

No. 94 – MS 3789/31

Daily allocation of bread and beer to deities, households and individuals, Early Dynastic/Early Sargonic, Adab. Pierced tablet.

obv. i	60 ninda < > dug	60 breads, < > jars (of beer):
	^{d}Inana	(goddess) Inana;
	60 ninda 1	60 breads, 1 (jar of beer):
	^{d}Iškur(LAK377)	(god) Iškur;
	60 ninda 1	60 breads, 1 (jar of beer):
	^{d}Nin-mug	(goddess) Ninmug;
	60 ninda 1	60 breads, 1 (jar of beer):
	$^{[d]}$⌜En⌝-ki	(god) Enki;
	[60] ⌜ninda⌝ 1	[60] breads, 1 (jar of beer):
	e_2-dam	the "House of the spouse";
ii	120 ninda 1	120 breads, 1 (jar of beer):
	^{d}Bara$_2$-En-lil$_2$-ĝar	Bara-Enlilĝar;
	60 ninda	60 breads:
	^{d}EN$_2$(ŠU$_2$+ḪAL).E$_2$-si	(deity) ENEsi;
	240 ninda	240 breads:
	e_2-dumu	the "House of the son";
	180 ninda 3	180 breads, 3 (jars of beer):
	e_2-AḪ	the E'AḪ;

	< > ⸢ninda⸣	< > breads, < > (jars of beer):
	PU$_3$.ŠA-^{d}Aš$_8$-⸢gi$_4$⸣	PUŠA-Ašgi;
	120 ninda 2	120 breads, 2 (jars of beer):
iii	Ma-U$_2$	MaU;
	120 ninda < >	120 breads, < > (jars of beer):
	Ur-$^{d.še3}$Šer$_7$-da	Ur-Šerda;
	120 ninda 2	120 breads, 2 (jars of beer):
	Ur-nu	Urnu;
	60 ninda	60 breads:
	Nu-mu-na	Numuna;
	120 ninda	120 breads:
	I$_3$-la-la	Ilala.
rev. i	(blank)	
	u$_4$ 20 *4*	Day 24.
	iti du$_6$-ku$_3$	Month Duku.
	180 ninda 3	180 breads, 3 (jars of beer).
	⸢e$_2$$^{?}$⸣-mi$_2$-še$_3$	Into the women quarters(?)
	an-de$_6$	it has been brought.
	^{d}Iškur-an-dul$_3$	To Iškur-andul
ii	an-na-šum$_2$	it has been given.
	(blank)	

No. 95 – MS 3789/33

Daily allocation of bread and beer to deities, households and individuals, Early Dynastic/Early Sargonic, Adab. Pierced tablet.

obv. i	[*ca.* 2 lines broken; uninscribed?]	
	120 [ninda n dug]	120 breads, [n jars (of beer)]:
	^{d}Inana	(goddess) Inana;
	120 *1* ninda 2	120 breads, 2 (jars of beer), "checked":
	^{d}Iškur(LAK377)	(god) Iškur;
	120 *1* ninda 2	120 breads, 2 (jars of beer), "checked":
	^{d}⸢Nin-mug⸣	(goddess) Ninmug;
	< > ⸢ninda⸣ <>	< > breads < > (jars of beer):
	^{d}En-ki	(god) Enki;
	120 *1* ninda 2	120 breads, 2 (jars of beer), "checked":
	e$_2$-dam	the "House of the spouse";
ii	[n *1* ninda n]	[n breads n (jars of beer), "checked":]
	[^{d}EN$_2$(ŠU$_2$+ḪAL).E$_2$-si]	[(deity) ENEsi;]
	[n+] 60 *1* ninda 1 [+n]	60+n breads 1+n (jars of beer), "checked":
	^{d}Bara$_2$-En-lil$_2$-ĝar	Bara-Enlilĝar;
	<> ninda [(n)]	< > breads [(< > (jars of beer))]:
	^{d}⸢Eš$_{23}$⸣-peš	(god) Ešpeš;
	<> ninda	< > breads:

	^{d}NI	(deity) NI;
	480 ninda *1*	480 breads, "checked":
	e$_{2}$-dumu	the "House of the son";
	< > ninda 6	< > breads, 6 (jars of beer):
iii	e$_{2}$-AḪ	the E'AḪ;
	120 *1* ninda 2	120 breads, 2 (jars of beer), "checked":
	PU$_{3}$.ŠA-^{d}Aš$_{8}$-gi$_{4}$	PUŠA-Ašgi;
	240 *1* ninda 2	240 breads, 2 (jars of beer), "checked":
	Ma-U$_{2}$	MaU;
	240 *1* ninda 4	240 breads, 4 (jars of beer), "checked":
	Ur-$^{d.še3}$Šer$_{7}$-da	Ur-Šerda;
	120 ninda 4	120 breads, 4 (jars of beer):
	Ur-nu	Urnu;
rev. i	60 ninda	60 breads:
	Nu-mu-na	Numuna;
	180 ninda 4	180 breads 4 (jars of beer):
	I$_{3}$-la-la	Ilala;
	3 dug	3 jars (of beer):
	e$_{2}$-kam	it is of the house.
	nu-banda$_{3}$	The supervisor.
	(blank)	
ii	u$_{4}$ 7	Day 7.
	iti ^{d}MUŠ$_{3}$×KUR.ZA	Month Šubanun.
	i$_{7}$-usan$_{x}$(AN.GU$_{2}$×PAP)-⌜du$_{6}$⌝	Canal Usandu.
	[x] ⌜x⌝ [...]	...
	[break]	

obv. i 3': The sign transliterated as *1* is a checkmark.

obv. ii 6: The sign in the divine name Ešpeš is an oblique "pointed" number 3. For the value eš$_{23}$, see MZL p. 141 no. 505.

obv. ii 8: The name of the deity may be *Il$_{3}$-i$_{3}$*. Alternatively, this may be a personal name AN-ne$_{2}$.

rev. i 6-7: Cf. e$_{2}$ nu-banda$_{3}$ in text No. 88 obv. ii 5.

rev. ii 3: See the commentary to text No. 250 obv. 7.

rev. ii 2: A mistake for iti ^{d}Šuba$_{3}$(MUŠ$_{3}$×ZA)-nun.

No. 96 – MS 3789/35

Daily allocation of bread and beer to deities, households and individuals, Early Dynastic/Early Sargonic, Adab. Pierced tablet.

obv. i	[n ninda n dug]	[... breads, ... jars (of beer)]:
	⸢^{d}Inana⸣	(goddess) Inana;
	⸢60⸣ ninda	60 breads:
	^{d}Iškur	(god) Iškur;
	60 ninda 1	60 breads, 1 (jar of beer):
	^{d}Nin-mug	(goddess) Ninmug;
	60 ninda	60 breads:
	^{d}En-ki	(god) Enki;
	60 ninda 1	60 breads, 1 (jar of beer):
	e$_2$-dam	the "House of the spouse";
	60 ninda	60 breads:
	^{d}EN$_2$(ŠU$_2$+ḪAL).E$_2$-⸢si⸣	(deity) ENEsi;
ii	[two lines broken]	...
	480 ninda ⸢2⸣	480 breads, 2 (jars of beer):
	e$_2$-⸢dumu⸣	the "House of the son";
	180 ninda 2	180 breads, 2 (jars of beer):
	e$_2$-AḪ	the E'AḪ;
	60 ninda 1	60 breads, 1 (jar of beer):
	PU$_3$.ŠA-⸢^{d}Aš$_8$⸣-[gi$_4$]	PUŠA-Ašgi;
	120 ninda 2	120 breads, 2 (jars of beer):
	⸢Ma⸣-[U$_2$]	MaU;
	60 [...]	60 [breads ...]:
	[break]	...
iii	[broken]	...
rev.	[broken]	...

No. 97 – MS 3789/39

Daily allocation of bread and beer to individuals, Early Dynastic/Early Sargonic, Adab. Pierced tablet.

obv. i	⸢120⸣ ninda 2	120 breads, 2 (jars of beer):
	⸢Ma⸣-U$_2$	MaU;
	60 [ninda] 1	60 breads, 1 (jar of beer):
	Ur-$^{d.še3}$Šer$_7$-da	Ur-Šerda;
	120 ⸢ninda⸣ 2	120 breads, 2 (jars of beer):
	I$_3$-la-la	Ilala.
ii	gu$_2$ DU tum$_2$-ma-ni-kam	It is his … that he has escorted.
	al-de$_6$	It is brought.
	iti ab-e$_3$-zi-ga	Month Ab-eziga,
	u$_4$ 20 7	Day 27.
rev.	(blank)	

obv. ii 1: The interpretation of the line is uncertain. For tum$_2$ as the singular perfective stem of the verb "to escort, to convoy" ("geleiten"), see Meyer-Laurin 2010: 11.

No. 98 – MS 3789/40

Daily allocation of bread and beer to households and individuals, Early Dynastic/Early Sargonic, Adab. Pierced tablet.

obv. i	120 ninda	120 breads:
	e$_2$-dumu	the "House of the son";
	180 ninda 3 dug	180 breads, 3 jars (of beer):
	e$_2$-AḪ	the E'AḪ;
	120 ninda ⸢2⸣	120 breads, 2 (jars of beer):
	e$_2$ Igi-si$_4$	the house of Igisi;
	120 ninda 2	120 breads, 2 (jars of beer):

	Ur-nu	Urnu;
ii	60 ninda	60 breads:
	⸢e$_2$⸣ ^{d}Nin-mug	the temple of Ninmug.
	⸢u$_4$ 20 *1*+n⸣-kam	It is day 21+n.
	[iti še]-kin-ku$_5$-kam	It is the [month] Šekinku.
	(blank)	
rev.	(blank)	

No. 99 – MS 3789/41

Expenditure of bread for (labor in) orchard(s), metalworkers and households, Early Dynastic/Early Sargonic, Adab. Pierced tablet.

obv. i	3(šar$_2$) / la$_2$ 1(ĝeš$_2$×u) 5(ĝeš$_2$) ninda /	
	½ ninda du$_8$	10500 breads; (each) bread (of) ½ (*sila* flour):
	^{ĝeš}kiri$_6$	(In) the orchard
	al-de$_6$	it is delivered.
	2(ĝeš$_2$×u) 5×ĝeš$_2$ ninda	1500 breads,
	2(ĝeš$_2$×u) ninda	1200 breads,
	[n+] 2(ĝeš$_2$×u) ninda	n+1200 breads,
	[...]	...
ii	4(ĝeš$_2$×u) ninda	2400 breads:
	e$_2$ nu-banda$_3$	the house of the supervisor.
	150 ninda	150 breads:
	tibira-me	they are metalworkers.
	1(ĝeš$_2$) ⸢la$_2$ 60 ninda⸣	540 breads,
	2(ĝeš$_2$) 60 ninda	1260 breads:
	e$_2$-dumu	the "House of the son."
	Lugal-bad$_3$	To Lugalbad
	an-na-šum$_2$	it has been given.
iii	(blank)	
	gu$_2$-an-še$_3$-bi 5(šar$_2$) 1(ĝeš$_2$×u) 120 ⸢ninda⸣	Its grand total: 18720 breads:
	al-zi	are expended.
	1(ĝeš$_2$×u) 120 [ninda] al-[x]	720 [breads]: are ...ed.

obv. i 1: See Brunke 2008: 98 for the metrology and proportions of ingredients in the preparation of bread.

No. 100 – MS 3789/44

Daily allocation of bread and beer to households and individuals, Early Dynastic/Early Sargonic, Adab. Pierced tablet.

obv. i	[n+] ⸢60⸣ ninda	x+60 breads:
	e$_{2}$-dumu	the "House of the son";
	180 ninda 3	180 breads, 3 (jars of beer):
	e$_{2}$-AḪ	the E'AḪ;
	120 ninda 2	120 breads, 2 (jars of beer):
	e$_{2}$ Igi-si$_{4}$	the house of Igisi;
	120 ninda 2	120 breads, 2 (jars of beer):
	Ur-nu	Urnu;
ii	60 [ninda 1] e$_{2}$ ^{d}Nin-[mug]	60 [breads, 1 (jar of beer)]: the temple of Ninmug;
	u$_{4}$ 20 *3*	Day 23,
	iti aša$_{5}$-il$_{2}$-šu-ĝar	month Aša'ilšuĝar.
	(blank)	
rev.	(blank)	

No. 101 – MS 3790/34

Daily allocation of bread and beer to deities, households and individuals, Early Dynastic/Early Sargonic, Adab. Pierced tablet.

obv. i	60 ninda 1 dug	60 breads, 1 jar (of beer):
	^{d}Inana	(goddess) Inana;
	60 ninda 1	60 breads, 1 (jar of beer):
	^{d}Nin-mug	(goddess) Ninmug;
	60 ninda 1	60 breads, 1 (jar of beer):
	^{d}En-ki	(god) Enki;
	60 ninda 1	60 breads, 1 (jar of beer):
	[break]	...
ii	e$_{2}$-dumu	the "House of the son";
	< > ninda 2	< > breads, 2 (jars of beer):
	e$_{2}$-AḪ	the E'AḪ;
	60 ninda	60 breads;
	PU$_{3}$.⸢ŠA-^{d}Aš$_{8}$-gi$_{4}$⸣	PUŠA-Ašgi;
	120 ⸢ninda⸣ 1	120 breads, 1 (jar of beer):
	[break]	
iii	< > ninda 1	< > breads, 1 (jar of beer):
	I$_{3}$-la-la	Ilala.
	(blank space)	
	u$_{4}$ 20 *1*	Day 21.
	iti ab-e$_{3}$-zi-ga	Month Ab-eziga.
rev.	(blank)	

No. 102 – MS 3790/62

Account of bread, beer and broth during the governor's stay in Agade, Early Dynastic/Early Sargonic, Adab.

obv. i	600 ninda-sig$_{15}$ 1(ban$_2$) 20 du$_8$	600 premium breads: 20 (loaves) baked (from) 1 *ban* (flour);
	600 ninda-še 1(ban$_2$) 20 du$_8$	600 barley breads: 20 (loaves) baked (from) 1 *ban* (flour);
	20 ⸢dug⸣	20 jars (of beer);
ii	10 ⸢tu$_7$⸣	10 (measures of) stew;
	e$_2$-[dumu/AḪ]	the "House [of the son]" (*or*: the E'[AḪ).]
	[u$_4$-ba] ⸢ensi$_2$⸣	[When] the governor
	⸢A-ga-de$_3$⸣^{ki}	(in) Agade
rev. i	u$_3$-mu-ti-la-a	lived.
ii	(blank)	

No. 103 – MS 3832

Account of bread, Early Sargonic, Adab.

obv. i	2400 ninda-še ne-saĝ	2400 barley *nesaĝ*-breads;
	720 ninda-sig$_{15}$ ne-saĝ	720 premium *nesaĝ*-breads;;
	720 ninda-gal-gal	720 large breads.
ii	(blank)	
rev.	(blank)	

obv. i 1–2: ne-saĝ is a term for offering to temples and is associated with calendrical festivals. See the commentary to CUSAS 23 no. 11 and SCTRAH no. 1 with further references.

1.1.7 – Beer

No. 104 – MS 3789/23

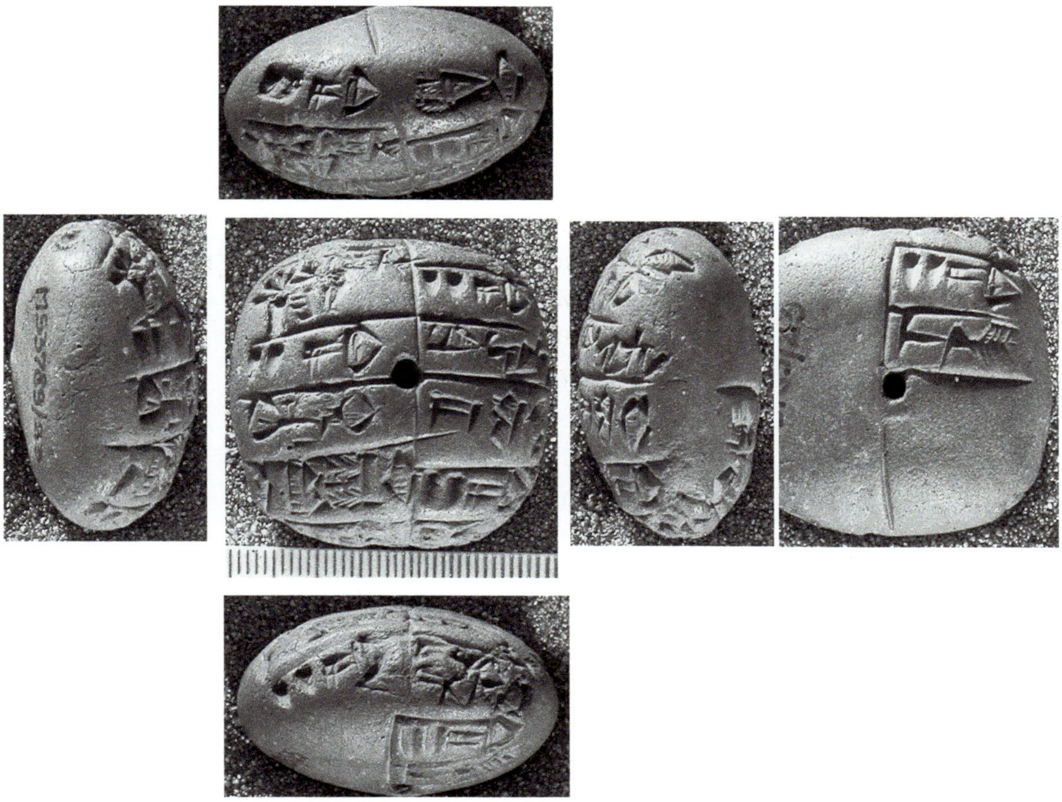

Allocation of beer to individuals from various locations, Early Dynastic/Early Sargonic, Adab. Pierced tablet.

obv. i	2N$_8$ dug	⅔ jar (of beer):
	^{d}Gi:bil-da	Gibilda;
	2N$_8$ dug	⅔ jar (of beer):
	dam-gara$_3$	the merchant
	UD-URI-SAR^{ki}	(from) …
	2N$_8$ dug	⅔ jar (of beer):
ii	Isin$_2^{ki}$	(an individual from) Isin;
	2N$_8$ dug	⅔ jar (of beer):
	lu$_2$-u$_5$	the shipping agent/courier(?)
	^{ĝeš}Ĝeša$_x$(UH$_{3\text{-}šeššig}$)^{ki}	(from) Ĝeša.
	2N$_8$ dug	⅔ jar (of beer):
ii	⌜x⌝ Urim$_5$(ŠEŠ.AB)^{ki}	... (from) Ur;
rev. i	2N$_8$ dug	⅔ jar (of beer):
	Me-zi	(for) Mezi.
ii	(blank)	

obv. i 1 f.: See Powell 1990: 506 for the dug "jar" of about 30 sila$_3$ that was subdivided into three vessels or units called gur$_4$-gur$_4$. Apparently, the sign 2N$_8$ is used here to designate ⅔ of the jar = two *gurgur*s. Powell 1990: 505 argues that this practice is attested only in texts from Ĝirsu. This statement should be reconsidered in the light of the present evidence. For the same notation in another text from Adab, see text No. 107 below.

obv. i 4: See Krebernik 2016: 119–20 for the reading dam-gara$_3$ instead of dam-gar$_3$.

obv. i 5: This geographical name is unidentified.

obv. ii 3: See FAOS 15/2 p. 598 for the discussion of this profession.

obv. ii 4: The two pairs of *šeššig*-strokes inside UḪ$_3$ in the writing of Ĝeša originate in KASKAL.

No. 105 – MS 3790/56

Allocation of beer, Early Dynastic/Early Sargonic, Adab.

obv. i	3 dug	3 jars (of beer):
	Ur-^{d}Nanše	Ur-Nanše;
	⌈6⌉ dug	6 jars (of beer):
	Ur-^{d}⌈*Er*$_x$⌉(KIŠ)-*ra*	Ur-Erra,
	ad-⌈KID$^?$⌉	the reed-worker;
ii	Šeš-tur	Šeštur,
	Ĝiri$_3$-ni zadim	(and) Ĝirini, the stonecutter;
	1 dug	1 jar (of beer):
	lu$_2$ ḪUB$_2$-BU-kam	it is (for) the man of ...;
	[break]	
rev. i	[n] ⌈dug⌉	x jars (of beer):
	Lugal-al-sa$_6$	Lugalalsa.
ii	(blank)	

obv. i 4: For this writings of the deity Erra, see Steinkeller 1987b: 165 fn. 23.

obv. ii 4: The line remains obscure. Cf. ḫub$_2$-bi = *ḫuppû* "acrobat"; CAD Ḫ 240.

No. 106 – MS 3790/70

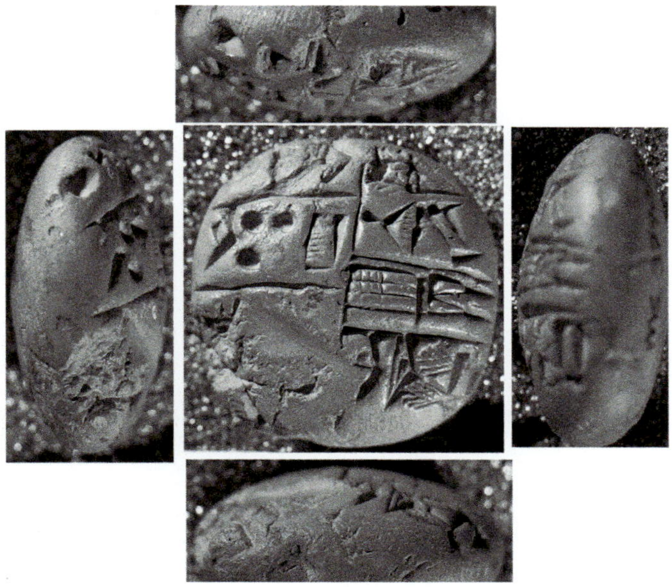

Account of beer, Early Dynastic/Early Sargonic, Adab.

obv. i	1 dug	1 jar (of beer):
	u$_4$ 30-še$_3$	for the 30th day.
	[...]-⸢da⸣	...
ii	in-na-gur$_{17}$(ĜIŠ$_{-tenû}$)	one has carried for him(?).
	e$_2$-dumu	The "House of the son."
	iti ni$_3$-kiri$_6$	Month Nikiri.
rev.	(blank)	

obv. ii 1: See Sallaberger 1994: 143–44 for ĜIŠ$_{-tenû}$ as a short form of IL$_2$ and its possible readings.

No. 107 – MS 4999

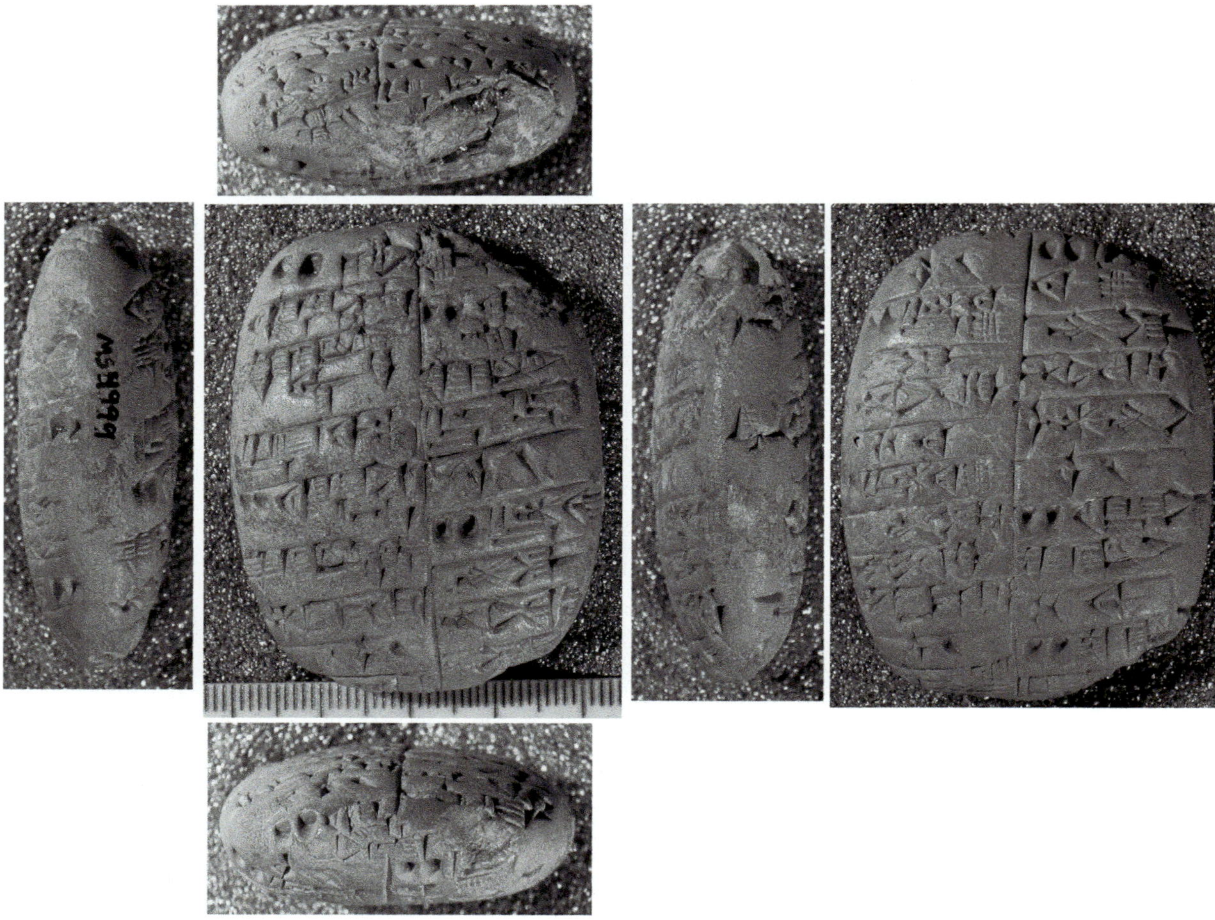

Record of beer for a reception of high-profile guests, including an official of the "king of Kiš," Early Dynastic/Early Sargonic, Adab.

The text records allocation of beer. The term for beer does not appear but the notation is the same as in text No. 104 above. The event for which the beer was distributed is the reception of two high-profile visitors from Kiš and Ĝirsu.

A notable detail is the reference to a "king of Kiš." Sargon is probably meant. The text seem to be dated to the "early career" of this ruler. At present it is known that Sargon became king long before he started on his conquest of Sumer. Importantly, an Ebla document provides a reference to an unnamed "king of Kiš," who was most likely Sargon. Later literary works suggest that Sargon succeeded the Kishite king Ur-Zababa through a coup. For a recent discussion of information on Sargon, see Schrakamp 2016: 1.

The present document offers another piece in the puzzle that is one of the most exciting events in Mesopotamian history: Sargon's rise to power and creation of an empire. The text hints at negotiations between representatives of Adab, the "king of Kiš" represented by his animal-manager, and the chief cook of Ĝirsu, probably as a representative of the Lagaš state. Such high-status dignitaries must have assembled because of some important matter. One can only speculate what was discussed during this beer-drinking event, for there are no direct clues. However, knowing the course of events, that those cities which joined Sargon prospered but those which refused the "offer which one cannot refuse" were defeated, one may suggest that the matter discussed was the question of whether to join or oppose Sargon. It is possible that the present document reports an attempt to draw Lagaš over to Sargon's side. Note that the document records beer for a second banquet, which lasted several days. This shows that there was much to discuss and/or it was hard to reach an agreement. A less probable interpretation of the text would be to relate "the king of Kiš" and the whole procedure to Iphur-Kiš, the king of Kiš promoted by the assembly of that city during the "Great Revolt" against Naram-Suen.

obv. i	2N$_8$ dug	⅔ jar (beer):
	PU$_3$.ŠA-Aš-tar$_2$	PUŠA-'Aštar,
	kuš$_7$ lugal Kiš^{ki}	the animal-manager of the king of Kiš.
	Ur-e$_2$-igi-nim	Ur-E'iginim (is responsible).
	2N$_8$ PU$_3$.ŠA-Aš-tar$_2$	⅔: PUŠA-'Aštar,
	kuš$_7$ lugal Kiš$^{:ki}$	the animal-manager of the king of Kiš.
	Diĝir-ĝa$_2$-ab-e	Diĝirĝabe (is responsible).
	2 u$_4$ *1*	2nd (time?), day 1.
	2N$_8$ PU$_3$.ŠA-Aš-tar$_2$	⅔: PUŠA-'Aštar.
ii	[Ur]-e$_2$-[igi-nim]	Ur-E'iginim (is responsible).
	2N$_8$ ⸢PU$_3$.ŠA⸣-Aš-tar$_2$	⅔: PUŠA-'Aštar,
	kuš$_7$ lugal	the animal-manager of the king.
	Ur-Šubur	Ur-Šubur (is responsible).
	(ras.) ⸢*1*?⸣ u$_4$ *1*	(erasure) 1st? (time?), day 1.
	2N$_8$ Ur-^{d}Ba-U$_2$	⅔: Ur-BaU,
	muḫaldim-gal	the chief cook
	Ĝir$_2$-su^{ki}	(of) Ĝirsu.
	Amar-GUL	AmarGUL (is responsible).
rev. i	2N$_8$ Ur-^{d}Ba-U$_2$	⅔: Ur-BaU,
	muḫaldim-gal	the chief cook
	Ĝir$_2$-su^{ki}	(of) Ĝirsu.
	Utu-diĝir-ĝu$_{10}$	Utudiĝirĝu (is responsible).
	u$_4$ *1*	Day 1.
	2N$_8$ PU$_3$.ŠA-Aš-tar$_2$	⅔: PUŠA-'Aštar,
	kuš$_7$ lugal	the animal-manager of the king.
	KUR-ba	KURba (is responsible).
	2N$_8$ kuš$_7$ ⸢lugal⸣	⅔: the animal-manager of the king.
	Ur-e$_2$-[igi-nim]	Ur-E'iginim.
ii	u$_4$ (ras.) *1*	Day 1 (2, erased).
	2N$_8$ Ur-^{d}Ba-U$_2$	⅔: Ur-BaU,
	muḫaldim-gal	the chief cook
	Ĝir$_2$-su^{ki}	(of) Ĝirsu.
	KUR-ba	KURba (is responsible).
	2N$_8$ Ur-^{d}Ba-U$_2$	⅔: Ur-BaU,
	muḫaldim-gal	the chief cook
	Ĝir$_2$-su^{ki}	(of) Ĝirsu.
	Diĝir-ĝa$_2$-ab-e	Diĝirĝabe (is responsible).
	u$_4$ *1*	Day 1.

	iti še-gur$_x$(|ŠE.ŠE|.KIN)-a	Month Šegura.
	ZA$_3$ *2*	The second reception.

rev. ii 7: The line is probably written on the erasure.

rev. ii 12: The meaning of ZA$_3$ in the present context may be "reception." For this meaning of za$_3$-gu$_2$-la$_2$, see Sallaberger 1993: 220 fn. 1051.

1.1.8 – Grain and Grain Products

No. 108 – MS 2191/2

Account of flour, beer and wooden objects, Early Dynastic/Early Sargonic, Adab.

obv. i	2 dabin gur	2 *gur* of barley flour;
	1 titab$_x$(ZI$_3$.LU$_3$) še dug	1 jar of barley ingredient *titab*;
	1 zi$_3$ za-tum dug	1 jar of flour *zatum*;
	1 zi$_3$ za-tum-sa$_6$-ga dug	1 jar of premium flour *zatum*;
ii	2(bariga) ⸢še x⸣	2 *bariga* … barley;
	10 ĝeš-⸢ur$_3$?⸣	10 wooden beams(?);
	36 ĝeš-⸢x⸣	36 wooden …;
	4 ĝeš-⸢al⸣-KA-⸢x⸣	4 wooden …
	2 ĝeš-[...]	2 wooden …;
	[n] ⸢ĝeš⸣-[x]-⸢al⸣-[x]	x wooden …;
rev. i	60 ninda	60 breads;
	13 dug	13 jars (of beer);
	3 dug (ras.)	3 jars (of <premium?> beer):
	nu-banda$_3$	The supervisor.
	1 dug	1 jar (of beer):
	Silim-^{d}Utu	Silim-Utu.

Texts Nos. 108 and 109 share the same hand. The provenance of both tablets is established by the presence of Silim-Utu, the supervisor.

obv. i 2: ZI$_3$.LU$_3$ is titab$_x$ according to the lexical list OB Diri Oxford 452 (*apud* DCCLT). Titab$_2$(LU$_3$.MUNU$_4$) is an ingredient for beer. For discussion, see Sallaberger 2012: 318–19 ("Treberkuchen").

obv. i 3: For the variety of flour zi$_3$ za-tum see the commentary to CUSAS 23 no. 100 obv. 6.

rev. i 3: The line is written over an erasure.

rev. i 4, 6: It is not certain that both lines refer to the same person.

No. 109 – MS 2191/8

Expenditure of a large amount of barley, Early Dynastic/Early Sargonic, Adab.

obv. i	120 la$_2$×7(gur) 3(ban$_2$) še gur	113 *gur* 3 *ban* of barley:
	⸢Ur⸣-kum-ke$_4$	Urkum,
	⸢Ur⸣-lu$_2$	to Urlu,
	⸢ma$_2$⸣-lah$_5$	the sailor,
	⸢in⸣-na-šum$_2$	he has given it to him.
ii	⸢x⸣-za-⸢x⸣	…
	al-⸢ĝa$_2$⸣	it is measured out.
	še zi-ga	Barley expended
	Ur-kum	(by) Urkum.
	Silim-^{d}Utu	Silim-Utu,
	nu-banda$_3$	the supervisor.
rev.	(blank)	

No. 110 – MS 2191/16

Allocation of grain and flour, Early Dynastic/Early Sargonic, Adab.

obv. i	2(bariga) dabin	2 *bariga* barley flour;
	2(bariga) še	2 *bariga* barley:
	Ur-a-da	Ur'a(ja)da,
	ugula-iri	the overseer over the city.
	[2(bariga)] dabin	[2 *bariga*] barley flour;
	[2(bariga)] še	[2 *bariga*] barley:
	Lugal-ĝar	Lugalĝar,
	dumu Sahar-ra-ni	son of Saharani.
ii	2(bariga) ⸢dabin⸣	2 *bariga* barley flour;
	2(bariga) še	2 *bariga* barley:
	Adab(NUN.UD)-ki:bi$_x$(DUG)	Adabkibi.
	2(bariga) dabin	2 *bariga* barley flour;
	2(bariga) še	2 *bariga* barley:
	A-ba-^{d}En-lil$_2$	Aba-Enlil,
	dumu Gi/Zi$_{-nutillû}$-ib	son of G/Zib.
	2(bariga) dabin	2 *bariga* barley flour;
	2(bariga) še	2 *bariga* barley:
	Ur-gu	Urgu,
iii	dumu Lugal-saĝ	son of Lugalsaĝ.
	2(bariga) dabin	2 *bariga* barley flour;
	2(bariga) še	2 *bariga* barley:
	Ĝessu	Ĝessu,
	dumu Ur-dam	son of Urdam.
	2(bariga) dabin	2 *bariga* barley flour;
	2(bariga) še	2 *bariga* barley:
	UŠ-*bum*	UŠ*bum*,

	dumu Šeš-tur	son of Šeštur.
rev. i	2(bariga) dabin gur	2 *bariga* barley flour;
	2(bariga) še	2 *bariga* barley:
	Šir$_3$(EZEN)-ra-ni	Širani,
	⸢arad$_2^{?}$⸣ Šeš-⸢tur⸣	the slave(?) of Šeštur.
	2(bariga) dabin	2 *bariga* barley flour;
	2(bariga) še	2 *bariga* barley:
	E$_2$-ur$_2$	E'ur,
	šeš Ur-gu	brother of Urgu.
	2(bariga) dabin	2 *bariga* barley flour;
ii	2(bariga) še	2 *bariga* barley:
	Ur-e$_2$-nim	Ur-Enim,
	šeš Nam$_2$-me	brother of Name.
	2(bariga) dabin	2 *bariga* barley flour;
	2(bariga) še	2 *bariga* barley:
	⸢Ur-zikum⸣	Urzikum.
	(blank)	
iii	(blank)	

obv. ii 3: Cf. Adab-ki-bi in CUSAS 11 no. 90 obv. ii 7 and in the present volume.

No. 111 – MS 3789/9

Account of barley groats, Early Dynastic/Early Sargonic, Adab. Pierced tablet.

obv. i	2 še ni$_3$-ar$_3$-ra gur	2 *gur* barley for groats:
	Ab-zu	to Abzu
	an-na-šum$_2$	it has been given.
	aša$_5$ ^{d}Dam-gal-nun-kam	It is of the Field (of) Damgalnun(a).
	iti a$_2$-ki-ti-kam	It is (the transaction) of the month Akiti.
ii	(blank)	
rev.	(blank)	

No. 112 – MS 3789/10

Account of barley for groats, Early Dynastic/Early Sargonic, Adab. Pierced tablet.

obv. i	1(gur) 2(bariga) še ni$_3$-ar$_3$-ra gur	1 *gur* 2 *bariga* barley for groats:
	Ab-zu	to Abzu
	an-na-šum$_2$	it has been given.
	aša$_5$ ^{d}Dam-gal-nun-kam	It is of the Field (of) Damgalnun(a).
	1(bariga) 2(ban$_2$) še ni$_3$-ar$_3$-ra	1 *gur* 2 *bariga* barley for groats:
ii	Ĝessu	to Ĝessu
	an-na-šum$_2$	it has been given.
	aša$_5$ e$_2$ Me-me	The field of the house (of) Meme.
	iti šu-ĝar-kam	It is (the transaction) of the month Šuĝar.
rev.	(blank)	

obv. ii 3: For this household in other ED/ES Adab texts, see CUSAS 11 nos. 220 and 259. Probably the same Meme occurs in text No. 17 obv. i 4; cf. also No. 115 obv. ii 2. These two references are clear examples of the communal ownership of land in contrast to the ownership by public households (palaces and temples).

No. 113 – MS 3789/11

Account of barley groats, Early Dynastic/Early Sargonic, Adab. Pierced tablet.

obv. i	2 še ni$_3$-ar$_3$-ra gur	2 *gur* of barley for groats:
	Ab-zu	to Abzu
	an-na-šum$_2$	it has been given.
	iti a$_2$-ki-ti-kam	It is (the transaction) of the month Akiti.
ii	aša$_5$ ^{d}Dam-gal-nun-kam	It is of the Field (of) Damgalnun(a).
rev.	(blank)	

No. 114 – MS 3789/15

Account of barley flour, Early Dynastic/Early Sargonic, Adab. Pierced tablet.

obv. i	2(bariga) dabin	2 *bariga* barley flour:
	Ur-^{d}En-ki	Ur-Enki;
	[n] Ne-saĝ	[n]: Nesaĝ;
	(blank space)	
ii	1(bariga) dabin	1 *bariga* barley flour:
	I$_3$-la-la	Ilala.
	(blank space)	
rev.	(blank)	

No. 115 – MS 3789/17

Account of barley and barley groats, Early Dynastic/Early Sargonic, Adab. Pierced tablet.

obv. i	1(gur) 2(bariga) še gur	1 *gur* 2 *bariga* barley:
	Ab-zu	to Abzu
	an-na-šum$_2$	it has been given:
	aša$_5$ ^{d}Dam-gal-nun	Field (of) Damgalnun(a).
	1(bariga) 2(ban$_2$) še ni$_3$-ar$_3$-ra	1 *bariga* 2 *ban* barley for groats:
ii	Ĝessu	(For) Ĝessu <it has been given>:
	e$_2$ Me-me	(the field of) the house (of) Meme.
	(blank space)	
	iti šu-ĝar-kam	It is (the transaction) of the month Šugar.

No. 116 – MS 3789/19

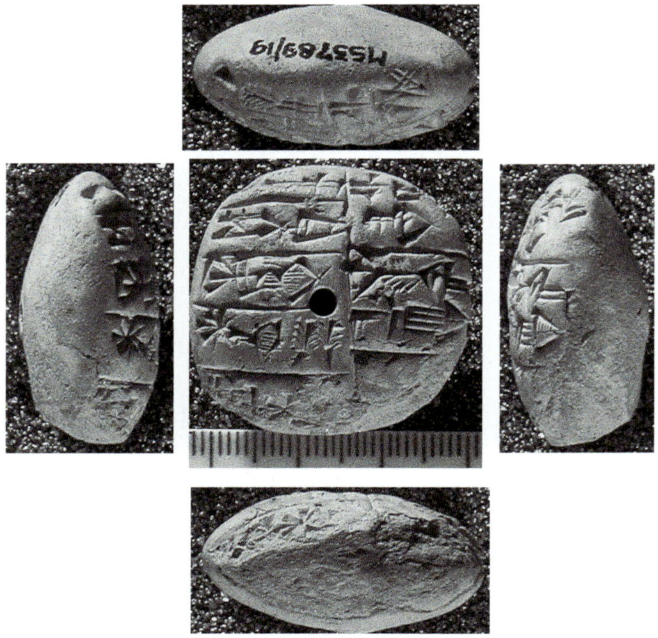

Account of barley, Early Dynastic/Early Sargonic, Adab. Pierced tablet.

obv. i	1 še gur	1 *gur* barley:
	Amar-ARAD	To AmarARAD,
	dam-gara$_3$	the merchant,
	an-na-šum$_2$	it has been given.
	⸢Ur⸣-^{d}⸢En⸣-[x]	Ur-En…
	maškim-bi$_x$(DUG)	(is) its commissioner.
	iti še-saĝ-sig$_{15}$-ga	Month Šesaĝsiga.
rev.	(blank)	

obv. i 2: For a merchant Amar-NI in ED/ES texts from Adab, see CUSAS 11 no. 122 rev. i 3 and, probably, BdI 1 no. 32 obv. ii 1, where the name is written Amar-NI-AN-AN(=nab?). In the present case the sign is ARAD (there are small stylus strokes that might even suggest ARAD×KUR = ARAD$_2$).

obv. ii 1: The sign DUG is consistently used instead of BI in the combination with maškim and in some other cases in ED/ES Adab. This could mean that DUG in the bread and beer texts above stands for kaš$_x$(DUG). Note, however, that in text No. 171 obv. i 2 the writing is kaš dug "jars of beer." Therefore, the sign DUG in these texts does actually signify the lexeme dug "pot," although beer is certainly implied.

No. 117 – MS 3789/24

Account of barley measured, Early Dynastic/Early Sargonic, Adab. Pierced tablet.

obv. i	1(ĝeš$_2$×u) 7(ĝeš$_2$) 40 ⸢3⸣(ras.) še gur	1060 (3, erased) *gur* barley
	sila$_3$ zabar$_x$(KA.BAR)^{uruda}-ta	by the bronze vessel (of one) *sila* (in capacity)
	al-bala	it is measured.
ii	Silim-^{d}Utu	Silim-Utu,
	nu-banda$_3$	the supervisor.
	(blank space)	
	aša$_5$ Mu-^{nu}nu$_{11}$-maḫ	Field Munumaḫ.
rev.	(blank)	

obv. i 3: Sallaberger 2016 esp. p. 246, argues that še … bala means "to measure barley (= to establish capacity)" in contrast to še … aĝ$_2$ "to measure out (= to issue) barley."

obv. ii 3: This field is recorded in ED/ES and CS texts from Adab, e.g., CUSAS 11 nos. 283 obv. 4, 284 obv. 4, CUSAS 13 no. 3 rev. 3.

No. 118 – MS 3789/25

Allocation of emmer to temple households, Early Dynastic/Early Sargonic, Adab. Pierced tablet.

obv. i	1 imĝaĝa$_{x}$(ZIZ$_{2}$.|AN.AN|) gur	1 *gur* emmer:
	e$_{2}$ ^{d}Aš$_{8}$-gi$_{4}$	the temple of Ašgi;
	3(bariga) e$_{2}$-SAR	3 *bariga*: (temple) E-SAR;
	2(bariga) e$_{2}$-GANA$_{2}$.IŠ	2 *bariga*: (temple) E-GANAIŠ.
ii	Šeš-ad$_{2}$-gal	Šešadgal,
	sagi	the cupbearer,
	maškim-bi$_{x}$(DUG)	(is) its commissioner.
	Silim-^{d}Utu	Silim-Utu,
	nu-banda$_{3}$	the supervisor.
rev. i	iti ^{d}Šuba$_{3}$(MUŠ$_{3}$×ZA)-nun	Month Šubanun.
ii	(blank)	

obv. i 1: This is the ED/ES Adab variant writing of /imĝaĝa/ "emmer," which is otherwise written imĝaĝa$_{3}$(ZIZ$_{2}$.AN), Akk. *kunāšu*.

No. 119 – MS 3789/32

Account of malt, Early Dynastic/Early Sargonic, Adab. Pierced tablet.

obv. i	1(gur) 2(bariga) munu$_{4}$ gur	1 *gur* 2 *bariga* malt:
	Igi-tur-tur	Igiturtur;
	1(gur) 1(bariga) 3(ban$_{2}$) Ur-^{d}Aš$_{8}$-gi$_{4}$	1 *gur* 1 *bariga* 3 *ban*: Ur-Ašgi;
	1(gur) la$_{2}$ 1(bariga) Zur-zur	1 *gur* minus 1 *bariga*: Zurzur;
	2(bariga) 3(ban$_{2}$) Lugal-u$_{4}$-su$_{13}$-še$_{3}$	2 *bariga* 3 *ban*: Lugalusuše;
	2(bariga) Nin-da-ti	2 *bariga*: Nindati;
	1(bariga) 3(ban$_{2}$) Da-ti	1 *bariga* 3 *ban*: Dati;
	1(bariga) 3(ban$_{2}$) A-ba-^{d}En-lil$_{2}$	1 *bariga* 3 *ban*: Aba-Enlil;
ii	1(bariga) 3(ban$_{2}$) Nin-amaš(LAK777)-zi	1 *bariga* 3 *ban*: Ninamašzi;
	1(bariga) AD-⸢KID$^{?}$⸣-zi	1 *bariga*: ADKIDzi;
	1(bariga) Ur-^{d}Nanše	1 *bariga*: Ur-Nanše;
	4(ban$_{2}$) ⸢n⸣ sila$_{3}$ Ur-pisaĝ	4 *ban* x *sila*: Urpisaĝ;
	2(gur) 3(ban$_{2}$) munu$_{4}$ ba-ba gur	2 *gur* 3 *ban* malt (for) the *baba*-product:
	Lugal-abba$_{2}$-ĝu$_{10}$	Lugalabbaĝu;
	1(gur) 2(bariga) munu$_{4}$ BU-RU	1 *gur* 2 *bariga* malt (for) ...:
	Lugal-abba$_{2}$	Lugalabba(ĝu);
rev. i	7(gur) 1(bariga) Lugal-abba$_{2}$-ĝu$_{10}$	7 *gur* 1 *bariga*: Lugalabbaĝu;
	4(gur) 3(ban$_{2}$) Bara$_{2}$-ga-ni-du$_{10}$	4 *gur* 3 *ban*: Baraganidu.
ii	(blank)	

obv. ii 5: For ba-ba, not "porridge," see Brunke 2008: 159 f.

obv. ii 7: Like ba-ba, BU-RU is a foodstuff produced from grain.

No. 120 – MS 3789/34

Issue of grain in a granary, Early Dynastic/Early Sargonic, Adab. Pierced tablet.

obv.	[n] 2(bariga) guru$_7$ gur	x *guru* 2 *bariga* (barley):
	[(x) ^{d}]En-lil$_2$-la$_2$	Enlila;
	[n+] 2(gur) Ur-pisaĝ	x+2 gur: Urpisaĝ;
	[n] Saĝ-zi	x: Saĝzi;
	2(gur) Ur-$^{⸢d⸣}$Eš$_{23}$-peš	2 *gur*: Ur-Ešpeš
rev.	[n+] ⸢2⸣(bariga) Ur-diĝir	x+2 *bariga*: Urdiĝir.
	⸢guru$_7$⸣-saĝ-ĝa$_2$	This is (the grain) in the main granary(?)
	⸢an⸣-na-šum$_2$-ma-am$_3$	(that) has been given to him.
	(blank)	

obv. 1, rev. 2: guru$_7$ means either "granary, silo" or a unit of capacity equal to 3600 gur-saĝ-ĝal$_2$ of 240 sila$_3$; see Powell 1990: 489. The absence of a term for grain is suspicious.

No. 121 – MS 3789/36

Monthly allocation of barley to two female workers and a child, Early Dynastic/Early Sargonic, Adab. Pierced tablet.

obv.	6(gur) 1(bariga) še gur ⸢x⸣	6 *gur* 1 *bariga* ... barley;
	2 geme$_2$ 1(bariga) 2(ban$_2$)-ta	2 women: 1 *bariga* 2 *ban* each;
	1 dumu 3(ban$_2$)	1 child: 3 *ban*.
	[iti] ⸢ĝa$_2$⸣-udu-ur$_4$-kam	It is of the [month] Ĝa'udu'ur.
	[break; uninscribed]	
rev.	(blank; stylus scratches)	

The photo shows a fragment attached to the tablet. It was absent at the time of the collation. The reverse of the tablet bears some scratches that seem to be ancient. They do not have any meaning, however.

No. 122 – MS 3789/38

Account of barley flour, Early Dynastic/Early Sargonic, Adab. Pierced tablet.

obv. i	1 dabin gur	1 *gur* of barley flour:
	ḫe$_2$-dab$_5$-me	these are *ḫedab*-workers,
	lu$_2$ *Iš-me-i$_3$-lum*	the people of *Yišme-'ilum*
	I$_3$-lum-(ras.)-*ra*-NI	(and) *'Ilum-ra*NI.
	1(ban$_2$) E$_2$-LUḪ-ge-si	1 *ban*: to ELUḪgesi;
ii	an-na-šum$_2$	it has been given.
	(blank space)	
	⸢iti⸣ aša$_5$-il$_2$-šu-ĝar	Month Aša'ilšuĝar.
	(blank)	
rev.	(blank)	

obv. i 2: For ḫe$_2$-dab, a category of low-ranking workers, see SCTRAH no. 244 commentary.

obv. i 5: For the same personal name in the Classical Sargonic Adab corpus, see PPAC 1 no. 632 obv. ii 2, no. 982 obv. i 3, CUSAS 19 no. 89 rev. 3, OIP 14 nos. 102 rev. 5, 152 rev. 3.

No. 123 – MS 3789/45

Account of barley, Early Dynastic/Early Sargonic, Adab. Pierced tablet.

obv. i	[n+] 60 še gur	x+60 *gur* barley
	⸢ĝanun$^{?}$⸣-ta	out of the storehouse(?)
	Ur-⸢x⸣-nam$_2$	Ur...nam,
	Na-ni	(to) Nani
	in-na-šum$_2$	he has given to him.
	⸢e$_2$⸣-dumu	The "House of the son."
ii	Silim-^{d}Utu	Silim-Utu,
	nu-banda$_3$	the supervisor.
	(blank space)	
rev.	(blank)	

obv. i 2: The sign ĜANUN is not without question, for there is an oblique wedge at the end which makes it resemble the end of a DA.

obv. i 4: The same individual appears in CUSAS 11 no. 126 obv. ii 4, no. 150 rev. i 2 and no. 334 obv. 2.

No. 124 – MS 3789/46

Account of barley, Early Dynastic/Early Sargonic, Adab. Pierced tablet.

obv. i	[n(gur)] 1(bariga) še gur	x *gur* 1 *bariga* barley:
	⸢tug$_2$⸣-du$_8$	it is (for) the felter(s)
	⸢Unug⸣^{ki}-kam	from Uruk.
	⸢Za$_3$⸣-mu sukkal	Zamu, the secretary,
	maškim-bi$_x$(DUG)	(is) its commissioner.
	11 geme$_2$ 2(ban$_2$)	11 female workers: 2 *ban* (barley each):
ii	e$_2$-dumu	the "House of the son."
	10 la$_2$ 1 ENGUR-TUM	9 (*gur* for) ... personnel.
	4(ban$_2$) ĜIR$_3$-⸢ĜIR$_3$⸣	4 *ban*: to ĜIRĜIR(?).
	še DU-[...]	Barley *delivered*(?).
	Na-[ni]	(to) Na[ni]
	⸢in⸣-[na-šum$_2$]	one has [given it].
rev.	[(blank space)]	
	[Silim-^{d}Utu]	[Silim-Utu,]
	nu-[banda$_3$]	the supervisor.
	(blank space)	
ii	(blank)	

obv. ii 2–3: The first term is obscure. See the commentary to Nos. 41 obv. i 3, 134 obv. ii 2. ĜIR$_3$-ĜIR$_3$ may be a personal name.

No. 125 – MS 3790/1

Account of barley flour, Early Dynastic/Early Sargonic, Adab.

obv. i	1 dabin gur	1 *gur* barley flour:
	Ur-e$_2$	to Ur-e,
	gala	the cult-singer,
	an-na-šum$_2$	it has been given.
	(blank space)	
ii	e$_2$-dumu	The "House of the son."
	iti ab-e$_3$-zi-ga	Month Ab-eziga.
	(blank space)	
rev.	(blank)	

No. 126 – MS 3790/2

Account of barley flour, Early Dynastic/Early Sargonic, Adab.

obv. i	1(bariga) dabin	1 *bariga* barley flour:
	Ur-ba-dab$_5$	Urbadab,
	nu-kiri$_6$	the gardener
	Ne-saĝ-kam	of Nesaĝ.
	Za$_3$-mu	Zamu
ii	maškim-bi$_x$(DUG)	(is) its commissioner.
	2(bariga) 3(ban$_2$) lu$_2$-tu-ra-me	2 *bariga* 3 *ban*: these are (for) the sick people.
	1(bariga) Ur-^{d}Aš$_8$-gi$_4$	1 *bariga*: Ur-Ašgi.
	zi$_3$ iti [...]	Flour of the month ...
	(blank space)	
rev. i	iti mu-tir	Month Mutir.
	zi$_3$ zi-ga	Flour expended.
	e$_2$-dumu	The "House of the son."
	(blank space)	

No. 127 – MS 3790/3

Account of wheat and emmer, Early Dynastic/Early Sargonic, Adab.

obv. i	20 la$_2$×1(bariga)+3(ban$_2$) kib$_3$ gur	20 *gur* minus 1 *bariga* 3 *ban* wheat:
	120 la$_2$ 1 ziz$_2$ gur	120 minus 1 *gur* emmer:
	e$_2$-dumu-saĝ	(to) the "House of the firstborn son,"
	Il$_2$	Il(a),
	dub-sar	the scribe,
ii	šu-a bi$_2$-gi$_4$	has turned over.
	Ur-^{d}Nin-mug-ra	To Ur-Ninmug
	<line erased>	
	an-na-šum$_2$	it has been given.
rev. i	iti a$_2$-ki-ti-kam	It is month Akiti.
	Silim-^{d}Utu	Silim-Utu,
	nu-banda$_3$	the supervisor.
	aša$_5$ Mar-MA-kam	It is of the field MarMA.

obv. i 3: This could be a fuller writing of e$_2$-TUR, an organization or building that is abundantly recorded in ED/ES texts from Adab; see Such-Gutiérrez 2005–6: 43–44. This fuller writing means "the house of the firstborn son" and may be a reference to the offspring of Diĝirmaḫ/

Ninḫursaĝa and Ašgi, the chief divine couple of the Adab pantheon. For a temple e$_2$-dumu-saĝ of the deity Ninti'uga at Nippur, see RIME 3/2 p. 396 1.6.1006 l. 6. Alternatively, the SAĜ at the end of the present writing could be a defective KA, thus producing e$_2$-dumu-ka$^!$ "in the 'House of the son'."

rev. i 4: For the same field, see PPAC 1 no. 940 obv. 3: [aša$_5$] Mar-ma-ta.

No. 128 – MS 3790/6

Account of barley flour mentioning a maid of the supervisor, Early Dynastic/Early Sargonic, Adab.

obv. i	1(bariga) dabin	1 *bariga* barley flour:
	E$_2$-nu-nu	to Enunu,
	geme$_2$ nu-banda$_3$	the maid of the supervisor,
	e$_2$-dumu-ta	out of the "House of the son"
	an-na-šum$_2$	it has been given to her.
ii	Ur-^{d}[...]	Ur... (is responsible).
	Aja$_2$-KA-du$_3$	AjaKAdu
	maškim-bi$_x$(DUG)	(is) its commissioner.
	iti še-kin-ku$_5$	Month Šekinku.
rev.	(blank)	

obv. i 2–3: The "supervisor" here is doubtlesly the well-known Silim-Utu.

No. 129 – MS 3790/7

Deliverey of premium flour to the "New Palace," Early Dynastic/Early Sargonic, Adab.

obv. i	[n+] 1 zi$_3$-sig$_{15}$ gur	x+1 *gur* of premium flour:
	⌜ni$_3$⌝-šu-gub-ba	in containers with handles.
	e$_2$-gal-gibil	(To) the New Palace
	an-de$_6$	it has been brought there.
	⌜Ur⌝-nu	Urnu,
ii	ugula-e$_2$	the overseer over the household,
	maškim-bi$_x$(DUG)	(is) its commissioner.
	iti ni$_3$-kiri$_6$	Month Nikiri.
	e$_2$-dumu	The "House of the son."
	[break; uninscribed]	
rev.	(blank)	

obv. i 5–6: This high official may be identical to the Ur-nu who appears without any title in numerous ED/ES texts from Adab.

No. 130 – MS 3790/10

Account of barley, Early Dynastic/Early Sargonic, Adab.

obv. i	1 še gur	1 *gur* barley:
	Lugal-giri$_x$(LAK85)-ĝal$_2$	Lugalgiriĝal,
	šita-iri	the city *šita*-official,
	E$_2$-zur-zur-kam	of (the town) Ezurzur,
ii	an-na-šum$_2$	it has been given to him.
	e$_2$-dumu	The "House of the son."
	iti mu-tir	Month Mutir.
rev.	(blank)	

obv. i 2: For the sign LAK85, see Krebernik 1998a: 275.

obv. i 4: Although an individual Zur-zur appears in ED/ES Adab texts (see in this volume), the phrase does not refer to his house. Instead, based on the reference in CUSAS 11 no. 141 Ad-da šita-iri E$_2$-zur-zur^{ki} "Adda, the city *šita*-official of Ezurzur," it is here a town or village.

No. 131 – MS 3790/11

Account of grain products, Early Dynastic/Early Sargonic, Adab.

obv. i	2(bariga) dabin	2 *bariga* barley flour;
	2(bariga) bappir	2 *bariga* sourdough;
	2(bariga) munu$_4$	2 *bariga* malt;
	2(bariga) ni$_3$-ar$_3$-ra	2 *bariga* groats:
	Lugal-[...]	to Lugal...,
ii	ma$_2$-laḫ$_4$	the sailor
	A-ga-de$_3$^{ki}	(from) Agade,
	an-na-šum$_2$	it has been given to him.
	iti šu-ĝar	Month Šuĝar.
rev. i	e$_2$-dumu	The "House of the son."
	A-ĝeštin	Aĝeštin,
	⸢sagi⸣	the cupbearer,
	maškim-bi$_x$(DUG)	(is) its commissioner.
ii	(blank)	

obv. i 2: See Sallaberger 2012: 308–10 for /bappir/ as a term for (dried/cooked) sourdough used in preparing beer.

No. 132 – MS 3790/13

Account of barley, Early Dynastic/Early Sargonic, Adab.

obv. i	2(gur) 2(bariga) še gur	2 *gur* 2 *bariga* barley:
	Lu$_{2}$-lugal-kam	of Lulugal(a);
	1 Ur-^{d}En-ki	1 *gur*: Ur-Enki,
	dumu Za$_{3}$	son of Za(mu ?).
	⸢an⸣-ne-[šum$_{2}$]	It has been given to them.
ii	še zi-ga	It is barley expended
	Ur-lu$_{2}$	by Urlu,
	dumu E$_{2}$-dam-si-kam	son of Edamsi.
rev.	[break]	...

No. 133 – MS 3790/16

Account of flour and grain products, Early Dynastic/Early Sargonic, Adab.

obv. i	1(bariga) zi$_{3}$ Ur-lu$_{2}$	1 *bariga* flour: Urlu,
	ma$_{2}$-laḫ$_{5}$	the sailor;
	2 aga$_{3}$-us$_{2}$ 1(bariga)	2 soldiers: 1 *bariga* (each);
	2(bariga) zi$_{3}$ 4(ban$_{2}$) bappir	2 *bariga* flour; 4 *ban* sourdough;
	4(ban$_{2}$) ni$_{3}$-ar$_{3}$-ra	4 *ban* groats;
ii	4(ban$_{2}$) munu$_{4}$	4 *ban* malt:
	A-[...]-⸢x⸣	A...,
	⸢dumu⸣ [...]-⸢x⸣-gal	son of ...gal.
	e$_{2}$-dumu	The "House of the son."
	Silim-^{d}Utu	Silim-Utu,
	nu-banda$_{3}$	the supervisor.
rev. i	iti a$_{2}$-ki-ti	Month Akiti.
	(blank)	

No. 134 – MS 3790/20

Account of barley bread, Early Dynastic/Early Sargonic, Adab.

obv. i	360 ninda-še	360 barley breads:
	tir ^{d}Aš$_{8}$-gi$_{4}$	the Forest of (god) Ašgi;
	180 ninda-še	180 barley breads:
ii	Ka$_{5}$-a	(to) Ka'a.
	ENGUR-TUM-me	They are ... personnel;
	600 ninda-še	barley breads:
	Aš$_{11}$-lum	(to) *Ašlum*
5	an-na-šum$_{2}$	it has been given.
rev. i	e$_{2}$ nu-banda$_{3}$	The house of the supervisor.
ii	(blank)	

obv. i 2: I am not aware of other references to this forest. However, "forests" of gods are well attested: cf., e.g., tir ^{d}Šara$_{2}$ and tir ^{d}Nin-dulum$_{2}$-ma in the Ur III documents from Umma.

obv. ii 2: The term appears in two other texts in this volume: Nos. 41 and 124, which also record beer, bread, and barley allocations. This fact and the copula =me(š) implies that the ENGUR-TUM-me was a category of personnel. The breads are allocated to workmen of this sort in the "Forest of Ašgi" and to those under the supervision of Ka'a.

No. 135 – MS 3790/21

Account of emmer, Early Dynastic/Early Sargonic, Adab.

obv. i	20 la$_2$×1(gur)+2(bariga) ziz$_2$ gur	20 minus 1 *gur* and 2 *bariga* emmer:
	Lugal-sila	to Lugalsila
	an-na-šum$_2$	it has been given.
	nu-banda$_3$	The supervisor (is in charge).
ii	e$_2$-dumu-kam	It is (the grain) of the "House of the son."
rev.	(blank)	

No. 136 – MS 3790/23

Account of premium barley, Early Dynastic/Early Sargonic, Adab.

obv. i	8 la$_2$ 1(bariga) še gur sig$_{15}$	8 *gur* minus 1 *bariga* of premium barley
	Ur-^{d}Zu:en	(to) Ur-Zu'en,
	^{lu2}lunga$_3$	the brewer,
	an-na-šum$_2$	it has been given.
ii	sa$_2$-du$_{11}$	The regular delivery.
	iti še-gur$_x$(|ŠE.ŠE|.KIN)-a	Month Šegura(m).
	e$_2$-dumu	The "House of the son."
rev.	(blank)	

No. 137 – MS 3790/25

Account of grain products, Early Dynastic/Early Sargonic, Adab.

obv. i	2(bariga) bappir	2 *bariga* sourdough;
	3(bariga) munu$_4$	3 *bariga* malt;
	2(bariga) ni$_3$-ar$_3$-ra	2 *bariga* groats:
	Gul-na$_2$	Gulna,
	nu-banda$_3$	the supervisor,
ii	a-de$_2$	has measured it out.
	ensi$_2$ [(x)]	(When) the governor
	A-za-bum-ta	from Azabum
	im-du-a	was on the way.
rev. i	iti še-kin-ku$_5$	Month Šekinku.
	e$_2$-dumu	The "House of the son."
ii	(blank)	

obv. i 4–ii 1: A supervisor of this name is unknown. It is not excluded that Gulna is the recipient of the grain products and the supervisor is Silim-Utu.

obv. ii 3: See text No. 161 in this volume for the same locality, and Schrakamp 2015a: 199 for references to it in other texts.

obv. ii 4: The distribution of writings with the verb ĝen "to go" in Adab texts edited in this volume shows that *hamṭu*-forms are written -ĝen-na whereas *marû*-forms appear as -du-a.

No. 138 – MS 3790/29

Account of barley flour, Early Dynastic/Early Sargonic, Adab.

obv. i	1(bariga) ⸢dabin⸣	1 *bariga* of barley flour:
	ĜIR$_3$-LUM	ĜIRLUM,
	sipa udu-niga	the shepherd of fattened sheep,
	A-ga-de$_3^{ki}$	(from) Agade,
ii	an-na-šum$_2$	it has been given to him.
	A-ĝeštin	Aĝeštin,
	i$_3$-du$_8$	the doorman,
	maškim-bi$_x$(DUG)	(is) its commissioner.
rev. i	e$_2$-dumu	The "House of the son."
	iti mu-tir	Month Mutir.

No. 139 – MS 3790/30

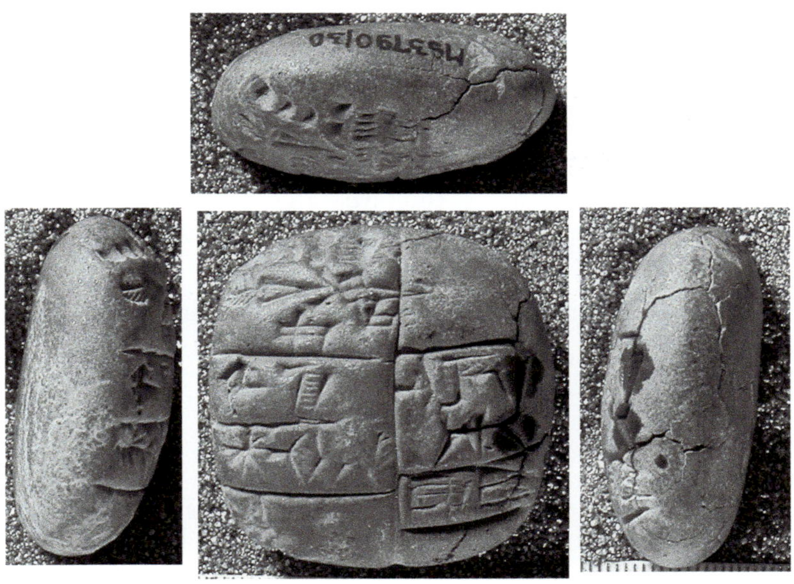

Account of GU.LUL seeds, Early Dynastic/Early Sargonic, Adab.

obv. i	3(gur) 2(bariga) 4(ban$_2$) še	3 *gur* 2 *bariga* 4 *ban*
	GU.LUL gur	of GULUL seeds:
	Igi-si$_4$	to Igisi
	an-na-šum$_2$	it has been given.
	(blank space)	

ii	(blank space)	
	iti a$_2$-ki-ti	Month Akiti.
	e$_2$-dumu	The "House of the son."
rev.	(blank)	

obv. i 1: The identification of the plant ^{u2}(GU.)LUL is uncertain. See SCTRAH p. 195 for a discussion, where Molina understands še GU.LUL of the present texts as the plant's "seeds."

No. 140 – MS 3790/36

Allocation of grain to personnel, Early Dynastic/Early Sargonic, Adab.

obv. i	[...] ⸢x x⸣	...:
	[...]-si	...si
	[n Aja$_2$]-⸢zu⸣-zu	n: Ajazuzu(?);
	[n ...]-men	n: ...men;
	[n I$_3$]-⸢la⸣-la	n: Ilala;
	2(bariga) Ur-ab-ba šu-ku$_6$	2 *bariga*: Ur-abba, the fisherman;
	2(bariga) Sa-DIŠ-ri engar	2 *bariga*: Sa..., the agricultural manager;
	2(bariga) Ur-pisaĝ engar	2 *bariga*: Urpisaĝ, the agricultural manager;
	3(bariga) Gala	3 *bariga*: Gala,
	dumu Aja$_2$-ne-da	son of Ajaneda
	Lugal-ra ugula	(and) Lugalra, the overseer;
	2(bariga) Nam-⸢x⸣-ga-ni	2 *bariga*: Nam...gani
	Ad-da-sila-si	(and) Addasilasi;
ii	2(bariga) Usar$_4$(LA$_2$×LAGAB)-re$_2$	2 *bariga*: Usare
	Amar-ḪA ad-KID	(and) Amar-ḪA, the reed-worker;
	1(bariga) 2(ban$_2$) Ur-Lum-ma	1 *bariga* 2 *ban*: Ur-Lumma,
	mušen-du$_3$ ĝiri$_3$	the bird-catcher: (for) the journey;
	2(bariga) Lugal-saĝ	2 *bariga*: Lugalsaĝ
	E$_2$-igi-nim	(and) E'iginim;
	2(bariga) ⸢Ad-da⸣ engar 2(bariga)	2 *bariga*: Adda, the agricultural manager: 2 *bariga*;
	2(bariga) ⸢Ga-x⸣	2 *bariga*: Ga...;
	⸢Lugal-x⸣ 2(bariga)	Lugal...: 2 *bariga*;
	⸢x-x-ki⸣ 2(bariga)	...ki: 2 *bariga*;
	Mu-ni-lal$_3$ 2(bariga)	Munilal: 2 *bariga*:
	⸢Saĝ⸣-ku$_5$ dumu šidim	Saĝku, the builders's apprentice,
	an-na-⸢šum$_2$⸣	it has been given to him.
	Ur-^{d}Nin-⸢x⸣ [...]	Ur-Nin...,
	Igi-[...]	Igi...,
iii	A-na-na-⸢x⸣	Anana...,
	⸢gala⸣	the cult-singer,
	Aja$_2$-zu-zu ugula	Ajazuzu, the overseer.
	ša$_3$ e$_2$-gal	(Those) within the palace.
	Saĝ-zi 2(bariga)	Saĝzi: 2 *bariga*;
	Ur-Šubur 2(bariga)	Ur-Šubur: 2 *bariga*;

	Im-⸢ta⸣ [2(bariga)]	Imta: [2 *bariga*];
	Ur-⸢^{d}⸣Aš$_8$-[gi$_4$]	Ur-Ašgi.
	e$_2$-AḪ	(Those of) the E'AḪ (household);
10–11	[2 lines defaced]	...
	Amar-^{d}⸢En-lil$_2$⸣	Amar-Enlil;
	Gal-zu [(x)]	Galzu;
	⸢x⸣-LUM-[...]	...;
15	[...]	...,
rev. i	mušen-du$_3$ ĝiri$_3$	the bird-catcher: (for) the journey;
	Lugal-ma-tum$_2$	Lugalmatum;
	Ur-⸢x-x⸣	Ur...;
	⸢x⸣-um	...um;
5–6	[2 lines defaced]	...
	⸢ĜAR$^{?}$⸣ [x] ⸢BI$^{?}$⸣	...
	saĝ-bi	its main amount
	an-na-šum$_2$	has been given to him.

obv. i 4: Cf. ^{d}Aš$_8$-gi$_4$-men, who appears in a document recording an allocation of barley (CUSAS 11 no. 260 obv. i 3).

obv. i 13: This is a full spelling of the abbreviated name Sila-si. Others include En-sila-si and Lugal-sila-si.

obv. ii 4: The sign ANŠE(LAK240) is unexpected here since mušen-du$_3$ is usually interpreted as a professional concerned with catching birds. However, references to a "bird-catcher of birds" (see FAOS 15/2 p. 84) imply that mušen-du$_3$ might have become a general term for a person who snared animals. In that case the sign refers not to a "journey" (reading ĝiri$_3$) but to "donkeys" (anše).

obv. ii 6: See the commentary to text No. 356 obv. i 13.

obv. ii 12: Alternatively, it is dumu DIM$_2$ "son of DIM."

obv. iii 4: The category of personnel ša$_3$ e$_2$-gal occurs alongside dumu e$_2$-gal in OB Proto-Lu$_2$ 78, MSL 12 p. 35. For a similar category of personnel ša$_3$-e$_2$ "those inside the 'house'," see CUSAS 26 no. 239 (CS Ur) rev. 1'.

No. 141 – MS 3790/38

Account of barley flour, Early Dynastic/Early Sargonic, Adab.

obv. i	1 dabin gur	1 *gur* of barley flour:
	Šeš-ad$_2$-⸢gal⸣	to Šešadgal,
	⸢sagi⸣	the cupbearer,
	an-na-šum$_2$	it has been given.
ii	e$_2$-dumu	The "House of the son."
	zi$_3$ zi-ga	Expended flour.
	Igi-si$_4$ ⸢maškim⸣-[bi]	Igisi (is) its commissioner.
	⸢iti ĝa$_2$⸣-[udu]-ur$_4$	Month Ĝa'udu'ur.
rev.	(blank)	

No. 142 – MS 3790/41

Account of barley flour, barley and flour for bread, Early Dynastic/Early Sargonic, Adab.

obv. i	1 dabin <gur>	1 <*gur*> of barley flour:
	Ur$_2$-ni	Urni;
	2(bariga) še gur	2 *bariga* (of a) *gur* barley:
	lu$_2$ Isin$_2^{ki}$-ta im-ĝen-na-me	(for) persons who have come from Isin;
	1(ban$_2$) zi$_3$ ninda	2 *ban* flour (for) bread;
ii	[break]	
	⸢x⸣ […]	…
	1(ban$_2$) […]	1 *ban* …
	1(ban$_2$) ⸢Ur$_2^{?}$⸣-[…]	1 *ban*: Ur…(?)
	e$_3$-a	Issued.
	Aja$_2$-KA-du$_3$	To AjaKAdu
rev. i	an-na-šum$_2$	it has been given.
	e$_2$-dumu	The "House of the son."
	iti še-kin-ku$_5$-kam	It was month Šekinku.
ii	(blank)	

No. 143 – MS 3790/42

Account of grain products, Early Dynastic/Early Sargonic, Adab.

obv. i	1 dabin ⸢gur⸣	1 *gur* barley flour;
	2(bariga) bappir	2 *bariga* sourdough;
	2(bariga) munu$_4$	2 *bariga* malt;
	2(bariga) ni$_3$-ar$_3$-ra	2 *bariga* groats:
	Ab-ba	(to) Abba
	an-na-šum$_2$	it has been given.
ii	Ur-^{d}[…]	Ur…
	maškim-bi$_x$(DUG)	(is) its commissioner.
	(ruling)	

	e$_2$-dumu	The "House of the son."
	iti du$_6$-ku$_3$	Month Duku.
rev.	(blank)	

No. 144 – MS 3790/44

Account of grain products, Early Dynastic/Early Sargonic, Adab.

obv. i	1 zi$_3$-sig$_{15}$ gur	1 *gur* of premium flour;
	1 bappir gur	1 *gur* sourdough;
	1 munu$_4$ gur	1 *gur* malt;
	1 ni$_3$-ar$_3$-ra gur	1 *gur* groats:
	⸢Šeš⸣-bad$_3$	Šešbad,
	⸢sagi⸣	the cupbearer,
ii	ki nu-banda$_3$	from/for/instead of the supervisor
	an-na-šum$_2$	it has been given to him.
	⸢e$_2$⸣-dumu	The "House of the son."
	iti še-saĝ-sig$_{15}$-ga	Month Šesaĝsiga.
rev.	(blank)	

No. 145 – MS 3790/45

Account of barley flour, Early Dynastic/Early Sargonic, Adab.

obv. i	[n] dabin gur	x *gur* of barley flour:
	⸢Lu$_2$⸣-pa$_3$-da	to Lupada,
	šeš Ur-TAR	brother of UrTAR,
	an-na-šum$_2$	it has been given.
ii	Šeš-lu$_2$-gi-na	Šešlugina
	maškim-bi$_x$(DUG)	(is) its commissioner.
	e$_2$-dumu	The "House of the son."
	iti ni$_3$-kiri$_6$	Month Nikiri.
	zi$_3$ zi-ga	Expended flour.
rev.	(blank)	

No. 146 – MS 3790/50

Account of emmer, Early Dynastic/Early Sargonic, Adab.

The provenance of this much damaged tablet is based on the paleography (especially the sign MAḪ) and the dimensions of the tablet, which match those of texts Nos. 164, 182, 197, 223 and 225. They derive from the office of the supervisor Silim-Utu.

obv. i	2(gur) 1(bariga) 3(ban$_2$) ziz$_2$ gur	2 *gur* 1 *bariga* 3 *ban* emmer:
	sa$_2$-⸢du$_{11}$⸣ [...]	the regular delivery...
	⸢x-x⸣	...
	⸢ensi$_2$⸣	(of) the governor.
	3(bariga) ziz$_2$ En-eden-ne$_2$	3 *bariga* emmer: Enedene,
	saĝĝa$_2$(LAK175)	the purification priest;
	2(bariga) ⸢Nin-da⸣-maḫ-di	2 *bariga*: Nindamaḫdi,
ii	agrig	the steward;
	1(gur) 1(bariga) Keš$_3$-da-maḫ-di	1 *gur* 1 *bariga*: Kešdamaḫdi;
	[n ...]	...
	⸢AN⸣-[x]	...
	⸢^{lu2}lunga$_3$⸣	the brewer.
	(blank)	
rev.	[partly destroyed]	
	⸢x⸣-[...]	...
	⸢x⸣-[...]	...
	ZA$_3$ ⸢x x⸣ MU TA	...

obv. i 5–6: A certain Enedene bears the title ugula mušen$^!$(RI)-du$_3$ in CUSAS 11 no. 77 obv. ii 8–9, and another occurs as a priest nu-eš$_3$ in CUSAS 11 no. 186 obv. ii 4–5. In our text Enedene bears a title that is written with the sign LAK175 and designates a purification priest; for the sign and its history, see Rubio 2013: 101–4. It is likely that CUSAS 11 no. 186 and the present text refer to a single individual who held various priestly offices during his career.

rev.: The reverse is unusual. Besides the lack of columns—a peculiarity of the ED IIIb "Umma" texts—there are no divisions between the lines. In addition, the shape of the damage is unusual, giving the impression that the upper part of the reverse was pressed against something hard and flat.

No. 147 – MS 3790/51

Account of large amounts of barley, Early Dynastic/Early Sargonic, Adab.

obv. i	[n] še gur	x *gur* barley:
	ga:eš$_8$	the long-distance trader
	Nibru^{ki}	(from) Nippur;
	427(gur) 2(bariga) lu$_2$-eše$_2$-aša$_5$-gid$_2$	427 *gur* 2 *bariga*: the field-surveyor;
	200 la$_2$ 2 Saĝ-ba	200 minus 2: Saĝba;
ii	200 la$_2$ 2 ⸢KUM⸣-KU-ŠE$_3$	200 minus 2: KUMKUŠE;
	200 la$_2$ 2 Ur-⸢^{d}⸣MUŠ	200 minus 2: Ur-MUŠ;
	155 Bar-tab$_{\text{-tenû}}$ simug	155: Bartab, the smith;
	45 sukkal-mah̯	45: the chief secretary;
	52(gur) 2(bariga) ma$_2$-lah̯$_5$-⸢gal⸣	52 *gur* 2 *bariga*: the chief sailor;
	90 ⸢x⸣ [...]	90: ...;
iii	Ba-za	Baza;
	120 la$_2$×5(gur)+2(bariga) Ur-^{d}Utu	120 *gur* minus 5 *gur* 2 *bariga*: Ur-Utu;
	135 Lugal-⸢zi⸣	135: Lugalzi;
	67(gur) 2(bariga) Saĝ-[x]	67 *gur* 2 *bariga*: Saĝ...;
	20 la$_2$ 2 [+n ...]	20 minus <2: ...;
	[break]	
rev. i	[break]	
	[n] ⸢KAL⸣-[...]	x: KAL...,

	lu$_2$-ma$_2$	the boatman;
	90 Mes-an-ne$_2$	90: Mesane,
	nu-banda$_3$	the supervisor
	^{ĝeš}Ĝeša$_x$(UḪ$_3$×KASKAL)^{ki}	(from) Ĝeša;
ii	1200+180[+n] aša$_5$-^{ĝeš}⸢peš$_3$$^?$⸣ [(x)]	1380+x: the Fig Field(?):
	Zur-zur	Zurzur,
	ugula-e$_2$	the overseer over the household,
	675 Lugal-šita / aša$_5$ ⸢IN$^?$-x-x⸣	675: Lugalšita: the field ...;
	900 aša$_5$ u$_6$(IGI.E$_2$)	900: the field U:
	Lugal-šita baḫar$_2$	Lugalšita, the potter;
	360 še gur	360 *gur* barley:
iii	aša$_5$ ki-sumun	the field “Old Place”:
	Zur-zur	Zurzur;
	840 ⸢Nu⸣-mu-na	840: Numuna;
	1800+420+30 Lugal-šita-ĝu$_{10}$	2250: Lugalšitaĝu;
	[break]	...

obv. ii 3: Bar-tab (or min?) is a rare personal name. It is attested in ED/ES Adab tablets, e.g., in CUSAS 26 no. 87.

No. 148 – MS 3790/52

Account of barley flour, Early Dynastic/Early Sargonic, Adab.

obv. i	1(ban$_2$) dabin	1 *ban* of barley flour:
	Ur-gu	(to) Urgu,
	ma$_2$-laḫ$_5$	the sailor.
	nu-banda$_3$	The supervisor
	an-na-šum$_2$	has given it to him.
	Za$_3$-mu sukkal	Zamu, the secretary,
ii	maškim-bi$_x$(DUG)	(is) its commissioner.
	iti še-gur$_x$(|ŠE.ŠE|.KIN)-a	Month Šegura(m).
rev.	[destroyed; blank]	

No. 149 – MS 3790/53

Account of barley flour, Early Dynastic/Early Sargonic, Adab.

obv. i	[n(bariga/ban$_2$)] ⸢dabin⸣	x ... of barley flour:
	⸢Lugal⸣-a-si	to Lugalasi,
	dub-sar	the scribe,
	an-na-šum$_2$	it has been given.
	u$_4$ *2*-kam	It is the 2nd day.
	⸢iti⸣ šu-ĝar	Month Šuĝar.
ii	(blank)	
rev.	(blank)	

No. 150 – MS 3790/54

Account of barley, emmer and grain products, Early Dynastic/Early Sargonic, Adab.

obv. i	1 še gur	1 *gur* of barley;
	1 ziz$_2$ gur	1 *gur* of emmer;
	2(bariga) zi$_3$-sig$_{15}$	2 *bariga* of premium flour;
	3(bariga) dabin	3 *bariga* of barley flour;
	2(bariga) ni$_3$-ar$_3$-ra	2 *bariga* of groats;
	[n(bariga)] bappir	[x *bariga*] of sourdough;
ii	2(bariga) ⸢munu$_4$⸣	2 *bariga* of malt;
	3(bariga) še ⸢kaš⸣-kam	3 *bariga* of barley: it is for (brewing) beer:
	ma$_2$-laḫ$_4$-ne	to the sailors
	an-ne-šum$_2$	it has been given.
	e$_2$-dumu-kam	It is (of) the "House of the son."
rev. i	(blank space)	
	iti ĝa$_2$-udu-ur$_4$	Month Ĝa'udu'ur.
	(blank space)	
ii	(blank)	

No. 151 – MS 3790/55

Account of barley allocation to individuals, Early Dynastic/Early Sargonic, Adab.

obv. i	1 še ⸢gur⸣	1 *gur* barley:
	Ur-^{d}⸢Am⸣-NE	Ur-Am(ma)NE;
	1 Saĝ-eš$_3$-⸢tuku⸣	1: Saĝeštuku;
	1 ⸢x⸣-[x]	1:...;
	1 Ab-⸢ba⸣	1: Abba;
	1 En-NE	1: EnNE;
ii	1 A-ba-^{d}En-lil$_2$	1: Aba-Enlil;
	[1] ⸢Na-ba-lu$_5$⸣	[1]: Nabalu;
	2 Ur-gu	2: Urgu;
	2 Ur-ĝiri$_2$-si	2: Urĝirisi;
	⸢2⸣ Ur-^{d}Am-NE	2: Ur-Am(ma)NE;
iii	1(gur) 2(bariga) Amar-^{d}⸢Ašnan⸣	1 *gur* 2 *bariga*: Amar-Ašnan
	ugula	the overseer.
	kaskal Igi-⸢si$_4$⸣-kam	It is (for) the journey of Igisi.
	e$_2$-⸢dumu⸣	The "House of the son."
	Silim-^{d}Utu	Silim-Utu,
	nu-banda$_3$	the supervisor.
rev. i	iti mu-tir	Month Mutir.
	e$_2$-dumu	The "House of the son."

obv. i 2, ii 5: TA×KUR is the writing for AM in ED/ES Adab. See also text No. 245 obv. 2, where the divine name in the personal name is written in full, spelled out as ^{d}Am-ma-NE-ra.

obv. iii 3: The text deals with the preparation for a journey by a certain Igisi. This individual appears without explicit bureaucratic title in several texts in this volume, but it is certain that he was a high-ranking dignitary. His house is mentioned in CUSAS 11 no. 189 obv. i 5.

No. 152 – MS 3790/57

Account of barley flour, Early Dynastic/Early Sargonic, Adab.

obv. i	[n(bariga/ban$_2$)] dabin	x … of barley flour:
	⸢x⸣-^{d}Sud$_3$-de$_3$-zu	…-Sudezu;
	⸢3⸣(ban$_2$) Ĝessu	3 *ban*: Ĝessu.
	⸢ašgab⸣-me	They are leather-workers.
	an-ne-šum$_2$	It has been given to them.
ii	⸢e$_2$⸣-dumu	The "House of the son."
	iti aša$_5$-il$_2$-šu-ĝar	Month Aša'ilšuĝar.
rev.	(blank)	

No. 153 – MS 3790/58

Account of emmer-wheat flour, Early Dynastic/Early Sargonic, Adab.

obv. i	5 zi$_3$ ziz$_2$ kib$_3$ gur	5 *gur* of emmer-wheat flour:
	gal$_5$-la$_2$-gal	the chief policeman;
	5 zi$_3$ ziz$_2$ kib$_3$ gur	5 *gur* of emmer-wheat flour:
	niĝir-gal	the chief herald.
	⸢e$_2$⸣-dumu-še$_3$	Into the "House of the son"
ii	an-de$_6$	it is brought.
	Ur-^{d}Nin-mug	To Ur-Ninmug,
	dub-sar-ra	the scribe,
	an-na-šum$_2$	it has been given.
	iti du$_6$-ku$_3$	Month Duku.
	ziz$_2$ ⸢kib$_3$⸣	Emmer (and) wheat
rev. i	e$_2$ ⸢nu$^?$⸣-[banda$^?$]	(of) the house of the supervisor(?).
ii	(blank)	

obv. i 1: This is evidently a mixture of emmer and wheat flour. The term appears as kib$_3$ ziz$_2$ in ED IIb Ĝirsu texts (FAOS 15/1 nos. 37, 39, etc.) and as ziz$_2$ kib$_3$ at Adab (CUSAS 11 nos. 40, 188, 313, CUSAS 20 no. 82, and PPAC 1 964, 1209).

No. 154 – MS 3790/59

Unfinished account of barley, Early Dynastic/Early Sargonic, Adab.

obv. i	2(gur) 2(bariga) 4(ban$_2$) še gur	2 *gur* 2 *bariga* 4 *ban* barley:
	120 < >	120 ...;
	2(gur) 2(bariga) 4(ban$_2$) še ⌜gur⌝	2 *gur* 2 *bariga* 4 *ban* barley:
	120 < >	120 ...;
ii	(blank)	
rev.	(blank)	

No. 155 – MS 3790/60

Account of barley flour, Early Dynastic/Early Sargonic, Adab.

obv. i	1 la$_2$ 3(ban$_2$) dabin gur	1 *gur* minus 3 *ban* barley flour:
	Il$_2$-^{d}Aš$_8$-gi$_4$	(to) Il-Ašgi (it has been given).
	Ad-da	Adda,
	dumu Inim-du$_{11}$	son of Inimdu,
obv. ii	maškim-bi$_x$(DUG)	(is) its commissioner.
	iti ab-e$_3$-zi-[ga]	Month Ab-eziga.
rev.	(blank)	

No. 156 – MS 3790/66

Account of emmer-wheat flour, Early Dynastic/Early Sargonic, Adab.

obv. i	[n zi$_3$] ziz$_2$ ⸢kib$_3$⸣ gur	x *gur* of emmer-wheat [flour]:
	⸢x⸣-me	they are ... (professionals).
	an-ne-šum$_2$	It has been given to them.
	2(bariga) *Bala-ba-um*	2 *bariga*: *Balaba'um*
ii	1(bariga) Ĝeštug-en	1 *bariga*: Ĝeštug-en,
	tug$_2$-kad$_4$	the textile worker.
	ba-de$_6$	They have taken it away.
	e$_2$-dumu	The "House of the son."
rev. i	iti ĝa$_2$-udu-ur$_4$	Month Ĝa'udu'ur.
ii	(blank)	

obv. ii 1–2: For this person, see CUSAS 11 nos. 40 rev. i 3, 271 obv. 6, 331 obv. i 3. For tug$_2$-kad$_4$, see MAD 1 no. 169 (Sargonic Ešnunna) obv. ii 3, where it designates a quality of a textile. Here the term refers definitely to a profession.

No. 157 – MS 3790/68

Account of grain and grain flour, Early Dynastic/Early Sargonic, Adab.

obv. i	10 še gur 2(bariga) dabin	10 *gur* barley, 2 *bariga* barley flour:
	Ur-ĝidru	Urĝidru,
	ma$_2$-laḫ$_5$	the sailor;
	1 še gur 2(bariga) dabin	1 *gur* barley, 2 *bariga* barley flour:
	Za$_3$-mu	Zamu:
	⸢ma$_2$-laḫ$_5$⸣	they are the sailors
ii	nu-banda$_3$-me	of the supervisor.
	Ur-lu$_2$ ma$_2$-laḫ$_5$	Urlu, the sailor,
	maškim-⸢bi$_x$(DUG)⸣	(is) its commissioner.
	⸢lu$_2$⸣ [...] ⸢NE⸣ [...]	The persons ...
	[...]	...
rev. i	šu [...]	...
	iti ⸢ĝa$_2$⸣-udu-ur$_4$	Month Ĝa'udu'ur.
	⸢e$_2$⸣-dumu	The "House of the son."
	še zi-ga	Barley expended
	Igi-si$_4$	(by) Igisi.
ii	(blank)	

No. 158 – MS 3790/71

Account of flour and bread, Early Dynastic/Early Sargonic, Adab.

obv. i	2(gur) 2(bariga) zi$_3$ [(x) gur]	2 *gur* 2 *bariga* of flour;
	4 BARA$_2$ dug	4 jars of …:
	aša$_5$ bar-kas$_4$	(to) the field Barkas
	nu-banda$_3$	with the supervisor
	am-da-de$_6$	it has been delivered.
	[..] ⸢x⸣ [...]	...
ii	[...]	...
	480 ⸢ninda⸣ [x]	480 ... breads:
	1(ban$_2$) 20 ⸢du$_8$⸣	(of the size) 20 (loaves) baked (from) 1 *ban* (flour).
	e$_2$-⸢gal⸣-[x]	(from/to) the palace
	[break: 2 lines]	...
rev. i	1(bariga) [...]	1 *bariga* ...;
	1 še gur	1 *gur* barley:
	⸢Ba⸣-ba	Baba,
	⸢x⸣-dab$_5$	the ...
	⸢x-x⸣-[...]	...
	Ur-e$_2$ [(x)]	Ur-e, (…),
ii	maškim-bi$_x$(DUG)	(is) its commissioner.
	(blank space)	
	e$_2$-⸢dumu⸣	The "House of the son."
	zi$_3$ zi-ga	It is flour expended
	Igi-si$_4$-kam	by Igisi.
	iti ĝa$_2$-udu-ur$_4$	Month Ĝa'udu'ur.

obv. i 2: For bara$_2$ as "sack," see texts No. 229 obv. i 3–4, 362 obv. 4. However, the presence of dug "pot" suggests that BARA$_2$ stands for a commodity. It might be a variety of flour or a related product.

rev. i 4: The broken sign is probably not GAN, so the professional title cannot be ḫe$_2$-dab$_5$.

No. 159 – MS 3799

Account of barley in connection to officials and households, Early Dynastic/Early Sargonic, Adab.

obv. i	[n(gur)] 2(bariga) še gur	[x] *gur* 2 *bariga* barley:
	[...]-⸢x⸣	...;
	3(gur) Lu$_{2}$-bara$_{4}$-bar	3 *gur*: Lubarabar;
	1(gur) i$_{3}$-du$_{8}$ ⸢ĝanun⸣-bar	1 *gur*: the doorman of the outer storehouse;
	1(gur) Du$_{11}$-ga-ni	1 *gur*: Dugani;
	5(gur) Lugal-ni$_{3}$-bara$_{4}$-du$_{10}$	5 *gur*: Lugalnibaradu,
ii	kiĝ$_{2}$-gal	the *labor manager*;
	10(gur) la$_{2}$ 1(bariga) e$_{2}$-SAR	10 *gur* minus 1 *bariga*: the (temple) E-SAR
	3(gur) 1(bariga) E$_{2}$-⸢GUR$^{?}$⸣ kuš$_{7}$	3 *gur* 1 *bariga*: EGUR(?), the animal-manager;
	3(bariga) ^{d}Ša-⸢ma-gan⸣	3 *bariga*: (the temple of) Šamagan;
	2(gur) 2(bariga) ⸢Igi$^{?}$⸣-tur-⸢tur⸣	2 *gur* 2 *bariga*: Igiturtur(?);
	[n] A-[x]	x: A...;
iii	1(gur) ugula-iri	1 *gur*: the overseer of the city;
	2(bariga) BU-KUR-DU-DU	2 *bariga*: the BUKURDUDU;
	3(gur) šatam(NAR)-gal	3 *gur*: the chief government auditor;

	4(gur) ⸢x⸣ -ni-⸢x⸣	4 *gur*: ...ni...;
	< > Ur-⸢saĝ⸣	< > Ursaĝ;
	[break]	
rev. i	[n x]-ḪUB$_2$-[x]	x ...ḪUB...;
	2(gur) baḫar$_2$-gal	2 *gur*: the chief potter;
	1(gur) 3(bariga) Ur$_2$-ni	1 *gur* 3 *bariga*: Urni;
	3(bariga$_2$) ⸢gal ša$_3$ ĝanun⸣	3 *bariga*: the head of the storehouse;
	2(gur) šandana	2 *gur*: the gardener;
	< > Za$_3$-mu	< >: Zamu;
	(blank space)	
ii	12(gur) unu$_3$	12 *gur*: cowherd;
	11(gur) 2(bariga) E$_2$-dam-si	11 *gur* 2 *bariga*: Edamsi;
	8(gur) ^{d}Aš$_8$-gi$_4$	8 *gur*: (the temple of the god) Ašgi;
	7(gur) 1(bariga) e$_2$-dumu	7 *gur* 1 *bariga*: the "House of the son."
	(blank)	

obv. ii 1: For the official kiĝ$_2$-gal, see SCTRAH p. 124, with further references. Molina suggests that the professional title UN-gal/gal-UN might be another spelling of the term.

obv. ii 5: See text No. 119 obv. i 2 for another attestation of Igiturtur in this volume.

obv. iii 2: The reading of this personal name or professional title is uncertain.

obv. iii 3: For the difficulty in differentiating between nar "musician" and šatam in pre-Ur III texts, see Civil 2013: 22.

rev. i 1: Cf. lu$_2$-ḪUB$_2$.BU-kam in text No. 105 obv. ii 4.

rev. i 4: The reading of this damaged line is uncertain. Cf. ša$_3$-ganun in CUSAS 11 no. 98 obv. i 7'.

rev. ii: This column was written on almost dry clay.

No. 160 – MS 3809

Account of emmer-wheat flour, Early Dynastic/Early Sargonic, Adab.

obv. i	1 zi$_3$ ziz$_2$ kib$_3$ gur	1 *gur* of emmer-wheat flour:
	E$_2$-dam-si	Edamsi
	I$_3$-la-la	(and) Ilala;
	1 UR	1 *gur*: UR
	1 Saḫar-ra-ni	1 *gur*: Saḫarani
	Ur-pisaĝ	(and) Urpisaĝ;
	1 E$_2$-(ras.)-nun-ne$_2$-si	1 *gur*: Enunesi
ii	Diri-⸢um?⸣	(and) Diri'um.
	iti ni$_3$-kiri$_6$	Month Nikiri.
	Ur-^{d}Nin-mug	Ur-Ninmug (is responsible).
	(blank space)	
rev.	(blank)	

obv. i 5, 7: These individuals appear in Molina 2014 no. 3 (ES Adab).

obv. ii 1: The restoration is tentative. This personal name is attested, e.g., in MVN 3 no. 30 obv. 4, CUSAS 13 no. 202 rev. 2, HSS 10 no. 107 obv. 8, etc.

No. 161 – MS 3815

Account of barley flour, Early Dynastic/Early Sargonic, Adab.

obv. i	1(bariga) dabin	1 *bariga* barley flour:
	Im-ta	(to) Imta,
	aga$_3$-us$_2$ nu-banda$_3$	the soldier of the supervisor,
	A-za-bum-še$_3$	for (the locality) Azabum
ii	an-na-šum$_2$	it has been given to him.
	Za$_3$-mu sukkal	Zamu, the secretary,
	maškim-bi$_x$(DUG)	(is) its commissioner.
	iti du$_6$-ku$_3$	Month Duku.
rev.	(blank)	

No. 162 – MS 3817

Account of barley, Early Dynastic/Early Sargonic, Adab?

obv. i	1 še gur	1 *gur* barley:
	Lugal-ḫe$_2$	Lugalḫe
	GA-IŠ-URUDA	(and?) ...;
	3(bariga) An-ta-ti	3 *bariga*: Antati,
	gala	the cult-singer;

	1(gur) 1(bariga) 2(ban$_2$) zi$_3$-ninda i$_3$-du$_8$	1 *gur* 1 *bariga* 2 *ban* of flour for bread: the doorman;
	4(ban$_2$) ni$_3$-ar$_3$-ra-kam	4 *ban*, it is of (= for) groats;
ii	3(bariga) še-kaš	3 *bariga* barley for (brewing) beer:
	e$_2$-gal	(for) the palace.
	1(bariga) 4(ban$_2$) zi$_3$-ninda	1 *bariga* 4 *ban* of flour for bread;
	1(ban$_2$) še-⌜kaš⌝	1 *ban* barley for (brewing) beer:
	1(bariga) 2(ban$_2$) še-⌜kaš⌝	1 *bariga* 2 *ban* barley for (brewing) beer:
	ĝa$_2$-udu-ur$_4$	(for) the sheep-plucking shed.
rev. i	2(bariga) 1(ban$_2$) zi$_3$-ninda	2 *bariga* 1 *ban* of flour for bread:
	10 tug$_2$-du$_8$	(for) 10 felters,
	8 simug	8 smiths,
	2 nagar	2 carpenters;
	5(ban$_2$) dumu Ur-$^{d.še_3}$Šer$_7$-da	5 *ban*: (for) the son of Ur-Šerda.
	šu-niĝin$_2$-bi	Its total:
rev. ii	5(gur) 2(bariga) 1(ban$_2$)	5 *gur* 2 *bariga* 1 *ban* (barley).

obv. i 3: Cf. a Semitic personal name *Ga-iš*-DU$_{10}$ in AAICAB 1/1, pl. 5, 1928-425 rev. 3 from ED/ES Kutha. Here the sign combination may be a professional title.

No. 163 – MS 3819

Account of an outstanding expenditure of barley, Early Dynastic/Early Sargonic, Adab.

obv. i	2(ĝeš$_2$×u) 2(ĝeš$_2$) 2(u) 5 1(bariga) še gur	1345 *gur* 1 *bariga* barley:
	še taka$_x$(LAK492) aga$_3$-us$_2$	the barley set aside (for) the soldier(s).
	Ur-^{d}Nin-mug	Ur-Ninmug,
	dub-sar	the scribe,
ii	Nin-ma-tum$_2$-ra	to Ninmatum

	i$_{3}$-na-šum$_{2}$	he has given it.
	600 še gur	600 *gur* barley:
	sila-ta	from the street (will follow).
rev.	(blank)	

obv. i 2: For the verb tak(a)$_{x}$, see SCTRAH p. 107, with further references. While some scholars maintain that the verb means "to leave, to set aside," others suggest that it refers to an amount left over from a previous transaction.

obv. ii 1: This individual is mentioned among recipients of grain in CUSAS 11 no. 186 obv. iii 9 and barley flour in CUSAS 11 no. 319. His/her professional title is unknown.

obv. ii 4: To quote SCTRAH p. 173, this "expression designates goods that were not on hand at the moment but whose delivery was expected in the near future (sila-a ĝal$_{2}$-la/ze$_{x}$-a) or that were finally collected (sila-ta e$_{3}$-a)." Cf. text No. 488 obv. ii 2 for sila-ta us$_{2}$-am$_{3}$ "that will follow from the street."

No. 164 – MS 3820

Account of barley flour and premium flour, Early Dynastic/Early Sargonic, Adab.

obv. i	2(ban$_{2}$) dabin	2 *ban* barley flour;
	4(ban$_{2}$) zi$_{3}$-sig$_{15}$	4 *ban* premium flour:
	Ur-eš$_{3}$	to Ur-eš,
	dam-gara$_{3}$	the merchant,
	an-na-šum$_{2}$	it has been given.
	(blank space)	
ii	iti aša$_{5}$:il$_{2}$-šu-ĝar	Month Aša'ilšuĝar.
	(blank space)	
rev.	(blank)	

No. 165 – MS 3826

Account of grain products, beer, cheese and butter, Early Sargonic, Adab.

obv.	10 zi$_{3}$ gur	10 *gur* flour;
	1(bariga) zi$_{3}$-sig$_{15}$	1 *bariga* premium flour;
	1(bariga) zi$_{3}$ za-tum	1 *bariga zatum*-flour;
	1(bariga) titab$_{x}$(ZI$_{3}$.LU$_{3}$)	1 *bariga* beer ingredient *titab*;
	300 ninda 5 kaš	300 breads; 5 (jars of) beer;
	1(ban$_{2}$) gamur$_{x}$(LAK490)^{ga} 1 i$_{3}$-nun umbin	1 *ban* of cheese, 1 *umbin*-measure of butter;
	1 ⸢x⸣-da	1…;
rev.	*Šu-Ma-ma*	*Šu-Mama,*
	Be-li$_{2}$-ṭāb(DUG$_{3}$)-ra	to *Bēlī-ṭāb*,
	šu i$_{3}$-na-šum$_{2}$	has put at his disposal.

obv. 3: See the commentary to text No. 108 obv. i 3 for this flour.

obv. 5: Note the sign BI = kaš "beer" here instead of dug. Cf. the writing umbin in obv. 6 without the inscribed LU.

obv. 6: The writing LAK490-GA stands for /gamur/ "cheese," where GA is likely a phonetic complement to let the reader know what this rare sign meant. This writing, from a paleographic perspective, stands between the earlier gamur$_{x}$(LAK490) and ga-mur(ḪAR). LAK490 here has a simplified form: 

No. 166 – MS 3831

Expenditure of grain from two fields, Early Dynastic/Early Sargonic, Adab?

obv. i	15 še gur	15 *gur* barley:
	še-sumun aša$_5$ Saman$_x$(ŠE.BU.NUN.EŠ$_2$)-sal-la-kam	it is the old barley of the field *Samansala*.
	15 še gur	15 *gur* barley:
	še-gibil aša$_5$-maḫ-kam	it is the new barley of the "Great field."
ii	Me-Unug^{ki}-ge-si	Me-Unugesi
	ba-de$_6$	has taken it away.
rev.	(blank)	

obv. i 2: This field appears in later Adab sources. Cf. the Classical Sargonic document OIP 14 no. 171 rev. 4' for exactly the same writing.

obv. i 4: aša$_5$-maḫ seems here to be a topographical name, since it occurs in a context with another field. In Sargonic texts from Ĝirsu and Umma it may be a general term rather than a topographical name. See CUSAS 20 no. 371 (Umma) obv. 2, where it is translated "superior field," with further references to the term in Umma texts.

No. 167 – MS 3835

Delivery of grain, Early Dynastic/Early Sargonic, Adab.

obv. i	14 (ras.) še gur	14 (erasure) *gur* barley:
	Ur-^{d}Zu:en	Ur-Zu'en
	mu-de$_6$	has brought.
ii	(blank)	
rev.	(blank)	

obv. i 2: See Nos. 2 rev. iv 2, 29 obv. i 3, for likely the same individual.

No. 168 – MS 3840

Account of barley of several months, Early Dynastic/Early Sargonic, Adab.

obv. i	1(gur) 1(bariga) še gur	1 *gur* 1 *bariga* of barley:
	iti ^{d}Šuba$_3$(MUŠ$_3$×ZA)-nun	month Šubanun;
	1(gur) 1(bariga) še gur	1 *gur* 1 *bariga* of barley:
	iti še-kin-ku$_5$	month Šekinku;
	1(gur) 1(bariga) še gur	1 *gur* 1 *bariga* of barley:
ii	iti še-gur$_x$(|ŠE.ŠE|.KIN)-gur$_x$(|ŠE.ŠE|.KIN)	month Šegurgur.
rev.	(blank)	

obv. ii 1: This remarkable spelling stands for the month name usually written še-gur$_x$(|ŠE.ŠE|.KIN)-a(m$_3$).

No. 169 – MS 3841

Account of barley flour, Early Dynastic/Early Sargonic, Adab.

obv. i	2(ban$_2$) dabin	2 *ban* barley flour:
	Ur-Šubur	(to) Ur-Šubur,
	aga$_3$-us$_2$ nu-banda$_3$	the soldier of the supervisor
	KA-NAGAR^{ki}	(stationed at the locality) KANAGAR,
ii	an-na-šum$_2$	it has been given to him.
	e$_2$ Mug-si	The house of Mugsi.
	iti ab-e$_3$-zi-ga	Month Ab-eziga.
rev.	(blank)	

obv. ii 2: See CUSAS 11 no. 189 obv. i 6 for barley of the house of a certain Mug-si. This house is the issuing organization in the present case.

No. 170 – MS 5033

Account of emmer-wheat flour, Early Dynastic/Early Sargonic, Adab. Pierced tablet.

obv. i	1(bariga) zi$_3$ ziz$_2$ kib$_3$	1 *bariga* of emmer-wheat flour:
	LAGAB-ḪU	(for) …;
	3(ban$_2$) dabin	3 *ban* of barley flour:
	Lu$_2$-ĝeš-gi	(for) Luĝešgi.
ii	(blank space)	
	iti ab-e$_3$-zi-ga	Month Ab-eziga.
rev.	(blank)	

The tablet is of the same format as the bread and beer texts mentioning the household E'AḪ.

obv. i 2: Probably a personal name; the interpretation is challenging.

1.1.9 – Various Foodstuffs

No. 171 – MS 3827

Account of various foodstuffs, Early Dynastic/Early Sargonic, Adab.

obv. i	120 šum$_2$ ⸢sa⸣	120 bundles of onions;
	4 [+n] ⸢kaš⸣ dug	4+x jars of beer;
	20 lu^{nisig} gu$_2$	20 loads of turnips;
	1 ĝeštin dug	1 jar of wine;
	1 i$_3$-nun ni$_3$-banda$_3$^{da} 2(BAN$_2$) umbin$_x$(UMBIN×LU)	1 *nibanda*-measure 2/x of the *umbin* measure of butter.
	52 *si-iš$_9$-qu$_3$-tum*	52 *sišqû*(-breads);
ii	180 ninda-sig$_{15}$ si	180 filled premium breads;
	6 ninda ki-an si šur (ras.)	6 filled Ki'an half-breads (erasure);
	1 udu-šum-ma	1 slaughtered sheep:
	Ama-eš$_3$-lil$_2$-ta	Ama'ešlil(a)ta (is responsible/received).

The selection of these delicacies suggests that the list relates to an offering or high-profile feast.

obv. i 5: See Powell 1990: 506 for a vessel ni$_3$-banda$_3$^{da} that functioned as a measure (ninda-banda$_3$ there, although it is preferable to interpret this lexeme as "little thing," thus referring to a container smaller than, e.g., dug "pot"). Powell argues that the ED IIIb Ĝirsu ni$_3$-banda$_3$^{da} was about the same size as kur$_2$, that is, about two liters. No direct evidence for the size of these vessels is available, however. The present text demonstrates that the units ni$_3$-banda$_3$^{da} and umbin were parts of the same system of mensuration. It was used for oil and similar products. The metrological value of the notation 2(BAN$_2$) umbin$_x$ is uncertain and requires further research. At any rate, it cannot refer to the actual measure ban$_2$ (= 10 *sila*), which would be too much. In fact, it must designate a fraction of the measure umbin$_x$.

obv. i 6: The spelling is SI-EŠ$_2$-GU-TUM. The form may be reconstructed as Akkadian */*siθqûtum*/ (following the reconstruction of the Sargonic Akkadian syllabary by Hasselbach 2005: 27 f.). It is a plural adjectival form of **siθqû* and must be identical to *sasqû*, a flour of a certain quality used for offerings; see CAD S 192–93. In our case, breads that are made of this flour are meant; therefore, the plural adjective, literally the "*sišqû*'ian (breads)." This interesting writing shows that the native language of the scribe was, in all likelihood, Akkadian, since he was unable to call to mind zi$_3$-eša(A.TIR), the Sumerian writing for the term.

obv. ii 1–2: The term si, literally "to fill," may refer to the filling of bread with extra ingredients.

obv. ii 2: See MSL 11 p. 119 l. 39 for a variety of bread ninda-ki-an-na, where ki-an-na may refer to a cultic location, a place of offering. For ninda-šur(SUR) "half-bread," see Brunke 2008: 146 with further references.

obv. ii 4: See text No. 11 obv. i 7 for this individual, who appears together with the prominent Me-Unugesi.

No. 172 – MS 3828

Account of provisions for a journey, Early/Middle Sargonic, Adab.

obv.	4 udu-niga	4 fattened sheep;
	40 zu$_2$-lum ⸢gurdub$_2$⸣	40 *gurdub*-baskets of dates;
	2(gur) 2(bariga) gazi(ĜA$_2$×ZIZ$_2$) [(x)]	2 *gur* 2 *bariga* mustard;
	1(bariga) 4(ban$_2$) gamun$_x$(LAK205)^{nisig}	1 *bariga* 4 *ban* cumin;
	45 peš$_2$-^{ĝeš}gi	45 thicket mice.
	A.BU.BU	To ABUBU,
rev.	A-ga-de$_3^{ki}$	(of) Agade,
	an-na-šum$_2$	it has been given.
	ĝiri$_3$-ĝen-na	It is (for the) the journey
	DA-GA-⸢*tum*-kam⸣	of *DAGAtum*.

obv. 5: See Heimpel 1990: 607 and CAD U/W s.v. *ušummu* for peš$_2$-^{ĝeš}gi, literally "thicket mouse." This animal was eaten and praised for its delicious taste.

obv. 6: This individual is probably identical to the "soldier of the governor" in text No. 278 rev. i 9'.

rev. 4: A "shepherd of *DAGAtum*" is mentioned in CUSAS 11 no. 268 obv. i 4. Obviously, the name is Akkadian and feminine. The selection of delicious and costly food implies that this woman was of high status and her journey was a high-profile enterprise. Her identity remains uncertain, however.

1.1.10 – Cattle and Sheep

No. 173 – MS 3789/14

Account of sheep, Early Dynastic/Early Sargonic, Adab. Pierced tablet.

obv. i	2 udu-niga	2 fattened sheep:
	Lugal-abba$_2$-ĝu$_{10}$	To Lugalabbaĝu
	Ti-bi$_2$-ra^{ki}	(of) Tibira
	an-na-šum$_2$	it has been given.
	Lugal-teš$_2$-ĝu$_{10}$	Lugaltešĝu
	⸢maškim-bi$_x$(DUG)⸣	(is) its commissioner.
ii	udu zi-⸢ga⸣	It is sheep expended
	Na-ni-kam	by Nani.
	iti še-saĝ-sig$_{15}$-ga	Month Šesaĝsiga.
	Silim-^{d}Utu	Silim-Utu,
	nu-banda$_3$	the supervisor.
rev.	(blank)	

No. 174 – MS 3789/16

Account of a goat for Inana, Early Dynastic/Early Sargonic, Adab. Pierced tablet.

obv. i	1 maš$_2$	1 goat:
	U$_3$-mu-NI-NI	UmuNINI.
	^{d}Inana-kam	It is of (the household of) Inana.
ii	(blank)	
rev.	(blank)	

No. 175 – MS 3790/14

Account of sheep, Early Dynastic/Early Sargonic, Adab.

obv. i	1 udu-niga	1 fattened sheep:
	Šuruppak(SU.KUR.RU)^{ki}	(from) Šuruppak
	A-ba-^{d}En-lil$_2$	to Aba-Enlil
	an-na-šum$_2$	it has been given.
ii	udu ⸢zi⸣-ga	Expended sheep.
	e$_2$-dumu	The "House of the son."
	iti mu-tir	Month Mutir.
rev.	(blank)	

obv. i 2–3: It is possible that the scribe meant "to Aba-Enlil (from) Šuruppak."

No. 176 – MS 3790/18

Account of sheep, Early Dynastic/Early Sargonic, Adab.

obv. i	3 udu-nita niga	3 male fattened sheep:
	^{d}En-⸢lil$_2$-la$_2$⸣(ras.)	to Enlilla,
	kaskal A-⸢ga⸣-de$_3$^{ki}-še$_3$	for the journey to Agade,
	an-na-šum$_2$	it has been given to him.
ii	iti ĝa$_2$-udu-ur$_4$-kam	It is of the month Ĝa'udu'ur.
	e$_2$-dumu	The "House of the son."
	Lugal-mi$_2$-du$_{11}$-ga	Lugalmiduga
rev. i	maškim-bi$_x$(DUG)	(is) its commissioner.

No. 177 – MS 3790/19

Account of sheep, Early Dynastic/Early Sargonic, Adab.

obv. i	1 udu-niga	1 fattened sheep:
	Nin-e$_2$-ke$_4$	Nin-e,
	e$_2$ ^{d}Inana-ka-še$_3$	to the household of Inana,
ii	i$_3$-de$_6$	has brought it.
	PU$_3$.ŠA-^{d}Aš$_8$-gi$_4$	PUŠA-Ašgi,
	dub-sar	the scribe,
	maškim-bi$_x$(DUG)	(is) its commissioner.
rev. i	udu zi-ga	It is a sheep expended
	Ur-^{d}Nin-mug-kam	by Ur-Ninmug.
	e$_2$-dumu	The "House of the son."
	Silim-^{d}Utu	Silim-Utu,
ii	nu-banda$_3$	the supervisor.
	iti še-kin-ku$_5$	Month Šekinku.

No. 178 – MS 3790/26

Account of sheep(?) on the occasion of a journey, Early Dynastic/Early Sargonic, Adab.

obv. i	[2 lines broken]	...
	[...]-ra	to ...
	an-na-šum$_2$	it has been given.
	Diĝir-lugal-kam	It is (the sheep?) of Diĝirlugal.
	1 e$_2$-ĝidru ^{d}Aš$_8$-gi$_4$	1 (sheep?): the "Scepter House" of (the god) Ašgi.
ii	e$_2$-dumu	The "House of the son":
	al-zi	it is expended.
	iti še-kin-ku$_5$-kam	It is month Šekinku.
	ĝiri$_3$-ĝen-na	It is (for) the journey
	Ur-^{d}Nin-mug	of Ur-Ninmug,
	dub-sar-kam	the scribe.

rev. i	(blank space)	
	Silim-^{d}Utu	Silim-Utu,
	nu-banda$_3$	the supervisor.
ii	(blank)	

obv. i 5: For the same individual, see BdI 1 no. 8 obv. i 2, CUSAS 20 no. 359 obv. i 2.

obv. i 6: For the temple e$_2$-ĝidru at Adab, cf. text No. 302 obv. 5 with commentary.

No. 179 – MS 3790/31

Account of sheep on the occasion of a journey, Early Dynastic/Early Sargonic, Adab.

obv. i	[n udu]-⸢niga⸣	x fattened [sheep];
	[n+] 1 maš$_2$-niga	x+1 fattened goats;
	⸢1⸣ gukkal	1 fat-tailed sheep:
	A-ga-de$_3$^{ki}	(to the city of) Agade
	al-laḫ$_5$	they are brought.
	e$_2$-dumu	The "House of the son."
	ĝiri$_3$-ĝen-na	This is (sheep for) the journey
ii	Ur-^{d}Nin-mug	of Ur-Ninmug,
	dub-sar-kam	the scribe.
	Silim-^{d}Utu	Silim-Utu,
	nu-banda$_3$	the supervisor.
	iti mu-tir	Month Mutir.
rev.	[broken; uninscribed]	

No. 180 – MS 3790/35

Account of sheep (*mašdari'a*), Early Dynastic/Early Sargonic, Adab.

obv. i	1 udu-nita 1 maš$_2$	1 male sheep, 1 goat:
	[I$_3$]-la-la	Ilala,
	[ugula$^?$]-e$_2$	[the overseer(?) of] the household
	[1] ⸢udu-nita⸣	[1] male sheep,
	[1] ⸢maš$_2$⸣	[1] goat:
	⸢unu$_3$⸣	the cowherd;
	1 udu-nita	1 male sheep,
	1 maš$_2$	1 goat:
	Al-mu	Almu,
ii	dub-sar	the scribe;
	1 ⸢x-x⸣	1 ...
	⸢Mu-x⸣	Mu...
	1 ⸢udu⸣-[nita]	1 [male] sheep:
	⸢x⸣	...;
	1 udu-nita	1 male sheep:
	Lugal-iti-da	Lugalitida:
	dub-sar-me	they are scribes;

	1 udu-nita	1 male sheep:
	[illegible]	…
iii	1 udu-nita	1 male sheep:
	Lugal-iti-da	Lugalitida;
	[1 udu]-nita	[1] male [sheep]:
	⸢Ur$_2$⸣-ni	Urni,
	šeš nu-banda$_3$	brother of the supervisor;
	1 udu-[nita]	1 [male] sheep,
	1 ⸢maš$_2$⸣	1 goat:
	E$_2$-⸢x⸣	E…;
	1 udu-[nita]	1 [male] sheep:
	[break]	…
iv	[break]	…
	⸢x⸣-[…]	…
	1 ⸢x⸣-[…]	1 …:
	⸢ĜIR$_3$⸣-[…]	ĜIR…,
	⸢e$_2$⸣-[…]	the … household;
	[…]-⸢^{d}En-lil$_2$⸣	…Enlil;
	1 udu-nita	1 male sheep:
	⸢Lugal⸣-[…]	Lugal…;
rev. i	1 maš$_2$	1 goat:
	E$_2$-da	Eda;
	1 u$_8$	1 ewe:
	Im-ta	Imta:
	sipa-me	they are herdsmen;
	[break]	…:
ii	engar e$_2$-dumu	the agricultural manager of the "House of the son";
	1 udu-nita	1 male sheep,
	2 ninni$_x$(|TIR.TIR|×U$_2$) gu$_2$	2 loads of *ninni*-rushes:
	Ur-^{d}En-lil$_2$	Ur-Enlil,
	lu$_2$-⸢EDIN⸣.GUR	the …;
	[…]	…:
	[Ur]-^{d}Nin-⸢mug⸣	Ur-Ninmug;
	1 udu-nita	1 male sheep:
	Me$^{?}$-^{d}Aš$_8$-gi$_4$	Me(?)-Ašgi;
iii	1 u$_8$	1 ewe:
	Lugal-šu	Lugalšu
	E$_2$-aša$_5$	(and) E'aša;
	1 udu-nita	1 male sheep:
	Igi-ta	Igita;
	[x] ⸢x⸣	…
	[…]	…
	⸢x x x⸣ u$_8$	… ewe(s);
	⸢15⸣ [udu]-nita	15 male [sheep];
	[n+] 3 [x]	x+3 …;

iv	maš-da-ri-am$_{3}$	It is a *mašdari'a*-contribution.
	⸢E$_{2}$⸣-gu-la	Egula (is in charge).
	⸢iti Šuba$_{3}$(MUŠ$_{3}$×ZA)⸣-[nun]	Month Šubanun.
	[Silim-^{d}Utu]	[Silim-Utu,]
	nu-banda$_{3}$	the supervisor.
	(blank space)	

rev. ii 5: The interpretation of the professional title lu$_{2}$-EDIN.GUR is uncertain. See SCTRAH, commentary to no. 243 rev. 1 for its discussion. For another attestation, see Nos. 6 obv. ii' 13' and 185 obv. i 4.

rev. ii 9: The sign is badly written. It might be UR.

rev. iii 3: Cf. an individual E$_{2}$-aša$_{5}$-i$_{7}$ in No. 330 rev. 2.

rev. iv 1: See SCTRAH p. 218 with additional references for this type of regular delivery by subordinates to a higher authority.

No. 181 – MS 3790/37

Account of sheep, Early Dynastic/Early Sargonic, Adab.

obv. i	[n] ⸢udu-nita⸣	x male sheep:
	Na-ni	(to) Nani
	an-na-šum$_{2}$	it has been given;
	3 udu-nita	3 male sheep:
	Na-ni	(to) Nani
	⸢an-na⸣-šum$_{2}$	it has been given.
ii	ĝiri$_{3}$-ĝen-na	(It is) the journey
	^{d}Utu-teš$_{2}$-ĝu$_{10}$	(of) Utu-tešĝu.
	e$_{2}$-dumu	The "House of the son."
	Silim-^{d}Utu	Silim-Utu,
	nu-banda$_{3}$	the supervisor.
	iti še-⸢kin⸣-ku$_{5}$-[kam]	[It is] the month Šekinku.
rev.	[broken; uninscribed]	

No. 182 – MS 3790/39

Account sheep for a journey, Early Dynastic/Early Sargonic, Adab.

obv. i	[...] ⸢x⸣	...
	[x]-ba	...
	[e$_{2}$]-dumu-kam	It is of the "House of the son."
	⸢20 la$_{2}$ 2⸣ udu-ḪAR	18 ... sheep.
	⸢iti ab-e$_{3}$-zi-ga⸣	Month Ab-eziga.
	[break]	...
ii	[...]	...
	Ur-[pisaĝ]	Urpisaĝ,
	engar [(x)]	the agricultural manager.

	⸢Silim-^{d}Utu⸣	Silim-Utu,
	nu-banda$_3$	the supervisor.
	ĝiri$_3$-⸢ĝen⸣-[na]	[It is] the journey
	[break]	[of PN].
rev.	(blank)	

obv. i 4: The interpretation of udu-ḪAR here is uncertain. Cf. CUSAS 23 no. 17 (ED IIIb Umma region) rev. i 2 ff. for udu ur$_5$-ra "the loaned sheep."

No. 183 – MS 3790/69

Account of sheep, Early Dynastic/Early Sargonic, Adab.

obv. i	1 udu-niga	1 fattened sheep:
	Lugal-teš$_2$-ĝu$_{10}$	to Lugaltešĝu,
	e$_2$ nu-banda$_3$-še$_3$	for the house of the supervisor,
	an-na-šum$_2$	he has been given it.
ii	udu zi-ga	It is sheep expended
	Ur-^{d}Nin-mug-kam	by Ur-Ninmug.
	e$_2$-dumu	The "House of the son."
	iti a$_2$-ki-ti	Month Akiti.
rev.	(blank)	

No. 184 – MS 3801

Account of sheep, Early Dynastic/Early Sargonic, Adab.

obv. i	1 udu-niga	1 fattened sheep:
	e$_2$-SAR	to (the temple) E-SAR
	a-ba-šum$_2$	it has been given.
	[ĝiri$_3$]-⸢ĝen⸣-[na]	It is the journey
	[Ur-^{d}]⸢Nin⸣-[mug]	of Urninmug,
ii	dub-sar-kam	the scribe.
	⸢Silim⸣-^{d}Utu	Silim-Utu,
	⸢nu-banda$_3$⸣	the supervisor.
	[break]	[Month?]
rev.	(blank)	

obv. i 3: Note the use of the form a-ba-šum$_2$ instead of an-na-šum$_2$ when referring to the inanimate recipient of goods.

No. 185 – MS 3816

Account of sheep, Early Dynastic/Early Sargonic, Adab.

obv. i	1 udu-nita	1 male sheep,
	1 maš$_2$	1 goat:
	Ur-^{d}En-ki	Ur-Enki,
	lu$_2$-EDIN.GUR	the ...;
	1 ⸢udu⸣-nita	1 male sheep:
	⸢Lugal⸣-ušum-gal	Lugalušumgal,
	⸢dumu⸣ Ur-^{d}En-ki	son of Ur-Enki;
	1 sila$_4$	1 lamb:
ii	Aja$_2$-ni-sikil	Ajanisikil;
	1 maš$_2$	1 goat:
	E$_2$-dam-si	Edamsi;
	1 maš$_2$	1 goat:
	Lugal-sa-par$_4$(KISAL)	Lugalsapar;
	1 maš$_2$	1 goat:
	Nin-da-⸢x⸣	Ninda...;
	1 [maš$_2$]	1 [goat:]
rev. i	[break]	...
	Ur-pisaĝ [(x)]	Urpisaĝ;
	1 maš$_2$	1 goat:
	Ti-tu-⸢tu⸣	Titutu,
	ugula su-bir$_x$(BAPPIR)-a	the overseer of Subareans;
	1 udu-nita	1 male sheep:
	(blank space)	
ii	[...] ⸢x⸣ [...]	...
	[...] ⸢x⸣ [...]	...
	(blank space)	

rev. i 3': The second TU may have been erased. Cf. U-mu-NI-NI dumu Ti-tu in a slightly later Adab document (CUSAS 13 no. 52 obv. 1–2).

No. 186 – MS 3834

Account of goats, Early Dynastic/Early Sargonic, Adab.

obv. i	4 maš$_2$	4 goats:
	Lugal-ša$_3$	(to) Lugalša,
	nu-banda$_3$	(by) the supervisor,
	e$_2$-⸢dumu(ras.)-še$_3$$^{?}$⸣ (ras.)	for(?) the house (of the son, erased).
ii	iti a$_2$-ki-ti	Month Akiti.
	ka ⸢i$_7$$^{?}$⸣-tur	The inlet of the "Small canal"(?).
rev.	(blank)	

obv. i 4: A rectangular sign was written over an erasure of TUR.

1.1.11 – Hides and Other Animal Products

No. 187 – MS 3789/12

Account of ewe hides, Early Dynastic/Early Sargonic, Adab. Pierced tablet.

obv. i	[n+] 1 kuš u$_8$	x+1 ewe hides:
	⸢šu⸣-a gi$_4$-⸢a⸣	turned over:
	Kar-ki-du$_{10}$	Karkidu.
	1 kuš la$_2$-a-bi	1 hide (is) its deficit.
ii	PU$_3$.ŠA-Ma-ma	PUŠA-Mama,
	dam-gara$_3$	the merchant,
	ba-de$_6$	has taken it away.
	iti še-saĝ̂-sig$_{15}$-ga	Month Šesaĝ̂siga.
rev.	(blank)	

obv. i 2: See SCTRAH p. 34 for the verb šu-a ... gi$_4$ "to turn over," referring to finished products delivered to warehouses.

No. 188 – MS 3789/20

Account of pig skins, Early Dynastic/Early Sargonic, Adab. Pierced tablet.

obv. i	13 kuš šaḫ$_2$	13 pig skins:
	Ĝ̂essu	to Ĝ̂essu,
	ašgab-ra	the leather-worker,
	e$_2$-dumu-ta	out of the "House of the son,"
ii	an-na-šum$_2$	it has been given to him.
	iti ni$_3$-kiri$_6$	Month Nikiri.
rev.	(blank)	

No. 189 – MS 3790/4

Account of a ewe hide and dried meat, Early Dynastic/Early Sargonic, Adab.

obv. i	1 kuš u$_8$	1 ewe hide;
	2 su-la$_2$	2 cuts of dried meat:
	šu-a gi$_4$-a	turned over
	Maš-kam	by Maš.
	iti du$_6$-ku$_3$	Month Duku.
ii	e$_2$-dumu	The "House of the son."
	Silim-^{d}Utu	Silim-Utu,
	nu-banda$_3$	the supervisor.
rev.	(blank)	

obv. i 2: See SCTRAH no. 7 commentary for su-la$_2$-(a) "dried and/or salted cut of meat," with further references.

No. 190 – MS 3790/5

Account of a lamb hide and dried meat, Early Dynastic/Early Sargonic, Adab.

obv. i	1 kuš sila$_4$-nita e$_3$-li	1 hide of a spring-born male lamb;
	1 su-la$_2$-a-bi	1 its cut of dried meat:
	šu-a gi$_4$-a	turned over
	Du-du	(by) Dudu,
ii	sipa	the shepherd.
	(blank space)	
	iti še-saĝ-sig$_{15}$-ga	Month Šesaĝsiga.
	e$_2$-dumu	The "House of the son."
rev.	(blank)	

No. 191 – MS 3790/8

Account of ewe hides and dried meat, Early Dynastic/Early Sargonic, Adab.

obv. i	2 kuš u$_8$	2 ewe hides;
	2 su-la$_2$	2 cuts of dried meat:
	šu-a gi$_4$-a	turned over
	Maš-kam	by Maš.
ii	iti a$_2$-ki-ti-kam	It is month Akiti.
	e$_2$-dumu	The "House of the son."
rev.	(blank)	

No. 192 – MS 3790/46

Account of sheepskins, Early Dynastic/Early Sargonic, Adab.

obv. i	⸢160⸣ kuš udu	160 sheep hides:
	e$_2$ nu-banda$_3$-še$_3$	into the house of the supervisor
	al-de$_6$	it is brought.
	Lugal-teš$_2$-ĝu$_{10}$	To Lugaltešĝu
	an-na-šum$_2$	it has been given.
	40 kuš udu	40 sheep hides:
ii	kuš Unug-še$_3$	the hides for Uruk(?),
	ĜIŠ-TUL$_2$(LAGAB×U)-*me-tum*	ĜIŠTUL*metum*
	an-si	has placed it(?);
	Amar-^{d}⸢Nisaba⸣	To Amar-Nisaba,
	⸢ašgab-gal⸣	the chief leather-worker,
	an-⸢na⸣-[šum$_2$]	it has been [given].
	10 ⸢kuš⸣ [udu]	10 [sheep] hides:
rev. i	kuš [...]	the hides for ...
	[break]	...
	Ur-^{d}⸢Nin⸣-[...]	Ur-Nin...
	iti še-saĝ-sig$_{15}$-⸢ga⸣	Month Šesaĝsiga.
	e$_2$-⸢dumu⸣	The "House of the son."
	⸢Silim-^{d}Utu⸣	Silim-Utu,
	⸢nu-banda$_3$⸣	the supervisor.

obv. ii 1–3: The writing of Uruk without the determinative is unexpected. An individual with the Akkadian name ĜIŠ-TUL$_2$(LAGAB×U)-*me-tum* appears also in text No. 194 obv. ii 2 below. The verb may be si.g "to place" instead of si "to fill." See an-si-ga in OSP 1 no. 100 iii 3'. For another reference in the corpus, see CUSAS 11 no. 72 rev. i 1. Despite this, the lines remain obscure.

No. 193 – MS 3790/49

Account of goat hides and dried meat, Early Dynastic/Early Sargonic, Adab.

obv. i	1 kuš LAK20	1 hide of a male goat;
	1 kuš maš$_2$ ša$_3$-⸢DUN⸣	1 hide of a kid goat ...;
	2 su-la$_2$-a-bi	2 cuts of their dried meat:
	šu-a gi$_4$-a	turned over
ii	Ur-^{d}*Ḫa*-⸢*ia*$_3$(NI)⸣	(by) Ur-Ḫaya.
	iti ni$_3$-kiri$_6$	Month Nikiri.
rev.	(blank)	

obv. i 2: The interpretation of the sign DUN (or ŠUBUR?) in the present context is difficult. The term that was used for animal sucklings is ša$_3$-du$_{10}$. For the latter, see FAOS 15/1, p. 419; FAOS 15/2, p. 198.

No. 194 – MS 3802

Account of waterskins and goat hides, Early Dynastic/Early Sargonic, Adab.

obv. i	21 ^{kuš}ummud$_{x}$(EDIN.A.SU)	21 leather waterskins:
	ki ensi$_{2}$-še$_{3}$	to the governor
	al-de$_{6}$	are brought.
ii	20 (ras.) kuš maš$_{2}$	20 (erasure) goat hides:
	ĜIŠ-TUL$_{2}$(LAGAB×U)-*me-tum*	(for) ĜIŠTUL*metum*.
	kuš zi-ga	These are hides expended
rev. i	Ur-^{d}Nin-mug-kam	by Ur-Ninmug.
	iti še-saĝ-⸢sig$_{15}$⸣-ga	Month Šesaĝsiga.
	(blank)	
ii	Silim-^{d}Utu	Silim-Utu,
	nu-banda$_{3}$	the supervisor.

obv. i 1: See SCTRAH p. 69 for a discussion of /ummud/ "waterskin" with additional references.

No. 195 – MS 3805

Delivery and receipt of animal horns, Early Dynastic/Early Sargonic, Adab.

obv. i	2 a$_{2}$ am-babbar$_{2}$	2 white bull horns;
	2 a$_{2}$ ab$_{2}$-babbar$_{2}$	2 white cow horns:
	Ur-saĝ-⸢x⸣-[x]	Ursaĝ…,
ii	dumu	son
	^{d}⸢Aš$_{8}$⸣-gi$_{4}$-an-dul$_{3}$	of Ašgi'andul,
	maškim-bi$_{x}$(DUG)	is its commissioner.
	mu-de$_{6}$	He has brought it.
rev. i	Ĝeštug-en	To Ĝeštug-en
	an-na-šum$_{2}$	it has been given.

obv. i 1: Note the unusual form of AM. The final wedge of KUR is placed outside the sign.

1.1.12 – Wooden Implements

Texts Nos. 198 and 199 record various parts of wagons and chariots. Text No. 196 is placed first in this section despite the fact that it does not record any object. This unique text is a blueprint of an Ešnunna-type chariot and may be the earliest cuneiform record describing the construction and measurements of a vehicle.

No. 196 – MS 1952/36

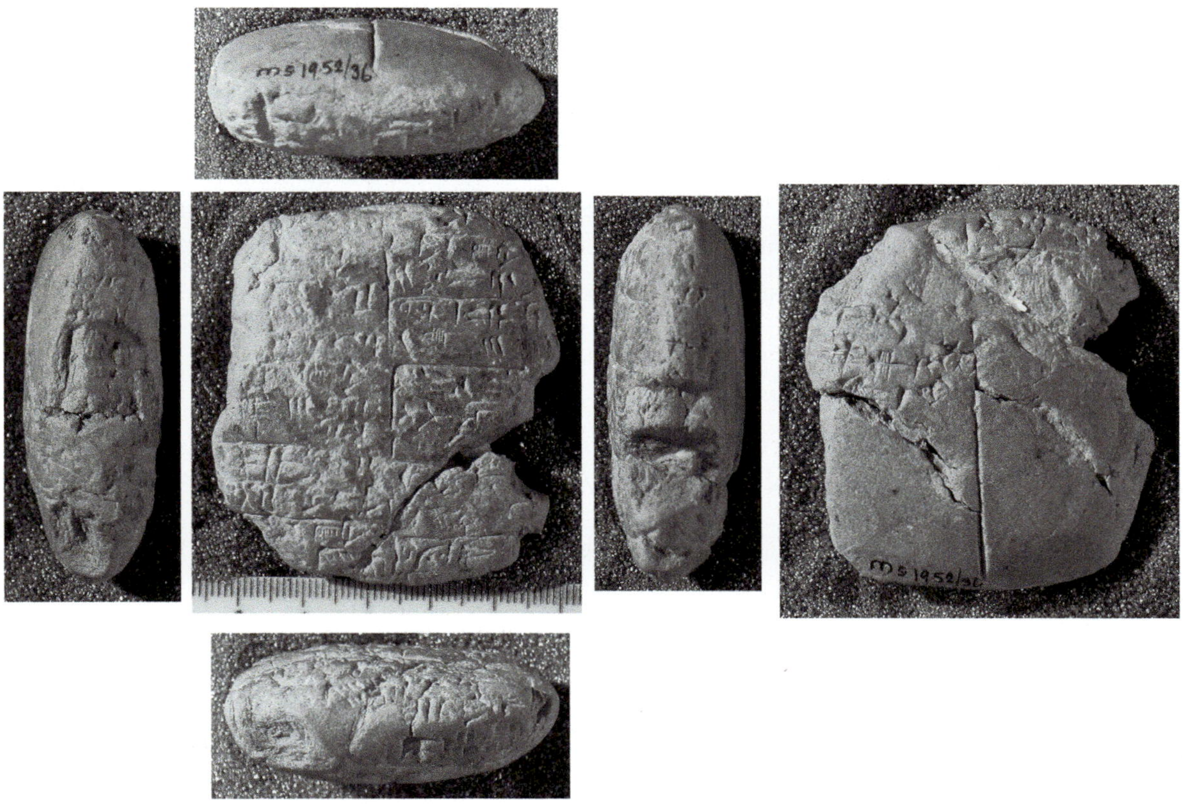

Description of the design of an Ešnunna-type chariot, Early Sargonic, Adab.

obv. i	[...]-⸢bi⸣	its ...
	[...] *6* ⸢šu⸣-si	... 6 fingers;
	[n ^{ĝeš}dal]-⸢dal⸣-ḫi-a	x wooden sideboards of the same length.
	[(x)] ⸢da⸣-bi	[(...)] its side:
	[*n*] kuš$_3$ *3* šu-si-am$_3$	it is x cubits 3 fingers.
	1 mar-⸢eše$_2$⸣ [(x)]	1 ...;
	ša$_3$-si-bi-ta	out of its crossbeam(?):
	⸢sukud$_x$⸣-bi [*n* kuš] la$_2$ *7* ⸢šu⸣-si	its height: [x cubits] minus 7 fingers;
ii	x-ba	...:
	sukud$_x$-bi *2* šu-du$_3$-a *1* šu-si	its height: 2 one-third-cubits 1 finger;
	daĝal mar-eše$_2$ *1* kuš *3* [šu]-⸢si⸣	the width of ...: 1 cubit 3 fingers.
	murgu(SIG$_4$) ⸢mar⸣-gid$_2$-⸢da⸣ [(x)]	The back of the wagon ...

	(illegible)	...
	⸢ni$_3$-ba⸣ i$_3$-⸢x⸣	...
	⸢E ŠIM$^?$⸣	...
rev. i	^{ĝeš}za-keš$_2$	...
	[1 line broken]	...
rev. ii	[(...)] ^{ĝeš}šubur Aš$_2$-nun-na⸢^{ki}-ka⸣-kam	It is a *šubur*-chariot of Ešnunna.

The tablet is unbaked and damages easily. Despite its poor state of preservation, it seems to record a blueprint of an Ešnunna-type transport or battle wagon.

obv. i 3: See the commentary to text No. 198 obv. ii 1. For -ḫi-a designating the same length/width of fields, see No. 496.

obv. i 6, ii 3: The meaning of mar-eše$_2$ is unclear. Cf. a type of chariot ^{ĝeš}mar.

obv. i 7: The interpretation is tentative. The phrase resembles ša$_3$-bi-ta "out of it," which occurs in the accounting of goods when a lesser amount is substracted from the principal amount. For $^{(ĝeš)}$ša$_3$-si/su$_3$ "crossbeams of the chariot body," see Civil 1968: 13.

obv. i 8, ii 2: sukud$_x$ "height" is written as TA×ŠE.

rev. i 1: Cf. ^{ĝeš}za-ra = Akk. *zarû* designating the axle of a wagon; CAD Z 70 *zarû* A.

No. 197 – MS 1952/43

Account of wooden implements, Early Dynastic/Early Sargonic, Adab.

obv. i	13 ^{ĝeš}u$_3$	13 planks;
	5 ^{ĝeš}al-kuš-⸢a$_2$⸣	5 wooden hoes with leather-(bound) handles;
	8 ^{ĝeš}⸢x⸣-ur-⸢x$^?$⸣	8 ...
	(blank)	
ii	(blank)	
rev.	(blank)	

obv. i 3: Unclear. The first sign is a narrow one. There are some traces after UR that may represent another sign.

No. 198 – MS 2365/15

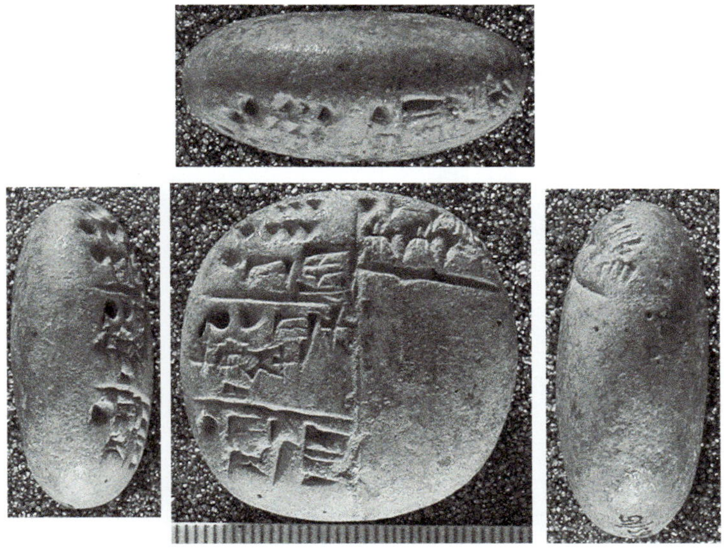

Account of wooden implements for chariots, Early Dynastic/Early Sargonic, Adab.

obv. i	26 ^{ĝeš}dib(LAGAB×PA)	26 wooden boards;
	11 ^{ĝeš}MAŠ-umbin	11 wheel fastener(?).
	1 ^{ĝeš}gub-taškarin(TUG$_2$)	1 boxwood stand(?);
ii	1 ^{ĝeš}*dal-dal-lum*	1 wooden sideboard.
	(blank)	
rev.	(blank)	

obv. i 1: ^{ĝeš}dib > Akk. *dibbu* B "board" and *dappu* "board"; CAD D 134, 106.

obv. i 2: Obviously, this is a part of a wheel: cf. ^{ĝeš}KA-umbin in EDPV A no. 239 p. 109 and ^{ĝeš}kak-umbin-gigir in MSL 6 p. 9 l. 55 (Ura V). The term may be present in the lexical entry ^{ĝeš}BAR-umbin mar-gid$_2$-da in MSL 6 p. 14 l. 98, since BAR and MAŠ were not distinguished in later periods. Based on the meanings of the MAŠ, many interpretations are possible. Ba$_7$ "half" and sa$_9$ are "half; middle." Cf., e.g., the famous Standard of Ur, where it can clearly be seen that the wheels of battle chariots were made from two pieces of wood. On the other hand, the form of the sign MAŠ is comparable graphically to the detail that fixes the wheel. The term ^{ĝeš}MAŠ-umbin appears also in CUSAS 20 no. 29. The same text mentions a charioteer and journey of a certain Ur-Ašgi. Although no interpretation is offered in the edition, see the commentary on this text for a reference to the Classical Sargonic text from Adab, A 636 obv. 10, PPAC 1 p. 123. *Contra* Pomponio and Visicato and in agreement with Yang, the term ^{ĝeš}gigir$_2$ e$_2$-umbin(UMBIN×LU)-*2* refers to a "two-wheeled chariot." See also EBPV A no. 230 p. 107, for a part of a chariot ^{ĝeš}E$_2$×AŠ-*tenû*-BAD-taškarin with additional references. Cf. also umbin maš ti-ḪAR (sumun) in DP 481 obv. ii 2, 482 rev. i 3.

obv. i 3: Cf. EDPV A no. 232 p. 107 for a vehicle implement ^{ĝeš}TUG$_2$-⸢x⸣. The correct sequence of the signs in the present text is uncertain. Cf. also ^{ĝeš}ĝiri$_3$-gub-gigir in MSL 6 p. 8 ll. 34–35 = *manzāzu* "floor of a chariot or wagon"; see CAD M^1 234.

obv. ii 1: See Civil 1968: 7 for ^{ĝeš}da-da, ^{ĝeš}ta-ta, ^{ĝeš}dal-dal as the "side(board)" of a chariot.

No. 199 – MS 3789/6

Account of wooden parts for chariots, Early Dynastic/Early Sargonic, Adab. Pierced tablet.

obv. i	1 ĝeš-saman$_x$(ŠE.BU.NUN.ŠE$_3$) ki-saĝ	1 wooden front side;
	100 ^{ĝeš}kak saman$_x$ ki-saĝ	100 wooden pegs (for) the tether of the front side;
	1 ĝeš-ti ^{ĝeš}gigir$_2$	1 wooden side of a chariot;
	30 ^{ĝeš}kak za$_3$-ga kak-ze$_2$	30 wooden pegs of the side, … wooden pegs.
ii	(blank space)	
	⸢nagar⸣-ne	To the carpenters
	saĝ iti ni$_3$-⸢kiri$_6$⸣	at the beginning of month Nikiri
	an-na-⸢šum$_2$⸣	it has been given to him (= them).
	e$_2$-dumu	The "House of the son."
	uš-bar [(x)]	Piece-work(?).
rev.	(blank)	

obv. i 1–4: For ki-saĝ, see ED Word List C 2, 89 (MEE 3 no. 47, pp. 155 ff.). See Civil 2013: 23–24 for ki-saĝ in Archaic Word List C and its interpretation as "assembly." That meaning does not fit the present context. Saman$_3$(ŠE.ŠE$_3$.NUN.BU) is "tether," Akk. *šummanu*. Here ĝeš-saman$_x$ may refer to the front part of a chariot where straps are attached, literally the "wood for the ropes." In this context, ki-saĝ could be taken quite straightforward as "front side." For ĝeš-ti mar-gid$_2$-da "rib/side of a *margida*-cart" = *ṣēlu*, see Hh V 84 (MSL 6, p. 12) and CAD Ḫ 124 f. The interpretation of kak-ze$_2$ is uncertain.

obv. ii 2: For saĝ iti, see Jagersma 2010: 146.

obv. ii 3: Note the incorrect prefix -na- instead of plural -ne- in the verbal form.

obv. ii 5: See USP p. 132 for this interpretation of uš-bar.

No. 200 – MS 3789/42

Account of wooden beams (exercise?), Early Dynastic/Early Sargonic, Adab. Pierced tablet.

obv. i	5 ^{ĝeš}ĝušur(UR$_3$)	5 wooden beams:
	Amar-ḪA	Amar-ḪA
	mu-de$_6$	has brought here;
	3 ^{ĝeš}ĝušur	3 wooden beams:
	Gala	Gala
ii	mu-de$_6$	has brought here;
	3 ^{ĝeš}ĝušur	3 wooden beams:
	Amar-ḪA	Amar-ḪA
	mu-de$_6$	has brought here;
	5 ^{ĝeš}ĝušur	5 wooden beams:
rev. i	Amar-ḪA	Amar-ḪA
	mu-de$_6$	has brought here;
	2 ^{ĝeš}ĝušur	2 wooden beams:
	Amar-[ḪA]	Amar-[ḪA]
	mu-de$_6$	has brought here;
	(blank)	
ii	(blank)	
	4 ^{ĝeš}ĝušur	4 wooden beams:
	Amar-ḪA	Amar-ḪA,
	Amar-⸢ḪA⸣	Amar-ḪA ...
	[break]	

Judging by its repetitive character, the text may be a student exercise.

obv. i 1 f.: The sign UR$_3$ of the present text has an archaic form and is not simply ĜA$_2$×|NUN.NUN| as in later texts.

obv. i 2: The reading of ḪA in this common personal name is uncertain because two or more geographical names may underlie it: A.ḪA = Tiwa/Tuwa(tuba$_2$), ḪA.A = (W)urum (see ELTS p. 41), and Ku'ara(ḪA.A)/Ku'ara$_2$(A.ḪA). See Schrakamp 2015a: 198 fn. 15.

No. 201 – MS 3790/47

Account of wooden implements, Early Dynastic/Early Sargonic, Adab.

obv. i	4 ^{ĝeš}ḫar-an	4 *ḫaran*-logs:
	Lugal-Ab-zu-da	to Lugal-Abzuda,
	nagar-ra	the carpenter,
	e$_2$-dumu-ta	out of the "House of the son"
	an-na-šum$_2$	it has been given to him.
	⸢E$_2$⸣-an-ne$_2$	E'anne,
ii	i$_3$-ra$_2$-ra$_2$	the oil-presser,
	e$_2$-gal-še$_3$	into the palace,
	i$_3$-de$_6$	he has brought it.
	iti šu-ĝar	Month Šuĝar.
	(blank space)	
rev.	(blank)	

obv. i 1: See SCTRAH p. 185 for ^{ĝeš}ḫar-(an) as a piece of wood used to produce the shafts of tools such as hoes and axes.

No. 202 – MS 3790/48

Account of wooden implements, Early Dynastic/Early Sargonic, Adab.

obv. i	[... ^{ĝeš}] i$_{-tenû}$-zi / 10 ⸢la$_2$ *1*⸣ gigir$_2$-šubur	x sideboards (for) 9 *šubur*-wagons;
	4 ^{ĝeš}mud	4 handles;
	3 ^{ĝeš}saĝ-apin	3 plough tops;
	[n] ^{ĝeš}erin$_2$	x yokes;
	[break]	[to PN it has been given.]
ii	e$_2$-dumu-kam	Into the "House of the son"
	an-de$_6$	it has been brought.
	(blank space)	
	iti ĝa$_2$-udu-ur$_4$-kam	It is month Ĝa'udu'ur.
	(blank space)	
rev.	(blank)	

obv. i 1: See MSL 5 p. 37 l. 38 for a ^{ĝeš}i-zi-X-gigir which is probably identical with the objects mentioned in the present text. See also ^{ĝeš}i-zi-na$_2$ = *amartu* "sideboard (of a bed)"; MSL 5 p. 166 l. 172; CAD A^2 3. Here, it is probably the sideboard of the *šubur*-wagon. The latter is usually written ^{ĝeš}šubur, however.

obv. i 2: Like ^{ĝeš}ḫar-an, ^{ĝeš}mud is a wooden handle for tools. See, e.g., lexical sections of the word *akkullu* "a hammer-like tool" in CAD A^1 276, and *aškuttu* "wedge" in CAD A^2 444.

obv. i 3: ^{ĝeš}saĝ-apin = *qaqqadu* "top (of a plow)"; MSL 6 p. 17 l. 135; CAD Q 100.

obv. ii 1: Note the use of copula instead of the locative or terminative case marker in this case.

1.1.13 – Metals and Metal Objects

No. 203 – MS 3790/64

Account of weapons, Early Dynastic/Early Sargonic, Adab.

obv. i	10 ur$_2$-gid$_2$ u$_3$-gibil	10 long shields (with) new planking:
	Ur-^{d}Dumu-zi-da	Ur-Dumuzida.
	[n] ĝeš-⸢x⸣	x … *weapons*:
ii	Aja$_2$-zu-zu	Ajazuzu
	Isin$_2^{ki}$	(of) Isin.
	⸢x$^?$⸣-SIG$_2$-⸢ta⸣ im-kas$_4$-e	From … he will run here(?).
rev. i	(blank)	
ii	5 ĝeš-gid$_2$-šub-ba	5 throwing spears:
	Aja$_2$-zu-zu	Ajazuzu
	Isin$_2^{ki}$	(of) Isin.

obv. ii 3: The line is unclear. The verbal form is in the imperfective.

No. 204 – MS 3803

Account of metal objects, Early Dynastic/Early Sargonic, Adab.

obv. i	1 zabar^{uruda}-saĝ-bar	1 mirror (with) the head on the outer side(?);
	1 zabar^{uruda}-šu	1 mirror (with) handle;
	1 nam^{uruda}	1 sieve(?);
	1 a-ĝa$_2$-UD-KUR^{uruda}	1 …
ii	ki-la$_2$-bi	their weight:
	1 la$_2$×7 giĝ$_4$ ma-na	1 mina minus 7 shekels.
	Lugal-ni$_3$-bara$_4$-du$_{10}$	Lugalnibaradu,
rev. i	dumu dam-gara$_3$-gal	son of the chief merchant.
ii	(blank)	

obv. i 2: For the identification of zabar-(šu) with "mirror (with handle)," see Steinkeller 1987a: 347–49.

obv. i 3: For ^{uruda}nam-zabar$_3$, see FAOS 15/1 p. 533 obv. i 4, with further references, where the meaning "sieve" is suggested.

No. 205 – MS 3821

Account of saws, Early Sargonic, Adab.

obv.	4(ĝeš$_2$) 4(u) 6(aš)	286;
	4(ĝeš$_2$) 4(u)	280;
	2(ĝeš$_2$) 3(u) 1(aš)	151:
	šum^{uruda}	saws.
rev.	(blank)	

Like texts Nos. 315–16, this text is largely of numerical nature. Its logic implies that a scribe calculated three batches of saws that were issued, received, or inventoried in storage. This document is another example of writing and management going hand in hand in early southern Mesopotamia.

No. 206 – MS 3822

Account of saws, Early Sargonic, Adab.

obv.	10 šum^{uruda} 5-ba	10 saws, its 5th:
	Ur-e$_2$	to Ur-e,
	dumu Amar-GUL	son of AmarGUL,
	kuš$_7$-⸢ra⸣(ras.)	the animal-manager,
	an-na-šum$_2$	have been given.
rev.	(blank)	

obv. 1: The construction *n*-ba is interpreted here as /N=bi=a(k)/, where the morpheme /=bi/ is either the possessive or the demonstrative particle. See Edzard 2003: 50, Jagersma 2010: 248 f. What exactly is meant by the "5th" is not certain. It may be the fifth receipt or allocation.

No. 207 – MS 3837

Account of a variety of copper (MUŠ$_3$-uruda), Early Dynastic/Early Sargonic, Adab.

obv. i	21 MUŠ$_3$-uruda ma-na	21 minas of … copper:
	Az(ZA.PIRIĜ) nu-banda$_3$	Az, the supervisor;
	20 ½ Lugal-ḫul$_2$	20 ½: Lugalḫul;
	10 ½ Lugal-ni$_3$-bara$_4$-du$_{10}$	10 ½: Lugalnibaradu;
	4 Lugal-ezen muḫaldim	4: Lugalezen, the cook;
	3 ½ Ama-Ab-zu$^!$(BA)-si	3 ½: Ama-Abzusi;
ii	3 E^{sic}-ki	3: Eki.
	uruda an-ta-e$_3$-am$_3$	It is copper that was issued.
	Inim-zi-da	Inimzida
	maškim-bi$_x$(DUG)	(is) its commissioner.
rev.	(blank)	

obv. i 1: See SCTRAH p. 178 for the discussion of this variety of copper. So far, the term has been identified exclusively in Adab texts.

obv. i 2: Az the supervisor is recorded in other Adab texts, e.g., BdI 1 no. 196 rev. i 5, CUSAS 20 no. 72 obv. 1. There was another nu-banda$_3$ by this name at Umma during the Sargonic period: see BIN 8 no. 314, Nik 2 nos. 58, 64.

obv. i 4: It is not certain whether one or more persons of the name Lugal-ni$_3$-bara$_4$-du$_{10}$ occur in the ED/ES texts from Adab. In this volume, he acts as a maškim, is a scribe, a son of the chief merchant, and a labor recruiter (kiĝ$_2$-gal). Theoretically, all these designations could apply to a single person, though that seems unlikely.

obv. i 6: See CUSAS 23 no. 96 obv. i 3 for the same individual.

1.1.14 – Oil

No. 208 – MS 3789/5

Issue of oil to a sailor, Early Dynastic/Early Sargonic, Adab. Pierced tablet.

obv.	4 i$_3$ umbin	4 *umbin*-measures of oil:
	Ur-lu$_2$	to Urlu,
	ma$_2$-laḫ$_4$	the sailor,
	an-na-šum$_2$	it has been given.
rev.	iti aša$_5$-il$_2$-šu-ĝar	Month Aša'ilšuĝar.

1.1.15 – Dates

No. 209 – MS 3790/43

Account of dates, Early Dynastic/Early Sargonic, Adab.

obv. i	1(gur) 2(bariga) ⸢zu$_2$-lum⸣ [gur]	1 [*gur*] 2 *bariga* of dates:
	Ur-[lu$_2$]	to Ur[lu],
	ma$_2$-laḫ$_5$-ra	the sailor,
	SAĜ-NAGAR^{ki}-še$_3$	for (the town) SAĜNAGAR
	an-na-šum$_2$	it has been given to him.
ii	[e$_2$-dumu]	[The "House of the son."]
	Silim-^{d}Utu	Silim-Utu,
	nu-banda$_3$	the supervisor.
	iti a$_2$-ki-⸢ti⸣	Month Akiti.
rev.	(blank)	

obv. i 4: Cf. KA.NAGAR in text No. 169 obv. i 4. The initial signs, KA in that document and SAĜ in the present, are clearly visible. Despite this discrepancy, both names must refer to the same location.

1.1.16 – Rushes

No. 210 – MS 3789/13

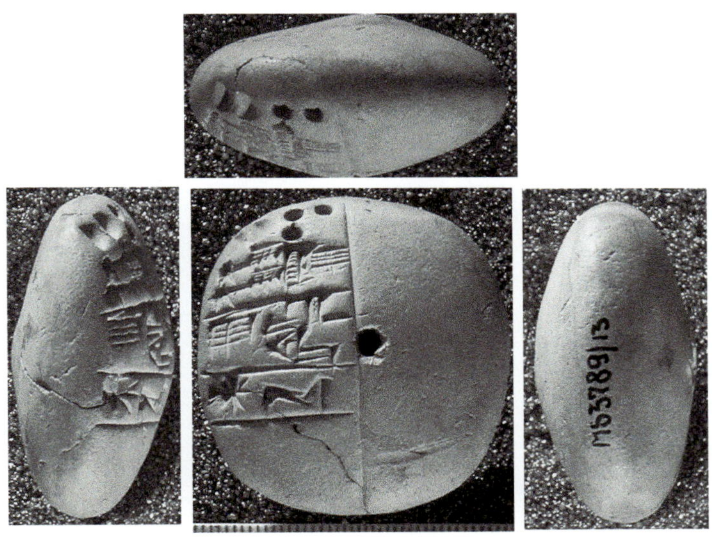

Account of rushes, Early Dynastic/Early Sargonic, Adab. Pierced tablet.

obv. i	150 |ZI.ZI|.ŠE$_3$ sa	150 bundles of rushes:
	e$_2$-iri-bar-ka$^!$(SAĜ)	in the "House of the outer city"
	an-de$_6$	it is brought.
ii	(blank)	
rev.	(blank)	

obv. i 1: See EDPV A p. 131 nos. 308–11 with additional references to this type of rush.

obv. i 2: e$_2$-iri-bar is literally the "house of the outer city" (e$_2$=iri=bar=(ak)), i.e., a building outside the main city enclosed by walls. The sign SAĜ is probably an unfinished KA.

1.1.17 – Reed and Reed Objects

No. 211 – MS 3790/9

Account of reed mats, Early Dynastic/Early Sargonic, Adab.

obv. i	12 kid ma$_2$-ša$_3$-ga	12 reed mats *mašaga*;
	12 kid bar-si	12 reed mats *barsi*:
	Ur-lu$_2$ ma$_2$-laḫ$_5$-ra	to Urlu, the sailor,
ii	an-na-šum$_2$	it has been given.
	iti aša$_5$-il$_2$-šu-ĝar	Month Aša'ilšuĝar.
	e$_2$-dumu	The "House of the son."
rev.	(blank)	

obv. i 1: See Civil 1994: 30–31 l. 69.

obv. i 2: The writing bar-si is usually a reference to the garment ^{tug_2}bar-si.g but here the term refers to a type of reed mat.

No. 212 – MS 3790/27

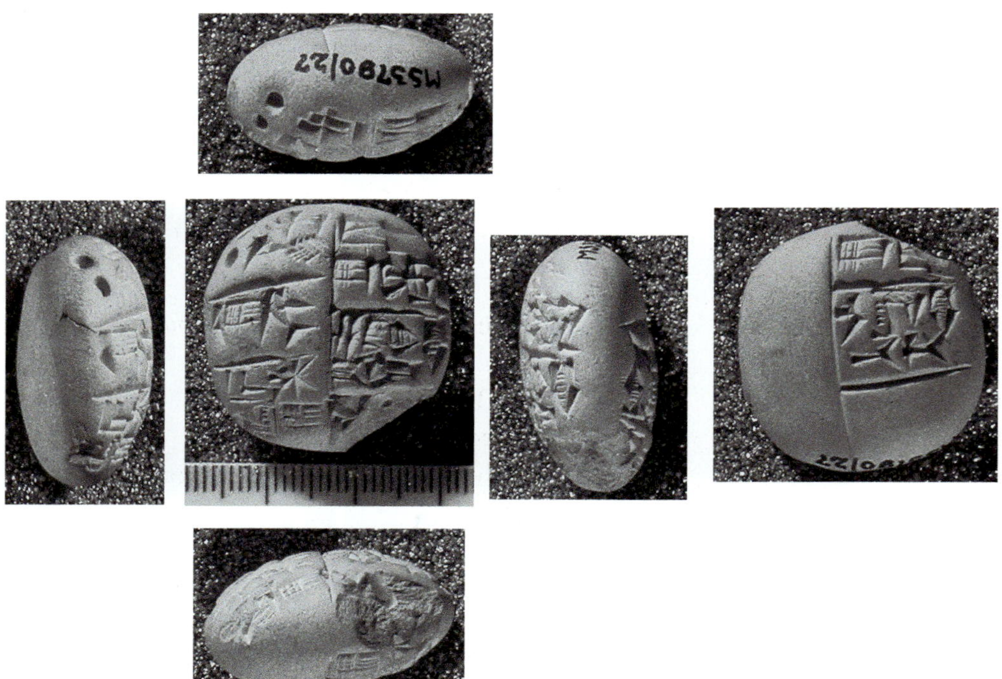

Account of reed *gur*-containers, Early Dynastic/Early Sargonic, Adab.

obv. i	20 gur-gi	20 reed (containers of one) *gur*:
	sa-ḫa	(with/for?) garden fruit:
	Ur-^{d}En-lil$_2$	(to) Ur-Enlil(a),
ii	dumu E$_2$-dam-si	son of Edamsi
	A-ga-de$_3^{ki}$	(of) Agade,

	⸢an⸣-[na-šum$_2$]	it has [been given to him]
	e$_2$-⸢dumu⸣	The "House of the son."
	iti a$_2$-ki-ti	Month Akiti.
ii	(blank)	

obv. i 1–2: ni$_3$-sa-ḫa is "garden fruits"; see SCTRAH nos. 168–69 with additional references. Here the term is certainly spelled sa-ḫa without ni$_3$. Since the similar texts below are accounts of containers and not of their contents, it is uncertain whether the subject of the present text is to be understood as "baskets of fruit" or "baskets for (collecting/storing) fruit."

No. 213 – MS 3790/32

Account of reed *gur*-containers, Early Dynastic/Early Sargonic, Adab.

obv. i	2 gur-gi	2 reed (containers of one) *gur*:
	Ka$_5$-a	to Ka'a,
	⸢šidim-gal⸣	the chief builder,
	an-na-šum$_2$	it has been given.
ii	e$_2$-dumu	The "House of the son."
	iti šu-ĝar	Month Šuĝar.
rev.	(blank)	

obv. i 3: The presence of the chief builder in this context suggests that the baskets in question may have been used in construction work.

No. 214 – MS 3790/63

Unfinished account of reed *gur*-containers and wooden implements, Early Dynastic/Early Sargonic, Adab.

obv. i	20 gur-gi	20 reed (containers of one) *gur*;
	20 ĝeš-⸢x⸣	20 ... wooden implements:
	Lugal-ni$_3$-bara$_4$-du$_{10}$	(to) Lugalnibaradu,
	dub-sar	the scribe,
ii	(blank)	<it has been given. The "House of the son." Month ...>
rev.	(blank)	

No. 215 – MS 3823

Account of reed *gur*-containers, Early Sargonic, Adab.

obv.	⸢50⸣ 5 gur-gi	55 reed (containers of one) *gur*:
	Amar-GUL	AmarGUL;
	36 Ur-kun	36: Urkun;
	10 Lugal-KA	10: LugalKA;
	10 A-ba-^{d}En-lil$_2$	10: Aba-Enlil;
	10 MI-A-MU	10: MIAMU;

	En-na-a-LUM	10: *'Enna*-LUM.
rev.	(blank)	

obv. 2: See Nos. 16 rev. i 2, 379 obv. ii 1, for the same individual.

obv. 6: See CUSAS 11 nos. 102 obv. iii 8, 201 obv. iv 2, for the same individual. The interpretation is probably MI-aja$_2$-ĝu$_{10}$ "… is my father".

obv. 7: This is a fuller writing of the name that occurs as *En-na*-LUM in ED/ES Adab texts CUSAS 11 nos. 75 obv. ii 2, 96 obv. ii 2 and *passim* in later Adab and elsewhere. This name is likely related to *En-num-i$_3$-li$_2$*, i.e., / *Ḫennum-'ili* / "By the grace of (my) god"; see Lipiński 1997: 255.

1.1.18 – Onions

No. 216 – MS 3790/15

Account of onions, Early Dynastic/Early Sargonic, Adab.

obv. i	2(gur) 2(bariga) 4(ban$_2$) gur šum$_2$-gaz	2 *gur* 2 *bariga* 4 *ban* of crushed onions:
	Al-mu	to Almu,
	lu$_2$-šum$_2$-ra	the onion farmer,
	aša$_5$ da-Kul-aba$_4^{ki}$-še$_3$	for the field "Vicinity of Kulaba,"
ii	an-na-šum$_2$	it has been given to him.
	e$_2$-dumu	The "House of the son."
	iti ab-e$_3$-zi-ga	Month Ab-eziga.
	ĝiri$_3$-ĝen-na	It is (for) the journey
rev. i	Ur-^{d}Nin-mug-kam	of Ur-Ninmug.
	Silim-^{d}Utu	Silim-Utu,
	nu-banda$_3$	the supervisor.
ii	(blank)	

No. 217 – MS 3790/22

Transfer of onions to a merchant from Ĝeša, Early Dynastic/Early Sargonic, Adab.

obv. i	1 šum$_2$ gur	1 *gur* onions
	½ ku$_3$ ma-na-kam	it is ½ mina in (*lit.* of) silver.
	dam-gara$_3$	To the merchant
	^{ĝeš}Ĝeša$_x$(UḪ$_3$×KASKAL)^{ki}	(from) Ĝeša,
	an-na-bala	it has been *measured* to him.
ii	⸢n⸣ šum$_2$ gur	x *gur* onions.
	A-ba-^{d}En-lil$_2$	Aba-Enlil,
	maškim-bi$_x$(DUG)	(is) its commissioner.
	šum$_2$ zi-ga	Expended onions.
	e$_2$-dumu	The "House of the son."
	Ur-nu	Urnu,
rev. i	ugula-e$_2$	the overseer over the household (is responsible).
ii	(blank)	

obv. i 5: See Sallaberger 2016 esp. p. 246 for še … bala "to measure barley." This meaning may apply here.

1.1.19 – Flax

No. 218 – MS 3790/65

Account of flax in bundles, Early Dynastic/Early Sargonic, Adab.

obv. i	90 gu sa	90 bundles of flax:
	Igi-si$_4$	to Igisi
	an-na-šum$_2$	it has been given.
ii	(blank space)	
	e$_2$-dumu	The "House of the son."
	iti ^{d}Šuba$_3$(MUŠ$_3$×ZA)-nun	Month Šubanun.
	(blank space)	
rev.	(blank)	

No. 219 – MS 3800

Account of flax in bundles, Early Dynastic IIIb, Adab?

To judge by its dimensions, this tablet may be from Adab. However, the form of the sign SA is not that of Adab, where it has the form ŠU$_2$+SA. The format of the tablet, with the broader first column, is also not typical of Adab. Accordingly the provenance of the document is uncertain.

obv. i	10 [+n gu] sa-la$_2$	10+x flax tied in bundles:
	u$_4$ *1*	day 1.
	22 gu sa-la$_2$	22 flax tied in bundles:
	u$_4$ *2*	day 2.
ii	gu umbin	The flax (for) …

1.1.22 – Fish

No. 225 – MS 3790/28

Account of fish, Early Dynastic/Early Sargonic, Adab.

obv. i	2(gur) 2(bariga) ku_6 gur	2 *gur* 2 *bariga* fish:
	Ur-^{d}Li$_9$-si$_4$	It is (for) Ur-Lisi,
	lu$_2$-nidba$_x$(GADA.ĜAR$^!$.MUŠ$_3$) ensi$_2$-kam	the man responsible for the governor's food offerings.
	Nibru^{ki}	(For) Nippur.
ii	(blank space)	
	iti še-<<še>>-kin-ku$_5$	Month Šekinku.
	e$_2$-dumu	The "House of the son."
	(blank space)	
rev.	(blank)	

obv. i 3: This sign combination is interpreted as a spelling for nidba(PAD.AN.MUŠ$_3$) "food offering." The sign after GADA has an extra wedge at the top right and in this way resembles SIG. The reference to Nippur in the following line suggests that the professional in question was responsible for making offerings at a sanctuary in Nippur on behalf of the governor.

obv. ii 1: Probably the scribe has confused two months: še-kin-ku$_5$ and še-gur$_x$(ŠE.KIN)-a(m$_3$).

No. 226 – MS 3838

Account of fish, Early Sargonic, Adab.

obv.	3(bariga) ku$_6$	3 *bariga* of fish
	gurdub$_2$ ab-šum$_2$	given (in) *gurdub*-baskets.
	Šu-Aš$_{11}$-tar$_2$	*Šu-'Aštar,*
	kuš$_7$ lugal	the animal-manager of the king.
	ĝiri$_3$ im-ši-er$_{14}$(DU.DU)-am$_6$	It is (when) they have taken the journey hither.
rev.	(blank)	

obv. 2: See discussion on the basket /gurdub/, here spelled gurdub$_2$(ĜA$_2$×GI$_4$), and the form ab-šum$_2$ in SCTRAH p. 83.

obv. 5: See an account of salt, CUSAS 23 no. 112 rev. 2, for the same plural verbal form im-ši-er$_{14}$(DU.DU)-a. A similar text, SCTRAH no. 69 rev. 3, has a form in the singular instead: im-ši-ĝen-na-am$_3$. In the present text, it seems that the verbal form records that Šu-'Aštar was accompanied on his journey by a number of unspecified individuals.

1.1.23 – Resins

No. 227 – MS 3842

Account of aromatics, Early Sargonic, Adab.

obv.	1 i$_3$ bulug$_x$(ŠIM×UḪ$_3$) dug	1 jar of *galbanum* oil;
	1 i$_3$ ŠIM×GIG dug	1 jar of *gig* oil;
	1 ir ^{šim}*ḫa-ra*-LUM dug	1 jar of aromatics *ḫaraLUM*:

	Ĝiri$_3$-ni	Ĝirini,
	dub-sar	the scribe,
rev.	⸢x⸣ an-gi$_4$	has returned it …(?).

obv. 1: For the aromatic substance bulug$_x$(ŠIM×UḪ$_3$), see MC 4 pp. 57–58, MZL p. 524, EDPV A p. 105. This resin was measured mostly by weight. Since its oil is mentioned, the resin could be processed into a liquid state that required storage in pots.

obv. 2: ŠIM×GIG is obviously an early writing for šim-gig, a tree and an aromatic product obtained from it, Akk. *kanaktu*; see CAD K 135.

obv. 3: Note the use of ir "aromatics" before the name of the substance. I am not aware of any other references to, or the identity of, the aromatic substance ^{šim}*ḫa-ra-LUM*.

1.1.24 – Garments

No. 228 – MS 3843

Account of garments, Early Sargonic, Adab.

obv. i	6 ni$_3$-lam$_2^{tug_2}$ suluḫu$_2$(SIKI.GID$_2$)	6 *nilam*-garments (with) long fleece;
	6 ib$_2$-ba-du$_3^{tug_2}$ suluḫu$_2$	6 *ibadu*-garments (with) long fleece;
	4 ni$_3$-⸢la$_2$⸣^{tug_2} suluḫu$_2$	4 *nila*-garments (with) long fleece;
	1 dul$_x$(DUN$_3$)-gi$_4^{tug_2}$ suluḫu$_2$	1 … garment (with) long fleece;
ii	13 ni$_3$-la$_2^{tug_2}$	13 *nila*-garments;
	7 ib$_2$-ba-du$_3^{tug_2}$	7 *ibbadu*-garments;
	2 ni$_3$-lam$_2^{tug_2}$	2 *nilam*-garments;
	4 *ḫa-la-um*^{tug_2}	4 *ḫala'um*-garments;
	2 aktum^{tug_2}	2 heavy garments.

rev. (blank)

obv. i 1: /suluḫu/ is a term for a long-fleeced breed of sheep, its fleece and fine garments made from its fleece. See *sulumḫû* in CAD S 371.

obv. i 4: This term is rare and its identification is uncertain. It is attested also in the present writing in CUSAS 11 no. 226 obv. i 4. The sign DUN$_3$ occurs in the writings of several garments and may be a writing for /dul/ "to cover." Cf. also DUL$_3^{tug_2}$ in EDPV A no. 177 p. 94.

obv. ii 4: This garment occurs regularly in ED/ES Adab and Nippur texts. Cf. MAD 3 p. 127, CUSAS 11 nos. 222 obv. i 1, 226 obv. ii 2, 325 obv. i 2; ECTJ nos. 103 obv. 1, 106 obv. 4, 107 obv. 2, 114 obv. 1, 148 obv. 4, 189 obv. 5. According to ECTJ no. 104 obv. ii 1–2, the average weight of one piece was about three minas.

1.1.25 – Miscellaneous Goods

No. 229 – MS 3812

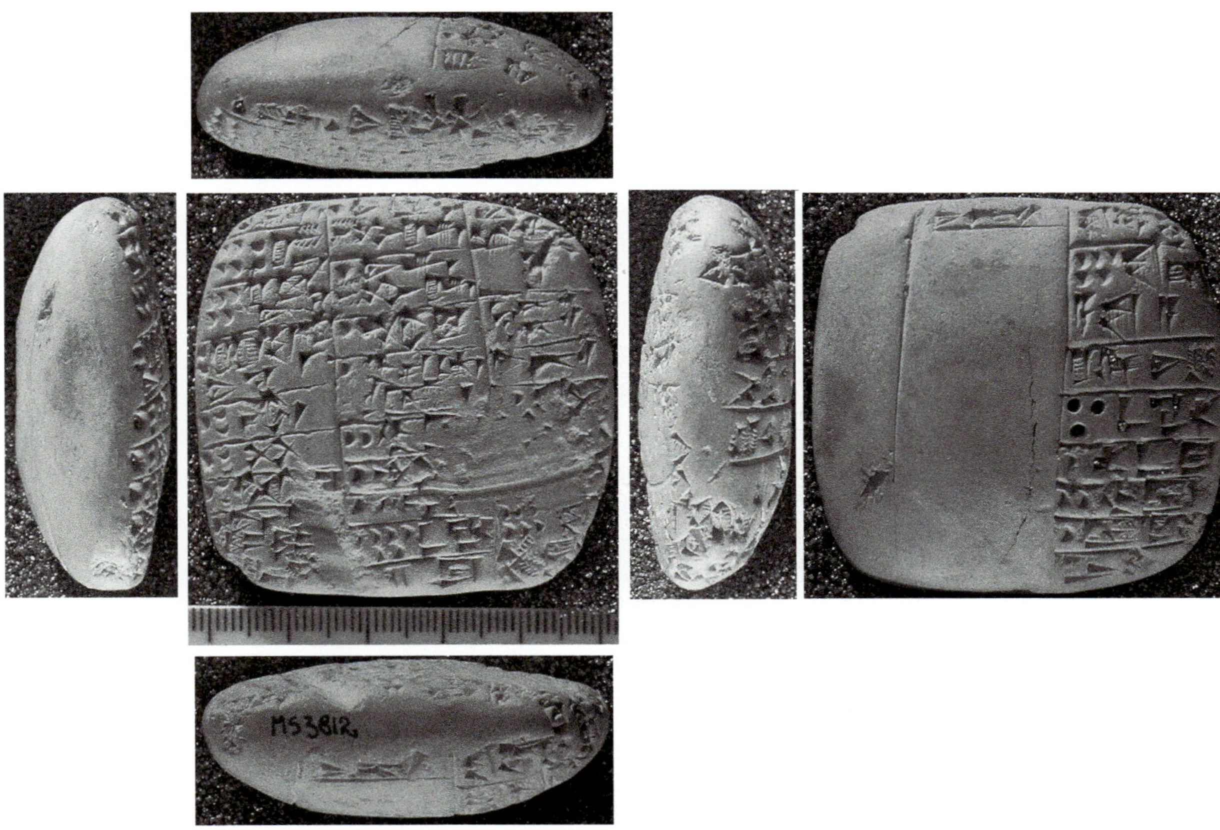

Account of miscellaneous goods brought by a sailor, Early Dynastic/Early Sargonic, Adab.

obv. i	10 še gur	10 *gur* barley;
	4(gur) 2(bariga) dabin gur	4 *gur* 2 *bariga* barley flour;
	5(gur) zi$_3$ bara$_2$ i$_3$-si	5 *gur* of flour poured into sacks;
	2(bariga) zi$_3$ bara$_2^{!}$ ^{kuš}a-⸢ĝa$_2$⸣-la$_2$ i$_3$-si	2 *bariga* of flour poured into leather *aĝala*-sacks;
	1(gur) 2(bariga) bappir	1 *gur* 2 *bariga* of sourdough;
	1(gur) 2(bariga) munu$_4$	1 *gur* 2 *bariga* of malt;
	1(gur) 2(bariga) ni$_3$-ar$_3$-ra	1 *gur* 2 *bariga* of barley groats;
	1 i$_3$ ⸢šim⸣-tur-tur ⸢saman$_x$⸣(ŠE.⸢BU⸣.ŠE$_3$.NUN)	1 flask of … oil;
ii	1 i$_3$ eren-babbar$_2$ saman$_x$	1 flask of the white cedar oil;
	1 i$_3$-nun saman$_x$	1 flask of clarified butter;
	1 ĝiri$_2$-udu	1 butcher's knife;
	1 ku$_6$ al-dar-⸢ra⸣ gurdub	1 basket of dried fish;
	2 ku$_6$ ⸢gurdub⸣	2 baskets of (fresh) fish;
	1 dim-⸢x⸣	1 …
	1 ⸢saĝ-šu$_2$⸣	1 head cover;
	7 bar-si-gada	7 linen *barsi(g)*-garments;
	[1] ⸢ni$_3$⸣-2^{tug_2}	[1] double(-layer) garment;
iii	Šeš-nam-lu$_2$-⸢ak$^{?}$⸣	Šešnamlu'ak(?),
	ma$_2$-laḫ$_4$	the sailor,
	i$_3$-de$_6$	has brought.
	2 ^{kuš}esir$_4$ ⸢x-du$_{10}$⸣-ga	2 fine … sandals;
	[...]-UD	…
	6 ^{kuš}esir$_4$ e$_2$-ba-kam	6 sandals in pairs
rev. i	kuš šaḫ$_2$-kam	(made) of pig skin.
	5 ^{kuš}ummud$_x$(EDIN.A.SU.A)	5 waterskins
	eše$_2$-sa i$_3$-šum$_2$	that have strings from sinews;
	30 bar-si-gada	30 linen *barsi(g)*-garments;
	1 ^{gada}bar-dul$_5$	1 linen *bardul*-garment;
	2 ku$_6$ gurdub	2 baskets of (fresh) fish;
	1 gurdub Bara$_2$-diĝir-ne$_2$	1 basket (for) Baradiĝir(a)ne:
	Ur$_4$-ša$_3$	Urša
ii	⸢i$_3^{!}$⸣-de$_6$	has brought.

obv. i 3–4: See CAD B 137 lexical section, for bara$_2$, Akk. *bašamu* "sack." See CAD N^1 379 lexical section, for ^{kuš}a-ĝa$_2$-la$_2$, Akk. *naruqqu* "sack, bag."

obv. ii 3: ĝiri$_2$-udu, literally "knife (to butcher) sheep," appears in contemporaneous practical vocabularies; see CUSAS 12 p. 206 l. 8:5'.

obv. ii 7: The usual writing of saĝšu "helmet, headgear" is U.SAĜ or ŠU$_2$.SAĜ.

1.1.26 – Unidentified Goods and Uncertain Contents

No. 230 – MS 3789/30

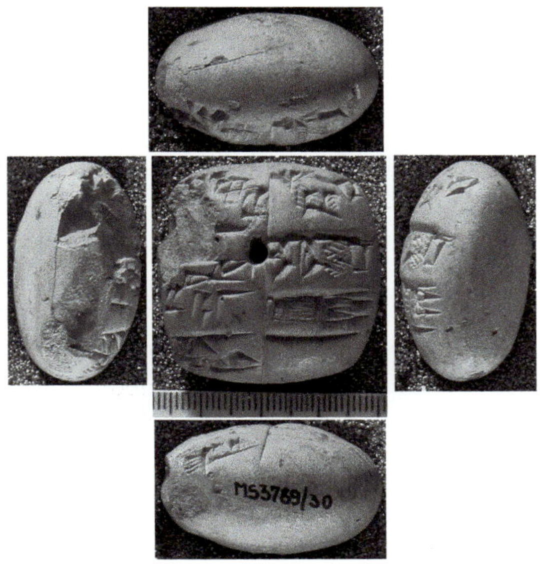

Account of uncertain items, Early Dynastic/Early Sargonic, Adab. Pierced tablet.

obv. i	2 MA$_2$×EŠE$_2$-⸢x⸣	2 …,
	⸢ma$_2$⸣ Dilmun$^?$ a-la$_2$	hung on a Dilmunite ship(?);
	Lu$_2$-lugal	to Lulugal(a)
ii	an-na-šum$_2$	it has been given.
	iti ni$_3$-kiri$_6$	Month Nikiri.
	e$_2$-dumu	The "House of the son."

obv. i 1: Cf. MA$_2$×EŠE$_2$-gid$_2$ in text No. 231. The latter text looks slightly younger than the present document. The traces of the broken sign in the present text do not resemble the gid$_2$ of No. 231, however. The reading of the sign MA$_2$×EŠE$_2$ is unknown. Based on the literal logographic meaning of its constituent parts ("ship/boat" with an inscribed "rope"), the sign may signify ropes used on a ship.

obv. i 2: The sequence of the two first signs and their interpretation are uncertain. The sign interpreted as DILMUN does not resemble the usual grapheme NI.TUKU. The sign is:

Its right-hand part resembles LAK483. Ships traveling to Dilmun appear regularly in Sargonic texts from various Sumerian cities. Cf., e.g., ITT 1 no. 1418 rev. 1; STTI 26 rev. i 10 (Ĝirsu); OSP 2 nos. 120 obv. 8, 128 obv. i 14, 132 ii 3 (Nippur); USP no. 2 rev. 8 (Umma); not to mention the famous inscription of Sargon, RIME 2, E2.1.1.11. Alternatively, the writing may refer to a ship of Dilmunite type. The interpretation of the grapheme a-la$_2$ is also challenging. ePSD claims that one of the words witten a-la$_2$ denotes "silt." I was unable to identify the source of this interpretation, however. ^{ĝeš}a-la$_2$ as timber appears in DP 483 obv. iii 4 among plants and varieties of wood. Another ED IIIb Ĝirsu text, VS 27 no. 35 obv. iii 1, mentions 12 ^{ĝeš}a-la$_2$ ma$_2$ "12 *ala* of a ship" in the context of wooden parts or equipment of ships. For a-la$_2$ as "balance" in irrigation gear, see Attinger 1997: 117 with additional references. This ^{ĝeš}a-la$_2$ was used for lifting water in irrigation. See EDPV A p. 73 fn. 157. Cf. also the term a-la$_2$ that appears in connection to boats in TCTI 2 no. 2747 (Ur III, Ĝirsu) rev. 3: ma$_2$ še ambar$^{!}$-Lagaš^{ki}-ta gid$_2$ a-la$_2$ "the boat with barley that is being punted from the Lagaš marshes ..."

obv. i 3: This is a personal name and not a "man of the king." For instances of this name, see OSP 1 nos. 54, 56, 154.

No. 231 – MS 3829

Account of an uncertain item, Early Sargonic, Adab.

obv.	1 MA$_2$×EŠE$_2$-gid$_2$	1 long ...
	Ur-^{d}En-ki	Ur-Enki,
	dub-sar	the scribe,
	Ga-ri$_2$-i$_3$-lum	(to) *Garyī-'ilum*,
5	an-na-šum$_2$	he has given it.
rev.	(blank)	

obv. 1: See the commentary to text No. 230 obv. i 1–2.

obv. 4: See, for the same individual, CUSAS 11 no. 259 obv. ii 1, CUSAS 20 nos. 20 rev. 1, 38 obv. 1, 173 rev. 3. The last-cited text bears a date formula with the name of this person, implying that he was of high status. For the personal name, see MAD 3 p. 119.

No. 232 – MS 3790/67

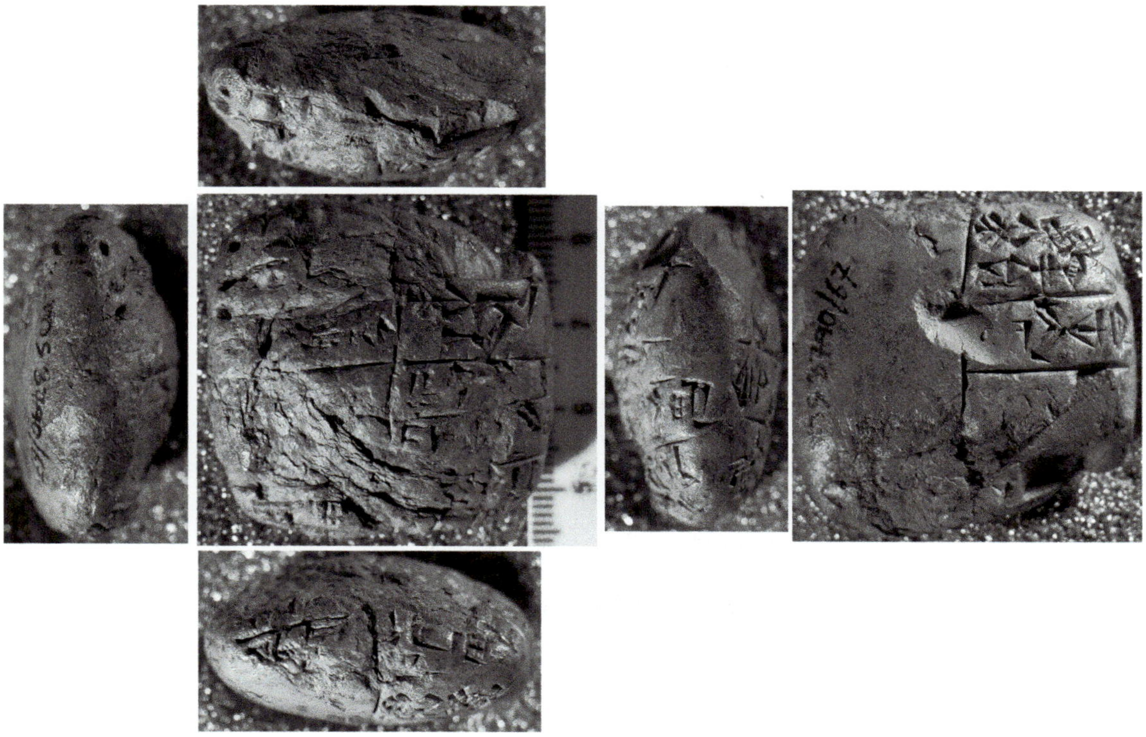

Account of uncertain goods dated by the "year when the brick of Karkara was placed in the mold," Early Sargonic, Adab.

obv. i	1 ˹…˺ […]	1 …
	1 […]	1 …
	[…] ˹aša$_5$-kam˺	… of the field;
	˹Lu$_2$˺-[…]	…
	ENGAR ˹x˺	…
	KA-˹x˺-[x]	…
ii	[2 lines missing]	…
	mu-laḫ$_5$	they have been brought.
	Ur-˹gu˺	Urgu
	˹Pu$_x$(LAGAB×TIL)-ta-pad$_3$˺-ra	to Putapad(a)
	[an-na]-šum$_2$	has given it to him.
rev. i	˹iti˺ ĝa$_2$-udu-˹ur$_4$˺ / mu šeg$_{12}$ / Karkara(IM)^{ki}	Month Ĝa'udu'ur. The year (when) the brick of the city of Karkara
	^{ĝeš}šub-ba ĝar	was placed in the brick mold.

obv. ii 3: Another possibility is mu-er$_{14}$ "they have come here." In both cases, the verb's subject is living beings.

rev. i 1–2: The writing in the second line is a short form of ^{ĝeš}u$_3$-šub "brick mold." The phrase is a year formula of an unknown Akkadian king. It implies a building or restoration project that took place in Karkara. See Powell 1980: 47–52 for the identification of IM^{ki} with the city of Karkara, now the massive mound of Tall Jidr to the north of Adab.

1.2 – Early Dynastic IIIb/Early Sargonic Bullae

No. 233 – MS 3181

Bulla-shaped letter-order, Early Dynastic/Early Sargonic, Adab

obv.	Ur-^{d}Nisaba	To Ur-Nisaba
	na-be$_2$-a	please say,
	Nin$_9$-nin$_9$-ĝu$_{10}$	(this is what) Ninninĝu (says):
	igi Nin-inim-zi-da	Nininimzida;
rev.	igi Nin-bur-šu-ma	Ninburšuma;
	igi Nin-ĝi$_6$-par$_4$-še$_3$	Ninĝiparše;
	igi ḫa-mu-ne-du$_8$	he should watch them!

obv. 3: Cf. text No. 273 rev. 2 for an individual Nin$_9$-nin$_9$.

No. 234 – MS 5018

Bulla recording bread and beer, Early Dynastic/Early Sargonic, Adab.

1	50 *2* ninda 1	52 breads, 1 (jar of beer):
2	^{d}Nin-mug	(goddess) Ninmug.
3	u_4 10 *2*	Day 12.
4	Lugal-iti-da	Lugalitida (is responsible).

No. 235 – MS 5019

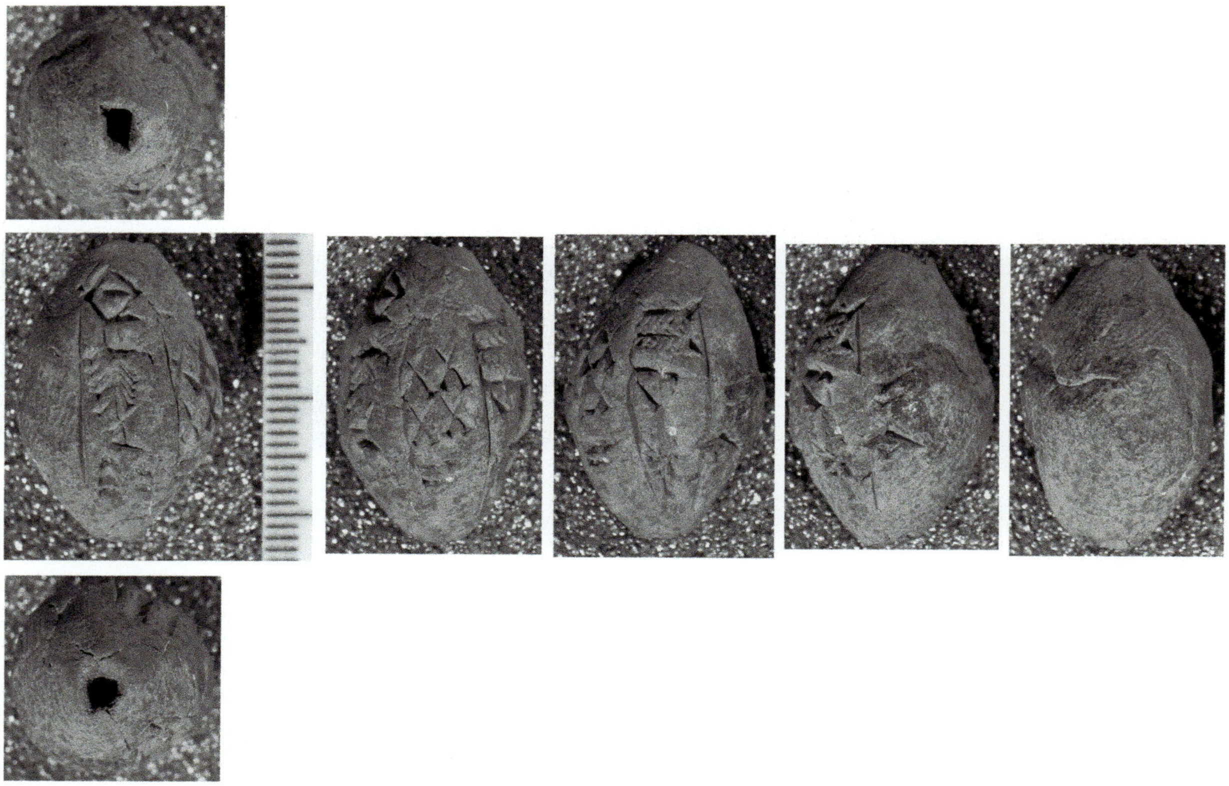

Bulla recording expenditure of reeds, Early Dynastic/Early Sargonic, Adab.

1	5 gi gu$_2$	5 loads of reed:
2	A.|BU$^!$.BU$^!$|	to ABUBU
3	an-na-šum$_2$	they have been given.
4	u$_4$ *2*	Day 2.

l. 2: The writing A.|BU$^!$.BU$^!$| may conceal a personal name Arina$_x$. BU appears here in the simplified shape of BULUĜ$_3$. BU itself is a simplification of the original |MUŠ.MUŠ|. This is one of the writings of the plant /a-/erina/, possibly sumaq (*Rhus coriaria*). See Molina 2014, commentary to no. 253 obv. 4 and Rudik 2011: 25, 91-92, 249 with further references.

No. 236 – MS 5020

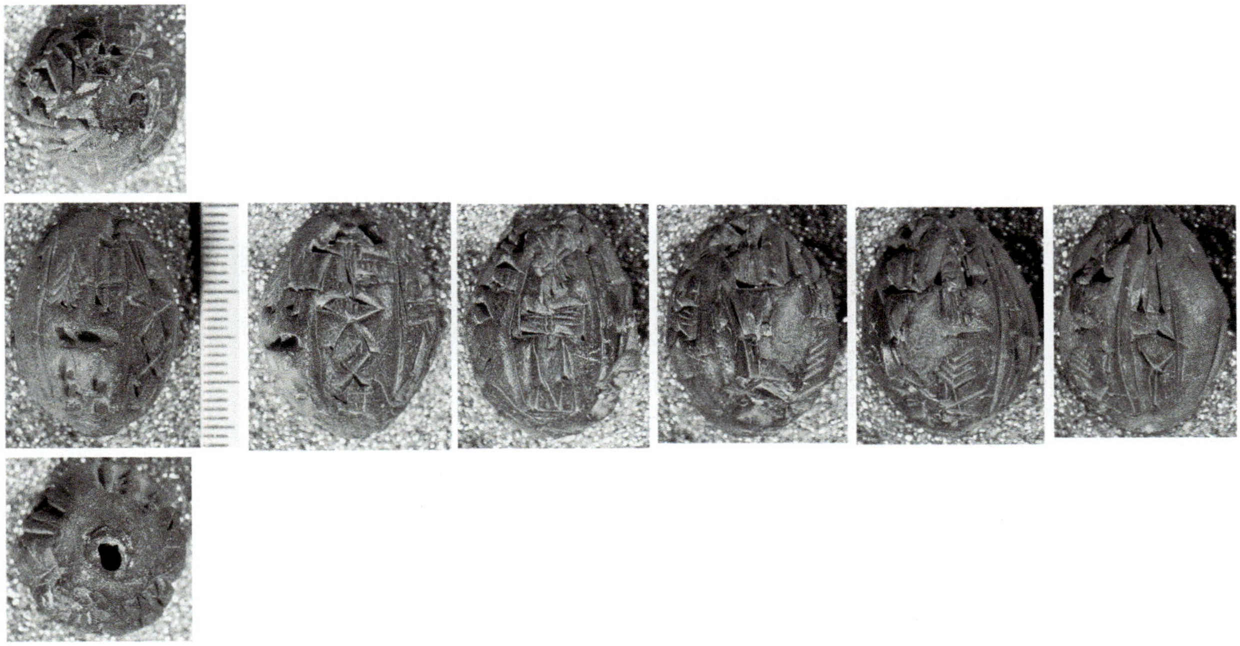

Bulla recording barley, Early Dynastic/Early Sargonic, Adab.

1	5(gur) 2(bariga) še gur	5 *gur* 2 *bariga* barley:
2	Eden-bi-še$_3$	Edenbiše,
3	dumu Za$_3$-mu	son of Zamu.
4	iti ab-e$_3$-zi-ga	Month Ab-eziga.
5	Na-ni ⸢x⸣	Nani …

l. 5: The last sign does not resemble -kam. It looks like the beginning of SILA$_3$.

No. 237 – MS 5021

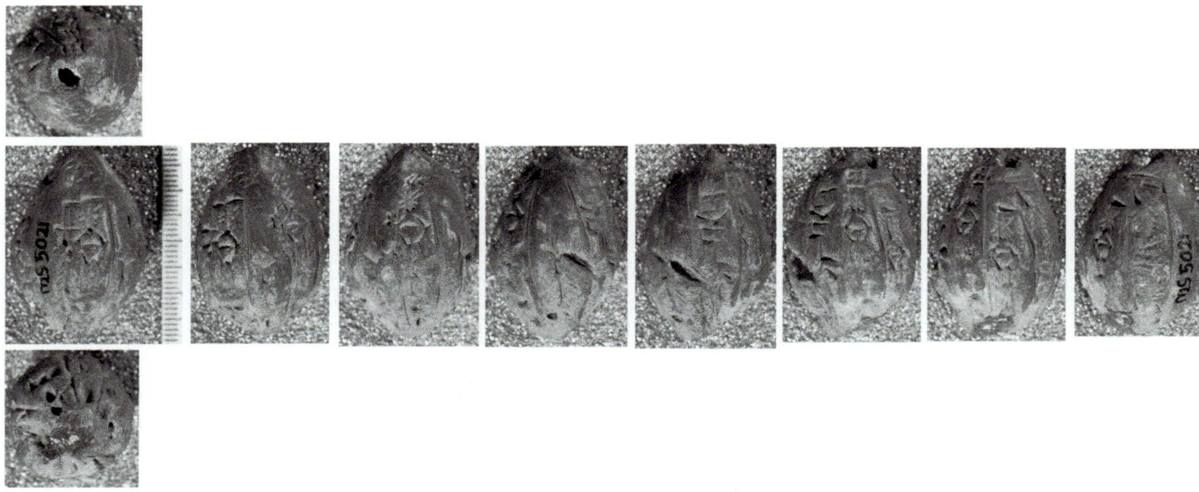

Bulla recording barley, Early Dynastic/Early Sargonic, Adab.

1	2(gur) 3(bariga) še gur gibil	2 *gur* 3 *bariga* of new barley;
2	1(gur) še-sumun	1 *gur* of old barley;
3	1(gur) 1(bariga) še-gibil	1 *gur* 1 *bariga* of new barley;
4	3(bariga) še-sumun	3 *bariga* of old barley:
5	⸢Gu⸣-ri$_2$-sa	Gurisa;
6	1(gur) 1(bariga) gibil-x	1 *gur* 1 *bariga*: new …
7	[n+] 2(bariga) še-gibil	x+2 *bariga* of new barley:
8	Nin-bara$_2$-ge-si	Ninbaragesi.

l. 5: Although the reading of the first sign is certain, this individual does not appear in the extant ED/ES Adab corpus or, to the writer's knowledge, elsewhere.

No. 238 – MS 5047/2

Bulla, flat on one side, that was attached to a tablet box, Early Dynastic/Early Sargonic, Adab.

obv.	pisaĝ-dub	The tablet box.
	e$_2$-dumu	The "House of the son."
	iti še-⸢kin-ku$_5$⸣	Month Šekinku.
rev.	(blank)	

obv. 1: The interpretation of the term pisaĝ-dub as "archivist" in the present context is unlikely because the sealing of a box is what is meant here.

No. 239 – MS 5047/3

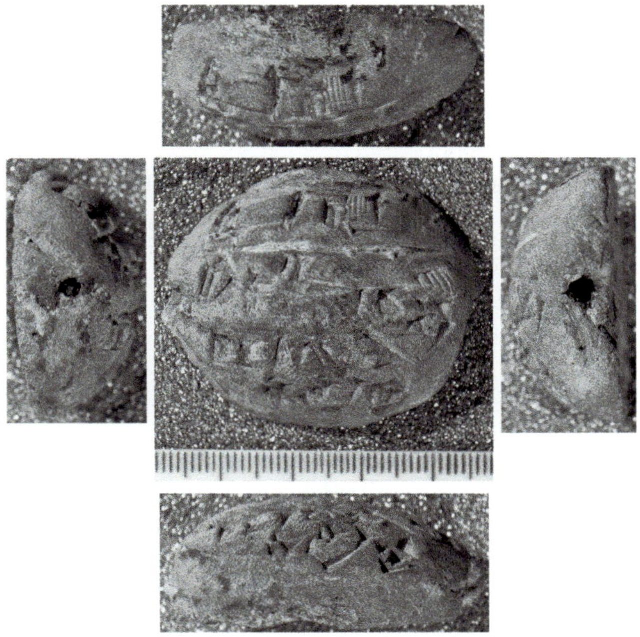

Bulla, flat on one side, that was attached to a tablet box, Early Dynastic/Early Sargonic, Adab.

obv.	pisaĝ̂-dub	The tablet box.
	ni$_3$ al-gi-na	Confirmed things
	e$_2$ lu$_2$-maḫ-kam	of the house of the *lumaḫ*-priest.
rev.	(blank)	

obv. 2: The expression probably refers to confirmed documents kept in the tablet box.

1.3 – Early to Middle Sargonic Tablets

1.3.1 – Personnel

No. 240 – MS 2724/6

Account of junior shepherds (gab$_2$-ra) in the service of individuals, Early/Middle Sargonic, Adab.

obv. i	4 gab$_2$-ra	4 junior shepherds:
	A-ba-mu-na	Abamuna;
	3 Ig-ge	3: Ige;
	3 Nam-maḫ-ni	3: Nammaḫ(a)ni;
	3 Aja$_2$-zu-zu	3: Ajazuzu;
	3 Igi-si$_4$	3: Igisi;
	3 E$_2$-amaš	3: E'amaš;
	3 IM-ki	3: IMki;
	⌜4⌝ En-gu$_2$-gal	4: Engugal;
ii	2 Ur-zikum	2: Urzikum;
	3 Ur-gu	3: Urgu;
	3 AN-na	3: ANna;
	3 Ša$_3$-ga-ni-su$_{13}$	3: Šaganisu;
	3 Gala(KU.ARAD)	3: Gala;
	4 Niĝir-Ab-zu	4: Niĝir-Abzu;
	2 Nam-maḫ	2: Nammaḫ;
	(ruling)	
	1 Ur-ĝidru	1: Urĝidru;
	1 Lu$_2$-lil-la	1: Lulila;
	1 Lu$_2$-bara$_2$-⌜ge⌝	1: Lubarage;
rev. i	2 A-^{ĝeš}rin$_2$-a	2: Arina;
	1 A$_2$-ni-ta	1: Anita;
	1 ugula-iri	1: the overseer of the city;
	1 dub-sar	1: the scribe;
	1 engar	1: the agricultural manager;
	(blank line)	
	2 Ur-a$_2$	2: Ur-a;
	3 Lugal-iri	3: Lugal-iri;
	3 Ur-$^{d⌜}$Aš$_8$-gi$_4$⌝	3: Ur-Ašgi.
ii	(blank)	

rev. i 1: This is another variant writing of the name /Arina/ that designates a plant. The present case with the determinative for plants and the phonetic complements /a/ confirm the phonemic structure /arina/.

No. 241 – MS 2724/10

Account of labor in the service of individuals, Early/Middle Sargonic, Adab.

obv.	12 E$_{2}$-amaš	12 (persons): E'amaš;
	8 Ur-e$_{2}$	8: Ur-e;
	8 Ur-a-da	8: Ur-ada;
	8 Lugal-e	8: Lugale;
	8 Saĝ-diĝir-tuku	8: Saĝdiĝirtuku;
	6 ŠIM-DU	6: ŠIMDU;
	6 Ur-^{d}TA	6: Ur-(AmmaNEra);
	8 Ur-^{d}En-ki	8: Ur-Enki;
	6 Igi-ni-še$_{3}$	6: Iginiše;
	4 En-me-na$_{2}$	4: Enme(a)na;
rev.	⸢4⸣ E$_{2}$-ur$_{2}$	4: E'ur;
	4 Ur-^{d}En-lil$_{2}$	4: Ur-Enlil;
	7 Lugal-sipa	7: Lugalsipa;
	6 Ad-da	6: Adda;
	6 Aja$_{2}$-KA-du$_{3}$	6: AjaKAdu;
	3 ^{d}En-lil$_{2}$-le	3: Enlile;
	10 la$_{2}$ 1 Ur-^{d}En-lil$_{2}$	9: Ur-Enlil;
	5 Ur-nin	5: Urnin;
	12 lu$_{2}$-eše$_{2}$-aša$_{5}$-<gid$_{2}$>	12: the field-surveyor;
l.e.	6 Ĝiri$_{3}$-ni	6: Ĝirini.

obv. 7: This writing is certainly an abbreviation of the personal name Ur-^{d}Am(TA×KUR)-ma-NE-ra of Nos. 245 obv. 2, 151 obv. ii 5.

No. 242 – MS 2724/11

Account of personnel, Early/Middle Sargonic, Adab.

obv.	1 Niĝir-Ab-zu	1 Niĝir-Abzu;
	1 Lugal-iri	1 Lugal-iri;
	1 Nam-maḫ-ni	1 Nammaḫ(a)ni;
	1 Aja$_{2}$-zu-zu	1 Ajazuzu;
	1 Igi-si$_{4}$	1 Igisi;
	1 E$_{2}$-amaš	1 E'amaš;
	1 IM-ki	1 IMki;
	1 En-gu$_{2}$-gal	1 Engugal;
	1 Ur-zikum-ma	1 Urzikuma;
rev.	1 Ur-^{d}Aš$_{8}$-gi$_{4}$	1 Ur-Ašgi;
	1 Ša$_{3}$-ga-ni-su$_{13}$	1 Šaganisu;
	1 AN-na	1 ANna;
	1 Gala(ARAD.KU)	1 Gala;
	1 Nam-⸢maḫ⸣	1 Nammaḫ;
	1 dub-sar	1 the scribe;

	1 Ur-ĝidru	1 Urĝidru;
	1 Lu$_{2}$-lil-la	1 Lulila;
	1 Lu$_{2}$-bara$_{2}$-ge	1 Lubarage;
	1 ugula-iri	1 the overseer of the city;
	1 engar	1 the agricultural manager.

obv. 6: The sign for /amaš/ is that found in text No. 240 obv. i 7, but without an inscribed "UDU" and with two wedges inside the rhombus where No. 240 has three.

1.3.2 – Land

No. 243 – MS 1952/35

Allocation of land, Early Sargonic, Adab.

obv. i	1(eše$_{3}$) Ur-^{d}Aš$_{8}$-gi$_{4}$	1 *eše*: Ur-Ašgi;
	1(eše$_{3}$) X-⸢x⸣	1 *eše*: …;
	1(eše$_{3}$) ⸢E$_{2}$-x⸣-[…]	1 *eše*: …;
	[…]	…
	1(eše$_{3}$) […]	1 *eše*: …;
	1(eše$_{3}$) ⸢Du⸣-[x]	1 *eše*: Du…,

	šidim	the builder;
ii	1(eše$_3$) [Aja$_2^?$-zu$^?$]-zu	1 *eše*: Ajazuzu(?)
	⸢1(eše$_3$)⸣ […]	1 *eše*: …;
	⸢1(eše$_3$)⸣ […]	1 *eše*: …;
	⸢1(eše$_3$)⸣ […]	1 *eše*: …;
	⸢1(eše$_3$)⸣ […]	1 *eše*: …;
	⸢x-x⸣	…
iii	*650*	650
rev. i	(blank space)	
	3(iku) ½(1N$_8$) ⸢aša$_5$⸣	3 ½ *iku* land:
	aša$_5$-*1*-<kam> eše$_2$ ⸢gid$_2$⸣	the first field measured.
	2(eše$_3$) (er.$^?$) 3(iku) aša$_5$-*2*-kam eše$_2$ gid$_2$	2 *eše* 3 ½ *iku*: the second field measured.
	1(eše$_3$) 4(iku) ½(1N$_8$) <aša$_5$>-*3*-kam <eše$_2$> gid$_2$	1 eše 4 ½ *iku*: the third <field> measured.
	⸢3(eše$_3$)⸣ [<aša$_5$> *4*-kam <eše$_2$> gid$_2$]	3 *eše*: [the fourth <field> measured.]
ii	2(iku) [+n] UD-[x]-⸢x⸣	2 *iku*: …;
	2(iku) ⸢Šeš⸣-šeš	2 *iku*: Šeššeš.
	aša$_5$-bala	Fields (on which water) is drawn.
	⸢4(iku)⸣ <aša$_5$> *5*-kam <eše$_2$>-gid$_2$	4 *iku*: The fifth <field> measured.
	(blank)	

The first column on the reverse is on the left. It summarizes four field mensurations. The right column, the second on the reverse, was added afterwards. It contains a record of two individuals each receiving two *iku* of land. This part is followed by a separate colophon and records the fifth mensuration.

obv. i 2: Uncertain. See the index of unidentified signs.

obv. iii 1: The meaning of this number is uncertain.

rev. ii 3: The interpretation of aša$_5$-bala is based on the meaning of bala "to pour out, draw water"; see PSD B[2] 49 s.v. bal D 3, CAD D 56 s.v. *dalû*.

1.3.3 – Sheep and Goats

No. 244 – MS 2724/1

Account of goats, Early Sargonic, Adab.

obv.	14 ud$_5$	14 nanny goats:
	Ur-Šubur	Ur-Šubur;
	12 Lu$_2$-bara$_2$-ge	12: Lubarage;
	16 Igi-ni-še$_3$	16: Iginiše;
	11 Ni$_3$-du$_7$	11: Nidu;
	10 la$_2$ 1 Inim-ma-ni-zi	9: Inimanizi;
	10 Ur-^{d}Iškur kuš$_7$	10: Ur-Iškur, the animal-manager.
	šu-niĝin$_2$ 73	Total: 73.
rev.	ud$_5$ u$_4$-de$_3$ ḫul-am$_3$	These are nanny goats one day ahead of the end of the

		month.
	<<Ur-^{d}En-lil$_2$>>	<<Ur-Enlil>>
	<<Lugal-mu-da-kuš$_2$>>	<<Lugalmudakuš>>
	<<e$_2$ ^{d}En-lil$_2$-la$_2$>>	<<The temple of Enlil>>
	<<vertical strokes>>	<<vertical strokes>>
	<<TUM TUM TUM TUM>>	<<(doodles)>>
l.e.	<<LUL LUL LUL>>	<<(doodles)>>

obv. 8: A mistake in calculations. The sum of all entries is 72.

rev. 1: See Sallaberger 1999: 233 for an expression u$_4$-de$_3$ gid$_2$-da "extended by one day." The basic meanings of the ḫul are "to destroy; (to be) bad." In the present context it may mean "to destroy = to shorten" and refers to an administrative procedure.

rev. ii–left edge: These lines, partly doodles, were added afterwards onto the dried clay.

No. 245 – MS 2724/7

Account of sheep and goats, Early/Middle Sargonic, Adab.

obv.	1 udu-nita E$_2$-⸢amaš⸣	1 male sheep: E'amaš;
	1 maš$_2$ Ur-^{d}Am-ma-NE-ra	1 goat: Ur-AmmaNEra;
	1 maš$_2$ Saĝ-diĝir-tuku	1 goat: Saĝdiĝirtuku;
	1 udu En-me-a-na$_2$	1 sheep: Enme'ana;
	1 udu Ur-a-da	1 sheep: Urada;
	1 udu ŠIM-DU	1 sheep: ŠIMDU;
	1 maš$_2$ E$_2$-ur$_2$	1 goat: E'ur;
	1 udu Ur-^{d}En-lil$_2$	1 sheep: Ur-Enlil;
	1 udu Ur-a$_2$	1 sheep: Ur-a;
rev.	1 sila$_4$ Lugal-ĝeš	1 lamb: Lugalĝeš;
	1 udu Ur-nu	1 sheep: Urnu.

obv. 2: The same individual appears in BdI 1 no. 25 (ES Adab) obv. i 7. The sign AM in both texts is TA×KUR. See Such-Gutiérrez 2005–6: 5 for the deity ^{d}AM.NE.RA. His/her temple is mentioned in the Adab corpus; see CUSAS 20 no. 131 obv. 2. The divine name is read there as ^{d}Am-ma-bi$_2$-ra without any explanation. However, it seems likely that -ra at the end shows that the sign NE has to be read bir$_9$, gir$_{10}$ or some other value that ends with /r/.

rev. 2: The sign for sheep (LU) tends to look like DIB in this line and less distinct in several lines above.

No. 246 – MS 2724/9

Expenditure of sheep, Early Sargonic, Adab.

obv.	10 la$_2$ 1 u$_8$	9 ewes;
	4 udu-nita	4 male sheep:
	udu Ma-ma	the sheep (of) Mama.
	Ur-^{d}Iškur	Ur-Iškur
	Ur-nu	(and) Urnu:
	an-ne-šum$_2$	it has been given to them.
rev.	(blank)	

obv. 3: See CUSAS 11 no. 152 obv. ii 3, an ED/ES text from Adab, for the same personal name.

No. 247 – MS 2724/13

Obverse: Account of sheep in connection to Lagaš. Reverse, written on dry clay: Allocation of barley from the temple E-SAR. Early Sargonic, Adab.

obv. i	5 udu Ĝiri$_3$-ni gu-la	5 sheep: Ĝirini, the senior;
	6 E$_2$-amaš-zi	6: E'amašzi;
	5 Ur-i$_7$-da	5: Ur-ida;
	5 ŠIM-⸢DU⸣	5: ŠIMDU;
	5 Ur-e$_2$	5: Ur-e;

	6 Saĝ-diĝir-tuku	6: Saĝdiĝirtuku;
	5 En-me-a-na$_{2}$	5: Enme'ana;
ii	5 Lugal-e	5: Lugale;
	5 Ur-^{d}En-ki	5: Ur-Enki;
	12 Tum-al	12: Tumal;
	6 Za$_{3}$-mu	6: Zamu.
	udu dab$_{5}$-ba	The sheep that have been taken.
	Lagaš(BURU$_{4}$.LA^{mušen})^{ki}	Lagaš.
rev. i	(blank space)	
	10 la$_{2}$ *1* še [gur]	9 gur barley:
	Ur-zikum	Urzikum;
	10 *4* Ur-^{d}Utu	14: Ur-Utu;
	10 Ur-^{d}Utu	10: Ur-Utu;
	10 Ur-ḪAR	10: UrḪAR.
	e$_{2}$-SAR-kam	It is (the barley) of the E-SAR (temple).

obv. i 1: See SCTRAH no. 302 for the same individual, and for the distinction between gu-la "senior" and tur "junior" in administrative texts. There is no doubt that SCTRAH no. 302 comes from Adab.

rev.: The reverse was inscribed when the clay was becoming dry.

No. 248 – MS 3818

Account of sheep, Early Sargonic, Adab.

obv.	1 udu-nita	1 male sheep:
	Ra-bi$_{2}$-i$_{3}$-lum	*Rabi-'ilum*,
	lu$_{2}$-u$_{5}$	the shipping agent
	Iri-saĝ-rig$_{x}$(SAL.ḪUB$_{2}$.DU)^{ki}	(from) Irisaĝrig;
	1 maš$_{2}$	1 goat:
	Ur-^{d}Dumu-zi-da	Ur-Dumuzida,
	lu$_{2}$ Ur-^{d}Nin-piriĝ	the man of Ur-Ninpiriĝ.
rev.	(blank)	

obv. 2, 6: A *Rabi-'ilum* and an Ur-Dumuzida appear in the sale document text No. 2, dated by the rule of the governor Ursaĝ-Keš of Adab (ED IIIb). They may be identical to the individuals of the present text. However, this text is certainly of a later date.

No. 249 – MS 4193

Account of sheep and pigs, Early/Middle Sargonic, Adab.

obv.	5 udu	5 sheep:
	⸢Lugal-zi⸣	Lugalzi;
	5 ⸢Lugal-ḫe$_2$⸣	5: Lugalḫe;
	3 Igi-si$_4^!$(SI)	3: Igisi;
	3 E$_2$-amaš	3: E'amaš.
	1 (ras.) šaḫ$_2$-niga	1 (erasure) fattened pig:
	Lugal-nita$_2$-zi	Lugalnitazi;
	1 šaḫ$_2$-niga	1 fattened pig:
rev.	Niĝir-Ab-zu	Niĝir-Abzu;
	1 šaḫ$_2$-niga	1 fattened pig:
	Aja$_2$-zu-zu	Ajazuzu;
	1 šaḫ$_2$-u$_2$ Lugal-zi	1 pig (fed with) grass: Lugal(nita)zi;
	2 šaḫ$_2$-u$_2$ Igi-si$_4$	2 pigs (fed with) grass: Igisi;
	2 šaḫ$_2$-niga	2 fattened pigs:
	IM-ki	IMki;
	1 šaḫ$_2$-niga	1 fattened pig:
	Ur-zikum$^!$(LAGAB×TIL)-ma	Urzikuma.

obv. 5: The sign is a graphic variant of LAK777 with two wedges inside the "body" instead of one:

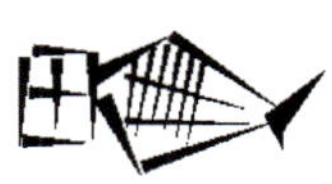

Texts from Sargonic Adab exhibit a considerable variation in the graphic representation of signs. Certainly not all of them should be regarded as temporal developments; some may, in fact, be synchronous graphic variants used by different scribes.

1.3.4 – Sheep and Wool

No. 250 – MS 2724/2

Account of wool and sheep, Early Sargonic, Adab.

obv.	12 siki gu$_2$ la$_2$ 7 ma-na	12 talents minus 7 minas wool:
	I$_3$-lum-GAR$_3$	*'Ilum*-GAR;
	200 udu-nita	200 male sheep;
	400 u$_8$	400 ewes;
	63 sila$_4$	63 lambs;
	15 siki gu$_2$ la$_2$ 8 ma-na	15 talents minus 8 minas wool:
	Usan$_x$(AN.GU$_2$×PAP)-du$_6$	Usandu;
rev.	195 udu-nita	195 male sheep;
	265 u$_8$	265 ewes;
	54 sila$_4$	54 lambs;
	13 siki gu$_2$ ma-na la$_2$ 2	13 talents minus 2 minas wool:
	Adab-ki-bi$_x$(DUG)	Adabkibi;
	240 la$_2$ 10 udu-nita	240 minus 10 male sheep;
	320 u$_8$ 60 sila$_4$	320 ewes, 60 lambs;
	14 <<la$_2$×10$^{!}$>> siki gu$_2$ ma-na la$_2$ 10	14 talents of wool minus 10 minas:
l. e.	⸢Za$_3$⸣-mu na-gada / Ur-^{d}Iškur kuš$_7$	Zamu, the herdsman, Ur-Iškur, the animal-manager.

r. e.	420 *40* udu / *52* sila$_4$	460 sheep, 52 lambs.

obv. 2: See the commentary in SCTRAH no. 145 obv. 5 for likely the same individual. The name is written Diĝir-GAR$_3$ there.

obv. 7: Cf. the sign combination AN.GU$_2$×KAK with the reading usan$_x$ in ePSD. In our case, the sign PAP is inscribed into GU$_2$ (GU$_2$×PAP = LAK552). It is possible that two signs are graphic variants. See text No. 95 rev. ii 3 for i$_7$ AN.GU$_2$×KAK-du$_6$ as the name of a canal.

rev. 8: A scribal mistake.

right edge: These lines were written on the drying clay. This is a characteristic trait of this dossier and the scribe who wrote it.

No. 251 – MS 2724/4

Account of sheep and wool, Early Sargonic, Adab.

obv.	600 la$_2$ 60 45 udu	495 sheep;
	50 la$_2$ 3 sila$_4$	47 lambs;
	14 siki gu$_2$ la$_2$ 6 ma-na	14 talents minus 6 minas wool:
	Ad-da	Adda
	E$_2$-zur-zur	(of/at the town) Ezurzur.
rev.	600 la$_2$ 4 udu	596 sheep;
	61 sila$_4$	61 lambs;
	17 siki gu$_2$ la$_2$ 6 ma-na	17 talents minus 6 minas wool:
	Ur-^{d}En-ki	Ur-Enki.

obv. 4–5: The same individual appears as the official šita-uru$_{18}$(URU×A) of the locality E$_2$-zur-zur^{ki} in CUSAS 11 no. 141 obv. i 1, ii 2 (ED/ES Adab).

No. 252 – MS 3814

Account of wool, Early Sargonic, Adab?

The upper edge is fake.

obv.	[n] ⸢siki⸣ [(x)] ma-na	x minas of … wool;
	450 siki-u$_8$ ma-na	450 minas of ewe wool.
	(blank line)	
	E$_2$-u$_6$-e	E'u'e (is in charge).
rev.	(blank)	

obv. 3: See CUSAS 11 no. 186 (Meskigala) obv. v 8 for an individual, a recipient of barley, with the same name.

1.3.5 – Cattle

No. 253 – MS 2724/12

Account of cattle of varying age, Early Sargonic, Adab.

For a similar text that probably originates in the same archive, see CUSAS 26 no. 290. Since the individual IM-ki of the present text appears in other Early to Middle Sargonic tablets from Adab, the date of CUSAS 26 no. 290 ("CS") has to be corrected.

obv.	16 ab$_{2}$-maḫ$_{2}$	16 mature cows;
	7 ab$_{2}$-*3*	7 cows of 3 (years);
	5 ab$_{2}$-*2*	5 cows of 2 (years);
	2 ab$_{2}$-*1*	2 cows of 1 (year);
	4 gu$_{4}$-*1*	4 bulls of 1 (year);
	1 gu$_{4}$-utua$_{2}$	1 stud-bull.
	(ruling)	(ruling)
	šu-niĝin$_{2}$ 35 ab$_{2}$	Total: 35 "cows" (= i.e. large cattle).
rev.	IM-ki	IMki (is responsible).

obv. 6: The sign designating "stud" /utua/ has here the form that differs from the one in the previous texts. It differs significantly from the form in LAK777. For the latter in ED IIIa texts, see Krebernik 1998a: 275. See also the commentary to text No. 249 obv. 5. For the etymology of the word for breeding ram as ⋆udu-a "seed-sheep," i.e., male sheep able to procreate, see Steinkeller 1995: 711 no. 609 f. Here the word is used together with gu$_4$ to denote a bull used for breeding.

1.3.6 – Hides

No. 254 – MS 4202

Account of hides, Early/Middle Sargonic, Adab.

obv.	16 kuš ab$_2$	16 cowhides:
	Niĝir-Ab-zu	Niĝir-Abzu;
	7 Lugal-ḫe$_2$	7: Lugalḫe;
	7 Aja$_2$-zu-zu	7: Ajazuzu.
	kuš šu-a gi$_4$-am$_6$	These are hides that have been turned over.
	⸢2⸣[+n] kuš Niĝir-⸢Ab⸣-zu	2+ hides: Niĝir-Abzu;
rev.	5 ⸢Lugal⸣-[ḫe$_2$]	5: Lugalḫe;
	5 Aja$_2$-⸢zu⸣-[zu]	5: Ajazuzu:
	kuš e$_2$-a ĝal$_2$-la	The hides are in the (store-)house.

obv. 5: Hides are turned over (šu-a…gi$_4$) to officials in charge of warehouses by craftsmen; see SCTRAH p. 34 for this construction and its meaning in the administrative context. The second section records the hides that are in the "house," where it is likely a short writing for "storehouse" e$_2$-ni$_3$-gur$_{11}$ (suggestion courtesy M. Molina). Both sections record the same persons.

1.3.7 – Milk Products

No. 255 – MS 4235

Account of cheese, Early/Middle Sargonic, Adab.

obv.	2(bariga) 3(ban$_2$) ga-ar$_3$	2 *bariga* 3 *ban* cheese:
	Niĝir-Ab-zu	Niĝir-Abzu;
	2(bariga) Lugal-zi	2 *bariga*: Lugalzi;
	1(ban$_2$) Lugal-zi	1 *ban*: Lugalzi;
	1(ban$_2$) Igi-si$_4$	1 *ban*: Igisi;
	1(ban$_2$) E$_2$-amaš	1 *ban*: E'amaš;
rev.	1(ban$_2$) Aja$_2$-zu-zu	1 *ban*: Ajazuzu;
	1(ban$_2$) IM-ki	1 *ban*: IMki;
	1(ban$_2$) Lugal-nita$_2$-zi	1 *ban*: Lugalnitazi.
	(blank)	

obv. 6: The sign is LAK777 without the final wedge in "UDU."

No. 256 – MS 4271

Turning over of cheese, Middle Sargonic, Adab.

obv.	1(gur) 1(bariga) ga-ar$_3$ gur	1 *gur* 1 *bariga* of cheese:
	Lugal-iri	Lugal-iri;
	2(bariga) E$_2$-amaš	2 *bariga*: E'amaš;
	1(gur) 2(bariga) la$_2$ 1(ban$_2$) AN-na	1 *gur* 2 *bariga* minus 1 *ban*: ANna;
	1(gur) la$_2$ 1(ban$_2$) IM-ki	1 *gur* minus 1 *ban*: IMki;
	1(gur) Nam-maḫ-ni	1 *gur*: Nammaḫ(a)ni;
	2(bariga) Niĝir-Ab-zu	2 *bariga*: Niĝir-Abzu;
	1(bariga) 3(ban$_2$) ga-ar$_3$ A-ba-mu-⸢na⸣	1 *bariga* 3 *ban* cheese: Abamuna.
rev.	(blank space)	
	ga-ar$_3$ šu-a gi-am$_6$	This is cheese that has been turned over.
	(blank space)	

obv. 3: The sign AMAŠ is similar to that in the preceding text, with the difference that the sign in the present text has two almost vertical wedges inside the "body."

1.3.8 – Grain and Grain Products

No. 257 – MS 2724/5

Account of grain, Early Sargonic, Adab.

obv.	10 še gur Ur-nu	10 *gur* barley: Urnu;
	8 E$_2$-nam	8: Enam;
	3(gur) 2(bariga) ^{d}En-lil$_2$-la$_2$	3 *gur* 2 *bariga*: Enlila;
	5 Inim-ma-ni-zi	5: Inimanizi;
	2(gur) 3(bariga) Lugal-ĝeš	2 *gur* 3 *bariga*: Lugalĝeš;
	2 E$_2$-ĝessu-bi	2 *gur*: Eĝessubi.
rev.	(blank)	

No. 258 – MS 2724/14

Account of barley arrears of shepherds, Early Sargonic, Adab.

obv. i	24 še gur	24 *gur* barley:
	Niĝir-Ab-zu	Niĝir-Abzu;
	110 Ur-nu	110: Urnu;
	20 dub-sar	20: the scribe;
	180 Ur-^{d}Iškur	180: Ur-Iškur;
	22(gur) 2(bariga) kuš$_{7}$	22 *gur* 2 *bariga*: the animal-manager;
	5 ugula-iri	5: the city overseer.
	sipa ud$_{5}$-me	They are goatherds.
ii	160 unu$_{3}$ ni$_{3}$-kas$_{4}$-me	160 (*gur* barley): they are the cowherds of …
	še Ur-mes-še$_{3}$	To the barley of Urmes
	ab-ši-du$_{7}$	it has been *fitted*.
	(ruling)	(ruling)
	šu-niĝin$_{2}$ 521(gur) 2(bariga) še gur	Total: 521 *gur* 2 bariga *barley*.
	(blank space)	(blank)
	110 la$_{2}$ 3 Lugal-e$_{2}$	107 *gur*: Lugal-e;
rev. i	5 aša$_{5}$ Me-e$_{2}$	5 *gur*: the field of Me'e:
	Ur-^{d}Eš$_{23}$-peš	Ur-Ešpeš;
	492(gur) 1(bariga) Lugal-ĝeš	492 *gur* 1 *bariga*: Lugalĝeš.
	(blank space)	

ii	(blank space)	
	še la$_2$-i$_3$	The barley arrears
	sipa-kam	of the shepherd(s).
	(blank space)	

obv. i 8: This statement implies that these high officials were involved in taking care of the palace's flocks.

obv. ii 1: See the commentary to text No. 283 rev. i 6.

obv. ii 2–3: The exact administrative implication of du$_7$ "to be fitting, suitable" is not certain in the present context. It may denote the addition of the amount.

rev. i 1: Cf. the individual E$_2$-me in No. 221 rev. i 1.

1.3.9 – Means of Payment (Silver and Grain)

No. 259 – MS 2724/3

Account of silver and barley, Early Sargonic, Adab.

obv.	*5* ku$_3$ giĝ$_4$ igi-*3*-ĝal$_2$	5 ⅓ shekels silver;
	40 še gur	40 *gur* barley:
	Gala(ARAD.KU)	Gala,
	dumu Al-mu	son of Almu.
	5 ku$_3$ giĝ$_4$ igi-*4*-ĝal$_2$	5 ¼ shekels silver;
	40 še gur	40 *gur* barley:
	Ur-eš$_3$	Ur-eš.
rev.	(blank)	

No. 260 – MS 3839

Account of silver, Early Sargonic, Adab.

obv. i	*2* ku$_3$ giĝ$_4$	2 shekels silver:
	Ur-mes	Urmes;
	1 Teš$_2$-teš$_2$	1: Tešteš;
	1 ^{d}En-lil$_2$-la$_2$	1: Enlila;
	1 Nam-dumu	1: Namdumu;
	1 Ad-da	1: Adda;
	1 Lugal-kur-ra	1: Lugalkura;
	1 Ur-^{d}Eš$_{23}$-peš	1: Ur-Ešpeš;
	1(N$_8$) Amar-girim$_x$(ḪA.DU)	1: Amargirim;
	1(N$_8$) Ur-mes	1: Urmes;
ii	1(N$_8$) Lugal-bad$_3$	1: Lugalbad;
	1(N$_8$) Lu$_2$-eše$_2$-ĝal$_2$-la	1: Lu'ešeĝala;
	1(N$_8$) Ur-^{d}Nin-sig$_x$(SAR)	1: Ur-Ninsig;
	1(N$_8$) Diĝir-⸢dub$_2$⸣(LAK632)	1: Diĝirdub;
	1(N$_8$) E$_2$-⸢šudu$_3$⸣	1: Ešudu;

	1(N_8) dumu ⸢Ad⸣-[da$^?$]	1: the son of Ad[da$^?$];
	1(N_8) En-⸢zi⸣ [(x)]	1: Enzi;
	1(N_8) Lu$_2$-⸢tuku$^?$⸣ [(x)]	1: Lutuku(?);
	1(N_8) En-me-[a-na$_2$]	1: Enme['ana];
	[break]	...
ii	[break]	...
	10 [...]	10 ...
	Ur-tur ⸢x⸣	Urtur, ...

obv. i 9: In all likelihood, the sign N_8 is a check-mark and does not have any numerical value. By this, the distinction between "*1*" and "1(N_8)" represents an administrative practice. ḪA.DU is another writing for the goddess of incantations ^{d}Nin-girim$_x$(A.BU.ḪA.DU etc.); see Such-Gutiérrez 2005–6: 25 with additional references.

obv. ii 3: For the reading of SAR as sig$_x$ "green" in the name of the deity, see Schrakamp 2015b: 197, with additional references.

1.3.10 – Copper

No. 261 – MS 3808

Record of copper, Early Sargonic, Adab.

obv.	[2 uruda ma-na]	[2 minas of copper].
	⸢dub *I$_3$*⸣-*lu-lu* a-ba-la$_2$	The tablet of *'Ilu(m)-lu...* has been hung:
	⸢Saĝ⸣-diĝir-tuku niĝir	Saĝdiĝirtuku, the herald.
	1 la$_2$ 10 uruda ma-na giĝ$_4$	1 mina minus 10 shekels copper:
	dub *I$_3$-lu-lu* a-ba-la$_2$	The tablet of *'Ilu(m)-lu...* has been hung:
	ḫa-zi Aja$_2$-ne-ne	The *hazi(n)*-axe (of) Ajanene.
	1 ^{šu2}1N_8 E$_2$-mes šu-i	1 ⅓ (mina): Emes, the barber.
	(blank space)	
rev.	(blank space)	
	šu-niĝin$_2$-pi	Its total:
	4 uruda ma-na	4 minas copper.
	(blank space)	

obv. 2, 5: See CUSAS 11 no. 354 obv. ii 1 for likely the same *I$_3$-lu-lu*.

1.3.11 – Miscellaneous Goods

No. 262 – MS 2724/8

Expenditure of miscellaneous goods, Early/Middle Sargonic, Adab.

obv.	5(gur) 2(bariga) še gur	5 *gur* 2 *bariga* barley:
	Ma$_{2}$-KA	MaKA;
	6(gur) 2(bariga) še gur	6 *gur* 2 *bariga* barley:
	Lugal-šudu$_{3}$	Lugalšudu;
	2(gur) 1(bariga) 2(ban$_{2}$) še gur	2 *gur* 1 *bariga* 2 *ban* barley:
	Nin-ŠE$_{3}$ ba-de$_{6}$	NinŠE has taken away.
	3 esir$_{4}$-kuš-la	3 sandals (with) leather belts;
rev.	2 sila$_{4}$ <ras.>	2 lambs;
	1 sila$_{4}$ A-rin$_{2}$-GIR	1 lamb: (for) ArinaGIR;
	1 ku$_{3}$ giĝ$_{4}$	1 shekel silver:
	Ur-eš$_{3}$ ba-de$_{6}$	Ur-eš has taken away.
	3 sa-KA	3 ...:
	Ur-gu	Urgu;
	1 ku$_{3}^{!}$ giĝ$_{4}$ gada-kam	1 shekel silver: it is (the price) of the flax/linen:
	Nin-ŠE$_{3}$ ba-de$_{6}$	NinŠE has taken away.

The document is similar to the "financial documents" in the section on ED/ES texts.

obv. 2: The reading of this personal name, otherwise unattested, is uncertain. KA(du$_{11}$) may be a mistake for DU, if the scribe intended the personal name Ma$_{2}$-laḫ$_{5}$(DU.DU) "sailor."

obv. 7: kuš-la may be indentical to kuš-la$_{2}$, probabaly a belt or sash; see CAD A^{I} 159 *sub aguḫḫu*.

rev. 5: The interpretation is unclear.

rev. 7: There are no strokes inside KU$_{3}$.

1.4 – Middle to Classical Sargonic Tablets

1.4.1 – Legal

No. 263 – MS 2465

Cumulative account briefly recording various transactions concerninig people, animals, and a house, Middle Sargonic, Adab. Pierced tablet.

The prosopography of the text suggests an either Early or Middle Sargonic date, but it is certainly younger than the Meskigala texts.

obv. i	1 saĝ	1 slave,
	Geme$_2$-^{d}En-lil$_2$	Geme-Enlil,
	dam Ur-tur	wife of Urtur,
	^{lu2}lunga$_3$	the brewer,
	NI-KA (i$_3$-du$_{11}$?)	.... (one has proclaimed ?)
	Ne-saĝ	Nesaĝ,
	1 ku$_3$ ma-na	1 mina silver,
	šu-du$_8$-a-pi i$_3$-de$_6$	has established the surety for it (the case);
	Bu-za	(with) Buza
	an-da-ti	she lives.
ii	1 Amar-in-nab	1 Amarinnab,
	nu-kiri$_6$	the gardener,
	ensi$_2$ Adab^{ki}	(with) the governor of Adab,
	i$_3$-da-ti	he lives.
	1 Šeš-gu-la	1 Šešgula
	Ĝiri$_3$-ni	with Ĝirini,
	pisaĝ-dub-da	the archivist,
	i$_3$-da-ti	he lives.
	(blank space)	
	2 gu$_4$	2 oxen
	Unug^{ki}	to Uruk
iii	ba-ši-⸢de$_6$?⸣	they have been brought(?).
	En-sila$_3$	Ensila,
	Ur-^{d}Sud$_3$-da	to Ur-Sudda
	E$_2$-kab$_2^{ki}$-ra	from Ekab,
	i$_3$-na-šum$_2$	he has given (them) to him.
	1 Keš$_3^!$-ta	1 (slave), Kešta
	mu-ni	his/her name,
	bar Ur-^{d}Gi:bil-ta	from Ur-Gibil
	^{d}Utu-gu$_2$-gal	Utu-gugal
	ba-ta-sa$_{10}$	has bought him/her.
rev. i	e$_2$	A house
	15 ku$_3$ giĝ$_4$	(for) 15 shekels of silver
	En-u$_2$	En-u
	i$_3$-sa$_{10}$	has purchased.
	1 Ur-Keš$_3$	1 Ur-Keš;
	1 Aja$_2$-ne-da	1 Ajaneda,
	e$_2$-pi	that house
	<gú> an-ne-ĝar	he has placed them (on the neck).
	1 Ur-^{d}En-lil$_2$ [(x)]	1 Ur-Enlil:
	lu$_2$-⸢ki-inim⸣-ma-pi-me	they are its witnesses.

ii	(blank space)	(blank space)
	1 Diĝir-sipa	1 Diĝirsipa.
	KAL-DI Diĝir-KA-*er*-me	They are the … of DiĝirKA(m)er.
	Adab^{ki}	In Adab
	i$_3$-durun(DUR$_2$)	they live.
	(blank space)	(blank space)
	Dam-maḫ$_2$	Dammaḫ,
	aga$_3$-us$_2$	the soldier
	lugal	of the king,
	mu-de$_6$	has brought (them) here.
iii	(blank)	

obv. i 2: The sign GEME$_2$ is written in an Early Dynastic IIIa Fara fashion with KUR inscribed inside the sign. This writing is also characteristic of some texts from Sargonic Nippur: e.g., OSP 1 no. 139. However, the present text is surely from Adab. First, there is a hole that is typical of ED/ES texts from Adab. Second, there is a prosopographical link: Dam-maḫ$_2$ in rev. ii 5–6 is likely the same person as in CUSAS 11 no. 275 obv. ii 2 and CUSAS 26 no. 85 obv. i 2.

obv. i 7–8: See Veenhof 2004: 442 for the construction šu-du$_8$-a … de$_6$ and Wilcke 2007: 113–14 for šu-du$_8$-a denoting surety. As suggested by Wilcke, it was meant to prevent a person of slave status from fleeing.

obv. i 10, ii 4, 8: Cf. the difference between the forms an-da-ti in the case with the slave and i$_3$-da-ti with two other individuals.

obv. iii 2: Notably, sila$_3$ appears here as a phonetic writing for sila "street" in the personal name En-sila-(si).

obv. iii 4: This locality appears in Classical Sargonic texts from Adab, Isin, and Nippur. See CUSAS 4 pp. 623–24 and Schrakamp 2015a: 212 fn. 153.

obv. iii 6: The grapheme is ŠU$_2$.GIR$_2$, probably a simplified form of Keš$_3$(ŠU$_2$.AN.ḪI×GADA).

rev. ii 2: For the personal name Diĝir-KA-*Me-er*, see the commentary to text No. 279 obv. 8. The reading and interpretation of the term KAL-DI that describes the individuals is uncertain. Since the sign KAL is used for ĝuruš starting from this period (MS), the phrase might be ĝuruš di "the male workers of the lawsuit," but this makes little sense.

1.4.2 – Personnel

No. 264 – MS 4208

Account of female workers with their supervisors, in service and "living in the field," Middle Sargonic, Adab (Mama-ummi's file).

obv.	3 geme$_2$	3 female workers:
	Ma-ma-um-mi	*Mama-'ummī;*
	5 Nin-ni$_3$-gi-bara$_4$	5: Ninnigibara;
	1 *Aš-tar$_2$*	1: *'Aštar;*
	2 *Ta$_2$-ni$_2$-a*	2: *Tāni(y)a;*
	1 Nin-ad$_2$-gal	1: Ninadgal;
	5 Ni$_3$-banda$_3^{da}$	5: Nibanda.
	(blank)	
	4 Nin-ni$_3$-zu	4: Ninnizu.
rev.	(blank space)	
	šu-niĝin$_2$ 21 geme$_2$	Total: 21 female workers.
	geme$_2$-gub-ba-me	They are female workers in service.
	8 geme$_2$-gu	8 spinners
	aša$_5$-ga mu-se$_{12}$	live in the field.

obv. 3: This female overseer appears as Nin-ĜAR in numerous texts from the same "file" that have been published in SCTRAH.

rev. 3: According to Waetzoldt 1980–83: 587, geme$_2$-gu were females working either on the production of strings or with flax. Later he interpreted the term as "spinners": see Waetzoldt 2011: 1. This fits well the contents of the texts in Mama-ummi's dossier.

rev. 4: This phrase may reflect the fact that these women were temporarily employed as agriculture workers.

No. 265 – MS 4233

Account of female workers in service with their supervisors, Middle Sargonic, Adab (Mama-ummi's file).

obv.	⸢25⸣ geme$_2$	25 female workers:
	Ma-ma-um-mi	*Mama-'ummī;*
	20 la$_2$ 1 Geme$_2$-^{d}En-lil$_2$-la$_2$	19: Geme-Enlila;
	41 Aš$_{10}$-tar$_2$	41: *'Aštar;*
	16 *Ta$_2$-ni$_2$-a*	16: *Tāni(y)a;*
	20 la$_2$ 1 Nin-ad$_2$-gal	19: Ninadgal;
	22 Ni$_3$-banda$_3^{da}$	22: Nibanda
	12 Me-niĝar-ta	12: Meniĝarta;
	14 Nin-ni$_3$-zu	14: Ninnizu;
	[4] *Si-bi-tum*	[4:] *Sibitum;*
rev.	(blank space)	
	[šu+niĝin$_2$] ⸢120⸣ 52 geme$_2$ gub-ba	[Total:] 172 female workers in service.

	uš-bar-me	They are weavers.
	Lugal-aja$_2$-ĝu$_{10}$	Lugalajaĝu,
	ensi$_2$	the governor.

rev. 3–4: See SCTRAH pp. 29–32 for the discussion of this governor, who served during the early reign of Naram-Suen. Before achieving the highest post in Adab, he was the chief administrator of the temple household of the god Iškur (saĝĝa ^{d}Iškur).

obv. 10: This Akkadian female name has been interpreted by Sommerfeld 1987: 58 tentatively as *šī-bītum*. He denies its comparison with *sipittum* "lamentation, mourning." Cf. also *sibittu* "seven (gods, stars, etc.)."

No. 266 – MS 4261

Account of personnel living in "reed thicket," Middle Sargonic, Adab.

obv.	1 ⸢Ĝessu⸣	1 Ĝessu;
	1 Lugal-⸢iti⸣	1 Lugaliti;
	1 Il$_2$	1 Il(a);
	1 Diĝir-kalag(ĜURUŠ)	1 Diĝirkalag(a).
	ĝeš-gi-a	In the reed thicket
rev.	mu-⸢se$_{12}$⸣	they dwell.
	(blank)	

obv. 5–rev. 1: This is likely a reference to a work assignment in a cane-brake. Less probably ĝeš-gi-a refers to a specific location. A field with this name appears in Ur III records from the Lagaš/Girsu province; see Studevent-Hickman 2006: 455. However, that must have been very far from Adab.

No. 267 – MS 4327

Account of workers (*ĝuruš*) together with their overseers, Middle Sargonic, Adab.

obv.	[break]	...
obv.	[...] ⸢x⸣ [...]	...
	⸢1⸣ Ur-^{d}Tu	1 Ur-Tu(da).
	ugula Ur-u$_4$-su$_{13}$	Overseer: Ur-usu.
	1 Ur-$^{d.ĝeš}$Ḫa-lu	1 Ur-Ḫalu(b);
	1 Bar-ra-ni-še$_3$	1 Baraniše.
	ugula Ur$_2$-maḫ	Overseer: Urmaḫ.
	1 Amar-SU	1 AmarSU,
	$^{[(ĝeš)]}$⸢gu⸣-za-la$_2$	the throne-bearer;
	[x]-⸢x⸣-ma-[x]	...ma..;
	[break]	...
rev.	[break]	...
	[1] ⸢Ur⸣-^{d}⸢Inana$^{?}$⸣	[1] Ur-Inana(?);
	1 Ur-^{d}En-lil$_2$	1 Ur-Enlil,
	⸢šu⸣-muš	the ...;

	2 sipa anše ^{ĝeš}šubur	2 shepherds of the donkeys (of) *šubur*-wagons.
	(blank space)	
	šu-niĝin$_2$ 10 la$_2$ 1 ĝuruš(KAL) [(x)]	Total: 9 *ĝuruš*-workers (...).
	[ugula$^?$] Ur-^{d}Utu [(x)]	[Overseer$^?$:] Ur-Utu.
	[...]-⌜x-na⌝-[...]	...
	[break]	

obv. 3': For Ur-usu, a high official responsible for the management of labor and goods, see SCTRAH no. 166 obv. 2 commentary. The present text witnesses several paleographic peculiarities. Note the unusual shape of the sign BU: 

obv. 4': Obviously the deified *ḫalub*-tree, ^{ĝeš}ḫa-lu-ub$_2$ = *ḫuluppu*.

obv. 5': The name is recorded in other MS/CS Adab texts. Note an unusual form of the sign ŠE$_3$:

obv. 6': See SCTRAH no. 166 obv. 4 commentry for this individual in other texts.

obv. 7'–8': Note that even such high officials as this throne-brearer could be conscripted as *ĝuruš*-workmen.

rev. 3': For šu-muš, a word or uncertain meaning, see the lexical list Niĝ$_2$-ga = *makkūru* 188, MSL 13 p. 101. The passage in the bilingual version is broken: see p. 119. The present context implies that this is a professional title.

No. 268 – MS 4761

Letter-order concerning the transfer of two persons, Middle Sargonic, Adab.

obv.	Lugal-aja$_2$-⌜ĝu$_{10}$⌝	This is what Lugalajaĝu
	na-be$_2$-a	says:
	šeš-ĝu$_{10}$	to my brother
	u$_3$-na-du$_{11}$	please tell it:
	1 dam-gara$_3$	1 the merchant,
	1 Ur-^{d}Eš$_5$-peš	1 Ur-Ešpeš,
	arad$_2$(NITA×KUR) lugal-[me]	[they are] servants of the king;
rev.	Lagaš(LA.⌜BURU$_4$⌝)$^{[ki]}$-[(a)]	in Lagaš
	ab-⌜durun$_x$(DUR$_2$.DUR$_2$)-ne$_2$-eš$_2$⌝	they are residing.
	ḫa-mu-ra-⌜ne⌝-šum$_2$-mu	He should hand them over to you.
	(blank)	

obv. 1: See SCTRAH pp. 30–32 for a discussion of Lugalajaĝu. He appears in administrative documents and letters, as well as in a votive inscription. Lugalajaĝu was the chief administrator of the temple of Iškur and afterwards became the governor of Adab. Molina argues this and other texts from the same group may be dated to the earliest part of Naram-Suen's reign, before the "Great Revolt."

rev. 2–3: These verbal forms are attested in ITT 1 no. 1100 (P213570) = FAOS 19 Gir 32, which is a letter-order in many respects very similar to the present document.

No. 269 – MS 5001

Assignment of personnel, Middle Sargonic, Adab.

obv.	1 Ur-e$_2$	1 Ur-e
	Lugal-si-⸢sa$_2$⸣	(assigned to) Lugalsisa,
	šu-⸢ku$_6$⸣ [(x)]	the fisherman;
	1 ^{d}En-lil$_2$-⸢la$_2$⸣	1 Enlila
	sagi	(to) the cupbearer;
	1 Du-du	1 Dudu
	Ur-lu$_2$ ⸢engar$^{?}$⸣	(to) Urlu, the agricultural manager(?);
	1 Ur-Nin-[x]	1 Ur-Nin…
rev.	Ur-e$_2$-igi-nim	(to) Ur-E'iginim.
	an-ne-šum$_2$	It (=they) have been given to them.
	Be-li$_2$-ṭāb(DUG$_3$)	*Bēlī-ṭāb* (is responsible).
	(blank)	

The document records the assignment of individuals to various professionals and officials.

No. 270 – MS 5003

Letter-order concerning the transfer of a woman, Middle Sargonic, Adab.

obv.	Ama-emeda$_x$(ME.UM)-zi	Ama'ededazi
	mu-ni	(is) her name,
	Šu-Sa-(ras.)-maš-da	with *Šu-Šamaš*
	e-da-ti	she lives.
	Ur-tur nab-be$_2$-a	This is what Urtur says:
	šeš-ĝu$_{10}$ du$_{11}$-ab	"Say to my brother:
	ḫa-mu-ra-šum$_2$-mu	He should hand over her to you!"
rev.	(blank)	

obv. 1: For the same woman, see CUSAS 23 no. 174 (most probably Middle Sargonic) and CUSAS 20 no. 286.

obv. 5: This spelling of the letter-opening formula nab-be$_2$-a is a temporal intermediary between the Early Dynastic IIIb na-e-a and Ur III na-ab-be$_2$-a.

No. 271 – MS 5004

Record concerning the residence of two women and a girl, Middle Sargonic, Adab.

obv.	1 Ama-emeda$_x$(ME.UM)-zi	1 Ama'emedazi;
	1 Nin-kur-ra	1 Ninkura,
	dumu-ni	her daughter;
	Lugal-ša$_3$	with Lugalša,
	aga$_3$-us$_2$-da	the soldier,
	an-da-ti	she lives.
	1 Nin-kala-ga	1 Ninkalaga,

rev.	Ur-u$_4$-su$_{13}$	with Ur-usu,
	šu-i	the barber,
	Lugal-abba$_2$-da	(and) with Lugalabba
	an-da-ti	she lives.
	(blank)	

Note that female individuals, with a child in one case, live in the households of men. This fact may reflect a socio-economic phenomenon widely recorded in early texts, whereby widows and low-ranking women with children live under the aegis of the central public households. Alternatively, these females are slaves.

obv. 3: The word dumu means "son/daughter," since Sumerian lacks grammatical gender. The extensions -nita/munus "male/female" are sometimes added, especially to clarify the biological sex of the individuals, but they are not obligatory.

rev. 1: For this individual, see the commentary to text No. 306 obv. 7.

1.4.3 – Land

No. 272 – MS 2191/27

A note concerning a field, Middle/Classical Sargonic, Adab.

obv.	1(eše$_3$) 1(iku) aša$_5$	1 *eše* 1 *iku* land:
	I$_7$-ki-gal	Ikigal.
	(blank space)	
	⌜engar⌝ Nita-zi-kam	He is the agricultural manager of Nitazi.
	i$_3$-da-ĝal$_2$	It (the land) is available with him (with Ikigal)
	naĝ-ku$_5$	(Situated at) the reservoir for flood control,
rev.	aša$_5$ ^{ĝeš}gigir$_2$	the field "Chariot."
	(blank)	

obv. 1: The personal name Ikigal "River (of) the Big Earth (= Underworld)" appears with and without the determinative for deities in other Early Dynastic and Sargonic texts: see, e.g., BIN 8 no. 250 rev. 2, OIP 14 no. 59 obv. i 1, ECTJ no. 88 obv. i 3.

rev. 1: This field appears elsewhere in the Adab corpus: see, e.g., CUSAS 11 no. 40 rev. ii 7.

1.4.4 – Grain and Grain Products

No. 273 – MS 2191/17

Expenditure of barley flour and *zidgu*-flour, Middle Sargonic, Adab.

obv.	1(bariga) dabin	1 *bariga* of barley flour;
	5 sila$_3$ zi$_3$-gu	5 *sila* of finely ground flour:
	A-ba-ga	to Abaga,
	aša$_5$ ^{d}Dam-gal-nun-še$_3$	for the field (of) Damgalnun(a),
rev.	an-na-šum$_2$	it has been given.
	1(bariga) 2(ban$_2$) Nin$_9$-nin$_9$	1 *bariga* 2 *ban*: to Ninnin,
	Pa$_x$(E×PAP)-unu$_5$(AB)^{ki}-še$_3$	for (the locality) Pa'unu,
	an-na-šum$_2$	it has been given.
	(blank/ruling)	
	iti še-saĝ-sig$_{15}$-ga-am$_3$	In the month Šesaĝsigam.

obv. 2: For zi$_3$-gu, a variety of premium flour, see FAOS 19 p. 242.

obv. 3: There is a vertical wedge after BA, which looks like an erasure.

rev. 3: The same locality appear as Pa$_5$-unu(UNUG)^{ki} in a CS text from Adab, CUSAS 13 no. 21 rev. 4.

No. 274 – MS 2191/24

Account of barley, Middle/Classical Sargonic, Adab.

obv.	90 še gur-saĝ-ĝal$_2$	90 *gursaĝĝal* barley:
	$^{ĝeš+}$A-rin$_2$ dub-sar-ra	to Arina, the scribe,
	i$_3$-na-šum$_2$	one has given.
	še ĝeš-ra-a	The barley (is) threshed.
	I-bir$_5$(NAM)*-ma-lik*	*Yibēr-malik* (is responsible).
rev.	(blank)	

obv. 2: It is a variant writing of the name /Arina/ written A-rin$_2$ and A-^{ĝeš}rin$_2$-a in the volume. Here the original GIŠ has merged with A, which results in a ligature.

1.4.5 – Bread and Beer

This dossier records bread and beer and may be compared to the large number of similar documents associated with the households E'AH and e$_2$-dumu of Early Dynastic/Early Sargonic date. The difference is that the latter are small and usually only one entity appears there. In contrast, this dossier gives a vivid impression of the hierarchy and professional structures within the central households in Sargonic Adab. A notable detail is the high frequency of references to officials and other persons immediately connected to the king. His son is mentioned in one of the texts. The king himself is never mentioned by name. The dates of the texts are not homogeneous in this group. Some tablets look older than others. For example, Nos. 275–78 may be in fact "Early Sargonic."[1] The other texts are definitely later. Both subgroups are edited together because their similar format demonstrates continuity in administrative practice.

Quantities of breads are written with "pointed" numerals whereas numbers of persons are recorded with "round" numerals.

No. 275 – MS 2109/1

Allocation of bread, Early/Middle Sargonic, Adab

obv. i	[n ninda]	[x breads:]
	[...]-⸢zi⸣-da	...zida,
	⸢gala⸣	the cult-singer;
	8 ^{d}En-lil$_2$-le	8: Enlile,
	lu$_2$ lu$_2$-maḫ	the man of the *lumaḫ*-priest;
	8 Sar-ru-e-li	8: *Šarru(m)-'eli*,
	lu$_2$ *Ib-ni-*^{d}Zu:en	the man of *Yibni-Su'en*;
ii	⸢4⸣ ugula *4*	4 overseers: 4 (breads each);
	7 lu$_2$-gub-ba *4*	7 *guards*(?): 4;
	3 ^{ĝeš}gu-za-la$_2$ *4*	3 throne-bearers: 4;

1 Other documents that belong to this subgroup are CUSAS 26 nos. 99–100. Westenholz ascribes them to the Middle Sargonic period.

	1 dub-sar *2*	1 scribe: 2;
	2 nar *6* 1 *4*	2 musicians: 6 (breads); 1 (musician): 4 (breads)
	1 u$_4$-da-tuš *4*	1 jester: 4;
	4 Niĝir-Ab-⸢zu⸣	4: Niĝir-Abzu,
iii	< > Gu$_3$-de$_2$-a	< >: Gude'a;
	1 a-zu anše *4*	1 veterinarian: 4;
	3 Lugal-saĝ	3: Lugalsaĝ;
	1 UR *4*	1 (man of) UR: 4;
	2 GIN$_2$-la$_2$	2: the *GINla*-professional.
	nisig mu-de$_6$	He has brought greens.
	8 Inim-ma-ni-zi	8: Inimanizi;
rev. i	1 i$_3$-du$_8$ *8*	1 doorman: 8;
	6 lu$_2$-ma$_2$-gur$_8$ *4*	6 boatmen: 4;
	2 lu$_2$-^{ĝeš}KAM *4*	2 …*guards*(?): 4;
	3 Za$_3$-mu *4*	3 (people of) Zamu: 4;
	1 sukkal *6* 1 *4*	1 secretary: 6 (breads); 1: 4 (breads);
	1 arad$_2$ zu-ni *4*	1 slave of …: 4;
	3 arad$_2$ ensi$_2$ *4*	3 slaves of the governor: 4;
	1 šu-i *2*	1 barber: 2;
	1 azlag$_7$ *2*	1 fuller: 2;
rev. ii	*4* lu$_2$ Diĝir-ĝa$_2$	4 (breads): the man of Diĝirĝa(be);
	1 šu-ku$_6$ *2*	1 fisherman: 2;
	3 Ur-nu	3: Urnu;
	3 Silim-eš$_3$	3: Silim-eš$_3$.
	ku$_6$ mu-de$_6$	He has brought fish.
	1 nu-kiri$_6$ *2*	1 gardener: 2;
	5 A-ba-^{d}En-lil$_2$	5: Aba-Enlil.
	gi-lam mu-de$_6$	He has brought *gilam*-baskets.
	2 lu$_2$-kiĝ$_2$-bar *3*	2 "people of the work outside": 3;
	⸢*2*⸣ Lugal-ĝeš	2: Lugalĝeš.
iii	udu mu-de$_6$	He has brought sheep.
	4 sipa anše *4*	4 donkey-herds: 4;
	1 (ras.)	1 (erased);
	(blank)	
	[šu-niĝin$_2$ n+] ⸢600⸣ 20 la$_2$ *3* [ninda ½] ⸢sila$_3$⸣	[Total x+] 620 minus 3 [breads of ½] sila.
	[...]-⸢x⸣	[Date]

obv. i 5: lu$_2$-maḫ is a high priest in cults of female deities; see Sallaberger and Huber Vulliet 2005: 628.

obv. ii 2: Based on the context with professionals connected to the court, lu$_2$-gub-ba in these texts does not exemplify the phrase lu$_2$ gub-ba "person in service." A lu$_2$-gub-ba can be associated with ecstatics and prophets, Akk. *maḫḫû*: CAD M[1] 90. Therefore, the term might refer to court prophets. Alternatively, taking the literal meaning of the term, lu$_2$-gub-ba may refer to a kind of doorman or bodyguard.

obv. ii 6: For u_4-da-tuš, a jester and probably a bear-tamer, see D'Agostino 2012: 89–99.

obv. iii 2: See CAD M^2 199 for references to the equation a-zu anše = Akk. *muna'išu* in lexical lists. The term is extremely rare in administrative records. It appears in ED Lu_2 B 22, MSL 12 p. 13.

obv. iii 5: GIN_2-la_2 is a professional term that appears rarely. Despite the brief discussions by Sallaberger 1994: 138 with n. 13 and Neumann 2001: 41 n. 20, the identity and functions of this professional remain enigmatic.

obv. iii 6: The same phrase with GIN_2-la_2 in the preceding line appears also in CUSAS 26 no. 99 iii 6–7. However, it is not certain whether the individuals who appear in the entries before the phrase "such and such goods mu-de_6" are the deliverers of these goods. It may be an impersonal statement "one has brought." Note the absence of numerals or measures in connection to these goods.

rev. i 3: Besides several texts in this volume and CUSAS 26 no. 99, the term lu_2-^{ĝeš}KAM appears in ECTJ no. 26 obv. i 2' and in OSP 1 no. 94 obv. ii 2, where it is written lu^{sic}-^{ĝeš}KAM. The term is neither translated nor commented on in both publications. An interpretation lu_2-ĝeš-kam (*lu_2=ĝeš=(a)k=am) is unlikely. The sign KAM with the determinative for wood appears in the word ^{ĝeš}$utul_2$(KAM), which is a large bowl, Akk. *dipāru*; see MC 4 pp. 16 f. However, an interpretation lu_2-^{ĝeš}$utul_2$ would be presumptuous. I tentatively suggest that lu_2-^{ĝeš}KAM are guards where the wooden object may be a sort of weapon. These persons appear side by side with lu_2-gub-ba, literally "people who stand."

rev. i 6: Cf. the personal names $ARAD_{(2)}$-*su-ni* in BIN 8 no. 160 rev. i 7, MVN 3 no. 102 obv. 5; and $ARAD_2$-zu-ni in CUSAS 27 passim. Here and in text No. 278 obv. ii 5, it could also be a personal name, despite the fact that the context does not favor this interpretation.

rev. ii 1: AN-$ĝa_2$ is likely an abbreviation of the personal name A_2-diĝir-$ĝa_2$-ta "By the strength of my god."

rev. ii 9: The interpretation of the professional title lu_2-$kiĝ_2$-bar, literally "persons (of) the work outside," is uncertain. The term appears in CUSAS 13 no. 86 obv. ii 3 as lu_2-$kiĝ_2$-bar-ra. Maiocchi's interpretation of kin bar as "to cut with the sickle" seems unlikely. Cf. also UTI 3 no. 1935 (Ur III, Umma) obv. i 2 for *ĝuruš*-workmen assigned to/for $kiĝ_2$-bar-ra. Similarly to $kiĝ_2$-gal, the term may refer to a professional concerned with labor ($kiĝ_2$).

No. 276 – MS 2109/2

Allocation of bread, Early/Middle Sargonic, Adab.

obv. i	*8* ninda	8 breads:
	PU$_3$.ŠA-*Aš$_{11}$-tar$_2$*	PUŠA-*'Aštar*,
	su-da-um	the *suda'um*;
	2 lu$_2$ *3*	2 (of his) people: 3 (breads);
	8 Lugal-ku$_3$	8 (breads): Lugalku,
	lu$_2$ Ad-da	the man of Adda,
	udu-niga	Fattened sheep
	mu-laḫ$_5$	he has brought.
	8 I$_8$(ENGUR)-*ba-um*	8 (breads): *Yiba'um*,
ii	lu$_2$ saĝ zaḫ$_3$	the fugitive free individuals and slaves,
	mu-laḫ$_5$-eš$_2$	he has brought them.
	8 EN.⌜PAP⌝-*il*	8 (breads): ENPAP-*'il*,
	dub-sar	the scribe
	lugal	of the king;
	5 NI-NI	5 (breads): NINI,
	aga$_3$-us$_2$ ensi$_2$	the soldier of the governor;
	8 Pu$_3$-i$_3$-li$_2$	8: *Pû-'ili*;
	8 Šu-Aš$_{11}$-tar$_2$	8: *Šu-'Aštar*.
iii	aga$_3$-us$_2$ lugal-me	they are the soldiers of the king;
	40 ugula-me ⌜*4*⌝	40 overseers: 4 (breads each);
	8 I$_3$-li$_2$-li$_2$	8: *'Il-'ili*,
	lu$_2$ Il$_2$	the man of Il(a),
	dumu lugal	son of the king;
	3 Lu$_2$-da-gi	3: Ludagi;
	5 Ama-Ab-zu-si	5: Ama-Abzusi;
	5 Gala	5: Gala;
rev. i	2 šu-i *6*-ta	2 barbers: 6 (breads) each;
	1 ḫe$_2$-dab$_5$ *8*	1 *ḫedab*-worker: 8;
	8 Lugal-a$_2$	8: Lugal'a;
	10 En-NE-la-ba	10: EnNElaba;
	7 ḫe$_2$-dab$_5$ *4* 1 5	7 *ḫedab*-workers: 4 (breads); 1 (worker): 5 (breads);
	Lugal-a$_2$	Lugal-a;
	8 I$_3$-li$_2$-en-nun	8: *'Ilī*-ennun;
	4 I-sar-ru	4: *Isarru*,
	azlag$_7$	the fuller;
ii	5 Ti-ĜAR-U	5: TiĜARU,
	a-zu$_5$	the physician;
	20 *6* aga$_3$-us$_2$ ensi$_2$-me	26 soldiers of the governor.
	ki-ḪA-ka i$_3$-na$_2$-am$_3$	They lie in the place of … (?)
	Aja$_2$-de$_5$-de$_5$	Ajadede
	maškim-bi$_x$(DUG)	(is) its commissioner.
	(blank space)	
iii	(blank space)	
	šu-niĝin$_2$-bi 240 la$_2$ 5 ninda	Total: 235 breads.

	u$_4$ 20 *4*	Day 24:
	A-ga-de$_3^{ki}$	Agade.
	u$_4$ *4*	Day 4:
	iti Šuba$_3$(MUŠ$_3$×ZA)-nun	month Šubanun.

obv. i 3: See SCTRAH no. 310 obv. 4, commentary p. 224 with additional references for *si/su/si$_{11}$-da-um*, an Akkadian term that refers to an occupation of uncertain function.

obv. ii 1–2: Cf. text No. 276 obv. i 7–8 for the same syntactical construction. Lu$_2$ saĝ zaḫ$_3$ is the object of the transitive verbal form mu=n=laḫ$_5$=eš$_2$, where /=eš$_2$/ marks the plurality of the individuals in contrast to the form without this marker, which refers to sheep.

obv. iii 4–5: It is not certain which king is meant. This person does not appear in Sargonic royal inscriptions.

rev. i 2: See SCTRAH no. 244 obv. 8 commentary for this low-ranking worker.

rev. ii 4: The line remains obscure.

rev. iii 2–5: This double date is notable.

No. 277 – MS 2109/3

Allocation of bread, Early/Middle Sargonic, Adab.

obv. i	10 *6* ninda	16 breads:
	A-ḫa-ḫa	Aḫaḫa;
	10 *6* BU-ra	16: BUra.
	aga$_3$-us$_2$ lugal-me	They are the soldiers of the king.
	6 Ur-pisaĝ	6: Ur-pisaĝ,
	lu$_2$ *Ga-ri$_2$-i$_3$-lum*	the man of *Garyī-'ilum*;
	6 E$_2$-šudu$_3$	6: Ešudu;
	1 šu-ku$_6$ *2*	1 fisherman: 2;
ii	2 šu-ku$_6$ *2*	2 fishermen: 2;
	5 Ur-Šubur	5: Ur-Šubur
	3 Ur-nu	3: Urnu;
	5 Igi-si$_4$ ugula	5: Igisi, the overseer;
	3 Ur-ki	3: Urki,
	lu$_2^!$-nisig	the vegetable grower;
	3 Eše$_2$-la$_2$	3: Ešela;
	3 Za$_3$-mu	3: Zamu;
	3 ^{d}Utu-i$_3$-kuš$_2$	3: Utu-ikuš;
	20 5 banšur	25 (for) the table;
	5 Ur-Šubur	5: Ur-Šubur,
	nu-kiri$_6$	the gardener;
iii	*8* Du-du	8: Dudu;
	8 Ur-^{ĝeš}gigir$_2$	8: Ur-gigir.
	aga$_3$-us$_2$ lugal-me	They are the soldiers of the king.
	8 EN.PAP-*il*	8: ENPAP-'*il*;
	8 NIM (ras.)	8: NIM:

	lu$_2$ *Iš-tup-pum*-me	they are the persons of *Ištuppum*.
	8 I-sar-⸢um⸣	8 *Isar'um*,
	aga$_3$-us$_2$ lugal	the soldier of the king;
rev. i	4 ⸢lu$_2$⸣ *Aš$_{11}$-⸢tar$_2$?⸣*-[...] ⸢*8*⸣	4 man of *'Aštar*-[...] 8 (breads each);
	8 Me-a	8: Me'a;
	8 Šu-Aš$_{11}$-tar$_2$	8: *Šu-'Aštar*;
	20 Lu$_2$-ni	20: Luni:
	kuš$_7$ lugal-me	they are the animal-managers of the king.
ii–iii	(blank)	

No. 278 – MS 2109/4

Allocation of bread, Early/Middle Sargonic, Adab.

obv. i	[n] ninda	x breads:
	[x]-NE-NE	…NENE;
	10 UŠ-*bum*	10: UŠ*bum*;
	10 *I*$_{3}$-*lu*-GAR$_{3}$	10: *'Ilu(m)*-GAR
	10 Ur-dub-la$_{2}$	10: Urdubla;
	10 *Pa*$_{2}$-*ša*$_{3}$-*ḫi-i*$_{3}$-*lum*	10: *Pašāhī-'ilum*;
	10 A-ba-^{d}En-lil$_{2}$	10: Aba-Enlil;
	10 Aš-da$^{?}$-X	10: …;
	10 Ensi$_{2}$-gal-zu	10: Ensigalzu;
ii	*8* Za-bad$_{3}$	8: Zabad;
	8 Diĝir-ab-gu	8: Diĝirabgu;
	8 *I*$_{3}$-*li*$_{2}$-en-nun	8: *'Ilī*-ennun;
	8 Ur-^{d}Inana	8: Ur-Inana,
	arad$_{2}$ zu-ni	the slave of …;
	1 arad$_{2}$ ensi$_{2}$ *8*	1 slave of the governor: 8 (breads);
	8 *E-li*-šilig(GIŠGAL×IGI)	8: *Eli*ŠILIG;
	8 Ur-^{d}Inana	8: Ur-Inana:
	sipa anše-me	they are donkey-herds.
	8 Za$_{3}$-mu	8: Zamu,
	dumu Ur-^{d}Nin-mug	son of Ur-Ninmug;
iii	*5* Ti-ĜAR-U	5: TiĜARU,
	a-zu$_{5}$	the physician;
	6 Diĝir-ab-ga	6: Diĝirabga;
	1 ad-KID *8*	1 reed-worker: 8 (breads);
	1 se$_{12}$ 10	1 blind worker: 10 (breads):
	ḫe$_{2}$-dab$_{5}$-me	they are *ḫedab*-workers;
	8 sagi *4* 4 *2*	8 cupbearers: 4 (breads); 4 (cupbearers): 2 (breads);
	3 ma$_{2}$-laḫ$_{5}$ *5*	3 sailors: 5 (breads);
	3 dub-sar *4*	3 scribes: 4 (breads);
	2 šu-i *6* 3 *2*	2 barbers: 6 (breads); 3 (barbers): 2 (breads);
	8 Lu$_{2}$-da-gi	8 (breads): Ludagi;
	10 sukkal-me [*n*]	10: they are secretaries: [x];
iv	20 ⌈x-x⌉ nu-banda$_{3}$-me [*n*]	20: they are … (of) the supervisor: [x];
	20 *3* sipa anše lugal-me *2*	23: they are the donkey-herds of the king: 2 (breads);
	3 šu-ku$_{6}$ *2*	3 fishermen: 2 (breads);
	5 ^{d}En-lil$_{2}$	5: Enlil:
	ku$_{6}$ mu-de$_{6}$	he has brought fish.
	20 la$_{2}$ *2* Ša$_{3}$-nu-ĝal$_{2}$	18: Šanuĝal;
	20 la$_{2}$ *2* Ni$_{3}$-du$_{7}$	18: Nidu:
	aga$_{3}$-⌈us$_{2}$⌉ [x-me]	[they are] the soldiers of …;
	[break]	…
rev. i	[break]	…
	⌈kuš$_{7}$⌉ [lugal$^{?}$]	the animal-manager [of the king?];
	40 la$_{2}$ *2* *A-li*$_{2}$-*li*$_{2}$	38: *'Al-'ilī*

	KU-lugal	the ... of the king;
	10 la$_2$ *1* Silim-^{d}Utu	9: Silim-Utu,
	nu-banda$_3$	the supervisor;
	10 la$_2$ *1* *I-bi$_2$-Il$_3$-a-ba$_4$*	9: *Yibbi-'Ilaba,*
	lu$_2$ ^{d}X-igi	the man of ..igi,
	sukkal	the secretary;
	10 la$_2$ *1* A.BU.BU	9: ABUBU,
	aga$_3$-us$_2$ ensi$_2$	the soldier of the governor;
ii	⸢10 la$_2$ *1*⸣ *I-bi$_2$-Il$_3$-a-ba$_4$*	9: *Yibbi-'Ilaba,*
	IB	the IB-official;
	5 ⸢Ama⸣-Ab-⸢zu⸣-si	5: Ama-Abzusi;
	5 Tum-al	5: Tumal;
	5 Nam-zi	5: Namzi;
	5 Lugal-ĝeš	5: Lugalĝeš;
	5 Ur-^{d}Eš$_{23}$-peš	5: Ur-Ešpeš;
	5 Ĝiri$_3$-ni	5: Ĝirini;
	5 Ur-diĝir	5: Urdiĝir:
	sa$_{12}$-du$_5$-me	they are land-recorders.
	⸢ĝeštin⸣ mu-de$_6$	He has brought wine.
	1 munus ḫe$_2$-dab$_5$ *8*	1 woman, the *ḫedab*-worker: 8 (breads).
iii	*Iš-tup-pum*	*Ištuppum*
	maškim-bi$_x$(DUG)	(is) its commissioner.
	3 šu-ku$_6$ *3*	3 fishermen: 3 (breads);
	5 Ur-Šubur	5: Ur-Šubur;
	3 šu-ku$_6$ *2*	3 fishermen: 2 (breads);
	5 Ur-u$_4$-su$_{13}$	5: Urusu:
	ḫa-mu-tum$_2$	he should bring it here.
	3 nu-kiri$_6$ *3*	3 gardeners: 3 (breads);
	5 Lu$_2$-lil-la	5: Lulila.
	gi-lam	*gilam*-baskets
	mu-de$_6$	he has brought.
	1080 la$_2$ 10 ninda	1070 breads:
	lu$_2$ ni$_3$-⸢dab$_5$⸣-me	they are requisitioners.
iv	(blank space)	
	šu-niĝin$_2$-bi 1620 *2* ninda	Its total: 1622 breads.
	u$_4$ 20 5	Day 25,
	iti a$_2$-ki-ti	month Akiti.

obv. iii 5: See SCTRAH p. 209 for se$_{12}$(SIG$_7$)-(a) "blind" or "blinded" workers with additional references.

rev. i 4'–5': The presence of the well-known supervisor Silim-Utu in this document may suggest that this and similar texts belong to the Early Sargonic period or that he held his post even after his former superior Meskigala had been already removed.

rev. ii 12: Note that women could also belong to the class of ḫe$_2$-dab$_5$ workers.

rev. iii 6: See the commentary to text No. 306 obv. 7 for this individual.

rev. iii 13: The term lu$_2$ ni$_3$-dab$_5$-(ba), literally "people who take things," is amply attested in the Ur III corpus and denotes the recipients of allocations from central households. Thus it is one of the general terms for household employees or dependents.

No. 279 – MS 2191/19

Account of bread and beer, Middle Sargonic, Adab.

The tablet was written by the same scribe as CUSAS 23 no. 112, SCTRAH no. 22 and other texts in SCTRAH.

obv.	1(ban$_2$) ninda 1 kaš	1 *ban* bread, 1 (jar of) beer:
	Sar-ru-us$_2$(ARAD)-GI	it is (for) *Šarrūs(su)-kēn*
	Ma$_2$-ad-ga^{ki}	(when) he was on the way
	im-du-am$_3$	to Madga.
	5 sila$_3$ ninda 5 sila$_3$ kaš	5 *sila* bread, 5 *sila* beer:
	Aja$_2$-de$_5$-de$_5$	Ajadede.
	5 sila$_3$ ninda 5 sila$_3$ kaš	5 *sila* bread, 5 *sila* beer:

	Diĝir-KA-*er*	DiĝirKA-*(M)er*.
rev.	še gur$_x$(|ŠE.ŠE|.KIN)-de$_3$	(When) they were going to harvest (crops).
	im-er$_{14}$(DU.DU)-am$_3$	
	(blank space)	
	iti eše$_2$-gar$_3$-ra-šu-ĝar-am$_3$	In the month Ešegarašuĝara.
	(blank space)	

obv. 3: For this locality located somewhere in the Transtigridian area, see Schrakamp 2015a: 238 fn. 459.

obv. 8–rev. 2: For the name (Diĝir)-KA-*Me-er*, see CUSAS 27 nos. 126 rev. i 19, 158 obv. 1, 159 obv. 4 and 174 rev. 7, and text No. 263 rev. ii 2 in this volume. Cf. Diĝir-KA-*Me-er* in the Maništusu Obelisk (ELTS no. 40) D v 3. The verb in the present text suggests that the subject of the action was plural.

No. 280 – MS 2191/21

Account of bread, Middle Sargonic, Adab.

obv.	*8* ninda	8 breads:
	lu$_2$ Za$_3$-mu-me	(for) the people of Zamu;
	5 ugula *4*	5 overseers: 4 (breads each);
	3 nar *6* 1 *8*	3 musicians: 6 (breads); 1 (musician): 8 (breads);
	1 mar-tu *8*	1 Amorite: 8;
	8 TUR-TUR *6*	8 children (minors): 6;
	10 Gu$_3$-de$_2$-a	10: Gude'a;
	<ras.> dub-sar < >	< > scribe(s) < >
rev.	<ras.> gu-za-la$_2$ < >	< > throne-bearer(s) < >
	1 aša$_5$-ga u$_4$-zal-⸢la⸣ 5	1 (person) in the field on the watch: 5 (breads).
	šita-iri	The *šita*-official of the city.
	(blank space)	
	šu-niĝin$_2$ 120 5 ninda ½ sila$_3$	Total: 125 breads of ½ sila.
	iti mu-tir	Month Mutir.

rev. 2: The line is not entirely clear, although it is certain that it records a single person who receives five breads. The term u$_4$-zal-la refers to the third watch of the night, the early morning.

rev. 3: This official is probably the commissioner (maškim) of the transaction.

No. 281 – MS 2250

Allocation of bread to a sick worker, Midde Sargonic, Adab.

obv.	1 lu$_2$-tu-ra	1 sick person:
	4 ninda sila$_3$-ta	4 breads of <1$^?$> *sila* each.
	ugula Aja$_2$-de$_5$-de$_5$	(His) overseer: Ajadede.
	iti Šuba$_2$(ZA.MUŠ$_3$)-nun	Month Šubanun.
rev.	(blank)	

obv. 3: See text No. 276 rev. ii 5 for the same individual in connection to bread.

No. 282 – MS 4189

Allocation of bread, Middle Sargonic, Adab.

obv. i	[1 line missing]	…
	[...]-⸢x *3*⸣ ninda sila$_3$	… 3: breads (of 1) *sila*;
	5 šandana	5 (breads): the orchard-administrator;
	20 la$_2$ 2 ĝuruš-tab(*2*) *3*	18 *ĝuruštab*-workers: 3 (breads each);
	5 Lu$_2$-^{d}Aš$_8$-gi$_4$	5 (breads): Lu-Ašgi;
	10 aga$_3$-us$_2$(ARAD) *3*	10 soldiers: 3 (breads each);
	5 Ur$_2$-maḫ	5: Urmaḫ;
	5 ugula *4*	5 overseers: 4 (breads each);
	11 lu$_2$-ma$_2$-gur$_8$ *3*	11 boatmen: 3;
	2 aga$_3$-us$_2$ *3*	2 soldiers: 3;
ii	[*n*] ⸢Ur⸣-^{d}Inana	x: Ur-Inana;
	1 lu$_2$ *3*	1 person: 3:
	A-bi$_2$-^{d}Tišpak(MUŠ$_2$)	(of) ʾ*Abī*-Tišpak;
	12 lu$_2$ ma$_2$-gal-gal *3*	12 crew of large ships: 3;
	1 ugula ma$_2$-gal-gal *5*	1 the overseer (of) large ships: 5;
	6 sagi *3*	6 cupbearers: 3;
	10 la$_2$ 1 i$_3$-ra$_2$-ra$_2$ *2*	9 oil-pressers: 2;
	4 ugula i$_3$-ra$_2$-ra$_2$	4: the overseer of the oil-pressers;
	1 nagar *2*	1 carpenter: 2;
	2 tug$_2$-du$_8$ *2*	2 fullers: 2;
rev. i	2 i$_3$-du$_8$ *2*	2 doormen: 2;
	2 šu-i$_2$ *3*	2 barbers: 3;
	⸢2⸣ [+n aga$_3$]-us$_2$(ARAD)	2+x (breads): the soldier;
	[*n* ...]-⸢zi⸣	x: …zi;
	[n] ⸢simug⸣ *2*	x smiths: 2;
	[n ...] *3*	…: 3
	[n nu]-kiri$_6$ *2*	x gardeners: 2;
	[...]-⸢ŠIM$^?$⸣	…,
	[... aga$_3$]-⸢us$_2$⸣(ARAD)	the soldier.
	10 ⸢ki⸣-[...]	10 …;
	6 dub-sar 5 4 *3* 6 *1*	6 scribes: 5 (breads), 4: 3 (breads); 6: 1 (bread each).

ii	(blank space)	
	[šu-niĝin$_2$] 430 [+n ninda] *1* ⸢sila$_3$⸣	[Total:] 430 [+n breads of] 1 sila.
	(blank space)	
	<iti> ĝa$_2$-udu-ur$_4$	<Month> Ĝa'udu'ur.
	u$_4$ 14-kam	It is (the allocation) of the 14th day.
	[break; nothing lost]	

obv. i 4: ĝuruš-tab is equated to Akk. *batūlu* "young adolescent man"; CAD B 174. This is an abbreviated writing of ĝuruš-tab-nu-zu, literally "young man who has not known a partner"; see Lu$_2$ III 81–82 = MSL 12 p. 126. In the present text, the meaning is different. Cf. a class of workers ĝuruš tab-ba that appears in Ur III documents. Their designation, literally "doubled" or "(with) companion," may imply that they worked in pairs. The term appears already in ED texts and is sometimes mistakenly transliterated ĝuruš-min as, e.g., in CUSAS 23 no. 52 from ED IIIb Umma.

obv. ii 4: See FAOS 15/1 p. 109 for this term, which designates crew members of large ships.

rev. i 7: The most probable restorations are either [nu]-kiri$_6$ "gardener" or [lu$_2$]-nisig "vegetable grower."

No. 283 – MS 4277/1

Allocation of bread, Middle Sargonic, Adab.

Note the appearance of a sister and a maid of the governor at the beginning of the document.

obv. i	10 *6* ninda ⸢x⸣-[x]	16 … breads:
	nin ensi$_2$	(for) the sister of the governor;
	8 Ma-ma-i$_3$-li$_2$	8 (for) *Mama-'ilī*,
	geme$_2$ ensi$_2$	the maid of the governor;
	1 ugula *4*	1 overseer: 4 (breads);
	4 dub-⸢sar⸣ [*n*]	4 scribes: [x];
	10 Gu$_3$-⸢de$_2$⸣-[a]	10: Gude'a;
	1 nar *4* 2 *8*	1 musician: 4 (breads); 2 (musicians): 8 (breads);
	1 u$_4$-da-tuš *6*	1 jester: 6;
	1 mar-tu *8*	1 Amorite: 8;
	4 Ur-ḪAR	4 (breads): UrḪAR;
	1 nagar *4*	1 carpenter: 4;
	4 Lugal-ĝeš	4: Lugalĝeš;
ii	*4* Ti-e$_2$	4: Ti'e;
	8 U$_2$-tuku	8: Utuku;
	6 Mu-⸢ni⸣-uri$_3$	6: Muni'uri;
	10 Ur-^{d}Iškur	10: Ur-Iškur;
	10 E$_2$-pu$_3$-li	10: Epuli;
	6 Saĝ-diĝir-tuku	6: Saĝdiĝirtuku;
	[n] sukkal *4*	x secretaries: 4;
	[*n*] Inim-gi	x: Inimgi;
	1 šu-ku$_6$ *5*	1 fisherman: 5;
	4 E$_2$-dam-si	4: Edamsi;

	8 dumu Az-me	8: the sons/daughters of Az;
	20 la$_2$ 2 ḫe$_2$-dab$_5$ *6*	18 *ḫedab*-workers: 6:
	Inim-ma-ni-zi	(of) Inimanizi.
rev. i	3 ḫe$_2$-dab$_5$ *6 6 4*	3 *ḫedab*-workers: 6 (breads each); 6 (workers): 4 (breads each):
	e$_2$-gal	(of) the palace.
	7 gu-za-la$_2$ *4*	7 throne-bearers: 4;
	5 sipa anše *4*	5 donkey-herds: 4;
	3 lu$_2$-^{ĝeš}KAM *4*	3 … *guards*(?): 4;
	6 saĝ ni$_3$-kas$_4$ *6*	6 slaves of …: 6;
	1 nagar *4*	1 carpenter: 4;
	1 lu$_2$-gub-ba *4*	1 *guard*(?): 4;
	5 šu-i *2*	5 barbers: 2;
	3 azlag$_7$ *2*	3 fullers: 2;
	2 Inim-ma-ni-zi *4*	2 (persons of) Inimanizi: 4;
	20 la$_2$ 1 Ur-ma-nu-gal *4* 1 *6*	19 (persons of) Urmanugal: 4 (breads); 1 (person): 6 (breads);
ii	[n] ⸢A⸣.BU.BU *4*	x (persons of) ABUBU: 4;
	[n] ⸢ad⸣-KID *4*	x reed-worker(s): 4;
	[n] ⸢ma$_2$⸣-laḫ$_5$ *4*	x sailor(s): 4;
	1 šidim *4*	1 builder: 4;
	1 EREN-da-ni *4*	1 (man/person of) ERENdani: 4 (breads);
	1 šu-ku$_6$ *2*	1 fisherman: 2;
	5 Ur-^{d}Inana	5: Ur-Inana:
	ku$_6$ mu-de$_6$	he has brought fish.
	1 lu$_2$-ma$_2$-gur$_8$ [*n*]	1 boatman: [x];
	(blank space)	
	šu+niĝin$_2$ 600 la$_2$ *3* ninda ½ / (ras.) sila$_3$	Total: 597 breads of ½ (erasure) *sila*.
	iti Šuba$_3$(MUŠ$_3$×ZA)-nun	Month Šubanun.
	u$_4$ *20* la$_2$ *2*	Day 18.

obv. i 1–4: The word nin "lady" may refer also to the wife of the governor. See CUSAS 26 no. 174 obv. i 6 where nin refers to the wife of Naram-Suen.

obv. ii 5: See SCTRAH no. 65 obv. 2 commentary p. 96 for this individual in other Adab texts. There the name is rendered in transliteration and translation ('Apuli) as Akkadian, although no etymology is provided.

obv. ii 11: Cf. Az nu-banda$_3$ in text No. 207 obv. i 2.

rev. i 6: The term ni$_3$-kas$_4$ of uncertain meaning appears in connection to several professional titles: sukkal "secretary" in text No. 1 rev. iii 8 and unu$_3$ "cowherd" in text No. 258 obv. ii 1. Here, saĝ "head," which usually means "slave" in this period, appears as the main element. Pomponio and Visicato interpret ni$_3$-kas$_4$ as "travel"; see their translation of CUSAS 20 no. 18. See also text No. 348 rev. 9, where the term appears as an element in a personal name. In Adab texts, the term seems to refer to an administrative unit.

No. 284 – MS 4277/2

Allocation of bread, Middle Sargonic, Adab.

obv. i	[*n* ninda x]-BU	x … [breads]:
	[nin] ⸢ensi$_2$⸣	[the sister of] the governor;
	[*n Ma*]-⸢*ma*⸣-*i$_3$-li$_2$*	x: *Mama-'ilī*,
	[geme$_2$] ⸢ensi$_2$⸣	[the maid] of the governor;
	[…]-⸢zi⸣	x …zi;
	[x]-⸢x⸣	…
	[…]-⸢x⸣	…
	[x]-⸢x⸣ *8*	…: 8 (breads);
	[…]-⸢ESIR$_4$⸣(GI%GI)	…;
	[…]-ki […]-ma	…;
	[…]-me	they are …;
	[…]-⸢x⸣	…
	⸢1 E$_2$⸣-[pu$_3$]-⸢li⸣ [*n*]	1: Epuli [x (breads)];
	6 Saĝ-[diĝir-tuku]	6: Saĝ[diĝirtuku];
ii	*5* Ur-^{d}Iškur	5: Ur-Iškur;
	1 ⸢nar⸣ 5 2 *6* 1 *8*	1 musician: 5 (breads); 2 (musicians): 6 (breads); 1 (musician): 8 (breads);
	1 ⸢u$_4$⸣-da-tuš *6*	1 jester: 6;
	4 ⸢Ur⸣-ḪAR	4: UrḪAR;
	1 mar-tu *8*	1 Amorite: 8;
	10 Gu$_3$-de$_2$-a	10 Gude'a;
	4 Ti-e$_2$	4: Ti'e;
	3 Lugal-saĝ	3: Lugalsaĝ;
	3 sukkal *4*	3 secretaries: 4;
	2 ugula *4*	2 overseers: 4;
	4 dub-sar *4*	4 scribes: 4;
	[…]-⸢IM⸣	…
	[n …] ⸢abba$_2$⸣ *4*	n … (of) the elder(s)(?): 4;
	[*ca.* 2 lines broken]	…
rev. i	[1 line missing]	…
	⸢3⸣ [… *n*]	3 [… x (breads)];
	5 sipa-[anše *n*]	5 [donkey]-herds: x;
	4 lu$_2$-⸢^{ĝeš}KAM⸣ *8*	4 … *guards*(?): 8;
	1 lu$_2$-gub-ba *8*	1 *guard*(?): 8;
	20 Ur-ma-nu-gal *8*	20 (persons of) Urmanugal: 8;
	14 lu$_2$-ma$_2$-gur$_8$ *4*	14 boatmen: 4;
	5 šu-i *4*	5 barbers: 4;
	2 azlag$_7$ *4*	2 fullers: 4;
	1 A.BU.BU *4*	1 (man of) ABUBU: 4;
	6 saĝ ni$_3$-kas$_4$ *6*	6 slaves of …: 6;
	1 Inim-ma-ni-zi *4*	1: Inimanizi: 4 (breads);
	4 Inim-gi	4: Inimgi;

	8 U$_2$-tuku	8: Utuku;
ii	*4* Lugal-ĝeš	4: Lugalĝeš;
	⸢20⸣ la$_2$ 2 ḫe$_2$-dab$_5$ *6*	18 *ḫedab*-workers: 6:
	⸢Inim⸣-ma-ni-zi	(of) Inimanizi;
	4 ḫe$_2$-dab$_5$ *6* 3 *4*	4 *ḫedab*-workers: 6; 3 (workers): 4:
	e$_2$-gal	(of) the palace.
	8 Ur-sipa-da	8: Ursipada,
	a-zu	the physician;
	10 ninda lu$_2$ Gu$_3$-de$_2$-a-me	10 breads: the people of Gude'a.
	(blank space)	
	šu+niĝin$_2$ 900 *2* ninda ½ sila$_3$	Total: 902 breads (of) ½ sila.
	⸢iti⸣ Šuba$_3$(MUŠ$_3$×ZA)-nun	Month Šubanun.
	[u$_4$] *11*	[Day] 11.

No. 285 – MS 4277/3

Allocation of bread, Middle Sargonic, Adab.

obv.	3 gu-za-la$_2$ *2*	3 throne-bearers: 2 (breads each);
	3 sipa anše *2*	3 donkey-herds: 2;
	1 lu$_2$-gub-ba *2*	1 *guard*(?): 2;
	4 lu$_2$-^{ĝeš}KAM *2*	4 … *guards*(?): 2;
	2 Inim-ma-⸢ni⸣-[zi *n*]	2 (persons of) Inimmanizi: [x];
	⸢4⸣ Ur-ma-[nu-gal *n*]	4 (persons of) Urmanugal [x];
	1 nagar [*n*]	1 carpenter: [x];
	4 šu-⸢i⸣ [x]	4 barbers: [x];
	1 ⸢azlag$_7$⸣ [x]	1 fuller: [x];
rev.	1 ⸢A⸣.BU.BU [x]	1 (man of) ABUBU: [x].
	(blank)	

The obverses of this and the following two documents are convex and their reverses are more or less flat.

No. 286 – MS 4277/4

Allocation of bread, Middle Sargonic, Adab.

obv.	2 gu-za-la$_2$ *2*	2 throne-bearers: 2 (breads each);
	2 sipa anše *2*	2 donkey-herds: 2;
	3 lu$_2$-^{ĝeš}KAM *2*	3 … *guards*(?): 2;
	⸢2⸣ lu$_2$-gub-ba *2*	2 *guards*(?): 2;
	16 Ur-ma-nu-gal *2*	16 (people of) Urmanugal: 2 (breads each);
	1 nagar 2	1 carpenter: 2;
	3 lu$_2$-ma$_2$-gur$_8$ *2*	3 boatmen: 2;
rev.	2 Inim-ma-ni-zi *2*	2 (persons of) Inimanizi: 2.
	(blank)	

No. 287 – MS 4277/5

Allocation of bread, Middle Sargonic, Adab.

obv.	[*n* …] ⸢x-x⸣ […]	…
	[šu]-i	the barber;
	8 Ur$_2$-ni	8 (breads): Urni,
	nar	the musician,
	5 E$_3$-gin$_7$	5 (breads): Egin,
	nar	the musician;
	5 sipa anše Ur-Ma-ma	5 (breads): the donkey-herd (of) Ur-Mama.
rev.	(blank)	

No. 288 – MS 4199

Allocation of bread, Middle/Classical Sargonic, Adab.

obv. i	[n ninda *n*] ⸢sila$_3$⸣	[x breads of x] *sila*:
	[...]-⸢da⸣	...da,
	maškim gada	the commissioner of flax;
	[10] la$_2$ *1* Ur-niĝar	9: Ur-niĝar;
	[10] la$_2$ *1* Ur-lu$_2$	9: Urlu:
	⸢aga$_3$⸣-us$_2$(ARAD) lugal-me	they are soldiers of the king;
	[n] Aja$_2$-KA-du$_3$	x: AjaKAdu,
	lu$_2$-kišib$_3$(DUB)	the cylinder-seal keeper;
	10 la$_2$ *1* Niĝir-kisal-le	9: Niĝirkisale,
	aga$_3$-us$_2$ lugal	the soldier of the king;
	10 la$_2$ *1* *I$_3$-li$_2$-a-ḫi*	9: *'Ilī-'aḫī*,
	lu$_2$ Me-luḫ	the man (of) Meluḫ(ḫa);
	10 la$_2$ *1* ⸢x⸣-ni-sig	9: ...nisig,
	⸢lu$_2$⸣-kišib$_3$	the cylinder-seal keeper;
ii	10 la$_2$ *1* ⸢Gala⸣(ARAD.⸢KU⸣)	9: Gala,
	maškim še	the commissioner of barley;
	10 la$_2$ *1* Gal-zu	9: Galzu,
	maškim ma$_2$ Dilmun	the commissioner of ships (from/to) Dilmun;
	10 la$_2$ *1* *Zaq-tum*	9: *Zaqtum*;
	20 la$_2$ *2* Du-du	18: Dudu,
	lu$_2$ *Sum-lum*	the man of *Šum(um-'i)lum*.
	2 lu$_2$ 10 la$_2$ *1*-ta	2 persons 9 each,
	lu$_2$ Du-du	they are the persons of Dudu
	mu *2*-me	of the 2nd year.
	20 la$_2$ *2* Ku$_3$-ga	18: Kuga;
	10 la$_2$ *1* Amar-^{d}Ašnan(ŠE.ŠE.NIR)	9: Amar-Ašnan,
	dumu Lugal-e	son of Lugale,
	lu$_2$ Me-⸢x⸣	the man of Me...;
	4 Ti-ĜAR-⸢U⸣	4: TiĜARU;
	4 Gala ⸢nagar⸣	4: Gala, the carpenter;
rev. i	10 la$_2$ *1* *Be-li$_2$*-GAR$_3$	9: *Bēlī*-GAR,
	lu$_2$-kišib$_3$	the cylinder-seal keeper;
	10 la$_2$ *1* *E-li-iš-ta$_2$-kal$_2$*	9: *'Eliš-takal,*
	sagi [*I*]-*mi*-diĝir	the cupbearer of *Yimit-'ilim*;
	10 la$_2$ *1* *Pa$_2$*-⸢*saḫ$_4$*⸣(GU%⸢GU⸣)-^{d}⸢x⸣	9: *Pasaḫ*...,
	lu$_2$-tukul [(x)]	the *bodyguard*;
	20 [...]-⸢x⸣ *4*	20 ... (professionals): 4 (breads each);
	4 [+n] ⸢ugula⸣ [*n*]	4+ overseers: x;
	7 dub-sar *4*	7 scribes: 4;
	6 ⸢nar⸣ *6* 1 *7*	6 musicians: 6; 1 (musician): 7;
	2 mar-tu *8*	2 Amorites: 8;
	6 sipa anše *4* [1] *6*	6 donkey-herds: 4; [1]: 6;
	2 lu$_2$-^{ĝeš}KAM [*n*]	2 *guards*(?): x;
	[n] gu-za-la$_2$ *4*	x throne-bearers: 4;

	[*n*] E$_2$-dam	x: Edam;
ii	[n šu]-i *4*	x barbers: 4;
	[n] ˹Nam-maḫ˺	x: Nammaḫ;
	[...]	...
	1 ma$_2$-laḫ$_5$ *6*	1 sailor: 6;
	1 sipa kurušda *4*	1 shepherd-fattener: 4;
	4 E$_3$-a *8*	4 (men of) E'a: 8;
	2 sukkal *4*	2 secretaries: 4;
	2 ˹x˺-zi *6*	2 (men of) ...zi: 6;
	[*n* Lum]-ma-zi	x Lummazi;
	6 Lugal-˹e˺	6: Lugale;
	[n] ugula ašgab *4*	x overseers of leather-workers: 4;
	[n] ^{d}En-lil$_2$-la$_2$	x: Enlila;
	[n] dam-gara$_3$ [*n*]	x merchant(s): x;
	[*n*] ˹Ur-e-pa$_3$˺ lu$_2$ *A-mur-*˹*um*˺	x Urepa, the man of *Amurrum*;
	[n] Lugal-dul$_5$	n: Lugaldul;
	[n+] *1* mušen-du$_3$ 10	n+1 catchers: 10;
	[n ...] *5*	n ...: 5.
	(ruling)	
	[šu-niĝin$_2$ n+] 10 ninda [...]	[Total: n+] 10 [...] breads.
	[break]	...

obv. i 3 f.: Note the presence of the rare titles maškim gada/še/ma$_2$ Dilmun.

obv. i 8: Cf. lu$_2$-kišib$_3$-ba in Nik 2 no. 14 obv. i 12 and Sommerfeld, Markina and Roudik 2005: 187. Cf. also lexical entries lu$_2$-DUB in ED Personal Names and Professions 179 and lu$_2$-kišib-UD.UD-ra = *kanniku* "official in charge of sealing" in CAD K 154 (Old Babylonian Lu$_2$).

obv. i 11–12: The person has an Akkadian name. Because of this, the attribute lu$_2$ Me-luḫ, "the man (of) Meluḫ(ḫa)," may refer not to his place of origin but to the place of his commision.

obv. ii 7: Cf. *Su-mu-lum* in Nos. 19 rev. ii 5, 32 obv. i 4. Both are variants of the name *Šumum-'ilum*.

obv. ii 14: The remains of the broken sign do not allow the restoration lu$_2$ Me-˹luḫ˺.

rev. i 6: For the discussion of lu$_2$-KU without a definite interpretation, see Sommerfeld, Markina and Roudik 2005: 188–90.

rev. ii 9: For Lum-ma-zi maškim, see BdI 1 no. 79 = CUSAS 26 no. 94 obv. 9, of the same date and provenance.

1.4.6 – Sheep and Cattle

No. 289 – MS 2191/26

Account of goats, Middle/Classical Sargonic, Adab.

obv.	[1 ud$_{5}$]-giggi(MI)	1 black [nanny goat];
	1 ud$_{5}$-si$_{4}$	1 brown nanny goat:
	Ur-pisaĝ kuš$_{7}$	Ur-pisaĝ, the animal-manager.
	1 LAK20	1 ram:
	Lugal-bad$_{3}$ sipa anše	Lugalbad, the donkey-herd.
	3 maš$_{2}$ ša$_{3}$-du$_{10}$	3 suckling kid goats:
	E$_{2}$-mu	Emu,
rev.	sipa	the shepherd.
	(blank space)	
	šu-niĝin$_{2}$ 6 udu-ḫi-a	Total: 6 various sheep.
	udu zi-ga	Expended sheep.
	Ur-^{d}Ištaran(KA.DI) sipa	Ur-Ištaran, the shepherd.
	(blank)	

obv. 2: See SCTRAH no. 267 for the wool of these goats.

No. 290 – MS 2227/2

Account of sheep, Early/Middle Sargonic, Adab.

obv.	830 udu-˹x˺	830 … sheep:
	˹Ama-Ab˺-zu-si	Ama-Abzusi.
	(blank space)	
rev.	(blank)	

obv. 2: See this volume for the same individual in Early/Middle Sargonic Adab texts. The name also occurs in other Early Sargonic and later Sargonic texts from Adab: see CUSAS 11 nos. 117 obv. ii 4, 271 rev. 1, CUSAS 13 no. 32 obv. 8.

No. 291 – MS 4224

Inventory of cattle, Middle Sargonic ("the year (when) the seed funnel was *erected*"), Adab.

obv.	50 ab$_2$-maḫ$_2$	50 mature cows;
	10 ab$_2$-*3*	10 three-year old cows;
	7 ab$_2$-*2*	7 two-year old cows;
	11 ab$_2$-*1*	11 one-year old cows;
	11 gu$_4$-*1*	11 one-year old bulls;
	2 gu$_4$-utua$_2$	2 stud-bulls.
	(ruling)	
	šu+niĝin$_2$ 90 ab$_2$	Total: 90 "cows" (=cattle).
rev.	Aja$_2$-zu-zu	Ajazuzu (is responsible).

	⸢*I*⸣-*mi*-diĝir-e	*Yimit-'ilim*
	⸢ka⸣ i$_7$ e$_2$-DUN-ka	at the inlet of the canal of the (town) E-DUN,
	⸢gurum$_x$⸣([IGI].ĜAR)-bi e-ak	has performed its inventory.
	iti a$_2$-ki-ti	Month Akiti.
	mu ^{ĝeš}inda(NINDA$_2$)	The year (when) the seed funnel
	al-du$_3$-am$_3$	was *erected*.

obv. 6: The writing of /utua/ corresponds exactly to the same sign in text No. 296 obv. i 6, that is, a sign like LAK777 but with additional "fins," a "tail," a second horizontal wedge inside the signs, and without the closing wedge of UDU at the beginning.

obv. 7: The sum of the individual entries is 91, not 90 as claimed by the total.

rev. 6–7: It is not certain to which Sargonic king this year date belongs. It is otherwise unattested to my knowledge. Rimuš, Maništusu or early Naram-Suen would be suitable candidates based on the paleography of the text. The lexeme ^{ĝeš}inda denotes the seed-funnel of the seeder plow. It was borrowed into Akkadian as *ittû*, CAD I/J 312 *ittû* B. A synonym in Akkadian is *abu* among other words. See e.g. in-da = NINDA$_2$ = *abum* in Ea = *nâqu* in CUSAS 12 p. 8 and CAD A^I 67 f. *abu*. The meaning of the verb in the year date is not certain.

No. 292 – MS 4243

Account of cattle, Middle Sargonic, Adab.

obv. i	1 ab$_2$-maḫ$_2$	1 mature cow;
	1 gu$_4$-*2*	1 ox of 2 (years):
	Lugal-iri	Lugaliri.
	2 ab$_2$-*2*	2 cows of 2:
	1 gu$_4$-*2*	1 ox of 2:
	Nam-maḫ-ni	Nammaḫ(a)ni.
	1 ab$_2$-*2*	1 cow of 2;
	1 gu$_4$-*3*	1 ox of 3:
	Niĝir-Ab-zu	Niĝir-Abzu.
	1 ab$_2$-maḫ$_2$	1 mature cow;
	1 ab$_2$-*2*	1 cow of 2:
	Aja$_2$-zu-zu	Ajazuzu.
	2 ab$_2$-*2*	2 cows of 2:
ii	E$_2$-amaš	E'amaš.
	1 ab$_2$-*3*	1 cow of 3;
	1 ab$_2$-*1*	1 cow of 1:
	IM-ki	IMki.
	1 gu$_4$-*2*	1 ox of 2:
	Igi-si$_4$	Igisi.
	1 ab$_2$-*3*	1 cow of 3:
	Ur-ĝidru	Urĝidru.
	1 ⸢ab$_2$⸣-*2*	1 cow of 2;
	1 gu$_4$-[*n*]	1 ox of x:

	Ur-^{d}Aš$_{8}$-gi$_{4}$	Ur-Ašgi.
	1 ab$_{2}$-*3*	1 cow of 3;
	1 gu$_{4}$-*2*	1 ox of 2:
	AN-na	ANna.
rev. i	1 ab$_{2}$-maḫ$_{2}$	1 mature cow;
	1 peš da-ba	1 … pregnant (cow):
	Ki-⌜ga$^{?}$-x⌝	Ki…(?).
	2 ab$_{2}$-*3*	2 cows of 3:
	Lugal-nita$_{2}$-zi	Lugalnitazi.
ii	(blank)	

rev. i 2: For amar da-ba cf. MAD 4 nos. 28 obv. 5, 38 obv. 5, 9. Since da-ba may apply to calves (amar), it is, unlike peš, not related to pregnancy.

rev. i 3: The sign after KI is GA or the beginning of IL$_{2}$, KAD$_{4}$ or KAD$_{5}$. I am not aware of personal names beginning with KI and one of these signs.

No. 293 – MS 4272

Account of "mountain" cattle, Middle Sargonic, Adab.

The document records that *I-mi*-diĝir (= Yimit-'ilim) collects herds of "mountain" cattle counted by the "yardman, animal-manager" (kuš$_{7}$) MIlulu in the cities of Akšak and Ereš. Part of the first herd is taken away by a Lagašite scribe.

obv.	240 la$_{2}$ 10 ab$_{2}$-kur gu$_{4}$-kur	230 mountain cows and mountain bulls
	Akšak(UD.KUŠU$_{2}$)^{ki}-ka	in Akšak
	MI-lu-lu kuš$_{7}$	MIlulu, the animal-manager,
	I-mi-diĝir-ra	to *Yimit-'ilim*
	e-na-šid	has counted.
	ša$_{3}$-bi-ta	Out of it:
	30 la$_{2}$ 2 ab$_{2}$-kur gu$_{4}$-kur	28 mountain cows and mountain bulls
	Ur-ĝidru	Urĝidru,
	dub-sar	the scribe
rev.	Lagaš(BURU$_{4}$.LA)^{ki}-ke$_{4}$	of Lagaš,
	⌜ba⌝-lah̬$_{5}$	has taken away.
	11 gu$_{4}$-kur	11 mountain bulls,
	10 [+n] ab$_{2}$-kur	10+x mountain cows,
	⌜MI-lu⌝-[lu] kuš$_{7}$	MIlulu, the animal-manager,
	⌜Ereš$_{2}$⌝^{ki}-a	in Ereš
	I-mi-diĝir-ra	to *Yimit-'ilim*
	e-na-šid	has counted.
	(blank)	

obv. 1: gu$_{4}$-kur-ra appears in l. 192 of the Nippur Forerunner to Hh XIII (*apud* DCCLT).

No. 294 – MS 4275

Expenditure of sheep, Middle Sargonic, Adab.

obv.	31 udu	31 sheep:
	udu zi-ga	these are sheep expended
	Be-li$_{2}$-ṭāb(DUG$_{3}$)-kam	by *Bēlī-ṭāb*.
	I-mi-diĝir-e	*Yimit-'ilim*
	E$_{2}$-dam-si	(for) Edamsi
rev.	^{ĝeš}kiri$_{6}$ Ur$_{5}^{!}$(AŠ$_{8}$)-du$_{2}$-^{d}Aš$_{8}$-gi$_{4}$	(for) the garden of Urdu-Ašgi
	ĝa$_{2}$-udu-ur$_{4}$	(from) the sheep-plucking shed
	in-na-zi	he has expended for him.
	(blank)	

1.4.7 – Hides

No. 295 – MS 4209

Expenditure of hides, Middle Sargonic, Adab.

obv.	[10+] 1 kuš-udu	11 sheepskins:
	Ur-^{d}Nu-muš-da	Ur-Numušda;
	10 kuš-udu	10 sheepskins:
	ensi$_{2}$	the governor;
	12 kuš-udu	12 sheepskins:
	Ĝessu	Ĝessu,
	sagi	the cupbearer
rev.	Karkara(IM)^{ki}	(from) Karkara.
	(blank space)	
	šu+niĝin$_{2}$ 33 kuš-udu	Total: 33 sheepskins:
	Ur-a$_{2}$	to Ur-a
	an-na-šum$_{2}$	it has been given.
	(blank space)	
	[iyi ĝa$_{2}$-udu-ur$_{4}$	[(Month)] Ĝa'udu'ur.

No. 296 – MS 4214

Delivery of hides, Middle Sargonic, Adab.

obv. i	[1] kuš gu$_{4}$	[1] oxhide:
	Lugal-en$_{8}$-tar-su$_{3}$	Lugalentarsu;
	1 Igi-si$_{4}$	1: Igisi;
	1 IM-ki	1: IMki;
	1 Ur-gu	1: Urgu;
	1 E$_{2}$-amaš	1: E'amaš;
	1 Ša$_{3}$-ga-ni-su$_{3}$	1: Šaganisu;
	1 Aja$_{2}$-zu-zu	1: Ajazuzu;
	1 En-gu$_{2}$-gal	1: Engugal.
	(blank space)	
	30 la$_{2}$ 2 ab$_{2}$ kuš	28 cowhides,
ii	7 kuš gu$_{4}$	7 oxhides:
	Ur-^{d}En-lil$_{2}$	Ur-Enlil;
	10 la$_{2}$ 1 kuš gu$_{4}$-⸢sig⸣	9 yellow oxhides:
	Ur-nu	Urnu,
	ka-guru$_{7}$	the granary superintendant;
	30 saĝ gu$_{4}$	30 ox heads.
	(ruling)	
	šu-niĝin$_{2}$ 82 kuš gu$_{4}$	Total: 82 oxhides.
	kuš gu$_{4}$	These are the hides
	A-ga-de$_{3}$^{ki}-še$_{3}$	to be brought to Agade.
	tum$_{3}$-dam	

	Ur-ḪAR	UrḪAR (is in charge).
rev.	(blank space)	
	3 kuš za$_3$ nu-šu$_2$	3 hides are not branded:
	e$_2$-gal-gibil	(for) the New Palace.
	Ur-^{d}En-lil$_2$-kam	It is (the responsibility) of Ur-Enlil.

obv. i 2: Note the interesting form of the sign SU$_3$, resembling BU in text No. 267 obv. 3'.

obv. i 6: The form of the sign AMAŠ is here the following: 

1.4.8 – Wool

No. 297 – MS 4232

Account of wool, Middle Sargonic, Adab.

obv.	3 siki gu$_2$ *1* ^{šu2}2N$_8$ ma-na	3 talents 1 ⅔ mina of wool:
	Ur-a$_2$	Ur-a,
	dub-sar	the scribe.
	3 siki gu$_2$ *42* ma-na	3 talents 42 minas of wool:
	Ur-^{d}Sug$_x$(^{su3}PA.SIKIL)	Ur-Sug.
rev.	*40* siki ma-na	40 minas of wool:
	Mu-ni	Muni.
	(blank)	
	šu+niĝin$_2$ 7 siki gu$_2$ *23* ^{šu2}2N$_8$ ma-na	Total: 7 talents 23 ⅔ minas of wool.

obv. 5: Both this individual and Muni in the following entry appear in CUSAS 20 no. 184. Bauer addressed the question of the sign combination PA.SU$_3$.EL/SU$_3$.PA.EL in Bauer 1982: 4–7 no. 19. It is a compound logogram with the reading sug$_x$, where the sign SU$_3$ is a phonetic complement. The word sug$_x$ denotes a ripe stalk of grain. See there for the deity of the ripe stalk ^{d}Ku$_3$-sug$_x$. Here the name appears simply as ^{d}Sug$_x$.

No. 298 – MS 4237

Account of wool in connection to shepherds, Middle Sargonic, Adab.

obv.	1 siki gu$_2$	1 talent of wool:
	Šeš-lu$_2$	Šešlu;
	1 E$_2$-amaš-zi	1 (talent of wool): E'amašzi;
	1 Du-du	1: Dudu;
	1 Ur-dam	1: Urdam;
	1 Ur-^{d}Ištaran(KA.DI)	1: Ur-Ištaran.
	(blank)	
	sipa-me	They are shepherds.
rev.	(blank space)	
	Adab^{ki}-ki	Adaki(du),
	dub-sar	the scribe,
	maškim	<its> commissioner.

1.4.9 – Textiles

The majority of the texts in this section belongs to the so-called "Mama-ummi's file." The title is owed to *Mama-'ummī* "(Goddess) Mama is my mother," a woman who appears at the beginning of most documents. She was one of the supervisors of female workers employed in textile production during the Middle Sargonic period. Pomponio and Visicato have suggested in the introduction to CUSAS 20 that these texts date to the governorship of Lugal-aja$_2$-ĝu$_{10}$. See there for a typology and overview of these documents.

No. 299 – MS 4049

Account of wool, Middle Sargonic, Adab (Mama-ummi's file).

obv.	*43* siki ma-na	43 minas wool:
	Ma-ma-um-mi	*Mama-'ummī*;
	1 siki gu$_2$ *20* ma-na	1 talent 20 minas wool:
	Geme$_2$-^{d}En-lil$_2$	Geme-Enlil;
	33 ma-na *Aš-tar$_2$*	33 minas: *'Aštar*;
	40 la$_2$ *3* *Ta$_2$-ni$_2$-a*	37: *Tāni(y)a*;
	1 gu$_2$ *1* ma-na Nin-ad$_2$-gal	1 talent 1 mina: Nin-adgal;
	1 gu$_2$ *11* ma-na	1 talent 11 minas:
rev.	Ni$_3$-banda$_3^{da}$	Nibanda;
	43 $^{\text{šu2}}$1N$_8$ Nin-ni$_3$-zu	43 ⅓ Ninnizu;
	2 Me-niĝar-ta	2: Meniĝarta;
	15 *Si-bi-tum*	15: *Sibitum*;
	15 Nin-ama-ĝu$_{10}$	15: Ninamaĝu.
	(blank space/ruling)	
	šu-niĝin$_2$ 6 siki gu$_2$ *40* $^{\text{šu2}}$1N$_8$ ma-na	Total: 6 talents 40 ⅓ minas wool.
	bar-ra ĝal$_2$-la	It is the outstanding (amount)
	ki-siki-ke$_4$-ne-kam	of (female) weavers.
	[iti] še-saĝ-sig$_{15}$-ga-a	In [the month] Šesaĝsiga.

obv.6: For *Ta$_2$-ni$_2$*(IM)*-a*, see SCTRAH no. 59 commentary.

rev. 7: See SCTRAH no. 122 commentary for the expression bar-ra ĝal$_2$-la, literally "what is available outside," with additional references.

rev. 8: See SCTRAH no. 59 commentary for ki-siki-(ak) as the abbreviation of geme$_2$ ki-siki-ka, literally "young woman of the wool-place."

No. 300 – MS 4195

Allocation of textiles, Middle Sargonic, Adab.

obv. i	⸢2⸣ bar-dul$_5$ u$_3$-la$_2$	2 … *bardul* garments:
	ensi$_2$-gal	the former governor;
	6 lu$_2$-eše$_2$-aša$_5$-gid$_2$	6: the field-surveyor;
	2 U$_3$-mu-NI-NI	2: UmuNINI;
	1 ^{d}En-lil$_2$-la$_2$	1: Enlila;
	1 Ur-Sumugan(ĜIR$_3$)	1: Ur-Sumugan;
	1 Lugal-ša$_3$	1: Lugalša;
	1 UR	1: UR;
	1 ⸢Ur-nu⸣ u$_2$-a	1: Urnu, the provisioner;
	1 Ur-sa$_6$-ga	1: Ursaga;
	1 Lugal-a$_2$	1: Lugal-a;
	[1] Ša$_3$-ge	[1:] Šage;
	[1 ...]-AN	[1:]…AN
	[1] ⸢Ur⸣-a$_2$ sukkal	[1:] Ur-a, the secretary;
	1 Ur-tum-al	1: Ur-tumal;
ii	[2 lines broken]	…
	1 ⸢x⸣ [...]	1: …;
	1 engar ⸢bala⸣-[a-ri$_2$]	1: the agricultural manager of the opposite side (of the river);
	1 Na-ba-lu$_5$	1: Nabalu;
	1 ma$_2$-laḫ$_5$-gal	1: the chief sailor;
	1 Lugal-saĝ sukkal	1: Lugalsaĝ, the secretary;
	2 sagi-maḫ	2: the chief cupbearer;
	1 enku	1: the tax-collector;
	3 ugula šu-ku$_6$	3: the overseer of fishermen;
	2 šita-iri	2: the *šita*-official of the city;
	1 Lugal-a$_2$	1: Lugal-a,
	lu$_2$-igi	the *courtier*;
	1 Du-du	1: Dudu,
	nu-banda$_3$	the (household) supervisor;
	1 Diĝir-kala	1: Diĝirkala(ga);
	2 Sila-si	2: Silasi;
iii	[*ca.* 3–4 lines broken]	…
	1 Ur-[...]	1: Ur…;
	1 Ur-^{d}⸢En⸣-[x]	1: Ur-En…;
	1 Az-⸢x⸣	1: Az…;
	1 ⸢Lugal⸣-[x]	1: Lugal…;
	2 Lu$_2$-⸢pa-da⸣	2: Lupada;
	1 kiĝ$_2$-⸢gal⸣	1: the labor recruiter;
	1 eš$_3$-du	1: the "He-walks-(in)-the-sanctuary" (a profession);
	2 saĝĝa e$_2$-maḫ	2: the chief temple-administrator of Emaḫ;
	2 saĝĝa ^{d}[...]	2: the chief temple-administrator of the (deity's) … (household);

	1 saĝĝa ^{d}[...]	1: 2: the chief temple-administrator of the (deity's) ... (household);
	1 Ur-[...]	1: Ur...
rev. i	Du$_{11}$-⸢ga⸣-[ni]	(and) Dugani;
	1 engar ⸢bala⸣-[a-ri$_{2}$]	1: the agricultural manager of the opposite side (of the river);
	[n] ⸢x⸣ [...]	[x:] ...;
	[n] Du-du	[n] Dudu
	⸢Ur⸣-mes	(and) Urmes;
	3 E$_{2}$-gal-[x]	3: Egal...;
	1 ensi$_{2}$-⸢gal⸣	1: the former governor;
	1 Pa$_{3}$-⸢da⸣	1: Pada;
	1 Ur-⸢mes⸣	1: Urmes;
	1 Ur-⸢x⸣-[x]	1: Ur...;
	2 Ur-[...]	2: Ur...;
	1 ⸢Saĝ⸣-[...]	1: Saĝ...;
	1 [...]	1: ...;
	[break]	...
ii	1 ⸢x⸣-ni	1: ...ni;
	1 ⸢x⸣-[x]-gal	1: ...gal;
	1 Lugal-šu	1: Lugalšu;
	1 Šeg$_{12}$-zi	1: Šegzi;
	1 Lugal-a	1: Lugala;
	1 baḫar$_{x}$(EDIN)-gal	1: the chief potter;
	1 A-ba-^{d}En-lil$_{2}$	1: Aba-Enlil;
	1 šandana	1: the orchard-administrator;
	1 *Ma*-SIKI	1: *MaSIKI*;
	1 lu$_{2}$-GIN$_{2}$-du$_{3}$-a	1: *the crown/ax holder*;
	1 Lugal-ša$_{3}$	1: Lugalša,
	ugula geme$_{2}$	the overseer of female workers;
	4 engar bala-a-ri$_{2}$	4: the agricultural manager of the opposite side (of the river);
	1 Ur-eš$_{3}$	1: Ur-eš;
	1 Ur$_{2}$-ni	1: Urni;
	1 šidim-[gal]	1: the [chief] builder;
	1 Saĝ-[...]	1: Saĝ...;
	1 ⸢x⸣-[...]	1: ...
iii	Ur-dam	(and) Urdam,
	⸢ugula ĝeš-kiĝ$_{2}$-ti x⸣	the overseer of craftsmen,
	⸢ugula ki⸣-siki-ta	the overseer of female weavers;
	[1] Ur-kun	[1:] Urkun;
	[1] ⸢Ur⸣-^{d}Na-ru$_{2}$-a	[1:] Ur'Naru'a,
	dub-sar	the scribe;
	1 šandana ugula	1: the orchard-administrator, the overseer;
	1 E$_{2}$-dam-si	1: Edamsi.

	(blank)	
	140 la$_2$ 3 bar-dul$_5$ u$_3$-la$_2$	137 … *bardul*-garments.

obv. i 1: Despite the multiple attestations in ED and Sargonic documents, the meaning of the term u$_3$-la$_2$ that is found with various textiles remains uncertain.

obv. i 2: ensi$_2$-gal may refer to the former governor in ED texts. Schrakamp 2012a: 280 no. 46 with additional references, doubts it. He proposes instead that the title denotes a cultic functionary or priest. However, cf. text No. 360 obv. i 4, where both ensi$_2$-gal and the field-surveyor are mentioned at the top of the governorate hierarchy. This favors an understanding of *ensigal* as former governor in Sargonic Adab.

obv. ii 4 f.: See SCTRAH p. 115 for bala-a-ri$_2$ as a variant writing of bala-a-ri "the opposite side (of the river)."

obv. ii 13: See the commentary to text No. 17 obv. ii 4. If it is a professional title, the term may refer to some sort of courtier. Lu$_2$-igi is literally the "person in front of (the high authority?)."

obv. iii 7: Cf. the profession eš$_3$-a-ab-du in FAOS 15/2 p. 274, FAOS 17 p. 81 with fn. 238; = Akk. *ešabdû*, CAD A^1 2 s.v. *ababdû*, to be corrected.

rev. ii 9: *Ma*-SIKI-(*be-li*$_2$) appears as an Akkadian personal name in several ED and Sargonic texts from Adab and Nippur: see ECTJ nos. 28 obv. ii 7, 35 obv. ii 4, and ELTS, Appendix to no. 32, p. 102 obv. vi 6.

rev. ii 10: Leaving aside the many Ur III occurrences of a professional title lu$_2$-GIN$_2$, there is no other attestation of the term in early sources. Cf. the compound verb al … du$_3$ "to hoe." Based on this, the literal meaning of the term lu$_2$-GIN$_2$-du$_3$-a may be either "one who holds the crown" (aga$_3$) (= crown-keeper) or "one who wields an ax" (giĝ$_4$) (= bodyguard?).

No. 301 – MS 4204

Account of produced garments with their weight indicated, Middle Sargonic, Adab (Mama-ummi's file).

obv.	[9 lines defaced]	…
	1 bar-⸢si sa-dab$_6$⸣	1 sash with laces to wrap around:
	ki-la$_2$-bi 5 ⸢giĝ$_4$⸣	its weight: 5 shekels:
	Ta$_2$-⸢*ni*$_2$-*a*⸣	*Tāni(y)a*;
rev.	2 bar-si sa-dab$_6$	2 sashes with laces to wrap around:
	ki-la$_2$-bi *10* giĝ$_4$	their weight: 10 shekels:
	Nin-ad$_2$-gal	Nin-adgal;
	1 bar-si sa-dab$_6$	1 sash with laces to wrap around:
	ki-la$_2$-bi 5 giĝ$_4$	its weight: 5 shekels:
	Ni$_3$-banda$_3$^{da}	Nibanda;
	3 bar-si sa-dab$_6$	3 sashes with laces to wrap around:
	ki-la$_2$-bi *15* giĝ$_4$	their weight: 15 shekels:
	Me-niĝar-ta	Meniĝarta;
	1 bar-dul$_5$ uš-bar	1 *bardul*-garment of low quality:
	ki-la$_2$-bi *3* ma-na	its weight: 3 minas:
	Nin-⸢ni$_3$⸣ PAP	Ninni(zu); (checked).

obv. 10: bar-si.g > Akk. *paršīgu* is a sash used as a headdress; see CAD P 203. For sa-dab$_6$ as "laces to wrap around" in this connection, see SCTRAH, commentary to no. 142 obv. 3.

rev. 12: PAP is written in the corner of the tablet as a check-mark.

No. 302 – MS 4207

Turning over and delivery of textiles, Middle Sargonic, Adab.

obv.	502 tug$_2$-ni$_3$-SU-a	502 … garments:
	tug$_2$ šu-a gi$_4$-a	these are the textiles that have been turned over
	azlag$_7$-e-ne-kam	by the fullers.
	240 la$_2$ 1 tug$_2$-ni$_3$-SU-a	239 … garments:
	tug$_2$ e$_2$-ĝidru-ka-kam	these are textiles of the "House of the scepter."
	tug$_2$ A-ga-de$_3$	These are textiles
	ba-de$_6$-am$_3$	that have been taken away to Agade.
rev.	(blank)	

obv. 1, 4: This garment remains unidentified. It is not connected to A.SU = aktum "heavy garment."

obv. 5: E$_2$-ĝidru is usually associated with a large temple household in Umma; see MC 5 no. 394. It appears as e$_2$-ĝidru Umma(GIŠ.KUŠU$_2$)^{ki}-ka in administrative texts and royal inscriptions alike, probably in order to avoid ambiguity. A building by the same name was situated in Adab: see Such-Gutiérrez 2005–6: 43. E$_2$-ĝidru ^{d}Aš$_8$-gi$_4$ is found in text No. 178 obv. i 6 and e$_2$-ĝidru e$_2$-gal appears in CS Adab texts CUSAS 13 no. 141 rev. 6, and text No. 356 obv. ii 1 in the present volume. This indicates firstly that the "Scepter House" in question was situated in Adab. Secondly, judging by the attributes, it was probably a shrine of Ašgi situated on the premises of the palace (e$_2$-gal).

obv. 6: Note the absence of the determinative ^{ki} after the geographical name. Agade is the final destination of the two batches of textiles, those produced by the fullers and those originating from the "House of the scepter."

No. 303 – MS 4229

Account of textiles in connection to female overseers, Middle Sargonic, Adab (Mama-ummi's file).

obv.	1 ^{tug2}ni$_3$-⸢lam$_2$⸣	1 *nilam*-garment:
	Ma-ma-um-mi	*Mama-'ummī*;
	1 Nin-ni$_3$	1: Ninni;
	2 *Aš-tar$_2$* 1 ⸢tug$_2$$^?$⸣	2: *'Aštar*, 1 textile(?);
	1 *Ta-ni$_2$-a*	1: *Tāni(y)a*;
	1 ^{tug2}ni$_3$-lam$_2$	1 *nilam*-garment,
	1 ^{tug2}ša$_3$-ga-du$_3$	1 *šagadu*-garment:
	⸢Nin⸣-ad$_2$-⸢gal⸣	Ninadgal;
rev.	1 Ni$_3$-banda$_3$^{da}	1: Nibanda;
	2 Me-niĝar-ta	2: Meniĝarta.
	(blank space)	
	tug$_2$ ⸢ab⸣-ta-si-ga-am$_3$	These are the garments that have been deposited.

No. 304 – MS 4276

Account of produced garments with weight indication, Middle Sargonic, Adab (Mama-ummi's file).

The top and bottom of the tablet were cut down in modern times in order to make the tablet look complete.

obv. i	[break]	…
	1 bar-dul$_5$ šabra	1 *bardul*-garment (of) "chief administrator" (quality):
	ki-la$_2$-bi *13*	their weight: 13 (minas).
	1 ^{tug_2}GI	1 *GI*-garment;
	3 bar-dul$_5$ uš-bar	3 *bardul*-garments of lower quality:
	ki-la$_2$-bi *12*	their weight: 12 (minas):
	Ma-ma-um-mi	*Mama-'ummī.*
	1 ^{tug_2}uš-bar bala	1 *ušbar*-garment (made from) *bala*-fabric;
	1 ^{tug_2}ni$_3$-lam$_2$ uš-bar	1 *nilam*-garment of lower quality;
	2 ^{tug_2}ša$_3$-ga-du$_3$ us$_2$	2 *šagadu*-garments of the following (quality);
	1 $^{⸢tug_2⸣}$[…]-⸢x⸣	1 … garment;
	[break]	…
ii	[break]	…
	1 $^{⸢tug_2⸣}$[…]	1 … garment;
	1 ^{tug_2}uš-⸢x⸣	1 … garment;
	4 ^{tug_2}uš-bar bala	4 *ušbar*-garments (made from) *bala*-fabric;
	1 ^{tug_2}ni$_3$-lam$_2$ uš-bar	1 *nilam*-garment of lower quality;
	1 (ras.) bar-dul$_5$ šabra	1 (erasure) *bardul*-garment (of) "chief administrator" (quality):
	ki-la$_2$-bi *35*	their weight: 35 (minas).
	2 ^{tug_2}GI	2 *GI*-garments;
	8 bar-dul$_5$ uš-bar	8 *bardul*-garments of lower quality:
	ki-la$_2$-bi *24 ½*	their weight: 24 ½ (minas):
	⸢*Aš*⸣-[*tar*$_2$]	*'Aštar.*
	[break]	…
rev. i	[break]	…
	⸢6⸣ […]	6 … garments:
	ki-la$_2$-bi ⸢*14*⸣	their weight: 14 (minas):
	⸢*Ta*$_2$⸣-*ni*$_2$-*a*	*Tāni(y)a.*
	4 ^{tug_2}ni$_3$-lam$_2$	4 *nilam*-garments:
	ki-la$_2$-bi *12*	their weight: 12 (minas).
	2 *2* bar-dul$_5$ uš-bar	2 (plus) 2 *bardul*-garments of lower quality:
	⸢ki⸣-la$_2$-bi *12*	their weight: 12 (minas):
	⸢Nin-ad$_2$⸣-gal	Ninadgal.
	2 ^{tug_2}uš-bar ⸢bala⸣	2 *ušbar*-garments (made from) *bala*-fabric;
	[break]	…
ii	[break]	…
	2 ^{tug_2}ni$_3$-lam$_2$ uš-bar	2 *nilam*-garments of lower quality;
	1 ⸢bar⸣-dul$_5$ šabra	1 *bardul*-garment (of) "chief administrator" (quality):
	ki-[la$_2$]-bi *10* la$_2$ *1*	their weight: 9 (minas);

	3 *1* bar-dul$_5$ uš-bar	3 (plus) 1 *bardul*-garment of lower quality:
	⸢ki⸣-la$_2$-bi *12*	their weight: 12 (minas):
	⸢Nin⸣-ni$_3$-zu	Ninnizu.
	4 ^{tug_2}ni$_3$-lam$_2$	4 *nilam*-garments:
	ki-la$_2$-bi *12*	their weight: 12 (minas);
	1 ^{tug_2}GI	1 *GI*-garment;
	1 *1* bar-dul$_5$ uš-bar	1 (plus) 1 *bardul*-garment of lower quality:
	⸢ki-la$_2$-bi *10* la$_2$ *1*⸣	their weight: 9 (minas).
	[break]	…
l. e. 1	*Si-bi-tum 2* $^{\text{šu}_2}$*2N$_8$*	Sibitum: 2 ⅔ (minas).
l. e. 2	*5 10* giĝ$_4$	5 (minas) 10 shekels.

Note the difference between the "round" and "pointed" numerals in the notation of garments. The former may record the garments that have been produced whereas the latter may designate those that have not yet been produced. It is unclear in this case, how the total weight could be calculated.

obv. i 1': See SCTRAH commentary to no. 4 obv. 1 for the quality gradations šabra and ensi$_2$ of garments.

obv. i 3': The garment GI^{tug_2} appears in EDPV A no. 178. The interpretation of the term is uncertain.

obv. i 7': For bala as a fabric, see SCTRAH commentary to no. 20 obv. 5.

No. 305 – MS 4450

Account of textiles with weight indication, Middle Sargonic, Adab (Mama-ummi's file).

obv.	1 bar-dul$_5$ uš-bar	1 *bardul*-garment of lower quality:
	⸢ki⸣-la$_2$-bi 3 ma-⸢na⸣ la$_2$ *5* giĝ$_4$	its weight: 3 minas minus 5 shekels.
	Ma-ma-um-mi	*Mama-'ummī.*
	1 bar-dul$_5$ uš-bar	1 *bardul*-garment of lower quality:
	ki-la$_2$-bi 3 ma-na	its weight: 3 minas:
	Nin-ni$_3$	Ninni.
	1 bar-dul$_5$ uš-bar	1 *bardul*-garment of lower quality:
	ki-la$_2$-bi 3 ma-na *5* giĝ$_4$	its weight: 3 minas 5 shekels:
	Aš-tar$_2$	*'Aštar.*
	1 bar-dul$_5$ uš-bar	1 *bardul*-garment of lower quality:
rev.	ki-la$_2$-bi 4 $^{\text{šu}_2}$1N$_8$ ma-na *5* giĝ$_4$	its weight: 4 ⅓ minas 5 shekels:
	Ta$_2$-ni$_2$-a	*Tāni(y)a.*
	1 bar-dul$_5$ uš-bar	1 *bardul*-garment of lower quality:
	ki-la$_2$-bi 3 ma-na la$_2$ *7* giĝ$_4$	its weight: 3 minas minus 7 shekels:
	⸢Nin⸣-ad$_2$-gal	Ninadgal.
	1 bar-dul$_5$ uš-bar	1 *bardul*-garment of lower quality:
	⸢ki⸣-la$_2$-bi 2 $^{\text{šu}_2}$2N$_8$ ma-na	its weight: 2 ⅔ minas:
	⸢Ni$_3$⸣-banda$_3$^{da}	Nibanda.
	1 bar-dul$_5$ uš-bar	1 *bardul*-garment of lower quality:
	⸢ki-la$_2$-bi⸣ 3 ⸢ma-na⸣ la$_2$ [*n*] ⸢giĝ$_4$⸣	its weight: 3 minas minus x shekels:
	[Nin]-ni$_3$	Ninni.

l.e.	2 bar-bul$_5$ uš-bar 7 ma-na Me-niĝar-ta	2 *bardul*-garments of lower quality: (their weight:) 7 minas: Meniĝarta.

1.4.10 – Bitumen

No. 306 – MS 2191/23

Account of bitumen, Middle Sargonic, Adab.

obv.	1(gur) 2(bariga) esir$_2$-e$_2$-duru$_5$ gur	1 *gur* 2 *bariga* of wet bitumen:
	Ur-^{d}Nu-muš-da	Ur-Numušda,
	lu$_2$-ma$_2$-gur$_8$	the boatman.
	1 esir$_2$-e$_2$-duru$_5$ gur	1 *gur* of wet bitumen:
	Igi-si$_4$ ad-KID	Igisi, the reed-worker.
	1(bariga) 1(ban$_2$) esir$_2$-e$_2$-duru$_5$	1 *bariga* 1 *ban* of wet bitumen:
	Ur-u$_4$-su$_{13}$	Ur-usu.
	[...]-sa	…
	[...]-bi	…
	[...]-⌜x⌝-še$_3$ al-de$_6$	to … it is brought.
	10 esir$_2$-ḫad$_2$ gu$_2$	10 talents of dry bitumen;
	⌜Niĝar⌝-[x nu$^?$]-⌜kiri$_6$⌝	Niĝar…, the gardener(?).
rev.	esir$_2$ [...]	The bitumen …
	(blank space)	
	Ur-^{d}Inana	Ur-Inana,
	dam-gara$_3$	the merchant,
	e$_2$-gal-še$_3$	to the palace
	in-de$_6$	he has brought it.
	iti ĝa$_2$-udu-ur$_4$	Month Ĝa'udu'ur.
	(blank)	

obv. 7: See SCTRAH no. 166 obv. 2 commentary for this individual in other texts.

rev. 2: See SCTRAH, no. 153 rev. 2 commentary for this notable merchant.

1.4.11 – Baskets

No. 307 – MS 4210

Tally of baskets in a warehouse, Middle/Classical Sargonic, Adab.

obv.	66 gurdub$_2^!$ 1	66 *gurdub*-baskets (of the) 1 (batch?).
	kiĝ$_2$ til-am$_3$	It is the completed work.
	e$_2$-ni$_3$-gur$_{11}$	(In) the warehouse
	mu-ĝal$_2$	it has been made available.
rev.	(blank)	

obv. 1: GI$_4$ of gurdub$_2$ is without multiple horizontal wedges at the beginning but the vertical wedge that should close them is present. The numeral 1 may refer to the number of assignment or a delivery.

obv. 3–4: See SCTRAH no. 151 for the same final clause. Unlike that text, the present document is undated.

1.4.12 – Sacrifical Animal Body-parts

No. 308 – MS 4211

Account of neck spines of sacrificial bulls, Middle/Classical Sargonic, Adab?

obv.	2 gu-mur gu$_2$	2 spines from neck:
	Ur-BI	UrBI;
	ugula Da-da gu$_4$-diĝir-ra	overseer: Dada; the oxen of the god.
	3 gu-mur gu$_2$	3 spines from neck:
	Mu-ni	Muni;
	ugula Ur-^{d}Šara$_2$	overseer: Ur-Šara;
rev.	gu$_4$-diĝir-ra	the oxen of the god.
	1 gu-mur gu$_2$	1 spine from neck:
	Aja$_2$-zi	Ajazi,
	ugula Niĝar gu$_4$-diĝir-ra	overseer: Niĝar; the oxen of the god.
	gu-NE-x	(unclear)

obv. 1: Gu-mur is an early writing for the word "spine." For a discussion of gu$_2$-mur$_7$ (Ur III) = mur$_7$-gu and murgu (afterwards), see Hallo 2001: 161–162. Gu$_2$ in the present context cannot denote anything but "neck." "The oxen of the god" are doubtlessly sacrificial animals. This text may be related to no. 354.

rev. 5: The element (or a separate sign) after NE looks similar to the element listed between LAK119 and LAK120, and resembles the end of LAK212.

1.4.13 – Flax

No. 309 – MS 4262

Delivery and expenditure of flax in bundles, Middle Sargonic, Adab.

obv.	600 gu sa	600 bundles of flax:
	Šeš-tur-e	Šeštur
	mu-de$_6$	has delivered.
	iti ĝa$_2$-udu-ur$_4$	Month Ĝa'udu'ur.
rev.	Mu-ni	To Muni
	an-na-šum$_2$	it has been given.

No. 310 – MS 4754

Arrears of flax, Middle Sargonic, Adab.

obv.	la$_2$-i$_3$ 1590 gu sa	Arrears: 1590 bundles of flax:
	gala-maḫ	the chief cult-singer;
	990 gu sa	990 bundles of flax:
rev.	E$_2$-zi	Ezi,
	gala Karkara(LAK377)$^{\ulcorner ki \urcorner}$	the cult-singer (from) Karkara.
	(bank)	

rev. 2: The frequent references to Karkara (most probably modern Tall Jidr, a huge tell stream north of Adab, see Powell 1980: 47–52) in Sargonic texts from Adab imply strong connections between these two cities.

1.4.14 – Onions

No. 311 – MS 4212

Calculations of onions associated with two plots of land and recorded with persons in charge, Middle/Classical Sargonic, Adab?

obv.	15 šum$_2$ sar	15 *sar* onions:
	šum$_2$-bi 2 gu$_2$	its onions: 2 loads;
	Lugal-ezen	Lugal-ezen.
	21 šum$_2$ sar	21 *sar* onions:
	šum$_2$-bi 8 gu$_2$	its onions: 8 loads;
	A$_2$-ni-ta	Anita.
rev.	(blank)	

During the Early Dynastic and Sargonic periods onions were measured in "loads," a primitive unit of mensuration, and not in talents, a standardized unit of weight. This "load" was divided into sa "bundles." Neither the weight of the "load" nor of the "bundle" was standardized in the 3rd millennium BC.

No. 312 – MS 4216

The price of onions, Middle/Classical Sargonic, Adab?

obv.	14 šum$_2$-saĝ gur	14 *gur* onion bulbs;
	ku$_3$-bi 4 giĝ$_4$ NINDA$_2$×ŠE.2N$_1$	its silver: 4 ⅔ shekels.
	Ur-kala-ga	It has been given to Urkalaga.
	an-na-šum$_2$	
rev.	(blank)	

1.4.15 – Oil

No. 313 – MS 4244

Receipt and expenditure of oil, Middle Sargonic, Adab.

obv.	3 lu$_2$	3 persons:
	1 i$_3$-ĝeš sila$_3$-ta	each 1 *sila* of sesame oil
	šu ba-ti	has received.
	lu$_2$ Ur-^{d}Aš$_8$-gi$_4$-ka-me	They are the people of Ur-Ašgi.
	1 i$_3$ sila$_3$	1 *sila* oil:
	Ma$_2$-laḫ$_5$-e	Malaḫ
	šu [ba]-ti	has received.
rev.	(blank space)	
	lu$_2$ ma$_2$-še	These are the people who punt
	ba-gid$_2$-da-me	boat(s carrying) barley.
	A-ga-de$_3^{ki}$-am$_3$	It is (for) Agade.
	(blank)	
	i$_3$ zi-ga-am$_3$	It is expended oil.
	iti Šuba$_3$(MUŠ$_3$×ZA)-nun	Month Šubanun.

The text records the receipt of sesame oil by a team of four people, a certain Malaḫ, alternatively "sailor," and three other crew members for a journey. Each receives one *sila* of oil. The purpose of the trip is also recorded.

1.4.16 – Salt

No. 314 – MS 4221

Turning over and allocation(?) of salt, Middle Sargonic, Adab.

obv.	10 la$_2$ 1 mun gur	9 *gur* salt:
	Ur-^{d}Imma$_x$(ĜA$_2$×SIG$_7$.ME)	Ur-Imma,
	šeš DI (ras.?)	brother of DI:
	šu-a gi$_4$-am$_3$	it is what has been turned over.
	ša$_3$-bi-ta	Out of it:
	5(gur) 2(bariga) mun gur	5 *gur* 2 *bariga* salt:
rev.	Inim-nin	Inimnin;

1(gur) Lugal-si-sa$_2$	1 *gur*: Lugalsisa;
2(bariga) En-ra	2 *bariga*: Enra,
ugula gu-kam	he is the overseer of flax (industry).
iti du$_6$-ku$_3$	Month Duku.

obv. 1–3: Ur-Imma is the one who turned over the salt. The following list of three individuals is a record of the distribution of a part of this amount. The sign combination ŠEŠ-DI does not occur as a personal name and, besides, another personal name would not be expected after the name of Ur-Imma. This leaves us with two possibilities. On the one hand, it could be a hitherto unattested professional title. On the other, the second sign may be an abbreviation of a personal name, e.g. Silim-Utu or Silim-eš$_3$.

rev. 3–4: Enra often appears in connection with the production of flax (gu) in Middle Sargonic Adab texts: see e.g. SCTRAH nos. 113–16, 308. In our text, it is explicitly recorded that he was in charge of this branch of the Adab economy. Alternatively, gu is an abbreviation of geme$_2$-gu "female spinner." In that case Enra is the overseer of these female workers.

1.4.17 – Timber

No. 315 – MS 2425/1

Numerical tablet recording deliveries of timber to a warehouse, Middle/Classical Sargonic, Adab.

obv. 1–6	*10.10.10 10.10.10*	60 × 6 = 360 (loads)
	(blank)	
obv. 7–8	*10.10.10 10.10.10*	60 × 2 = 120 (loads)
rev. 1	*10.10.10 10.10.10*	60 × 1 = 60 (loads)
	(blank)	

See the following document.

No. 316 – MS 2425/2

Account recording deliveries of timber to a warehouse, Middle/Classical Sargonic, Adab.

obv. 1–7	*10.10.10 10.10.10*	60 × 7 = 420 (loads)
obv. 8	*10.10.10* ĝeš-ME-SIG	30 (loads of) … … wood:
rev.	e$_2$-ni$_3$-gur$_{11}$	into the warehouse
	ba-ku$_4$(ŠE.ŠU)	has entered.
	(blank)	

These two texts[1] provide evidence that a scribe observed and controlled deliveries of timber, most likely measured in "loads," into a storage facility. He marked each tenth delivery with the sign U = "ten." The numerical system is sexagesimal: note that the number of deliveries in each line is 60.

[1] For another text belonging to this group, see CUSAS 23 no. 206. The obverse and reverse are confused in the original edition. The obverse is where the numerical notations ("doodles") are placed. The beginning of the reverse may have the reference to e$_2$-ni$_3$-gur$_{11}$. The first line should be corrected: […]-⌜tu⌝ > [ba]-⌜ku$_4$⌝.

This text demonstrates that writing was deeply embedded into everyday managerial routine. These and similar administrative texts unequivocaly show that at least some administrative records were composed while the actual transaction took place.

obv. 8: The variety of timber ĝeš-ME-SIG is unidentified.

rev. 2: The provenance of the numerical tablets Nos. 315–16 as Adab can be established by the writing of KU$_4$ as ŠE.ŠU. For this, see CUSAS 13 p. 285 signlist no. 579.

1.4.18 – Miscellaneous Goods

No. 317 – MS 2191/25

Account of gypsum, potash and aromatic substances, Middle Sargonic, Adab.

obv.	1 im-babbar$_2$ gu$_2$	1 talent of gypsum;
	1 naĝa gur	1 *gur* of potash:
	bur-gul	the stonecutter;
	1 *I$_3$-li$_2$-be-li$_2$*	1 (*gur* potash): *'Ilī-bēlī*;
	2(bariga) Lugal-iti-da	2 *bariga*: Lugalitida;
	2(bariga) AN-na	2 *bariga*: ANna;
	2(bariga) *Šu-i$_3$-li$_2$-su*	2 *bariga*: *Šu-'ilīšu*.
	3 sila$_3$ šim-gig	3 *sila* of *gig*-aromatics;
	½ gi ma-na	½ mina of *sweet-reed*;
rev.	½ bulug$_x$(ŠIM×UH$_3$) ma-na	½ mina of *galbanum*:
	Ur-pisaĝ	Urpisaĝ.
	3 sila$_3$ šim-gig	3 *sila* of *gig*-aromatics;
	2 gi ma-na	2 minas of *sweet reed*;
	½ bulug$_x$(ŠIM×UH$_3$) ma-na	½ mina of *galbanum*:
	Ur-^{d}MUŠ	Ur-MUŠ.
	Ur-^{d}Inana	Ur-Inana,
	ga:eš$_8$	the traveling merchant.

obv. 9: The term appears as gi-i$_3$, gi or ^{šim}gi in third-millennium sources: see Brunke and Sallaberger 2010: 50 for a discussion. The Akkadian equivalent of the term is *qanû ṭābu* "sweet reed," attested in later texts: see CAD Q 85, 88–89.

rev. 1, 5: As in other ED/ES Adab texts, the sign UH$_3$, inscribed inside ŠIM, is LAK304 with additional strokes. These wedges are the result of the further development of the sign LAK304×KASKAL = Ĝeša$_x$. A similar graphical process is observed for the sign KAS$_4$. Originally, the sign was DU×KASKAL. Starting about the Middle Sargonic period, the sign is written as DU$_{\text{-šeššig}}$.

rev. 7: This ga:eš$_8$ may be identical with the dam-gara$_3$ of text No. 306 rev. 2.

No. 318 – MS 4194

Account of miscellaneous goods, Middle Sargonic (early Naram-Suen), Adab.

obv.	1 ⸢tug$_2$-us$_2$ bala⸣	1 garment of secondary quality (made from) *bala*-fabric;
	1 i$_3$-ĝeš ĝeš-šum$_2$-ma ^{ĝeš}ni$_3$-*1*-sila$_3$	1 oil … *processed*(?) (in a) 1-*sila* wooden container;
	1 ^{kuš}esir$_4$ e$_2$-ba	1 pair of shoes;
	1 ze$_2$-na-ĝešimmar	1 midrib of date-palm frond:
	A$_2$-GA-LUM	*AGALUM* (is responsible).
	(blank)	
rev.	(blank)	

obv. 2: See SCTRAH no. 27 obv. 2 commentary, for the oil referred to as ĝeš šum$_2$-ma sila$_3$; Molina suggests that it refers to a method of processing oil and fat. For ^{ĝeš}niĝ$_2$ as a wooden container of certain capacity, see, e.g., an Ur III text, CDLI P105800 obv. ii 19.

obv. 4: See CAD Z 123 for *zinû* "midrib of the frond of the date palm" which was used as cheap wood for implements.

obv. 5: The name *A$_2$-GA-LUM* (interpretation uncertain; see MAD 3 p. 21) appears in a number of Classical Sargonic texts from Umma. This name is absent from the Adab corpus to my knowledge. However, cf. a similar text from Adab, SCTRAH no. 27, identified by Molina as dating to the early reign of Naram-Suen, where both sandals and oil in a wooden container are also mentioned. The present text belongs to the same group and so also comes from Adab.

No. 319 – MS 4238

Expenditure of food: barley flour, oil, fish and sheep for meat, Middle/Classical Sargonic, Adab.

obv.	3(ban$_2$) dabin	3 *ban* barley flour;
	1(ban$_2$) i$_3$ sila$_3$	1 *ban* oil (as 10) *sila*;
	2(ban$_2$) ku$_6$	2 *ban* fish:
	Ur$_2$-ni	To Urni,
	sagi	the cupbearer,
	udu ni$_3$-šum-ma-še$_3$	(when) for the sheep that had been slaughtered
rev.	im-ši-ĝen-na-am$_3$	he had come,
	an-na-šum$_2$	it has been given to him.
	(blank space)	
	(blank line)	
	iti še-kin-ku$_5$	Month Šekinku.

obv. 6: ni$_3$-šum-ma = *ṭabḫu* "slaughtered, butchered," CAD Ṭ 6.

1.5 – Classical to Late Sargonic Tablets

1.5.1 – Grain and Grain Products

No. 320 – MS 1952/21

Allocation of barley, Classical Sargonic, Adab.

obv.	2(ban$_2$) še A-ga-de$_3^{ki}$	2 *ban* barley (by the gur of) Agade:
	Ur-^{d}Aš$_8$-gi$_4$	Ur-Ašgi.
	1(bariga) še *Sar-ru-iš-ta$_2$-kal$_2$*	1 *bariga* barley: *Šarriš-takal.*
rev.	[...]	...
	[n+] 2(ban$_2$) še	x+2 *ban* barley:
	⸢x-x⸣	...
	[...]	

obv. 2: The personal name suggests Adab as provenance.

obv. 3: Cf. a tablet of similar format but uncertain provenance, CUSAS 26 no. 211 obv. 3, that mentions a person with a similar name, *Be-li$_2$-iš-ta$_2$-kal$_2$*. Note the "broken" writing *Sar-ru-iš* instead of *Sar-ri$_2$-iš* (MAD 3: 287).

No. 321 – MS 2191/35

Account of barley, Classical Sargonic, Adab?

obv.	10 še gur-saĝ-ĝal$_2$	10 *gursaĝĝal* barley:
	Ur-gu$_2$	Urgu;
	12(gur) 1(bariga) 2(ban$_2$) še gur / sila$_3$-zabar-ta	12 *gur* 1 *bariga* 2 *ban* barley by the bronze *sila*-vessel.
rev.	Ne-saĝ kuš$_7$	Nesaĝ, the animal-manager.
	4 še gur	4 *gur* barley:
	lu$_2$ *Ma*-SIKI-*su*	the man of *Ma*SIKI*šu*.
	(blank)	

rev. 3: Cf. *Ma*-SIKI in text No. 300 rev. ii 9.

No. 322 – MS 2365/1

Account of barley, Classical Sargonic, Adab.

obv.	20 še gur	20 *gur* barley:
	saĝ še-kam(ḪI×TIL)	it is the main amount of the barley:
	ki gi$_4$-gi$_4$-bi-še$_3$	it has to be restored.
	40 še gur	40 *gur* barley:
	Lu$_2$-^{d}En-lil$_2$	for Lu-Enlil,
	dam-gara$_3$-ra	the merchant.
rev.	Ur-zikum-ma	With Urzikuma,
	dub-sar-da	the scribe,

	an-da-tuku	he has it.
	še lu$_2$ Nubru^{ki}-ka-kam	It is the barley of the person from Nippur.

obv. 3: See Thomsen 1984: 303 for the compound verb ki-bi-(še$_3$) … gi$_4$ "to restore," and Wilcke 1976: 58 for ki-gi$_4$-gi$_4$-ba "bei seiner Rückgabe."

No. 323 – MS 2365/2

Expenditure of barley for bread and beer, Classical Sargonic, Adab.

obv.	60 ninda *6* ninda-gu	60 breads; 6 breads from the finely ground flour;
	3 kaš	3 (jars of) beer:
	PU$_3$.ŠA-*Er$_3$-ra*	PUŠA-Erra,
	ugula ⸢šu⸣-gal$_5$:la$_2$	the overseer of *šugalla'um*-professionals;
	60 ninda *6* ninda-gu	60 breads; 6 breads from the finely ground flour;
	3 kaš	3 (jars of) beer:
rev.	En-ra-ra	Enrara.
	(blank space)	
	šu-niĝin$_2$ 1(bariga) 3(ban$_2$) *4* sila$_3$ ^{šu2}1N$_8$^{ša} še / A-ga-de$_3$^{ki}	Total: 1 *bariga* 3 *ban* 4 ⅓ *sila* barley (by the *gur* of) Agade.
	zi-ga	Expended
	Ur-zikum-ma	(by) Urzikuma.
	iti mu-tir	Month Mutir.

obv. 1: See Milano 1993: 26 for (zi$_3$-)gu, a common variety of flour, probably a finely ground variety.

obv. 4: See MAD 3 p. 266 and Krecher 1973: 251 for references to the unidentified profession *šugalla'um* and its various writings.

No. 324 – MS 2365/3

Expenditure of grain for bread and beer, Classical Sargonic, Adab.

obv.	60 ninda-^{šu2}*1N$_8$*	60 breads of ⅓ (*sila*);
	6 ninda-imĝaĝa$_3$(AŠ$_3$.AN)	6 breads from processed emmer;
	3 kaš	3 (jars of) beer:
	2(ban$_2$) še anše gu$_7$	2 *ban* barley (as) donkey fodder:
	Pu$_x$(LAGAB×TIL)-ta	Puta,
rev.	dub-sar-maḫ	the chief scribe
	^{ĝeš}KUŠU$_2$^{ki}	of Umma.
	(blank space/ruling)	
	šu+niĝin$_2$ 1(bariga) 1(ban$_2$) še A-ga-de$_3$^{ki}	Total: 1 *bariga* 1 *ban* barley (by the *gur* of) Agade.
	šu+niĝin$_2$ *2* sila$_3$ zi$_3$-imĝaĝa$_3$	Total: 2 *sila* flour from processed emmer.
	zi-ga Ur-zikum-ma	Expended (by) Urzikuma.
	[iti] a$_2$-⸢ki⸣-[ti]	[Month] Akiti.

rev. 2: The sign for Ĝeša is no longer UḪ$_3$×KASKAL or UḪ$_3$-*gunû*, as in ED/ES Adab texts, but consists of a simplified sign UḪ$_3$ rotated 90° counter-clockwise: 

Accordingly the sign is transliterated KUŠU$_2$ instead of UḪ$_3$.

No. 325 – MS 2365/4

Expenditure of barley flour, Classical Sargonic, Adab.

obv.	4(ban$_2$) dabin A-ga-de$_3$^{ki}	4 *ban* of barley flour (by the gur of) Agade;
	1(ban$_2$) zi$_3$-gu	1 *ban* of finely ground barley flour:
	Ib-ni-lugal	*Yibni-šarrum*,
	šu-gal$_5$:la$_2$	the *šugalla'um*-official.
rev.	(blank space)	
	šu-niĝin$_2$ 5(ban$_2$) *1* sila$_3$ dabin A-ga-de$_3$^{ki}	Total: 5 *ban* 1 *sila* of barley flour (by the *gur* of) Agade.
	zi-ga	Expended
	Ur-zikum-ma	(by) Urzikuma.
	iti šu-ĝar	Month Šuĝar.

rev. 1: Curiously, there is no prior mention of the total's "1 *sila*" in the main body of the document.

No. 326 – MS 2365/5

Receipt of barley, Classical Sargonic, Adab.

obv.	23(gur) 1(bariga) še gur-si-sa$_2$	23 *gur* 1 *bariga* (by) the standard *gur*:
	ma$_2$ Arad$_2$(NITA$_2$×KUR)-lugal-ta	from the ship of Aradlugal(a),
	Ur-zikum-ma-ke$_4$	Urzikuma
	šu ba-ti	has received.
rev.	ša$_3$-bi-ta	Out of it:
	1 še gur	1 *gur* barley:
	Za$_3$-mu ma$_2$-GIN$_2$	(for) Zamu, the *caulker*;
	1(gur) Ur-^{d}Inana	1 *gur*: Ur-Inana;
	1(gur) la$_2$ 1(ban$_2$) 5 sila$_3$ Lugal-ĝeš	1 *gur* minus 1 *ban* 5 *sila*: Lugalĝeš.

obv. 2: Alternatively, "from the ship of the servant(s) of the king." Arad$_2$-lugal is a well-attested name but it does not appear in the Adab corpus.

rev. 3: For the profession ma$_2$-GIN$_2$/DUN$_3$/ŠU$_2$.DUN$_3$ associated with ships and sailing, see ED Lu$_2$ E 42, FAOS 17 p. 255, FAOS 15/2 p. 198 with additional references.

rev. 5: The scribe cancelled this entry by striking it out.

No. 327 – MS 2365/6

Expenditure of barley flour, Classical Sargonic, Adab.

obv.	1(bariga) dabin A-ga-de$_3^{ki}$	1 *bariga* of barley flour (by the *gur* of) Agade:
	arad$_2$(NITA×KUR) Lu$_2$-sa$_6$	they are the slaves of Lusa,
	sagi-me	the cupbearer.
	zi-ga	Expended
rev.	Ur-zikum-ma	(by) Urzikuma.
	(blank space)	
	iti eše$_2$-gar$_3$-šu-ĝar	Month Ešegaršuĝar.

No. 328 – MS 2365/7

Expenditure of barley, processed emmer and groats, Classical Sargonic, Adab.

obv.	60 ninda-^{šu_2}*1N$_8$* *6* ninda-imĝaĝa$_3$	60 breads of ⅓ (*sila*); 6 emmer breads;
	3 kaš	3 (jars of) beer;
	1(ban$_2$) *3* sila$_3$ ^{šu_2}*1N$_8$* še	1 *ban* 3 ⅓ *sila* barley:
	Ur-^{d}Nemur$_x$(⌜PIRIĜ⌝.TUR)	Ur-Nemur,
	dub-sar	the scribe;
	1(ban$_2$) zi$_3$ imĝaĝa$_3$	1 *ban* of emmer flour;
rev.	*2* sila$_3$ ni$_3$-ar$_3$-ra imĝaĝa$_3$	2 *sila* of emmer groats:
	i$_7$-ensi$_2$ ḫaš-de$_3$	to divert the "Canal of the Governor,"
	Lugal-e$_2$ šu ba-ti	Lugal-e has received.
	(blank space/ruling)	
	šu-niĝin$_2$ 1(bariga) *3* sila$_3$ ^{šu_2}*1N$_8$* še A-ga-de$_3^{ki}$	Total: 1 *bariga* 3 ⅓ *sila* (by the *gur* of) Agade.
	šu-niĝin$_2$ 1(ban$_2$) *4* sila$_3$ imĝaĝa$_3$	Total: 1 *ban* 4 *sila* of processed barley.

	zi-ga Ur-zikum-ma	Expended (by) Urzikuma.

rev. 2: For a … ḫaš(TAR) "to divert (water)," see De Maaijer and Jagersma 1997–98: 279. Here the verb may refer to work to be performed at the canal. For the same canal, see text No. 56 obv. i 3. The flour and groats were likely for distributing to the laborers working on this project. As recipient of the goods Lugal-e is an overseer of some kind.

No. 329 – MS 2365/8

Expenditure of barley, emmer flour and peas, Classical Sargonic, Adab.

obv.	150(gur) 3(bariga) 5(ban$_2$) *2* sila$_3$ / še gur A-ga-de$_3^{ki}$	150 *gur* 3 *bariga* 5 *ban* 2 *sila* of barley (by) the *gur* of Agade;
	10(gur) 2(bariga) 4(ban$_2$) *3* sila$_3$ zi$_3$ imĝaĝa$_3$ gur / A-ga-de$_3^{ki}$	10 *gur* 2 *bariga* 4 *ban* 3 *sila* of emmer flour (by) the *gur* of Agade;
	3(bariga) *7* sila$_3$ gu$_2$-gu$_2$	3 *bariga* 7 *sila* of peas.
rev.	zi-ga	Expended
	Ur-zikum-ma	(by) Urzikuma.
	(blank space)	
	iti ezen ^{d}Nin-mug	Month Ezen-Ninmug.
	u$_4$ *12* al-zal	12 days passed.
	ni$_3$-kas$_7$(ŠID)-bi ba-ak	Its balanced account has been done.

No. 330 – MS 2365/9

Turning over and receipt of processed emmer and peas, Classical Sargonic, Adab.

obv.	8(gur) 2(bariga) 1(ban$_2$) imĝaĝa$_3$ gur	8 *gur* 2 *bariga* 1 *ban* of processed emeer;
	9(gur) 1(bariga) 4(ban$_2$) gu$_2$-gu$_2$ gur	9 *gur* 1 *bariga* 4 *ban* of peas;
	10(gur) la$_2$ 2(bariga) bappir gur	10 *gur* minus 2 *bariga* of sourdough.
	šu-a gi$_4$-a	Turned over:
rev.	lu$_2$-eše$_2$-gid$_2$	the field-surveyor.
	E$_2$-aša$_5$-i$_7$	E'aša'i
	šu ba-ti	has received.

rev. 3: This is a personal name. Cf. the similar name Lugal-aša$_5$-i$_7$ in CUSAS 20 no. 161, CUSAS 23 no. 102. The same E$_2$-aša$_5$-i$_7$ appears in a similar text concerning barley, PPAC 1 no. 718 rev. 5.

No. 331 – MS 2365/10

Account of barley in connection to a merchant, Classical Sargonic, Adab.

obv.	1(gur) 2(bariga) 2(ban$_2$) še gur	1 *gur* 2 *bariga* 2 *ban* barley:
	Ur-mes	Urmes,
	šabra dumu-dumu-me	the chief administrator of the (royal) children('s household);
	6 še gur	6 *gur* barley:
rev.	Da-da	Dada,
	ĜIR$_3$-ERIN$_2$	…;
	10 še gur	10 *gur* barley:
	Ur-diĝir šu-i	Ur-diĝir, the barber.
	Gala dam-gara$_3$	Gala, the merchant.

obv. 3: Cf. CUSAS 11 no. 173 for a similar term ib-tur-tur-me, inaccurately translated as "they are of the small IB." Compare the ED IIIb Ĝirsu terms di$_4$-di$_4$-la-ne, TUR-TUR-ne, nam-dumu, and lu$_2$-tur(-ra) that are used as synonyms and refer to the governor's children and their domain. This document from Adab refers to a high official that manages the manor of the governor's offspring at Adab.

No. 332 – MS 2365/11

Issue of barley, Classical Sargonic, Adab.

obv.	5 še gur	5 *gur* barley:
	ašgab-gal	the chief leather-worker;
	3 še gur	3 *gur* barley:
	gu$_4$ udu	(for) cattle and sheep;
rev.	3 A$_2$-ni-ta	3 (*gur*): Anita;
	1 ⸢La⸣-[x]	1 (*gur*): La….
	(blank space)	
	e$_2$-maḫ-ta	Out of Emaḫ
	am$_3$-ta-e$_3$	it has been issued.

rev. 4: The writing A-AN-ta-e$_3$ shows that at least some forms of AN- (excluding an-na-/ne-) in earlier Adab texts may be reconstructed as a verbal chain that includes the ventive am$_6$-, /a=m=/.

No. 333 – MS 2365/12

Turning over and delivery of malt, Classical Sargonic, Adab.

obv.	3(bariga) 1(ban$_2$) munu$_4$ A-ga-de$_3^{ki}$	3 *bariga* 1 *ban* malt (by the *gur* of) Agade.
	šu-a gi$_4$-am$_3$	It has been turned over:
	Lu$_2$-$^{d.aš}$Aš$_7$-gi$_4$-am$_3$	It is of Lu-Ašgi,
rev.	munu$_4$-mu$_2$	the maltster.
	(blank space)	
	e$_2$-ni$_3$-gur$_{11}$-ra	Into the warehouse
	ba-ku$_4$	it has entered.

rev. 2: See FAOS 15/1 p. 73 for this lexeme designating a storage depot (e$_2$-ni$_3$-ga-ra there).

No. 334 – MS 2365/13

Allocation of barley flour and groats, Classical/Late Sargonic, Adab.

obv.	1 dabin gur	1 *gur* of barley flour:
	Ur-^{d}Za$^!$(A)-ba-ba ma$_2$-GIN$_2$	Ur-Zababa, the *caulker*;
	1 nagar-gal	1: the chief carpenter;
	1 niĝir$^!$(DUN$_3$)-gal	1: the chief herald;
	1 Lu$_2$-⸢lil⸣-la	1: Lulila;
	1 azlag$_4$(ĜIŠ.TUG$_2$.KAR.DU)-gal	1: the chief fuller;
	1 La-NI lu$_2$ A-⸢x-la⸣	1: LaNI, the man of A…la;
	1 KAM$_4$-mu	1: KAMmu;
	1 (ras.$^?$) Si-du$_3$	1: (erasure?) Sidu;
	2(bariga) ^{d}En-lil$_2$-la$_2$	2 *bariga*: Enlila,
	sagi-maḫ	the chief cupbearer;
	1 šidim-gal	1 (*gur*): the chief builder;
	2 Ur-sa$_6$ lu$_2$ […]	2: Ursa, the man of …;
	1 ⸢ni$_3$-ar$_3$-ra gur⸣(?)	1 *gur* of groats(?):
	E$_2$-dam-⸢si⸣	Edamsi;
rev.	1 $^{d.aš}$Aš$_7$-gi$_4$-pa-e$_3$	1: Ašgi-pa'e;
	1 Ur-^{d}Iškur	1: Ur-Iškur,
	dub-sar	the scribe;
	1 <…>	1 <…>
	(blank space)	
	1 ni$_3$-ar$_3$-ra gur	1 *gur* of groats:
	Uzug$_x$(AN.ZAG)-še$_3$	Uzugše;
	1 E$_2$-ušumgal(GAL.UŠUM)	1: E'ušumgal.

obv. 8: Cf. KAM$_4$-mu-e$_3$ in CUSAS 11 no. 103 (Meskigala). The person in our text should be a different individual considering the interval in time between these two texts.

rev. 6: Cf. the name Lugal-uzug$_x$(AN.ZAG)-še$_3$ in ECTJ no. 54 (ED IIIa Nippur) obv. iii 3. Cf. also Uzug$_x$(AN.ZAG) in texts similar to the present one, CUSAS 26 nos. 182 obv. 6, 183 obv. 5. Both documents are of Classical Sargonic date and uncertain provenance.

No. 335 – MS 2642

Account of barley, Classical Sargonic, Adab?

obv.	48(gur) 2(ban$_2$)⸢še$^!$ gur⸣	48 *gur* 2 *ban* barley:
	Nam-maḫ-ni	Nammaḫ(a)ni;
	15(gur) 1(bariga) 4(ban$_2$) Lugal-iti-da	15 *gur* 1 *bariga* 4 *ban*: Lugalitida;
	21(gur) 2(bariga) Šu-na	21 *gur* 2 *bariga*: Šuna;
	8(gur) 2(bariga) Gala	8 *gur* 2 *bariga*: Gala.
rev.	(blank)	

No. 336 – MS 4190

Account of barley measured by the large *gur*, Classical Sargonic, Adab?

obv.	⸢80⸣ še gur-maḫ	80 large *gur* of barley:
	a-ra$_2$ *1*-kam	it is of the 1st time.
	50 a-ra$_2$ *2*-kam	50: it is of the 2nd time.
	60 a-ra$_2$ *3*-kam	60: it is of the 3rd time.
	11 a-ra$_2$ *4*-kam	11: it is of the 4th time.
rev.	(blank space)	
rev.	šu+niĝin$_2$ 201 še gur-maḫ	Total: 201 large *gur* of barley.
	(blank space)	

No. 337 – MS 4201

Inventory of barley and emmer available in a field and a storehouse, Classical Sargonic, Adab?

obv.	3 guru$_7$ / 2(ĝeš$_2$×u) 6(ĝeš$_2$) / 5(u) 5(aš) 1(bariga) še gur	3 *guru* 1615 *gur* 1 *bariga* barley
	sila$_3$-zabar-ta	by the bronze *sila*-vessel.
	še aša$_5$-ga ĝal$_2$-la-am$_3$	It is the barley that is available in the field.
rev.	2 še guru$_7$ (ras.) gur	2 *guru* (erasure) (= 7200) *gur* barley
	1 ziz$_2$ guru$_7$ gur	1 *guru* (= 3600) *gur* emmer:
	ĝanun	(in) the storehouse.
	(blank)	
l.e.	[...]-⸢a$^?$⸣	...

Note the impressive amounts of barley in the field (3×3600+1615 $^1/_5$ gur = 12,415 $^1/_5$ gur = 3,724,560 *sila*, if one assumes the "Akkadian" *gur* of 5 *bariga* and 300 *sila* here), and of both barley and emmer in the storehouse (together 10,800 gur = 3,240,000 *sila*). This text is likely an inventory of barley and emmer in a whole large household. A remarkable fact is that the first amount is attributed to "barley in the field." This implies that the barley had not yet been delivered to the storehouse. Accordingly, the first part of the document may record grain that had been recently harvested or even give a calculation of grain that had not yet been harvested.

rev. 1–2: The use of two terms for measures in one entry should not be confusing. Cf. writings ^{šu2}1N$_8$^{ša} giĝ$_4$, literally "⅓ mina (mina as 20) shekel(s)" in some ED and Sargonic texts. The explanation of this phenomenon lies in scribal practice and not in metrology. If one rules out a scribal mistake, the reason to mention two measures in one entry may be that the first measure was perceived as a numeral by the scribes. In the case of weight measures, the notation $^{\text{šu2}}$1N$_8$^{ša} has the numerical value 20. Similarly, guru$_7$ is a logogram for the number 3600 when used with capacity measures.

No. 338 – MS 4222

Receipt of groats, Classical/Late Sargonic, Adab.

obv.	*1(gur) 2(bariga)* ni$_3$-ar$_3$-ra gur-maḫ	1 *gur* 2 *bariga* groats (by) the large *gur*:
	Ur-lugal	Ur-lugal;
	1(gur) ni$_3$ Ur-LUḪ	1 *gur* gr<oats>: UrLUḪ;
	3(bariga) 1(ban$_2$) 5 sila$_3$ ni$_3$ Maš-tur	3 *bariga* 1 *ban* 5 *sila* gr<oats>: Maštur;
	2(bariga) ni$_3$ Ur-$^{\text{d.aš}}$Aš$_7$-<gi$_4$>	2 *bariga* gr<oats>: Ur-Aš(gi);
	2(bariga) 3(ban$_2$) ni$_3$ AB-⸢e⸣	2 *bariga* 3 *ban* gr<oats>: AB-e;
	2(bariga) ni$_3$ E$_2$-saḫar-ta	2 *bariga* gr<oats>: Esaharta;
	1(bariga) 2(ban$_2$) Ur-mes	1 *bariga* 2 *ban*: Urmes;
rev.	*1(bariga) 2(ban$_2$)* ni$_3$ E$_2$-saḫar-ta unu$_3$	1 *bariga* 2 *ban* gr<oats>: Esaharta, the cowherd;
	5(ban$_2$) ni$_3$ Ur-^{d}Nin-zu	5 *ban* gr<oats>: Ur-Ninzu;
	3(bariga) 4(ban$_2$) ni$_3$ nagar-gal	3 *bariga* 4 *ban* gr<oats>: the chief carpenter;
	2(bariga) ni$_3$ Ur-^{d}Dumu-zi-da	2 *bariga* gr<oats>: Ur-Dumuzida;
	2(bariga) ni$_3$ Ur-eš$_3$-lil$_2$-la$_2$ sipa	2 *bariga* gr<oats>: Ur-ešlila, the shepherd.
	(ruling)	
	šu+niĝin$_2$ *7(gur) 2(bariga) 5(ban$_2$)* ni$_3$-ar$_3$-ra / gur-maḫ	Total: 7 *gur* 2 *bariga* 5 *ban* groats (by) the large *gur*.
	(ruling)	
	Šu-Ma-ma	*Šu-Mama*
	šu ba-ti	has received.

obv. 1: gur-maḫ, literally "large gur," was the main unit of mensuration during the Fara period and was equal to 480 *sila*. Thus it was two times bigger than the standard *gur* (gur-saĝ-ĝal$_2$-si-sa$_2$) of the Early Dynastic IIIb period. The "*gur* of *Agade*" was introduced at some time during the Sargonic period. Powell 1990: 498 states that "in the Ur III period, maḫ probably denotes any standard higher than the normal (Akkad) standard." Owing to the good state of preservation, it is possible to calculate the capacity of the gur-maḫ in this text and learn whether this measure was larger than the Akkadian *gur*. The sum of the individual numbers in the text is 2 *gur*, 20 *bariga*, 17 *ban* and 5 *sila*. The sum of the numbers in accordance to the the standard gur-saĝ-ĝal$_2$ of 4 *bariga* gives a total of 7 *gur* 2 *bariga* 5 *ban*. This number appears in the total of the document, if one disregards 5 *sila* in obv. 4, which the scribe has obviously forgotten to add to the total. This shows that the gur-maḫ of the present text was equal to the normal gur-saĝ-ĝal$_2$ of 4 *bariga* and 240 *sila* of the ED IIIb period, and in turn that the Sargonic "large *gur*" was in fact smaller than the Akkad *gur* of 5 *bariga* and 300 *sila*.

obv. 3 f.: ni$_3$ is an abbreviation for ni$_3$-ar$_3$-ra "groats." Note its absence in obv. 8; probably a mistake of the scribe.

No. 339 – MS 4240a

Account of barley and emmer, Classical Sargonic, Adab.

MS 4240 consists of two fragments of different tablets put together in modern times. The thin fragment on the right side is fake.

obv.	4(gur) 2(bariga) 2(ban$_2$) še gur-maḫ	4 *gur* 2 *bariga* 2 *ban* barley (by) the large *gur*.
	KA-bi 1(gur) la$_2$ 1(ban$_2$) *1* sila$_3$ gur	Its …: 1 *gur* 1 *ban* 1 *sila*.
	5(gur) la$_2$ 4(ban$_2$) ziz$_2$ gur-maḫ	5 *gur* minus 4 *ban* emmer (by) the large *gur*.
	KA-bi 1(gur) *1* ^{šu2}*2N$_8$* sila$_3$ ⸢gur⸣	Its …: 1 *gur* 1 ⅔ sila.
	šu+niĝin$_2$ 5(gur) 2(bariga) 1(ban$_2$) la$_2$ 1(sila$_3$) še [gur]	Total: 5 *gur* 2 *bariga* 1 *ban* minus 1 *sila* barley.
	šu+niĝin$_2$ 5(gur) 3(bariga) ⸢1⸣(ban$_2$) [+n ziz$_2$ gur]	Total: 5 *gur* 3 *bariga* 1 *ban* [+x emmer].

	[break]	…
rev.	[break]	…
	šu+niĝin$_2$-šu+niĝin$_2$ ⸢40⸣ [+n … še gur]	Grand total: 40+x [*gur* barley].
	šu+niĝin$_2$-šu+niĝin$_2$ 14 [+n … ziz$_2$ gur]	Grand total: 14+x [*gur* emmer].
	AB-[…]	…
	mu-[x-x]	has …ed.
	(blank)	
	En-e$_2$	En-e.

obv. 2, 4: The meaning of KA-bi "its …" in the present context is uncertain. It appears in other texts from the same "file," CUSAS 19 nos. 84, 109. Maiocchi and Visicato tentatively suggest that it denotes a difference between various *gur* measures. As for the present document, in the case of barley, the total corresponds to the sum of two amounts, the normal and the one preceded by KA-bi. Note that in this text, the gur-maḫ of barley is actually a *gur* of 5 *bariga* corresponding to the normal Akkadian *gur* of 300 *sila*. In the case of emmer, the calculations are not clear and require further study.

rev. 1'–2': See the commentary to text No. 363 rev. ii 1 for "grand total."

rev. 5': See CUSAS 13 nos. 71, 76, 104, 113, CUSAS 19 nos. 83–84, 94, 99, 108, 177, CUSAS 20 no. 348, and BdI 1 no. 110 for the same scribe. See also CUSAS 19, commentary to no. 84.

No. 340 – MS 4240b

Offering of grain to gods, Classical Sargonic, Adab.

obv.	[break]	…
	PAP *2*(gur) *2*(bariga) [(x)] ^{d}Inana	(checkmark) 2 *gur* 2 *bariga*: Inana;
	PAP *1*(gur) *2*(bariga) ^{d}En-⸢ki⸣	(checkmark) 1 *gur* 2 *bariga*: Enki;
	PAP *2*(gur) *1*(bariga) ^{d}Mes-lam-ta-[e$_3$]	(checkmark) 2 *gur* 1 *bariga*: Meslamta'e(a);
	PAP *2*(bariga) *3*(ban$_2$) e$_2$-dam	(checkmark) 2 *bariga* 3 *ban*: the "House of the spouse";
	3(bariga) ^{d}Bara$_2$-^{d}En-lil$_2$-ĝar [(x)]	3 *bariga*: Bara-Enlilĝar(a);
	1(gur) ^{d}DUB.⸢ME⸣	1 *gur*: DUBME;
	1(gur) ^{d}Nisaba(NAGA)	1 *gur* Nisaba;
	2(gur) PAP ^{d}Nin-mug	2 *gur* (checkmark): Ninmug;
rev.	PAP *2*(bariga) *3*(ban$_2$) ^{d}Dam-gal-nun	(checkmark) 2 *bariga* 3 *ban*: Damgalnun(a);
	⸢n⸣ PAP ^{d}NI	x: (checkmark) (deity) NI;
	1(gur) ^{d}Utu	1 *gur*: Utu;
	PAP *2*(bariga) *3*(ban$_2$) ^{d}Nin-⸢x⸣-[x]	(checkmark) 2 *bariga* 3 *ban*: Nin…;
	PAP *3*(gur) ⸢^{d}⸣[x]-⸢x⸣	(checkmark) 3 *gur*: …;
	PAP *3*(bariga) ^{d}Eš$_{23}$-peš	(checkmark) 3 *bariga*: Ešpeš.
	(blank)	
	šu+niĝin$_2$ *51* *1*(bariga) še gur […]	Total: 51 *gur* 1 *bariga* barley …
	[break]	…

obv. 6': See CUSAS 23 no. 167 for a similar offering list that includes this deity.

obv. 7': The name of the goddess is written with the same sign as the word naĝa "potash" in text No. 317 obv. 2.

No. 341 – MS 4249

Receipt and arrears of barley, Classical/Late Sargonic, Adab.

obv.	1(gur) 2(bariga) la$_2$ 2(ban$_2$) 5 sila$_3$ še gur sa$_2$-du$_{11}$	1 *gur* 2 *bariga* minus 2 *ban* 5 *sila* barley (by) the "tithe *gur*":
	ki KA-[x]-⸢x⸣	from …;
	3(bariga) 1(ban$_2$) ĝanun-gal-ta	3 *bariga* 1 *ban*: out of the big storehouse;
	2(bariga) e$_2$-ni$_3$-gur$_{11}$	2 *bariga*: (out of) the warehouse;
	1(bariga) 3(ban$_2$) a-ra$_2$ *1*	1 *bariga* 3 *ban*: the 1st time;
	1(bariga) 1(ban$_2$) a-ra$_2$ *2*	1 *bariga* 1 *ban*: the 2nd time;
	2(bariga) a-ra$_2$ *3*	2 *bariga*: the 3rd time:
	ki Nin-nir-zi-ta	from Ninnirzi.
	šu+niĝin$_2$ 3(gur) 2(bariga) 2(ban) 5 sila$_3$ še gur	Total: 3 *gur* 2 *bariga* 2 *ban* 5 *sila* barley.
	šu ti-a-am$_3$	It is what has been received.
	la$_2$-i$_3$ 1(gur) 2(ban$_2$) še gur	Arrears: 1 *gur* 2 *ban* barley:
rev.	En-bara$_2$	Enbara;
	1(gur) 2(bariga) *7* sila$_3$ še gur	1 *gur* 2 *bariga* 7 *sila* barley:
	Ki-inim-ma	Ki'inima;
	1(gur) 1(ban$_2$) 5 sila$_3$ Abba$_2$ dub-sar	1 *gur* 1 *ban* 5 *sila*: Abba, the scribe;
	1(gur) ⸢4(ban$_2$)⸣ Lu$_2$-ni	1 *gur* 4 *ban*: Luni(zu);
	1(bariga) 1(ban$_2$) *2 ½* sila$_3$ Tu-tu	1 *bariga* 1 *ban* 2 ½ *sila* Tutu;
	5(ban$_2$) Nin-nir-zi	5 *ban*: Ninnirzi;
	šu+niĝin$_2$ 4(gur) 1(bariga) 1(ban$_2$) *4 ½* sila$_3$ še gur	Total: 4 *gur* 1 *bariga* 1 *ban* 4 ½ *sila* barley.
	(ruling)	
	šu ti-a ninda-bi du$_8$	Received. Its bread (to) bake.
	[la$_2$]-⸢i$_3$⸣ *1(bariga) 2(ban$_2$)* še ⸢gur⸣	Arrears: 1 *bariga* 2 *ban* barley.
	iti še-gur$_x$(|ŠE.ŠE|.KIN)-am$_3$	Month Šeguram.

obv. 1: See Powell 1990: 507 for the capacity measure for sa$_2$-du$_{11}$, literally "tithe." According to him, the measure was either 18 or 24 *sila* during the Sargonic period. The "tithe *gur*" (gur sa$_2$-du$_{11}$) was based on the measure sa$_2$-du$_{11}$ and was probably equal to 160 *sila* (160 *sila* = 16 *ban* = 4 *sadu(g)* = 1 *gur sadu(g)*).

obv. 8: See CUSAS 20 no. 204 rev. 2' for likely the same individual.

No. 342 – MS 4258

Account of grain and grain products with price relations in barley and silver, Classical Sargonic, Adab?

obv.	[n še gur]	[x *gur* of grain];
	2(bariga)⌜dabin⌝	2 *bariga* barley flour;
	2(gur) ni$_3$-ar$_3$-⌜ra⌝ [(x)]	2 *gur* groats;
	2(gur) bappir ⌜x⌝ [...]	2 *gur* … sourdough;
	3 ninda 1 [kaš]	3 breads, 1 (jar of) [beer]:
	Ur-^{d}Utu	Ur-Utu.
	1 še gur	1 *gur* of grain:
	šandana-SAR	the … gardener.
	1 giĝ$_4$ ku$_3$ še-bi 2(bariga) [(x)]	1 shekel silver; its barley: 2 *bariga*.
rev.	1 ^{tug2}bar-dul$_5$	1 *bardul*-garment;
	še-bi 3(bariga)	its barley: 3 *bariga*.
	5(ban$_2$) še	5 *ban* barley:
	Lugal-en-nu	Lugal-ennu.
	1(gur) 2(ban$_2$) imĝaĝa$_3$(AŠ$_2$.AN) gur	1 *gur* 2 *ban* of processed emmer.
	(blank space)	
	šu+niĝin$_2$ 13(gur) la$_2$ 5(ban$_2$) še ⌜zi$_3$⌝ [...]	Total: 13 *gur* minus 5 *ban* barley (and) flour …
	Ur-^{d}[...]	Ur…
	[1 line missing]	…

obv. 5: The fragment with the signs ninda 1 is glued to the tablet upside-down but is authentic.

obv. 8: See the commentary to text No. 360 obv. iii 10.

1.5.2 – Bread and Beer

No. 343 – MS 4192

Expenditure of beer, Classical Sargonic, Adab.

See CUSAS 13 nos. 92–102 for similar texts. Both Šu-ilišu and Mesag appear in the present text and the CUSAS 13 texts but should not be confused with the eponymous individuals of the "Mesag" and "Šu-ilišu" archives.

obv.	2 kaš-sag$_{10}$	2 (jars of) premium beer;
	2 kaš-ĝiri$_{3}$	2 (jars of) *traveler's* beer:
	Šu-i$_{3}$-li$_{2}$-su	*Šu-'ilīšu*,
	sagi lugal	the cupbearer of the king.
	1 kaš-sag$_{10}$ 1 kaš-ĝiri$_{3}$	1 (jar of) premium beer, 1 (jar of) *traveler's* beer:
	Da-da *šu* šabra-e$_{2}$	Dada, the man of the chief administrator of the household.
	[1] kaš-sag$_{10}$ 1 kaš-ĝiri$_{3}$	1 (jar of) premium beer, 1 (jar of) *traveler's* beer:
	[E$_{2}$]-da-mu	Edamu,
	[dub]-sar	the scribe.
rev.	[3] kaš-sag$_{10}$	[3] (jars of) premium beer,
	[3] kaš-ĝiri$_{3}$	[3] (jars of) *traveler's* beer:
	[A]-bi$_{2}$-i-sar	*Abī-yisar.*
	(blank space)	
	šu+niĝin$_{2}$ 7 kaš-sag$_{10}$	Total: 7 (jars of) premium beer,
	šu+niĝin$_{2}$ 7 kaš-ĝiri$_{3}$	Total: 7 (jars of) *traveler's* beer.

	zi-ga Me-^{sag3}sag$_7$(GAN)	Expended (by) Mesag.
	iti ĝa$_2$-udu-ur$_4$	Month Ĝa'udu'ur.

obv. 2: The interpretation of kaš-ĜIR$_3$ remains uncertain: see CUSAS 13 no. 92 commentary and Schrakamp 2012a: 283 sub nos. 92–93. One possibility is that the sign ĜIR$_3$ denotes the quality of beer allocated for journeys (ĝiri$_3$), thus "traveler's beer."

obv. 6: The Akkadian pronoun appears here instead of the usual Sumerian lu$_2$.

obv. 8–9: See CUSAS 13 no. 100 obv. 3–4 for the same individual.

rev. 3: There is room only for a very narrow sign, e.g. A.

No. 344 – MS 4196

Allocation of bread and beer, Classical Sargonic, Adab?

obv.	[2$^?$] ninda ⸢ne⸣-[saĝ] umbin$_x$(UMBIN×LU)	[2$^?$] offering breads (of 1) *umbin*-measure (flour each);
	24 [ninda] ne-saĝ *1* sila$_3$	24 offering breads (of) 1 *sila* (each);
	3 kaš	3 (jars of) beer:
	Ni$_3$-^{li}liš-da	Nilišda;
	4 ninda ne-saĝ umbin$_x$(UMBIN×LU)	4 offering breads (of 1) *umbin*-measure (each);
	10 ninda ne-saĝ *1* sila$_3$	10 offering breads (of) 1 *sila* (each);
	[break]	. . .
rev.	[break]	. . .
	5 lu$_2$ *Ša-ma-*⸢*si*$^?$*-in*$^?$⸣	5 persons of *Šamašin*:
	1 kaš *Šu-Ma-ma*	1 (jar of) beer: *Šu-Mama*;
	1 kaš Da-da	1 (jar of) beer: Dada;
	1 kaš ^{ĝeš}Gigir$_x$(LAGAB×TIL)-e	1 (jar of) beer: Gigire;
	1 kaš *Ma-sa-nin-su*	1 (jar of) beer: *Ma(n)-šāninšu*
	1 kaš Ur-mes	1 (jar of) beer: Urmes.
	(ruling)	
	[šu+niĝin$_2$] 6 ninda ne-saĝ ⸢umbin$_x$⸣	[Total:] 6 offering breads (of 1) *umbin*-measure (each);
	⸢34 ninda ne⸣ -[saĝ *1* sila$_3$]	34 offering breads (of) 1 *sila* (each);
l.e.	[n] kaš u$_4$ 7	x (jars of) beer. Day 7.

For similar texts, see CUSAS 13 no. 90 and text No. 345 below.

obv. 4: This is probably a personal name. The sign LI is likely a phonetic complement to help the reader take LIŠ as /liš/. Cf. also a bread ninda-LIŠ-da in MSL 11 p. 118 6.1 l. 2 (Nippur Forerunner to Hh XXIII–XXIV).

rev. 1': For this Akkadian name, which often appears in Classical Sargonic texts from Umma, see Schrakamp 2012b: 151 no. 16, with additional references.

rev. 5': Cf. BdI 1 no. 257 obv. 5 for likely the same individual. Because of him, the text may be attributed to Adab.

No. 345 – MS 4197

Allocation of bread and beer, Classical Sargonic, Adab?

obv.	31 ninda ne-saĝ	31 offering breads:
	Niĝir-AB	Niĝir-AB;
	6 ninda Lugal-lu-ni ⸢x⸣	6 breads: Lugalluni, the…;
	6 ninda Lu$_2$-sa$_6$ šu-i	6 breads: Lusa, the barber;
	4 ninda Du-du nar	4 breads: Dudu, the musician;
	3 ninda (ras.)	3 breads: (erasure)
	2 ninda i$_3$-du$_8$-gal	2 breads: the chief doorman;
	2 ninda Lugal-ḫa-ma šu-i	2 breads: Lugalhama, the barber;
	2 ninda ma$_2$-laḫ$_5$-gal	2 breads: the chief sailor;
	2 [ninda] Pu$_3$-zu$_2$-ru-sa	2 [breads]: Puzurusa;
	[n ninda] dumu Ur-^{d}Inana ⸢ugula⸣	[x breads]: the son of Ur-Inana, the overseer;
	[break]	…
rev.	[break]	…
	2 […]	2:

	2 ⸢I$_3$⸣-[...]-⸢x⸣	2: I...;
	2 Lugal-ḫa-ma šu-i	2: Lugalhama, the barber;
	2 Pu$_3$-zu$_2$-ru-sa	2: Puzurusa;
	2 Lugal-⸢ezen⸣ Ur-eš$_3$	2: Lugalezen (and) Ur-eš;
	2 ninda Saĝ-ku$_5$ 2 ninda i$_3$-⸢du$_8^?$⸣	2 breads: Saĝku; 2 breads: the doorman(?);
	10 ninda 10 kaš sila$_3$	10 breads; 10 *sila* beer:
	Lagaš$_x$(BUR.NU$_{11}$)^{ki}	Lagaš;
	10 ninda 10 kaš sila$_3$	10 breads; 10 *sila* beer:
	Na-ir-ru-um	*Na'irrum*;
	x *3* ninda NIM lu$_2$ $^{⸢ĝeš⸣}$[Gigir$_2$-(e)]	... 3 breads: NIM, the man of [Gigir(e)].
	šu-niĝin$_2$ 90 ninda	Total: 90 breads.
	u$_4$ *2*-kam	It is the 2nd day.
l.e.	[n] ninda Amar-ki nagar	x breads: Amarki, the carpenter.

Several individuals in this text appear in other Classical Sargonic texts: see CUSAS 13 nos. 105–9, CUSAS 23 no. 121. Although the respective editors claim the texts are from Adab, some of them may belong to the "Lugal-ra" archive.

obv. 2: Cf. Niĝir-AB in CUSAS 26 no. 203 obv. 2, which Westenholz attributes to the "Lugal-ra" archive."

rev. 11': Cf. CUSAS 13 no. 109 rev. 3: 3 ninda NIM lu$_2$ ^{ĝeš}Gigir$_2$-e.

No. 346 – MS 4248

Allocation of bread and beer, Classical Sargonic, Adab.

obv.	60 ninda ne-saĝ umbin$_x$(UMBIN×LU)	60 offering breads of (1) *umbin*-measure;
	40 ninda ne-saĝ *1* sila$_3$	40 offering breads of 1 *sila*;
	10 sila$_3$ kaš-sig$_5$ 2 kaš	10 *sila* of fine beer, 2 (jars of regular) beer:
	Ur-niĝar lu$_2$ Unug^{ki}	Urniĝar, the Urukean.
	15 ninda 1 kaš	15 breads, 1 (jar of) beer:
	KU-lugal	KUlugal.
	3 ninda 1 kaš Ur-ĝar	3 breads, 1 (jar of) beer: Urĝar.
	2 ninda baḫar$_2$	2 breads: the potter.
	10 ninda *10* sila$_3$ kaš	10 breads, 10 *sila* beer:
	lu$_2$ abba$_2$-iri Saman$_x$(ŠE.BU.NUN.ŠE$_3$)-na^{ki}	the man of the city elder of (the town) Saman(a).
	1 ninda ne-saĝ umbin$_x$	1 offering bread of (1) *umbin*-measure:
	$^{d.aš}$Aš$_7$-gi$_4$-a$_2$-na ^{ĝeš}gu-za-la$_2$	Ašgi'ana, the throne-bearer.
	10 ninda Da-da nar	10 breads: Dada, the musician.
	1 ninda-si Mu-ni-maḫ	1 filled bread: Munimaḫ.
rev.	(blank)	

obv. 6: The first sign is written over erasure. See OIP 14, 179 (CS Adab) for the same personal name.

No. 347 – MS 4252

Account of bread and beer, Classical Sargonic, Adab.

obv.	[n ninda ne]-⌜saĝ⌝ umbin$_x$(UMBIN×LU)	x offering [breads] (baked from 1) *umbin*-measure (of flour);
	[n] ninda ne-saĝ *1* sila$_3$	x offering breads (baked from) 1 *sila* (of flour);
	3 kaš	3 (jars of) beer:
	Ni$_3$-^{li}liš-da	Nilišda;
	120 ninda ne-saĝ *1* sila$_3$	120 offering breads (baked from) 1 *sila* (of flour);
	6 kaš	6 (jars of) beer:
	Pu-ša$_3$-ti-U$_3$	Pušati'U;
	20 ⌜ninda⌝ 1 kaš	20 breads, 1 (jar of) beer:
	lu$_2$ Ur-^{d}Utu	the man of Ur-Utu;
rev.	5 ninda lu$_2$ Pu$_3$-sa	5 breads: the man of Pusa;
	5 ninda tibira	5 breads: the metalworker;
	10 ninda Me-^{sa2}sag$_7$ sukkal	10 breads: Mesag, the secretary;
	3 ninda ne-saĝ umbin$_x$	3 offering breads (baked from 1) *umbin*-measure (of flour):
	[n ^{ĝeš}banšur$_x$(GIŠGAL×IGI)] ensi$_2$-ka	[x breads: the table] of the governor.
	(blank space)	
	šu+niĝin$_2$ 63 ninda ne-saĝ umbin$_x$	Total: 63 offering breads (baked from 1) *umbin*-measure (of flour);
	šu+niĝin$_2$ 185 ninda ne-saĝ *1* sila$_3$	Total: 185 offering breads (baked from) 1 *sila* (of flour);
	[šu+niĝin$_2$] 10 kaš	[Total]: 10 (jars of) beer.
	[...] u$_4$ *3*-kam	This is the … of the 3rd day.

rev. 1: Pu$_3$-sa may be an abbreviation of the name Pu$_3$-zu$_2$-ru-sa, for which see text No. 348 obv. 8.

No. 348 – MS 4256

Account of bread and beer, Classical Sargonic, Adab.

obv.	6 ninda ne-saĝ *1* sila$_3$	6 offering breads (baked from) 1 *sila* (of flour);
	A$_2$-na sagi	Ana, the cupbearer;
	2 E$_2$-ĜAR-bi šidim	2: EĜARbi, the builder;
	20 ^{ĝeš}banšur$_x$(GIŠGAL×IGI) ensi$_2$-ka	20: the table of the governor;
	2 gala-maḫ	2: the chief cult-singer;
	2 gala e$_2$-maḫ	2: the cult-singer of the Emaḫ (temple);
	2 [x]-mu šidim	2: …mu, the builder;
	2 Pu$_3$-zu$_2$-ru-sa	2: Puzurusa;

	⸢4⸣ šandana	4: the orchard-administrator;
	2 E$_{2}$-sa$_{6}$ baḫar$_{x}$(EDIN)	2: Esa, the potter;
	½ maš-maš	½: the incantation priest;
	1 ½ ereš-diĝir Bara$_{2}$-^{d}En-⸢lil$_{2}$⸣-[ĝar]	1 ½: the high priestess of Bara-Enlilĝar(a);
	3 ninda 1 kaš	3 breads, 1 (jar of) beer:
	⸢SAĜ$^{?}$⸣-ĜAR-⸢x⸣	…;
rev.	15 ninda 1 ⸢kaš⸣	15 breads, 1 (jar of) beer:
	lu$_{2}$ Lagaš(BURU$_{4}$.LA)[^{ki}-(me)]	the people from Lagaš;
	5 ninda 5 sila$_{3}$ [kaš]	5 breads, 5 *sila* [beer]:
	Lu$_{2}$-^{d}Su-la-[at]	Lu-Sulat;
	2 E$_{2}$-lu$_{2}$ gu$_{2}$-za-la$_{2}$	2: Elu, the throne-bearer;
	2 E$_{2}$-LUḪ-ge-⸢si x⸣	2: ELUḪgesi, the …;
	1 En-kisal nar	1 Enkisal, the musician;
	6 A$_{2}$-na sagi	6: Ana, the cupbearer;
	4 En-ni$_{3}$-kas$_{4}$ NI-x-KU	4: Ennikas, the …;
	2 mar-tu *Na-aḫ-šum-sa-na-at*	2: the Amorite *Naḫšum-sanat.*
	1 ninda ne-saĝ umbin$_{x}$(UMBIN×LU)	1 offering bread (baked from 1) *umbin*-measure (of flour):
	Mu-ni-maḫ	Munimaḫ.
	(ruling/blank space)	
	šu+niĝin$_{2}$ 1 ninda ne-saĝ umbin$_{x}$	Total: 1 offering bread (baked from 1) *umbin*-measure (of flour);
	šu+niĝin$_{2}$ 86 ninda ne-saĝ *1* sila$_{3}$	Total: 86 offering breads (baked from) 1 *sila* (of flour);
	šu-niĝin$_{2}$ 2 kaš	Total: 2 (jars of) beer.

obv. 4: The sign is LAK650 with an extra vertical closing wedge. For the same sign, see CUSAS 13 p. 256 sign no. 79, variant c.

rev. 5: Note the writing gu$_{2}$-za-la$_{2}$ instead of the usual gu-za-la$_{2}$.

rev. 10: This Amorite name appears in Ur III texts as *Na-ah-šum*-BALA. See *Na-ah-šum-(sa-na-at)* in CUSAS 27 nos. 48, 148, 193, which belong to the "Šu-ilišu" archive from Maškan-ili-Akkade. The present text does not seem to belong to that archive.

1.5.3 – Cattle and Sheep

No. 349 – MS 2191/28

Inventory of dead cattle, Classical Sargonic, Adab.

obv.	2 ⸢gu$_{4}$⸣	2 oxen;
	1 ab$_{2}$-*1*	1 cow of 1 (year):
	ba-ug$_{7}$	they have died.
	ni$_{3}$-kas$_{7}$(ŠID) ba-ak	The balanced account has been done.
	bar-bi-ta	*Out of what is left …*
rev.	(blank)	

obv. 5: The document is probably not fishished because it ends with an administrative term bar-bi-

ta, literally "out of its outside." Cf. ša$_3$-bi-ta that designates a part of an amount. See CUSAS 23 no. 99 obv. 4.

No. 350 – MS 2191/29

Account of sheep and goats, Middle/Classical Sargonic, Adab.

obv.	1 ⸢udu⸣	1 sheep;
	1 maš$_2$	1 goat:
	Ur-^{d}Ištaran(KA.⸢DI⸣)	Ur-Ištaran;
	1 udu 1 maš$_2$	1 sheep, 1 goat:
	ni$_3$-gur$_{11}$ ⸢Šu-i$_2$⸣	the property of Šu'i;
	2 maš$_2$	2 goats:
	^{d}⸢Aš$_8$-gi$_4$⸣-[x-x] sukkal	Ašgi…, the secretary;
rev.	2 udu	2 sheep:
	Ḫi-li-za	Ḫiliza.
	(blank space)	
	Gala	Gala,
	dam-gara$_3$	the merchant.

No. 351 – MS 2301

Delivery of a goat, Classical/Late Sargonic, Adab.

obv.	1 maš$_2$	1 goat:
	I$_3$-li	*Ili*,
	gu-ti-um	the Gutean.
rev.	(blank space)	
	mu-de$_6$	He brought.

See OIP 14 for texts of similar format and content.

No. 352 – MS 2365/14

Account of sheep, Classical Sargonic, Adab.

obv.	2 udu-nita	2 male sheep:
	Inim-ma	Inima;
	1 Diĝir-zu-a	1: Diĝirzu'a;
	1 udu a-ra$_2$ *1*	1 sheep: the 1st time;
	1 udu a-ra$_2$ *2*-kam-ma	1 sheep: the 2nd time;
	2 udu a-ra$_2$ *3*-kam-ma	2 sheep: the 3rd time;
	[1] udu a-ra$_2$ *4*-kam-ma	[1] sheep: the 4th time.
rev.	lu$_2$-ĝanun-ke$_4$	The warehouseman
	in-laḫ$_5$	has brought them.
	2 Diĝir-ĝa$_2$	2: Diĝirĝa;
	1 Ur-^{d}Dumu	1: Ur-Dumu.

	šu+niĝin$_2$ 11 udu	Total: 11 sheep.
	⸢x-saĝ$^?$⸣-an-na	...

rev. 1: The professional lu$_2$-ĝanun-(na) "person (in charge) of the storehouse" appears in another CS Adab text, CUSAS 19 rev. 1.

rev. 3: This is an abbreviated form of the name Diĝir-ĝa$_2$-ab-e. For the name, see OSP 1 no. 108 rev. 4, CUSAS 26 no. 76 obv. v 2.

rev. 6: This is likely a personal name, maybe Ur-saĝ-an-na.

No. 353 – MS 4076

Account of sheep, Classical Sargonic, Adab.

obv.	2 udu 1 sila$_4$	2 sheep, 1 lamb:
	ki Aja$_2$-sa$_6$-ta	from Ajasa
	Nam-aga$_3$	Nam-aga
rev.	i$_3$-x	has ...ed.
	(blank space)	
	iti šu-ĝar	Month Šuĝar.

obv. 2: See CUSAS 27 no. 79 (= BdI 1 no. 240) obv. 3 for likely the same individual (Aja$_2$-sa$_6$-ga).

No. 354 – MS 4203

Allocation of sheep's heads and hearts to high priests and priestesses, Classical Sargonic, Adab.

obv.	4 saĝ-du udu	4 sheep's heads,
	4 ša$_3$ udu	4 sheep's hearts:
	en Diĝir-maḫ-me	they are high priests of (the goddess) Diĝirmaḫ;
	1 saĝ-du 1 ša$_3$ udu	1 sheep's head, 1 sheep's heart:
	Lal$_3$-la	Lala;
	2 saĝ-du 2 ša$_3$ udu	2 heads, 2 sheep's hearts:
	ereš-diĝir ^{d}Nin-⸢šubur⸣	the high priestess of Ninšubur;
	2 ša$_3$ udu ^{d}Iškur	2 sheep's hearts: Iškur;
	[1] ⸢saĝ-du⸣ 1 ša$_3$ udu	[1] head, 1 sheep's heart:
rev.	$^{[d]}$Gu$_2$-la$_2$	Gula;
	⸢4⸣ ša$_3$ udu e$_2$-[maḫ$^?$]	4 sheep's hearts: the E[maḫ-temple ?];
	7 ša$_3$ udu ĝal$_2$-⸢la-am$_3$⸣	7 sheep's hearts are (still) available.
	(blank space)	
	šu+niĝin$_2$ 8 saĝ-du udu	Total: 8 sheep's heads.
	šu+niĝin$_2$ 21 ša$_3$ udu	Total: 21 sheep's hearts.
	iti ni$_3$-^{ĝeš}kiri$_6$	Month Nikiri.

obv. 3: Note the plural. It is usually assumed that there was only one *en*-priest or *en*-priestess in the cult of a deity. The present text offers an indication that there were several *en*-priests active in the cult of the goddess Diĝirmaḫ. For en and ereš-diĝir below, see Sallaberger and Huber Vulliet 2005: 626–27. Alternatively, the line implies the men of the high priest.

obv. 3, 8: Note a clear differentiation between male (en) and female (ereš-diĝir) high priestess.

obv. 5: Although lal$_3$-(la) was a designation of a priest (see Sallaberger and Huber Vulliet 2005: 635–36), here it is certainly a female personal name, "Honey." The same Lala appears in CUSAS 19 no. 141 obv. 3, another CS Adab text that also mentions high priestesses. See PPAC 1 no. 632 obv. i 2, where Lala is placed at the top of the list. See text No. 362 rev. 17–18, asserting that she was the "wife (dam) of the god Ašgi," i.e. a priestess playing the role of this god's spouse. Note the difference between the terms dam and ereš-diĝir. The latter appears in relation to the gods Ninšubur, Irḫan and Bara-Enlilgar(a) in Nos. 363 obv. i 6, 354 obv. 7, and 348 obv. 12 respectively.

rev. 1: See CUSAS 13 no. 143 obv. 9 for saĝĝa ^{d}Gu$_2$-la$_2$. That text also belongs to the group of Classical Sargonic texts from Adab that records allocations to high priests and priestesses.

No. 355 – MS 4257

Account of sheep and meat, Classical Sargonic, Adab?

obv.	[1 line missing]	…
	Ur-zikum-ma	Urzikuma.
	3 sila$_4$-nim	3 lambs born in autumn;
	2 maš$_2$-nim	2 goats born in autumn;
	1 maš$_2$-e$_3$-li	1 goat born in spring:
	Lugal-an-dul$_3$	Lugal-andul.
	1 su-la$_2$-a udu-nita	1 cut of dried meat of a male sheep;
	2 udu-nita	2 male sheep;
	1 sila$_4$-nim	1 lamb born in autumn:
	Lugal-i$_3$-nun	Lugal-inun.
	3 udu-nita 1 u$_8$	3 male sheep, 1 ewe:

	[n] maš$_2$-nim	x goat(s) born in autumn:
	⸢x⸣-tur	…tur.
	[n] maš$_2$-ga	x suckling kid goat(s);
	[n] ⸢sila$_4$⸣ Ur-nu [(x)]	x lambs: Urnu.
	[break]	…
rev.	[1 line missing]	…
	[…] ⸢KUM x⸣ ab-laḫ$_5$	… have been brought.
	1 ud$_5$ 3 su-la$_2$-a ud$_5$	1 nanny goat, 3 dry cuts of nanny goat;
	1 su-la$_2$-a LAK20	1 dry cut of a ram:
	U$_3$-mu-NI-NI Ur-gal-[ra$^?$]	UmuNINI [to] Urgal
	in-na-laḫ$_5$	he has brought them to him.
	1 ud$_5$ 1 sila$_4$-ga	1 nanny goat, 1 suckling lamb:
	Iri-ki-⸢x⸣	Iriki…
	2 su-la$_2$-a maš$_2$-ga	2 dried cuts of suckling kid's meat:
	U$_3$-mu-NI-NI	UmuNINI.
	1 maš$_2$-ga Lugal-an-dul$_3$	1 suckling kid: Lugal-andul.
	1 maš$_2$-ga Šu-i$_2^!$(*6*)	1 suckling kid: Šu'i.
	1 udu-nita E$_2$-[…]	1 male sheep: E…
	1 udu-nita UŠ-[…]	1 male sheep: UŠ…
	[break]	…
l.e.	[n] ⸢la$_2$ 4⸣ su-la$_2$-a udu til$_3$-⸢am$_3$⸣	x minus 4 dried cuts of meat. This is the living sheep.

obv. 13: The broken sign may be one of the "Tierkopfzeichen" depicting an animal's head.

rev. 8: For the name Iri-ki, see, e.g., CUSAS 26 no. 56 rev. 2. The broken sign does not resemble ḪI (= du$_{10}$).

left edge: The phrase udu TI-am$_3$ is not entirely clear. It may refer to the living sheep in contrast to the dried pieces of meat. The absence of a total for the sheep is unusual.

No. 356 – MS 4748

Offering of sheep to gods and temples, Classical Sargonic, Adab.

obv. i	[3 lines broken]	…
	[…]-⌈gi$_4$⌉	…
	[…]-LU	…
	[… $^{d.(aš)}$]Aš$_7$-gi$_4$	…: (for the god) Ašgi;
	[1] udu-⌈niga⌉ 1 sila$_4$	[1] fattened sheep, 1 lamb:
	⌈e$_2$⌉-GANA$_2$.IŠ	(temple) E-GANAIŠ;
	1 udu-niga ^{d}Inana	1 fattened sheep: Inana;
	1 udu-niga 1 sila$_4$	1 fattened sheep, 1 lamb:
	^{d}Nin-šubur	Ninšubur;
	1 udu ⌈1 sila$_4$⌉ ^{d}En-lil$_2$	1 sheep, 1 lamb: Enlil;
	1 udu e$_2$-igi-nim	1 sheep: (temple) E'iginim;
	[1 udu] ^{d}Ašnan(ŠE.ŠE.NIR)	[1 sheep]: Ašnan;
	[1 udu] ^{d}Iškur(LAK377)	[1 sheep]: Iškur;
	[1 udu ^{d}]⌈Nin⌉-mug	[1 sheep]: Ninmug;
ii	1 udu e$_2$-⌈ĝidru e$_2$⌉-gal	1 sheep: the Scepter House (of) the palace;
	1 udu Bara$_2$-gu$_2$-la$_2$	1 sheep: the Great Dais;
	1 udu ^{d}Utu	1 sheep: Utu;
	1 udu-niga ^{d}En-ki	1 fattened sheep: Enki;
	1 udu ^{d}Za$^{!}$(A)-ba-ba	1 sheep: Zababa;
	1 udu ^{d}Nisaba	1 sheep: Nisaba;
	1 udu ^{d}Mes-lam-ta-e$_3$-a	1 sheep: Meslamta'e'a;
	1 udu ^{d}En-lil$_2$	1 sheep: Enlil;
	1 udu e$_2$-dam	1 sheep: the House of the Spouse;
	1 udu ^{d}Ĝeš-du$_3$-a / ^{d}Nergal(KIŠ)$^{eri_{12}}$	1 sheep: Nergal-the-Breeder;
	1 udu ^{d}Dam-gal-nun	1 sheep: Damgalnun(a);
	1 udu ^{d}En-lil$_2$ eš$_3$-igi-nim	1 sheep: Enlil of the Upper Sanctuary;
	1 udu e$_2$-saĝ-šu$_4$	1 sheep: Esaĝšu (temple);
	1 udu ^{d}MUŠ	1 sheep: Irḫan(or Niraḫ);
rev. i	1 udu ^{d}Imma$_x$(ĜA$_2$×SIG$_7$.ME)	1 sheep: Imma;
	1 udu ^{d}Ĝeštin-an-[na]	1 sheep: Ĝeštinana;
	1 udu Unu$_2$(TE.UNUG)-X-UD-a-a-si-ga	1 sheep: (shrine?) Unu…a'asiga;
	1 udu Ĝa$_2$-sipa-ca	1 sheep: (shrine?) Ĝasipada;
	⌈1⌉ udu ^{d}Nin-sumun$_2$	1 sheep: Ninsumun;
	[1] ⌈udu⌉ ^{d}Zu:en	[1] sheep: Su'en;
	< > udu ^{d}Iškur(LAK377) Karkara(LAK377)^{ki}	< > sheep: Iškur (of) Karkara;
	< > udu tir-ku$_3$	< > sheep: the Holy Forest;
	1 udu e$_2$-maḫ	1 sheep: the Great House (Diĝirmaḫ's temple).
	(blank)	
ii	(blank)	

obv. i 8: See SCTRAH p. 94 with additional references. E$_2$-GANA$_2$.IŠ, of uncertain interpretation, was the second most important temple in Early Dynastic and Sargonic Adab after e$_2$-maḫ/e$_2$-SAR.

obv. i 13: See Such-Gutiérrez 2005–6: 43 for this temple, literally "Upper House."

obv. ii 2: Bara$_2$-gu$_2$-la$_2$ may be identical to the shrine of Enlil that otherwise appears in the Adab corpus as $^{(d)}$Bara$_2$-^{d}En-lil$_2$-ĝar.

obv. ii 9: See Such-Gutiérrez 2005–6: 42–43 for e$_2$-dam.

obv. ii 10: The term ĝeš-du$_3$-a means "breeder" when referring to animals: see Heimpel 1993: 130. Here it probably denotes an aspect of Nergal as procreator. This chief deity of Kutha is usually associated with pestilence, the exact opposite of procreation.

obv. ii 13: A building of the same name appears also in a Sargonic document from Umma: see Sommerfeld, Markina and Roudik 2005: 208–9 no. 15 obv. 2. See also the commentary to text No. 83 obv. i 2.

rev. i 3: Probably the name of a shrine. Detailed photo:

rev. i 8: tir-ku$_3$ "Holy Forest," besides being well attested in documents from Ĝirsu, seems to be a generic term for a cultic locality.

1.5.4 – Hides and Related Products

No. 357 – MS 4268

Allocation of sandals, Middle/Classical Sargonic, Adab.

obv.	1 ^{kuš}esir$_4$-ERIN$_2$ e$_2$-ba	1 pair of ... sandals:
	PU$_3$.ŠA-*Il$_3$-a-ba$_4$*	PUŠA-*'Ilaba*,
	maškim Lugal-dul$_5$-maḫ	the commissioner of Lugaldulmaḫ.
	1 Zu-zu maškim-še	1: Zuzu, the commissioner of barley.
	1 Maš *šu-gal$_5$-la$_2$-um*	1: Maš, the *šugalla'um*-official.
	1 *Iš-me*-diĝir	1: *Yišme-'ilum*,
	ḪU-še$_3$ im-ši-du-a	who is going to ...(?)
	1 Da-da	1: Dada,
	lu$_2$-uz-ga	*uzga*-professional,
	maškim Ti-bi$_2$-ra	the commissioner of (the city Bad)-Tibira.
	(blank line)	
rev.	1 Ur-^{d}Utu	1: Ur-Utu,
	šu-gal$_5$-la$_2$-um	the *šugalla'um*-official.
	(blank space)	
	iti mu-tir	Month Mutir.

obv. 1: The variety of sandals ^{kuš}esir$_4$-ERIN$_2$ is otherwise unattested.

obv. 4: See a Middle Sargonic document SCTRAH no. 41 obv. 2 for the same individual.

obv. 7: The interpretation of the logogram ḪU is uncertain, but it is clearly a locality, for the construction R-še$_3$ im-ši-DU-a often occurs in Sargonic and Ur III records describing the transfer of individuals and labor teams.

obv. 9: See Schrakamp 2012b: 154 sub Nr. 24 with additional references for a profession uz-ga. The full writing of this professional term is lu$_2$-uz-ga, as, e.g., in BdI 1 no. 184 obv. 6.

1.5.5 – Lard and Oil

No. 358 – MS 4228

Account of lard and oil, Classical Sargonic, Adab?

obv.	44 sila$_3$ i$_3$-šaḫ$_2$	44 *sila* lard:
	Gu$_3$-de$_2$-a	Gude'a;
	1 dug 1 sila$_3$ i$_3$	1 jar 1 *sila* oil.
rev.	Lu$_2$-ni-zu	Lunizu;
	5 sila$_3$ i$_3$	5 *sila* oil:
	In-ta-pa-e$_3$	Intapa'e.

The syntax of the goods and measures shows that the text was composed in Akkadian.

obv. 1, 3: Only two standards of a dug, 20 *sila* and 30 *sila*, appear in early records: see Powell 1990: 504–5. It is unclear why the scribe decided to write 44 sila$_3$ instead of 1 dug 14 sila$_3$. The occurrence of 1 dug 1 sila$_3$ in obv. 3 is thus notable. Why did the scribe not write 31 sila$_3$ instead? One possibility is that lard and oil were recorded differently. Another possibility is that i$_3$ in obv. 3 and rev. 2 is an abbreviation of i$_3$-šaḫ$_2$. This would imply a jar of at least 50 *sila* capacity, theoretically possible but unlikely.

1.5.6 – Wooden Implements

No. 359 – MS 4264

Expenditure of agricultural tools, Classical Sargonic, Adab?

obv.	5 ^{ĝeš}eme	5 wooden plow-shares;
	20 ^{ĝeš}zu$_2$ ^{ĝeš}GAN$_2$-ur$_3$	20 wooden points of the harrow;
	60 ^{ĝeš}kak-al	60 wooden nails for hoes:
	E$_2$-lu$_2$	To Elu
	an-na-šum$_2$	it has been given.
rev.	(blank)	

obv. 1: This term, literally "tongue," can refer to several tools. Most scholars interpret it as a plow-share or harrow. Here it cannot be the latter, for that occurs in the next line.

obv. 2: See ^{ĝeš}GAN$_2$-ur$_3$ = *maškakātum* "harrow"; CAD M^{1} 368.

obv. 3: See PSD A^{3} 141 for gag-al "nail for the hoe." Thus the text records exclusively pointed parts of agricultural tools.

1.5.7 – Miscellaneous Goods

No. 360 – MS 4206

Account of gold and silver in connection to high dignitaries, Classical Sargonic, Adab.

The text is written in Akkadian and records amounts of gold and silver received from(?) a number of individuals. They are the highest dignitaries in the Adab governorate during the reign of Naram-Suen. The governor himself is not mentioned. Rev. iii 8 offers an abbreviated writing of a year date of Naram-Suen; see Sallaberger and Schrakamp 2015: 46 for its full writing. The defeat of the land Aḫuzinnum in the eastern Ḫabur region may have taken place shortly after the king had put down the "Great Revolt"; see RIME 2 p. 86 with additional references.

obv. i	[n giĝ$_4$ ku$_3$-sig$_{17}$]	[x shekels of gold]:
	dub-sar-maḫ	the chief scribe;
	⸢24⸣ [+n] lu$_2$-eše$_2$-gid$_2$	24+x: the field-surveyor;
	⸢n ensi$_2$⸣-gal	x: the former governor;
	[n] šabra-e$_2$	x: the chief administrator of the household;
	[n] saĝĝa e$_2$-maḫ	x: the chief temple-administrator of Emaḫ (temple);
	[n] saĝĝa ^{d}Iškur	x: the chief temple-administrator of Iškur's (temple);
	[n] ⸢saĝĝa⸣ ^{d}Aš$_7$-gi$_4$	x: the chief temple-administrator of Ašgi's (temple);
	[n] ⸢sagi⸣-maḫ	x: the chief cupbearer;
	[n] sukkal-maḫ	x: the chief secretary;
	[n] abba$_2$-iri	x: the city elder;
	[n gal$_5$]-la$_2$-gal	x: the chief policeman;
	[n] ⸢KUN⸣-ŠE$_3$	x: …;
	[n] ⸢niĝir⸣-gal	x: the chief herald;
	[n] ⸢gu⸣-gal	x: the canal inspector;
	[n x]-gal	x: the chief …;
	[2 lines broken]	…
ii	[1 line broken]	…
	2 DUN$_3$-[x]	2: DUN…;
	2 Il$_2$	2: Il(a);
	2 Lugal-e$_2$-maš-e	2: Lugal-emaše,
	engar-maḫ-me	they are the chief agricultural managers;
	1 Nita-zi	1: Nitazi;
	1 Ad-da	1: Adda;
	1 A$_2$-ni-ta	1: Anita;
	1 Lu$_2$-^{d}Aš$_7$-gi$_4$	1: Lu-Ašgi:
	engar-tur-me	they are junior agricultural managers;
	2 Inim-ma	2: Inima;
	2 Ur-a$_2$	2: Ur-a;
	2 Ur-^{d}Inana	2: Ur-Inana:
	nu-banda$_3$ eden-na-me	they are the supervisors of the "steppe";
	2 lu$_2$-gu$_4$-mu$_2$-da	2: the cattle-raiser;
	4 ka-⸢guru$_7$⸣	4: the granary supervisor;
	1 pisaĝ-dub ĝanun	1: the archivist of the storehouse;
	1 Lugal-nam	1: Lugalnam;
	1 šidim-gal	1: the chief builder;
	1 sukkal e$_2$-⸢ḪI$^{?}$⸣-[x]	1: the secretary of … "house."
iii	[3 lines broken]	…

	1 saĝĝa ^{d}Inana	1: the chief temple-administrator of Inana's (temple);
	1 saĝĝa ^{d}En-ki	1: the chief temple-administrator of Enki's (temple);
	1 lu$_2$-ni$_3$-bara$_2$-ga	1: *the person of the barag-garment* (occupation);
	1 Lugal-^{d}⸢Sud$_3$-de$_3$⸣	1: Lugal-Sude;
	1 lu$_2$-⸢x⸣	1: …;
	10 ga:eš$_8$	10: the traveling merchant;
	2 ½ šandana-SAR	2 ½ the … gardener;
	1 muḫaldim-gal	1: the chief cook;
	1 la$_2$×igi-*3* ka-⸢dug⸣	1 minus ⅓: the keeper of jars;
	1 A$_2$-ni-ta	1: Anita;
	1 *A-mur-*⸢*ru-um*⸣	1: *Amurrum*;
	½ Bi-da-⸢x⸣	½: Bida…;
	2 lu$_2$-kiĝ$_2$-⸢du$_3$-a⸣	2: the *work organizer*;
	½ ugula ^{ĝeš}⸢gigir$_2$⸣	½: the overseer of the (governor's) chariot;
	1 ugula ^{ĝeš}gu-[za]	1: the overseer of the throne;
	2 ⸢x⸣ […]	2: …;
	[1 line broken]	…
rev. i	[3 lines broken]	…
	2 […]	2 …;
	2 ⸢En⸣-[…]	2: En…;
	2 E$_2$-⸢maḫ⸣	2: Emaḫ;
	2 Abba$_2$	2: Abba;
	½ Lugal-zi	½: Lugalzi;
	½ Ur-e$_2$-maš	½: Ur-emaš;
	½ Ur-ŠE$_3$	½: UrŠE;
	1 la$_2$×igi-*3* Im-ta	1 minus ⅓: Imta;
	1 a-zu-gal	1: the chief physician;
	½ ugula a-ga-⸢am?⸣	½: the overseer of (the labor on) the lake (for disposing of flood waters);
	2 ⸢enku⸣	2: tax-collector;
	1 Lugal-[…]	1: Lugal…;
	1 la$_2$×igi-*3* ⸢Lugal⸣-[…]	1 minus ⅓: Lugal…;
	1 ⸢la$_2$×igi-*3*⸣ […]	1 minus ⅓: …;
	1 […]	1: …;
	[break]	…
ii	*1* saĝĝa e$_2$-[…]	1: the chief temple-administrator of the temple…;
	1 ašgab-[gal]	1: the [chief] leather-worker;
	1 tug$_2$-du$_8$-gal	1: the chief felter;
	1 ad-KID-gal	1: the chief reed-worker;
	1 igi-du	1: the "foremost" (a legal official);
	1 la$_2$×igi-*3* baḫar$_x$(EDIN)-gal	1 minus ⅓: the chief potter;
	1 *ra-bi* e$_2$-gal	1: the majordomo of the palace;
	2 ma$_2$-laḫ$_5$-gal	2: the chief sailor;
	2 Ur-a$_2$ ašgab	2: Ur-a, the leather-worker.
	(ruling)	

šu+niĝin$_2$ 3 ma-na ^{šu2}1N$_8^{ša}$ *17* la$_2$×igi-*6* ku$_3$-sig$_{17}$	Total: 3 ⅓ minas 17 minus ^{1}/6 shekels gold;
^{šu2}1N$_8^{ša}$ la$_2$×*1* giĝ$_4$ ku$_3$-babbar	⅓ (mina) minus 1 shekel silver.
lu$_2$-BI×A-me	They are ….
12 ½ En-li	12 ½: Enli
u$_3$ Ša$_3$-zu	and Šazu.
10 ugula saĝ-(ras.)-LAGAB×*U*	10: the overseer of … slaves;
(blank space)	
iii (blank space)	
[^{šu2}N$_8$]⌜^{ša} la$_2$⌝×[*n*] giĝ$_4$ ku$_3$	⅓ (or ⅔ mina) minus x shekels silver.
[ku$_3$]-⌜sig$_{17}$⌝-bi *14* ½ giĝ$_4$	Its gold: 14 ½ shekels.
[n+] 2 ma-na ^{šu2}⌜2N$_8^{ša}$ [n] ⌜giĝ$_4$ ku$_3$⌝-sig$_{17}$	x+2 ⅔ minas x shekels gold.
[...]-ĜAR-e	…GAR,
[...]-AB	…
[x]-⌜x-x⌝	…
(blank)	
in 1 mu	In the year (when Naram-Suen was victorious in battle against Subir)
⌜*A*⌝-*zu-ḫi-nim*$^{⌜ki⌝}$	at Azuḫinnum (and captured Tahišatili).
(blank)	

obv. i 13: The profession KUN-ŠE$_3$ remains open to interpretation. The term appears in Adab texts PPAC 1 no. 863 obv. 2, CUSAS 13 no. 2 obv. 3, CUSAS 20 no. 282 obv. ii 6. The two latter documents belong to the same group as the present text.

obv. i 15: Gu-gal is another writing of gu$_2$-gal "canal inspector." Note that the sign in question cannot be MU, thus excluding muḫaldim-gal "chief cook." Besides, the latter appears in obv. iii 11.

obv. ii 14: The term nu-banda$_3$ eden-na "supervisor of the steppe" refers most probably to officials who administered the "steppe," i.e., the uncultivated regions outside the settlements. Other attestations of the term are ITT 1 no. 1288 obv. 5, ITT 4 no. 7076 obv. 8. In the latter case the term appears in connection to workmen, ĝuruš.

obv. ii 15: Lu$_2$-gu$_4$-mu$_2$(mud$_6$)-da means literally a "person who makes oxen grow" and apparently refers to the fattener of oxen. Cf. lu$_2$-gu$_4$-udu-niga = *mārû* "fattener"; see CAD M^{I} 316. The term lu$_2$-gu$_4$-mu$_2$(mud$_6$)-da appears in several other CS Adab texts: PPAC 1 nos. 719+ rev. i 2, 892 obv. 6, CUSAS 13 no. 2 rev. 1, CUSAS 20 no. 282 obv. ii 4 "cattle breeder."

obv. iii 6: The element ^{tug2}ni$_3$-bara$_{3/4}$ appears in personal names with the elements lugal and nin. Krebernik 2002: 34 fn. 180 suggests that these names allude to the use of this textile in the cult. For another attestation of this professional or priestly title, see CUSAS 11 no. 21 (ED IIIb Adab) obv. ii 3–5: Lugal-abba$_2$-ĝu$_{10}$ lu$_2$-ni$_3$-bara$_4$-ga-da an-da-tuku "it is available with Lugalabbaĝu, the … professional."

obv. iii 7: For the same Lugal-^{d}Sud$_3$-de$_3$, see Adab texts PPAC 1 no. 1209 obv. ii 9, CUSAS 20 nos. 18 obv. ii 2, 58 obv. 5', 117 obv. 3, CUSAS 23 no. 133 obv. 3.

obv. iii 10: Interpretations of the term šandana-SAR include -kiri$_6$ "garden" and -nisig "(responsible for) greens."

obv. iii 12: Attested in both ED and Sargonic texts, the rare professional title ka-dug is constructed on the pattern ka+object. In the present case, it cannot refer to anyone but a person in charge of jars. Note that "KA-bi" in CUSAS 20 no. 18 obv. i 3 is the same term. In our case, the sign is certainly DUG and differs considerably from BI, for which see obv. iii 15.

obv. iii 16: See discussion in CUSAS 20 no. 18 commentary.

obv. iii 17–18: See CUSAS 20 no. 18 obv. ii 4–5 for the restoration.

rev. i 13: See FAOS 15/1 pp. 61–62 for a discussion of the professional title a-ga-am in ED IIIb texts from Ĝirsu. Literally a-ga-am is a "lake" used to dispose of flood water. The ugula in our case was most likely responsible for supervising this lake and managing labor connected to it.

rev. ii 5: For igi-du, see the commentary to text No. 3 obv. vii 16.

rev. ii 12: The interpretation of lu$_2$-BI×A-me is uncertain, although it is clear from the context that it is an umbrella term for the dignitaries and professionals related to the palace via a payment in gold and silver. Note that the sign in question is not DUG.

rev. ii 15: The interpretation of saĝ-LAGAB×U is uncertain. The writing PA-saĝ-LAGAB×U may be a personal name.

No. 361 – MS 4223

Offering of sheep and bread, Classical/Late Sargonic, Adab.

obv.	[1] udu	[1] sheep,
	[n ninda] ⌜ne⌝-saĝ ½ sila$_3$	[x] offering [breads] of ½ *sila*:
	⌜e$_2$⌝-maḫ	(for) the Emaḫ (temple);
	[1 udu] 10 ninda ne-saĝ ½ sila$_3$	[1 sheep], 10 offering breads of ½ *sila*:
	$^{[d]}$En-lil$_2$	Enlil;
	[1] ⌜udu⌝ 5 ninda ne-saĝ ½ sila$_3$	[1] sheep, 5 offering breads of ½ *sila*:
	$^{⌜d⌝.aš}$Aš$_7$-gi$_4$	Ašgi;
	[1] ⌜udu 10⌝ ninda ne-saĝ ½ sila$_3$	[1] sheep, 10 offering breads of ½ *sila*:
	$^{⌜d⌝}$Inana	Inana;
	⌜1⌝ udu 10 ninda ne-saĝ ½ sila$_3$	1 sheep, 10 offering breads of ½ *sila*:
	^{d}Iškur	Iškur;
	1 udu 10 ninda ne-saĝ ½ sila$_3$	1 sheep, 10 offering breads of ½ *sila*:
rev.	^{d}Nin-šubur	Ninšubur;
	1 udu 10 ninda ne-saĝ ½ sila$_3$	1 sheep, 10 offering breads of ½ *sila*:
	^{d}Ašnan(ŠE.ŠE.⌜NIR⌝)	Ašnan;
	[1 udu] 10 ninda ne-saĝ ½ sila$_3$	[1 sheep], 10 offering breads of ½ *sila*:
	$^{[d]}$En-ki	Enki;
	[1 udu] 10 ninda ne-saĝ ½ sila$_3$	[1 sheep], 10 offering breads of ½ *sila*:
	$^{[d]}$Utu	Utu;
	[1 udu 10] ninda ne-saĝ ½ sila$_3$	[1 sheep, 10] offering breads of ½ *sila*:
	$^{[d]}$Zu:en	Su'en.
	(ruling)	
	[šu-+niĝin$_2$ n] udu	[Total: x] sheep;
	[šu+niĝin$_2$ n] ninda ne-saĝ ½ sila$_3$	[Total: x] offering breads of ½ *sila*.
	[mu]-de$_6$	Delivered.

No. 362 – MS 4255

Accounts of metals, textiles and wool as presents, Classical Sargonic, Adab.

obv.	2 zabar$_x$(UD.KA×BAR)^{uruda}	2 bronze (vessels);
	1 ^{tug2}*na-aš$_2$-pa$_2$-ru-um*	1 *našparum*-garment;
	1 ^{tug2}bala-*4*	1 4-(tiered) *bala*-garment;
	30 bara$_2$ še	30 sacks (of) barley:
	Ur-^{d}Utu	Ur-Utu.
	2 ku$_3$-ĝeštug-min e$_2$-ba	2 pairs of silver earrings;
	1 ^{tug2}ni$_3$-lam$_2$	1 *nilam*-garment:
	Še-muš	Šemuš.
	1 ^{tug2}bala-*3*	1 3-(tiered) *bala*-garment:
	Ur-gal	Urgal.
	1 ^{tug2}ni$_3$-lam$_2$	1 *nilam*-garment;
	1 ^{tug2}ša$_3$-ga-du$_3$	1 *šagadu*-garment:
	Ama-Abzu-si	Ama-Abzusi.
	1 ^{tug2}ni$_3$-lam$_2$	1 *nilam*-garment:

	Šu-NE-ka	ŠuNEka.
	½ ku$_3$ giĝ$_4$	½ shekel siver:
	Inim-ku$_3$ gala	Inimku, the singer.
	3 siki ma-na	3 minas wool:
	Du-du	Dudu.
rev.	*3* ma-na	3 minas:
	U$_3$-u$_3$	U'u.
	3 ma-na PA-⌜x-x⌝	3 minas: …
	3 ma-na	3 minas:
	Iš-*te*$_4$-*li*$_2$	*'Ište'(i)li* ("From the God").
	1 ma-na	1 mina:
	dumu Šu-NE-ka	the son of ŠuNE.
	1 ma-na	1 mina:
	dumu Ur-gu	the son of Urgu.
	3 ma-na	3 minas:
	Šu-NE	ŠuNE.
	(blank space)	
	šu+niĝin$_2$ 12 tug$_2$-ḫi-a	Total: 12 various garments.
	šu+niĝin$_2$ 20 la$_2$ 3 siki ma-na	Total: 17 minas of wool.
	šu+niĝin$_2$ 2 zabar^{uruda}	Total: 2 bronze (vessels).
	šu+niĝin$_2$ 2 ½ ku$_3$ giĝ$_4$	Total: 2 ½ shekels of silver.
	ni$_3$-ba	The present(s)
	Lal$_3$-la	(for) Lala,
	dam ^{d}Aš$_8$-gi$_4$	wife of the god Ašgi.

The text records valuable gifts from a number of individuals to Lala, a priestess embodying the wife of the god Ašgi in the cult at Adab.

obv. 1: See SCTRAH no. 305 commentary to rev. 5 with additional references for zabar$^{(uruda)}$. Depending on context, it designates a "mirror" (zabar-(šu)) or a bronze cup of 1 *sila*. In the present case, it is not certain which of these objects is meant. Note how the term is written in this line and compare it to the usual writing in rev. 14.

obv. 3: See SCTRAH no. 20 obv. 5 commentary with additional references. However, do the terms ^{tug_2}pala(NAM.LUGAL) and ^{tug_2}bala denote the same garment? "4," as well as "3" below, may refer to the "tiers" of the garments that one can observe on seals and other artifacts depicting clothing. See Foster 2010: 123 f.

obv. 6: Cf. a similar 1 ku$_3$ giĝ$_4$ ĝeštug in OSP 2 no. 76 (Sargonic Nippur) obv. 2. The total of silver in the present document illustrates that these items of ear jewelry also weighed one shekel apiece.

obv. 8: Še-muš, Akk. *šigūšu*, a variety of barley, appears here as a personal name.

rev. 17–18: See the commentary to text No. 354 obv. 5.

1.5.8 – Unidentified Goods

No. 363 – MS 4213

Allocation of unidentified goods to temple personnel, Classical Sargonic, Adab.

obv. i	4 sila$_3$ X-A	4 *sila* of liquid(? duru$_5$)…:
	e$_2$-gal-am$_3$	it is (for) the palace;
	2 lu$_2$-mah̬	2 (*sila*): the *lumah̬*-priest;
	1 TU	1: the *TU*-priest;
	1 a-tu	1: the *atu*-priestess;
	1 ereš-diĝir ^{d}MUŠ	1: the high priestess of Irh̬an(or Nirah̬);
	2 saĝĝa	2: the chief temple-administrator;
	1 dub-sar-mah̬	1: the chief scribe;
	2 šu-luh̬-h̬a-me	2: the purification priests;
	1 agrig-MU	1: the ... steward;
	1 agrig	1: the steward;
	1 i$_3$-du$_8$	1: the doorman;
	1 sukkal	1: the secretary;
	1 ^{lu2}lunga$_3$-me	1: the brewers;
	1 u$_2$-a	1: the provisioner;
	1 bah̬ar$_x$(EDIN)	1: the potter.
ii	šu+niĝin$_2$ 21 sila$_3$ X-A	Total: 21 *sila* of …:
	e$_2$-mah̬	the Emah̬ (temple).
	10 la$_2$ 1 sila$_3$ X-A	9 *sila* of …:
	[e$_2$]-gal-⸢am$_3$⸣	it is for the palace;
	2 lu$_2$-[mah̬]	2: the *lumah̬*-priest;
	2 dub-sar-[mah̬]	2: the [chief] scribe;
	2 šu-⸢luh̬⸣-[h̬a-me]	2: [the] purification priest[s];
	1 Ur-⸢sa$_6$⸣	1: Ursa;
	1 ^{lu2}⸢lunga$_3$⸣-[me]	1: [the] brewer[s];
	1 u$_2$-⸢a⸣	1: the provisioner;
	1 i$_3$-du$_8$	1: the doorman;
	1 bah̬ar$_x$	1: the potter.
	(ruling)	
	šu+niĝin$_2$ 20 sila$_3$ X-A	Total: 20 *sila* of …:
	e$_2$-GANA$_2$.IŠ	The E-GANAIŠ (temple).
	10 la$_2$ 1 sila$_3$ X-A	9 *sila* of …:
rev. i	e$_2$-gal-am$_3$	it is for the palace;
	1 Lal$_3$-la	1: Lala;
	1 išib $^{d.aš}$Aš$_7$-gi$_4$	1: the incantation priest of (the god) Ašgi;
	2 saĝĝa $^{d.aš}$Aš$_7$-gi$_4$	2: the chief temple-administrator of Ašgi's (temple);
	1 šu-luh̬-h̬a	1: the purification priest;
	1 agrig	1: the steward;
	1 i$_3$-du$_8$	1: the doorman;
	1 sukkal	1: the secretary;
	1 ^{lu2}⸢lunga$_3$⸣	1: the brewer;
	1 u$_2$-[a]	1: the provisioner;
	1 ⸢bah̬ar$_x$⸣	1: the potter.
	(ruling)	

	šu+niĝin$_2$ ⸢20 sila$_3$⸣ X-A	Total: 20 *sila* of …:
	[e$_2$] $^{d.aš}$Aš$_7$-gi$_4$	[the temple] of Ašgi
ii	(blank)	
	šu+niĝin$_2$-šu+niĝin$_2$ 61 sila$_3$ X-A	Grand total: 61 *sila* of …
	(blank)	

This text presents a vivid picture of the high priests, dignitaries, and professionals of three importmant temple households in Sargonic Adab: e$_2$-maḫ, e$_2$-GANA$_2$.IŠ and e$_2$ ^{d}Aš$_7$-gi$_4$. The number of *sila* a person receives is doubtless related to his or her status. Note that saĝĝa, the chief temple-administrator, lu$_2$-maḫ, the high priest (= en elsewhere), and the chief scribe are at the top of the hierarchy. By contrast, the priests šu-luḫ-ḫa and brewers are referred to not individually but as a group.

obv. i 1: The sequence "measure unit – measured goods" implies that the text was written and read in Akkadian. Apart from this feature, these are no Akkadian elements in the document. The sign in doubt is unidentified:

It is a vessel "TA" with extra horizontal wedges, like GA, and the sign ŠE$_3$ inscribed inside. Based on the context, the allocation of this commodity to high profile individuals, it was a luxury product.

obv. i 4–5: These lines match the beginning of the lexical list ED Lu$_2$ C (SF 47). The function of the profession TU is uncertain. However the appearance of both terms among priests (see Sallaberger and Huber Vulliet 2005: 626) makes it very probable that both were cultic personnel. For a-tu as a priestess of the mother goddess, see Stol 2000: 76.

obv. i 10–11: The term agrig-MU does not appear elsewhere as far as I know. Here, it appears in the company of a normal agrig, the temple steward.

rev. i 2: See the commentary to text No. 354 obv. 5.

rev. ii 1: Note the term for "grand total." It seems that by this date gu$_2$-an-še$_3$ was no longer used in Adab. It is not certain whether šu+niĝin$_2$-šu+niĝin$_2$ is "good" Sumerian or an artificial logogram introduced by Akkadian-speaking scribes.

Part 2 – Documents from Isin

2.1 – Early Sargonic Documents from Isin

No. 364 – MS 4273

Receipt of miscellaneous goods, Early Sargonic, Isin.

obv. i	2(gur) la$_2$ *2(ban$_2$)* še gur	2 *gur* minus 2 *ban* barley:
	ba ĝiri$_3$-ta	out of the allocation for trips(?);
	1(bariga) 1(ban$_2$) zi$_3$ ba ĝiri$_3$-ta	1 *bariga* 1 *ban* flour out of the allocation for trips(?);
	1 ḫa-zi^{uruda}	1 *ḫazi(n)*-axe:
	ki-la$_2$-bi	its weight:
	1 uruda ma-na la$_2$ 5 giĝ$_4$	1 mina minus 5 shekels copper.
ii	½(BAR) ku$_3$ giĝ$_4$	½ shekel silver
	ni$_3$-sa$_{10}$	(is) the price
	zabar$_x$(^{zu2}UD^{bar})^{uruda}	of bronze.

	e$_2$-duru$_5$-ta	Out of the village
	A$_2$-diĝir-zi-ga	Adiĝirziga,
	Inim-ku$_3$-ga-ni	Inimkugani,
	Aga$_3$-⸢lugal⸣	(and) Agalugal.
	⸢x⸣ [...] ⸢x⸣	...
rev. i	mu-de$_6$ [(x)]	He has brought here.
	šu ba-ti [(x)]	He has received.
	(blank)	
ii	(blank)	

obv. ii 1: The writing of the half shekel with the sign BAR appears almost exclusively in Early Dynastic and Sargonic texts from Isin. The matter is discussed in detail by the present author in a forthcoming book on the Sumerian system of weight measures.

obv. ii 3: The sign for copper is UD with two phonetic complements, here KA.UD.BAR = $^{\text{zu2}}$zabar$_x$(UD)^{bar} and elsewhere UD.KA.BAR = zabar$_x$(UD)$^{\text{zu2-bar}}$.

obv. ii 4 f.: The interpretation remains tentative.

No. 365 – MS 4274

Witnessed document concerning silver, Early/Middle Sargonic, Isin?

obv.	[n] ⸢x⸣ Ur$_5$-du$_2$	[n] ... Ur$_5$-du$_2$;
	$^{\text{šu2}}$1N$_8$ la$_2$×*2("ban$_2$")* $^{\text{ša-na}}$ giĝ$_4$ ku$_3$	⅓ (mina) silver minus x (in) shekels,
	Lugal-a$_2$-zi-da kuš$_7$	Lugalazida, the animal-manager,
	Ĝeš-Kul-aba$_4$^{ki}-⸢ta⸣	from Ĝeš-Kulaba
	mu-de$_6$	he has brought.
	1 igi En-⸢ne$_2$⸣-ne$_2$	1 (in) front of Ennene
	1 igi Ne-saĝ aga$_3$-us$_2$	1 (in) front of Nesaĝ, the soldier,
	A$_2$-kal-le ugula-e$_2$	(the man of) Akale, the overseer of the household.
	1 igi Lugal-dul$_5$	1 (in) front of Lugaldul.
rev.	1 igi Aja$_2$-ki-aĝ$_2$-še$_3$	1 in front of Ajaki'aĝ.
	1 igi A$_2$-ni-ta-še$_3$	1 in front of Anita.
	1 igi Ur-^{d}Inana zadim-še$_3$	1 in front of Ur-Inana, the stone-cutter.
	1 igi Ur-ḪAR šu-i$_2$-še$_3$	1 in front of UrḪAR, the barber.
	zi$_3$ ĝiri$_3$ ba kuš$_7$ ba	The flour distributed for trips (and) distributed to the animal-manager.
	ib$_2$-ba-du$_3$ ab-dab$_6$(URUDA)	...
	e$_2$-ta ba-ta-e$_3$	It has been issued out of the household.
	⸢inim⸣-pi	This matter
	[al]-til	is settled.

obv. 2: This writing, usually associated with the capacity measure "2 *ban*," is not expected with weight measures. The author is not aware of its occurrence with weight measures in Early Dynastic and Sargonic documents. It may be a mistake for la$_2$×½ giĝ$_4$ "minus ½ shekel."

obv. 4: There are various opinions on the location of this settlement. While some scholars identify it with the Kulaba district in Uruk, others argue that Ĝeš-Kul-aba$_4$^{ki} was a settlement in northern Babylonia. See Schrakamp 2015a: 198 fn. 11 with additional references.

rev. 6: The line is not clear. Ib$_2$-ba-du$_3$^{tug_2} is a well-attested garment, a sort of waistband or skirt. Ab-URUDA may be a verbal form (cf. dab$_6$ "to wrap around").

rev. 8: The writing of the possessive suffix /=bi/ with the sign PI may speak in favor of Isin or Nippur as the provenance of this tablet.

2.2 – A Private Archive from Middle and Classical Sargonic Isin

For the identification and partial publication of this private archive from Isin, see Westenholz, CUSAS 26 nos. 45–59. In addition to the nine tablets mentioned there, more documents have been identified by the present author in the Schøyen Collection. Several temples play a legal role in these texts: the Egalmaḫ, the temple of the goddess Ninisina, and a temple dedicated to her husband, Pabilsag. The content of the texts is typical for legal documents of this period: purchases of immobilia, contesting these purchases, contesting slave status, etc.

Some tablets belonging to the archive are of blackish clay. The thickness of almost all the tablets falls between 20 and 23 mm. Another characteristic feature of many of these tablets is that the left edge is usually inscribed.

No. 366 – MS 4200

Weighing out of silver to a number of individuals, Classical Sargonic, Isin.

obv.	1 ⸢Ur-ĝidru dub-sar⸣	1 Urĝidru, the scribe,
	lu$_2$ Dab$_4$(DUB)-si-ga-ke$_4$	the man of Dabsiga,
	Inim-zi-da-ra	to Inimzida,
	1 *Šu-Aš$_{11}$-tar$_2$*	1 *Šu-'Aštar*,
	Mu-ni	he is of Muni,
	lu$_2$-tukul-la$_2$-kam	the *bodyguard*.
	maškim-še$_3$ mu-na-de$_6$	For the commissioner he has brought it here.
	15 ku$_3$-babbar giĝ$_4$	15 shekels silver
	Inim-zi-da	Inimzida
	1 Ur-ĝidru dub-sar	1 to Urĝidru, the scribe,
	lu$_2$ Dab$_4$-si-ga-ra	the man of Dabsiga,
	i$_3$-na-la$_2$	has weighed it out.
	u$_4$ še ku$_3$-ga 2(gur) 2(bariga) še gur	When one measured 2 *gur* 2 *bariga* barley in silver (= for 1 shekel of silver)
	al-aĝ$_2$-ĝa$_2$	
rev.	37(gur) 2(bariga) še gur-saĝ-ĝal$_2$-la	37 *gur* 2 *bariga* (by) the "*gur* over the brim"
	šu ba-ti-eš$_2$	they have received.
	1 *'Id$_3$-lul-il*	1 *Yidlul-'il*,
	kuš$_7$ e$_2$ Dab$_4$-si-ga	the animal-manager of the household of Dabsiga,
	U$_3$ NE-MU-DIM$_2$-DU	…
	1 igi Lu$_2$-kisal-le-še$_3$	1 in front of Lukisale.
	1 igi Il$_2$-še$_3$	1 in front of Il(a).
	1 igi Lu$_2$-diĝir-ra-še$_3$	1 in front of Ludiĝira:
	dumu sa$_{12}$-du$_5$-me	they are sons of the land-recorder.
	1 igi Ur-ĝidru Diĝir-*ba-ni*-še$_3$	1 in front of Urĝidru (the man/son of) *'Ilum-bani*.
	⸢1⸣ [E$_2$]-⸢dub⸣ šu-i$_2$-še$_3$	1 in front of Edub, the barber.
	⸢Lu$_2$⸣-[na]-⸢nam⸣ simug	Lunanam, the smith.
	⸢x⸣-[....]-⸢x⸣-bi	… its
	[2 lines broken]	…

obv. 2: For Dab$_4$-si-ga, cf. CUSAS 13 no. 163; Schrakamp 2012a: 287 with additional references. Cf. especially OAIC no. 3 pp. 193–94 for the variants Tab-si-ga/Dab$_4$(DUB)-si-ga.

obv. 6: See the commentary to text No. 82 obv. i 4.

obv. 7: For the form maškim-še$_3$ mu-de$_6$, see CUSAS 26 no. 46 obv. 8.

rev. 4: The fact that the "house" of Dabsiga had an animal-manager suggests that Dabsiga was a wealthy and influential person with plenty of livestock.

rev. 5: The reading of the line is uncertain. Akkadian language is not expected in a text that uses Sumerian verbal forms. Therefore *u$_3$* "and" is not expected. The sign combination DIM$_2$-DU appears in geographical (i$_7$-piriĝ-gin$_7$-DU in a CS Ĝirsu text, CUSAS 26 no. 173 rev. i 1') and personal names (Ur-me-DIM$_2$-DU in an ED IIIb "Umma" text, CUSAS 26 no. 155 obv. i 3).

rev. 11–12: Cf. a barber E$_2$-dub in another document from Isin, CUSAS 13 no. 163 rev. i 7, and a smith Lu$_2$-na-nam in MAD 4 no. 71 rev. 3 (probably from Isin). Suggestions courtesy J. Hernández.

No. 367 – MS 4205

Purchase of land, Classical Sargonic, Isin.

obv. i	[3 or 4+] 3(iku) aša$_5$	x+3 *iku* land
	⸢pa$_5$⸣ Da-na an-ĝal$_2$	available at the ditch Dana.
	ni$_3$-sa$_{10}$-bi	Its price:
	½ ku$_3$ ma-na	½ mina silver:
	Nin-sa$_6$	Ninsa,
	dam Lugal-ni$_3$-zu	wife of Lugalnizu.
	Me-šeš-šeš	Mešeššeš,
	dumu sa$_{12}$-du$_5$	son of the land-recorder,
	šu-ne-⸢ne⸣	their hands
	⸢ab⸣-[si]	were [filled (with silver)].
	Da-da simug	Dada, the smith,
	i$_3$-ne-la$_2$	has weighed it them out.
	⸢Me⸣-šeš-šeš	Mešeššeš,
	[dumu] sa$_{12}$-du$_5$-ke$_4$	[son] of the land-recorder,
ii	na-be$_2$-a	(that is what) he indeed has said:
	aša$_5$-ba lu$_2$ u$_3$-ma-du$_3$-a	"(If) someone else happens to hold this field,
	aša$_5$-ab-ba	the field of (my) father
	ga-ši-ĝar	I shall place (instead of it)."
	inim-ma am$_3$-ĝal$_2$	It was put into the agreement.
	mu lugal-še$_3$	By the name of the king (he/they swore).
	a alur$_x$(SIG$_4$)-ra ab-ta-de$_2$	Water was poured out on the brick.
	[inim-bi] al-til	[The contract relating to it] is concluded.
	Nin-sa$_6$	Ninsa,
	dam Lugal-ni$_3$-zu	wife of Lugalnizu,
	Me-šeš-šeš	(and) Mešeššeš,
	dumu sa$_{12}$-du$_5$	son of the land-recorder,
rev. i	lu$_2$ ni$_3$-sa$_{10}$ gu$_7$-a-me	are those who accepted the price (= sellers).
	Da-da simug	Dada, the smith,
	lu$_2$ ni$_3$-sa$_{10}$ ak-am$_3$	is the one who offered the price (= buyer).
	1 Ad-da	1 Adda,
	dumu Inim-zi-da	son of Inimzida;
	1 Ad-da	1 Adda,
	dumu Du$_{11}$-ga-ni	son of Dugani;
	1 Ur-^{d}Inana ugula	1 Ur-Inana, the overseer,
	dumu A$_2$-ni-ta	son of Anita;
	1 U$_3$-NI-NI	1 UNINI,
	dumu *Su*$_4$-^{c}MUŠ	son of *Šu*-MUŠ;
	1 Nam-maḫ	1 Nammaḫ,
	dumu Ur-saĝ nar	son of Ursaĝ, the musician;
	1 Me-sa$_6$	1 Mesa,
ii	[dumu] ⸢Mes⸣-kisal-e	[son] of Meskisale;
	[1 Ur]-⸢sa$_6$⸣ dam-gara$_3$	[1 Ur]sa, the merchant;

1 Lugal-iti-da	Lugalitida,
dumu Ad-da	son of Adda;
1 Du-du simug	1 Dudu, the smith;
1 Iri-ku$_3$-ki-du$_{10}$	1 Irikukidu,
dumu Lugal-en-nu	son of Lugalennu(g);
1 Nidba$_2^!$(PAD)-DI dumu Du-du	1 NidbaDI, son of Dudu;
1 Lugal-ni$_3$-sa$_6$	1 Lugalnisa,
nar dumu A-rin$_2$-GIR	the musician, son of ArinaGIR,
1 Lugal-^{d}En-lil$_2$-le	1 Lugal-Enlile,
arad$_2$(NITA$_2$×KUR) Me-šeš-šeš	the slave of Mešeššeš;
1 Nin-ḪAR-ni sagi-a-maḫ	1 NinḪARni, the chief cupbearer.
(blank)	
lu$_2$ ki-inim-ma-bi-me	They are its (the deal's) witnesses.

obv. i 2: For the ditch pa$_5$ da-na at Isin, see Wilcke 1976: 47 f. obv. iv 21, v 25 (courtesy J. Hernández).

obv. i 9–10: For the same form, see MAD 4 no. 77 obv. 6 (courtesy J. Hernández).

obv. ii 2: See MAD 4 no. 151 obv. 10 for the same eviction clause, written u$_4$ aša$_5$-ga lu$_2$ u$_3$-ma-a-du$_3$-a. For its interpretation, see FAOS 17 p. 55–56.

obv. ii 7: See CUSAS 26 no. 53 obv. 5' for the same construction, Wilcke 2007: 173 for its interpretation.

rev. ii 8: For Nidba$_2$(PAD.MUŠ$_3$)-DI, son of Dudu the smith, cf. text No. 376 rev. i 5.

rev. ii 13: The writing sagi(SILA$_3$.ŠU.DU$_8$)-a for /šagi'a/ "cupbearer" with an extra A is a spelling typical of Classical Sargonic texts from Isin. Contrary to Taylor 2002, this writing is well attested before the Ur III period.

No. 368 – MS 4217

Inventory of the treasure of a person, Classic/Late Sargonic, Isin? (or Adab?).

obv.	[1(bariga)] zu$_2$-lum	[1] *bariga* dates;
	5 ^{ĝeš}peš$_3$ nindan-DU	5 fig tree rods
	5 ^{ĝeš}peš$_3$ nindan-DU	5 fig tree rods;
	½ ĝeš-ḫi-a *1* li sila$_3$	½ (*sila*) of various wood (resins), 1 *sila* of juniper (resin):
	⸢ki⸣ Diĝir-gu-⸢la⸣	from Diĝirgula.
	1(bariga) zu$_2$-lum	1 *bariga* dates;
	5 ^{ĝeš}kab-peš$_3$ nindan-DU	5 *crooked* fig tree rods;
	½ ĝeš-ḫi-a *1* sila$_3$ li	½ (*sila*) of various trees (resin), 1 *sila* of juniper (resin):
	1 i$_3$-nun sila$_3$	1 *sila* of butter oil;

	1 i$_3$-eren-babbar sila$_3$	1 *sila* of white cedar oil;
	½ i$_3$-ḪI-nun sila$_3$	½ sila of ... oil;
	4 siki ma-na	4 minas wool,
	siki tug$_2$-ĝar-ra-kam$^?$	it is the wool of the ... textile;
	1 siki ma-na	1 mina wool:
rev.	Ĝeš-gu-la$_2$	Ĝešgula.
	7 kin 2 gurdub	7 sickles, 2 *gurdub*-baskets;
	7 ^{ĝeš}kid-da-du$_3$	7 woven ... baskets;
	1 kid 1 ^{ĝeš}dar-du$_3$	1 reed mat, 1 wooden mooring pole;
	^{d}Šuba$_3$(MUŠ$_3$×ZA)-nun	Šubanun.
	1(bariga) zu$_2$-lum	1 *bariga* dates;
	5 ^{ĝeš}kab-peš$_3$ nindan-DU	5 *crooked* fig tree rods;
	½ ĝeš-ḫi-a *1* sila$_3$ li	½ (*sila*) of various trees (resin), 1 *sila* of juniper (resin):
	1 i$_3$-nun sila$_3$	1 *sila* of butter;
	1 i$_3$-eren-babbar sila$_3$	1 *sila* of white cedar oil;
	½ i$_3$-ḪI-nun sila$_3$	½ *sila* of ... oil;
	7 kin 2 gurdub	7 sickles, 2 *gurdub*-baskets;
	2(bariga) < > x-x ^{d}Šuba$_3$-nun	2 *bariga* < > ... Šubanun.
	1 i$_3$-nun sila$_3$	1 *sila* of butter;
	½ ĝeš-ḫi-a *1* sila$_3$ li	½ (*sila*) of various trees (resin), 1 *sila* of juniper (resin):
	6 gi gu$_2$ 7 kid gu$_2$	6 loads of reeds, 7 loads of (reed) mats (or "fibers"?);
	1(bariga) [+n] zu$_2$-lum	1+x *bariga* dates.
l.e.	gil Ur-^{d}Eš$_5$-⌜peš⌝	(It is) the treasure of Ur-Ešpeš.

For a text of similar format and date, see CUSAS 13 no. 164, which M. Maiocchi attributes to Isin. Although that is possible, there is no definite proof for his assertion. Rather, both this text and CUSAS 13 no. 164 may be from Adab.

obv. 2, 3, 7, rev. 7: The writing nindan-DU usually refers to a measure of length of *ca.* 6 m. Here it is used in its literal meaning "rod."

obv. 7, rev. 7: The proposed interpretation of the term as ^{ĝeš}kab-peš$_3$ "crooked(?) fig tree" is tentative.

obv. 13: The meaning of siki tug$_2$-ĝar-ra-kam$^?$ is not certain. The final sign is somewhat unusual for KAM and resembles neither ḪI×DIŠ nor ḪI×TIL.

rev. 3: See a similar term ^{ĝeš}kid-da ĝešimmar "a small basket made of woven palm fronds," Akk. *tuḫallu*; CAD T 451. For the interpretation of the term as a variety of basket placed around date palms when harvesting them, see Volk 2004: 287. In our case, the verb du$_3$ in ^{ĝeš}kid-da-du$_3$ may mean "to do, perform."

rev. 4: For dar-du$_3$ as "mooring pole," cf. Powell 1992: 118 with additional references.

rev. 13: The first sign(?) is a diagonal wedge starting from the right, which is unusual in cuneiform. The second looks like a TUG$_2$ or similar.

No. 369 – MS 4234

Legal document of uncertain nature concerning silver, Classical Sargonic, Isin.

obv.	[break]	…
	⸢x⸣-[…] ⸢x⸣	…
	Nin-⸢ĝessu-e⸣ šu ba-ti	Ninĝessu has received.
	mu [Da]-da	Instead of/because of(?) Dada,
	⸢x⸣-na-ni-KAS$_4$.DU	…
	ku$_3$-ta še-ta ku$_3$ 2 giĝ$_4$-kam	It is 2 shekels silver in silver and grain,
	[šu] ba-ti	he has received.
	⸢½⸣ ku$_3$ giĝ$_4$ e$_2$-gi$_4$-a	½ shekel silver: it is the bride(-price)
	Zaq-tum-kam	of *Zaqtum*.
	ku$_3$ igi-3-ĝal$_2$ Lugal-ĝeš	⅓ (shekel) silver: Lugalĝeš.
	½ ku$_3$ giĝ$_4$ Lugal-diĝir-ku$_3$-ge	½ shekel silver: Lugaldiĝirkuge.
	ku$_3$ igi-4-ĝal$_2$ Ur-^{d}Gu$_2$-la$_2$	¼ (shekel) silver: Ur-Gula,
	⸢saĝ⸣ Lugal-ĝeš-še$_3$	As the main amount (of) Lugalĝeš
	[šu] ⸢ba⸣-ti-eš$_2$	they have received it.
	[…]-⸢x⸣-[…]	…
	[…]	…
rev.	[…]	…
	[Da]-da [(simug)]	Dada, (the smith),
	[Lugal]-ĝeš-ra i$_3$-na-la$_2$-a	out of what he has weighed it out for Lugalĝeš,
	[ša$_3$]-bi-ta	
	KA-ba	KAba (and)
	Lugal-en-nu dumu Pu$_x$(LAGAB×TIL)-ta	Lugalennu(g), son of Puta,
	6 ku$_3$ giĝ$_4$	6 shekels silver

	⸢šu⸣ ba-ta-ti-eš$_2$	they have received.
	ku$_3$-egir-pi 4 giĝ$_4$	Its inheritance silver 4 shekels,
	Nin-ĝessu-e šu ba-ti	Ninĝessu has received.
	1 giĝ$_4$ ur$_5$-še$_3$ Da-da i$_3$-na-šum$_2$	1 shekel as a loan (to) Dada he has given.
	1 bar-dul$_5$ 1 giĝ$_4$ ku$_3$-kam	It is 1 *bardul*-garment of 1 shekel silver (value).
	1(gur) 2(bariga) še gur 1 giĝ$_4$ ku$_3$-kam	It is 1 *gur* 2 *bariga* barley of 1 shekel silver (value).
	še-ta zu$_2$-lum-ta igi-3-ĝal$_2$-kam	⅓ (shekel silver) in barley and dates.
	[break]	…
l.e. 1	[…]-⸢x⸣	[If …]
l.e. 2	2 še gur al-aĝ$_2$-ĝa$_2$-a […]	one measured 2 *gur* barley …
l.e. 3	nam-erim$_2$!(<NE>.RU)-pi in-na!(KI)-ku$_5$-eš$_2$	They swore to him.

obv. 4': The line is unclear. The sign combination KAS$_4$.DU is attested once in the canal name pa$_5$ ^{d}Saman-KAS$_4$.DU (Ur-Nanše of Lagaš; see RIME 1 E1.9.9.2/3/10).

rev. 5: For the same KA-ba son of Lu$_2$-maḫ, see CUSAS 26 no. 46 rev. 8.

rev. 9: ku$_3$-egir, literally "silver (left) behind," means most likely "inheritance silver." See egir = *arkatu* 3 in CAD A^2 274 f.: "estate, inheritance, family fortune."

left edge 3: Interpretation courtesy J. Hernández.

No. 370 – MS 4239

Witnessed document. Contents uncertain, Classical Sargonic, Isin.

obv.	*1* Da-da dumu En-ne$_{2}$	1 Dada, son of Ene;
	1 Amar-bad$_{3}$	1 Amarbad,
	dumu ⸢sagi⸣-a-maḫ	son of the chief cupbearer;
	1 Ur-⸢x⸣ dumu Ur-⸢si$_{4}$⸣	1 Ur…, son of Ursi;
	1 E$_{2}$-li-li	1 Elili
	1 Ur-gu dumu Lugal-⸢ša$_{3}$⸣	1 Urgu, son of Lugalša;
	1 Saĝ-a-DU šu-ku$_{6}$	1 Saĝ-aDU, the fisherman;
	1 Ad-da	1 Adda,
	lu$_{2}$ nin	the man of the lady;
	1 U$_{2}$-u$_{2}$ engar	1 U'u, the agricultural manager;
	1 Ad-da	1 Adda,
rev.	dumu Lu$_{2}$-kisal-[le]	son of Lukisale;
	1 Ur-sa$_{6}$	1 Ursa,
	dumu Kur-re$_{2}$	son of Kure;
	1 Ur-TUR-TUR dumu-ni	1 UrTURTUR, his son;
	1 RU-RU-ki	1 RURUki,
	sukkal i$_{7}$-da	the secretary of the River;
	1 Ur-LI dumu Kur-re$_{2}$	1 UrLI, son of Kure;
	1 Amar-ku$_{3}$ dumu E$_{2}$-bar-⸢bi⸣	1 Amarku, son of Ebarbi;
	1 E$_{2}$-uri$_{3}$ igi-du-bi	1 E-uri, its (the matter's) *legal court official*;
	1 Saĝ-diĝir sagi-a	1 Saĝdiĝir, the cupbearer;
	1 Ur-eš$_{3}$ šandana	1 Ur-eš, the gardener.
	KAL$^{?}$ MA AN SI$^{?}$ IN X	…
l.e.	*1* Ur-^{d}Nisaba dub-sar maškim-bi	1 Ur-Nisaba, the scribe, its legal commissioner.

obv. 5: For a Semitic name E$_{2}$-LI-LI, see Sommerfeld 2010: 145 and *passim* there.

obv. 6: For the same person, see CUSAS 26 no. 52 rev. 9.

obv. 7: Cf., e.g., the Saĝ-a-DU who frequently appears in the "Mesaĝ archive"; see Bridges 1981.

obv. 9: It is unclear from the context who the nin "lady" might be. One might consider reading ereš with similar meaning or nin "sister." Another possibility is to understand Nin as an abbreviated personal name.

rev. 3: For a full form of the same name, see text No. 371 obv. i 2 (KA-ku$_{3}$-kur-re$_{2}$).

rev. 5: Cf. CUSAS 26 no. 57 (CS Isin) rev. 1' for RU-RU-[(ki)].

rev. 6: See OSP 2 no. 136 (MS/CS Nippur) rev. 6' for PN sukkal i$_{7}$-da, "vizier of the Divine River." If Westenholz's interpretation is correct, this person may be connected to the river as a place of ordeal.

rev. 12: Uncertain. Detailed photo:

No. 371 – MS 4242

Purchase of a field, Classical Sargonic, Isin.

The top and bottom have been glued together, with about one third of the tablet missing from the middle.

obv. i	aša$_5$ A$_2$-ni-ta	The field of Anita,
	dumu KA-ku$_3$-kur-re$_2$-ka	son of KAkukure,
	Da-da simug	which Dada, the smith,
	i$_3$-sa$_{10}$-a	has bought,
	Lugal-[...]	Lugal...
	[break]	...
	[...] ⌜ŠID?⌝	...
	Bar-ra-ni-še$_3$	Baraniše,
	dumu Mes-kisal-e	son of Meskisale,
	Za$_3$-mu	Zamu,
	dumu sagi-maḫ	son of the chief cupbearer,
	Qu$_2$-ra-dum	*Qurādum* ("Strong"),
ii	dumu *Zaq-tum*	son of *Zaqtum*,
	ka e$_2$-gal-maḫ-ka	at the entrance of the Egalmaḫ temple
	di-bi si bi$_2$-sa$_2$-eš$_2$	they rendered justice in this case.
	Da-da [simug]	Dada, [the smith],
	[break]	...
	[1 ...]-^{d}Šara$_2$	[1] ...Šara,
	lu$_2$-^{ĝeš}tukul-ku$_3$-sig$_{17}$	the *man of the golden weapon*;
	1 *Da-num$_2$* kuš$_7$	1 *Dannum*, the animal-manager;
	1 *Zaq-tum*	1 *Zaqtum*;
	1 *Sa$_2$-lim-be-li$_2$*	1 *Šalim-bēlī*,
	dumu Sipa-*ni-se$_{11}$*	son of *Rē'i-nišē*;
	1 E$_2$-gal-gi	1 *Ekal-kēn*,
	dumu *Šu-i$_3$-li$_2$-su*	son of *Šu-'ilīšu*:
rev. i	aga$_3$-us$_2$ lugal-me	they are soldiers of the king.
	1 Ur-^{d}En-lil$_2$-la$_2$ išib	1 Ur-Enlila, the *išib*-priest;
	1 Ur-sa$_6$	1 Ursa,
	dumu Ne-saĝ	son of Nesaĝ;
	1 Lu$_2$-^{d}En-lil$_2$-la$_2$	1 Lu-Enlila,
	dumu saĝĝa	son of the chief temple-administrator;
	1 Ĝessu kuš$_7$	1 Ĝessu, the animal-manager;
	1 KA-[...]	1 KA...;
	[break]	...
	1 Il$_2$ [(x)]	1 Il(a);
	1 Na-ba-lu$_5$	1 Nabalu,
	sagi-a	the cupbearer;
	1 Ur-LI	1 UrLI,
	šeš-ni	his brother;
	1 E$_2$-li-li	1 Elili

ii	1 Ur-ĝidru	1 Urĝidru,
	dumu Nin-ERIN$_2$-zi	son of NinERINzi;
	1 Ur-ĝidru dub-sar	1 Urĝidru, the scribe;
	1 Ur-gu šu-i$_2$	1 Urgu, the barber;
	1 Nam-maḫ-ni simug	1 Nammaḫ(a)ni, the smith;
	[break]	…
	1 *Šu-Aš$_{11}$-[tar$_2$]*	1 *Šu-'Aštar*,
	si-da-um	the *sida'um*.
	nu-banda$_3$ *Sar-ru-dan*	The supervisor (of) *Šarrum-dān*('s household)
	maškim-bi	(is) its commissioner.
	1 Lugal-ni$_3$-zu šu-i$_{\textit{-tenû}}$	1 Lugalnizu, the barber,
	igi-du-bi	(is) its legal official.

The following fragment (not necessarily of the same tablet) was glued upside-down on to MS 4242 when photographed. It is now missing and could not be located.

[1] ⌜x⌝-ku$_3$ […]	[1] …ku, …;
1 Ur-^{d}Nin-⌜x⌝	1 Ur-Nin…;
1 Amar-⌜x⌝	1 Amar…;

obv. i 2: See BIN 8 no. 167 rev. 7 for the same individual. Cf. also KA-ku$_3$-ga-ni dumu Kur-re$_2$-[…] in MAD 4 no. 170 l. 8 (reference courtesy J. Hernández).

obv. ii 2: E$_2$-gal-maḫ was the temple of Gula as Ninisina in Isin: see MC 5, p. 88 no. 318.

obv. ii 6': Cf. lu$_2$-tukul-la$_2$-kam in text No. 366 obv. 6. Here and elsewhere the title may refer to high-ranking bodyguards.

obv. ii 10': See CUSAS 26 no. 123 (Adab) rev. i 10 for the same name.

rev. ii 6: For the same person, see CUSAS 26 no. 46. Restoration courtesy J. Hernández.

rev. ii 7': For this term of uncertain meaning, see SCTRAH no. 310 obv. 4 commentary, with additional references.

rev. ii 11': The term igi-du and palil(IGI.DU) = *ašarēdu* "foremost" is, like maškim, a legal function rather than a professional title. The function of igi-du is not certain. In CUSAS 26 no. 46 obv. 11–12, the professional *si-da-um* is the "foremost" of the legal case.

No. 372 – MS 4245

Self-sale into slavery, Classical Sargonic, Isin.

obv.	Lugal-ša$_3$	For Lugalša,
	dumu Ur-sa$_6$-ra	son of Ursa,
	u$_4$ še ku$_3$ 1 giĝ$_4$	when one measured
	1(bariga) 2(ban$_2$) al-aĝ$_2$	1 *bariga* 2 *ban* barley for 1 shekel silver,
	4 ku$_3$ giĝ$_4$	4 shekels silver
	ni$_3$-sa$_{10}$-a-ni-še$_3$	as his price
	Diĝir-igi-du dam-gara$_3$	Diĝirigidu, the merchant,
	Ur-du$_6$-<ku$_3$>-ga dam-gara$_3$	(and) Urdu<ku>ga, the merchant,
	in-ni-ĝar-e-eš$_2$	they have established it.
	Da-da simug	Dada, the smith,
	6 ku$_3$ giĝ$_4$-še$_3$	for 6 shekels silver,
	Lugal-ša$_3$	Lugalša,
	Ur-sa$_6$ ad-da-ni	Ursa, his father,
	U$_3$-ma-ni ama-ni	Umani, his mother,
	Lugal-sila (ras.) šeš-a-ni	Lugalsila (erasure), his brother,
rev.	UN-ĝa$_2$ dam-ni	UNĝa, his wife,
	ĝeš i$_3$-na-ta-bala	he let him pass by the wooden (pestle).

	inim-ma-ni al-til	The contract relating to him is concluded.
	1 Me-sa$_6$ dumu Mes-kisal-e	1 Mesa, son of Meskisale;
	1 Ur-lu$_2$ dumu Lugal-ša$_3$	1 Urlu, son of Lugalša;
	1 Ad-da dumu Du$_{11}$-ga-ni	1 Adda, son of Dugani;
	1 U$_2$-u$_2$ engar	1 U'u, the agricultural manager;
	1 Ur-diĝir-ra šeš Ama-bara$_2$-si	1 Urdiĝira, brother of Amabarasi;
	⸢1⸣ Lugal-⸢KA⸣	1 LugalKA,
	dumu ⸢Ama⸣-tur-ra	son of Amatura;
	1 Du-⸢du⸣ simug	1 Dudu, the smith:
	(blank/ruling)	
	lu$_2$ ki-inim-ma-bi-me	They are its witnesses.
	ni$_3$!-ba še 7(gur) 2(bariga) gur	The "present": it is 7 *gur* 2 *bariga* barley
	zu$_2$-lum igi-*4* ku$_3$ ĝal$_2$-kam	(and) dates worth ¼ (shekel) silver.
l.e.	gu$_2$ i$_3$-ĝar	He put it on (his) neck.

rev. 2: See Wilcke 2007: 79 for this expression signifying that the person or movable goods in question come into possession of the buyer.

left edge: See FAOS 15/2 pp. 402–3 rev. i 5 f. for the expression gu$_2$-possessive suffix … -ĝar "auf das Schuldkonto setzen," i.e., to charge, to score, to mark up.

No. 373 – MS 4246

Purchase of miscellaneous goods, Classical Sargonic, Isin.

obv.	1 [...] ki-⸢la$_2$⸣-bi ^{šu_2}*2N$_8$*$^{ša-na-bi}$	1 …, its weight: ⅔ (mina);
	3 siki ma-na	3 minas of wool
	1 ku$_3$ giĝ$_4$-kam	of (the value) 1 shekel silver;
	1 ud$_5$ šu-la$_2$-am$_3$	1 nanny goat …,
	ni$_3$-U$_6$ zabar$_x$(UD.KA×BAR)^{uruda}	… bronze,
	ku$_3$ NINDA$_2$×ŠE.2N$_1$ ma-na	(of the value) 2 little minas (= ⅔ shekel);
	1 zabar$_x$^{uruda} ki-la$_2$-bi	1 bronze (drinking vessel), its weight:
	[break]	…
rev.	[break]	[name and affiliation of a person to be sold into slavery]
	Da-da i$_3$-sa$_{10}$	Dada has bought.
	ni$_3$-sa$_{10}$-ma-ni	His price,
	6 ku$_3$ giĝ$_4$	6 shekels silver,
	Ur-^{d}Nin-sig$_x$(SAR) šu ba-ti	Ur-Ninsig has received.
	6 ku$_3$ giĝ$_4$	6 shekels silver
	E$_2$-lu$_2$ šu ba-ti	Elu has received.
	(blank)	

obv. 4: The interpretation is uncertain. šu-la$_2$^{uruda} denotes a metal vessel. Variant writings of the term — mostly šu-(ša/še$_3$)-la$_2$^{uruda} — point to the phonemic shape ★/šušla/ for this Sumerian word. Its capacity lay in the range ¼–1 sila. See MC 4 p. 48.

obv. 5: The interpretation of the term ni$_3$-U$_6$ zabar$_x$^{uruda} is challenging. Whereas the latter part may refer to a bronze drinking vessel (zabar^{uruda}), the lexeme ni$_3$-U$_6$ remains problematic. This sign combination appears in a god's name, ^{d}Ni$_3$-u$_6$-di-du$_{10}$: see Cavigneaux and Krebernik 1999.

obv. 7: See EDPV A p. 85 no. 133.

No. 374 – MS 4247

Witnessed document recording a purchase(?) of mostly metal objects. Classical Sargonic, Isin. The lower two-thirds of a tablet.

obv.	[break]	...
	[1] ⸢x⸣-sa$_6$-ga ⸢x⸣-al-U$_2$^{uruda}	[1] premium bronze ...
	[1] ⸢ĜAR$^{?}$⸣ banšur	[1] ... of the table;
	[1 (x)] ⸢banšur⸣ zu$_2$-lum ga-ar$_3$	[1] table (for) dates (and) cheese;
	1 zabar^{uruda}	1 bronze (cup);
	1 za-ḫa-da^{uruda}	1 bronze *zaḫada*-ax;
	1 LU-TIL-ku$_3$	1 silver ...:
	ku$_3$ ka-ka-na	silver on his/her mouth
	u$_3$ ku$_3$ ur$_2$-ra-na	and silver on his/her lap.
	igi Du-du simug	(In) front of Dudu, the smith;
rev.	igi Lugal-ĝar šu-i$_2$	(in) front of Lugalĝar, the barber;
	igi Ur-ĝidru	in front of Urĝidru,
	dumu Nin-ERIN$_2$-zi-še$_3$	son of NinERINzi;
	igi E$_2$-li-li-še$_3$	in front of Elili;
	igi Ad-da	in front of Adda,
	dumu Du$_{11}$-ga-ni-še$_3$	son of Dugani;
	igi Lugal-ĝar engar	in front of Lugalĝar, the agricultural manager,
	dumu Inim-ma-ni-zi-še$_3$	son of Inimanizi.
	igi-ne-ne-ta	In front of them
	Da-da simug	Dada, the smith,
	[break]	[has ...ed, etc.]

obv. 5': For this type of ax, see Schrakamp 2010: 214.

obv. 6'–8': This is likely a description of a figurine of an animal (sheep, if LU is read as udu) or an anthropomorphic being.

No. 375 – MS 4260

Contesting the purchase of a garden, resolved by the *saĝĝa* of Isin in the temple of Ninisina, Classical Sargonic, Isin.

obv.	^{ĝeš}kiri$_6$ ⸢Ad⸣-[da]	(For) the garden of Adda,
	dumu Du$_{11}$-⸢ga⸣-[ni]	son of Dugani,
	Da-da [simug]	Dada, [the smith,]
	i$_3$-⸢aĝ$_2$⸣	has measured (barley as price).
	Ur-eš$_3$ šandana	Ur-eš, the gardener,
	gu$_3$ i$_3$-da-ĝar	has lodged a claim.
	Lu$_2$-diĝir-ra	Ludiĝira,
	saĝĝa Isin$_2$$^{⸢ki⸣}$	the chief temple-administrator of Isin,
	[break]	…
rev.	[break]	…
	1 […]	1 …
	1 Ur-saĝ dumu ^{d}En-lil$_2$-[la$_2$]	1 Ursaĝ, son of Enlila;
	1 Lugal-ša$_3$ E$_2$-maḫ-da	1 Lugalša (of) Emaḫda;
	1 *Sa$_2$-lim-*^{d}Utu šeš-ni	*Šalim-Šamaš*, his brother.
	1 Ur-ĝidru sukkal	1 Ur-ĝidru, the secretary;
	1 Da-da dumu En-ne$_2$-⸢ke$_4$?⸣	1 Dada, son of Enne;
	1 Ur-gu sipa ⸢anše⸣	1 Urgu, the donkey-herd;
	1 ⸢Nita⸣ dumu ^{d}En-[lil$_2$-la$_2$]	1 Nita, son of En[lila].
l.e. 1	[…] e$_2$-gal-maḫ-a	in the Egalmaḫ (temple)
l.e. 2	di-bi al-til	this case has been resolved.

obv. 6: Gu$_3$ (or/and inim) … ĝar = Akk. *ragāmu* "to lodge a claim, to sue, to bring a legal complaint, to claim something by lawsuit" (CAD R 62).

No. 376 – MS 4265

Purchase of immovable property, Classical Sargonic, Isin.

obv. i	[1 line missing]	…
	ŠU-[…]	…
	80 […]	80 …
	12 [+n…]	12+x …
	^{ĝeš}[kiri$_6$ …]	[the garden(?) …]
	ku$_3$ ⸢x⸣-[…]	the silver …
	ki ⸢Da⸣-[da$^?$ simug$^?$-ta]	from Da[da, smith(?)],
	Ur-sa$_6$	Ursa,
	dumu KA-ku$_3$-ke$_4$	son of KAku,
	šu ba-ti	has received.
	inim-bi al-[til]	This matter is [settled].
	Nam-⸢maḫ⸣	Nammaḫ,
	šandana-[SAR]	the … gardener,
	lu$_2$ ni$_3$-⸢sa$_{10}$⸣ [ak]-am$_3$	is the person who [did] the price (= buyer).
ii	[*1*] Lugal-maḫ$_2$	[1] Lugalmaḫ,
	lu$_2$ Še-ĝeš-i$_3$	the man of Šegeš-i ("Sesame");
	1 Nita	1 Nita,

	dumu ^{d}En-lil$_2$-la$_2$	son of Enlila;
	1 Lugal-ĝeš	1 Lugalĝeš;
	[dumu Pu$_x^?$]-⸢ta⸣	[son of Pu$^?$]ta;
	[*1* Ur]-tur	[1 Ur]tur,
	[dumu] ⸢Ur⸣-si$_4$	[son of] Ursi;
	1 E$_2$-li-li	1 Elili;
	1 Al-si$_4$	1 Alsi,
	lu$_2$ Pu$_x$(LAGAB×TIL)-ta	the man of Puta;
	1 Ur-⸢eš$_3$⸣	1 Ur-eš,
	dumu A-ba-an-da	son of Aba'anda;
	1 Saĝ-diĝir-tuku	1 Saĝdiĝirtuku,
	dumu Ur-LI	son of UrLI;
rev. i	*1* Ur-^{d}Inana	1 Ur-Inana
	šandana-SAR *Tu-ṭa-na-ab-šum*	the … gardener of *Tuṭṭanab-šum*;
	1 Nita	1 Nita,
	dumu sa$_{12}$-du$_5$	son of the land-recorder;
	1 Du-du simug	1 Dudu, the smith;
	1 Nidba$_2$-DI	1 NidabaDI,
	dumu Du-du simug	son of Dudu, the smith;
	1 ⸢x⸣-MU-DU-zu	1 …MUDUzu,
	gala	the cult-singer;
	1 Bar-ra-⸢ni-še$_3$⸣	1 Baraniše;
	1 Me-^{sa2}[sag$_7$]	1 Mesag,
	dumu Ur-eš$_3$	son of Ur-eš.
	šandana-SAR-me	They are … gardeners.
	1 E$_2$-ki	1 Eki,
	⸢dumu⸣ E$_2$-zi	son of Ezi.
ii	(blank space)	
	lu$_2$ ki-inim-ma-bi-me	They are its witnesses.
	(blank space)	

obv. ii 13: Cf. A-ba-an-da-sa$_2$ in CUSAS 26 no. 47 rev. i 8.

rev. i 1: Cf. a high priestess and daughter of Naram-Suen by the same name. See RIME 2 p. 175 E2.1.4.2017. For the new interpretation of the name *Tu-ta$_2$-na-ap-šum* as *Tu-ṭa-na-ab-šum* = *Tuṭṭanāb-šum* "Sie (die Göttin) bereitet ihm (dem König) immer wieder Gutes," i.e., "She (the goddess) is constantly preparing good for him (the king)," see Sommerfeld 2011: 290–92.

No. 377 – MS 4266

Witnessed receipt of barley and silver, Middle Sargonic, Isin.

obv.	20 še gur su$_7$(LAĜAR×SUM)-⸢kam⸣	20 *gur* barley of the threshing floor:
	e$_2$ ^{d}Pa-bil$_2$-saĝ	(in) the temple of Pabilsaĝ,
	Ur-lu$_2$-ba-da	Urlubada,
	dumu Lu$_2$-ĝeš-ke$_4$	son of Luĝeš,
	šu ba-ti	has received.
	5 ku$_3$ giĝ$_4$	5 shekels silver:
	saĝ ku$_3$-kam	it is the initial amount of silver.
	2 ½(BAR) ku$_3$ giĝ$_4$	2 ½ shekels silver:
	A ku$_3$-ga-kam	it is the *"father"* of silver.
	saĝ Ur-lu$_2$-ba-da	The initial amount (of) Urlubada,
	⸢Lu$_2$$^{?}$⸣-ḫe$_2$-ĝal$_2$	Luheĝal(?),
rev.	dam-gara$_3$	the merchant
	Nibru^{ki}-ke$_4$	(from) Nippur,
	šu ba-ti	has received.
	igi Ur-si$_4$ Nin-GAN$_2$	(In) front of Ursi (of) NinGAN;
	igi Lugal-ĝuruš(KAL)-zi	(in) front of Lugalĝuruszi;
	igi Inim-ma-ni-zi a-zu	(in) front of Inimanizi, the physician;
	igi Il$_2$	(in) front of Il(a);
	igi Inim-ma-ni-zi	(in) front of Inimanizi,
	dam-gara$_3$	the merchant.
	(blank/ruling)	
	igi-ne-ne-ta	In front of them
	šu ba-ti	he has received it.

obv. 1: The term (ki-)su$_7$ is interpreted mostly as "threshing floor" and sometimes as "fallow land" (see Civil 1994: 94 sub 94). Thus, the barley in question originates either directly from threshing or from a fallow field, the latter being less likely. However, several texts suggest a different interpretation of gur su$_7$. BIN 8 no. 85 (MS/CS Isin?) rev. 2 and CUSAS 19 no. 164 (CS Adab according to editors) obv. 3' have še gur su$_7$-ta "barley by the *gur* of the threshing floor" and zu$_2$-lum gur su$_7$-ta "dates by the *gur* of the threshing floor" respectively (*contra* the interpretation in CUSAS 19). This could be evidence of another standard of the capacity measure *gur*. It is unknown whether this *gur* was larger than, equal to, or smaller than the usual Akkad *gur*. Theoretically, this measure could be equal to the usual *gur* but since grain after threshing is fresh, its weight and capacity diminishes in the course of time due to drying. For su$_7$ du$_8$-a in connection to barley, see Maekawa 1986: 94 (text no. 32 p. 116). He argues that the term refers to threshing with the help of cattle, which was done separately from threshing expressed by the form še ĝeš ra-a. Accordingly, the two terms refer to barley threshed by different methods.

obv. 2: The god Pabilsaĝ is the consort of the goddess Gula/Ninisina and appears as a resident of the temple of Gula as Ninisina, e$_2$-gal-maḫ in Isin: see MC 5 p. 88 no. 318. His own temple bears the name e$_2$-rab-ri-ri in liturgical texts (ibid. p. 136 no. 935). It is likely that this temple is meant here.

obv. 7, 9: The usual meaning of saĝ is "capital"; see CAD R 277 *rēšu* 5: "first installment, original amount, capital assets." For saĝ ku$_3$-bi as "initial silver (= price)," see Middeke-Conlin and Proust 2014: 7. The meaning of A ku$_3$-ga is uncertain.

rev. 4: Like Nin-GAN$_2$-a in CUSAS 11 no. 37 obv. ii 4, Nin-GAN$_2$ of the present text is a feminine name. There was also a deity ^{d}Nin-GANA$_2$: see Cavigneaux and Krebernik 2000b.

No. 378 – MS 4270

Purchase of a house, Classical Sargonic, Isin.

This text should be studied together with CUSAS 26 no. 52, a document that records the same legal case.

obv.	*1* ⸢Ama⸣-bara$_2$-ge	1 Amabarage;
	1 E$_2$-bar-bi	1 Ebarbi;
	1 Na-ba-lu ⸢sagi-a⸣	1 Nabalu, the cupbearer;
	1 Lu$_2$-diĝir-ra sa$_{12}$-du$_5$	1 Ludiĝira, the land-recorder;
	1 Me-šeš-šeš	1 Mešeššeš,

šeš-ni	his brother;
1 KA-ku$_3$	1 KAku,
dumu Lugal-ĝuruš(KAL)-zi	son of Lugalĝuruszi;
1 Me-sa$_6$	1 Mesa,
dumu Mes-kisal-e	son of Meskisale;
1 Lugal-ĝeš	1 Lugalĝeš,
dumu Kur-re$_2$	son of Kure.
igi-ne-ne-ta	In front of them,
rev. ĝeš-⸢kiĝ$_2$⸣-ti e$_2$-gal-ka	in the workshop of the palace,
Da-da simug	Dada, the smith,
Lugal-ĝeš dumu Ur-saĝ niĝir-da	together with Lugalĝeš, son of Ursaĝ, the herald,
u$_3$ Nin-ĝessu dam-ni-bi	and with (= bi-(da)) Ninĝessu, his wife,
ni$_3$-sa$_{10}$ e$_2$-na	on the price of his house
ni$_3$-kas$_7$(ŠID)-bi i$_3$-da-ak	he has made an account (= purchase contract).
ku$_3$-ta še-ta 7 ku$_3$ giĝ$_4$-kam	It is 7 shekels silver in silver and barley.
sa$_{10}$-diri e$_2$-še$_3$	The remainder (*lit.* extra price) for the house
Da-da simug	Dada, the smith,
gu$_2$ in-ni-ĝar	has put it on (his) neck (= charged him).
(blank)	

Part 3 – Documents from the Umma Region

3.1 – ED IIIb Documents from the Umma Region

3.1.1 – Personnel

No. 379 – MS 2466

Account of workers (*ĝuruš*) listed in groups, Early Dynastic IIIb, Umma region.

obv. i	15 ĝuruš-dub$^!$(MES) Gala	15 (teams of) *ĝuruš*-workers of the tablet (= regular workers): Gala;
	5 Lugal-a$_2$-maḫ	5: Lugal-amaḫ;
	5 Lugal-nir-ĝal$_2$	5: Lugal-nirĝal;
	5 ⸢x-x⸣	5: …
ii	4 Amar-GUL	4: AmarGUL;
	6 la$_2$ ¼ Lugal-šudu$_3$-du$_{10}$	6 minus ¼ (teams; = 23 individuals): Lugalšududu;
	5 Saĝ-diĝir-tuku	5: Saĝdiĝirtuku;
	3 ½ Saĝ-eš$_3$-tuku	3 ½ (= 14 individuals): Saĝ-eštuku;
iii	5 Nam$_2$-[…]	5: Nam…
	53 ¼ ĝuruš-dub	(Total): 53 ¼ (teams = 213 individuals) of *ĝuruš*-workers of the tablet.
rev.	(blank)	

ĝuruš-workmen are recorded in teams of four with their respective supervisors. The numeral N_8×*AŠ* (usually "½") here stands for ¼ whereas N_8×*DIŠ* means "½." The term ĝuruš-dub "the workmen of the tablet" may be related to the term saĝ-dub in ED IIIb documents from Ĝirsu, where it designates a permanent worker in contrast to temporary conscripted workers; see Bauer 1998: 543.

No. 380 – MS 3791/3

Account of personnel, Early Dynastic IIIb, Umma region.

obv. i	1 Maḫ-an-dab$_6$(URUDA)-e	1 Maḫandabe;
	1 Ur-Šubur	1 Ur-Šubur;
	1 E$_2$-giri$_x$(LAK85)-ni	1 Egirini;
	1 Lugal-šu-sikil	1 Lugalšusikil;
	1 *En-ne-nu-um*$^!$(DUB)	1 *Ennenum*;
ii	1 E$_2$-ur$_2$-bi-du$_{10}$	1 E-urbidu,
	sipa ama-gan	the herder of jenny-(asses).

	1 Amar-ki-ku$_3$	1 Amarkiku;
	1 Amar-ki-ku$_3$	1 Amarkiku;
	1 Utu-šeš-ĝu$_{10}$	1 Utušešĝu;
rev. i	1 Lugal-u$_4$	1 Lugal-u;
	1 Gu-la	1 Gula.
	(rest blank)	
ii	(blank)	

obv. i 5: Cf. the Ur III personal name *En-ne-nu-um* in NATN 567 (Ur III, Nippur) obv. 6.

obv. ii 2: The animals referred to are likely female donkeys. See Waetzoldt 1975: 422 for sipa anše ama-gan-na "Hirte der Eselinen, die geworfen haben," i.e., shepherds of jenny-asses that have given birth.

No. 381 – MS 3791/8

Craftsmen of the palace in teams with their supervisors, Early Dynastic ED IIIb, Umma region.

obv. i	[n ...]	[n: ... professionals]:
	⸢Lugal⸣-Abzu-a	Lugal-Abzu'a;
	4 ad-KID	4 reed-workers:
	Ur-tilla$_x$(|AN.AN|)	Urtilla;
	1 tug$_2$-du$_8$	1 felter:
ii	⸢x⸣-[...]	[personal name];
	4 ma$_2$-⸢laḫ$_4$⸣	4 sailors:
	Amar-Ku'ara(ḪA.A)	Amar-Ku'ara.
	(blank)	
rev.	ĝeš-kiĝ$_2$-ti	The craftsmen
	ša$_3$ e$_2$-gal	(those) inside the palace.
	ĝeš-gaba-tab(*2*)	Manual seeding.
	u$_8$ sila$_4$-⸢bi-da⸣	Ewes and lambs.

rev. 3: The term ĝeš-du$_8$ tab-bi appears in CUSAS 27 no. 10 (= BdI 1 no. 220) obv. 5 and no. 11 (= BdI 1 no. 221) obv. 6. The correct reading is likely ĝeš-gaba-tab-bi. Ĝeš-gaba-tab was a seeding tool operated by workers; see Heimpel 1995: 125, Studevent-Hickman 2006: 117. If this reading is correct, the text records craftsmen under the supervision of named individuals working on the fields as seeders. It remains unclear how to relate this activity to the "ewes and lambs" in the next line.

3.1.2 – Land

No. 382 – MS 2191/31

Inventory of land in possession of elders, Early Dynastic IIIb, Umma region.

obv. i	1(eše$_3$) 3(iku) ⸢Ne-saĝ⸣	1 *eše* 3 *iku*: Nesaĝ
	KA-LI-LI	(and) KALILI;
	2(iku) Ur-^{d}Dulum$_2$	2 *iku*: Ur-Dulum;
	4(iku) Ur-^{d}Dulum$_2$	4 *iku*: Ur-Dulum,
ii	gal$_5$-la$_2$-gal	the chief policeman;
	4(iku) ⸢AB⸣.KID.KID	4 *iku*: ABKIDKID
	E$_2$-maḫ-da	(and) Emaḫda;
	4(iku) Lugal-inim-du$_{10}$	4 *iku*: Lugalinimdu,
	Nita E$_2$-ušum-⸢gal⸣	Nita (and) E'ušumgal.
iii	4(iku) Ne-saĝ	4 *iku*: Nesaĝ
	Kar-du$_3$	(and) Kardu;
	2(eše$_3$) Si-ĝar	2 *eše*: Siĝar
	En-kalam	(and) Enkalam
rev.	aša$_5$ u$_2$-rum / lu$_2$ / da-ba / bur-šu-ma	
		The land (is) the property. The "holders." The elder(s).

obv. i 2: This is probably a personal name. Cf. KA-LI-LI = *šegû* "rabid, raging" in a "philological" composition published in CUSAS 12 p. 252 no. 7.1: 176.

rev.: The translation "property" for u$_2$-rum is conventional and refers to the domain of a temple household or ruler. The term lu$_2$ da-ba may be compared to ED IIIb Ĝirsu individuals designated lu$_2$ šuku dab$_5$-ba. They were holders of parcels of land that were the property of central organizations. Bur-šu-ma, literally "senior," appears as person in charge of administrative tasks in ED IIIa Fara texts; see Visicato 1995: 44–45. The socio-economic interpretation of the document depends largely on the interpretation of the colophon. A similar colophon, text No. 385 rev. ii 1, has aša$_5$ u$_2$-rum without any specification as to who are the recipients of the plots.

No. 383 – MS 2661/1

Account of land, Early Dynastic IIIb, Umma region.

Note the peculiarities of texts Nos. 383 and 384 in regard to the color of the clay, onomastics, numerical signs, and the absence of a "*mu-iti*" dating formula. Despite this, the documents are certainly from the Umma region, for they share spelling and onomastics with other "Umma" tablets of the same date.

obv. i	aša$_5$ 3(iku) Lugal-pa-e$_3$	3 *iku* land: Lugalpa'e;
	3 ½ ¼(iku) Lugal-šita-ĝu$_{10}$	3 ¾ *iku*: Lugalšitaĝu;
	[n] Lugal-[...]-ki$^?$-gi-[...]-⸢x⸣-ma	n *iku*: Lugal...;
	1(bur$_3$) 1(eše$_3$) Lugal-nemur$_x$(PIRIĜ.TUR)	1 *bur* 1 *eše*: Lugalnemur;
	[...]-⸢x⸣	
ii	1(bur$_3$) Lugal-ša$_3$-diĝir-zu	1 *bur*: Lugalšadiĝirzu;
	1(eše$_3$) Lugal-aja$_2$-nun	1 *eše*: Lugalajanun;
	1(bur$_3$) 1(eše$_3$) Lugal-šu-sikil	1 *bur* 1 *eše*: Lugalšusikil;
	1(bur$_3$) (ras.) Lugal-aga(MIR)	1 *bur*: Lugalaga;
iii	3 1/8(iku) Lugal-da-kuš$_2$	3 1/8 iku: Lugaldakuš;
	1(bur$_3$) 1(eše$_3$) Lugal-nagar-zi	1 *bur* 1 *eše*: Lugalnagarzi;
	1(bur$_3$) 1(eše$_3$) Lugal-ib$_2$-ta-e$_3$	1 *bur* 1 *eše*: Lugalibta'e;
	1(bur$_3$) Ur-⸢a$_2$⸣-zi	1 *bur*: Urazi;
iv	13 [2("bariga")] Ur-[...]	13 (*gur*?) [2 *bariga*]: Ur...;
	13 / 13 [n("bariga")] Ur-^{d}Inana	13 (*gur*?) / 13 (*gur*?) [+x]: Ur-Inana;
	13 2("bariga") Igi-diĝir-še$_{3\text{-}tenû}$	13 *gur* 2 *bariga*(?): Igidiĝirše;
	13 ⸢2⸣("bariga") Ur-[...]	13 *gur* 2 *bariga*(?): Ur...
rev.	[(...)] Lugal-e-pa$_5$	Lugalepa.

obv. ii 2: The numerical sign was added after the name was written down.

obv. iv: The numerical signs in this column, especially the *bariga*-like sign, are difficult to explain as notations of area measure. They may represent units of the capacity system. Their uniformity is suspicious, however. Note the peculiar notation "13 / 13" in obv. iv 2.

No. 384 – MS 2661/2

Account of land, Early Dynastic IIIb, Umma region.

Note the number of rare divine names as elements in the personal names.

obv. i	1(bur$_3$) aša$_5$ Ǝ$_2$-ḫur-saĝ	1 *bur* land: Eḫursaĝ;
	1(eše$_3$) Lugal-ezen	1 *eše*: Lugalezen;
	2(iku) AN-ur-saĝ	2 *iku*: AN-ursaĝ;
	1(eše$_3$) Ur-^{d}Nin-Dulum$_2$	1 *eše*: Ur-Nindulum;
ii	1(eše$_3$) ½ ¼(iku) Ur-^{d}Ĝidru	1 *eše* ¾ *iku*: Ur-Ĝidru;
	2(iku) Ur-^{d}Nin-gal	2 *iku*: Ur-Ningal;
	4(iku) Ur-^{d}Hendur-saĝ	4 *iku*: Ur-Hendursaĝ;
	1(bur$_3$) Ur-^{c}Nin-ĜA$_2$×MUŠ	1 *bur*: Ur-Nin...;
5	1(iku) 1N$_8$ Ur-ĝidru	1 *iku* + *x*: Urĝidru;
iii	2(eše$_3$) E$_2$-maḫ$_2$-da	2 *eše*: Emaḫda;
	1(bur$_3$) Ur-^{d}Nin-⸢x⸣	1 *bur*: Ur-Nin...;
	[...]	...
	1(bur$_3$) [Ur$^{?}$]-⸢^{d}⸣[...]-⸢MUŠ⸣	1 *bur*: ...;
iv	1(bur$_3$) 2(iku) Ur-e$_2$	1 *bur* 2 *iku*: Ur-e;
	1(eše$_3$) 3 ½ ¼(iku) Ur-tilla$_3$(AN.DIŠ.AN)	1 *eše* 3 ¾ *iku*: Urtilla;
	4(iku) Ur-^{d}Nin-girim$_x$(A.BU.ḪA.DU)	4 *iku*: Ur-Ningirim(a);
	2(bur$_3$) 5(iku) Ur-ĝidru	2 *bur* 5 *iku*: Urĝidru.
rev.	(blank)	

obv. i 3: An-ur-saĝ "(God) An is the hero" is one of the possible readings of this personal name. Although An is a rather passive deity in later literary sources, his original character may have been different. This name and the name ^{d}Inana-ur-saĝ in the Umma tablets speak in favor of a close connection between the cults of these two deities, whose cults were combined in the city of Uruk.

obv. ii 4: See Cavigneaux and Krebernik 2000c for this deity. The reading of the sign ĜA$_2$×MUŠ is unknown.

obv. ii 5: The metrological meaning of the sign N_8 here is uncertain. It is used in ED IIIa Fara texts to denote ½ *iku*. However, that unit is written 1N_8×*DIŠ* in Umma texts. The writing in the present text may be a scribal mistake for ½ *iku*.

obv. iv 3: For Ningirima, a goddess associated with incantations, see Krebernik 2000.

No. 385 – MS 2824

Account of land, Early Dynastic IIIb (governor Me'anedu), Umma region.

This is a large tablet with twelve columns on the obverse, the largest extant ED IIIb Umma tablet. The obverse is badly eroded, so many readings remain tentative. The document records the allocation of parcels of land to a number of individuals, many of whom are priests and temple officials. Note that several individuals are qualified by the names of gods instead of professional titles. This is an indication that they were associated with the cults of the respective deities. Badly damaged or uncertain entries have not been indexed.

obv. i	[break]	…
	[n+] 1(eše$_3$) 3(iku) ⸢x-x⸣	x+1 *eše* 3 *iku*: …;
	⸢x-x⸣	…
	⸢gu-gal?⸣	…
	2(eše$_3$) KA-SAR	2 *eše*: KASAR;
	3 ½(iku) x-bur-x	3 ½ *iku* …;
	3 ½(iku) Nin-⸢x⸣	3 ½ *iku*: Nin…;
	1(eše$_3$) 1 ½(iku) Ur$_2$-x	1 *eše* 1 ½ *iku*: Ur…;
	⸢x-x-x⸣	…
	⸢n x-x-x⸣	…

ii	[...]	...
	⌜3⌝ ½(iku) [E$_2$]-⌜ušum⌝-gal	3 ½ *iku*: E'ušumgal;
	3 ½(iku) ⌜Ki-nu-ni-il$_2$⌝	3 ½ *iku*: Kinuni'il;
	4(iku) A$_2$-ni-⌜x⌝	4 *iku*: Ani... (not Anita);
	8(bur$_3$) ⌜x-x⌝	8 *bur* ...;
	1(bur$_3$) la$_2$ ½(iku) E$_2$-na	1 *bur* minus ½ *iku*: Ena;
	3 ½(iku) ⌜Gu⌝-la	3 ½ *iku*: Gula;
	⌜7⌝(bur$_3$) [x]-RU-⌜x-x⌝	7 *bur*: ...;
	3(iku) ⌜x⌝-Abzu	3 *iku*: ...Abzu;
	6 ½(iku) [...]	6 ½ *iku*: ...;
	[traces]	...
	⌜7⌝(bur$_3$) ⌜x-x-x⌝	7 *bur*: ...,
	[...]	...
	[...]	...
iii	2(eše$_3$) ⌜x-x⌝	2 *eše*: ...;
	1(bur$_3$'u) 2(bur$_3$) Mu-ni-a-da-šid	12 *bur*: Muni'adašid;
	3(bur$_3$) 1(eše$_3$) Amar-šuba$_3$(MUŠ$_3$.ZA$_7$)	3 *bur* 1 *eše*: Amaršuba,
	lu$_2$ ⌜x-x⌝	the man of ...;
	1(eše$_3$) ⌜Lugal-^{d}Tu⌝	1 *eše*: Lugal-Tu(da),
	⌜igi-nu-du$_8$⌝	the *iginudu*-worker;
	1(eše$_3$) ½(iku) ⌜Lugal⌝-maḫ	1 *eše* ½ *iku*: Lugalmaḫ
	A.ḪA.NE	(and) AḪANE;
	1(eše$_3$) 1 ½(iku) Pa$_4$-en-ni	1 *eše* 1 ½ *iku*: Pa'en(a)ni;
	1(bur$_3$) 1(eše$_3$) 1(iku) ⌜x-x-x⌝ / ⌜Abzu-x⌝ / nagar	
		1 *bur* 1 *eše* 1 *iku* ..., the carpenter;
	1(eše$_3$) ⌜E$_2$⌝-DU-DU	1 *eše*: EDUDU,
	⌜x⌝-NE	the ...;
	1(eše$_3$) 1(iku) Lugal-⌜ḫur-saĝ⌝	1 *eše* 1 *iku*: Lugalḫursaĝ;
	⌜2⌝(bur$_3$) Ama-[...]	2 *bur*: Ama...;
	2(bur$_3$) 1(eše$_3$) 3(iku) U$_2$-⌜x-x⌝	2 *bur* 1 *eše* 3 *iku*: U...;
	⌜1(eše$_3$) 1(iku) x-x⌝	1 *eše* 1 *iku*: ...;
	1(bur$_3$) 1(eše$_3$) ⌜Lugal⌝-x-si	1 *bur* 1 *eše*: Lugal...si,
iv	ugula nu-banda$_3$ gu$_4$	the overseer of the supervisors of oxen;
	5(bur$_3$) Lu$_2$-^{d}Lamma	5 *bur*: Lu-Lamma(r),
	^{d}En-ki	(of the god) Enki;
	1(bur$_3$) 1(eše$_3$) 1(iku) Pag-ga	1 *bur* 1 *eše* 1 *iku*: Pagga,
	^{ba15}⌜baḫar$_2$⌝	the potter;
	4(iku) Ur-⌜x⌝-ĜA$_2$×NUN	4 *iku*: Ur...;
	⌜n⌝ 1 ½(iku) Lu$_2$-nu-mu-⌜da-sa$_2$⌝	x 1 ½ *iku*: Lunumudasa;
	⌜n Lugal$^?$:ib$_2^?$-x-x⌝	x Lugalib...(?);
	1(eše$_3$) 1 ½(iku) ⌜Ki-x⌝ A-⌜x-x⌝-ĝal$_2$	1 *eše* 1 ½ *iku*: ...;
	2(eše$_3$) De$_5$-de$_5$	2 *eše*: Dede
	A-ba-da-sa$_2$	(and) Abadasa;
	3(bur$_3$) Ur-⌜^{d}⌝Dulum$_2$	3 *bur*: Ur-(Nin)dulum,
	A-KALAM$^?$-⌜x⌝	...;

	4 ½(iku) Lugal-⸢x-x⸣	4 ½ *iku*: Lugal…;
	2(bur$_3$) Silim-⸢Utu⸣ ensi$_2$-gal	2 *bur*: Silim-Utu, the former governor;
	3(bur$_3$) 1(eše$_3$) ⸢x-x⸣	3 *bur* 1 *eše*: …;
	2(bur$_3$) ⸢Lu$_2$?-x-x⸣	2 *bur*: …;
v	1(eše$_3$) x-x	1 *eše* …;
	3(bur$_3$) 1(eše$_3$) Ur-saĝ x-ŠID	3 *bur* 1 *eše* Ursaĝ …;
	3(bur$_3$) A-la-x	3 *bur* Ala…;
	[2 lines broken]	…
	1(bur$_3$) […]-NAGAR	1 *bur* …,
	i$_3$-du$_8$	the doorman;
	1(bur$_3$) ⸢x-x⸣	1 *bur* …;
	⸢x x x x⸣ SU$_3$	…
	4 ½(iku) Me-an-nu-si	4 ½ *iku*: Me'annusi,
	ugula ⸢BI⸣	the overseer of …;
	1(eše$_3$) ⸢Lugal-ad?-da⸣	1 *eše*: Lugal-adda;
	3(bur$_3$) 1(eše$_3$) En-ne$_2$-mud	3 *bur* 1 *eše*: Enemud;
	1(bur$_3$) […]-⸢x⸣	1 *bur*: …;
	1(eše$_3$) 1(iku) ⸢x-x⸣	1 *eše* 1 *iku*: …;
	1(bur$_3$) ⸢x-ba?-x-a⸣	1 *bur*: …;
	[traces]	…
	[…] KAL TA?	…
vi	1(eše$_3$) ⸢3⸣(iku) ⸢x-šeš-x⸣	1 *eše* 3 *iku*: …;
	2(eše$_3$) 3(iku) E$_2$-ḫur-saĝ	2 *eše* 3 *iku*: Eḫursaĝ;
	4(bur$_3$) ⸢1⸣(eše$_3$) 2(iku) ⸢GAN$_2$-x⸣	4 *bur* 1 *eše* 2 *iku*: …;
	2(eše$_3$) Saĝ-⸢x-x⸣	2 *eše*: Saĝ…;
	⸢2⸣(eše$_3$) [x]-⸢maḫ⸣-di	2 *eše*: …maḫdi;
	3 ½(iku) […]	3 ½ *iku*: …,
	⸢x-da⸣	the …;
	2(bur$_3$) 1 eše$_3$ Du-du	2 *bur* 1 *eše*: Dudu,
	⸢x-x⸣	the …;
	3(bur$_3$) 1(eše$_3$) ⸢x-x⸣	3 *bur* 1 *eše*: …;
	4(bur$_3$) 1(eše$_3$) ⸢Lugal⸣-an-⸢dul$_3$⸣	4 *bur* 1 *eše*: Lugalandul;
	1(bur$_3$) 2(eše$_3$) En-⸢ne$_2$-mud⸣	1 *bur* 2 *eše*: Enemud;
	1(bur$_3$) Ak-⸢x-x⸣	1 *bur*: Ak…;
	2(eše$_3$) ⸢x-x⸣	2 *eše*: …;
	⸢1(eše$_3$?) 3 ½(iku)⸣ […]	1 *eše* 3 ½ *iku*: …;
	⸢n x-x-x⸣	…;
vii	2(eše$_3$) 4(iku) Lugal-ezen	2 *eše* 4 *iku*: Lugalezen;
	2(eše$_3$) Niĝir-⸢x⸣-na	2 *eše*: Niĝir…;
	⸢2⸣(bur$_3$) ⸢2⸣(eše$_3$) ⸢x⸣-en-⸢x⸣	2 *bur* 2 *eše*: …;
	2(eše$_3$) Ur-⸢d⸣LAGAB×⸢x⸣	2 *eše*: Ur…;
	4 ½(iku) AN-LUL	4 ½ *iku*: ANLUL;
	1(eše$_3$) 1(iku) Aja$_2$-zu-zu	1 *eše* 1 *iku*: Ajazuzu,
	sipa	the shepherd;
	1(eše$_3$) Ur-dTu	1 *eše*: Ur-Tu(da);

2(eše$_3$) ⸢x-da⸣	2 *eše*: …da;
3(iku) ⸢Ama-bara$_2$⸣-si	3 *iku*: Amabarasi;
2(eše$_3$) Utu-mu-⸢kuš$_2$⸣	2 *eše*: Utumukuš,
⸢x⸣	the …;
⸢2⸣(eše$_3$) […]	2 *eše*: …;
2(bur$_3$) ⸢x-x-x⸣	2 *bur*: …;
2(eše$_3$) ⸢x-x-x⸣	2 *eše*: …;
⸢n⸣ 1(bur$_3$) [x]-^{d}⸢Dulum$_2$ x-x⸣	n+1 *bur*: …Dulum …;
viii 1(eše$_3$) Ur-$^{d?}$Utu	1 *eše*: Ur-Utu(?);
1(eše$_3$) Mes-Utu-ba	1 *eše*: Mes-Utuba;
1(eše$_3$) Gu-la	1 *eše*: Gula;
1(eše$_3$) 3(iku) Ur-saĝ-Utu	1 *eše* 3 *iku*: Ursaĝ-Utu;
1(eše$_3$) 3(iku) Bara$_2$-sag$_3$-nu-di	1 *eše* 3 *iku*: Barasagnudi;
2(bur$_3$) Ki-⸢x⸣-me	2 *bur* Ki…;
1(eše$_3$) 3(iku) ⸢x⸣-ak	1 *eše* 3 *iku*: …ak,
^{d}En-lil$_2$	(of the temple? of the god) Enlil;
1(eše$_3$) 3(iku) Ur-^{d}Inana	1 *eše* 3 *iku*: Ur-Inana;
3(bur$_3$) gal-nagar	3 *bur*: the chief carpenter;
3(iku) Si-du$_3$	3 *iku*: Sidu (and)
Lum-ma	Lumma (*or*: (of the god) Lumma);
1(eše$_3$) 3(iku) ⸢U$_4$⸣-bi-kur-ra	1 *eše* 3 *iku*: Ubikura;
2(eše$_3$) Lam:saĝ-du$_3$	2 *eše*: Lamsaĝdu;
3(iku) Pa$_4$-⸢x-x⸣	3 *iku*: Pap…;
2(bur$_3$) 2(eše$_3$) ⸢n(iku) x⸣	2 *bur* 2 *eše* …:
⸢KA$^{?}$-LI-LI⸣	KALILI(?)
1(eše$_3$) ⸢Ama-bara$_2$⸣-si	1 *eše*: Amabarasi;
2(eše$_3$) ⸢Lu$_2$-x⸣	2 *eše*: Lu…;
2(eše$_3$) E$_2$-DU-DU	2 *eše*: EDUDU,
ix $^{ba15?}$baḫar$_2$	the potter;
2(bur$_3$) ⸢Mes⸣-pa$_3$	2 *bur*: Mespa,
gala	the cult-singer;
1(bur$_3$) 1(eše$_3$) E$_2$-DU-DU	1 *bur* 1 *eše*: EDUDU
AN-BU	(and) ANBU;
1(bur$_3$) 1(eše$_3$) ⸢x-na⸣-DU	1 *bur* 1 *eše*: …;
1(eše$_3$) 3(iku) ⸢A$_2$⸣-ni-kur-ra	1 *eše* 3 *iku*: Anikura;
2(bur$_3$) Mes-Utu-ba	2 *bur*: Mes-Utuba;
3(bur$_3$) AN-⸢x-(x)⸣	3 *bur*: …;
1(eše$_3$) Ad-da	1 *eše*: Adda
Aja$_2$-ne-ne	(and) Ajanene;
2(bur$_3$) Diĝir-en-ne$_2$ ugula-e$_2$	2 *bur*: Diĝir-en(a)ne, the overseer of the household;
1(bur$_3$) 1(eše$_3$) ⸢x-DU⸣ ŠID	1 *bur* 1 *eše*: …;
2(eše$_3$) Ur-⸢pisaĝ⸣	2 *eše*: Urpisaĝ
Šubur	(and) Šubur;
1(bur$_3$) Ur-^{d}Dulum$_2$	1 *bur*: Ur-Dulum
⸢x-x⸣	(and) …;

	1(eše$_3$) 1(iku) Saĝ-diĝir$^?$-⸢tuku$^?$⸣	1 *eše* 1 *iku*: Saĝdiĝirtuku(?);
	1(eše$_3$) E$_2$-⸢DU-DU⸣	1 *eše*: EDUDU,
	⸢nar⸣	the musician;
	⸢n Ama-bara$_2$⸣-si	x: Amabarasi;
x	1(eše$_3$) 3(iku) ⸢x-x⸣	1 *eše* 3 *iku*: …;
	1(eše$_3$) Mes-pa$_3$	1 *eše*: Mespa;
	2(bur$_3$) Gu$_2$-gal	2 *bur*: Gugal;
	3(bur$_3$) ⸢Da-da$^?$⸣	3 *bur*: Dada(?)
	⸢x⸣-x	(and) …;
	1(eše$_3$) 1(iku) ⸢Amar⸣-TUM	1 *eše* 1 *iku*: AmarTUM;
	1(eše$_3$) 3(iku) URU×A-DU-DU-⸢x⸣	1 *eše* 3 *iku*: …;
	4(iku) Ak zadim	4 *iku*: Ak(a), the stone-cutter;
	1(eše$_3$) 3(iku) Utu-⸢mu⸣-kuš$_2$	1 *eše* 3 *iku*: Utumukuš,
	⸢gala⸣	the cult-singer;
	1(eše$_3$) 2(iku) Lugal-šudu$_3$-du$_{10}$	1 *eše* 2 *iku*: Lugalšududu;
	1(bur$_3$) Me-zu-an-da	1 *bur*: Mezu'anda,
	Be-li$_2^?$-⸢KU$_3$⸣	*Bēlī*KU(?);
	2(bur$_3$) Lugal-a$_2$-na-tum$_2$-⸢ma⸣	2 *bur*: Lugal-anatuma;
	1(bur$_3$) Bara$_2$-ga-ni-du$_{10}$	1 *bur*: Baraganidu;
	2(eše$_3$) Bara$_2$-sag$_3$-nu-di	2 *eše*: Barasagnudi
	⸢x⸣-NIR	(and) …;
	1(bur$_3$) ⸢x-x-x-x⸣	1 *bur*: …;
xi	1(eše$_3$) 3(iku) Lugal-x-si	1 *eše* 3 *iku*: Lugal…;
	1(eše$_3$) Ama-bara$_2$-si	1 *eše*: Amabarasi
	URU×A	(from) Uru'a(?);
	3(iku) Du$_{11}$-ga-ni	3 *iku*: Dugani;
	1(eše$_3$) Ur-Šubur	1 *eše*: Ur-Šubur,
	šidim	the builder;
	1(bur$_3$) la$_2$ 1(iku) Maš-da$_3$ dub-sar	1 *bur* minus 1 *iku*: Mašda, the scribe;
	⸢3⸣(iku) ⸢Mes⸣-Utu-ba	3 *iku*: Mes-Utuba,
	gal-SAR	the manager of vegetables(?);
	2(eše$_3$) *I$_x^?$*(EZEN×AN)-*lum$_x$*(LAK218)-*sar*	2 *eše*: '*Ilum-šar(rum)*(?);
	1(eše$_3$) Lugal-^{d}Tu	1 *eše*: Lugal-Tu(da)
	a-zu$_5$	the physician;
	1(eše$_3$) 3(iku) Ur-^{d}Dulum$_2$	1 *eše* 3 *iku*: Ur-Dulum
	Amar-^{ĝeš}peš$_3$	(and) Amarpeš;
	1(bur$_3$) Pa$_4$-si-lugud$_2$(LAGAB)-da	1 *bur*: Papsiluguda;
xii	⸢n x-li-BU⸣	n: …;
	1(eše$_3$) x-ama-ušum-x	1 *eše*: …;
	4(iku) Ur-Šubur	4 *iku*: Ur-Šubur;
	1(eše$_3$) x-šeš	1 *eše*: …šeš;
	1(eše$_3$) la$_2$ ¼(iku) Pa$_4$-nam$_2$ dub-⸢sar⸣	1 *eše* minus ¼ *iku*: Panam, the scribe;
	1(eše$_3$) x-piriĝ$^?$ Pa$_4$-nam$_2$	1 *eše* … (and) Panam;
	2(bur$_3$'u) Numun Amar-TUM	20 *bur*: Numun (and) AmarTUM;
	1(eše$_3$) Ur-[…]	1 *eše*: Ur…;

	1(bur$_3$) ⸢1⸣(eše$_3$) Maš-⸢da$_3$ KA-LI-LI⸣	1 *bur* 1 *eše*: Mašda (and) KALILI;
rev. i	[destroyed/blank]	…
ii 1	gu$_2$-an-še$_3$ / 4(šar$_2$) 9(bur$_3$) / 2(eše$_3$) 1(iku) / aša$_5$ u$_2$-rum	4495 *iku* (*ca.* 161,82 ha.): the land (is) the property (of the household).
2	Kar-na$_4$ / Ukur$_3$-gi / Da-^{ĝeš}kiri$_6$-ka / du$_6$ NU$_{11}$$^{⸢mušen⸣}$.SU-⸢LAK248$^{?}$⸣	(In the domains) Karna, Ukurgi, Dakiri ("Side of the garden"), and the mound "Suburu" …
3	saĝ-apin	Plowmen.
4	⸢Silim⸣-Utu saĝĝa / ⸢Zabala$_6$⸣([AB].⸢MUŠ$_3$⸣)	Silim-Utu, chief temple-administrator of Zabala.
5	[…]-TUR / […] ⸢x⸣ / […] ⸢gu⸣:[sur]	………, field administrator.
middle	Me-an-ne$_2$-du$_{10}$ / ensi$_2$	Me'anedu, governor.

obv. ix 5: For attestations of the personal name AN-BU, see CUSAS 33 no. 240 p. 211, with additional references. It is possibly to be read An-nun$_3$, a reference to the *Annuna*-deities. See CUSAS 23 no. 201 obv. i 1 for An-nun$_3$-na in a school exercise. For a high priestess AN-BU ereš in a ED IIIa text from "Umma," see CUSAS 26 no. 150 rev. iii 2–3.

obv. xi 3: The sign may refer to the person's origins, "(from) Uru'a." However, the absence of the determinative ^{ki} is suspicious. For URU×A^{ki}, a locality on the border of Elam, see Schrakamp 2015a: 203 fn. 70 with additional references.

obv. xi 9: This professional title appears in ED Lu$_2$ A 109. For this occupation in connection to the management of harvested vegetables, see OSP 2 p. 91. The reading of the sign SAR may be nisig but this is not confirmed.

obv. xi 10: The sign EZEN×AN has a phonetic reading *u*$_9$ at Ebla and Abu Salabikh; see Krebernik 1982: 186, id. 1998a: 297. I draw the interpretation of the sign EZEN×AN as i$_x$ from the comparison of two writings of the same personal name /Iḫaḫa/. It appears as EZEN×AN-ḫa-ḫa in an ED IIIa text from the Umma region AAICAB 1/1, pl. 001, 1924-455 + photo, pl. 1 = P222314 and as NI-ḫa-ḫa in an ED IIIb Umma region text CUSAS 33 no. 5 obv. i 2. The tentative interpretation of the name in the present text is "The god is king."

rev. ii 2: Ukur$_3$(LAL$_2$×DU)-gi and other geographical names in this subscript are the "domains" that often appear in ED IIIb Umma documents. The locality du$_6$ NU$_{11}$^{mušen}.SU is probably identical to du$_6$ Su-buru$_4$(NU$_{11}$.BUR)^{mušen} in text No. 391 obv. i 1. However, in the present case, the sign SU is followed not by BUR but by a damaged "Tierkopfzeichen," probably LAK248.

rev. ii 3: saĝ-apin, literally "plowman," is used here to designate the category of individuals who receive these plots of land as holders.

rev. ii 4: Silim-Utu (DI-UD), sometimes erroneously transliterated Sa$_2$-laḫ, was the chief temple-administrator of the temple household of Inana during the governorship of Me'anedu. See Monaco 2015: 163.

No. 386 – MS 3791/11

Account of land, Early Dynastic IIIb, Umma region.

obv. i	2(eše$_3$) 2(iku) aša$_5$ Ur-Šubur	2 *eše* 2 *iku* land: Ur-Šubur;
	1(eše$_3$) Ki-nu-ni-il$_2$	1 *eše*: Kinuni'il,
	munu$_4$-mu$_2$	the maltster;
	1(eše$_3$) Me-zu-an-da	1 *eše*: Mezu'anda,
ii	šeš saĝĝa	brother of the chief temple-administrator;
	1(eše$_3$) ½(iku) Amar-ki-ku$_3$ kuš$_7$	1 *eše* ½ iku: Amarkiku, the animal-manager.
	šu-bad nu-e$_3$-a	*Pledge* that has not (yet) been issued.
rev.	(blank)	

obv. ii 3: The literal meaning of šu … bad is "to spread open the hand." Šu-bad is recorded lexically, although its Akkadian equivalent is broken; see MSL 13 pp. 101 l. 201, 119 l. 175. In texts Nos. 389 obv. ii 3, 387 obv. iv 4, šu-bad-me designates the recipients of the parcels, literally "(those) who spread the hand." The writing šu-bad appears in ED IIIa Fara documents and was interpreted by Pomponio and Visicato as "to take into possession," in opposition to negated verbs (EDATŠ p. 178 n. 56). However, in the present case, šu-bad occurs with a negated verbal form. For the meaning "to pledge" of šu … bad, see Steinkeller 1981a: 25.

No. 387 – MS 3791/14

Account of land, Early Dynastic IIIb, Umma region.

obv. i	1(bur$_3$) 2(eše$_3$) 1(iku) aša$_5$ še-UD	1 *bur* 2 *eše* 1 *iku* land (with) ... barley:
	Ur-Šubur sipa	Ur-Šubur, the shepherd;
	1(eše$_3$) De$_5$-de$_5$	1 *eše*: Dede;
	3(iku) Lugal-sa$_6$-ga	3 *iku*: Lugalsaga;
	3(iku) Ki-ni-mu-zu	3 *iku*: Kinimuzu,
	lu$_2$ ⸢x⸣-UNUG	the man (of) ...;
	1(eše$_3$)	1 *eše*:
ii	Lugal-a$_2$-maḫ	Lugal-amaḫ;
	4 ½(iku) Ur-⸢UN-ga⸣	4 ½ *iku*: Ur-UNga,
	gala	the singer;
	2(eše$_3$) Abzu-ki-du$_{10}$	2 *eše*: Abzukidu;
	1(eše$_3$) E$_2$-⸢ezen IB⸣	1 *eše*: E'ezen, the *IB*-official;
	2(iku) E$_2$-ĝessu-⸢bi-du$_{10}$⸣	2 *iku*: Eĝessubidu,
iii	EGIR	the ...;
	2(eše$_3$) ⸢Šubur⸣-tur	2 *eše*: Šuburtur;
	[...]	...

	1(eše$_3$) ⸢x-x⸣	1 *eše*: ...,
	nu-kiri$_6$	the gardener;
	3(iku) Lugal-šeš	3 *iku*: Lugalšeš,
	⸢x⸣-ir$^?$	the ...;
	[n ...]	n ...,
iv	⸢x⸣ [...] ⸢x⸣	...
	⸢1(eše$_3$) Ab-ba-tur⸣	1 *eše*: Abbatur;
	lu$_2$ ⸢E$_2^?$-na$^?$⸣	the man (of) Ena(?);
	šu-bad-me / saĝĝa / Du$_6$-a / gu:sur	They are the *pledgers*. <PN>, the chief temple-administrator; Du'a, the land-surveyor.
v	*30* la$_2$ *3* mu / iti *8*	Year 27, month 8.
rev.	[destroyed/blank]	

obv. i 1: Cf. še-UD-a at Umma: see Foster 1982: 82.

obv. i 6, iv 3: The final sign seems to be UNUG. Note that in the Umma corpus "elder" is written ab-ba-iri instead of abba$_2$; therefore, the sign cannot be ABBA$_2$.

obv. iii 1: The meaning of the professional title EGIR is uncertain. The same individual bears the same title in text No. 389 obv. i 4.

No. 388 – MS 3791/15

Account of land, Early Dynastic IIIb, Umma region.

obv. i	3(iku) aša$_5$ Utu-a$_2$-maḫ	3 *iku* land: Utu'amaḫ;
	2 ½ Lugal-a-ĝi$_6$	2 ½ *iku*: Lugal-aĝi;
	4 ½ Ur-pu$_x$(LAGAB×TIL)-saĝ	4 ½ *iku*: Urpusaĝ,
	gal-nagar	the chief carpenter;
	2 ½ Du$_6$-a	2 ½ *iku*: Du'a;
	3 De$_5$-de$_5$	3 *iku*: Dede;
	½ Lugal-Abzu-si	½ *iku*: Lugal-Abzusi;
	5 Bi$_2$-za$_7$	5 *iku*: Biza;
	3 E$_2$-⸢ĝessu⸣-bi-du$_{10}$	3 *iku*: Eĝessubidu,
	ab-ba-iri	the city elder;
	2 ½ Bi$_2$-za$_7$	2 ½ *iku*: Biza;
ii	3 Bi$_2$-za$_7$	3 *iku*: Biza;
	1 ½ Ur-Abzu	1 ½ *iku*: Ur-Abzu;
	1 ½ Bi$_2$-za$_7$	1 ½ *iku*: Biza;
	3 Zi-ni-ŠE$_{3\text{-}tenû}$	3 *iku*: ZiniŠE;
	1(eše$_3$) 3(iku) Lugal-šudu$_3$-du$_{10}$	1 *eše* 3 *iku*: Lugalšududu;
	2 ½ De$_5$-de$_5$	2 ½ *iku*: Dede;
	1(eše$_3$) 1 ½(iku) Lugal-šudu$_3$-du$_{10}$	1 *eše* 1 ½ *iku*: Lugalšududu;
	½ Ki-ni-mu-zu	½ *iku*: Kinimuzu;
	2(eše$_3$) 1(iku) Ur-ĝanun	2 *eše* 1 *iku*: Ur-ĝanun;
	2 Ša$_3$-nu-ĝal$_2$	2 *iku*: Šanuĝal;
	1 ½ Ša$_3$-nu-ĝal$_2$	1 ½ *iku*: Šanuĝal;
	2 Ur-^{d}Nin-Dulum$_2$	2 *iku*: Ur-Nindulum;

iii	1 Lugal-šudu$_3$-du$_{10}$	1 *iku*: Lugalšududu;
	5 Ur-ĝanun	5 *iku*: Ur-ĝanun;
	2 Gu-la	2 *iku*: Gula
	2 E$_2$-ĝessu-bi-du$_{10}$	2 *iku*: Eĝessubidu;
	1 ½ Munus-a$_2$-na	1 ½ *iku*: Munus-ana.
	(blank)	
iv-v	(blank)	
rev.	4(bur$_3$) 2(eše$_3$) ½(iku)	(Total:) 4 *bur* 2 *eše* ½ *iku*.

obv. ii 9, iii 2: ĜANUN is written LAGAB×NUN instead of ĜA$_2$×NUN in both cases.

No. 389 – MS 3791/18

Account of land, Early Dynastic IIIb, Umma region.

obv. i	2(eše$_3$) aša$_5$ še-UD	2 *eše* land (with) ... barley:
	Abzu-ki-du$_{10}$	Abzukidu;
	1(eše$_3$) E$_2$-ezen IB	1 *eše*: E'ezen, the *IB*-official;
	2(iku) E$_2$-ĝessu-bi-du$_{10}$	2 *iku*: Eĝessubidu,
	EGIR	the …;
ii	1(eše$_3$) Šubur-tur	1 *eše*: Šuburtur,
	ab-ba-iri	the city elder.
	šu-bad-me / *30* la$_2$ *3* mu / iti *8*	They are the *pledgers*. Year 27, month 8.
rev.	(blank)	

obv. i 1: See text No. 387 obv. i 1 for a discussion of this term.

obv. i 3: The stroke after EZEN is probably a slip of the stylus. See Molina 1991: 144 for the professional title IB.

obv. i 5: For the same individual with the same title, see text No. 387 obv. iii 1.

obv. ii 3: See discussion of texts Nos. 386 obv. ii 3, 387 obv. iv 4.

No. 390 – MS 3791/19

Account of land, Early Dynastic IIIb, Umma region.

obv. i	6(bur$_3$) aša$_5$ ugula nu-banda$_3$	6 *bur* land: the overseer of the supervisors;
	6(bur$_3$) 3(iku) Ama-bara$_2$-si	6 *bur* 3 *iku*: Amabarasi;
	6(bur$_3$) 4 ½(iku) ⸢Ur⸣-tilla$_x$(AN.AN)	6 *bur* 4 ½ *iku*: Urtilla;
	[n+] 1(bur$_3$) 1(eše$_3$) Lugal-[...]	... 1 *bur* 1 *eše*: Lugal...;
	[1–2 lines missing]	...
ii	Lugal-igi-tab(*2*)-ĝu$_{10}$	Lugal-igitabĝu.
	2(bur$_3$) 1(eše$_3$) 4 ½(iku) aga$_3$-us$_2$	2 *bur* 1 *eše* 4 ½ *iku*: the soldier;
	2(bur$_3$) 2(eše$_3$) 3(iku) dub-sar	2 *bur* 2 *eše* 3 *iku*: the scribe;
	2(eše$_3$) ugula	2 *eše*: the overseer;
	2(bur$_3$) 4 ½(iku) Ba-lu$_5$	2 *bur* 4 ½ *iku*: Balu;
	2(bur$_3$) 3(iku) Niĝir-Abzu	2 *bur* 3 *iku*: Niĝir-Abzu;
	⸢2(bur$_3$)⸣ 1(eše$_3$) Šeš-pa$_3$	2 *bur* 1 *eše*: Šešpa;

iii 2(bur$_3$) 2(eše$_3$) Mes-Utu-ba — 2 *bur* 2 *eše*: Mes-Utuba;
1(bur$_3$) Mar-ku$_7$ — 1 *bur*: Marku;
1(bur$_3$) 1(eše$_3$) 1 ½(iku) nagar — 1 *bur* 1 *eše* 1 ½ *iku*: the carpenter;
1(eše$_3$) 3(iku) ašgab — 1 *eše* 3 *iku*: the leather-worker;
2(eše$_3$) simug — 2 *eše*: the smith;
2(eše$_3$) 1 ½(iku) tug$_2$-du$_8$ — 2 *eše* 1 ½(iku): the felter;
rev. i 2(eše$_3$) 1 ½(iku) ad-KID — 2 *eše* 1 ½(iku): the reed-worker;
1(eše$_3$) 1 ½(iku) ⸢x-maḫ?-AN-x⸣ — 1 *eše* 1 ½ *iku*: ...;
[3 lines defaced]
ii (blank)
rev. iii (colophon) [...]-a / [...]-da / ⸢*n* mu / iti *n*⸣...... Year ..., month ...

obv. ii 2: 3 iku is written over an erasure of ½ iku.

No. 391 – MS 3791/23

Account of land, Early Dynastic IIIb, Umma region.

This document records parcels of land in various fields (aša$_5$) and estates (e$_2$). The numbers are too small to be the measurements of these fields and estates themselves.

obv. i	4(bur$_3$) 3(iku) aša$_5$ / naĝ-ku$_5$ du$_6$ / Su-^{mušen}buru$_4$(NU$_{11}$.BUR)	4 *bur* 3 *iku*: the field (at) the flood reservoir (at) the mound Suburu.
	1(eše$_3$) 2(iku) aša$_5$ ^{d}Šara$_2$-šeš	1 *eše* 2 *iku*: the field (of) Šarašeš;
	2(iku) aša$_5$ Bar-bar	2 *iku*: the field (of) Barbar;
	1(bur$_3$) 5(iku)	1 *bur* 5 *iku*:
ii	e$_2$ Lugal-a$_2$-mah	the house (of) Lugal-amah;
	3(bur$_3$) 1(eše$_3$) aša$_5$ Ab-ba saĝĝa	3 *bur* 1 *eše*: the field (of) Abba, the chief temple-administrator;
	2(eše$_3$) Na-ru$_2$-a	2 *eše*: (the field of) Naru'a (*or*: Field of the Stele);
rev. i	1(eše$_3$) ⌜e$_2$ UMBIN⌝-*LUM*	1 *eše*: (the field of) the house of …*lum*;
	2(bur$_3$) 2(iku) Kar-na$_4$	2 *bur* 2 *iku*: (domain) Karna.
	(blank)	
ii	(blank)	

obv. i 1: For the divine name ^{d}UD-su-buru$_4$^{mušen}, see SF 1 rev. ii 25. For a discussion of the mound du$_6$ SU.MUŠEN.NU$_{11}$.BUR in ED IIIb Umma documents, see CUSAS 33 no. 139 commemtary. Doubts about identifying this writing with the city of Lagaš are justified on the one hand by the presence of the phonetic complement su instead of la, and on the other hand by the absence of the determinative ^{ki}. Besides, what would "mound of Lagaš" mean when that city was intact and flourishing during the period under consideration?

obv. i 2: This personal name is amply attested in Ur III records.

obv. i 3: The same field appears in Ur III sources: see, e.g., a list of fields BPOA 1 no. 1001 obv. 6.

No. 392 – MS 3791/27

Account of land, Early Dynastic IIIb, Umma region.

obv. i	5 ½(iku) Su-bir$_x$(BAPPIR)	5 ½ *iku*: Subir;
	½(iku) Lugal-ša$_3$-su$_3$	½ *iku*: Lugalšasu;
	1 la$_2$ ¼(iku) Ne-saĝ IB	1 minus ¼ *iku*: Nesaĝ, the *IB*-official;
	1(iku) Lugal-šudu$_3$-du$_{10}$	1 *iku*: Lugalšududu;
	1(iku) Gu-la	1 *iku*: Gula;
	1(iku) E$_2$-na	1 *iku*: Ena;
	2(iku) E$_2$-mah$_2$-da am-me	2 *iku*: Emahda, the …;
ii	1(iku) ⌜x-x-x⌝	1 *iku*: …;
	1(iku) ⌜x-x⌝	1 *iku*: …;
	1(iku) Aja$_2$-zu-zu	1 *iku*: Ajazuzu;
	1(iku)[1]	1 *iku*: …;
iii	1 ½(iku) ⌜De$_5$-de$_5$⌝	1 ½ *iku*: Dede;

1 This and the rest of the column is erased by the scribe.

	3 ½(iku) kuš$_7$	3 ½ *iku*: the animal-manager;
	1(iku) E$_2$-maḫ$_2$-da	1 *iku*: Emaḫda;
	1 ¼(iku) Ur-^{d}Dulum$_2$	1 ¼ *iku*: Ur-Dulum
	Ur-^{d}Sumugan(ĜIR$_3$)	(and) Ur-Sumugan;
	1(iku) ⸢Ur⸣-la	1 *iku*: Urla;
	1(iku) Du$_6$-a gala	1 *iku*: Du'a, the cult-singer;
	2(iku) Ak-lu$_2$	2 *iku*: Aklu;
	1(iku) En-šita	1 *iku*: Enšita;
iv	[1(iku)] ⸢Eden$^?$-gi$^?$⸣	[1 *iku*]: Edengi(?);
	1(iku) Lugal-⸢šudu$_3$⸣-du$_{10}$	1 *iku*: Lugalšududu;
	1(iku) ^{d}Amar-^{d}Ašnan$_x$(TIR)	1 *iku*: Amar-Ašnan;
	1(iku) Teš$_2$-teš$_2$ ⸢x⸣-nun	1 *iku*: Tešteš (and) …nun;
	[1(iku)] x-x⸣	[1 *iku*:] …
	(blank)	
rev.	(defaced; traces of a colophon and *mu–iti* date formula)	

obv. i 1: See CUSAS 33, 240 obv. i 5 for a chief sailor by the same name.

obv. i 7: The professional title(?) am-me is obscure. The first sign cannot be a graphic variant of GEME$_2$ written SAL×KUR, since there are two horizontal wedges at the beginning.

No. 393 – MS 3791/28

Allocation of lease land (aša$_5$ apin-la$_2$) at the temple household of Inana, Early Dynastic IIIb (Silim-Utu, chief temple-administrator), Umma region.

obv. i	2(iku) aša$_5$ še-UD	2 *iku* land (with) ... barley:
	Lugal-Abzu-si	Lugal-Abzusi;
	1(iku) E$_2$-^{d}Inana	1 *iku*: E'Inana;
	3 ½(iku) Ab-ba-tur	3 ½ *iku*: Abbatur;
	4 ½(iku) Bi$_2$-za$_7$	4 ½ *iku*: Biza;
	1(iku) Ur-Abzu	1 *iku*: Ur-Abzu;
	1(iku) Lugal-šita-ĝu$_{10}$	1 *iku*: Lugalšitaĝu;
	2 Ur-^{d}Inana	2 *iku*: Ur-Inana;
	2 ½ Bara$_2$-ga-ni-du$_{10}$	2 ½ *iku*: Baraganidu;
	4 ½ Me-^{d}En-lil$_2$-da	4 ½ *iku*: Me'Enlilda;
ii	1 ½ Utu-mu-kuš$_2$	1 ½ *iku*: Utu-mukuš;
	1(eše$_3$) 1(iku) A-DU-mu-še$_3$-ti	1 *eše* 1 *iku*: ADUmušeti;
	1(eše$_3$) 1(iku) Silim-Utu	1 *eše* 1 *iku*: Silim-Utu;
	1(eše$_3$) Lugal-Anzu$_2^{mušen}$	1 *eše*: Lugal-Anzu
	2(iku) Ur-^{d}Nin-Dulum$_2$	2 *iku*: Ur-Nindulum;
	2(iku) Nam-maḫ	2 *iku*: Nammaḫ;
	1(eše$_3$) DU-LUL-bi	1 *eše*: DULULbi;
	1(eše$_3$) 3(iku) Maš-da$_3$	1 *eše* 3 *iku*: Mašda;
	2(eše$_3$) ½(iku) A-DU-mu-še$_3$-ti	2 *eše* ½ *iku*: ADUmušeti;
	1(bur$_3$) 5(iku) ⸢Ak$^?$-lu$_2$⸣	1 *bur* 5 *iku*: Aklu(?);
iii	3(iku) Lugal-Dulum$_2$	3 *iku*: Lugal-Dulum;

	3(iku) Ur-^{d}Nin-Dulum$_2$	3 *iku*: Ur-Nindulum;
	4 ½(iku) Inim-ma	4 ½ *iku*: Inima;
	1(eše$_3$) Aja$_2$-nu-zu	1 *eše*: Ajanuzu;
	1(eše$_3$) Šubur-tur	1 *eše*: Šuburtur;
	1(eše$_3$) Lugal-Dulum$_2$	1 *eše*: Lugal-Dulum;
	1(eše$_3$) 3 ½(iku) *Il-su*-ḪA	1 *eše* 3 ½ *iku*: *'Ilšu*-ḪA
	Be$_2$-li	(and) *Bēlī*;
	1(eše$_3$) 4 ½(iku) gu:sur	1 *eše* 4 ½ *iku*: the land-surveyor;
	1(eše$_3$) ½(iku) ⸢x-x⸣	1 *eše* ½ *iku*: ...;
	1(eše$_3$) 1(iku) ⸢x-NE⸣	1 *eše* 1 *iku*: ...NE;
	1(eše$_3$) ⸢x⸣ [...]	1 *eše*: ...;
iv	1 ½(iku) Lugal-^{d}Tu	1 ½ *iku*: Lugal-Tu(da);
	1 ½(iku) Unug-ga-ĝal$_2$	1 ½ *iku*: Unuga-ĝal;
	1 ½(iku) Saĝ-diĝir-tuku	1 ½ *iku*: Saĝdiĝirtuku;
	1(iku) Aja$_2$-nu-zu	1 *iku*: Ajanuzu;
	3 ½(iku) Utu-e$_2$-ḪA	3 ½ *iku*: Utu'eḪA;
	1(eše$_3$) Lugal-^{d}Tu	1 *eše*: Lugal-Tu(da);
	1(eše$_3$) Nita	1 *eše*: Nita;
	4 ½(iku) Ab-ba-tur	4 ½ *iku*: Abbatur;
	1(iku) Ki-⸢ni⸣-mu-zu	1 *iku*: Kinimuzu;
	3 ½(iku) Lugal-diĝir-ĝu$_{10}$	3 ½ *iku*: Lugaldiĝirĝu;
	1 ½(iku) Lugal-ša$_3$-diĝir-zu	1 ½: Lugalšadiĝirzu;
	3(iku) Lugal-ḫe$_2$	3 *iku*: Lugalḫe;
	1(eše$_3$) ⸢Lugal⸣-[...]	1 *eše*: Lugal...;
	2(eše$_3$) ⸢x-x-x⸣	2 *eše*: ...;
	5(iku) ⸢Saĝ-x-x⸣	5 *iku*: Saĝ...;
v	4(iku) Ba-gar$_3$	4 *iku*: Bagar;
	3 ½(iku) Igi-Dulum$_2$-še$_{3\text{-}tenû}$	3 ½ *iku*: Igi-Dulumše;
	1(eše$_3$) 3(iku) Lugal-⸢ib$_2$⸣	1 *eše* 3 *iku*: Lugal-ib;
	2(eše$_3$) la$_2$ 1(iku) Ab-ba-tur	2 *eše* minus 1 *iku*: Abbatur;
	1(iku) AN-da-lu	1 *iku*: ANdalu;
	3(iku) Bara$_2$-ga-ni-du$_{10}$	3 *iku*: Baraganidu;
	2(iku) Ne-saĝ	2 *iku*: Nesaĝ;
	½(iku) ⸢E$_2$⸣-zi	½ *iku*: Ezi;
	1(eše$_3$) ⸢Lugal-bi$^?$-x⸣	1 *eše*: Lugalbi...;
	5(iku) Ab-ba-tur	5 *iku*: Abbatur;
	1(eše$_3$) Niĝar-⸢mud⸣	1 *eše*: Niĝarmud;
	4 ½(iku) Lugal-ḫe$_2$	4 ½ *iku*: Lugalḫe;
	1(eše$_3$) ⸢E$_2$-maḫ⸣-da	1 *eše*: Emaḫda;
	(blank)	
	Uš$_x$(LAK672)-du$_3$-a-maḫ	(Domain) Ušdu'amaḫ;
vi	1(bur$_3$) la$_2$ 1(iku) Si-ĝar	1 *bur* minus 1 *iku*: Siĝar;
	3(iku) Me-sag$_3$-nu-di	3 *iku*: Mesagnudi;
	3(iku) Saĝ-diĝir-tuku	3 *iku*: Saĝdiĝirtuku;
	3(iku) Saĝ-^{d}Šara$_2$-da	3 *iku*: Saĝ-Šarada;

	1(eše$_3$) ½(iku) Lugal-šudu$_3$-du$_{10}$	1 *eše* ½ *iku*: Lugalšududu;
	5 ½(iku) Lugal-da-maḫ-di	5 ½ *iku*: Lugaldamaḫdi;
	4(iku) Mes-ki-nu-zu	4 *iku*: Meskinuzu;
	4(iku) Utu-maḫ-maḫ	4 *iku*: Utumaḫmaḫ;
	1(eše$_3$) Silim-Utu ugula	1 *eše*: Silim-Utu, the overseer;
	1(eše$_3$) 3(iku) Šubur-tur	1 *eše* 3 *iku*: Šuburtur;
	2 ½(iku) Ur-⸢pu$_x$(LAGAB×TIL)⸣-saĝ	2 ½ *iku*: Urpusaĝ;
	1(eše$_3$) 3(iku) Lugal-šudu$_3$-du$_{10}$	1 *eše* 3 *iku*: Lugalšududu;
	4(iku) En-gar-zi	4 *iku*: Engarzi;
	2(iku) De$_5$-de$_5$	2 *iku*: Dede;
vii	1 ½(iku) Lugal-ḫe$_2$	1 ½ *iku*: Lugalḫe;
	3(iku) KA-ki-bi-še$_3$	3 *iku*: KAkibiše;
	4(iku) Ur-pu$_x$(LAGAB×TIL)-saĝ	4 *iku*: Urpusaĝ;
	1(eše$_3$) 2(iku) Utu-aja$_2$-ĝu$_{10}$	1 *eše* 2 *iku*: Utu'ajaĝu;
	3(iku) Gu-ru$_7$-usar$_x$(LAL$_2$×TUG$_2$)-du$_{10}$	3 *iku*: Guru'usardu;
	1(eše$_3$) Diĝir-nu-me-a	1 *eše*: Diĝirnume'a;
	1 ½(iku) i$_3$-du$_8$ ĝanun	1 ½ *iku*: the doorman of the storehouse;
	2 ½(iku) Inim-Utu-zi	2 ½ *iku*: Inim-Utuzi;
	1(eše$_3$) 1(iku) Amar-šuba$_3$(MUŠ$_3$.ZA$_7$)	1 *eše* 1 *iku*: Amaršuba;
	½(iku) Me-šeš-šeš	½ *iku*: Mešeššeš;
	2(iku) Ur$_2$-ni	2 *iku*: Urni;
	2(iku) Me-^{d}En-lil$_2$-da	2 *iku*: Me'Enlilda;
	1(iku) Ad-da	1 *iku*: Adda;
viii	2(iku) Ab-ba-tur	2 *iku*: Abbatur;
	2(iku) Gu-[ni-DU]	2 *iku*: GuniDU;
	½(iku) Ur-^{d}Nam$_2$-nun	½ *iku*: Ur-Namnun;
	1(iku) Nin-an-si	1 *iku*: Ninansi;
	5(iku) Lugal-ezen	5 *iku*: Lugalezen;
	4(iku) Aja$_2$-nu-zu	4 *iku*: Ajanuzu;
	1 ½(iku) Ur-^{d}Nin-Dulum$_2$	1 ½ Ur-Nindulum;
	1(iku) Nin-an-si	1 *iku*: Ninansi;
	5(iku) gu:sur	5 *iku*: the land-surveyor;
	4 ½(iku) Lugal-saĝ-dilmun	4 ½ *iku*: Lugalsaĝdilmun;
	3 ½(iku) Lugal-ḫe$_2$	3 ½ *iku*: Lugalḫe;
	[...]	...
rev. i	½(iku) Lu$_2$-zi	½ *iku*: Luzi;
	5(iku) Maḫ-an-dab$_6$(URUDA)-e	5 *iku*: Maḫandabe
	Šubur-tur	(and) Šuburtur;
	3 ½(iku) Ur-^{d}En-lil$_2$	3 ½ *iku*: Ur-Enlil
	Igi-Dulum$_2$-še$_{3\text{-}tenû}$	(and) Igi-Dulumše;
	1 ½(iku) A$_2^{!}$(DA)-ni-kur-ra	1 ½ *iku*: Anikura;
	2(iku) Si-du$_3$	2 *iku*: Sidu;
	2(iku) gu:sur	2 *iku*: the land-surveyor;
	1 ½(iku) Šubur-tur	1 ½ *iku*: Šuburtur;
	2(iku) Ab-ba-tur	2 *iku*: Abbatur;

	2(iku) Lugal-ḫe$_2$	2 *iku*: Lugalḫe;
	1 ½(iku) Lugal-ḫur-saĝ	1 ½ *iku*: Lugalḫursaĝ;
	2(iku) Ur-^{d}Inana	2 *iku*: Ur-Inana;
ii	2 ½(iku) Nam$_2$-aja$_2$-ĝu$_{10}$	2 ½ *iku*: Namajaĝu;
	1(eše$_3$) 2(iku) Kur-še$_3$-ur-saĝ	1 *eše* 2 *iku*: Kurše'ursaĝ;
	1 ½(iku) E$_2$-ĝessu$_x$(MI)-bi-du$_{10}$	1 ½ *iku*: Eĝessubidu;
	4(iku) Ša$_3$-ni-si	4 *iku*: Šanisi;
	(blank)	
	Mar-da	(Domain) Marda.
	2(iku) Teš$_2$-teš$_2$	2 *iku*: Tešteš;
	2 ½(iku) Ur-eš$_3$	2 ½ *iku*: Ur-eš;
	2(iku) Gu-la	2 *iku*: Gula;
	3 ½(iku) U$_2$-u$_2$ IB	3 ½ *iku*: U'u, the *IB*-official;
	3(iku) Diĝir-šita	3 *iku*: Diĝiršita;
	1(iku) Lugal-igi-še$_{3\text{-}\textit{tenû}}$	1 *iku*: Lugal-igiše;
	½(iku) Ĝanun-nam$_2$-maḫ	½ *iku*: Ĝanunnammaḫ;
	2 ½(iku) Lugal-ki-gal-la	2 ½ *iku*: Lugalkigala;
iii	5(iku) E$_2$-nam-kalam-ma	5 *iku*: Enamkalama;
	3(iku) E$_2$-maḫ-da	3 *iku*: Emaḫda
	Diĝir-lu$_2$-maḫ	(and) Diĝirlumaḫ;
	2(iku) Ur-^{d}Šara$_2^{!}$	2 *iku*: Ur-Šara;
	2(iku) Lugal-aja$_2$-ĝu$_{10}$	2 *iku*: Lugalajaĝu;
	1 ½(iku) Gala-tur	1 ½ *iku*: Galatur;
	1(iku) Me-an-ne$_2$-si	1 *iku*: Me'anesi;
	3(iku) Ur-^{d}Nin-Dulum$_2$	3 *iku*: Ur-Nindulum;
	2 ½(iku) E$_2$-ĝessu$_x$(MI)-bi-du$_{10}$	2 ½ *iku*: Eĝessubidu;
	1(iku) En-kalam-du$_{10}$	1 *iku*: Enkalamdu;
	1(iku) Lugal-ezen	1 *iku*: Lugalezen;
	2(iku) Lugal-igi-še$_{3\text{-}\textit{tenû}}$	2 *iku*: Lugaligiše;
iv	(blank)	
	KA-^{ĝeš}gi	(Domain) KAgi.
	5(iku) Ur-^{d}Nin-Dulum$_2$	5 *iku*: Ur-Nindulum;
	Kar-na$_4^{!}$(UD)	(Domain) Karna.
	Du$_6$-a gu:sur	Du'a, the land-surveyor.
	(blank)	
v	gu$_2$-an-še$_3$ / 1(bur'u) 5(bur$_3$) la$_2$ ½(iku) / Uš$_x$(LAK672)-du$_3$-a-maḫ	
		Grand total: 15 *bur* minus ½ *iku*: (domain) Ušdu'amaḫ;
	1(bur'u) 1(eše$_3$) 4(iku) Mar-da	10 *bur* 1 *eše* 4 *iku*: (domain) Marda;
	2(bur$_3$) 2(eše$_3$) la$_2$ 1(iku) KA-^{ĝeš}gi	2 *bur* 2 *eše* minus 1 *iku*: (domain) KAgi;
	[n+] 2(iku) (ras.) ⌜gu⌝:[sur]	... 2 *iku*: the land-surveyor.
	aša$_5$ / apin-la$_2$ / ^{d}Inana / Silim-Utu / saĝĝa	
		The land (in) lease (at the temple household of) Inana. Silim-Utu (is) the chief temple-administrator.
vi	*26* mu / iti *13*	Year 26, month 13.
	Ba-li lu$_2$-eše$_2$-gid$_2$	*Ba'lī*, the field-surveyor.

Note that some individuals appear many times in the document.

obv. iii 4: Like Aja$_2$-nu-zu "(One who) does not know a father," A-zu-zu is probably Aja$_2$-zu-zu "(One who) shall know (his) father," throughout this volume.

obv. iii 9, viii 9, rev. i 8: The land-surveyor mentioned here is likely identical to Du'a of rev. iv 5.

obv. v 15: See Powell 1978: 14 for LAK672-du$_3$-a and LAK672-du$_3$-a-tur as "domains" in the Zabala region.

obv. vii 5: This may be the full writing of the name Usar$_x$(LAL$_2$×TUG$_2$)-du$_{10}$, attested in the ED Umma text corpus as a governor (ensi$_2$) of Umma. For this governor, see Monaco 2015: 161. Judging by the date formula, the present text itself can be dated to the time of Me'anedu. The chief temple-administrator (saĝĝa) of the Inana household in Zabala mentioned in this text is Silim-Utu. He was in office during the governorships of both Me'anedu and Usardu.[2] Therefore, the Guru$_7$-usar$_x$(LAL$_2$×TUG$_2$)-du$_{10}$ of this text may be identical to the successor of Me'anedu.

obv. vii 9: MUŠ$_3$.ZA$_7$ is a graphic variant of šuba$_3$, written MUŠ$_3$.ZA in later periods and MUŠ$_3$×ZA in ED and Sargonic Adab.

obv. viii 3: See Krebernik 1998b for the goddess ^{d}NAM$_2$.NUN.

obv. viii 10: The name is read as Lugal-saĝ-dilmun(NI.TUKU) "The king is the head (of) the important" (dilmun = *kabtu*; see CAD K 25a) instead of Lugal-saĝ-ni-tuku "The king has his slave." This interpretation is favored by the presence of the logograms DILMUN and MAḪ$_2$ in an Akkadian personal name containing the element *šarrum* "king" (Andersson 2012: 215).

rev. ii 6, iv 2: For these domains, see Powell 1978: 14, 26.

rev. v 4: According to rev. iv 4–5, the land-surveyor is the only person who receives land in the domain Karna.

No. 394 – MS 3791/31

Account of land, Early Dynastic IIIb (governor Šubur), Umma region.

obv. i	1(eše$_3$) 1 ½(iku) aša$_5$ Me-an-si	1 *eše* 1 ½ *iku*: Me'an(e)si
	Ama-en-ne$_2$	(and) Ama'en(a)ne;
	1(eše$_3$) 2(iku) Gan-tilla$_x$(|AN.AN|)	1 *eše* 2 *iku*: Gantilla;
	4(iku) ⸢Me-kalam⸣-si	4 *iku*: Mekalamsi;
ii	4(iku) E$_2$-men-na-u$_4$-su$_3$	4 *iku*: Emena'usu;
	3 ¼(iku) Me-kalam-si	3 ¼ *iku*: Mekalamsi,
	Ur-^{d}Nin-Dulum$_2$	Ur-Nindulum
	Ur-^{d}*Er*$_x$(KIŠ)-*ra*	(and) Ur-*Erra*;
iii	1(eše$_3$) 3(iku) TAB-ba-am$_6$	1 *eše* 3 *iku*: it is the ... (land);
	1(eše$_3$) 2(iku) aša$_5$ šeš Aja$_2$-AN-da	1 *eše* 2 *iku*: land: the brother of Aja'ANda
	Diĝir-en-ne$_2$	(and) Diĝiren(a)ne;
	1(eše$_3$) 2(iku) Teš$_2$-⸢teš$_2$ x⸣-[x]	1 *eše* 2 *iku*: Tešteš ...;

[2] See Monaco 2015: 163 for a historical reconstruction of the sequence of tenures of the principal Umma officials.

rev. i	[n …]	…,
	gu:sur	the land-surveyor;
	4 ½(iku) Nir-ĝal$_2$	4 ½ *iku*: Nirĝal
	En-kalam-du$_{10}$	(and) Enkalamdu,
	ugula-e$_2$	the overseer of the household;
	4 ½(iku) E$_2$-nun-ne$_2$	4 ½ *iku*: Enune;
	3(iku) Gu-ni	3 *iku*: Guni(DU)
ii	Ur-^{d}Šara$_2$ tug$_2$-du$_8$	(and) Ur-Šara, the felter;
	2(iku) Me-kalam-si	2 *iku*: Mekalamsi;
	2(iku) aša$_5$ AN-ne-si	2 *iku* land: ANnesi;
	4 ½(iku) Saĝ-diĝir-tuku	4 ½ *iku*: Saĝdiĝirtuku;
	4 ½(iku) Lugal-saĝ-ku$_5$-su$_3$	4 ½ *iku*: Lugalsaĝkusu,
iii	Si-du$_3$	Sidu
	Lugal-maḫ-di	(and) Lugalmaḫdi;
	2(iku) Me-sag$_3$-nu-di	2 *iku*: Mesagnudi
	E$_2$-an-da gala	(and) E'anda, the cult-singer;
	5(iku) aša$_5$ Aja$_2$-AN-da	5 *iku* land: Aja'ANda,
	lu$_2$ Bara$_2$-si	the man of Bara(ge)si.
	Šubur ensi$_2$	Šubur, the governor.
	⌜*30*?⌝ la$_2$ *2* mu	Year 28(?).

obv. iii 1: TAB-BA is a grapheme that appears often in connection to land in ED IIIb texts from the Umma region. It is left without interpretation in Powell 1978. It appears side by side with the term EŠ$_{16}$-BA. Because of that, the reading *tab-ba is not confirmed. Both terms may, in fact, contain references to numerals: *2*-ba and *3*-ba. The writing in the present text is found much later in a document of Ur III date, as a-ša$_3$ tab-ba-am$_6$, CUSAS 3 no. 1502 rev. 1.

rev. iii 7–8: A governor by the name of Šubur is as yet unattested in Early Dynastic documents from Umma. Šubur may be a previously unknown ruler. If so, the historical reconstructions of Marchesi 2015: 141–43 and Monaco 2015: 163, 165 should be revised. The present text looks older than the majority of texts edited here, which were composed during the latter part of the rule of the governor Me'annedu.

No. 395 – MS 3824

Account of land in connection to issued silver, Early Dynastic IIIb, Umma region.

obv. i	1(bur$_3$) la$_2$ ½(iku) aša$_5$ Lugal-šudu$_3$-du$_{10}$	1 *bur* minus ½ *iku* land: Lugalšududu,
	dub-sar	the scribe;
	5(iku) E$_2$-ĝessu-bi-du$_{10}$	5 *iku*: Eĝessubidu,
ii	ab-ba-iri	the city elder.
	ku$_3$ e$_3$	The silver (is) issued.
rev.	(blank)	

The entries of the document deal with plots of land, but the colophon apparently records an issue of silver, suggesting a connection between them. The silver is probably a sort of tax or payment, but the fact that it leaves the organization instead of entering it is hard to explain at present.

3.1.3 – Grain and Grain Products

No. 396 – MS 1952/6

Allocation of barley flour, Early Dynastic IIIb/Early Sargonic, Umma region.

obv. i	1(bariga) 2(ban$_2$) dabin	1 *bariga* 2 *ban* barley flour:
	⸢Lugal-da-lu⸣	Lugaldalu;
	1(bariga) 2(ban$_2$) *I-mud-il*	1 *bariga* 2 *ban*: *Yimud-'il*;
	1(bariga) 2(ban$_2$) Diĝir-aga$_3$-zi	1 *bariga* 2 *ban*: Diĝiragazi;
	1(bariga) 2(ban$_2$) Diĝir-lu$_2$-maḫ	1 *bariga* 2 *ban*: Diĝirlumaḫ;
ii		[2 lines broken]...
	[1(bariga) 2(ban$_2$) Ur]-^{d}⸢x⸣-[x]	[1 *bariga* 2 *ban*: Ur]...,
	sipa ud$_5$	the goatherd;
	1(bariga) 2(ban$_2$) Lugal-mu-da	1 *bariga* 2 *ban*: Lugalmuda
	Saĝ-Utu-da	(and) Saĝ-Utuda;
	1(bariga) 2(ban$_2$) Za$_3$-nin-mu-ta	1 *bariga* 2 *ban*: Zaninmuta
	Kaskal-ni-du$_{10}$	(and) Kaskalanidu;
iii	[...]	...
	⸢x-x⸣-[...]	...
	1(bariga) 2(ban$_2$) Lugal-a$_2$-zi-da	1 *bariga* 2 *ban*: Lugalazida
	Amar-Ku'ara(ḪA.A)	(and) Amar-Ku'ara;
	1(bariga) 2(ban$_2$) Lugal-men	1 *bariga* 2 *ban*: Lugalmen
	RI-TI	(and) RITI;
rev. i	1(bariga) 2(ban$_2$) E$_2$-ur$_2$-bi-du$_{10}$	1 *bariga* 2 *ban*: E'urbidu;
	1(bariga) 2(ban$_2$) *Gar*$_x$(NUN$_{\text{-tenû}}$)*-il*	1 *bariga* 2 *ban*: *Gar-'il*;
	1(bariga) 2(ban$_2$) Lugal-sipa na-gada	1 *bariga* 2 *ban*: Lugalsipa, the herdsman;
	1(bariga) 2(ban$_2$) Lugal-sipa [...]	1 *bariga* 2 *ban*: Lugalsipa, the ...,
	⸢A$_2$⸣-[...]	(and) A...
		(rest blank)

rev. i 2: The sign NUN$_{\text{-tenû}}$ written vertically here has either a reading agargara, designating a fish, or a syllabic value gar$_x$, used in the writing of the same fish (MZL p. 75 no. 144; PSD A^3 58 f.; CAD A^1 145–46). This reading may apply here too: cf. the name *Ga-ri*$_2$*-i*$_3$*-lum* in this volume.

No. 397 – MS 2191/7

Delivery of bread to the palace, Early Dynastic IIIb, Umma region.

obv. i	240 ninda / Lugal-diĝir-ĝu$_{10}$ / saĝĝa-ĜAR / e$_{2}$:gal / de$_{6}$	240 breads. Lugaldiĝirĝu, the chief temple-administrator. Brought (to) the palace.
ii	*16* mu *13* iti	Year 16, month 13.
	(blank)	
rev.	(blank)	

No. 398 – MS 3791/1

Allocation of barley to herders, Early Dynastic IIIb, Umma region.

obv. i	1(bariga) 2(ban$_{2}$) ⸢x⸣-[x]	1 *bariga* 2 *ban*: ...;
	1(bariga) 2(ban$_{2}$) Za$_{3}$-nin-mu-ta	1 *bariga* 2 *ban*: Zaninmuta;
	1(bariga) 2(ban$_{2}$) NIM	1 *bariga* 2 *ban*: NIM;
	2(bariga) Utu-aja$_{2}$-ĝu$_{10}$	2 *bariga*: Utu'ajaĝu;
	1(bariga) 2(ban$_{2}$) Ur-Ab-U$_{2}$	1 *bariga* 2 *ban*: Ur-AbU;
	2(bariga) NIM	2 *bariga*: NIM;
	1(bariga) 2(ban$_{2}$) Šeš-ama-na	1 *bariga* 2 *ban*: Šeš-amana;
ii	[1(bariga) 2(ban$_{2}$) x]-⸢na⸣-na$_{2}$	[1 *bariga* 2 *ban*: ...]nana;
	1(bariga) 2(ban$_{2}$) Ur-^{d}Dulum$_{2}$	1 *bariga* 2 *ban*: Ur-Dulum;
	1(bariga) 2(ban$_{2}$) Ša$_{3}$-nu-ĝal$_{2}$	1 *bariga* 2 *ban*: Šanuĝal;
	1(bariga) 2(ban$_{2}$) Ur-e$_{2}$	1 *bariga* 2 *ban*: Ur-e;
	1(bariga) 2(ban$_{2}$) Igi-ig-gal-še$_{3\text{-}tenû}$	1 *bariga* 2 *ban*: Igi'iggalše;
	1(bariga) 2(ban$_{2}$) Diĝir-lu$_{2}$-maḫ	1 *bariga* 2 *ban*: Diĝirlumaḫ;
iii	⸢2(bariga)⸣ Šeš-an-da-lu	2 *bariga*: Šešandalu.
	gab$_{2}$-ra še-ba	Herder(s). Barley allocation.
rev.	*30* la$_{2}$ *2* mu / iti *4*	Year 28, month 4.

No. 399 – MS 3791/9

Account of bread, beer and beer ingredients, Early Dynastic IIIb, Umma region.

obv. i	40 ⸢ninda-UD-sa$_{6}$-ga⸣	40 ... premium breads;
	7 UKKIN×GUG$_{2}$ kaš sila$_{3}$ uš-bar	7 *sila* of ... (for) beer;
ii	3 šim-⸢x⸣ sila$_{3}$ u$_{2}$-u$_{2}$-la	3 *sila* of ... beer malt;
	5 DIN.ŠE kaš sila$_{3}$	5 *sila* of ... (for) beer;
	10 kaš-sag$_{8}$(KAL) sila$_{3}$	10 *sila* of premium beer.
	(blank)	
rev.	(blank)	

obv. i 1: See the discussion of the possible readings of ninda-UD in CUSAS 23 no. 30.

obv. i 2: For UKKIN×GUG$_{2}$, see the sign LAK720 = UKKIN×(MUNU$_{4}$.GUG$_{2}$). This entry refers most probably to a sort of beer. The term uš-bar usually denotes a textile of some kind but its meaning in the present context is uncertain.

obv. ii 1: The term u$_{2}$-u$_{2}$-la is obscure.

obv. ii 2: For a discussion of the term ŠE.DIN "barley beverage," see FTP p. 59, with additional references.

obv. ii 3: The interpretation of the sign KAL as sag$_{8}$ "good" is conventional. Damerow 2012: 5 proposed reading kaš-sig$_{15}$ "golden(?) beer."

No. 400 – MS 3791/13

Account of barley, Early Dynastic IIIb, Umma region.

obv. i	70 še gur	70 *gur* barley:
	Ur-^{d}Dulum$_{2}$	Ur-Dulum;
	70 Inim-Utu-zi	70: Inim-Utu-zi;
	26 Amar-ki-ku$_{3}$ kuš$_{7}$	26: Amarkiku, the animal-manager;
ii	20 Mar-ku$_{7}$	20: Marku;
	11 $^{ba_{15}}$baḫar$_{2}$	11: the potter;
	13 nu-kiri$_{6}$	13: the gardener.
	(blank)	
iii	(blank)	
rev.	(blank)	

obv. ii 2: The writing is BAR plus LAK742(BAḪAR$_{2}$). Obviously, BAR is the phonetic complement: $^{ba_{15}}$baḫar$_{2}$. See Krebernik 1998a: 283 fn. 524 for the difference between LAK742 = baḫar$_{2}$ and LAK747 = eden.

No. 401 – MS 3791/21

Account of barley, Early Dynastic IIIb, Umma region.

obv. i	68 še gur-saĝ-ĝal$_{2}$	68 *gursaĝĝal* barley:
	Ša$_{3}$-nu-ĝal$_{2}$	Šanuĝal;
	63 Lu$_{2}$-na-nam	63: Lunanam;
	64 Lugal-mu-da-zu	64: Lugalmudazu;
ii	64 De$_{5}$-de$_{5}$	64: Dede.
	(blank)	
iii	(blank)	
rev.	(blank)	

3.1.4 – Livestock

No. 402 – MS 3791/4

Contribution of sheep (*mašdari'a*), Early Dynastic IIIb, Umma region.

obv. i	1 maš$_{2}$ bar-dul$_{5}$ da-ri Aja$_{2}$-zu-zu	1 *bardul*-kid brought at the side: Ajazuzu;
	1 udu-babbar 1 maš$_{2}$-ga ⸢Ur$^{?}$⸣-ki	1 white sheep, 1 milk kid: Urki(?);
	1 dub-sar-maḫ	1 (kid): the chief scribe;
	1 Amar-saĝ-ku$_{5}$	1 (kid): Amarsaĝku;
	1 ⸢x⸣-si	1 (kid): ...si.
ii	(blank)	
rev.	⸢maš$_{2}$⸣ da-ri	*Mašdari(a)*-contribution.
	[(n+$^{?}$)] *3* mu	Year 3 [+n?].

obv. i 1: maš$_{2}$ bar-dul$_{5}$ is otherwise unattested. The interpretation of bar-dul$_{5}$ as a garment seems unlikely in the present context. For the compound verb da ... ri "to lead at one's side," see Selz 1995b: 251 f.

No. 403 – MS 3791/5

Account of sheared sheep, Early Dynastic IIIb, Umma region.

obv. i	24 u$_8$	24 ewes;
	13 sila$_4$	13 lambs;
	10 ⸢udu mu⸣-*2*	10 2-year-old sheep;
	10 udu Gu-gu-u$_2$	10 (other) sheep: Gugu'u;
5	2 (ras.) maš$_2$-saĝ	2 bellwethers:
ii	De$_5$-⸢de$_5$⸣	Dede.
	30 la$_2$ *3* udu Maš-da$_3$	27 sheep: Mašda.
	udu kurušda / ĝanun-maḫ / ur$_4$ /*30* la$_2$ *3* mu / iti *7*	Sheep (of) the fattener. The main storehouse. Plucked. Year 27, month 7.
iii	(blank)	
rev.	(blank)	

obv. i 4: Gu-gu-u$_2$ may be a variant of or mistake for the personal name Gu$_2$-u$_2$-u$_2$. For the latter, cf. Bramanti, *Three Administrative Texts from the Time of Me'annedu* (forthcoming).

obv. i 5: The erased sign is UDU. See FAOS 6 p. 231 for maš-saĝ-ĝa$_2$ "Leitbock."

No. 404 – MS 3791/7

Account of sheep, Early Dynastic IIIb, Umma region.

obv. i	16 u$_8$ / 10 la$_2$ *1* udu-nita / 8 ud$_5$ / 6N$_8$ sila$_4$-sig / 4 maš$_2$	16 ewes; 9 male sheep; 8 nanny goats; 6 (juvenile?) lambs introduced into the flock; 4 billy goats:
ii	Ad-da-da	Addada.
	Eden-Hu-bu$_7$^{bu}	Eden-Hubur(um):
	šu-ne$_2$ šid-da	That is what has been counted into his hand.
rev.	udu u$_2$-rum	The sheep (are) the property.
	Gu-na	Guna,
	ugula nu-banda$_3$ gu$_4$	the overseer of the supervisors of oxen (is responsible).
	25 mu / iti *11*	25th year, month 11.

obv. i 1: Compare the term -sig to si.g. This stage follows suckling (amar-ga) and separation from mother (amar-ku$_5$), and denotes introduction to the rest of the flock (amar-sig). See Bauer 1989–90: 88–89. Note the use of the numerical sign N$_8$ instead of N$_1$ in connection to animals, as also in texts below.

obv. ii 2: For a recent discussion of the geographical name ḪU.DUR$_2$.BU(.NE.RU = rum$_2$), see Krebernik, Steible and Yildiz 2014: 349–50 with additional references. It occurs as personal name on its own or as an element in personal names in documents from ED I–II until the Ur III period inclusive. For the reading Ḫu-bu$_7$^{bu}-(rum$_2$), see Steible 2015: 160, Schrakamp 2015a: 206, 238.

No. 405 – MS 3791/10

Account of sheep, Early Dynastic IIIb, Umma region.

obv. i	*33* utua$_2$	33 breeding rams:
	Ur-^{d}Tu	Ur-Tu(da);
	20 la$_2$ *3* Diĝir-aja$_2$-zi	17: Diĝirajazi;
ii	*20* Lugal-mu-da-kuš$_2$	20: Lugalmudakuš.
	⸢*n* mu *n* iti⸣	Year ..., month ...
rev.	[destroyed/blank]	

obv. i 1: The sign for /utua/ "breeding ram" (see Green 1980: 4) resembles more closely the form of ZATU578 than that of LAK777.

obv. i 2: ^{d}Tu is most likely an abbreviation of ^{d}Tu-da, the titulary deity of the town KiAN: see ll. 212–14 of the *Zami*-Hymn Collection in OIP 99 p. 52. Krebernik 2014: 152–53 is of the same opinion.

No. 406 – MS 3791/12

Account of sheep and goats, Early Dynastic IIIb, Umma region.

obv. i	11 u$_8$ / 10 4N$_8$ udu-nita	11 ewes; 10 (and) 4 (juvenile?) male sheep;
	5 kir$_{11}$ / 2N$_8$ sila$_4$-nita-nim	5 female lambs; 2 (juvenile?) male lambs born in autumn;
	2 ud$_5$ / 8 ^{munus}aš$_2$:gar$_3$	2 nanny goats; 8 female kids;
ii	5 maš$_2$ / 1N$_8$ maš$_2$ bar-dul$_5$	5 billy kids; 1 (juvenile?) *bardul*-kid;
	20 la$_2$ *3* maš$_2$ ša$_3$-du$_{10}$	17 suckling kids.
	udu u$_2$-rum Nagar-ša$_3$	The sheep (are) the property (of) Nagarša.
rev. i	Ur-Šubur sipa	Ur-Šubur, the shepherd (is responsible).
	šid-da / e$_2$-gal-ta / šum$_2$-ma / *30* la$_2$ *2* mu / *4* iti	(Ac)counted. Given out of the palace. Year 28, month 4.
ii	(blank)	

obv. i 1: The numerical value of the sign N$_8$ in the present context is uncertain. The sign cannot refer to castrated males since it is used also with female animals: cf. text No. 413 obv. ii 1. It is likely that here, as in Late Uruk IV accounts of animals, the sign is used to designate young animals. See Bartash 2015b: 131 with additional references.

obv. i 2: For nim "born in autumn," see Selz 1993 no. 50. Sila$_4$-nim is interpreted as "spring lamb" by CAD; see MC 4 p. 35.

obv. ii 1: See text No. 402 obv. i 1 for maš$_2$ bar-dul$_5$.

obv. ii 3: Nagar-ša$_3$ is chief temple-administrator (saĝĝa) according to text No. 409 rev. i 1.

obv. ii 3–rev. i 2: That the sheep are issued out of the palace, but are the property of the chief temple-administrator Nagarša, suggests that the term u$_2$-rum does not refer to private property in the modern sense; the term requires further study.

No. 407 – MS 3791/16

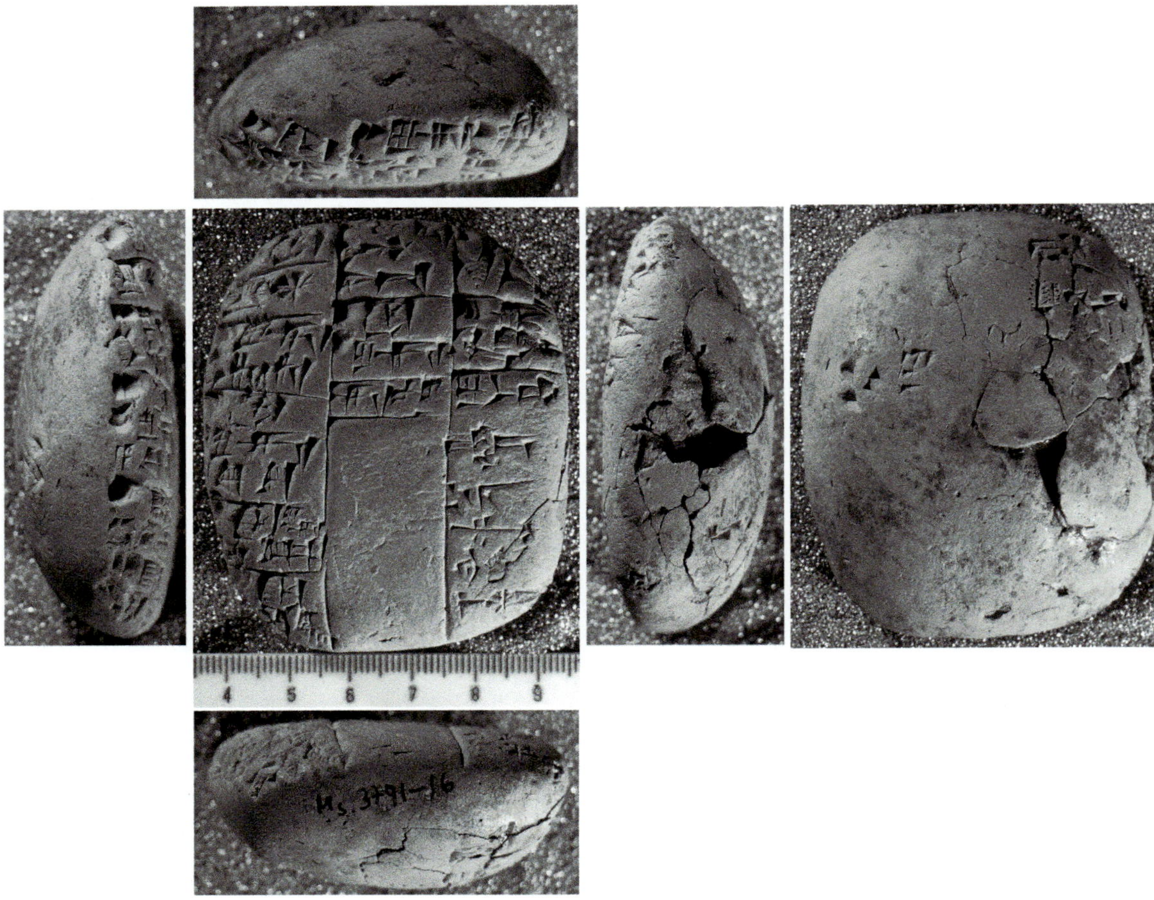

Account of sheep and goats, Early Dynastic IIIb, Umma region.

obv. i	2 u$_8$	2 ewes:
	Uzug(ZAG.AN)	Uzug;
	2 udu-nita Ki-de$_5$-de$_5$	2 male sheep: Kidede;
	2 u$_8$ 2N$_8$ udu-nita Aja$_2$-zu-zu	2 ewes, 2 (juvenile?) male sheep: Ajazuzu;
5	1 u$_8$ 1N$_8$ udu-nita Ur-Abzu	1 ewe, 1 (juvenile?) male sheep: Ur-Abzu;
	2 u$_8$ Amar-ki-ku$_3$	2 ewes: Amarkiku;
ii	2 udu-nita Gu-ni-DU	2 male sheep: GuniDU;
	1 u$_8$ 1N$_8$ udu-nita	1 ewes, 1 (juvenile?) male sheep:
	Nita sipa	Nita, the shepherd.
	(blank)	
iii	1 LAK20 En-sila-si	1 male goat: Ensilasi;
	3 ud$_5$ Du$_{11}$-ga-ni	3 nanny goats: Dugani;
	udu sila-ta / LAK617×ḪI / *30* la$_2$ *1* mu / iti ⸢*4*⸣ / Me-an-ne$_2$-⸢du$_{10}$⸣	
		The sheep that will follow (and the sheep that are) ....
		Year 29, month 4. Me'anedu,
rev. i	kurušda / šum$_2$-ma	the fattener: provided.
ii	*22* udu	22 sheep.

obv. iii 1: For an animal written LAK20, see Krebernik 1998a: 275 with additional references. Interpretations include "male goat" and "sow" ("Mutterschwein").

obv. iii 3: Although this text dates to the reign of the governor Me'anedu, the fattener Me'anedu here is a different person. He appears as kurušda in other documents from Umma: see CUSAS 33 nos. 6, 11, 13, 52, 70, 72.

For the expression sila-ta, see the commentary to text No. 163 obv. ii 4. The sign in question looks like BAD$_3$ but with an inscribed ḪI instead of AN. The horizontal wedge inside the beginning of the sign is probably a slip of the stylus and has no significance (unless it is ZATU44a = EZEN$_b$×*AŠ*). This sign appears instead of the verb e$_3$ in the construction sila-ta e$_3$. Consequently, it is probably also a verb, if it indeed refers to the udu sila-ta. P. Notizia suggests (personal communication) that the sign in question may be a variant of ug$_5$ (EZEN×UŠ$_2$) "to die" (plural). However, in this case it would be difficult to explain the phonetic(?) indicator ḪI. Besides, dead animals are denoted in the usual fashion uš$_2$/ug$_7$, for which see below.

No. 408 – MS 3791/17

Account of plow oxen, Early Dynastic IIIb, Umma region.

obv. i	3 gu$_4$-apin	3 plow oxen:
	En-sila-si	Ensilasi;
	1 Ĝiri$_3$-ni	1: Ĝirini;
	3 Mi-tum-ma-ni	3: Mitumani;
ii	2 Lugal-kur-ra-diri	2: Lugalkuradiri;
	1 sagi	1: the cupbearer;
	1 sukkal	1: the secretary;
	1 ma$_2$-laḫ$_4$	1: the sailor;
	2 Maš	2: Maš;
	1 ab-ba-iri	1: the city elder;
iii	1 Lu$_2$-na-nam	1: Lunanam;
	1 Ur-pu$_x$(LAGAB×TIL)-saĝ	1: Urpusaĝ;
	1 Ad-da-bi	1: Addabi;
	1 e$_2$ Ur-e$_2$	1: the house of Ur-e.
rev.	(blank)	

obv. iii 4: For the same household, see CUSAS 33 no. 88 and especially no. 96, where the "house" has an administrative function as the place of accounting.

No. 409 – MS 3791/22

Delivery of dead sheep to the palace, Early Dynastic IIIb, Umma region.

obv. i	1 u$_8$-uš$_2$ Ur-e$_2$ sagi	1 dead ewe: Ur-e, the cupbearer
	Ur-Abzu sipa	(and) Ur-Abzu, the shepherd;
	1 u$_8$-uš$_2$ Gu-ni-DU ⸢x⸣-DU	1 dead ewe: GuniDU (and) …;
ii	1 u$_8$-uš$_2$ Lugal-ezen šeš ugula nu-banda$_3$	1 dead ewe: Lugalezen, brother of the overseer of the supervisors,
	Nita sipa	(and) Nita, the shepherd;
	1 udu-nita-uš$_2$ Lugal-ša$_3$-su$_3$ sukkal	1 dead male sheep: Lugalšasu, the secretary;
	⸢Lu$_2$⸣-[...]	(and) Lu...;
iii	1 udu-nita-uš$_2$ ul$_3$-la Mes-Utu-ba	1 dead male *harnessed* sheep: Mes-Utu-ba,
	Aja$_2$-zu-zu ⸢sipa⸣	(and) Ajazuzu, the shepherd;
rev. i	[(n)] ⸢udu⸣ / e$_2$-gal / de$_6$ / Nagar-ša$_3$ / saĝĝa	[(x)] sheep delivered (to) the palace. Nagarša, the chief temple-administrator.
rev. ii	*30* la$_2$ *2* mu / *11* iti	Year 28, month 11.

obv. iii 1: The term ḫul$_3$-la refers to sheep harnessed with cloth rings: see CUSAS 33 no. 15 commentary to obv. i 1, and below, text No. 510 obv. 2 and commentary.

No. 410 – MS 3791/24

Account of sheep, ready for plucking or dead, and of hides, Early Dynastic IIIb, Umma region.

obv. i	111 sila$_4$-ur$_4$ / *10* kuš	111 lambs ready for plucking, 10 hides,
	20 la$_2$ *3* sila$_4$-ug$_7$ e$_2$-gal de$_6$	17 dead lambs, delivered (to) the palace:
	Ur-Šubur	Ur-Šubur;
	2 sila$_4$-ur$_4$ *1* kuš	2 lambs ready for plucking, 1 hide,
	4 kuš e$_2$:gal de$_6$	4 hides, delivered (to) the palace:
	Lugal-šeš	Lugalšeš;
	8 sila$_4$ *10* la$_2$ *1* kuš	8 lambs, 9 hides:
	Lugal-ḫe$_2$	Lugalḫe;
	10 sila$_4$-ur$_4$ *3* kuš	10 lambs ready for plucking, 3 hides:
ii	Lugal-Anzu$_2^{mušen}$	Lugal-Anzu;
	16 sila$_4$ *3* kuš	16 lambs, 3 hides:
	I-da-il	*Yida-'il;*
	3 sila$_4$ Amar-ki-ku$_3$	3 lambs: Amarkiku;
	4 sila$_4$-ur$_4$ *3* kuš	4 lambs ready for plucking, 3 hides:
	^{ĝeš}Ĝiškim-nu-ti	Ĝiškimnuti;
	1 sila$_4$-ur$_4$ Ad-da-tur	1 lamb ready for plucking: Addatur.
	sila$_4$ bar-⸢ĝal$_2$⸣ / e$_2$ ^{d}⸢Ištaran⸣(⸢KA⸣.[DI]) ⸢ur$_4$⸣-[ra]	Lambs with fleece. The temple of Ištaran. Plucked.
iii	1 ⸢sila$_4$⸣ *I-da-il* ⸢x⸣	1 lamb: *Yida-'il …*
(colophon)	*30* la$_2$ *2* mu / iti *11* / *165* sila$_4$ / [n+] *10* kuš	Year 28, month 11. 165 lambs, ...+10 hides.
rev.	(blank)	

No. 411 – MS 3791/25

Account of sheep. Early Dynastic IIIb, Umma region.

obv. i	114 u$_8$	114 ewes,
	32 utua$_2$	32 rams,
	65 udu mu-*2*	65 sheep of 2 years:
	Aja$_2$-zu-zu	Ajazuzu;
	65 u$_8$	65 ewes,
	30 la$_2$ *1* utua$_2$	29 rams,
ii	53 udu mu-*2*	53 sheep of 2 years:
	(blank space)	
	Amar-ki-ku$_3$	Amarkiku;
	93 u$_8$ / 30 la$_2$ *3* utua$_2$	93 ewes, 27 rams:
	(blank space) / Uzug	Uzug;
iii	83 u$_8$ / 25 utua$_2$	83 ewes, 25 rams:
	(blank space)	
	Nita	Nita;
	80 la$_2$ *2* u$_8$ / 23 utua$_2$	78 ewes, 23 rams:
	(blank space)	
	Ur-[...]	Ur...;
iv	43 u$_8$ / 20 utua$_2$	43 ewes, 20 rams:
	(blank)	
	Utu-mu-⌜kuš$_2$⌝	Utu-mukuš;
	[break]	
rev. i	[break]	[n ewes, n rams:]
	(blank space)	
	Gu-ni-DU	GuniDU;
	94 udu-nita	94 male sheep:
	(blank space)	
	Ḫur-saĝ-Ebiḫ$_2$	Ḫursaĝ-Ebiḫ.
ii (colophon)		
	7 / udu zuḫ(KA) / kur$_2$ bala	7 sheep stolen(?): *the difference has been included in the account*(?).
	dub si-sa$_2$-a / udu-ur$_4$ zu$_2$-si	The regular tablet. Sheep ready for plucking (to be) plucked.
	30 la$_2$ *2* mu / iti *6* / ^{d}Inana / Zabala$_5$	Year 28, month 6. Inana('s household in) Zabala.

obv. ii 1: The interpretation of the grapheme PAP-bala is tentative, although it is clear from the indentation that it refers to these seven sheep. The sign PAP is usually a "checkmark" and often appears in entries with goods or personnel. Here it must be a lexeme instead. The verb bala "to turn" is used in several compound verbs with reference to various administrative practices, e.g., dub ... bala "to go over an account." The matter is complicated by the uncertainty in the interpretation of the grapheme udu-KA. According to the present reading of the text, seven animals were stolen and this led to the need to recalculate the account. These changes are noted by the expression (or compound verb) kur$_2$ bala, literally "to turn the difference." For a discussion of dub si-sa$_2$-a, see CUSAS 33 no. 66 commentary.

No. 412 – MS 3791/29

Account of sheep(?), Early Dynastic IIIb, Umma region.

obv. i	13 ⸢Si-du$_3$⸣	13: Sidu;
	30 la$_2$ *3* Ur$_2$-ni	27: Urni;
	25 ugula nu-banda$_3$	25: the overseer of supervisors;
	20 Ur-^{d}Nin-Dulum$_2$	20: Ur-Nindulum;
	15 Ur-saĝ-Utu	15: Ursaĝ-Utu;
ii	12 Du$_{11}$-⸢ga⸣-ni-du$_{10}$	12: Duganidu;
	11 E$_2$-⸢kur⸣-nu-⸢si⸣	11: Ekurnusi;
	20 la$_2$ *1* ⸢Ur⸣-en-⸢nun⸣	19: Ur-ennun.
	(blank)	
rev.	*152*	152 (animals)

No. 413 – MS 3791/30

Account of sheep, Early Dynastic IIIb, Umma region.

obv. i	20 (ras.) u$_8$	20 ewes,
	4 u$_8$ kurušda *1* udu-nita	4 ewes (of) the fattener, 1 male sheep:
	Saĝ-eš$_3$-tuku	Saĝeštuku;
	15 sila$_4$	15 lambs,
	[...] ⸢x⸣ [...] sila$_4$	... lambs;
	[...] ⸢x⸣	...
ii	2 sila$_4$-nita / 3N$_8$ kir$_{11}$ bar-li	2 male lambs, 3 (juvenile?)...female lambs:
	(blank)	
	De$_5$-de$_5$	Dede;
	7 kir$_{11}$-ur$_4$ / ⸢*3* udu kurušda⸣	7 female lambs ready for plucking, 3 sheep (of) the fattener:
iii	Saĝ-eš$_3$-tuku	Saĝeštuku;
	⸢10⸣ u$_8$ / 15 sila$_4$-nita-ur$_4$ / Maš-da$_3$	10 ewes, 15 male lambs ready for plucking: Mašda.
	De$_5$-de$_5$ / kurušda šum$_2$-⸢ma⸣	Dede, the fattener: provided.
rev.	[(...)] ⸢ĝanun⸣-maḫ / [(...)] ⸢ur$_4$⸣-ra / ⸢*30*⸣ la$_2$ *3* mu / *7* iti	
		... the main storehouse. Plucked [...]. Year 27, month 7.

obv. ii 1: The meaning of the term bar-li is unknown. Bar designates "fleece" in the context of plucking. Cf. also a term e$_3$-li qualifying animals born in spring shortly after the beginning of the year: see Selz 1993; Sallaberger 1994: 146.

No. 414 – MS 3791/32

Account of sheep and hides, Early Dynastic IIIb, Umma region.

obv. i	*65* Aja$_2$-zu-zu *14* kuš	65 (animals): Ajazuzu: 14 hides;
	50 la$_2$ *2* Amar-ki *11* kuš	48: Amarki: 11 hides;
	20 E$_2$-⸢maḫ⸣ *8* kuš	20: Emaḫ: 8 hides;
	11 Uzug(ZAG:AN$^!$) *3*	11: Uzug: 3 (hides);

	8 Nita *4*	8: Nita: 4;
	10 Ur-Abzu *4*	10: Ur-Abzu: 4;
ii	*7* Utu-mu-kuš$_2$ *1*	7: Utumukuš: 1;
	8 Ni$_3$-babbar$_2$-pa-e$_3$ *1*	8: Nibabbarpa'e;
	1 Lugal-pa-e$_3$	1: Lugalpa'e: (0);
	2 Gu-ni *1*	2: Guni(DU): 1;
	10 U$_2$-u$_2$-a *1 6* la$_2$	10: U'u'a: 1, 6 arrears;
	4 Ni$_2$	4: Ni(zu): (0);
	4 Ur-^{d}En	4: Ur-En(ki): (0);
iii	*3* Ḫur *2*	3: Ḫur(saĝ-Ebiḫ): 2.
	e$_3$:li / e$_2$ ^{d}Ištaran(KA.DI) / ur$_4$-ra / *30* la$_2$ *3* mu	Spring. The temple of Ištaran. Plucked. Year 27.
rev.	(blank)	

No. 415 – MS 3791/33

Account of sheep and hides, Early Dynastic IIIb, Umma region.

obv. i	72 sila$_4$ *5* kuš	72 lambs, 5 hides:
	Aja$_2$-[zu]-zu	Ajazuzu;
	35 sila$_4$ *7* kuš	35 lambs, 7 hides:
	Amar-ki-ku$_3$	Amarkiku;
	50 la$_2$ *3* sila$_4$ *4* kuš	47 lambs, 4 hides:
	E$_2$-a-a	E'aja;
	45 sila$_4$ Uzug *12* kuš	45 lambs, 12 hides: Uzug;
	54 sila$_4$ 10 la$_2$ *1* kuš *2* la$_2$	54 lambs, 9 hides, 2 (hides) arrears:
ii	Nita	Nita;
	41 sila$_4$ *10* kuš Ur-Abzu	41 lambs, 10 hides: Ur-Abzu;
	31 sila$_4$ *12* kuš Utu-mu-kuš$_2$	31 lambs, 12 hides: Utumukuš;
	55 sila$_4$ *5* kuš Lugal-pa-e$_3$	55 lambs, 5 hides: Lugalpa'e;
	34 sila$_4$ *4* kuš Ni$_3$-babbar$_2$-pa-e$_3$	34 lambs, 4 hides: Nibabbarpa'e;
	56	56 (lambs),
iii	*8* kuš U$_2$-u$_2$-a	8 hides: U'u'a;
	16 sila$_4$ *10* la$_2$ *1* kuš Ur-^{d}En-ki	16 lambs, 9 hides: Ur-Enki;
	12 *6* kuš Ni$_2$-zu	12 (lambs), 6 hides: Nizu;
	6 *3* kuš Gu-ni-DU	6 (lambs), 3 hides: GuniDU;
	(blank)	
iv	*505* sila$_4$ / igi-du$_8$	505 lambs: inspected(?);
	120 la$_2$ *6* kuš	114 hides.
	2 sila$_4$ Lugal-*si$_4$-LUM*	2 lambs: Lugal-*siLUM*.
rev.	[10+] *16* mu / ⸢iti⸣ *12*	Year 26, month 12.

obv. iv 1: The term igi-du$_8$ is attested as a professional title designating a cult specialist; see SCTRAH no. 230 commentary to obv. 3. Here it is an administrative procedure. Based on the literal meaning of the verb igi … du$_8$ "to behold, observe," it must be a sort of inspection. The same term appears in the colophon of another text about animals from ED IIIb Umma, CDLI P271237 (unpublished) rev. ii 1.

No. 416 – MS 4929

Account of sheep, Early Dynastic IIIb, Umma region.

obv. i	444 u$_8$ 50 la$_2$ *2* [x]	444 ewes, 48 ...;
	[break filled with fake]	...
	[n+] 22 ⌜udu⌝-nita	... 22 male sheep;
ii	16 u$_8$	16 ewes;
	4N$_8$ udu mu-*2*	4 (juvenile?) sheep, 2 years old.
	(blank)	
rev.	(blank)	

3.1.5 – Financial Documents

No. 417 – MS 3791/6

Account of loans in barley, Early Dynastic IIIb, Umma region.

obv. i	15 še gur-saĝ-ĝal$_2$	15 *gursaĝĝal* barley;
	Ur-^{d}Dulum$_2$	Ur-Dulum,
	dumu E$_2$-nu-si	son of Enusi;
	10(gur) Inim-ma-ni-zi	10: Inimanizi,
	e$_2$ Ur-e$_2$	(of) the house (of) Ur-e;
	3(gur) Amar-^{d}Nanše	3: Amar-Nanše;
	10(gur) Mes-dab$_6$	10: Mesdab;
	15(gur)	15:
ii	Lugal-pa-e$_3$	Lugalpa'e,
	sipa	the shepherd;
	5(gur) ⸢Silim⸣-Utu	5: Silim-Utu
	Mu-ni-ḫur-saĝ	(and) Muniḫursaĝ;
	6(gur) Kar-ki-du$_{10}$	6: Karkdu;
	1(gur) E$_2$-DU-DU	1: EDUDU,
	nagar	the carpenter;

	1(gur) 2(bariga) ḪU-TAR	1 *gur* 2 *bariga*: ḪUTAR;
	1(gur) Ki-ni-mu-zu	1 *gur*: Kinimuzu,
	lu$_2$ A$_2$-ag̑$_2$-ni-du$_{10}$	man (of) A'ag̑nidu;
iii	1(gur) 2(bariga) Nin-gal-zu	1 *gur* 2 *bariga*: Ningalzu;
	2(bariga) Um-mi-pa$_3$	2 *bariga*: Ummipa;
	1(gur) Ba-lu$_5$	1 *gur*: Balu,
	dumu Šes-ama-na	son of Šešamana;
	2(bariga) *Il-su*-ḪA	2 *bariga*: *'Ilšu*-ḪA
	G̑AR-RU-RU	(and) G̑ARRURU;
	2(bariga) G̑AR-DIN	2 *bariga*: G̑ARDIN;
	2(bariga) Ama-bara$_2$-ge	2 *bariga*: Amabarage;
	2(bariga) Igi-^{d}Dulum$_2$-še$_{3\text{-}tenû}$	2 *bariga*: Igi-Dulumše;
iv	2(bariga) Šeš-pa$_3$ i$_3$-du$_8$	2 *bariga*: Šešpa, the doorman;
	2(bariga) Lugal-gaba-g̑al$_2$	2 *bariga*: Lugalgabag̑al;
	(blank)	
v	(blank)	
	[n+] 30 še gur-sag̑-g̑al$_2$	[n+] 30 *gursag̑g̑al* barley:
	u$_4$ E$_2$-maḫ-da ⸢še ag̑$_2$⸣	When Emaḫda measured barley.
	(blank)	
rev. i	gu$_2$-an-še$_3$ / 55(gur) 2(bariga) / še gur-sag̑-g̑al$_2$	Grand total: 55 *gursag̑g̑al* 2 *bariga* barley.
	še ḫa-mul / Gu-na / šum$_2$-ma	Loan barley. Guna: provided.
	20 la$_2$ *3* mu	Year 17.
	(blank)	

obv. iii 6: The grapheme is interpreted here as a personal name.

obv. iii 7: See CUSAS 23 no. 62 (ED IIIb or earlier, Umma region) obv. i 2 for the same name of uncertain reading.

rev. i 2: For še ḫa-mul-(le), which appears in other Umma region texts (e.g., in BIN 8, 63 obv. ii 4) as "loan barley," see CUSAS 33 no. 234 with commentary and previous literature. Guna is certainly the ugula nu-banda$_3$ gu$_4$ who appears in BdI 2/1 no. 48 obv. i 2–3, CUSAS 14 no. 89 rev. i 1–2, and above, text No. 404 rev. 2.

No. 418 – MS 3791/26

Loan of barley and metal, Early Dynastic IIIb, Umma region.

This document shows that beside loans provided in barley, there were also loans issued in ^{uruda}ni$_3$-UD, literally "white substance" (^{uruda}ni$_3$-babbar), probably a variety of copper alloy.

obv. i	3(gur) 2(bariga) še gur-saĝ-ĝal$_2$	3 *gursaĝĝal* 2 *bariga* barley:
	Amar-^{ĝeš}peš$_3$	Amar-peš,
	^{lu_2}lunga$_3$	the brewer;
	1(gur) Lugal-an-dul$_3$	1 *gur*: Lugal-andul,
	dumu Amar-ig-gal	son of Amar-iggal;
ii	2(bariga) Si-du$_3$	2 *bariga*: Sidu
	2(bariga) Igi-ur-rib-ba	2 *bariga*: Igi'urriba;
	2(bariga) ĜAR-DIN	2 *bariga*: ĜARDIN;
	1(gur) i$_3$-du$_8$ ^{d}Uraš $^{ĝeš.ki}$Ĝeša$_x$(KUŠU$_2$)	1 *gur*: the doorman of Uraš('s temple at) Ĝeša.
	1(gur) E$_2$-DU-DU PI-bar	1 *gur*: EDUDU, the ...;
	2(bariga) Lugal-gaba-ĝal$_2$	2 *bariga*: Lugalgabaĝal;
iii	2(bariga) Amar-⸢Ku'ara(ḪA.A)⸣	2 *bariga*: Amar-Ku'ara;
	6 [...]	6 *gur*: ...;
	[...] ⸢x-x⸣	...;
	1(gur) ⸢*Il*-x-x-x⸣-na$^?$	1 *gur*: *Il*...;
	2(bariga) ⸢šu$^?$⸣-gaba (ras.?)	2 *bariga*: ... (entry erased?),
	2(bariga) še gur	2 *bariga* barley (in) *gur*,
iv	5 ^{uruda}ni$_3$-UD ma-na Amar-ki-ku$_3$	5 minas of ...: Amarkiku,
	ma$_2$-laḫ$_4$	the sailor;
	3 ^{uruda}ni$_3$-UD ma-na Lu$_2$-^{d}Lamma	3 minas of ...: Lu-Lamma;
	14 [+n] Amar-⸢Isin$_2$⸣	14: Amar-Isin;
rev. i	35 ^{uruda}ni$_3$-UD ma-na Utu-mu-kuš$_2$	35 minas of ...: Utu-mukuš,
	dam-gara$_3$	the merchant.
	(blank)	

ii (colophon) še ḫa-mul / Gu-na / šum$_2$-ma / *30* la$_2$ ⸢*1*⸣ mu

Barley as loan. Guna: provided. Year 29.

obv. ii 2: Cf. the same personal name Igi-ur-rib-ba at ED IIIb Ĝirsu, e.g., VS 25 no. 69 obv. vi 4. Note that IGI.UR may be read as ḫul(u).

obv. ii 5: The meaning of PI-bar, probably a professional title, is uncertain.

No. 419 – MS 3794

Account of silver and sheep, Early Dynastic IIIb, Umma region.

obv. i	½$_{\text{Umma}}$ ku$_3$-luḫ giĝ$_4$	½ shekel of pure silver:
	Ba-NI	BaNI;
	1 udu-nita Lugal-ezen	1 male sheep: Lugalezen;
	1 ku$_3$ giĝ$_4$ Lu$_2$-⸢x⸣-[...]	1 shekel of silver: Lu...;
ii	2N$_8$ ku$_3$ ⸢NINDA$_2$×ŠE⸣ giĝ$_4$	⅔ shekel of silver:
	2N$_8$ ku$_3$ ⸢NINDA$_2$×ŠE⸣ giĝ$_4$ Diĝir-lu$_2$-⸢maḫ$_{2b}$⸣	⅔ shekel of silver: Diĝirlumaḫ,
	⸢2N$_8$ ku$_3$ ⸢NINDA$_2$×ŠE giĝ$_4$⸣ / Ur-pu$_x$(LAGAB×TIL)-saĝ	⅔ shekel of silver: Urpusaĝ;
	2N$_8$ ku$_3$ ⸢NINDA$_2$×ŠE giĝ$_4$⸣	⅔ shekel of silver:
iii	Silim-Utu	Silim-Utu
	Lugal-ezen	(and) Lugalezen;
	$^{\text{šu}_2}$1N$_8$ NINDA$_2$×ŠE giĝ$_4$ Ur-saĝ-Utu	⅓ shekel of silver: Ursaĝ-Utu;
	[n] ku$_3$ giĝ$_4$ [...]	... shekels of silver ...
rev. i	⸢x-x⸣	...
	4 ⸢$^{\text{šu}_2}$1N$_8$⸣ ku$_3$ giĝ$_4$ / Ab-ba-tur	4 ⅓ shekel of silver: Abbatur;
	2 ⸢maš$_2$⸣	2 kids.
	(rest blank)	
ii	(blank)	

The text uses a unique notation for the fractions "one-third" and "two-thirds" of the shekel. The usual notations of the shekel's fractions during the ED IIIb period are::

	one third	*two thirds*
Mina	$^{\text{šu}_2}$1N$_8$^{ša} = šušana	$^{(\text{šu}_2)}$2N$_8$$^{\text{ša-(na-bi)}}$ = šanabi
Shekel	NINDA$_2$×ŠE+1N$_1$ (ma-na)	NINDA$_2$×ŠE+2N$_1$ (ma-na)

The scribal tradition of the Early Dynastic state of Umma was different. It used the notation $^{(\text{šu}_2)}$N$_8$ (giĝ$_4$) for both the shekel's and the mina's fractions "one-third" and "two-thirds" (see lexical text CUSAS 12, 6.3.1 and commentary to CUSAS 33 no. 222 rev. ii 3).

The idiosyncrasy in this text is a hybrid writing that mixes the original ED IIIa practice to notate the fractions "one-third" and "two-thirds" of the shekel as NINDA$_2$×ŠE.N$_1$ (ma-na) "n little mina(s)" with the local tradition of Umma. This results in the unique notation 2N$_8$ NINDA$_2$×ŠE giĝ$_4$ of the fractions "one-third" and "two-thirds" of the shekel.

obv i 1: The sign that is transliterated ½$_{\text{Umma}}$ is a combination of the sign N$_8$("bariga") and a vertical pointed wedge ("*DIŠ*"). This is a typical writing of the fraction one half of the mina and shekel that was used in the Umma region during the Early Dynastic and Sargonic periods. In other parts of southern Mesopotamia, the usual sign (1N$_8$×*AŠ*) was in use.

obv. ii 2: The personal name Diĝir-lu$_2$-maḫ is usually written with the sign MAḪ in the Umma corpus. The sign here is different, being the same as in CUSAS 26 no. 150 obv. iii 2 in the same name. Judging by the paleography of the sign, it is a graphic variant of AL(= maḫ$_2$) rather than of MAḪ.

No. 420 – MS 3796

Inventory of property and goods, Early Dynastic IIIb, Umma region.

This text and its duplicate (No. 421) are lists of property and goods including land, slaves, agricultural tools, items of women's clothing, lard, and wool. The reference to the "price of the house" and the fact that the text has copies suggest its legal nature. However, because witnesses are absent, it is placed in this section rather than in a section of legal documents. The uncertain meaning of the verb written ŠU precludes a proper understanding of the procedure. The document concludes with the statement that Ur-Nindulum takes the goods away. The text cannot be an exercise since it mentions people who appear in other documents from the same archive.

obv. i	1(bur$_3$) 1(eše$_3$) še aša$_5$ mu$_2$	1 *bur* 1 *eše* land (where) barley grows;
	60 še gur	60 *gur* barley;
	15 ziz$_2$ gur	15 *gur* emmer;
	2 saĝ-nita	2 male slaves;
	2 saĝ-munus	2 female slaves;
	20 ĜAR-utua$_2$(LAK777)	20 ... rams;
	4 udu-suluḫu$_2$	4 sheep with long fleece;
	30 ĝeš-ur$_3$	30 beams;
ii	2 dug i$_3$-šaḫ$_2$	2 jars of lard;
	10 i$_3$-sig$_{15}$ sila$_3$	10 *sila* of premium oil;
	5 kib$_3$(GIG) gur	5 *gur* wheat;

	1 tug$_2$-munus	1 woman's dress;
	1 ku$_3$ ma-na	1 mina silver;
	12 ku$_3$ giĝ$_4$	12 shekels silver:
	[sa$_{10}$ e$_2$]	[(it is) the price of the house.]
	[1 mar]	[1 shovel;]
	[1 GUR$_8$-da]	[1 ...]
iii	1 saĝ-⸢munus⸣	1 female slave;
	2N$_8$ ku$_3$ giĝ$_4$	⅔ mina silver (is her price?);
	1 ^{uruda}šen	1 cauldron:
	12 ku$_3$-bi giĝ$_4$	its silver (= price): 12 shekels;
	1 ⸢zabar⸣	1 cup;
	1 ^{uruda}za-ḫum	1 copper basin;
	[3 bur]	[3 stone bowls]
iv	1 ⸢x-šudul⸣	1 ... yoke(?):
	E$_2$-DU-DU	EDUDU
	e-ŠU	has ...ed.
	2 saĝ$^!$-munus	2 slave women;
	3 ni$_3$-SAL-la$_2$:saĝ	3 headbands;
	1 [i$_3$-šaḫ$_2$ dug]	1 [jar of lard;]
	[6 siki-garig$_x$-ak ma-na]	[6 minas of combed wool.]
v	Nin-sa$_6$-sa$_6$	Ninsasa
	e-ŠU	has ...ed.
	Ur-^{d}Nin-Dulum$_2$	Ur-Nindulum
	ba-de$_6$	has taken it away.
rev.	(blank)	

obv. i 6: ĜAR-utua$_2$ is probably a variety of ram. See CUSAS 33 no. 252 commentary to rev. ii 2.

obv. iv 2–3, v 1–2: e-ŠU is a verbal form. The same verb can appear in reduplicated form as ŠU-a-(ŠU-a): cf. the discussion in CUSAS 23 no. 30.

obv. iv 5: See CUSAS 33 no. 226 rev. iii 2 with commentary and additional references for this headgear.

No. 421 – MS 3810

Inventory of property and goods, Early Dynastic IIIb, Umma region.

obv. i	1(bur$_3$) 1(eše$_3$) aša$_5$ še mu$_2$	1 *bur* 1 *eše* land (where) barley grows;
	60 še gur	60 *gur* barley;
	15 ziz$_2$ gur	15 *gur* emmer;
	2 saĝ-nita	2 male slaves;
	2 saĝ-munus	2 female slaves;
	20 ĜAR-utua$_2$	20 ... rams;
	4 udu-suluḫu$_2$	4 sheep with long fleece;
	⸢30⸣ ĝeš-ur$_3$	30 beams;
ii	2 dug i$_3$-⸢šaḫ$_2$⸣	2 jars of lard;
	10 i$_3$-sig$_{15}$ ⸢sila$_3$⸣	10 *sila* of premium oil;
	5 kib$_3$(GIG) gur	5 *gur* wheat;
	1 tug$_2$:munus	1 woman's dress;
	1 ku$_3$ ma-na	1 mina silver;

	12 ku$_3$ giĝ$_4$	12 shekels silver:
	sa$_{10}$ e$_2$	(it is) the price of the house;
	1 mar	1 shovel;
	1 GUR$_8$-da	1 ...;
iii	1 saĝ-munus	1 female slave;
	2N$_8$ ku$_3$ giĝ$_4$	⅔ mina silver (is her price?);
	1 ^{uruda}šen	1 cauldron:
	12 ku$_3$-giĝ$_4$-bi	its silver (= price): 12 shekels;
	1 zabar	1 cup;
	1 ^{uruda}za-ḫum	1 copper basin;
	3 bur	3 stone bowls;
	1 ⌜x-šudul⌝	1 ... yoke(?):
iv	E$_2$-DU-DU	EDUDU
	e-⌜ŠU⌝	has ...ed.
	2 saĝ-munus	2 slave women;
	3 ni$_3$:SAL-la$_2$-saĝ	3 headbands;
	1 i$_3$-šaḫ$_2$ dug	1 jar of lard;
	6 siki-garig$_x$(ZUM×KASKAL)-ak ma-na	6 minas of combed wool:
v	Nin-sa$_6$-sa$_6$	Ninsasa
	e-ŠU	has ...ed.
	Ur-^{d}Nin-Dulum$_2$	Ur-Nindulum.
	ba-de$_6$	has taken it away.
rev.	(blank)	

obv. iv 6: The word /garig/ "comb" is written with the sign ZUM×LAGAB in ED IIIb texts from Ĝirsu. At Umma, the sign has the form ZUM×KASKAL.

No. 422 – MS 3797

Account of silver, sheep, and goats, Early Dynastic IIIb, Umma region.

obv. i	12 ku$_3$ giĝ$_4$	12 shekels silver:
	Ur-^{d}En-⌜lil$_2$⌝	Ur-Enlil,
	unu$_3$ Adab^{ki}	cattle herder (from) Adab.
	13 ⌜ku$_3$⌝ giĝ$_4$	13 shekels silver:
ii	Ur-šeš-maš	Uršešmaš.
	Lugal-si-ĝar	Lugalsiĝar
	maškim$_x$(DU$_{-šeššig}$.PA)	(is) the legal commissioner (of the transaction).
	13 ku$_3$ giĝ$_4$	13 shekels silver:
iii	Mes-du$_7$-na$_2$ kuš$_7$	Mesduna, the animal-manager;
	Lugal-ezen	Lugalezen,
	maškim$_x$(DU$_{šeššig}$.PA)	(is) the legal commissioner.
	2 A-[x] ku$_3$ ⌜su⌝-ga	2 (shekels) of silver: ... repaid(?):
iv	[break]	...
	[...] UD [...]	...
	[x] še Ur-saĝ-a$_2$-na	... barley: Ursaĝ-ana

rev. i	[n+] 10 ˹udu˺-siki	... 10 sheep for wool;
	5N$_8$ ud$_5$	5 (juvenile?) nanny goats:
	Mes-[...]	Mes....
	(blank)	
ii	[*n* mu iti *n*]	[... year, month ...]

obv. iii 4: There is no room for the writing giĝ$_4$ "shekel" in this line, which is suspicious. The interpretation of the line is uncertain. For su-ga as "compensation" ("Ersatz"), see FAOS 19 p. 236. Cf. CUSAS 33 no. 244 obv. vi 7 with commentary, for the writing su$_3$-ga for the same verb.

3.1.6 – Ropes, Nets, Implements

No. 423 – MS 2247

Account of ropes and a net, Early Dynastic IIIb, Umma region.

obv. i	4 eše$_2$-UR$^{?}$-ŠID e$_2$-ba	4 pairs of ... rope;
	1 sa-za$_3$-lu	1... net:
ii	Lugal-^{a}aga-na$_2$	Lugalagana.
	e$_2$-gal de$_6$	Brought (to) the palace.
rev.	*30* la$_2$ *2* mu / iti *12*	Year 28, month 12.

Judging by the initial signs eše$_2$ and sa, the document records the delivery of ropes and a net to the palace.

No. 424 – MS 2249

Account of covers and a plow for ox teams, Early Dynastic IIIb, Umma region.

obv. i	2 ni$_3$-dul$_5$ gu$_4$-apin gibil	New covers (for) 2 ox plow teams (= 8 oxen):
	Ur-saĝ	(for) Ursaĝ;
	2 1N$_8$ <ni$_3$-dul$_5$> gu$_4$-apin Ab-ba-tur	<Covers> (for) 2 ¼ ox plow teams (= 9 oxen): (for) Abbatur;
	1 apin	1 plow:
	[x]-⌜gu$^{?}$⌝	(for) ...gu;
ii	1 1N$_8$ ni$_3$-dul$_5$ gu$_4$-apin	Covers for 1 ¼ ox plow teams (= 5 oxen):
	Šudu$_3$-ni-du$_{10}$	(for) Šudunidu;
	1 apin	1 plow:
	Lugal-kiĝ$_2$-gal-zu	(for) Lugalkiĝalzu.
	(blank)	
	Lugal-^{a}aga-na$_2$	Lugalagana,
	tug$_2$-du$_8$-gal	the chief felter (provided).
iii	*30* la$_2$ *3* mu iti *6*	Year 27, month 6.
rev.	(blank)	

3.1.7 – Unidentified Goods

No. 425 – MS 4259

Account of unidentified goods, Early Dynastic IIIb, Umma region.

obv. i	*10* Igi-še$_3$	10: Igiše;
	7 Kar-du$_3$ *1 1 1*	7 Kardu: (3 checkmarks);
	8$_{strikethrough}$ Ur$_2$-ni	~~8~~: Urni;
	7$_{horizontal,strikethrough}$ Maš ugula	~~7~~: Maš, the overseer;
	6$_{strikethrough}$ ugula nu-banda$_3$	~~6~~: the overseer of supervisors;
	7 En-sila-si	7: Ensilasi;
	3 sukkal	3: the secretary;
	2$_{strikethrough}$ Ab-ba-tur	~~2~~: Abbatur;
ii	*2*$_{strikethrough}$ Ur-saĝ	~~2~~: Ursaĝ;
	2 Šudu$_3$-ni-du$_{10}$	2: Šudunidu;
	2 (erasure: Gu-x)	2: (erasure)
	3 Ur-saĝ-Utu	2: Ursaĝ-Utu;
	3 Mu-ni	3: Muni;
	3 E$_2$	3: E;
	3 Ur-Abzu	3: Ur-Abzu;
rev. i	*4* Ur-Šubur Ša$_3$-nu$^{!}$-ĝal$_2$	4: Ur-Šubur (and) Šanuĝal;
	4 Ur-en-nun	4: Urennun;
	4 Nin-igi-tab-ĝu$_{10}$	4: Ninigitabĝu;
	3 Ur-$^{d!}$	3: Ur...
ii	šu-niĝin$_2$ *73*	Total: 73.

This remarkable text employs three different ways to write numerals. The way they are written relates to some administrative procedures. First, obv. i 2 etc. have oblique wedges. Second, obv. i 3 etc. offer striking through the numerals. Third, obv. i 4 uses numerals written horizontally.

rev. i 4: AŠ is the beginning of an unfinished sign, probably an AN.

3.2 – Early to Middle Sargonic Documents from the Umma Region

The majority of the Early Sargonic tablets from Umma in this section date to the time of the governor *Šurus-kēn*, who administered the province of Umma during the reign of Sargon. Based on the paleography, some texts in the section may be of slightly later date.

3.2.1 – Legal

No. 426 – MS 1952/2

Sale of a house, Early Sargonic (governor *Šurus-kēn*), Umma region.

obv. i	[n+] 2 $^{\text{šu2}}$1N$_8$ 5 [giĝ$_4$] ⸢e$_2$⸣ sar	n+ 2 ⅓ *sar* 5 shekels of house area.
	[n+] 1 ku$_3$ giĝ$_4$ ⸢ma⸣-na	n+1 mina ... shekels silver:
	sa$_{10}$ e$_2$	the price of the house.
	2 ku$_3$ giĝ$_4$	2 shekels silver;
	1 ni$_3$-SAL-la$_2$-saĝ	1 headband;
	1 i$_3$ sila$_3$ šaḫ$_2$	1 *sila* lard:
	ni$_3$-ba e$_2$	the gift for the house.
	1 Ur-^{d}Tu sagi-maḫ	1 Ur-Tu(da), the chief cupbearer,
	Ama-tir	Amatir,
	AN^{ki}-ki-du$_{10}$	ANkidu,
ii	[...]	...
	[...]-⸢da/a$_2$-DAM⸣	...
	⸢Ama⸣-bara$_2$-si	Amabarasi
	I$_2$-bi$_2$-⸢bi$_2$⸣	(and) *Ibibi*,
	e$_2$ e-⸢ne⸣-še$_3$-⸢sa$_{10}$⸣	payed them for the house.
	inim-bi e-til	This matter is settled.
	1 Nin-sa$_6$-ga	1 Ninsaga,
	dam Ur-^{d}Tu sagi-maḫ	spouse of Ur-Tu(da), the chief cupbearer;
	1 Nagar-ša$_3$	1 Nagarša;
	[1] ⸢Mes⸣-e$_2$-zi-da	1 Mes-ezida;
iii	[...]	...
	1 ⸢Niĝar⸣	1 Niĝar;
	1 Ur-[^{d}Nin]-⸢Dulum$_2$⸣	1 Ur-Nindulum,
	dumu Ur-[^{d}Tu] ⸢sagi⸣-[maḫ]	son of Ur-Tuda, the chief cupbearer;
	1 Ur$_2$-[ni$^?$]	1 Urni(?);
	1 Ur-^{d}[x]	1 Ur...;
	1 A.BU.[BU$^?$] ⸢sagi⸣	1 ABUBU(?), the cupbearer;
	1 Šubur [dam$^?$]-gara$_3$	1 Šubur, the merchant(?);
	1 Amar-[x]	1 Amar...;
	1 ⸢Du$^?$⸣-[du] ⸢šeš⸣ [...]	1 Dudu(?), brother of ...;
rev. i	[...]	...
	1 Lu$_2$-[x]-⸢ga⸣	1 Lu...ga;
	1 Šeš-[x]	1 Šeš...;
	1 ⸢Sig$_5$⸣-[x]	1 Sig...;
	1 Lugal-[x]	1 Lugal...;
	1 KA-AN-[x]	1 ...;
	1 UD-⸢x⸣-še [(x)]	1 UD...;
	1 Ur-^{d}⸢Nagar⸣ šidim	1 Ur-Nagar, the builder;
	1 ⸢Ama-emeda(UM.ME)⸣-[(zi)]	1 Ama'ededazi;
	[*ca.* 3 lines broken]	...:
ii	lu$_2$-[ki-inim]-ma-[bi-me]	they are its witnesses.
	1 A$_2$-kal-le um-⸢mi⸣-a	1 Akale, the master scribe;
	1 Ak ⸢um-mi-a⸣	1 Ak(a), the master scribe;
	1 Ur-^{d}Nagar dub-sar	1 Ur-Nagar, the scribe;

	1 Ĝiri$_2$-nun niĝir	1 Ĝirinun, the herald;
	1 Nin-⸢^{d}⸣En-⸢lil$_2$-x⸣ dub-sar	1 Nin-Enlil..., the scribe;
	1 Ama-kur-⸢ra⸣	1 Amakura;
	1 Me-me-⸢x⸣	1 Meme...:
	e$_2$-gi$_4$-a Ur-sa$_6$-ga-me	they (the last two persons) are daughters-in-law of Ursaga.
	(blank/ruling)	
	u$_4$-ba uruda ⸢ma-na⸣	When a mina of copper,
	ku$_3$-bi [...]	its silver [n was weight out].
iii	u$_4$-ba ⸢*Su$_4$-ru-us$_2$*-GI⸣ / ensi$_2$-⸢ke$_4$$^?$⸣	When *Šurus-kēn* (was) the governor.
	330 ninda-banšur	330 table breads;
	1 kaš dug	1 jar of beer;
	10 ku$_6$-dar-ra	10 split fish;
	1 ku$_6$ saĝ-⸢keše$_2$⸣	1 string of fish.
	[n+] *3* mu	Year n+3.

obv. i 5: For this item, see CUSAS 33 no. 226 commentary to rev. iii 2.

obv. i 6: The signs I$_3$+SILA$_3$ are written as ligature.

obv. i 9: This person appears in documents from the time of Lugalzagesi. See, e.g., BIN 8 no. 49 obv. i 2, where he/she is associated with the household/building e$_2$-saḫar.

obv. i 10: AN$^{(ki)}$ is a writing for the town Ki'AN in the Umma region; see CUSAS 14 p. 2.

rev. iii 1: *Šurus-kēn* was the governor who ruled the province of Umma during the reigns of Sargon and Rimuš. He was a contemporary of Meskigala, the governor of Adab: see Visicato 2012: 169–74, esp. 170, 172; Marchesi 2015: 151.

No. 427 – MS 1952/3

Sale of house, Early Sargonic, Umma region.

The text is similar to the preceding and also belongs to the time of *Šurus-kēn*.

obv. i	[... e$_2$] ⸢sar x⸣	... *sar* of house area:
	[... ^{d}Aš$_8$]-gi$_4$-[ur$_5$]-⸢du$_2$⸣	... Ašgi'urdu.
	1 ku$_3$ [...]	1 [mina] silver ...
	[rest of the column defaced]	...
ii	[*ca.* 5 lines defaced]	...
	⸢2 siki ma-na⸣	2 minas of wool:
	⸢Pu$_x$(LAGAB×TIL)⸣-ta	Puta;
	⸢2 siki⸣ ma-na	2 minas of wool:
	⸢Sa$_6$⸣-da	Sada;
	[2] ⸢siki⸣ ma-na	[2] minas of wool:
	Ama-bara$_2$-ge	Amabarage;
	[break]	...
iii	[break]	...
	⸢1N$_8$ x⸣-ga	1 ...ga;
	⸢1N$_8$ Ur-x-x-AN-ne$_2$	1 Ur...;

	⸢1N$_8$ Ur-^{d}x⸣	1 Ur...;
	[1N$_8$ ...]-ni	[1] ...ni;
	⸢1N$_8$ Ad-da⸣	1 Adda,
	dumu Ĝeš-ša$_3$ ⸢x⸣ KA ⸢x⸣	son of Ĝešša, ...;
	[...] ⸢AN⸣ [...]	...
	1N$_8$ Lugal-[x]	1 Lugal...,
	⸢dumu Gan⸣-[x]	son of Gan...,
	maškim	the commissioner;
	1N$_8$ Ur-⸢^{d}Nin$^{?}$⸣-[...]	1 Ur-Nin...;
rev. i	[...]	...,
	šu-⸢i$_{tenû}$⸣	the barber;
	1N$_8$ Šeš-⸢x⸣ Igi-diĝir-še$_3$ ⸢x⸣	1 Šeš... (and) Igidiĝirše, ...;
	1N$_8$ Silim-⸢^{d}⸣[Utu]	1 Silim-[Utu],
	dumu Šeš-[x]	son of Šeš...;
	[3 lines broken]	...
	1 ku$_3$ ⸢giĝ$_4$⸣	1 shekel silver:
	Ur-⸢saĝ$^{?}$-zi$^{?}$⸣	Ursaĝzi(?)
	Gu-nun	(and) Gunun
	[x] igi-*3*-⸢ĝal$_2$⸣	... ⅓ (shekel):
	[2 lines broken]	...
	PA-[...]	...
ii	[...]-kar	...kar;
	[...]-⸢x⸣-ŠE$_3^{?}$-BU	...,
	ugula šu-ku$_6$-ne	the overseer of fishermen;
	1N$_8$ E$_2$-ki	1 Eki,
	lu$_2$ E$_2$-kisal	the man of Ekisal;
	1N$_8$ ⸢Ur⸣-da-da	1 Urdada;
	[...]-⸢x⸣	
	1N$_8$ ⸢^{d}⸣[x]-⸢x⸣-da	1 ...da,
	šu-i$_{-tenû}$	the barber;
	1N$_8$ Ur-e$_2$-maḫ nar	1 Ur-emaḫ, musician;
	1N$_8$ Ĝeš-ša$_3$	1 Ĝešša;
	1N$_8$ Ur-^{d}[...]-⸢x⸣	1 Ur...;
	[...] Ur-^{d}Nin-tu	... Ur-Nintu.
	⸢lu$_2$⸣-ki-inim-ma-me	They are the witnesses.
	ki ĝeš-rin$_2$-bi i$_3$-ak	He made the place of weighing scales (i.e. established the silver's weight).
	ša$_3$-bi i$_3$-su	He reimbursed its amount.
	[...]-nagar [...]	...nagar ...;
iii	[...]	...
	[...]-⸢kam⸣	It is ... of ...
	[n+] 60 ninda-banšur	n+60 table breads;
	90 saĝ-ninda	90 *saĝ*-breads;
	1 1/2$_{Umma}$ kaš dug	1 ½ jars of beer;
	1 tu$_7$ utul$_2$	1 bowl of soup.
	10 mu *3* ⸢iti⸣	Year 10, month 3.

rev. ii 15: The compound verb ki ĝeš-rin$_2$-bi ... ak must refer to the process of weighing. The next line also refers to silver.

rev. iii 4: For this type of bread, see USP p. 15.

rev. iii 6: Both signs are KAM(ḪI×TIL): cf. MC 4 pp. 15–19 for a discussion of this and similar signs.

No. 428 – MS 1952/12

Record contesting the purchase of a slave, Middle Sargonic, Umma region?

obv.	Ĝiri$_3$-⸢x-x⸣	Ĝiri...
	mu-[ni]	his name,
	arad$_2$	the slave
	Ur-^{d}Nisaba	(of) Ur-Nisaba (he is).
	aš$_2$-de$_3$	from
	⸢Lugal-x-x⸣	Lugal...,
rev.	šeš	brother
	Du^{sic}-ga-ni	(of) Dugani
	u$_3$-la sa$_{10}$	has not purchased(?).
4–5	(indistinct traces of signs written on dry clay)...	

rev. 2: Note the unorthographic writing Du-ga-ni instead of the usual Du$_{11}$-ga-ni. This fact, the crude large writing, and the use of Akkadian language suggest that the tablet was written in a private context.

rev. 3: *u$_3$-la* = /'ulā/ is an Old Akkadian particle of negation: see Hasselbach 2005: 288.

rev. 4: The beginning of the line may have the sign combination PA.TE.SI = ensi$_2$.

No. 429 – MS 1952/13

Legal document concerning a person contesting his slave status, Early/Middle Sargonic, Umma region.

obv.	[...]-⸢x⸣-pa-e$_3$	...pa'e (personal name?);
	[x] ⸢e$_2$⸣-du$_7$-e	[son of] ... (personal name?):
	KAL-KIŠ(LAK248) dumu Ĝir$_2$-⸢su⸣^{ki}-ke$_4$	KALKIŠ, the citizen of Ĝirsu,
	ir$_{11}$(UŠ×KUR)-ĝu$_{10}$ bi$_2$-du$_{11}$	he has said: "(This is) my slave"
	Za-bum$_2$-ma ba-de$_6$	(and) has taken him for himself at *Zabum*.
	ki-⸢tuš⸣-ni ⸢x⸣-saĝ	His place of residence ...
	⸢x-x⸣-[...]	... (personal name)
	maškim-bi	its commissioner.
	u$_4$ nam-ir$_{11}$-ra-ni	If his slave status
rev.	nu-gi-na	cannot be confirmed,
	KAL-KIŠ nu-du$_{11}$-am$_3$	KALKIŠ should not claim it (anymore).
	(blank)	
	1 mu *10* la$_2$ *1* iti	Year 1, month 9.

3.2.2 – Personnel

No. 430 – MS 1952/1

Withdrawal of workers (saĝ-dub, šeš-sur$_x$-ra) in teams, Early/Middle Sargonic, Umma region.

obv. i	1N$_8$ Saĝ-lu$_2$	1 (team): Saĝlu,
	⸢Lu$_2$⸣-ulu$_3$(ĜIŠGAL)-ni	Lu'uluni,
	A$_2$-ni-ta	(and) Anita.
	1N$_8$ Lugal-e-su$_3$	1: Lugalesu,
	Ur-a$_2$	Ur-a,
	Lugal-a$_2$	Lugal-a.
	1N$_8$ E$_2$-ki-aĝ$_2$	1: Eki'aĝ,
	Ur-^{d}⸢x-x⸣	Ur...,
	Ur-^{d}Nin-Dulum$_2$	Ur-Nindulum.
	1N$_8$ Amar-Ku'ara(ḪA.A)	1: Amar-Ku'ara,
	Lu$_2$-ma-DU	LumaDU.
	(blank)	
	1N$_8$ Du$_{11}$-ga-ni	1: Dugani,
	E$_2$-ḫa-lu-ub$_2$	Eḫalub,
	Ur-⸢e$_2$⸣	Ur-e.
	1N$_8$ Ur-^{d}[Nin]-⸢Dulum$_2$⸣	1: Ur-Nindulum,
	Ad-⸢da⸣	Adda.
	(blank)	
	1N$_8$ Ur-ama-⸢na⸣	1: Ur-amana,
	(illegible)	…
	(illegible)	…
ii	1N$_8$ Lugal-zi	1: Lugalzi,
	Ĝeš-ša$_3$ saĝ Ur-^{d}Nin-dulum$_2$-še$_3$	Ĝešša, in place of Ur-Nindulum,
	Niĝar	Niĝar,
	Ur-^{d}Šubur	Ur-Šubur.
	1N$_8$ Lugal-nir-ĝal$_2$	1: Lugalnirĝal,
	Lugal-⸢x⸣-me-zi	Lugal...mezi,
	E-ta	Eta.
	1N$_8$ Ur-tur	1: Urtur,
	Si-du$_3$	Sidu.
	(blank)	
	1N$_8$ ⸢Ur-^{d}x-še$_3$⸣	1: Ur...,
	Ur-⸢x-IM$^{?}$⸣	Ur...,
	⸢Mu⸣-ni	Muni.
	[1N$_8$ …]-ša$_3$	1: ...ša,
	[Ur-^{d}]⸢En⸣-ni-zu	Ur-Ennizu,
	Lugal-KA	LugalKA.
	1N$_8$ Lugal-nagar-zi	1: Lugalnagarzi,
	⸢Dub-saĝ-e⸣	Dubsaĝe,
	[4 lines broken]	…
iii	⸢Lugal-en⸣-tar-su$_3$	Lugalentarsu.
	1N$_8$ E$_2$-si	1: Esi,
	Lugal-ni$_3$	Lugalni,
	Šeš-kur-ra	Šeškura.

	1N$_8$ Ur-^{d}*Er*$_x$(LAK248)-*ra*	1: Ur-*Erra*,
	E$_2$-ḫa-lu-ub$_2$	Eḫalub.
	1N$_8$ Ur-^{d}Muš-nu-de$_3$	1: Ur-Mušnude,
	E$_2$-kur	Ekur,
	E$_2$-zi-diri	Ezidiri.
	1N$_8$ ⸢Lugal⸣-Dulum$_2$	1: Lugal-Dulum,
	Ur-^{ĝeš}gigir$_2$	Urgigir,
	Ur-^{d}Nin-⸢Dulum$_2$⸣	Ur-Nindulum.
	1N$_8$ Ur-^{d}[x]-ma-[x]	1: Ur...ma...,
	E$_2$-⸢x⸣	E...,
	⸢x-x⸣	...,
	Ur-⸢x⸣-[...]	Ur...
	1N$_8$ [...]	1: ...
	[*ca.* 5 lines broken]	...
iv	1N$_8$ Tir-⸢ku$_3$⸣	1: Tirku,
	Lugal-kur	Lugalkur,
	Lugal-zi	Lugalzi.
	1N$_8$ Lugal-tir	1: Lugaltir,
	Ur-^{d}Ur$_3$	Ur-(Nin)ur,
	E$_2$-⸢kur⸣	Ekur.
	1N$_8$ Ur-[...]	1: Ur...,
	Ur-[...]	Ur...
	(blank)	
	1N$_8$ Saĝ-⸢x⸣	1: Saĝ...,
	⸢x x⸣	...,
	⸢Ĝir$_2$⸣-[...]	Ĝir...
	1N$_8$ [...]	1: ...;
	[*ca.* 10 lines broken]	
rev. i	šu+niĝin$_2$ 30 saĝ-dub	Total: 30 permanent workers,
	53 šeš-sur$_x$(ERIN$_2$)-ra	53 team workers:
	erin$_2$ Ne-saĝ nu-banda$_3$-ta	The working troops that have been taken away,
	⸢ba⸣-de$_6$-a	from (the labor of) Nesaĝ, the supervisor.
	Ur$_2$-mud	Urmud
	⸢maškim⸣-bi	(is) its commissioner.
	ensi$_2$ ĝanun-⸢maḫ⸣	The governor has *assigned them*(?) (to/from) the main grain store.
	ba-⸢SAR$^{?}$⸣-SAR	
	(blank space)	
	4$^{?}$ mu iti *10*	Year 4, month 10.

The text shows that two to four workers made up a team. Notably, the term erin$_2$ "people" (= crown dependents or similar) is used here as an umbrella term for two categories of workers, saĝ-dub and šeš-sur$_x$-ra.

obv. iii 7: The deity is probably different from ^{d}Nu-muš-da.

obv. iv 5: For the temple of ^{d}Nin-ur$_3$, see text No. 507 obv. 3.

rev. i 1–2: See FAOS 15/2 pp. 230–31 for a discussion of these terms for workers.

rev. i 8 : The damaged sign in the middle has slight traces of what might be another SAR. The interpretation is tentative and is based on the verb sar "to write down."

rev. i 9: The first numeral may instead be 13.

No. 431 – MS 1952/4

Withdrawal of people who "went to the city," Early Sargonic, Umma region.

obv. i	[1N$_8$] ⸢x-x-x⸣	...
	[1N$_8$ Ur-^{d}]Nagar	... Ur-Nagar;
	[1N$_8$] Sa$_6$-[da]	... Sada;
	[1N$_8$] ⸢Ak$^{?}$⸣ nu-banda$_3$-⸢bi⸣	1 Ak(?), their supervisor;
	1N$_8$ KUM-DUR$_2$-še$_3$	1 KUMDURše;
	1N$_8$ E$_2$-⸢da⸣ ugula-⸢iri⸣ / ⸢Ur$^{?}$⸣-^{d}Nin-sig$_x$(SAR)	
		1 Eda, the overseer of the city, (and) Ur-Ninsig;
	⸢1N$_8$⸣ Da-da nu-banda$_3$-bi	1 Dada, their supervisor;
	1N$_8$ Du$_{11}$-ga-ni	1 Dugani;
	1N$_8$ Amar-ki	1 Amarki(ku);
ii	[...]	...
	1N$_8$ Pu$_x$(LAGAB×TIL)-[ta]	1 Puta;
	1N$_8$ Ad-da-⸢gi/zi⸣	1 Adda...;
	Ad-da-[x]	(and) Adda...
	1N$_8$ ⸢Az⸣-[x]	1 Az...
	(blank)	
	šu-niĝin$_2$ 10 la$_2$ 1 ⸢lu$_2$⸣	Total: 9 persons.
	lu$_2$ zi-⸢ga⸣ iri ere$_x$(DU.DU)-me	The persons (are) withdrawn. They are (those who) went (to) the city.
	(rest blank)	
rev.	(blank)	

obv. i 4 f.: The suffix =bi is used here to refer to the individuals belonging to the team of each respective supervisor or "captain," if the text describes the recruitment of military men.

obv. ii 7: Alternatively, lu$_2$ ... iri gub-gub-me "these are persons who are at service in the city."

No. 432 – MS 1952/5

Transfer of craftsmen (ĝeš-kiĝ$_2$-ti), Middle/Classical Sargonic, Umma region.

obv. i	1N$_8$ Lugal-⸢kas$_4^?$⸣	1 Lugalkas(?);
	A$_2$-kal-le	Akale,
	um-mi-a mu-de$_6$	the master scribe, has brought him here.
	1N$_8$ *Be$_6$-li$_2$-li$_2$*	1 *Bēl-'ilī*:
	Amar-lu$_2$ ⸢ba⸣-laḫ$_5$-ḫe	Amarlu has taken them away.
	1N$_8$ Lugal-igi	1 Lugaligi,
	1N$_8$ Amar-^{d}Ašnan$_x$(TIR)	1 Amar-Ašnan:
	⸢Gal⸣-zu ku$_3$-dim$_2$-e	Galzu, the goldsmith:
	[ba]-laḫ$_5$-ḫe	has taken them away.
	[1N$_8$] Kur-ra	[1] Kura,
	[(1N$_8$) x]-DU-a	[1$^?$] ...DUa:
	[(x)] ⸢Sa$_6$⸣-ga ba-laḫ$_5$-ḫe	Saga has taken them away.
	[1N$_8$...]-ta	...
	[break]	
ii	1N$_8$ Lu$_2$-mu-⸢x⸣	1: Lumu...:
	Ne-saĝ ašgab	Nesaĝ, the leather-worker,
	ba-laḫ$_5$	has taken them away.
	A$_2$-kal-le	Akale,
	um-mi-a mu-de$_6$	the master scribe, has brought him here.
	šu-niĝin$_2$ 8 ĝeš-kiĝ$_2$-ti ba-laḫ$_5$-ḫe	Total: 8 craftsmen. They have been taken.
	1N$_8$ Ur-^{d}Ab-⸢U$_2$⸣	1: Ur-Ab-U:
	Ur-^{d}Šara$_2$ (ras.)	Ur-Šara,
	dumu ensi$_2$-ka-ke$_4$	son of the governor,
	ba-de$_6$	has taken away.
	1N$_8$ ĜA$_2$-NE$^?$-nam-munus	1: ...
	Ur-^{d}Nin-aga$_3$-da	Ur-Ninagada,
	x [...]	...
	[break]	...
rev. i	[...] ⸢x⸣ [...]	...
	[n] lu$_2$ um-mi-a mu-laḫ$_5$-a-me	These are x persons who were brought here by the master scribe.
	(blank space)	
	ensi$_2$ ⸢x-x⸣	The governor ...,
	e-⸢x-ne⸣-[x]	has ...ed [them] to them.
	3 mu *11* ⸢iti⸣	Year 3, month 11.

obv. ii 13: The unidentified sign looks like ŠE plus a ŠUBUR-like sign. See the index of unidentified signs.

No. 433 – MS 2191/13

Record of two persons residing with another, Early/Middle Sargonic, Umma region.

obv.	[(x)] Du-du	Dudu,
	[(x)] Ur-saĝ	Ursaĝ:
	(blank space)	
	gan-durun$_x$(DUR$_2$.DUR$_2$)-⸢me⸣	they are tenants.
	Lugal-bara$_2$-[da]	With Lugalbara
	e-da-se$_{12}$	they live.
rev.	*8* iti	Month 8.

obv. 3: See Jagersma 2010: 130 for gan-tuš/ga-an-tuš "tenant."

No. 434 – MS 2191/38

Account of erin$_2$-people, Early/Middle Sargonic, Umma?

obv.	erin$_2$ mu-sar-ra	The *eren*-people that were written down;
	ša$_3$-bi-ta	out of them:
	1 Lugal-ezen	1 Lugalezen;
	1 Lugal-aja$_2$	1 Lugalaja:
	nu-se$_{12}$	they do not dwell (there);
	1 Ur-emeda(UM.ME)-ga	1 Ur-emedaga:
	tu-⸢ra⸣-am$_3$	he is sick.
	[...]-am$_3$	he is …
edge	[...]-⸢gi$_4$⸣	…
rev.	⸢Ur⸣-^{d}Sumugan(ĜIR$_3$)	Ur-Sumugan,
	⸢SAĜ?⸣-ra	(to) …,
	i$_3$-na-šum$_2$	he has given.
	(blank space)	

obv. 1: For erin$_2$ as a class of free royal dependents owing labor to the crown during the Ur III period, see Steinkeller 2013b: 350 f. Mu-sar-ra is here a verbal form and not related to the word "inscription," mu-sar-ra = Akk. *musarû*.

obv. 6: The name Ur-emedaga appears in Nik 2 no. 88 obv. 4 from Umma.

3.2.3 – Grain and Grain Products

No. 435 – MS 1952/7

Expenditure (si) of emmer to a number of individuals, Middle Sargonic, Umma.

obv. i	2 imĝaĝa$_3$(AŠ$_2$.AN) gur	2 *gur* emmer:
	Ma$_2$-gur$_8$	Magur;
	1(gur) 2(bariga) En-ki-aĝ$_2$	1 *gur* 2 *bariga*: Enki'aĝ;
	1(gur) 2(bariga) Niĝir-kisal	1 *gur* 2 *bariga*: Niĝirkisal
	1(gur) 2(bariga) Ur-^{d}Nagar ⸢x-AD⸣	1 *gur* 2 *bariga*: Ur-Nagar, the …;
	1(gur) ⸢Mes⸣-e$_2$	1 *gur*: Mes-e;
	1(gur) 2(bariga) Ur-⸢^{d}Nagar engar⸣	1 *gur* 2 *bariga*: Ur-Nagar, the agricultural manager;
	1(gur) Ur-^{d}Nagar E$_2$-⸢me⸣-kam	1 *gur*: Ur-Nagar, he is of Eme;
	1(gur) 2(bariga) Lugal-⸢inim-gi⸣ / ⸢x⸣ UNUG⸢^{ki}-x⸣	1 *gur* 2 *bariga*: Lugalinimgi …;
	1(gur) 2(bariga) ⸢Du-du⸣ lu$_2$-eše$_2$-gid$_2$	1 *gur* 2 *bariga*: Dudu, the field-surveyor
	[1(gur) 2(bariga)] ⸢Ĝeš⸣-ša$_3$ u$_2$-il$_2$	[1 *gur* 2 *bariga*]: Ĝešša, the carrier;
	[1(gur) 2(bariga)] ⸢Lugal⸣-du$_{11}$-ga-ni	[1 *gur* 2 *bariga*]: Lugaldugani;
	[1(gur) 2(bariga) x]-^{d}Gašam$_x$(TAG.NUN)	[1 *gur* 2 *bariga*]: ...Gašam;
ii	[2 lines broken]	…
	⸢x⸣-[…]	…
	[1(gur)] 2(bariga) Ur-[...]	[1 *gur*] 2 *bariga*: Ur...;
	1(gur) 2(bariga) Ur-e$_2$-sir$_2$-ra	1 *gur* 2 *bariga*: Ur-esira;
	1(gur) 2(bariga) Lugal-Abzu-⸢a⸣	1 *gur* 2 *bariga*: Lugal-Abzu'a;
	1(gur) 2(bariga) Lugal-kur	1 *gur* 2 *bariga*: Lugalkur;
	1(gur) 2(bariga) Ad-da Lugal-ni$_3$	1 *gur* 2 *bariga*: Adda (and) Lugalni;
	1(gur) 2(bariga) Ur-TAR U$_2^?$-ba$^?$	1 *gur* 2 *bariga*: UrTAR…;
	1(gur) Ur-^{d}E$_2$-mi-la-zu	1 *gur*: Ur-Emilazu.
	(blank)	
	šu-niĝin$_2$ 30 la$_2$ 1	Total: 29 *gur*.
rev. i	imĝaĝa$_3$ dub-sar-kam	It is emmer of the scribe.
	⸢e-ne⸣-si	He has filled it for them.
	[x]-da sa$_{12}$-du$_5$-ka	... the land-recorder,
	[maškim]-bi	(is) its commissioner.
ii	[*n* mu iti *n*]	[Year *n*, month *n*].
	(blank)	

obv. i 1: imĝaĝa$_3$ "emmer" is written AŠ$_2$.AN at Umma, unlike the writing ZIZ$_2$.AN of the Adab documents.

obv. ii 9: Cf. the Ur III period name Ur-TAR-luḫ-ta. The last sign here cannot be TA, however. Cf. also the name Ur-TAR-KID$^?$ in Umma texts BIN 8 nos. 105 obv. 5, 107 obv. i 2, 4, 234 obv. i 6.

rev. i 3: The sign KA at the end is unexpected.

No. 436 – MS 1952/9

Allocation of barley flour to individuals native to Zabala, Early/Middle Sargonic, Umma region.

obv. i	[1(bariga)] ⸢dabin⸣	1 *bariga* barley flour:
	⸢Lugal⸣-mes-e niĝir	Lugalmese, the herald;
	1(bariga) Da-da	1 *bariga*: Dada,
	lu$_2$ Ur-si [(x)]	the man of Ursi;
	1(bariga) Lugal-⸢nagar⸣-zi	1 *bariga*: Lugalnagarzi,
	dumu Ama-⸢bara$_2$⸣-si	son of Amabarasi;
	1(bariga) Ama-bara$_2$-si	1 *bariga*: Amabarasi,
	dumu Tir-ku$_3$ niĝir	son of Tirku, the herald;
	[1(bariga)] ⸢x⸣-DIŠ-MU	1 *bariga*: …,
	[dumu] Tir-ku$_3$ niĝir	[son of] Tirku, the herald;
	[...]-Abzu	[1 *bariga*] ...-Abzu;
	[...]-ga	...
	[...]-an-ne$_2$	...
ii	1(bariga) [..]	1 *bariga*: ...,
	dumu Ša$_3$-TAR	son of ŠaTAR;
	1(bariga) Gala	1 *bariga*: Gala,
	dumu Ur-a$_2$	son of Ur-a;
	1(bariga) Lugal-ša$_3$	1 *bariga*: Lugalša,
	dumu KA×ŠU-la-ni	son of Šu'ilani.
	(blank)	
	dumu Zabala$_5^{ki}$-me	They are citizens of Zabala.
	Inim-zi-da-ke$_4$	Inimzida
	e-PA-X-ne	…
	Zabala$_5^{ki}$-ta	They have left
	e-er$_x$(DU.DU)-re-eš$_2$	Zabala.
rev. i	[Inim-zi]-⸢da⸣	[Inimzi]da
	[maškim]-bi	(is) its [commissioner].
	(blank)	
	4 mu *13* iti / ⸢u$_4^?$ n⸣	Year 4, month 13, day(?) …

obv. ii 2: See SCTRAH commentary to no. 216 obv. 5 for this personal name.

obv. ii 6: The reading here of KA×ŠU, usually šudu$_3$ "prayer," is uncertain. In view of the final consonant /l/ and the similar name šu-il$_2$-la-ni (PPAC 1 nos. 685+734 obv. 9; Sargonic Adab), KA×ŠU may have the reading /šu'il/ "hand-raising = prayer."

obv. ii 10: The sign after PA is uncertain. The line may be a verbal form.

rev. 3: The form of ITI is typical of the Early Sargonic texts from Umma.

No. 437 – MS 1952/10

Account of large amounts of barley, Early/Middle Sargonic, Umma region.

obv. i	60 še gur-saĝ-ĝal$_2$	60 *gursaĝĝal* barley:
	I$_3$-lu-sar nu-banda$_3$	*'Ilu(m)-šar*, the supervisor;
	60 Maš nu-banda$_3$	60: Maš, the supervisor;
	60 Gi-nun-ba	60: Ginunba;
	60 A-da-da	60: Adada;
	60 Eš$_3$-me-gara$_2$	60: Ešmegara;
	60 Dulum$_2$	60: Dulum;
	50 Ur-^{d}Nagar	50: Ur-Nagar;
	[(n+)] 20 Teš$_2$-teš$_2$	n + 20: Tešteš;
	[n] ⸢Tir⸣-ku$_3$	n: Tirku;
	[break]	
ii	<n> Ur-si-ĝar	<n> Ursiĝar;
	<n> Lugal-Utu-am$_6$	<n> Lugal-Utu'am;
	<n> nu-banda$_3$ kalam-ĜIR$_3^?$ ⸢(x)⸣	<n> the supervisor of …;
	<n> ugula-e$_2$ ^{d}Nin-ur$_4$	<n> the overseer of the household of (the deity) Nin-ur;
	<n> Ur$_{4\text{-}gun\hat{u}}$-ša$_3$	<n> Urša;
	<n> Lugal-kur	<n> Lugalkur;
	40 Ad-da	40: Adda;
	60 Gu$_2$-en	60: Gu'en;
	(blank)	
	šu-niĝin$_2$ < > [(x)]	Total: < >

rev. i–ii [*n* mu iti *n*][Year ..., month ...]

obv. ii 5: The sign UR$_4$ has several wedges inside that resemble *gunû*-strokes.

No. 438 – MS 1952/28

Receipt of barley, Early Sargonic, Umma region.

obv.	4(ban$_2$) zi$_3$ A-ga-de$_3^{ki}$	4 *ban* flour (by the *gur* of) Akkade;
	Gan-tu-da nu-banda$_3$-ke$_4$	Gantuda, the supervisor,
	šu ba-ti	has received.
	⸢x⸣-a-gal	...agal
	⸢maškim-bi⸣	(is) its commissioner.
rev.	5 mu 7 iti	Year 5, month 7.

No. 439 – MS 1952/31

Delivery and receipt of beer and bread, Early Sargonic, Umma region.

obv.	[...] sa$_2$-du$_{11}$ gur$_8$-⸢gur$_8^?$⸣	n *gurgur*-jars of ... as regular offerings;
	[...] ⸢x⸣ gur$_8$-gur$_8$	n *gurgur*-jars of ...;
	[n] ninda 6 saĝ-ĝar	n breads, 6 *saĝĝar*-breads;
	⸢UŠ$^?$⸣-*bum*	UŠ*bum*(?)
	⸢x-kar-KA$^?$⸣-URUDA	...
	Zabala$_6^{ki}$-ta	from Zabala
	⸢mu⸣-de$_6$	he has brought here.
rev.	šu ba-ti	He has received it.
	En-ḪU-ni-ĝal$_2$	EnḪUniĝal,
	aga$_3$-us$_2$ *I$_3$-li$_2$-be$_6$-li$_2$*	the soldier of *'Ilī-bēlī*,
	maškim-bi	(is) its commissioner.
	En-⸢maḫ$^?$-x / x-x⸣	En...
	[n] mu iti *7*	year x, month 7.

obv. 1–2: See Sallaberger 1996: 51–52, 56, for this vessel, a variety of jar used for liquids. Sa$_2$-du$_{11}$ of the first line might refer to its capacity: 40 sila$_3$ during the Sargonic period (ibid. p. 56).

obv. 3: For ninda-saĝ-ĝar, see MSL 11 p. 120 l. 59.

rev. 5: Indistinct signs, which must have been added after the tablet was finished.

3.2.4 – Livestock

No. 440 – MS 1952/16a

Record of oxen living with a herdsman, Middle Sargonic, Umma region.

obv.	4 gu$_4$	4 oxen:
	Ur-i$_7$ unu$_3$-da	with Ur-i(da), the cowherd,
	e-da-se$_{12}$	they live.
	[break]	
rev.	[break]	
	(blank)	

No. 441 – MS 1952/17

Account of sheep, Early/Middle Sargonic, Umma region.

obv.	*60* udu-nita	60 male sheep;
	100 la$_2$ *2* u$_8$	98 ewes;
	20 kir$_{11}$ e$_3$-li bar-ĝal$_2$-la	20 female spring-born lambs with fleece;
	20 la$_2$ *1* sila$_4$ ⸢x-x-x-x⸣	19 ... (male) lambs;
	[n+] *126* siki ⸢ma-na⸣	x+126 minas wool.
	(blank)	
	⸢A$_2$⸣-kal-le sipa-bi	Akale (is) their shepherd.

rev.	udu ur$_4$-ra e$_2$ Gala kuš$_7$	Sheep that are ready for plucking; (in) the house(hold) of Gala, the animal-manager.
	udu X ⸢x⸣-kam	The sheep are the … of …
	3 mu iti *7*	Year 3, month 7.

rev. 2: The unidentified sign X after udu looks like a suspicious U$_2$ finished by a diagonal wedge.

No. 442 – MS 1952/20

Expenditure of hides, Middle Sargonic, Umma region.

The top corners are fake.

obv.	[n+] 4 kuš [x]	x+4 … hides;
	25 kuš-⸢ab$_2$⸣	25 cowhides.
	kuš e$_2$-⸢kešda$^?$⸣	The hides of the spinning workshop(?).
	Šubur dub-⸢sar-e⸣	Šubur, the scribe,
rev.	Da-da	to Dada,
	dub-sar-ra	the scribe,
	i$_3$-na-šum$_2$	has given.
	6 mu *10* iti	Year 6, month 10.

obv. 3: The reading of the broken sign is uncertain. For the building e$_2$-kešda-a, see commentary to No. 23 rev. ii 3.

3.2.5 – Textiles

No. 443 – MS 1952/15

Allocation of textiles to high-ranking persons from Nippur and Irisaĝrig by the governor *Šurus-kēn* in the temple household Eĝidru; Early Sargonic, Umma region.

obv.	1 ^{tug_2}ša$_3$-ga-du$_3$	1 *šagadu*-garment;
	1 ^{tug_2}ni$_3$-la$_2$	1 *nila*-garment;
	1 ^{tug_2}ni$_3$-lam$_2$	1 *nilam*-garment;
	1 ^{tug_2}DUL$_3$	1 DUL-garment:
	tug$_2$ uš-[bar$^?$] -⸢am$_3$$^?$⸣	these are garments of *ušbar* quality(?).
	A-ba-^{d}En-lil$_2$ šeš ⸢ensi$_2$⸣ / Nibru$^{[ki]}$-ka-⸢kam⸣	It is for Aba'Enlil, brother of the governor of Nippur.
	1 ^{tug_2}ša$_3$-⸢ga-du$_3$⸣	1 *šagadu*-garment;
	1 ^{tug_2}ni$_3$-lam$_2$	1 *nilam*-garment:
	⸢Lugal⸣-kar-si lu$_2$-⸢mah$^?$⸣ Nibru^{ki}	(for) Lugalkarsi, the *lumah*-priest(?) of Nippur.
	1 $^{[tug_2]}$⸢ša$_3$⸣-ga-du$_3$	1 *šagadu*-garment;
	1 ^{tug_2}ni$_3$-la$_2$	1 *nila*-garment;
rev.	1 ^{tug_2}ni$_3$-lam$_2$	1 *nilam*-garment:
	Ur$_5$-du$_2$ lu$_2$-u$_5$ [(x)] / Iri-saĝ-rig$_{12}$(DU.HUB$_2$)^{ki}	(for) Urdu, the shipping agent (from) Irisaĝrig.
	⸢tug$_2$⸣ uš-bar-⸢am$_3$⸣	These are garments of *ušbar* quality.

	Su$_4$-ru-us$_2$-GI	*Šurus-kēn*,
	ensi$_2$ ^{ĝeš}KUŠU$_2$^{ki}-ke$_4$	the governor of Umma,
	e$_2$-ĝidru ^{ĝeš}KUŠU$_2$^{ki}-⸢ka⸣	in the Eĝidru of Umma,
	e-ne-ba	has allocated to them.
	I$_3$-li$_2$-a-hi	*'Ilī-'aḫī*
	maškim-bi	(is) its commissioner.
	6 mu ⸢*1*$^?$ iti⸣	Year 6, month 1$^?$.

obv. 5: The interpretation of the line is uncertain. The last sign is probably not AN, and there is hardly space for BAR.

rev. 2: For lu$_2$-u$_5$ as "Spediteur(?)" or "courier," see FAOS 15/2 pp. 597–98 with additional references.

No. 444 – MS 1952/25

Account of textiles belonging to a scribe and available with a fuller, Early Sargonic, Umma region.

obv.	[...] ⸢x x⸣ [...]	...
	⸢tug$_2$⸣ Bara$_2$-ga-ni dub-sar-kam	These are textiles of Baragani, the scribe.
	Lugal-⸢nir⸣-ĝal$_2$ azlag$_4$(ĜIŠ.TUG$_2$.KAR.DU)-da	With Lugalnirĝal, the fuller,
	e-da-ĝal$_2$	it is available.
rev.	5 mu iti *10*	Year 5, month 10.

No. 445 – MS 1952/27

Account of a *mašdari'a*-contribution in textiles, Early Sargonic, Umma region.

obv.	10 ⸢x-tug$_2$⸣	10 ... textiles;
	1 ⸢x-tug$_2$⸣	1 ... textile;
	1 da-⸢ba-tum⸣ [...]	1 *dabatum*-textile.
	⸢maš$_2$⸣-da-ri-a	The *mašdari'a*-contribution
	⸢x⸣ dam-gara$_3$	(of) ..., the merchant
	⸢Zabala$_6$^{ki}⸣	(from) Zabala.
	[break]	...
rev.	[break]	...
	[n+] 30 ĝeš-[...]	30 ...
	[x] GAZ [x]	...
	⸢x dam⸣-[gara$_3$]	..., the merchant,
	E$_2$-zi [x]	Ezi...
	[...]-⸢x⸣	

No. 446 – MS 1952/29

Allocation of a garment to a *karkid*-woman, Early Sargonic, Umma region.

obv.	1 ^{tug_2}ni$_3$-lam$_2$ uš-bar	1 *nilam*-garment of *ušbar* quality:
	Me-Aš$_{10}$-tar$_2$ kar-kid$_3$(AK)^{kid}	For Me'Aštar, the *karkid*-woman
	ensi$_2$ Zabala$_5$^{ki}-še$_3$	for/to the governor of Zabala,
	⸢še$^{?!}$⸣ kiĝ$_2$ ku$_5$-še$_3$	(when) *for the harvesting of barley*(?)
	i$_3$-ĝen-na-a	she went,
rev.	ĝanun-maḫ-a	in the main storehouse
	e-ba	to her one has allocated it.
	I$_3$-li$_2$-a-hi	*'Ilī-'aḫī*
	maškim-bi	(is) its commissioner.
	6 mu ⸢iti⸣ [*n*]	Year 6, month ...

obv. 4: The damaged sign at the beginning does not resemble ŠE since it has a final vertical wedge. However, I do not see any possibile interpretation of the term in question other than še-kin-ku$_5$ "to reap grain with a sickle."

No. 447 – MS 1952/30

Receipt of garments by Subareans at the outlet of Zabum, Early Sargonic, Umma region.

obv.	10 la$_2$ 1 ^{tug_2}ni$_3$-[la(m)$_2$] uš-bar	9 *nila(m)*-garments of *ušbar* quality:
	su-bir$_x$(BAPPIR)-a-ne	the Subareans
	ka Za-bum$_2$-ma-ka	at the outlet of (the canal) Zabum
	šu ba-ti	have received.
rev.	*4* mu iti ⸢5⸣ [+n]	Year 4, month 5+.

obv. 2–3: On Subareans at the outlet of canal Zabum in Sargonic texts from Umma, cf. Steinkeller 1987c: 186–87. For other references to this location, see Schrakamp 2015a: 258.

No. 448 – MS 1952/47

Account of textiles mentioning a king's wife, Early Sargonic, Umma region.

obv.	1 ^{tug_2}ša$_3$-ga-du$_3$	1 *šagadu*-garment;
	1 ^{tug_2}ni$_3$-la$_2$	1 *nila*-garment;
	1 ^{tug_2}ni$_3$-lam$_2$	1 *nilam*-garment.
	tug$_2$ uš-bar-am$_3$	These are garments of *ušbar* quality.
	⸢x⸣-lu$_2$ dam ⸢lugal⸣	...lu, the king's wife.
	[break]	
rev.	[break]	
	⸢*3*⸣-kam-⸢ma⸣ munus tug$_2$ ba	For the 3rd time, allocation of garments to women.
	5 mu *2* iti	Year 5, month 2.

No. 449 – MS 2191/14

Allocation of textiles, Early/Middle Sargonic, Umma region.

obv.	1 ^{tug_2}ša$_3$-ga-du$_3$	1 *šagadu*-garment;
	1 ^{tug_2}ni$_3$-la$_2$	1 *nila*-garment;
	1 ^{tug_2}ni$_3$-lam$_2$	1 *nilam*-garment.
	tug$_2$ uš-bar-am$_3$	These are garments of *ušbar*-quality.
	Lugal-nesaĝ-ni nar	(For) Lugalnesaĝni, the musician,
	Adab^{ki}-ta	(when) Adab
	e-ĝen-na-a	he left,
	ki udu-še$_3$ ĝa$_2$-ĝa$_2$	to establish …
	Be$_6$-li$_2$-lu-sa-⌜ri$^?$⌝	*Bēlī-lū-šarrī*(?)
rev.	e-ba	has allocated it.
	I$_3$-li$_2$-a-hi	*'Ilī-'aḫī*
	maškim-bi	(is) its commissioner.
	5 mu *10* la$_2$ *1* iti	Year 5, month 9.

3.2.6 – Metals and Metal Objects

No. 450 – MS 1952/16b

Arrears of metal objects, Early/Middle Sargonic, Umma region.

obv.	[break]	…
	⌜47⌝ ^{uruda}tu-kul$_2$-tur-tur	47 small (metal) "weapons";
	50 la$_2$ 1 ^{uruda}tu-kul$_2$-gal-gal	49 large (metal) "weapons";
	1 uruda sal-la-um	1 (piece of) copper wire:
	2 kuš$_3$-numun 5 šu-si / uruda sal-la-um	2 seed-cubits 5 fingers (*ca.* 2.1 m) (of) copper wire.
rev.	(blank)	
	la$_2$-i$_3$ ĝal$_2$ *2*-kam-ma-kam	These are the current arrears of the second time.
	ĝeš-kiĝ$_2$-ti-a	In the workshop.
	la$_2$-i$_3$ ⌜x⌝-[...]	The arrears ...
	[break]	

obv. 1'–2': ^{uruda}tu-kul$_2$ is likely a syllabic writing of tukul(KU) "weapon." The determinative shows that it was a metal weapon.

obv. 3'–4': For a similar term for copper wire ^{uruda}a-ru$_{12}$-da sal-la-um-ma, see RTC 24 obv. i 1. See Powell 1990: 462 for kuš-numun "seed-cubit," a length measure of about 1 m.

No. 451 – MS 1952/26

Weighing of copper, Early Sargonic, Umma region.

obv.	⸢16⸣ uruda ma-na	16 minas of copper:
	⸢KA⸣-ki sukkal-e	Kaki, the secretary,
	Ad-da dub-sar	(to) Adda, the scribe,
	e-na-la$_2$	weighed it out for him.
	Nagar-zi	Nagarzi (is responsible).
rev.	5 mu iti *2*	Year 5, month 2.

obv. 3: This scribe appears often in Sargonic Umma texts in the context of weighing out copper to smiths; cf., e.g., CHEU 53 and CST 11.

No. 452 – MS 1952/32

Receipt of silver, Early Sargonic, Umma region.

obv.	6 ku$_3$ ⸢giĝ$_4$⸣	6 shekels silver:
	Lugal-bur:⸢gul?⸣ sukkal-e	Lugalburgul(?), the secretary,
	šu ba-ti	has received.
	Ĝeš-ša$_3$ ab-ba-iri	Ĝešša, the city elder,
	maškim-bi	(is) its commissioner.
	4 ku$_3$ giĝ$_4$	4 shekels silver:
rev.	ĜIŠ-NAM$_2$-e	Ĝešnam(?)
	ba-de$_6$	has taken away.
	5 mu [*n* iti]	Year 5, [month n].

rev. 1: A mistake for Ĝeštug$_3$(ĜIŠ.PI.TUG$_2$)? The sign in question is narrower than a usual TUG$_2$.

3.2.7 – Weapons

No. 453 – MS 2191/15

Account of arrows, Early Sargonic, Umma region.

obv.	50 la$_2$ 3 ^{uruda}gag ^{ĝeš}ḫašḫur	47 copper arrowheads (with) apple-wood (shafts);
	360 ^{uruda}gag gi-šul-ḫi	360 copper arrowheads (with) *gišulḫi*-reed (shafts);
	Ad-⸢da⸣ dub-⸢sar⸣-e	Adda, the scribe,
rev.	sur$_x$(ERIN$_2$)-re ba-ta-⸢x⸣	has ...ed to the troops.
	5 ⸢mu⸣ *10* ⸢iti⸣	Year 5, month 10.

No. 454 – MS 2227/1

Delivery of weapons, Early Sargonic, Umma region.

obv.	8 ^{ĝeš}šukur(IGI.GAG)	8 spears;
	2 ^{ĝeš}eme-ĝiri$_2$	2 dagger blades:
	saĝĝa Zabala$_6^{ki}$	the chief temple-administrator of Zabala
	⸢e$_2$⸣ Ša$_3$-ge-pa$_3$-da / ⸢^{ĝeš}KUŠU$_2^{?}$⸣[$^{ki?}$ x]-⸢x⸣	(in?) the house of Šagepada (in) Ĝeša(?) ...
	⸢x⸣ [...]	...
rev.	[Ur]-^{d}Saman$_x$(ŠE$_3$.NUN.BU)-kam	It is of [Ur]-Saman.
	Lugal-kur dub-sar	Lugalkur, the scribe,
	mu-de$_6$	has brought it here.
	⸢7⸣ mu iti *12*	Year 7, month 12.

3.2.8 – Wood and Wooden Objects

No. 455 – MS 1952/48

Delivery of beams to the palace, Early Sargonic, Umma region.

obv.	42 ^{ĝeš}ĝušur(UR$_3$)	42 beams,
	ĝeš e$_2$-a-<<ta>>	timber that into(!) the "house" (storage)
	de$_6$-(ras.)-a	has been brought.
	a-ra$_2$ *3*-kam-ma	(The wood) that for the 3rd time
	e$_2$-gal-la ku$_4$-ra$_2$	has entered the palace.
rev.	*6* mu *3* iti	Year 6, month 3.

obv. 2: E$_2$ "house" is a storage here. See No. 254 rev. 3. The writing e$_2$-a-ta is a mistake for e$_2$-a "into the storage." An erasure in the following verbal form shows that the scribe was unsure. In the case of issue, the form e$_2$-ta e$_3$-a "issued out of the 'house'" is expected.

No. 456 – MS 2191/10

Delivery of timber from the governor's house in Agade with its subsequent receipt in a workshop, Early Sargonic, Umma region.

obv.	70 ⸢x⸣ [...]	70 ...;
	40 ^{ĝeš}⸢asal$_2$ x-x⸣	40 poplar ...;
	40 la$_2$ 2 ⸢x⸣ ma-nu gag	38 willow pegs;
	⸢Šul⸣-me ugula-e$_2$	Šulme, the overseer of the household,
	A-ga-de$_3^{ki}$-ta	from Agade,
	e$_2$ ensi$_2$-ka-ta	out of the house of the governor,
	mu-de$_6$	brought.
rev.	ĝeš-kiĝ$_2$-ti-a	In the workshop
	ba-ku$_4$	it has entered.
	⸢x-x⸣ šu ba-ti	... (personal name) has received it.
	6 mu *6* iti	Year 6, month 6.

obv. 3: The sign after the numeral may be the beginning of an erased ASAL$_2$, as in the line before. In any case, the traces do not allow a ĜIŠ.

obv. 5–6: Note the double use of the ablative case. This passage also offers a reference to the seat of the governor in the capital city, Agade.

3.2.9 – Bricks

No. 457 – MS 2191/30

Account of bricks produced as obligation, Early Sargonic, Umma region.

The document records the amount of bricks produced by or under the supervision of a number of individuals.

obv. i	[n+] 10 [...]	... 10 ...:
	⸢*I_3*⸣-*lu*-⸢*sar*⸣	*'Ilu(m)-šar*;
	[n+] 20 Maš	... 20: Maš;
	[n] la$_2$ 10 Mes-e$_2$	... minus 10: Mes-e;
	160 A-da-da	160: Adada;
	680 Ur-^{d}Nagar	680: Ur-Nagar;
	20 Dulum$_2$	20: Dulum;
	640 Ad-da	640: Adda;
ii	[n+] 10 ⸢x⸣	... 10 ...;
	60 U$_2$-ru$_{14}$(URU×A)	60: Uru;
	400 Ĝeš-ša$_3$-šeš-gal	400: Ĝeššašešgal;
	200 E$_2$-muš$_3$	200: Emuš;
	1520 Lugal-si-sa$_2$	1520: Lugalsisa;
	1320 Lugal-gal-⸢zu⸣	1320: Lugalgalzu;
rev. i	1000 Lugal-kur enku	1000: Lugalkur, the tax-collector;
	600 Teš$_2$-teš$_2$	600: Tešteš.
	(blank)	
ii	šu-niĝin$_2$ šu-niĝin$_2$ 4800 šeg$_{12}$-⸢x⸣	Grand total: 4800 ... bricks.
	a$_2$ ⸢x⸣ [...]	The work ...
	(blank)	
	[*n*] ⸢mu *6*⸣ iti	Year ..., month 6.

3.2.10 – Miscellaneous Goods

No. 458 – MS 1952/11

Expenditure of rings and textiles in connection to a high-profile mission at different localities, Early/Middle Sargonic, Umma region.

The document records the expenditure of goods to high officials with the purpose of giving them as presents to VIP persons at several localities.

obv. i	[n ḫar]-ḫul$_3$-la-[ku$_3$] e$_2$-ba	x pairs of rings:
	⸢ki⸣-la$_2$-bi 15 giĝ$_4$	their weight: 15 shekels:
	I$_3$-lu-lu	(for) *'Ilu(m)-lu...*,
	lu$_2$ lugal	the man of the king,
	ma$_2$-še$_3$ e-še$_3$-ĝen-na	who went to the boat.
	Gara$_2$^{ki}-a e-ba	He has given it as present at (the locality) Gara.
	2 ḫar-ḫul$_3$-la-ku$_3$ e$_2$-ba	2 pair of rings:
	ki-la$_2$-bi 1 ma-na	their weight: 1 mina;
	[n] ⸢^{tug_2}⸣ni$_3$-lam$_2$	x *nilam*-garments;
	[n ^{tug_2}]DUL$_3$	x *cloaks*:
ii	U$_3$-mu-mu	Umumu,
	lu$_2$-ma$_2$-gur$_8$	the boatman;
	1 ^{tug_2}ni$_3$-lam$_2$	1 *nilam*-garment:
	⸢*Sar*⸣*-su$_2$-a-ri$_2$-ik*	(for) *Šar(rus)su-'arik,*
	sagi lugal	the cupbearer of the king.
	Der$_x$(BAD$_3$.AN)^{ki}-a e-ba	He has given it as present at (the locality) Der.
	1 ^{tug_2}ni$_3$-lam$_2$	1 *nilam*-garment;
	1 ^{tug_2}ša$_3$-ga-du$_3$	1 *šagadu*-garment;
	1 ^{tug_2}DUL$_3$	1 *cloak*;
	⸢Za⸣-ḪI×X IB lugal	..., the *IB*-official of the king.
	1 ḫar-ḫul$_3$-la ku$_3$-babbar e$_2$-ba	1 pair of silver rings:
	ki-la$_2$-bi 14 giĝ$_4$	their weight: 14 shekels;
rev. i	1 ^{tug_2}ni$_3$-lam$_2$	1 *nilam*-garment;
	1 ^{tug_2}ša$_3$-ga-du$_3$	1 *šagadu*-garment:
	⸢ *Qer$_x$*(ĜIR$_3$)⸣*-bi-šum*	*Qerbī-šum*,
	⸢sagi⸣ lugal	the cupbearer of the king.
	1 ⸢^{tug_2}⸣ni$_3$-⸢lam$_2$⸣	1 *nilam*-garment;
	1 ^{tug_2}ša$_3$-⸢ga⸣-du$_3$	1 *šagadu*-garment;
	1 ^{tug_2}⸢DUL$_3$⸣	1 *cloak*;
	E$_3$-zu-zum	*Ezuzum*,
	šeš *Qer$_x$-bi-šum*	brother of *Qerbī-šum*.
	1 ^{tug_2}⸢ni$_3$⸣-lam$_2$	1 *nilam*-garment;
	1 ^{tug_2}ša$_3$-ga-du$_3$	1 *šagadu*-garment:
	Za-qar-su	*Zaqaršu*,
	lu$_2$ ensi$_2$ Aš$_2$-nun-na^{ki}-ka	the man of the governor of Ešnunna;
ii	[...]-mu [...]-⸢x⸣-a	...
	[1 ^{tug_2}ni$_3$]-lam$_2$	1 *nilam*-garment;

	[1 ^{tug_2}]ša$_3$-ga-du$_3$	1 *šagadu*-garment:
	[...]-⸢x⸣	...
	[lu$_2$] ⸢ensi$_2$⸣ [...]-⸢ka⸣	[the man of] the governor of [the land/city *x*]
	[2 lines broken]	...
	[...]-⸢x⸣	...
	[n ḫar-ḫul$_3$-la-ku$_3$ e]-ba	n pairs of [silver rings]
	[n ^{tug_2}ni$_3$]-⸢lam$_2$⸣	1 *nilam*-garment:
	NE-NE	NENE,
	lu$_2$ Ki-AN^{ki}	the man (from) Ki'AN.
	[...] ⸢10$^?$ ba/iti$^?$ *2*⸣	...
	[...]-⸢gar$_3$⸣ maškim-bi	...gar (is) its commissioner.
	[*n* mu] *8* ⸢iti$^?$⸣	Year *n*, month 8(?).

obv. i 10: See EDPV A no. 177 for DUL$_3$^{tug_2} "cover."

No. 459 – MS 2191/9

Luxury goods sent by a governor of Subir, Early Sargonic, Umma region.

obv.	[n ...] ⸢dug⸣	n jars of ...;
	[n ...] ⸢ĜIŠ$^?$⸣ nindan-DU	n ... wood rods:
	1 [x]-⸢KA×ŠE-x⸣ ^{kuš}a-ĝa$_2$-la$_2$	1 leather bag of ...;
	La-NI ensi$_2$ Su-bir$_x$(BAPPIR)^{ki}-a-ke$_4$	LaNI, the governor of the land Subir,
	ensi$_2$-ra šu mu-na-us$_2$	sent it to the governor.
	Šu-Aš$_{11}$-tar$_2$ aga$_3$-us$_2$ ensi$_2$-ka-ke$_4$	*Šu-'Aštar*, the soldier of the governor,
	mu-de$_6$	has brought it here.
	Bara$_2$-ga-ni	Baragani
rev.	šu ba-ti	has received it.
	⸢*2*⸣ [+n] ⸢mu⸣ *11* iti	Year n+2, month 11.

The text reports the remarkable information that the land of Subir, Akk. *Subartum*, in northern Mesopotamia had its own governor and that this governor sent goods to Umma.

obv. 3: See EDPV A no. 266 for the interpretation "leather bag (for solids)."

No. 460 – MS 2191/34

Expenditure of miscellaneous commodities, Early Sargonic, Umma region.

obv. i	1 maš$_2$-nita	1 male kid;
	1 ^{uruda}zabar	1 bronze vessel;
	1 ni$_3$-tug$_2$-bar-ba suluḫu$_2$(SIKI.GID$_2$)	1 garment with outer fleece;
	1 tug$_2$-gid$_2$	1 long garment;
	[1] ^{ĝeš}na$_2$	[1] bed;
	[1] tug$_2$-kuš	[1] leather garment;
ii	1 ^{uruda}zabar	1 bronze vessel;
	1 gada	1 linen (garment);

	1 tug$_2$-kuš	1 leather garment;
	1 ni$_3$-saĝ-la$_2$	1 headdress:
	Sa$_6$-da ba-de$_6$	Sada has taken it away.
rev.	(partly destroyed, partly blank)	

No. 461 – MS 5048/17

Receipt of baskets(?), Middle(?) Sargonic, Umma region.
Read from photographs.

obv.	⸢x⸣ dupsik	x *dupsik*-baskets(?):
	⸢Ne-saĝ (x?)⸣	Nesaĝ,
	⸢sagi-e?⸣	the cupbearer
	šu ⸢ba⸣-ti	has received.
	Mu-ka-ge-du$_{10}$	Mukagedu
	⸢maškim⸣-bi	(is) its commissioner.
rev.	(blank space)	
	⸢*3*?⸣ mu 7 iti	Year 3$^?$, month 7.

obv. 1: The first sign does not look like a numeral.

obv. 2–3: For the cupbearer Nesaĝ, see BIN 8 no. 341 obv. 4, and USP p. 116, where Foster assigns this text to "group C," i.e., the Classical Sargonic period. The present tablet looks somewhat older.

3.2.11 – Uncertain Goods

No. 462 – MS 2191/4

Inspection of unidentified goods (AŠ$_2$-SA), Early/Middle Sargonic, Umma region.

obv.	[n] ⸢AŠ$_2$⸣-SA la$_2$-i$_3$ Niĝir-⸢x⸣	n …: the arrears of Niĝir…;
	[n+] 1 *I$_3$-lu-sar*	n+1 *'Ilu(m)-šar*;
	8 Maš nu-banda$_3$	8: Maš, the supervisor;
	20 la$_2$ 1 Gi-nun-ba	19: Ginunba;
	5 A-da-da	5: Adada;
	6 Dulum$_2$	6: Dulum;
	2 Eš$_3$-me-gara$_2^!$(BI)	2: Ešmegara;
	4 Ur-^{d}Nagar nu-banda$_3$	4: Ur-Nagar, the supervisor;
	4 Tir-ku$_3$ nu-banda$_3$	4: Tirku, the supervisor;
	5 Lugal-kur enku	5: Lugalkur, the tax-collector;
rev.	3 Lugal-Utu-⸢am$_6$⸣	3: Lugal-Utu'am;
	4 Ur-⸢x⸣ […]	4: Ur…;
	4 Ĝeš-⸢ša$_3$⸣ […]	5: Ĝešša, …;
	2 Ur-^{d}⸢NAGAR⸣[.(BU)]	2: Ur-Nagar (or Ur-Dulum);
	(blank)	
	šu-niĝin$_2$ 80 ⸢4⸣ AŠ$_2$-⸢x-x⸣	Total: 84 ….
	AŠ$_2$-SA la$_2$-i$_3$ ⸢x⸣-ne-kam	…: these are the arrears of ….
	Ad-⸢da⸣ dub-sar-e	Adda, the scribe,
	⸢E⸣-ma-⸢ra-an⸣^{ki}-na	at Emaran
	gurum$_x$(IGI.ĜAR)-bi e-ak	did its inspection.
	[10] la$_2$ *1* mu *2* iti	Year 9, month 2.

obv. 1, rev. 6: The interpretation of the term AŠ$_2$-SA is not certain. "Emmer in bundles" (ziz$_2$ sa) would not make sense.

rev. 5: The traces do not resemble a SA.

rev. 8: Cf. the locality Im-ma-ra-an^{ki} at Ebla (ARET 13 no.14 obv. ii 19).

No. 463 – MS 2191/12

Arrears of a material measured by weight, Early Sargonic, Umma region.

obv.	la$_2$-i$_3$ / 2 ½$_{Umma}$ ma-na	Arrears: 2 ½ minas.
	⸢*Ri$_2$*-ZUM-*tum*$^?$⸣ /⸢dam-gal$^?$⸣ [(x)]	*Ri…tum* …
	mu-da-ĝal$_2$	is available with him/her.
rev.	E$_2$-gal-i$_3$-si / saĝĝa Zabala$_6^{ki}$	Egal-isi, the chief temple-administrator of Zabala.
	1 mu iti *7*	Year 1, month 7.

obv. 2: The line is greatly damaged. Detailed photo:

3.3 – Classical to Late Sargonic Documents from the Umma Region

3.3.1 – A Letter Concerning Barley and Land

No. 464 – MS 2044

Letter concerning the transfer of barley and occupation of land, Classical Sargonic, Umma region.

This remarkably detailed and lively letter concerns a delivery of barley and the occupation of land. The addressee of the letter may be the famous Mesaĝ, who held an estate in the Lagaš region and may have assumed the governorship of Umma (see Foster 2016: 72–73).

obv.	UN-il$_2$-e	That is what UNil
	na-be$_2$-a	says:
	Me-^{sag_3}sag$_7$-ra	To Mesag
	u$_3$-na-du$_{11}$	please say (the following):
	A ŠI E$_2$ i$_3$-ma-ak	"... you have done to me.
	še-ĝu$_{10}$ 4 še gur-sag-ĝal$_2$-bi	My barley, its 4 *gursaĝĝal* barley,
	ma$_2$-a u$_3$-mi-si	after you have loaded on to the ship,
	šu ḫa-ma-ab-us$_2$-e	you should send it to me.
	šu+niĝin$_2$-tur-bi šu na-ma-ab-e	You should not touch its *lesser total* for me.
	⸢x⸣-ĝu$_{10}$ u$_3$-mu-na-bala	After you have measured my ... for me,
	⸢x⸣-ĝu$_{10}$ ḫe$_2$-ma-tum$_3$	you should bring my ... to me.
	[x]-ĝu$_{10}$ a-ša$_3$ ki-ĝir$_2$-⸢nun⸣	My ... (on) the field Kiĝirnun
rev.	⸢x⸣ gu [...]	...
	⸢2⸣(bur'u) 6(bur$_3$) aša$_5$-bi	Its 26 *bur* of land
	ḫa-ma-ab-ni-ib-gi-ne$_2$	you should confirm there for me.
	a-ša$_3$ sa$_6$-ga ḫe$_2$-am$_3$	It should be a good field!
	[a-ba] šeš-ĝu$_{10}$-gin$_7$	[Who is] like my brother!"
	(blank)	

obv. 5: The similar expression A-ŠI-DIĜIR i$_3$-ma-ak is discussed in CUSAS 13 no. 171 rev. 4 commentary (CS Umma). There are diverse opinions on how to interpret it. However, the present text, which most likely comes from CS Umma too, provides a parallel, but with a "house" (e$_2$) taking the place of a god (diĝir). It seems to be part of an idiomatic expression or an element in a personal name.

obv. 10–11: The doubtful sign is the same in both lines: not ŠE but a sign with a prolonged angular shape at the end.

obv. 12: The same field appears in a CS Umma text, CST no. 27 obv. iii 3, rev. ii 2 (agar$_4$ ki-ĝir$_2$-nun).

rev. 5: For this formula in letters, see Sallaberger 2015: 22.

3.3.2 – Personnel

No. 465 – MS 1952/18

Adding two persons to a list, Classical Sargonic, Umma region.

The document draws a clear-cut line between two classes of people, slaves of the king (arad$_2$ lugal) and free citizens (dumu-gi$_7$.r).

obv.	1 Gala	1 Gala,
	arad$_2$ lugal-kam	he is a slave of the king.
	1 Lugal-⌜bad$_3$⌝	1 Lugalbad,
	dumu E$_2$-e	he is the son of E'e,
	dumu-gi$_7$-am$_3$	a free citizen.
	ugula Ur-^{d}Nagar	The(ir) overseer (is) Ur-Nagar,
rev.	gu-za-la$_2$	the throne-bearer.
	im-si-sa$_2$-a	On to the regular roster,
	ba-taḫ-e	they have been added.
	(blank)	
	5 [iti]	[Month] 5.

For a similar document, see Nik 2 no. 71 and discussion in USP p. 124. Foster interprets the document as recording persons placed on a list of people who received monthly rations.

3.3.3 – Bricks

No. 466 – MS 1952/19

Account of baked bricks, Classical/Late Sargonic, Umma region.

obv.	7 sar šeg$_{12}$	7 *sar* (= *ca.* 252 m^2) bricks.
	šeg$_{12}$ du$_8$-a	Baked bricks.
	a$_2$ *1* u$_4$-a	The work of the 1st day.
rev.	gal$_5$-la$_2$-gal	The chief policeman (is responsible).
	(blank)	
	7 mu 5 iti	Year 7, month 5.

Part 4 – Documents from Other Locations

4.1 – Ebla (Early Dynastic IIIb)

No. 467 – MS 5091

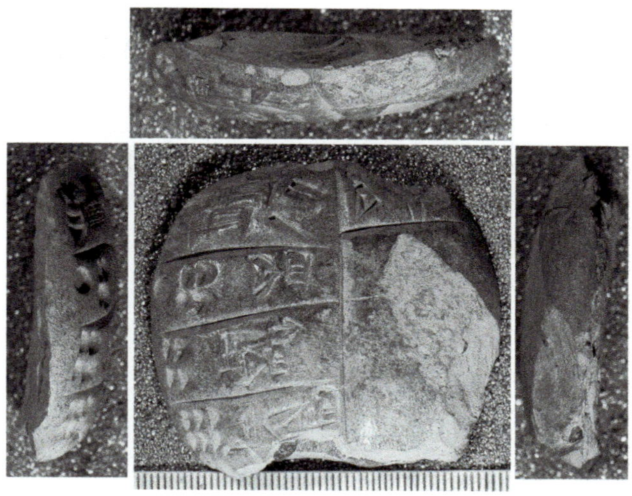

Account of garments, Early Dynastic IIIb, Ebla.

One side is completely destroyed. It is not certain if the extant side is the obverse.

obv.? i	2N$_1$ e$_2$ *2* / 2N$_8$ e$_2$ *1*	……
	14 SAL^{tug_2}	14 *fine* garments;
	4 gu-mug^{tug_2}	4 garments from shoddy wool;
	6 ib$_2$×3^{tug_2}-⸢gunu$_3$?⸣	6 multicolored(?) … waistbands;
ii	⸢x⸣-[…] ni$_3$-⸢ba⸣	… the allocated goods.
	(rest blank)	
rev.?	[destroyed]	

obv. i 1: The meaning of the first line is uncertain. Evidently, it has something to do with the delivery or allocation of textiles in a household, e$_2$.

obv. i 2–4: See Biga 2010: 158–60 for these textiles at Ebla. The garment ib$_2$×3^{tug_2} appears with numerous qualifiers in Ebla texts: Ar-mi^{ki}, gada-tug$_2$, Ma-ri^{ki}, -babbar, -gunu$_3$, -saĝ, -sal, -sa$_6$-(gunu$_3$/-saĝ), -u$_2$-ḫab$_2$-(u$_2$), etc. It is not certain which of these suits the traces of the damaged sign. The meaning of the numerals, from 1 to 5, that are inscribed inside ib$_2$ or following it is debated.

4.2 – Sagub (Classical Sargonic)

No. 468 – MS 4544

List of women not present at work, Classical Sargonic, Sagub ("Mesag archive").

obv.	nu Geme$_2$-⸢d⸣[Utu]	Not (present): Geme-[Utu];
	nu Nin-⸢en⸣ [(x)]	not (present): Nin-en;
	nu Nin-uĝ$_3$(LAK730)-ĝa$_2$	not (present): Nin-uĝa.
	(blank)	
rev.	(blank)	

For similar texts, see NBC 7008 = Bridges 1981: 467, MC 4 no. 45, BIN 8 no. 243. The document originates from the so-called "Mesag archive," which Steinkeller attributes to the ancient town of Sagub. See MC 4 pp. 8–10 for discussion; further CUSAS 27 pp. 26–27, where Westenholz argues that Sagub was situated near Zabala.

obv. 1–2: A person called Nin-en geme$_2$-maš is mentioned in NBC 7008 = Bridges 1981: 467 rev. 10'. Geme$_2$-^{d}Utu also appears in the text, which permits the restoration of her name here.

obv. 3: The same person appears in MC 4 no. 45 rev. 14.

4.3 – ŠURUPPAK/FARA (EARLY DYNASTIC IIIA)

No. 469 – MS 1718

Purchase of a field, Early Dynastic IIIa, Šuruppak (Fara).

For a very similar sale contract, see MVN 10 no. 86.

obv. i	22 ½ uruda ma-na	22 ½ minas copper:
	sa$_{10}$ aša$_5$	the price of the field.
	2(eše$_3$) 3(iku) aša$_5$-bi	2 *eše* 3 *iku* its area.
	40 la$_2$ 3 uruda ma-na	40 minus 3 minas copper:
	ni$_3$-diri	its additional payment.
	36 uruda ma-na	36 minas copper,
ii	1 še lid$_2$-ga	1 *lidga* barley:
	ni$_3$-ba	the "present."
	8 siki ma-na	8 minas wool,
	(ras.) tug$_2$	(for) a garment;
	60 ninda	60 breads;
	60 gug$_2$	60 cakes;
	10 kur$_2$ tu$_7$(ḪI×AŠ)	10 *kur* of stew;
	10 kur$_2$ adaku'a$_x$(GA$_2$×ḪA.A)	10 *kur* of fish soup;
	1 i$_3$ sila$_3$	1 *sila* of oil:
	Su$_4$-a(ZA)*-bi*	*Šu-'abi*;
iii	1 tug$_2$-šu	1 … garment,
	10 ½ uruda ma-na-kam$_4$	it is of (value) 10 ½ minas copper.
	za$_3$ Mu-ni ba-us$_2$(ARAD)	… Muni …
	Nin-šu-a(ZA)	Ninšu'a,
	lu$_2$ sa$_{10}$ gu$_7$	(is) the person (who) accepted the price (= seller).
	2(bariga) še	2 *bariga* barley;
	10 ninda	10 breads;
	10 gug$_2$	10 cakes;
iv	2 kur$_2$ tu$_7$	2 *kur* of stew;
	2 kur$_2$ adaku'a$_x$(GA$_2$×ḪA.A)	2 *kur* of fish soup:
	Ur-^{d}En-saḫar-ra	(for) Ur-Ensaḫara
	Ur$_2$-ni	(and) Urni,
	lu$_2$ Ki-ur$_3$	the man of Ki'ur.
	1 Ur-^{d}Sud$_3$	1 Ur-Sud,
	um-mi-a	the master scribe;
	1 Ur-^{d}Gu$_2$-la$_2$	1 Ur-Gula,
	dub-sar	the scribe;
v	1 Nin-ad$_2$-gal	1 Nin-adgal,
	ugula	the overseer;
	1 Dumu-$^{d.mušen}$Anzu(MI.IM)	1 Dumu'Anzu,
	munu$_4$-mu$_2$	the maltster;
	1 Ki-ni-mu-zu	1 Kinimuzu
	Ur-^{d}Sud$_3$	(and) Ur-Sud,
	i$_3$-du$_8$	the doorman;
rev. i	1 Du$_{11}$-ga-ni	1 Dugani,
	a-ru	the consecrated person;
	(ras.) Aja$_2$-ne-ne	(erasure) Ajanene,

	ĝuruš-tab	the *ĝuruštab*-worker;
	1 E$_2$-zi	1 Ezi,
	^{d}Gu$_2$-la$_2$	(and) Gula;
	1 ^{d}Sud$_3$-ur-saĝ	1 Sud-ursaĝ,
	maškim	the legal commissioner;
ii	1 Mu-ni-eš$_3$	1 Muni'eš,
	sagi	the cupbearer:
	lu$_2$-ki-inim	(they are) the witnesses.
	2 ku$_3$ giĝ$_4$	2 shekels silver;
	10 ninda	10 breads;
	10 gug$_2$	10 cakes;
	2 kur$_2$ tu$_7$	2 *kur* of stew;
	2 kur$_2$ adaku'a$_x$(GA$_2$×ḪA.A)	2 *kur* of fish soup:
	Ur-^{d}Nin-Unug	(for) Ur-Nin-Unug,
	dub-sar aša$_5$ (DUB GAN$_2$ SAR)	the scribe of the field (sale).
	(blank space)	
iii	Ur-^{d}En-lil$_2$	Ur-Enlil,
	gal$_5$-la$_2$-gal	the chief policeman,
	lu$_2$ aša$_5$ sa$_{10}$	(is) the person (who) bought the field.
	bala	The term of office
	Nam-maḫ	(of) Nammaḫ.
	Ambar-tur	(Locality) "The Small Marsh."

obv. ii 8: See MC 4 p. 19 for the writings of a dish /adaku'a/ or /edaku'a/, probably a fish soup.

obv. iii 3–4: See Thomsen 1984: 322 for the interpretation "to border on, to stand by, to set aside" of the compound verb za$_3$ … us$_2$. The sign combination za$_3$-us$_2$, literally "leaning on the side," occurs as a term for the back or armrests of a chair (SCTRAH no. 99 obv. 5 commentary). Its meaning in the present context is uncertain.

rev. i 2: For individuals dedicated to temples a-ru-a, literally "donated," see Gelb 1972.

rev. i 4: See ĝuruš-tab = *batūlu* "young adolescent man"; CAD B 174. Ĝuruš-tab-(nu-zu) "young man who has not known a partner" appears in Lu$_2$ III 81–82 = MSL 12 p. 126. Accordingly, ELTS p. 184 (nos. 32 v 8, 33 i 5) translates the term "bachelor." Ur III texts mention ĝuruš tab-ba as a class of workers; cf., e.g., MVN 10 no. 120 rev. i 8. Since "unmarried man" is not a professional title, the term ĝuruš-tab is likely a specific type of workman.

rev. i 6: This is an abbreviated name. For another person ^{d}Gu$_2$-la$_2$, see DP 33 (ED IIIa, Šuruppak?) obv. iii 1.

rev. iii 6: The sign LAGAB×A(ZA) = ambar (or sug) "marsh" appears in the colophons of NTSŠ 92 and TSŠ 303, where it designates a locality where fields are situated.

No. 470 – MS 2725

Purchase of a house, Early Dynastic IIIa, Šuruppak (Fara).

obv. i	7 ku$_3$-luḫ-ḫa giĝ$_4$	7 shekels of pure silver:
	sa$_{10}$ e$_2$	the price of the house.
	2 e$_2$-bi sar giĝ$_4$ 10	Its house: 2 *sar* 10 shekels (area).
	11 ku$_3$-luḫ-ḫa giĝ$_4$	11 shekels of pure silver:
	ni$_3$-diri	the additional payment.
	2 še lid$_2$-ga	2 *lidga* barley:
	ni$_3$-ba	the "present."
	2 siki ma-na	2 minas wool
ii	tug$_2$	(for) a garment;
	1 me:ĝal$_2$tug$_2$	1 *meĝal*-garment;
	4(ban$_2$) še ninda	4 *ban* barley for (baking) bread;
	40 gug$_2$	40 cakes;
	5 kur$_2$ tu$_7$(ḪI×DIŠ)	5 *kur* of stew;
	5 kur$_2$ adaku'a$_x$(GA$_2$×ḪA)	5 *kur* of fish soup:
	1 i$_3$ sila$_3$	1 *sila* oil:
	Ur-^{d}En-ki	Ur-Enki,
	^{d}En-lil$_2$-mu-šum$_2$	Enlilmušum,
	E$_2$-ĝessu-bi-du$_{10}$	(and) Eĝessubidu
iii	lu$_2$ sa$_{10}$ gu$_7$	(are) the persons who accepted the price (= sellers).
	1(bariga) še	1 *bariga* barley;
	10 gug$_2$	10 cakes:
	Gan-e$_2$-gibil	Gan-egibil.
	3(ban$_2$) še	3 *ban* barley;
	10 gug$_2$	10 cakes:
	Nin-ra	Ninra.
	1(bariga) še	1 *bariga* barley;
	10 gug$_2$	10 cakes:
	Nin-gaba-ĝal$_2$-Abzu	Ningabaĝal-Abzu.
	1(ban$_2$) še	1 *ban* barley;
	10 gug$_2$	10 cakes:
iv	Gan-ki-ku$_3$	Gankiku.
	2(ban$_2$) še	2 *ban* barley;
	10 gug$_2$	10 cakes:
	Gan-^{d}*E-lum*	Gan-*Ellum*.
	3(ban$_2$) še	3 *ban* barley;
	10 gug$_2$	10 cakes:
	Nin-šu-mu-gi$_4$	Ninšumugi
	Nin-lu$_2$	(and) Ninlu;
	1 Si-ĝar	1 Siĝar;
	1 Ki-tuš-me-te	1 Kitušmete;
	1 Bar-tab	1 Bartab;
v	1 Lugal-e$_2$-gub	1 Lugal-egub;
	1 E$_2$-teš$_2$-ĝu$_{10}$	1 Etešĝu;
	1 ^{d}Nin-PA-men	1 NinPAmen;

	1 Saĝ-a-DU-ba-šum$_2$	1 Saĝ-aDUbašum,
	^{ba15}baḫar$_x$(EDIN)	the potter;
	1 ^{d}Sud$_3$-ra-mu-gi$_4$	1 Sudramugi;
	1 Utu-mu-kuš$_2$	1 Utumukuš,
	gala(ARAD.KU)	the singer;
rev. i	1 Utu-mu-kuš$_2$	1 Utumukuš,
	dumu Niĝin$_6$(AB×ḪA)-ki-du$_{10}$	son of Niĝinkidu;
	1 Ur-^{d}Dumu-zi	1 Ur-Dumuzi,
	dub-sar	the scribe:
	lu$_2$-ki-inim	(they are) the witnesses.
	1 uruda ma-na	1 mina copper;
	40 ninda$^!$	40 breads;
	40 gug$_2$	40 cakes;
	2 kur$_2$ tu$_7$	2 *kur* of stew;
ii	2 kur$_2$ adaku'a$_x$(GA$_2$×ḪA)	2 *kur* of fish soup:
	Ur-^{d}Inana	(for) Ur-Inana,
	um-mi-a	the master scribe,
	lu$_2$ e$_2$ eše$_2$ ĝar	the person who measured the house.
	10 ninda	10 breads;
	10 gug$_2$	10 cakes:
	Ur-^{d}E$_2$-saman$_3$(ŠE$_3$.ŠE.NUN.BU)	Ur-Esaman,
	niĝir:sila	the street herald.
	1 ku$_3$ giĝ$_4$	1 shekel silver,
	ku$_3$ E$_2$-mud	the silver (for) Emud,
	ugula lu$_2$-<x>	the overseer of … professionals.
	(blank space)	
iii	AN-na-ne-saĝ	ANnanesaĝ,
	dumu Niĝin$_6$-ki-du$_{10}$	son of Niĝinkidu,
	sipa	the shepherd,
	lu$_2$ e$_2$ sa$_{10}$	(is) the person who bought the house.
	bala	The term of office
	Ur-^{d}En-lil$_2$	(of) Ur-Enlil.
	Ki-uzug$_2$(KA.U$_2$)	(In the quarter) Ki'uzug.

obv. ii 2: This textile appears in other Fara contracts. Cf., e.g., ^{tug2}me-ĝal$_2$, Molina and Sanchiz 2007: 2 no. 1 obv. ii 3 and commentary on p. 4 with additional references.

obv. iii 4: See WF 31 rev. ii 3, 74 rev. iv 2 for the same person.

obv. v 4: Despite the writing with -ba after DU in this and similar names it is not certain whether to read gub-ba. Cf. the name A-DU-mu-še$_3$-ti in text No. 393 obv. ii 2 f., which might suggest that the sign BA is the verbal prefix /ba=/ in these names.

rev. ii 4: Literally, "person who placed the rope on/in the house."

rev. ii 11: One sign is omitted due to the lack of space in the column. Cf. ugula lu$_2$-gu$_4$ (TSŠ 24 obv. ii 3), ugula lu$_2$-ad (WF 7 rev. iii 6), and ugula lu$_2$-DI (WF 9 obv. iii 2).

rev. iii 7: For the locality Ki-uzug$_2$, probably a quarter in Šuruppak, see MC 4 p. 21 sub x 4. This was the "address," intended to locate the house in question in a large city.

Part 5 – Documents of Uncertain Provenance

5.1 – Early Dynastic I–II Documents

No. 471 – MS 2522

Contents uncertain, ED I–II, uncertain provenance.

The numerals are the same as in ED I–II texts from Ur.

obv. i	[2 lines broken]	
	⸢4⸣ Ur-maš$_{2}$-da	4 (gur?): Urmašda;
	4 RU	4: …;
	4 x-saĝ	4: …saĝ;
ii	[4] ⸢DAR-ḪU⸣	[4]: …;
	[4] ⸢DA$^{?}$⸣-GA	[4]: …;
	4 Amar-en-⸢ba⸣	4: Amar-enba;
	2 E$_{2}$-su$_{3}$-aĝ$_{2}$	2: Esuaĝ
iii	(blank)	
	[…] AĜ$_{2}$ [..]	… measured(?) …
	[rest destroyed]	

obv. i 5: The sign is similar to ED IIIa ĜURUŠ. C. Lecompte informs me (personal communication) that the ED I–II predecessor of this sign has not yet been identified. However, the sign is not S.327 of the UET 2 sign list, since the vertical wedge remains within the sign and does not cross it as it does in S.327.

No. 472 – MS 2523

Account of personnel, ED I–II, uncertain provenance.

This text is more recent than the previous one, but older than the ED IIIa Fara texts. Note the rounded form of NU and the numerals resembling those of ED I–II Ur documents. The text records individuals, probably workers, who are accounted in groups. Each section ends with a double ruling very similar to a text of the same date (ED I–II) from Fara published as Krebernik, Steible and Yildiz 2014 no. 2.

obv. i	1 ⸢x-gi⸣	1 …;
	1 ŠITA×ḪI$^{?}$	1 …;
	1 Ur:lugal	1 Urlugal.
	(double ruling)	
	1 ⸢Šeš-ama-na⸣	Šešamana;
	[1] ⸢LUL⸣-[x]	[1] LUL…
	[1 …]	[1 …]
ii	[1 …]-⸢GUM⸣	[1 …] …
	1 Amar:⸢x⸣	1 Amar…
	(double ruling)	
	1 Du_{11}-ga:ni	1 Dugani;

	1 Diĝir-nu-me	1 Diĝirnume.
	(double ruling)	
	1 Amar:Abzu	1 Amar-Abzu;
	1 Ama-DIM(LAK53)-kalam	1 AmaDIMkalam;
	[1 ...]	[1 ...]
iii	[1 ...]	[1 ...]
	(double ruling)	
	1 KU-li-li	1 KUlili.
	(double ruling)	
	1 Nin	1 Nin.
	(double ruling)	
	1 Diĝir-nu-me	1 Diĝirnume.
	(double ruling)	
	(blank space)	
	UD-ARAD-KI	(Personal name)
rev.	(blank)	

obv. i 2: The sign inscribed inside ŠITA is a diamond with a final vertical wedge.

obv. ii 2: The damaged sign is from the "family" of animal head signs. It begins with an element resembling the strokes of ŠE, but the sign is probably neither ŠEG$_9$ nor DARA$_3$.

obv. iii 2: The same name is attested in ED IIIa (e.g., WF 18 rev. vii 7) and later sources (e.g., HSS 10 no. 52 obv. i 4' from CS Gasur). Like early names such as *Bi-li-li* and *E*$_{(2)}$*-li-li* (see Sommerfeld 2010 *passim*), the name may be Semitic.

obv. iii 5: This locality is attested in the lexical list ED Geography A. See CUSAS 12 6.2.5 l. 267 for UD.UŠ^{ki}. The Ebla variant has ĜIŠ.NE-ru$_{12}$(EN)^{ki}. See MEE 3 pp. 238 l. 267, 224 rev. i 16. It appears in the context of unlocated towns such as *A-lu*^{ki} and Pa$_4$-NAM$_2$^{ki}. See Steible 2015: 157–58 for these localities in the ED IIIa material. UD.UŠ^{ki} remains unlocated. C. Lecompte drew the author's attention to the fact that this sign combination is a personal name in an ED I–II text from Ur, UET 2 no. 112 obv. vi 12. Here it is probably the name of an administrator in charge of these personnel. The sign UŠ is written with its graphic variant ARAD.

No. 473 – MS 4928

Account of sheep, ED I–II, uncertain provenance (Ur?).

obv. i	126 udu	126 sheep:
	[fake restoration with imitation of cuneiform]...	
	Amar:Nanna(ŠEŠ.KI)	(to) Amar-Nanna.
ii	(blank)	
rev.	[...]	

Note the reference to the chief deity of Ur in the personal name.

The reverse has at least one damaged column filled with mud. Reading will be possible only after a thorough cleaning of the tablet. It is possible that what is presently believed to be the obverse is actually the reverse of the tablet.

5.2 – Early Dynastic IIIA Documents

No. 474 – MS 1384

Account of land sown with mottled barley and of irrigated land, Early Dynastic IIIa, uncertain provenance.

The documents differentiates between plots that have crops on them (še aša$_5$) and those that are are still wet (ki-duru$_5$ aša$_5$). Thus, the text partly records the agriculture cycle on the fields, for which see Hruška 1990: 109.

The reverse is occupied with a different matter and its interpretation is challenging. The numerals used are N$_1$ and N$_8$. Their usual metrological meanings in the context of land are 1 and ½ *iku*. However, note the notation 1N$_{34}$ 4N$_1$ in rev. ii 1, which is alien to the system of area measures. The numerical meaning of the sign N$_8$ is also uncertain. Rev. ii 3 with 7N$_8$ may imply that N$_8$ could be a fraction (1/8 or 1/10) of N$_1$. It could be evidence of a hitherto unknown mensuration system that was probably concerned with grain.

The sign of an object of mensuration on the reverse resembles GAN$_2$ but does not have the lower horizontal wedge protruding. It looks exactly like the sign ŠE$_{3\text{-}tenû}$ in ED IIIb texts from the Umma region. Note however the same sign turned 45° clockwise in rev. i 6, which may imply that the sign is KAR$_2$. The text is remarkable in many respects and requires further study.

obv. i	⸢6(bur$_3$) 1(eše$_3$)⸣ še-gunu$_3$ aša$_5$	6 *bur* 1 *eše* land (with) mottled barley:
	sa$_{12}$-du$_5$	(for) the land-recorder
	ZIZ$_2^{ki}$	of (the locality) ZIZ.
	⸢1(bur$_3$) 2(eše$_3$) še-gunu$_3$⸣	1 *bur* 2 *eše* (with) mottled barley;
	1(eše$_3$) 1(iku) ki-⸢duru$_5$⸣	1 *eše* 1 *iku* of wet land:

	⸢x⸣-na	…na.
	(blank space)	
ii	2(bur$_3$) še aša$_5$	2 *bur* of land (with) barley;
	2(eše$_3$) ki-duru$_5$ aša$_5$	2 *eše* of wet land:
	Lugal-e$_2$-a	Lugal-e'a.
	1(bur$_3$) še aša$_5$	1 *bur* of land (with) barley:
	⸢*Sar*⸣-GAR$_3$	*Šar(rum)*-GAR.
	[n+] 2(iku) še aša$_5$	x+n *iku* of land (with) barley:
rev. i	1(eše$_3$) 2(iku) ki-duru$_5$ / Ki-bi	1 *eše* 2 *iku* of wet land: Kibi.
	3N$_1$ ŠE$_{3\text{-}tenû}^{?}$	3 …:
	Lugal-e$_2$-(ras.)-ki	Lugal-eki.
	1N$_1$ ŠE$_{3\text{-}tenû}^{?}$	1 …:
	Ur-$^{d:}$Dam$_{\text{-}nutillû}$-gal-nun	Ur-Damgalnun(a).
	1N$_1$ 5N$_8$ ŠE$_{3\text{-}tenû}^{?}$	1 5/8 …:
	Zu-zu	Zuzu.
ii	1N$_{34}$ 4N$_1$ ŠE$_{3\text{-}tenû}^{?}$	x+4 …:
	E$_2$-ĝessu-gal	Eĝessugal.
	1N$_1$ 7N$_8$ ŠE$_{3\text{-}tenû}^{?}$	1 7/8 …:
	Ze$_2$-na	Zena.

obv. i 1: še-gunu$_3$, lit. "speckled barley," may be identical with še-gu-nu = *šegunû*, *ṣaḫḫaru*; CAD Š^2 260, Ṣ 61.

obv. i 3: The locality ZIZ$_2^{ki}$ remains unidentified. Cf. Aš$_2$-DI^{ki} in OIP 99 no. 494 (ED IIIa, Abu Salabikh) obv. ii 2.

obv. i 4: The line was erased by the scribe.

obv. i 6: The damaged sign is not the same as in Ze$_2$-na below. It resembles the base for GU$_2$ or DUR and may be any of the signs LAK544 ff. On the other hand, it might be an Umma-looking MAḪ.

obv. ii 3: The sign A is written over an erasure.

rev. i 5: The sign DAM lacks the initial MUNUS part. Cf. LAK46a. The actual sequence of the signs on the tablet is GAL-DAM$_{nutillû}$-UR-AN-NUN.

No. 475 – MS 2076

Assignment of workers (*ĝuruš*) to a number of professionals, Early Dynastic IIIa, uncertain provenance (Abu Salabikh?).

For a similar document, see OIP 99 no. 490 from ED IIIa Abu Salabikh. The present text may have the same origin. It records workers with their overseers, professionals of all sorts. Each overseer has about ten workmen under his command.

obv. i	160	160 (*ĝuruš*-workers),
	27 ugula	27 overseers:
	nagar	carpenters;
	142	142,
	14 ugula	14 overseers:
ii	šidim	builders:
	40 ĝuruš	40 *ĝuruš*-workers,
	5 ugula	5 overseers:
	simug	smiths;
	26 ĝuruš	26 *ĝuruš*-workers,
rev. i	5 ugula	5 overseers:
	bur-gul	stone-cutters;
	13 ĝuruš	13 *ĝuruš*-workers,
	4 ugula	4 overseers:
	tug$_2$-du$_8$	felters.
ii	gu$_2$:an:še$_3$	Grand total:
	382 ĝuruš	382 *ĝuruš*-workers,
	55 ugula	55 overseers.

rev. ii 2: The sum of all entries with *ĝuruš*-workers should be 381.

No. 476 – MS 2190

Account of miscellaneous commodities, Early Dyastic IIIa/IIIb, uncertain provenance.

obv. i	2(gur) 3(bariga) še gur-saĝ-ĝal$_2$	2 *gursaĝĝal* 3 *bariga* barley:
	Gan-^{d}NE	Gan-NE.
	10 ⸢SUM⸣ ma-na ni$_3$-sa$_{10}$	10 minas … (is) the price(?).
ii	½ ku$_3$ šu	½ *silver hand*;
	12 siki ma-na	12 minas of wool;
	1 kaš	1 (jar of) beer;
	1 saĝ	1 slave;
	$^{\text{šu}_2}$1N$_8$ suluḫu$_2$(SIKI.GID$_2$)	⅓ (mina) fleece;
iii	50 ḫašḫur	50 apples:
	Gan-^{d}NE	Gan-NE.
	4(ban$_2$) ziz$_2$	4 *ban* emmer;
	30 ḫašḫur	30 apples;
	10 aktum	10 heavy garments;
iv	10 ninda 1 za$_3$ ku$_6$	10 breads, 1 measure of fish.
	(rest blank)	
rev.	(blank)	

obv. iv 1: See FAOS 15/1 p. 357 for the fish measure za$_3$.

No. 477 – MS 2899

Allocation of fleece and copper, Early Dynastic IIIa, uncertain provenance (Lagaš region?).

The document is inscribed on stone, which suggests that it was important. Despite that, it seems to be an allocation of fleece in pieces and copper in minas, and does not resemble a sale contract or land grant ("*kudurru*"). Based on the shape of the numerals and the paleography, the text's date is ED IIIa at the earliest. The reference to the town Niĝin/Nina in rev. i 3 may provide a clue to the provenance of this interesting document.

obv. i	[n bar-udu] ⸢siki⸣	[…] fleece;
	[n] uruda ⸢ma-na⸣ […]	x minas of copper …;
	[break]	[PN]
ii	[n] uruda ⸢ma-na⸣	x minas of copper:
	⸢lu$_2$⸣-[(eše$_2$)]-⸢gid$_2$⸣	Lugid (*or*: the field-surveyor).
	[n] ⸢bar-udu⸣ siki	x fleece;
	4 ⸢uruda⸣ [ma-na]	4 [minas] of copper:
iii	[…]-⸢x⸣	… (PN).
	[n] bar-udu siki	x fleece;
	2 uruda ma-[na]	2 minas of copper:
	[break]	
rev. i	[…] ⸢x⸣ / ⸢x-x⸣-me	…
	ezen(LAK611) še ⸢ĜAR⸣ […]	The festival of barley …
	[x] ⸢PA Niĝin$_6$(AB×KU$_6$)^{ki}⸣ […]	… (of/in the town) Niĝin …
ii	[…]	…
	⸢x⸣-[…]	…
	[…]	…
	[…]-⸢x⸣-NAM$_2$	…NAM (PN)
	[…]-⸢x⸣	…
iii	(destroyed/blank)	

No. 478 – MS 3790/33

List of brewers, Early Dynastic IIIa, uncertain provenance (Umma region?).

Another list of personnel of the same date and appearance is text No. 479, which includes several names that appear in the present text. A similar text is CUSAS 23 no. 2, which the present author tentatively attributed to the Umma region. The word "potter" is usually written $^{ba_{15}}$baḫar$_2$ in ED IIIb Umma texts. This does not exclude Umma as a possible place of provenance, since synchronous variations are quite possible in documents from the same city, and even the same archive. The present document records the professionals that were employed by a central organization.

obv. i	1 Ba-za	1 Baza;
	1 Teš$_2$-teš$_2$	1 Tešteš;
	1 Lugal-⸢URU×KUR⸣-da	1 Lugal…da;
	1 Dam-kur-ra	1 Damkura;
	1 Ur-kisal	1 Urkisal;
	1 E$_2$-saĝ-⸢ki⸣	1 Esaĝki;
	1 ⸢x-x⸣	1 …;
ii	1 Utu-ak	1 Utu'ak;
	1 E$_2$-lu$_2$-da	1 Eluda;
	1 ^{d}En-lil$_2$-ak	1 Enlil-ak;
	1 Silim-Utu	1 Silim-Utu;
	1 Ur-saĝ-pa-e$_3$	1 Ursaĝpa'e;
	1 Ušumgal-Abzu	1 Ušumgal-Abzu;
	1 PA-PA	1 PAPA,
	i$_3$-du$_8$	the doorman;
iii	1 Amar:eden	1 Amar-eden,
	baḫar$_2$	the potter;
	1 E$_2$-saḫar-ta	1 Esaḫarta,
	agrig	the *agrig* manager
	^{lu2}lunga$_3$	(of) brewers;
	1 Igi-si$_4$	1 Igisi;
	1 Mi-⸢tum⸣-[ma]-ni	1 Mitumani;
	1 Pa$_4$-⸢nam$_2$⸣	1 Panam;
	1 Pa-bil$_2$-ga-⸢x⸣	1 Pabilga…;
iv	1 ⸢KA-x-x⸣	1 KA…;
	1 [x]-KASKAL.⸢DU?⸣	1 …kas(?);
	1 ⸢En⸣-[…]	1 En…;
	1 Engar-⸢x⸣	1 Engar…;
	1 ⸢UN-il$_2$⸣	1 UNil;
	1 Gu$_2^?$-ni-ĝa$_2$	1 Guniĝa(?);
rev. i	[mostly destroyed]	…
	(blank space)	
ii	^{lu2}lunga$_3$	(They are) brewer(s).
	(rest blank)	

obv. iii 7: Cf. this name in an Umma text, No. 408 obv. i 4.

obv. iv 6: The first sign is uncertain. The name might instead be X-ĝa$_2$-ni.

No. 479 – MS 4746

List of personnel. Early Dynastic IIIa, uncertain provenance (Umma region?).

The text was published and discussed in Bartash 2015c.

obv. i	1 Šubur	1 Šubur,
	KA-gul	(the man of) KAgul;
	1 E$_2$-UD-pa-⌜e$_3$⌝	1 E'UDpa'e;
	1 Šeš-ĝeštin	1 Šešĝeštin;
	1 ^{d}En-lil$_2$-ak	1 Enlilak;
	1 Amar-Saman$_x$(ŠE.BU.NUN)	1 Amar-Saman;
ii	1 Ba-za	1 Baza,
	Ur:^{d}Šara$_2$	(the man of) Ur-Šara;
	1 En-ḫe$_2$(AŠ.GAN):ĝal$_2$	1 Enheĝal;
	1 Ur:Nin-ĝir$_2$-su	1 Ur-Ninĝirsu;
	1 Nagar	1 Nagar;
	1 ⌜ḪAR$^?$⌝-ĝeštin	1 ...ĝeštin;
	1 Šubur	1 Šubur,
	Sa(ŠU$_2$.SA)-du$_8$-du$_8$	(the man of) Sadudu;
	1 Pa$_4$-nam$_2$	1 Panam;
iii	1 Ak	1 Ak(a),
	nagar	the carpenter;
	1 ⌜NE⌝-nu-si	1 NEnusi;
	1 E$_2$-na	1 Ena;
	1 ⌜U$_4$⌝-bi-kur-ra	1 Ubikura;
	1 Ig-nu-gi$_4$	1 Ignugi
	SAĜ-ZA-SI^{ki}	(from) SAĜZASI;
	1 *Al*$_6$(MAḪ)-*lu*$_5$	1 *'Al-('i)lu(m)*;
iv	1 Ni$_3$-ti	1 Niti
	Ĝir$_2$-su^{ki}	(from) Ĝirsu;
	1 A:zu$_5$	1 Azu
	Lagaš(BURU$_4$:LA^{mušen})^{ki}	(from) Lagaš;
	1 Šeš:tur	1 Šeštur,
	simug	the smith;
	1 Lu$_2$-gid$_2$	1 Lugid,
	E$_2$-*la:lum*$_x$(LAK218)	(the man of) *Ḫalalum*
	UB-me^{ki}	(from) UBme.
rev. i	⌜gu$_2$:an-še$_3$⌝	Total:
	22 ⌜Ka$_5$⌝:a	22 (persons under) Ka'a.
	(rest blank)	

Many of the personal names in this document occur in Fara texts, but other evidence suggests that Šuruppak was not its provenance. For instance, SA in obv. ii 8 has a writing ŠU$_2$.SA uncharacteristic of Fara texts. Judging by personal names, such as Ur-Šara and Ur-Ninĝirsu, and the geographical names Ĝirsu, Lagaš and UBme (if indeed that is the Early Dynastic city of Umma), the text could have been excavated in the Umma or Lagaš regions. As stated above, there are clear prosopographic links with text No. 478. Both are probably from the Umma region.

obv. iii 5: Cf. the same name in a later document from Umma, text No. 385 obv. viii 13.

obv. iii 6: The strokes at the beginning of GI$_4$ are oblique.

obv. iii 7: The place name SAĜ-ZA-SI^{ki} remains unidentified. The sequence of the signs is uncertain. One should take into account the fact that ZA interchanges with A in Early Dynastic IIIa texts. Therefore, Saĝ-diri(SI.A(ZA))^{ki} is also possible.

obv. iii 8: The interpretation of the name *Al*$_6$(MAḪ)-*lu*$_5$/*lul* is tentative. For its many variants, see EDATŠ Indices, p. 11.

obv. iv 4: The writing is LA.NU$_{11}$.BUR.ḪU.KI.

obv. iv 8: See Krebernik 1998a: 275 fn. 457 with additional references for the reading /lum/ of the sign LAK218.

No. 480 – MS 3791/20

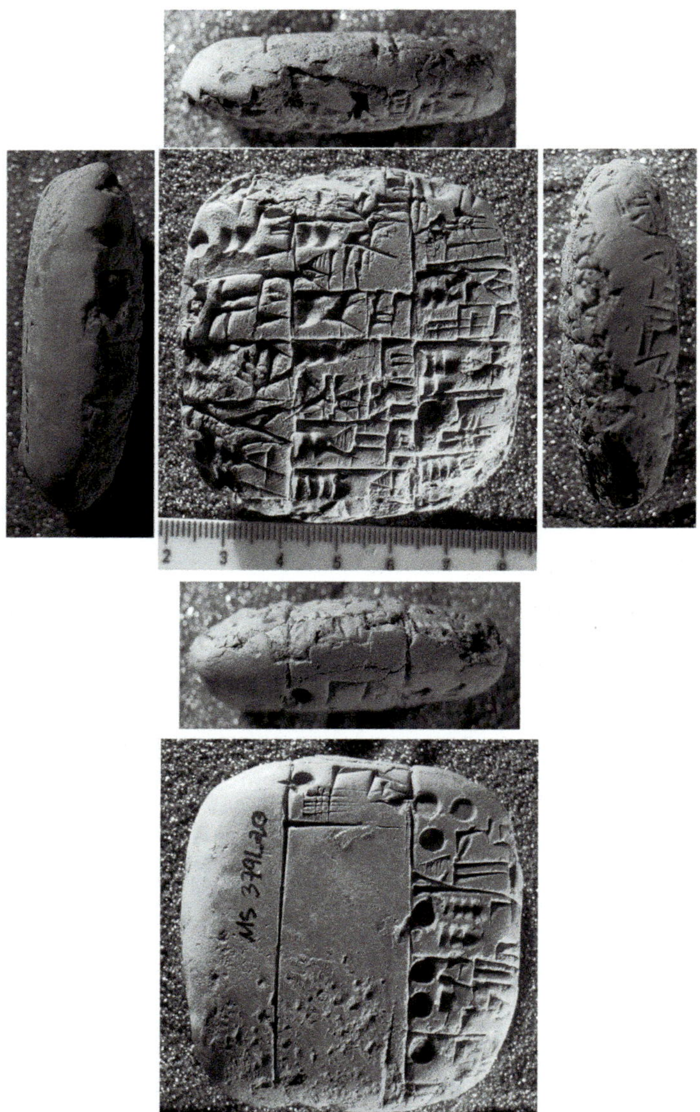

Account of textiles and other goods, Early Dynastic IIIa, uncertain provenance (Umma region?).

obv. i	12 ⸢gada-x⸣^{tug_2}	12 linen ... garments;
	⸢10⸣ la_2 *1* bar-bul_5	9 *bardul*-garments;
	5 *3*-ĜAR	5 ... garments;
	7 gada ib_2-du_3	7 linen loincloths;
ii	[n+] 2 ⸢ni_3⸣-lam_2^{tug_2}	n+ 2 *nilam*-garments;
	2 gada $aktum_2$(SU:A)	2 heavy linen garments;
	1 gada tug_2	1 linen garment;
	3 $^{kuš?}$$tug_2$-⸢ĜAR$^?$⸣-aktum-TUR	3 heavy linen .... garments;
	2 dul_3^{tug_2}	2 covers;
	4 ^{kuš}DU-⸢x⸣	4 leather ...;
iii	2 si-ĝar-duḫ-eren	2 cedar bolt-openers (= handles?);
	4 ^{kuš}gul-⸢x⸣	4 leather ...;
	5 LAK490	5 ...;
	10 gaba:la_2	10 ...;
	7 ⸢x⸣-[x]	7 ...;
rev. i	30 ni_3-DUL_3:la_2	30 ... garments;
	17 ni_3-SUḪUŠ:la_2	17 ... garments;
	21 ni_3-saĝ:la_2	21 headdresses;
	10 ni_3-saĝ:la_2	10 headdresses;
	(blank space)	
ii	10 ni_3-u_2:la_2	10 ... garments.
	(rest blank)	
iii	(below: several damaged signs?)	

obv. i 3: See ED Vessels and Garments 125 for tug_2-3(AŠ)+ĜAR.

obv. i 4: This is an abbreviated spelling of the garment ^{tug_2}ib_2-ba-du_3. See MEE 4 p. 297 l. 863 for ib_2-du_3^{tug_2} = *ma-ša-gu-um*. See Foster 2010: 129 for the identification of ^{tug_2}ib_2-ba-du_3 with "loincloth, kilt." See EDPV A p. 96 sub no. 188 for "waist garment."

obv. ii 5: See EDPV A no. 177 for this garment.

obv. iii 3: See EDPV A no. 88 for a discussion of /ga'ar/ "cheese." Food is not expected in this context. The sign may designate a garment or similar.

rev. i 1–2, ii 1: Unidentified. The terms obviously denote items of clothing.

rev. i 3–4: See EDPV A no. 28 for this term denoting a type of headgear.

No. 481 – MS 4735

Delivery of silver to the palace, Early Dynastic IIIa, uncertain provenance (Umma region?).

The handwriting of the document is similar to that of text No. 479.

obv. i	^{šu_2}*1N*$_8$ 5 ku_3	⅓ (mina) 5 (shekels) silver:
	Na-u_2-u_2	Na'u'u;
	^{šu_2}*1N*$_8$ Šubur-ak	⅓ (mina): Šubur-ak;
	^{šu_2}*1N*$_8$ KUM-e_2:gibil	⅓ (mina): …egibil;
ii	⸢^{šu_2}*1N*$_8$ *4* ½⸣ Da-⸢ti⸣	⅓ (mina) 4 ½ (shekels): Dati;
	5 Pa_4-a_2-gal-⸢tuku⸣	5 (shekels): Pa'agaltuku
	⸢^{šu_2}*1N*$_8$ ⸢NE⸣-nu-a	⅓ (mina): NEnu'a.
	10 5 ⸢x⸣	15 (shekels): …
iii	[broken/blank]	…
rev.	e_2:gal de_6	Delivered to the palace.

rev.: This subscript is typical of ED texts from the Umma region.

No. 482 – MS 5008

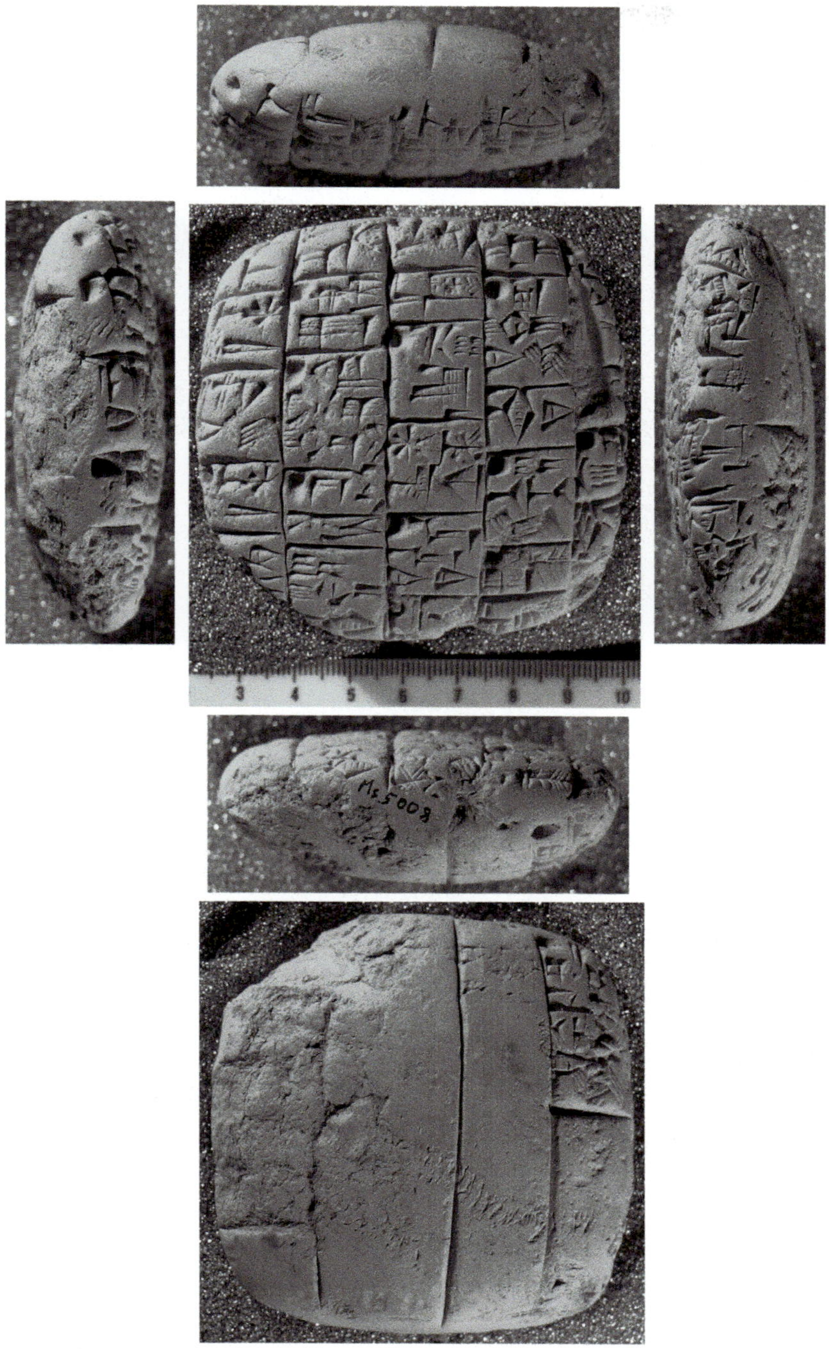

List of personnel, Early Dynastic IIIa, uncertain provenance (many Semitic names).

obv. i	1 Me-me	1 Meme;
	1 Me-^{d}Nisaba	1 Me-Nisaba,
	A-ḫu$^{!}$(RI)*-i*$_3$*-lum*	(and) *'Aḫu(m)-'ilum*;
	1 Me-^{d}Nisaba	1 Me-Nisaba;
	1 ⌜Gan⌝-[x]	1 Gan…;
	[1 line broken]	…
ii	Ur-Ab-⌜zu⌝	(and) Ur-Abzu;
	1 Gan-e$_2$	1 Gan-e,
	PU$_3$.ŠA-*Sa*(ŠU$_2$.SA)*-rum*$_2$(NE.RU)	(and) PUŠA-*šarrum*;
	1 ^{ĝeš}ERIN$_2$*-tum*	1 *Damiqtum*,
	I-bi$_2$*-su*$_x$(TAG)	(and) *Yibbi-šu*;
iii	1 Me-Aš-tar$_2$	1 Me'Aštar,
	Ur-ĜA$_2$×GI$_4$	(and) Ur…;
	1 *Si-mi-um*	1 *Simi'um*,
	^{d}*Su-mu*-Zu:en	(and) *Šumu(m)-Su'en*;
	1 *Ma-ma-i*$_3$*-li*$_2$	1 *Mama-'ilī*;
	1 A-⌜šeš⌝-mu-⌜ak⌝	1 Ašešmu'ak,
iv	Lugal-ezen	(and) Lugal-ezen;
	1 *Ra-bi*$_2$*-i*$_3$*-lum*	1 *Rabi-'ilum*,
	Na-ni	(and) Nani;
	1 *I-di*$_3$*-lum*	1 *'Id(ī)-'ilum*;
	1 E$_2$-zi	1 Ezi,
	⌜Engar⌝-zi	(and) Engarzi;
v	1 Lugal-eden-⌜ne$_2$⌝-si	1 Lugaledensi,
	[x]-zi	(and) …zi;
	1 *La-mi-um*	1 *Lami'um*,
	Ša$_3$-NE-da-nu	(and) ŠaNEdanu;
rev. i	1 *A-lu*$_{\text{-nutillû}}$*-lu*$_{\text{-nutillû}}$	1 *'Alu(m-'i)lu(m)*,
	Damiq(SIG$_5$)*-i*$_3$*-lum*	(and) *Damiq-'ilum*.
	(rest blank)	
ii–iii	(blank)	
iv	[colophon destroyed]	…

rev. i 1: For the same sign LU$_{\text{-nutillû}}$ in the same name, but in a slightly different spelling, *Al*$_6$*-lu*$_{\text{nutillû}}$*-lu*$_{\text{-nutillû}}$, see CUSAS 23 no. 1 (ED IIIa Umma region). However, judging by its many Semitic names, the text either comes from the north or records workers of Semitic origins brought to the Umma region.

obv. ii 4: For ĜIŠ.ERIN$_2$ as a graphic variant of SIG$_5$ = *damqum*, see the commentary to ELTS p. 105 ii 9.

obv. v 4: For this name, see Pomponio 1987: 224.

5.3 – Early Dynastic IIIb/Early Sargonic Document

No. 483 – MS 3825

Expenditure of barley as fodder for animals and allocations to workers and children, Early Dynastic/Early Sargonic, uncertain provenance.

obv. i	1(bariga) še	1 *bariga* barley:
	anše gu_7	(for) the donkeys to consume.
	7 ĝuruš	7 *ĝuruš*-workers:
	2(ban_2)-ta	2 *ban* (barley) each.
	8 TUR-TUR	8 children (minors):
ii	1(ban_2) 5 $sila_3$-ta	1 *ban* 5 *sila* each.
	4(ban_2) X 5 $sila_3$	4 *ban* … 5 *sila*.
	(blank space)	
	1(gur) 2(bariga) igi-3-$ĝal_2$ / šu-$niĝin_2$-bi	1 *gur* 2 *bariga* ⅓ its total.
	ni_3 zi-ga / ĝanun-kam	These are goods expended. It is of the storehouse.
rev.	(blank)	

A beautifully formed round tablet. The complete absence of personal names precludes any attempts to link the document to any known "archive." The shape of the document may be a clue to its provenance when similar tablets are identified.

obv. i 4: Two *ban* (*ca.* 20 l.) of barley as a monthly allowance is very low for an adult *ĝuruš*-worker. The usual amount for this category is 1 *bariga*, and even more in Early Dynastic IIIb and Sargonic records. Note, however, that *ĝuruš*-workmen receive two *ban* of flour in WF 98 rev. iii 1–2 as allotments (ED IIIa, Fara). The difference in the amount of rations may reflect the age categories among the class of ĝuruš. Whereas some of them were adults and even elderly, the term was applied to adolescents and some probably even younger.

obv. i 5: An even lesser amount of rations suggests that these are definitely minors. See Bartash (forthcoming), "Sumerian 'Child'" for the terminology for "child, minor" in Sumerian records. TUR-TUR may be either tur-tur or di$_4$-di$_4$(-la), both meaning "children, minors."

obv. ii 2: The sign X is unknown and the reading of the line uncertain. At any rate, it cannot be LAGAB, for which cf. obv. ii 4. Neither can it be ĜIŠ$_{\textit{-tenû}}$, for which see Sallaberger 1994: 143–44, because of the two wedges in each of the vertical lines of the present sign.

obv. ii 3: The use of the construction igi-*n*-ĝal$_2$ for fractions is very unusual with capacity measures.

No. 484 – MS 1952/51

Account of reeds, Early Sargonic, uncertain provenance.

Read from photographs.

obv. i	3 gi gu$_2$ ⸢x⸣	3 loads of reeds …;
	⸢x⸣ […] ⸢lu$_2$⸣ ŠU$^?$ AN	…
	⸢2⸣ […] ⸢x⸣ […]	2: …
ii	(blank)	
rev.	(blank)	

5.4 – Middle Sargonic Documents

5.4.1 – "Northern Deliveries" File

Texts Nos. 485 and 486 are written by the same scribe and their measurements are similar. References to Gasur and Keš(?) are clues to their provenance. Note the consistent use of Sumerian language and Sumerian personal names. The "file" cannot be from central or northern Mesopotamia. Museum numbers suggest that these two texts may come from Umma.

No. 485 – MS 1952/23

Delivery of food to Gasur, Middle/Classical Sargonic, uncertain provenance.

obv.	6 zi$_3$ gur A-⸢ga-de$_3$⸣$^{[ki]}$	6 *gur* of flour (by the *gur* of) Agade;
	[n+] 1(gur) 4(ban$_2$) ⸢bappir⸣ [gur]	x+1 *gur* 4 *ban* of sourdough;
	1(gur) 4(ban$_2$) ⸢munu$_4$⸣ [gur]	1 *gur* 4 *ban* of malt;
	3(gur) 4(ban$_2$) ⸢ni$_3$-ar$_3$-ra⸣ gur	3 *gur* 4 *ban* of groats;
	1 i$_3$ ⸢dug⸣-gal	1 large jar of oil;
	70 i$_3$ sila$_3$ i$_3$-ak	70 *sila* oil …;
	1(gur) 1(bariga) ku$_6$ gur-saĝ-⸢ĝal$_2$⸣	1 *gursaĝĝal* 1 *bariga* of fish;
	[n x]-NI-⸢x⸣	…;
	[n+] 6 dupsik	x+6 *dupsik*-baskets.
rev.	la$_2$-i$_3$	These are the arrears
	[x] An-na-⸢num$_2$⸣-e	that Annanum
	Ga-sur$_2^{ki}$-⸢a⸣	has brought to Gasur.

mu-de$_6$-a-kam
(blank)
(no month name written)

No. 486 – MS 1952/44

Delivery and receipt of grain at Keš(?), Middle/Classical Sargonic, uncertain provenance.

obv.	68 [x gur] / A-[ga-de$_3$^{ki}]	68 *gur* of … (by the *gur* of) Agade:
	⸢zi$_3$$^{?}$⸣ Ur-⸢x⸣ dumu Ne-[saĝ] / nu-banda$_3$-⸢ke$_4$⸣	it is the flour(?) that Ur…, son of Ne[saĝ], the supervisor,
	⸢mu⸣-de$_6$-am$_3$	has brought.
	[n+] ⸢43⸣(gur) 1(bariga) ⸢x⸣ gur A-ga-de$_3$^{ki}	x+43 *gur* 1 *bariga* of … (by the *gur* of) Agade;
	12 la$_2$ 1(bariga) ⸢še⸣ gur A-ga-de$_3$^{ki}	12 *gur* minus 1 *bariga* of barley (by the *gur* of) Agade:
	[x] Ur-SAĜ×ḪA ugula-e$_2$	… Ur…, the household overseer,
	[mu]-de$_6$-⸢x⸣	has delivered.
rev.	[…] ⸢Keš$_3$$^{?}$⸣^{ki}-a	… in Keš(?)
	[šu] ba-ti	has received it.
	(blank)	

obv. 6: For the reading ḫu$_x$ of the sign SAĜ×ḪA in the word ḫu$_x$-mul "interest (of a loan)," see Civil 1983: 564. See ibid. p. 566 for this sign in early personal names. The reading of the sign in names remains uncertain.

5.4.2 – Other Middle Sargonic Documents

No. 487 – MS 1952/24

Account of butter, oil, lard and wine, Middle Sargonic, uncertain provenance. This document may be from Umma.

obv.	4 dug i$_3$-nun	4 jars of butter;
	2 dug i$_3$-udu	2 jars of sheep lard;
	5 <dug> i$_3$-šaḫ$_2$	5 <jars> of pig lard;
	2 dug ĝeštin	2 jars of wine;
	1 dug i$_3$-ir	1 jar of perfumed oil.
	En-nu-[...]	Ennu…
rev.	ĜIŠ-⸢x⸣-[…] / [(mu)]-de$_6$-⸢am$_3$⸣	It is what one has brought …
	(blank space)	

No. 488 – MS 2191/36

Cumulative record of various transactions in silver, Middle Sargonic, uncertain provenance.

For another text from the same dossier, see CUSAS 26 no. 161, which also records the individuals Ajaguba(bara) and Ninirida(kuš). That text is attributed to the Umma region by Westenholz, but the reason for this is not explicitly stated. The name Ninirida occurs also in the Middle Sargonic text

CUSAS 20 no. 204, a list of women receiving lard. Although Pomponio and Visicato believe the text to be from Adab, this is yet to be substantiated.

The two main topics of the document are loans with interest in silver to several individuals and the purchase of slaves.

obv. i	1 ku$_3$ ma-na	1 mina silver:
	dam E$_2$-muš	the wife of Emuš.
	^{šu_2}1N$_8$ la$_2$ *3* ku$_3$ Aja$_2$-gub-ba-am$_3$	⅓ (mina) minus 3 (shekels): Ajagubam.
	^{šu_2}1N$_8$ *6* Lugal-Keš$_3$	⅓ (mina) 6 (shekels): Lugal-Keš.
	1 la$_2$ *6* En-me-te-na	1 (mina) minus 6 (shekels): Enmetena.
	4 addir$_x$(ĜIŠGAL×A.GADA)^{dir} / anše-kam	4 (shekels): it is the hire of donkeys:
	Nin-ga-zi	Ningazi.
	4 Nin-amaš-zi	4: Ninamašzi.
	4 Usar$_4$(LA$_2$×LAGAB)-re$_2$ dam-gara$_3$	4: Usare, the merchant.
	2 Ki-na$_4$	2: Kina
	Nin-ga-zi	(and) Ningazi.
ii	šu+niĝin$_2$ 3 ku$_3$ ma-na la$_2$ *3* giĝ$_4$	Total: 3 minas minus 3 shekels silver.
	2N$_8$^{ša} sila-ta us$_2$(ARAD)-am$_3$	⅔ (mina): it is (what) *follows from the street* (i.e. is on the way and will be available soon).
	1 ½ maš ku$_3$-ga-kam	1 ½ (shekel): it is the interest of the (loaned) silver.
	(ruling)	
	ša$_3$-bi-ta	Out of it:
	(ruling)	
	½ ku$_3$ giĝ$_4$	½ shekel silver:
	ni$_3$-sa$_{10}$	It is the price
	Ḫa-la-lum-⸢kam⸣	of *Ḫalalum*.
	7 ku$_3$ giĝ$_4$	7 shekels silver:
	ni$_3$-sa$_{10}$ Za-⸢gin$_3$$^?$⸣-[kam$^?$]	[it is] the price of Zagin(?).
	2N$_8$ ku$_3$ ⸢^{ša} ni$_3$-sa$_{10}$⸣	⅔ mina silver: the price
rev. i	[break]	of …
	[…]-kam	it is …
	10 [ni$_3$]-sa$_{10}$	10 (shekels): it is the price
	Nin-iri-da-kam	of Nin-irida.
	15 ku$_3$ giĝ$_4$	15 shekels silver:
	ni$_3$-sa$_{10}$	it is the price
	I$_3$-[lum-ba]-ni-kam	of *'Ilum-bani*.
	1 [+n ku$_3$ n] giĝ$_4$ ni$_3$-⸢sa$_{10}$⸣	1+x [minas x] shekels [silver]: it is the price
ii	arad$_2$ geme$_2$-kam	of male (and) female slaves.
	(ruling)	
	šu+niĝin$_2$ 3 2N$_8$ [ku$_3$^{ša}] ma-na	Total: 3 ⅔ minas [silver].
	an-na-[x]	he has [weighed/given] to him.
	⸢Maḫ-x⸣-[…]	Maḫ…
	⸢x⸣-[…]	…
	ni$_3$-sa$_{10}$ Nin-bur-šu-ma-kam	It is the price of Ninburšuma.
	6 ku$_3$ giĝ$_4$	6 shekels silver:
	ni$_3$-sa$_{10}$	it is the price

	Nin-iri-da-kam	of Ninirida.
	UN-il$_2$-da	With UNil
	an-da-ĝal$_2$	it is available.
l.e.	*6* En-me-te-na	6 (shekels for) Enmetena.

obv. ii 2: See the commentary to text No. 163 obv. ii 4 for this expression.

obv. ii 5: Half a shekel is too low to be the price of an adult person. Was *Ḫalalum* a child? The name is likely the same as in the writing E$_2$-*la-lum*$_{(x)}$.

No. 489 – MS 2191/37

Weighing of wool, Middle Sargonic, uncertain provenance.

obv.	21 siki gu$_2$ *20* ma-na	21 talents 20 minas wool:
	⸢Lu$_2$⸣-pa$_3$-da	Lupada
	i$_3$-la$_2$	has weighed.
rev.	(blank)	

5.5 – Classical and Late Sargonic Documents

5.5.1 – The "ANIza Archive"

The interpretation of the name of the protagonist of this archive, A-NI-za, requires further study. Other texts that belong to the same archive are CUSAS 19 nos. 185–91. Although the texts witness almost exclusively Sumerian names and are written in Sumerian, they employ an ancient Semitic calendar that is well attested at Ebla and in northern Mesopotamia. This fact is puzzling. Maiocchi and Visicato suggest that the archive originates in the "Adab region" (CUSAS 19, Introduction 1.6), but there is no clear evidence for this suggestion. Month names in the text suggest an area from Ešnunna in the north to Ĝirsu in the south, which is, essentially, the whole of central and lower Mesopotamia.

No. 490 – MS 1952/49

Receipt of barley, Classical Sargonic, uncertain provenance.

obv.	1(bariga) še A-ga-de$_3^{ki}$	1 *bariga* barley (by the *gur* of) Agade:
	ki Lu$_2$-^{d}Šara$_2$-ta	from Lu-Šara,
rev.	A-NI-za	ANIza
	šu ba-ti	has received.
	(blank/ruling)	
	iti *za-lul*	Month *Zalul.*

rev. 3: For this month and its linguistic interpretations, see Cohen 2015: 16.

No. 491 – MS 1952/50

Expenditure of barley, Classical Sargonic, uncertain provenance.

obv.	5 sila$_3$ še anše gu$_7$	5 *sila* barley (as) donkey fodder:
	UD-re$_2$	(for) UDre.
rev.	⸢še⸣ zi-ga	Barley expended.
	A-NI-za	ANIza (is responsible).
	iti *ba-ḫi-ir*-EGIR	Month "Late (*lit.* back) Hot Season."

obv. 2: Cf. the same personal name in OSP 1 no. 23 (Nippur) obv. ii 17' f. It has the form UD-URU-na in Ur III texts.

rev. 3: As observed by Maiocchi and Visicato, the month *ba-ḫi-ir* does not appear at Ebla but is attested at Ešnunna, Nippur, Adab and even as far south as Ĝirsu (CUSAS 19, Introduction 1.6). Relying on CAD, Westenholz interprets the month name iti *Ba-ḫi-ir* IGI-*me* as "Month of the Early Hot Season" (OSP 2 no. 9 and p. 202).

5.5.2 – The "*Qa'u* Archive"

Four texts comprise a single dossier recording transactions of grain and female workers. All texts mention the same individuals. The provenance of this dossier is uncertain. Some of the personal names are unusual. On the basis of paleography, the texts can be dated to the Classical Sargonic period.

No. 492 – MS 4269/1

Allocation of barley, Classical Sargonic, uncertain provenance.

obv.	1(bariga) maš 1(*ban$_2$*) še	1 *bariga* 1 *ban* barley:
	Ba-al-la	Ba'ala;
	1(bariga) Sim$_x$(GIG)-ma-AN	1 *bariga*: SimmaAN;
	1(bariga) 1(ban$_2$) *Qa-u*	1 *bariga* 1 *ban*: *Qa'u*;
	5(ban$_2$) *Ḫi-ir-tu*	5 *ban*: *Ḫīrtu(m).*
rev.	(blank)	

obv. 3: The interpretation of the name is uncertain. Sim$_x$(GIG)-ma as "wound" or similar is recorded only in the literary composition *Lugal-e* 177 f. Note that personal names from the Lagaš region end on -an instead of the usual writing …a-ni (see Westenholz in CUSAS 26, Introduction to the "Lugal-ra Archive").

No. 493 – MS 4269/3

Account of barley flour, Classical Sargonic, uncertain provenance.

obv.	5(ban$_2$) dabin	5 *ban* barley flour:
	Ba-⌜al⌝-la	Ba'ala;
	1(bariga) Sim$_x$(GIG)-ma-⌜AN⌝	1 *bariga*: SimmaAN;
	5(ban$_2$) *Qa-u*	5 *ban*: *Qa'u*;
	1(ban$_2$) *Ḫi-ir-tu*	1 *ban*: *Ḫirtu(m)*.
rev.	(blank)	

No. 494 – MS 4269/2

Assignation of female workers, Classical Sargonic, uncertain provenance.

obv.	*4* geme$_2$	4 female workers:
	Ba-al-la	Ba'ala;
	6 Sim$_x^!$(MI)-ma-AN	6: SimmaAN;
	3 *Qa-u*	3: *Qa'u*.
(rev.)	(blank)	

obv. 3: The sign GIG is not finished, thus resulting in MI.

No. 495 – MS 4269/4

Allocation of barley to female workers mentioning their overseers, Classical Sargonic, uncertain provenance.

obv.	*6* geme$_2$ *3*(ban$_2$)	6 female workers 3 *ban* (grain each):
	Ba-al-la	Ba'ala;
	6 geme$_2$ *3*(ban$_2$)	6 female workers 3 *ban*:
	Sim$_x$(GIG)-ma-AN	SimmaAN;
	7 geme$_2$ *3*(ban$_2$)	7 female workers 3 *ban*:
	Qa-u	*Qa'u*;
	⸢*3*⸣ geme$_2$ 3(ban$_2$)	3 female workers 3 *ban*:
rev.	A-ba-a-ne-gin$_7$	Aba'anegin ("Who is like him?")
	1 geme$_2$ 3(ban$_2$)	1 female worker 3 *ban*:
	E$_2$-gu-la	Egula.
	(ruling)	
	šu+niĝin$_2$ *2*(gur) *1*(bariga) še gur / A-ga-de$_3$^{ki}	Total: 2 *gur* 1 *bariga* grain (by) the *gur* of Akkad.
	u$_4$ *2*-kam	It is of the 2nd day.

5.5.3 – Land

No. 496 – MS 4219

Account of fields, Classical/Late Sargonic, uncertain provenance.

The upper left corner is faked.

This and the following land texts are of similar format and share the same terminology. The author is grateful to Robert Middeke-Conlin for making these documents more lucid to him. For a discussion of similar documents of Sargonic date, see Friberg 2007: 402.

Saĝ is here "front (side of the field)" and us$_2$ is "side." The second numeral after each term designates the length of the second "front" or "side." The marker -ḫi-a with either saĝ or us$_2$ refers to two edges of the same length. In most cases, only length measures appear. The basic unit of length is either gi = *ca.* 3 m or nindan = *ca.* 6 m. If a calculation of area is present, it has the following structure: first, edges of various lengths are averaged: $(N_1+N_2)/2$. Then, the "front" is multiplied by the "side" to arrive at the area. The term du$_3$ in the second text is obscure.

Many of the fields are trapezoidal, most likely because their "fronts" lay on the banks of ditches or canals. Others are rectangular, and so were probably not situated on canals.

obv. i	[2 lines broken]	. . .:
	⸢Ur⸣-pisaĝ	Urpisaĝ,
	lu$_2$-tir	the forester.
	[n] saĝ *4 ½*	(The first) front x (*nindan*), (the second front) 4 ½ (*nindan*),
	[n+] *20* us$_2$-ḫi-a	both sides: 20+x:
	Lul-gu-ak	Lulgu'ak.
	13 ½ saĝ *16*	Fronts: 13 ½ (and) 16 (*nindan*),
	30 la$_2$ *3* us$_2$ *40* la$_2$ *3*	sides: 27 (and) 37:
	Ur-nu	Urnu,
	dam-gara$_3$	the merchant.
	20 saĝ *20* la$_2$ *3*	Fronts: 20 (and) 17;
	42 saĝ *40*	fronts: 42 (and) 40:
	E$_3$-mu-da	Emuda.
ii	*10* saĝ *10*	Fronts: 10 (and) 10;
	⸢*30*⸣ us$_2$-ḫi-a	both sides: 30;
	[n] saĝ *6*	Fronts: x (and) 6;
	[n+] *½* us$_2$ *10*	sides: x+½ (and) 10:
	Lugal-ni$_3$-bara$_4$-du$_{10}$	Lugalnibaradu.
	2 saĝ *1* kuš$_3$ *3*	Fronts: 2 (*nindan*) 1 cubit (and) 3 (*nindan*);
	40 us$_2$	(both) sides: 40:
	Ur-^{d}Dumu	Ur-Dumu.
	3 ½ saĝ *1* kuš$_3$	Fronts: 3 ½ (*nindan* and) 1 cubit;
	40 la$_2$ *1* us$_2$	(both) sides: 39:
	Ur-zikum-ma	Urzikuma.
	7 ½ saĝ *6 ½*	Fronts: 7 ½ (and) 6 ½;
	43 us$_2$-ḫi-a	both sides: 43;
	3 ½ saĝ *3*	fronts: 3 ½ (and) 3;
	23 us$_2$	(both) sides: 23:
rev. i	Ur-^{d}Ištaran(KA.DI)	Ur-Ištaran,
	mušen-du$_3$	the bird-catcher.
	6 saĝ *4 ½*	Fronts: 6 (and) 4 ½;

	24 us$_2$ *20*	sides: 24 (and) 20:
	Ur-e$_2$	Ur-e.
	6 ½ saĝ *7*	Fronts: 6 ½ (and) 7;
	20 la$_2$ *2* us$_2$ *16*	sides: 18 (and) 16:
	Ur$^!$-e-ga	Urega.
	12 saĝ-ḫi-a	Both fronts: 12 fronts,
	16 us$_2$ *13 ½*	sides: 16 (and) 13 ½:
	Lugal-a$_2$-maḫ	Lugal-amaḫ.
	6 saĝ *5 ½*	Fronts: 6 (and) 5 ½;
	23 us$_2$ *25*	sides: 23 (and) 25:
	Lu$_2$-gid$_2$	Lugid(a).
	4 ½ saĝ *2 ½*	Fronts: 4 ½ (and) 2 ½;
	24 ⸢us$_2$⸣-ḫi-a	both sides: 24:
	A$_2$-⸢zi-da⸣	Azida.
	⸢*4* saĝ⸣ [...]	Fronts: 4 (and) x;
ii	*30* la$_2$ *3* us$_2$ *24*	sides: 27 (and) 24:
	^{d}Utu-an-zu	Utu'anzu.
	15 saĝ *5*	Fronts: 15 (and) 5;
	60+10 us$_2$-ḫi-a	both sides: 70:
	Bar-ra-ni-še$_3$	Baraniše.
	4 saĝ-ḫi-a	Both fronts: 4;
	60+20 us$_2$-ḫi-a	both sides: 80:
	A$_2$-zi-da	Azida.
	4 saĝ-ḫi-a	Both fronts: 4;
	60+20 us$_2$	both sides: 80:
	^{d}Utu-an-zu	Utu'anzu.
	⸢*4*⸣ saĝ-ḫi-a	Both fronts: 4;
	60+20 us$_2$	both sides: 80:
	E$_3$-mu-da	Emuda,
	dumu Diĝir-en-nun	son of Diĝir-ennun.
	⸢ša$_3$$^{?}$⸣ aša$_5$ Lugal-[...] ⸢gur⸣-maḫ	From(?) the field of Lugal..., (the grain? in) the large *gur*.

No. 497 – MS 4226

Account of fields, Classical/Late Sargonic, uncertain provenance.

obv. i	*5 ½* saĝ *7 ½*	Fronts: 5 ½ (and) 7 ½ (*nindan* length),
	10 us$_2$	(both) sides: 10;
	7 ½ saĝ *10*	fronts: 7 ½ (and) 10;
	10 saĝ *5 ½*	fronts: 10 (and) 5 ½;
	23 ½ us$_2$	(both) sides: 23 ½;
	2 ½ saĝ *2 ½*	fronts: 2 ½ (and) 2 ½;
	21 us$_2$	(both) sides: 21:
	^{d}En-lil$_2$-le	Enlile.
	20 saĝ *13*	Fronts: 20 (and) 13;
	23 us$_2$ *30*	sides: 23 (and) 30;

	3 saĝ *6*	fronts: 3 (and) 6;
	10 us$_2$	(both) sides: 10;
	6 saĝ *10*	fronts: 6 (and) 10;
ii	*10* us$_2$-ḫi-a	both sides: 10;
	10 saĝ *10*	fronts: 10 (and) 10;
	20 us$_2$	(both) sides: 20;
	2 ½ saĝ *1*	fronts: 2 ½ (and) 1;
	10 us$_2$	(both) sides: 10:
	Ur-zu	Urzu
	u$_3$ Amar-^{c}Ašnan	and Amar-Ašnan.
	aša$_5$ (ras.) ereš-diĝir	The field {erasure} (of) the high priestess.
	4 saĝ *4*	Fronts: 4 (and) 4;
	40 us$_2$	(both sides): 40:
	Da-da	Dada.
	4 saĝ	(Both) fronts: 4;
	40 us$_2$	(both) sides: 40:
rev. i	E$_2$-mes	Emes.
	du$_3$ saĝ *11*	Fronts: *du* (and) 11,
	15 us$_2$-ḫi-a	both sides: 15;
	11 saĝ *11*	fronts: 11 (and) 11;
	30 us$_2$ *30*	sides: 30 (and) 30;
	1 ½ saĝ *1 ½*	fronts: 1 ½ (and) 1 ½;
	20 us$_2$ *3(AŠ)* aša$_5$	(both) fronts: 20; (= $^{?}$) 3 (*iku*) area:
	Šu-i$_3$-li$_2$-su	*Šu-'ilīšu.*
	20 saĝ *25*	Fronts: 20 (and) 25;
	34 us$_2$ *34*	sides: 34 (and) 34;
	2 ½ saĝ *2 ½*	fronts: 2 ½ (and) 2 ½;
	10 la$_2$ *1* us$_2$-ḫi-a	both sides: 9,
	10 la$_2$ *1* saĝ du$_3$	fronts: 9 (and) *du*;
	20 us$_2$	(both) sides: 20;
ii	*20* us$_2$	(both) sides: 20;
	12 saĝ-ḫi-a	both fronts: 12;
	14 us$_2$ ⸢du$_3$⸣	sides: 14 (and) *du*;
	6 saĝ *5*	fronts: 6 (and) 5;
	50 us$_2$	(both) sides: 50;
	2 ½ saĝ *2*	fronts: 2 ½ (and) 2;
	10 us$_2$-ḫi-a	both sides: 10;
	3 ½ saĝ *3 ½*	fronts: 3 ½ (and) 3 ½;
	35 us$_2$-ḫi-a	both sides: 35:
	E$_2$-saḫar-ta	Esaḫarta.
	5 ½ saĝ *7*	Fronts: 5 ½ (and) 7;
	40 us$_2$	(both) sides: 40:
	Ur-zikum-ma	Urzikuma.
	aša$_5$ ^{d}Utu-nu-ba	The field of Utunuba.

obv. ii 2: Due to lack of space the sign A appears in the column to the right (col. i of the reverse).

No. 498 – MS 4253

Account of fields with calculations of area, Classical/Late Sargonic, uncertain provenance.

obv.	*12 ½* saĝ-ḫi-[a]	Both fronts: 12 ½;
	50 la$_2$ *2 ½* us$_2$-ḫi-a	both sides: 47 ½:
	a-ša$_3$-bi *1(eše$_3$)* še-kur TAB-ba	its area: 1 *eše* (to be sown with) *mountain barley*; the *taba*-(land):
	Da-da *u$_3$* E$_2$-sa$_6$-ga	Dada and Esaga.
	60+20 la$_2$ *2* saĝ *60 la$_2$ 2*	Fronts: 78 (and) 58;
	60+30 us$_2$ *60+24*	sides: 90 (and) 84;
	10 saĝ-ḫi-a	both fronts: 10;
	30 us$_2$-ḫi-a	both sides: 30:
	a-ša$_3$-bi *3(bur$_3$) 1(eše$_3$) 2(iku)* TAB-ba	its area: 3 *bur* 1 *eše* 2 *iku*: the *taba*-(land):
	⸢dub⸣-sar-maḫ	the chief scribe.

	⸢*20*⸣ saĝ *10*	Fronts: 20 (and) 10;
	65 us$_2$-ḫi-a	both sides: 65:
	[a-ša$_3$]-bi *2(eše$_3$) 1(iku)* EŠ$_{16}$-ba	its [area]: 2 *eše* 1 *iku ešba*-(land):
	[Me]-^{sa2}sag$_7$ dub-sar	[Me]saĝ, the scribe.
	⸢x⸣-DU-DU-⸢x⸣	…
	[x] Ur-niĝar-⸢ta?⸣	… (of?) Urniĝarta,
rev.	[x]-tu	…
	[*n*] saĝ *54*	Fronts: x (and) 54;
	[*n*]+*15* us$_2$ *120+20* la$_2$ *2 ½*	sides: x+15 (and) 137 ½:
	a-ša$_3$-bi *4(bur$_3$)* še-kur maš$_2$ *3(AŠ)* ki	its area: 4 *bur* (to be sown with) mountain barley; *the irrigation tax (of) the 3 ki-(land)*(?):
	Šu-ni-diĝir	Šunidiĝir,
	Inim-ma	Inima,
	⸢Lugal⸣-uri$_3$	(and) Lugaluri.
	[*n* a-ša$_3$?] še-kur maš$_2$	… (to be sown with) mountain barley, *the irrigation tax.*
	[....] dub-sar	…, the scribe.
	1(eše$_3$) EŠ$_{16}$-ba ŠID-ni-⸢bi⸣ [x]-⸢ak?⸣	1 *eše*: *ešba*-(land): *its account has been done*(?)
	(blank space)	
	aša$_5$ ĜIŠ-⸢SAĜ?⸣	Field …
	im-*1*-⸢*x*⸣	…

obv. 3: For a variety of grain še-kur, literally "mountain barley," see USP p. 87 = Nik 2 no. 69 from Sargonic Umma. For TAB-ba and EŠ$_{16}$-ba, which appear in connection to fields in numerous ED IIIb documents from the Umma region, see the commentary to text No. 394 obv. iii 1. These documents may originate in the Umma region.

rev. 12: The writing may represent an Akkadian verbal form where *1* stands for U(*šu$_4$*).

5.5.4 – Personnel

No. 499 – MS 4241

Assignation of workers (*ĝuruš*) to a number of individuals, Classical Sargonic, uncertain provenance.

obv.	*13* ĝuruš	13 *ĝuruš*-workers:
	Lu$_2$-banda$_3$^{da}	Lubanda;
	14 Ur-^{d}Inana	14: Ur-Inana;
	15 Lugal-e$_2$	15: Lugal-e;
	10 la$_2$ *1* Da-da	9: Dada;
	12 Lugal-šu-maḫ	12: Lugalšumaḫ;
	12 ^{ĝeš}gu-za-la$_2$	12: the throne-bearer;
	<n> azlag$_3$(ĜIŠ.TUG$_2$.PI.KAR.DU)	< >: the fuller;
	30 ^{d}Ašnan(ŠE.ŠE.NIR)-ur-saĝ	30: Ašnan-ursaĝ;
	⌜*x*⌝+*6* Lugal-⌜x-x⌝	26: Lugal…;
	30 la$_2$ *3* Ur-saĝ	27: Ursaĝ;
	12 (ras.) nagar	12: (erasure) the carpenter;
	10 la$_2$ *1* ⌜simug⌝	9: the smith;
rev.	*11* ⌜ašgab⌝	11: the leather worker;
	7 tug$_2$-du$_8$	7: the felter;
	1 ad-KID	1: the reed-worker;
	10 la$_2$ *1* azlag$_3$	9: the fuller;
	10 Lu$_2$-^{d}⌜Inana⌝	10: Lu'Inana.
	(blank space)	
	šu-niĝin$_2$ *204* lu$_2$	Total: 204 persons.
	erin$_2$ gub-ba	The *erin*-individuals in service.

obv. 6: Cf. Lugal-šu-maḫ in a text of the same date and script, CUSAS 26 no. 179. The sign ŠU is written exactly as there. The present account is likely from the same archive.

rev. 6–7: See the commentary to text No. 434 obv. 1 for erin$_2$ as a class of individuals. Notable here is that *ĝuruš*-workers are referred to as both lu$_2$ "(free) persons" and erin$_2$, a class of free royal dependents. In this way the text offers an example of the use of free individuals in conscripted work. They are under the supervision of a number of professionals and persons that are known only by their personal names, probably officials.

5.5.5 – Silver

No. 500 – MS 1893

Receipt of silver designated "i$_3$-bi$_2$-za of the house," Classical Sargonic, uncertain provenance.

obv. i	Lugal-ša$_3$ ugula	Lugalša, the overseer,
	Iri-(ras.)-ga-ki	(and) Irigaki,
	$^{\text{šu}_2}$1N$_8$ ku$_3$ 3 giĝ$_4$	⅓ (mina) 3 shekels silver,
	i$_3$-bi$_2$-za e$_2$-kam	it is the compensation of the "house,"
	šu ba-ti	received.
	½ ku$_3$ ma-na 6 giĝ$_4$	½ mina 6 shekels silver
	Ĝiri$_3$-ni Lugal-ba	Ĝirini (and) Lugalba,
	i$_3$-bi$_2$-za e$_2$-kam	it is the compensation of the "house,"
	šu ba-ti	received.
	13 ku$_3$ giĝ$_4$	13 shekels silver

	Lugal-mu	Lugalmu,
	i$_3$-bi$_2$-za e$_2$-kam	it is the compensation of the "house,"
	šu ba-ti	received.
ii	^{d}Nin-dam-gal-nu^{sic}	(For the deity) Nindamgalnu
	^{ĝeš}kiri$_6$-a ba-du$_3$-a	that was erected in the garden,
	15 ku$_3$ giĝ$_4$	15 shekels silver
	Lugal-ša$_3$ Za-za-la	Lugalša (and) Zazala
	šu ba-ti	received.
	^{šu_2}|1N$_8$.1N$_8$| ku$_3$ 2 giĝ$_4$	⅔ (mina) 2 shekels silver
	Me-Unug^{ki} dub-sar	Me'Unug, the scribe,
	i$_3$-bi$_2$-za e$_2$-kam	it is the compensation of the "house,"
	šu ba-ti	received.
	(blank/ruling)	
	šu-niĝin$_2$-bi 2 ma-na la$_2$ 11 giĝ$_4$	Its total: 2 minas minus 11 shekels.
	saĝ Šeš-šeš-maḫ	Instead of Šeššešmaḫ,
	Zur-re$_2$-re$_2$	(to) Zurere,
	⸢x⸣-ŠID-ni	his …,
rev. i	Ama-ni$_3$-tu	(to) Amanitu,
	saĝ Ur-e$_2$-še$_3$	instead of Ur-e,
	ba-šum$_2$	it was given.
	(rest blank)	
ii	(blank)	

obv. i 4 f.: i$_3$-bi$_2$-za = *ibissû*: "financial loss; damages (i.e., restitution of losses sustained)"; CAD I/J 3. Cf., however, OSP 2 no. 46 p. 63, where the term does not refer to a loss. The same may apply to the present text. The term may mean "compensation." As for e$_2$ "house," this could be a reference to a public or a private household, as, e.g., in the "Enlilemaba archive" from Nippur (see OSP 2).

obv. ii 1: Cf. the deity ^{d}Nin-dam-gal-nun-na in TCL 2 no. 5482 (Ur III, Puzriš-Dagan) rev. i 19. The sign NU in the present writing is used as a syllabic spelling of /nu(n)/.

obv. ii 2: The interpretation is tentative.

5.5.6 – Jewelry

No. 501 – MS 1952/14

Account of beads, Classical Sargonic, uncertain provenance (Umma?).

obv.	[n za$_7$]-⸢gid$_2$⸣-da	x elongated [beads];
	[n za$_7$-(tur$_5$)] ⸢*u$_3$*⸣ za$_7$-gid$_2$-da	x [(translucent)] and elongated beads;
	2 za$_7$-tur$_5$ *u$_3$* za$_7$-gal-gal	2 translucent and large beads;
	2 za$_7$-tur$_5$ *u$_3$* za$_7$-tur-tur	2 translucent and small beads;
	1 za$_7$-sa *u$_3$* za$_7$	1 jewelry bead and bead;
	(blank/ruling)	
	za$_7$ si$_3$-si$_3$-de$_3$	The beads to be mounted.
	$^{\check{s}u_2}$2N$_8^{\check{s}a}$ 5 giĝ$_4$ [...]	⅔ (mina) 5 shekels [silver/gold].
	ĜIŠ-⸢x⸣-[...]	...
	(blank)	
rev.	SAĜ MA-⸢x⸣-de$_3$	in order to ...
	KUM-DUR$_2$-ŠE$_3$	to KUMDURŠE
	e-na-šum$_2$	one has given it.
	(rest blank)	

obv. 1 ff. For a recent discussion of the paleography of the sign ZA$_7$, see Bramanti and Notizia in CUSAS 35 pp. 309–11.

obv. 3 f.: For tur$_5$(TU) instead of duru$_5$ in describing gemstones, see text No. 7 obv. iv 3, 6.

obv. 5: Cf. (gil)-sa = *šukuttu* "jewelry"; CAD Š^3 237.

obv. 6: The verb si$_3$(.g) = *šakānu* probably refers here to the mounting of gems on to a piece of jewelry.

5.5.7 – Grain and Grain Products

No. 502 – MS 2191/11

Grain as payment for different purposes, Classical Sargonic, uncertain provenance.

obv.	*20* še gur A-ga-de$_3^{ki}$	20 *gur* of barley (by) the *gur* of Akkad:
	a$_2$ lu$_2$ ḫuĝ-ĝa$_2$	the wages of the hired men.
	2 gur	2 *gur*:
	addir$_x$(PA.DUG.ĜIŠ.PAD)^{dir}	the ferriage.
rev.	*1*(gur) *2*(bariga) *3*(ban$_2$) [še] gur	1 *gur* 2 *bariga* 3 *ban* barley:
	a$_2$ $^{\hat{g}e\check{s}}$gigir$_2$	the wages of the chariot(eers).
	1(bariga) ⸢dabin⸣	1 *bariga* of barley flour:
	zi-ga	expended.
	Lu$_2$-^{d}Inana	Lu'Inana.

obv. 4: See Selz 1995a: 197 f. for addir$_x$ as "ferriage, ferry toll."

No. 503 – MS 2251

Expenditure of emmer on the occasion of a festival of Dumuzi, Classical Sargonic, uncertain provenance.

obv.	[n+] 5 ziz$_2$ gur-saĝ̂-si-⸢sa$_2$⸣	x+5 standard *gur* of emmer:
	ki ezen ^{d}[Dumu]-zi-da	for the place of the festival of Dumuzi,
	[Me]-^{sag_3}sag$_7$	Mesag,
rev.	[...]	...
	[x]-⸢x⸣-la-a	...
	[...]-da	...
	[x]-an-ne$_2$	..anne,
	[...]	...

obv. 1: For this writing of the "normal *gur*" (gur-si-sa$_2$) of 240 *sila*, see Powell 1990: 496–97.

No. 504 – MS 2252

Account of regilar food delivery, Classical Sargonic, uncertain provenance.

obv.	[n+] 5 sila$_3$ <i$_3$>-nun	x+5 *sila* of butter;
	[n+] ⸢1⸣(bariga) 3(ban$_3$) ni$_3$-ar$_3$-ra	x+1 *bariga* 3 *ban* of groats;
	3(bariga) munu$_4$	3 *bariga* malt.
	sa$_2$-du$_{11}$	The regular delivery.
	⸢ba⸣-da-⸢ĝen⸣	With it he went(?);
rev.	Ku'ara(A.⸢ḪA⸣)^{ki}	Ku'ara.
	(rest blank)	

obv. 5: Likely a verbal form. However, there is no reference to the person with whom (-da) these goods were brought, unless Sa$_2$-du$_{11}$ is a personal name.

No. 505 – MS 2253

Account of beer, Classical Sargonic, uncertain provenance (Umma?).

obv.	1 kaš gur$_8$-gur$_8$ Igi-GAM-GAM	1 *gurgur*-jar of beer: IgiGAMGAM;
	1 kaš gur$_8$-gur$_8$ Ĝiri$_3$	1 *gurgur*-jar of beer: Ĝiri.
rev.	sa$_2$-du$_{11}$	The regular delivery.
	1 kaš nesaĝ$_2$(ŠID)	1 (jar of) *nesaĝ*-beer:
	aga$_3$-us$_2$	the soldier
	A-ga-de$_3^{ki}$	(from) Agade.

obv. 1: This is another writing of /gurgur/, usually gur$_4$-gur$_4$, a standardized vessel for wine, beer, and oil, of capacity ½ or ⅓ of a dug "jar": see Powell 1990: 506. The writing gur$_8$-gur$_8$ appears in numerous Sargonic texts from Umma.

No. 506 – MS 4218

Expenditure of barley, Classical Sargonic, uncertain provenance.

A fake is attached to the right edge to make the tablet look complete.

obv.	40 še gur	40 *gur* barley:
	a-ra$_2$ *1*-a-kam	it is of the 1st time;
	8 a-ra$_2$ *2*-kam	8 *gur*: it is of the 2nd time:
	^{d}Ḫa-ia$_3$-an-⸢dul$_3$⸣	Ḫaya'andul;
	10 la$_2$ 2(bariga) Nin-⸢x⸣	10 *gur* minus 2 *bariga*: Nin…;
	3 še ni$_3$-ar$_3$-ra ⸢Lu$_2$⸣-[x]	3 *gur* barley (for) groats;
	2 Amar-ḪA	2: AmarḪA;
	3 Ur-a$_2$	3: Ur-a;
	2(bariga) 3(ban$_2$) Lugal-da-lu	2 *bariga* 3 *ban*: Lugaldalu;
rev.	1(bariga) 3(ban$_2$) Ne-⸢saĝ⸣	1 *bariga* 3 *ban*: Nesaĝ

	16(gur) 2(bariga) dabin [gur]	16 *gur* 2 *bariga* barley flour.
	(blank space)	
	šu-niĝin$_2$ 83 še gur	Total: 83 *gur* barley.
	še zi-ga	Expended barley
	Lu$_2$-du$_6$-a	(by) Ludu'a.

obv. 4: For this divine element, cf. the personal name from Sargonic Adab Lu$_2$-^{d}Ḫa-NI in CUSAS 20 no. 347 obv. 4'.

rev. 5: Cf. this personal name in an ED/ES texts from Adab, CUSAS 26 no. 76 iv 7.

No. 507 – MS 4230

Calculation of an unspecified commodity, probably grain, in connection to a temple; Classical Sargonic, uncertain provenance (Ĝirsu or Umma?).

obv.	*6* 4(ban$_2$)	6 (times?) 4 *ban* (= 24 *ban*).
	(blank space)	
	šu-niĝin$_2$ 3(bariga) 2(ban$_2$) gur	Total: 3 *bariga* 2 *ban* (= 20 *ban*)
	e$_2$ ^{d}Nin-ur$_3$	Temple of Ninur.
	E$_2$-zi	Ezi (is responsible).
rev.	(blank)	

obv. 1–2: If the "pointed" number 6 at the beginning represents the factor, the correct total would be 4 *bariga*. The document's actual total requires the factor 5.

obv. 3: ^{d}Nin-ur$_3$ appears often in ED IIIb texts from Ĝirsu. For this deity, often paired with ^{d}Nin-duba, see Cavigneaux & Krebernik 2000a, 2000d. Both deities were related to the cult of Nanše at the town Niĝin/Nina. Ninur appears also as an element in personal names in Ur III documents from Umma. This speaks in favor of a southern provenance for the present text.

No. 508 – MS 4231

Allocation of bread, Classical Sargonic, uncertain provenance.

obv.	120 ninda	120 breads:
	I-ba-tum	*'Ibatum*;
	120 *I-bi$_2$-bi$_2$*	120: *Yibbībi*;
	100 ninda	100 breads:
	dub-sar-me	the scribes;
	80 ninda	80 breads:
	Mu-uz-ga	Muzga;
	182 ninda	182 breads:
rev.	^{d}Zu:en-al-ba	Su'en-alba.
	(blank)	

obv. 2: I. J. Gelb connected this personal name with the verb *buā'um* "to come"; MAD 3 p. 86.

obv. 3: This name appears almost exclusively in Classical Sargonic texts from northern Babylonian sites such as Kiš, Ešnunna, and the Himrin area. Cf. also this name in a document from Maškan-ili-Akkade written in Akkadian, BdI 2 no. 59 = CUSAS 27 no. 209 obv. 2.

obv. 7: The line is problematic. The name *Mu-uz-ga is not attested. For uz-ga as a profession, see Schrakamp 2012b: 154 *sub* no. 24 with additional references. The full writing of this occupation is lu$_2$-uz-ga, as, e.g., in BdI 1 no. 184 obv. 6.

rev. 1: The appearance of a Sumerian name in this text is notable. It may be an abbreviation of *^{d}Zu:en-al-ba-ni-du$_{11}$: cf. Aja$_2$-al-ba-ni-du$_{11}$ in an Ur III seal (CDLI P454377).

No. 509 – MS 4427

Expenditure of beer, Classical Sargonic, uncertain provenance (Adab?).

obv.	*121* kaš *10* sila$_3$ kaš-sag$_{10}$	121 (jars of) beer, 10 *sila* of premium beer;
	10 kaš a-da-gur	10 (jars of) *adagur*-beer;
	23 kaš-sag$_{10}$	23 (jars of) premium beer:
	Me-^{sa_2}sag$_7$	(for) Mesag.
	91 kaš-sag$_{10}$	91 (jars of) premium beer;
	15 kaš-gin	15 (jars of) medium quality beer;
	30 la$_2$ *3* kaš a-da-gur	27 (jars of) *adagur*-beer:
	e$_2$-kurun$_x$(DIN.KAŠ)	(for) the "beer house" (tavern?).
	⌜zi⌝-ga	Expended.
rev.	$^{[lu_2]}$lunga$_3$	The brewer.
	(blank)	

obv. 1 f.: kaš-sag$_{10}$-ga = *našpu*, a qualification of beer; CAD N^2 78. See also the lexical list OB Forerunner of Hh XX–XXI C 179–83, for a gradation of beer quality kaš-sag$_{10}$, kaš-gin, kaš-us$_2$, etc.

obv. 2: Cf. a vessel for libations $^{(dug)}$a-da-gur$_4$ in the lexical list Ešbarkin, MEE 15 no. 53 rev. i' 6' ; CUSAS 12. 3.2.1 OB Hh 5:46 = Hh X 204. Here, it could designate a specific type of beer.

obv. 8: Cf. lu$_2$-^{kaš}kurun-na = *sābûm* "innkeeper, beer merchant" in CAD S 5, and his house e$_2$ lu$_2$ ^{kaš}kurun$_2$-na in OB Kagal 67. For a discussion of DIN.KAŠ = kurun$_x$, see Waetzoldt 2006: 183–184.

5.5.8 – Wool

No. 510 – MS 1952/22

Expenditure of wool for a donkey's neck-ring, Classical Sargonic, uncertain provenance.

obv.	*11* ma-na siki	11 minas of wool:
	ḫul$_3$(LAK276)-la anše-nita$_2$ ur$_3$-še$_3$	(for) a neck ring to pull a male donkey.
	Lugal-ni$_3$	Lugalni,
rev.	tug$_2$-du$_8$-e	the felter,
	šu ba-ti	has received it.
	siki zi-ga	Wool expended.

obv. 2: The word ḫul$_3$-la = *ḫullu* designates a neck ring for animals made of wool. See the commentary to NISABA 9 no. 316 obv. 4. For ur$_3$ "to drag (over the ground)," see Thomsen 1984: 321.

5.5.9 – Livestock

No. 511 – MS 2045

Account of livestock classified as males, females, and sucklings, Classical Sargonic, uncertain provenance.

obv.	371 [+n ĝeš-munus]	371+x [female working animals];
	23 ⸢ĝeš⸣-[nita]	23 [male] working animals;
	136 ĝeš-ša$_3$-du$_{10}$	136 sucklings of working animals:
	Lugal-gub	Lugalgub.
	⸢240⸣ ĝeš-munus	240 female working animals;
	64 ĝeš-nita	64 male working animals;
	61 ĝeš-ša$_3$-du$_{10}$	61 sucklings of working animals:
	KA-ku$_3$	KAku.
	312 ĝeš-munus	312 female working animals;
	14 ĝeš-nita	14 male working animals;
	[n+] 24 ⸢ĝeš-ša$_3$-du$_{10}$⸣	x+24 sucklings of working animals:
rev.	[Ur]-^{d}Inana	[Ur]-Inana.
	430 ĝeš-munus	430 female working animals;
	31 ĝeš-nita	31 male working animals;
	185 ĝeš-ša$_3$-du$_{10}$	185 sucklings of working animals:
	Iri-nam-zu	Irinamzu.
	428 ⸢ĝeš-munus⸣	428 female working animals;
	5 ĝeš-nita	5 male working animals;
	461 ĝeš-ša$_3$-du$_{10}$	461 sucklings of working animals;
	Lugal-ni	Lugalni.
	(blank)	

The text records the assignation of unidentified animals to a number of individuals. The interpretation of ĜIŠ is uncertain, but the reference to females, males, and young (ša$_3$-du$_{10}$) makes it very likely that some variety of animal is recorded. Cf. gu$_4$-ĝeš "yoke bull," anše-ĝeš "yoke donkey" and ĝeš as "yoke" in Heimpel 1995: 86–87. The high number of animals is notable, as is the low proportion of males in comparison to females and young.

rev. 5: The name Iri-nam-zu appears in Classical Sargonic texts from various sites. See Foster 1989 no. 2 obv. 2 for the same name in a text concerning sheep and goats. The same name may appear in ITT 1 no. 1101 from CS Ĝirsu, about timber. The wife of an Iri-nam-zu appears in a CS Adab text, OIP 14 no. 167 obv. 5, in connection to sheep.

5.5.10 – Onions

Two tablets with similar script concern the harvesting of onions from fields of a certain size. In the second document the anaphoric pronoun and the syntax of measure and commodity confirm that it was written in Akkadian. By contrast, the first document has the typically Sumerian syntax of "measured – measure" and not *vice versa*. For that reason these two texts must originate in different localities.

No. 512 – MS 2191/5

Account of the yield of an onion plot, Classical Sargonic, uncertain provenance.

obv.	600 šum$_2$-GU$_4$-us$_2$ sa	600 bundles of medium spring onions;
	580 šum$_2$-GU$_4$-gal sa	580 bundles of large spring onions;
	⌈120⌉ šum$_2$-GU$_4$-tur sa	120 bundles of small spring onions;
	18 šum$_2$-sa$_6$	18 bundles of sweet onions.
rev.	šu+nigin$_2$ 1320 la$_2$ 2 šum$_2$ sa	Total: 1318 bundles of onions.
	a-ša$_3$-bi 1 iku	Its field area: 1 *iku*.

obv. 1 f.: For šum$_2$-GU$_4$ as spring onions, see FAOS 15/2 pp. 412–13. The specifications -gal "large," -us$_2$ "medium" (lit. following (the large)), and -tur "small" in the present text probably relate to the size of the bulb.

No. 513 – MS 2191/6

Account of the yield of an onion plot, Classical Sargonic, uncertain provenance.

obv.	616 sa šum$_2$-GU$_4$	616 bundles of spring onions:
	a-ša$_3$-bi 1 ½(1N$_8$×*DIŠ*) iku ½ sar	its field area: 1 ½ *iku* ½ *sar*.
	šu 2 u$_4$	That is of the 2nd day.
rev.	(blank)	

5.5.11 – Resins
No. 514 – MS 2191/3

Account of the ingredients for five jars of aromatic oil, Classical Sargonic, uncertain provenance (Umma region?).

The text is not from Ĝirsu, where cypress is spelled ^{šim}šu-me, not ^{ĝeš}EREN$^{\text{šu-me}}$. Cf. BIN 8 no. 319 from Umma, which has $^{\text{šu-me}}$EREN. Also in contrast to the present text, the Ĝirsu texts have ^{šim}ba$_5$-lu-ḫum for "galbanum(?)," rather than ^{šim}ba-lu-ḫum.

obv.	2 ^{ĝeš}⌜eren⌝ gu$_2$	2 talents of cedar (resin);
	1 ^{ĝeš}šurmen$_x$(EREN$^{\text{šu-me}}$) ⌜gu$_2$⌝	1 talent of cypress (resin);
	1 ^{ĝeš}eren zu$_2$-ba-lum gu$_2$	1 talent of pine (resin);
	30 ^{ĝeš}ad$_2$ ma-na	30 minas of myrtle (resin);
	30 ^{šim}gi ma-na	30 minas of sweet reed;
	30 ^{šim}ba-lu-ḫum ma-na	30 minas of galbanum(?);
	20 diri-*um* ma-na	20 minas of ...*um* resin;
rev.	2(bariga) šim-gig	2 *bariga* of *gig*-resin;
	2(bariga) šim-GAM-GAM-ma	2 *bariga* of terebinth resin;
	2(bariga) ^{šim}su-DI-ḪI-nun	2 *bariga* of ... resin;

2(bariga) ^{šim}gu-gu-ru-⸢um⸣	2 *bariga* of … resin.
(blank space)	
^{šim}eren	These are aromatic substances (*lit.*"cedar resin")
5 i$_3$-dug-kam	for 5 jars of oil.

rev. 2: See Brunke and Sallaberger 2010: 51 for this substance.

rev. 3: This unidentified term appears as ^{šim}su-DI-ir-nun in ED IIIb Ĝirsu texts. See, e.g., DP 511 obv. ii 4.

rev. 4: This is another spelling of the substance *kuk(u)ru*, for which see Brunke and Sallaberger 2010: 51.

5.5.12 – Ropes

Nos. 515 and 516 – MS 4220a and b

Expenditure of ropes for yokes measured by weight, Late Sargonic, uncertain provenance (Umma?).

The top right-hand corner of MS 4220 has been patched with an upside-down fragment of a blackish tablet. The two pieces are edited here in turn, as Nos. 515 and 516. Text No. 515 has personal names typical of the Ur III period, and so may be dated to the Late Sargonic or "Gutian" period. Based on the onomastics, the provenance may be Umma.

obv.	1 eše$_2$ ab$_2$-saĝ [ki-la$_2$-bi n] ⸢ma⸣-[na]	1 rope (to attach) the front ox; [its weight: x] mina;
	8 DI-ki-[...]	8 ...:
	Ur-^{d}⸢Nagar⸣-[e šu ba-ti]	Ur-Nagar [has received].
	1 eše$_2$ ab$_2$-saĝ [...]	1 rope (to attach) the front ox; [its weight: x mina];
	1 eše$_2$ saĝ-⸢x⸣-[...]	1 ... rope;
	ki-la$_2$-bi *10* [+n] ma-na	its weight: 10+x minas:
	1 Ur-⸢x⸣-DI	1 Ur...DI (and)
	Ur-^{d}Nagar-e šu ba-ti	Ur-Nagar received.
	1 eše$_2$ ab$_2$-ur$_2$ 1 eše$_2$ ab$_2$-saĝ	1 rope (to attach) the rear ox, 1 rope (to attach) the front ox;
	ki-la$_2$-bi 5 ma-na	their weight: 5 minas:
	Lugal-^{ĝeš}gigir$_2$-e dumu Ama-bara$_2$	Lugalgigire, son of Amabara.
	4 eše$_2$-ḫul$_3$-la 1 eše$_2$-maš-da / 1 eše$_2$-u$_3$-X ki-la$_2$-bi 5 ma-<na>	4 neck-ropes, 1 ... rope, 1 ... rope; their weight: 5 minas:
	Niĝar-ĝiri$_3$-DUR$_2$	Niĝarĝiri...;
	6 eše$_2$ ^{ĝeš}TAR ki-la$_2$-[bi n ma-na]	6 ... ropes; [their] weight [... minas]:
	AN-na dub-sar	ANna, the scribe.
rev.	*6* ma-na Ša$_3$-⸢ad-⸣-[da$^?$]	6 minas: Ša'adda(?),
	šabra Lu$_2$-i-[...]	the chief administrator of Lu'i...
	3 ma-na Ur-^{d}[...] tug$_2$-⸢du$_8$⸣	3 minas: Ur..., the felter.
	6 ma-na Maš sagi	6 minas: Maš, the cupbearer.
	(line erased)	(line erased)
	4 [eše$_2$-ḫul$_3$]-la 1 eše$_2$-maš-da / 1 [eše$_2$ u$_3$]-X ki-la$_2$-bi 5 ma-na	4 neck ropes, 1 ... rope, 1 ... rope; their weight: 5 minas.
	Za-⸢NE lu$_2$⸣-KU-a	ZeNE, the ....
	4 ⸢eše$_2$-ḫul$_3$⸣-la 1 eše$_2$-maš-da / 1 [eše$_2$ u$_3$]-⸢X⸣ ki-la$_2$-bi 4 [ma-na]	4 neck ropes, 1 ... rope, 1 ... [rope]; their weight: 4 [minas]:
	Lu$_2$-⸢x⸣-[...]	Lu...
	1 eše$_2$ ab$_2$-[saĝ/ur$_2$ ki-la$_2$-bi]	1 rope (to attach) the [front/rear] ox; [its weight:]
	1 Ma-⸢x⸣-[...]	1 Ma... (PN)
	Da-[...]	Da... (PN).
	(blank/ruling)	
	šu-niĝin$_2$ 1 gu$_2$ [...]	Total: 1 talent [x minas of ropes].
	zi-ga [...]	Expended.

obv. 1 f.: For eše$_2$ ab$_2$-saĝ and eše$_2$ ab$_2$-ur$_2$, ropes to attach the front and rear oxen to the plow, see OB Nippur Hh V 424 and EDPV A nos. 282–83.

obv. 5: Cf. OB Nippur Hh V 423.

obv. 12 f.: For eše$_2$-ḫul$_3$-la, see the commentary to text No. 510 obv. 2. The term eše$_2$-maš-da remains uncertain. The writing in rev. 4 proves that the sign is MAŠ. Another unclear term is eše$_2$-u$_3$-X. The sign X may be KEŠ$_2$: 

obv. 14: The term appears also in UET 9 no. 413 (Ur III, Ur) obv. 3.

rev. 7: Alternatively, "the man of KUa." Cf. the name KU-a-a in CDLI P275266 (Ur III, Umma) obv. 3.

The fragment No. 516 is of an earlier date than is the tablet to which it has been attached. Judging by the script it belongs to an Early Sargonic tablet. It is the left-hand bottom corner of a multi-columned tablet. The reverse of the fragment is blank. The transliteration is as follows:

obv. i 1'	[n] la$_2$ *3* maš$_2$ Nir-an-da-ĝal$_2$	x minus 3 male goat kids: Nir-andaĝal.
	30 la$_2$ *3* $^{munus:}$aš$_2$-gar$_3$	27 female kids.

obv. i 1': For this personal name in the Sargonic period, see, e.g., OSP 2 no. 23 obv. ix 3.

5.5.13 – A Letter Concerning a Boat

No. 517 – 2191/1

Letter-order concerning a boat, Classical Sargonic, uncertain provenance.

obv.	BU-bal	That is what BUbal
	na-be$_2$-a	says:
	Lugal-iti-da-ra	"To Lugalitida
	u$_3$-na-du$_{11}$	please say (the following):
	ma$_2$ ḫe$_2$-BU-le	You should *caulk*(?) the boat."

rev. (blank)

obv. 1: Cf. the personal name A-BU-bal in Nik 2 no. 35 obv. ii 9.

obv. 5: The verb that is written with the sign BU should refer to either caulking (du$_8$, *peḫû*) or punting (gid$_2$/BU, *šadādu*). However, since the final consonant of the verb in the present form is /l/, gid$_2$ can be excluded. The only reading with a final /l/ for the sign BU is dul$_{10}$, which appears solely in the writing ^{ĝeš}ma-dul$_{10}$ "pole." Cf. the boat-related occupation ma$_2$-DUN$_3$ (dul$_x$), for which see Bauer 1989–90: 82.

5.6 – Early Dynastic and Sargonic School Exercises

No. 518 – MS 3793

Exercise, Early Dynastic IIIb, uncertain provenance.

obv. i	IN EGIR DIRI	...
	Ad-<da>-sa$_6$-⸢ga⸣	Ad<da>saga (PN)
ii	(blank)	
rev.	(blank)	

No. 519 – MS 1902

School tablet listing fruit trees and sweets, Early Dynastic/Early Sargonic, uncertain provenance.

obv.	^{ĝeš}ḫašḫur / munu$_4$-du$_{10}$ gug$_2$-tur	Apple (tree), sweet malt, small cake,
	lu$_2$ ša$_3$ ^{ĝeš}kur-ḫašḫur	person, heart, "mountain apple tree."
rev.	(blank)	

obv. 2: A mistake for ^{ĝeš}ḫašḫur-kur-(ra) of lexical lists.

No. 520 – MS 1952/46

School exercise listing cattle, Sargonic, uncertain provenance.

obv.	13 gu$_4$	13 oxen;
	4 ab$_2$	4 cows;
	2 amar-nita	2 male calves;
	1 amar-munus	1 female calf.
rev.	(blank)	

No. 521 – MS 2191/18

Exercise, Early Sargonic, uncertain provenance (Adab?).

obv. i	MAR ŠA$_3$	. . .
	X AŠ$_2$ LAK131	. . .
	ŠAB ZIZ$_2$ ḪI	. . .
	Gan-^{d}En-lil$_2$	Gan-Enlil.
	AMA KUR KIŠ E$_2$	. . .
	⸢Lugal⸣-abba$_2$-ĝu$_{10}$	Lugalabbaĝu.
	⸢ŠAB⸣-pum [(x)]-gal	. . .
	⸢Ĝiri$_{2\text{-}gun\hat{u}}$⸣-nun	Ĝirinun.
	eš$_3$(AB)	/eš/ ("shrine")
ii	še$_{22}$(EREN)	/še/ (syllabic value)
	še	/še/ ("barley")
	še$_x$(SIG$_7$)	/še/ ("to live")
	(rest blank)	
rev.	(blank)	

obv. i 6: This name in this spelling is recorded in a number of ED/ES Adab texts. See the commentary to CUSAS 23 no. 94 obv. i 2.

obv. ii: The scribe set down homophonous signs that have the same syllabic value. Note also /eš/ in obv. i 9.

References

Almamori, H. O. 2014. Ĝišša (Umm Al-Aqarib), Umma (Jokha), and Lagaš in the Early Dynastic III Period. *Al-Rāfidān* 35: 1–37.

Andersson, J. 2012. *Kingship in the Early Mesopotamian Onomasticon 2800–2200 BCE*. Studia Semitica Upsaliensia 28. Uppsala.

Attinger, P. 1997. Review of PSD A². *Zeitschrift für Assyriologie und Vorderasiatische Archäologie* 87/1: 112–22.

Bartash, V. 2014. E_2-mi_2 "Women's Quarters": The Earliest Written Evidence, in: F. Buccellati, T. Helms and A. Tamm (eds.), *Household and Household Economies in 3rd Millennium B.C. Syro-Mesopotamia*. BAR International Series 2682. Oxford: 9–20.

Bartash 2015a. Children in Ancient Sumer: How Much Do We Know? *The Ancient Near East Today*, ASOR Blog (http://asorblog.org/2015/06/09/children-in-ancient-sumer-how-much-do-we-know/).

Bartash, V. 2015b. Children in Institutional Households of Late Uruk Period Mesopotamia. *Zeitschrift für Assyriologie und Vorderasiatische Archäologie* 105/2: 131–38.

Bartash, V. 2015c. On the Sumerian City UB-me[ki], the Alleged "Umma". *Cuneiform Digital Library Bulletin* 2015:2. (http://cdli.ucla.edu/pubs/cdlb/2015/cdlb2015_002.html).

Bauer, J. 1982. Die Göttin ^{d}kug-su_3(g). *Altorientalische Notizen* 19. Höchberg (Im selbstverlag des Verfassers): 4–7.

Bauer, J. 1989–90. Altsumerische Wirtschaftsurkunden in Leningrad. *Archiv für Orientforschung* 36–37: 76–91.

Bauer, J. 1998. Die vorsargonische Abschnitt der Mesopotamischen Geschichte, in: J. Bauer, R. K. Englund and M. Krebernik, *Mesopotamien. Späturuk-Zeit und Frühdynastische Zeit*. Orbis Biblicus et Orientalis 160/1. Fribourg–Göttingen: 431–585.

Biga, M. G. 2010. Textiles in the Administrative Texts of the Royal Archives of Ebla (Syria, 24th century BC) with Particular Emphasis on Coloured Textiles, in: C. Michel and M.-L. Nosch (eds.), *Textile Terminologies in the Ancient Near East and Mediterranean from the Third to the First Millennia BC*. Oxford: 146–72.

Bramanti, A. (forthcoming). Three Administrative Texts from the Time of Me'annedu.

Bridges, S. J. 1981. The Mesag Archive: A Study of Sargonic Society and Economy. Ph.D. dissertation, Yale University.

Brunke, H. 2008. *Essen in Sumer. Metrologie, Herstellung und Terminologie nach Zeugnis der Ur III-zeitlichen Wirtschaftsurkunden*. Munich.

Brunke, H. and Sallaberger, W. 2010. Aromata für Duftöl, in: A. Kleinerman and J. M. Sasson (eds.), *Why Should Someone Who Knows Something Conceal It? Cuneiform*

Studies in Honor of David I. Owen on His 70th Birthday. Bethesda, Md.: 41–74.

Cavigneaux, A. and Krebernik, M. 1999. Niĝ-udidu. *Reallexikon der Assyriologie und Vorderasiatischen Archäologie* 9/3–4: 313.

Cavigneaux, A. and Krebernik, M. 2000a. Nin-duba. *Reallexikon der Assyriologie und Vorderasiatischen Archäologie* 9/5–6: 339–40.

Cavigneaux, A. and Krebernik, M. 2000b. ^{d}Nin-GANA$_2$. *Reallexikon der Assyriologie und Vorderasiatischen Archäologie* 9/5–6: 360.

Cavigneaux, A. and Krebernik, M. 2000c. ^{d}Nin-GA$_2$×MUŠ. *Reallexikon der Assyriologie und Vorderasiatischen Archäologie* 9/5–6: 360.

Cavigneaux, A. and Krebernik, M. 2000d. Nin-ur$_3$. *Reallexikon der Assyriologie und Vorderasiatischen Archäologie* 9/5–6: 510.

Civil, M. 1968. Išme-Dagan and Enlil's Chariot. *Journal of the American Oriental Society* 88/1: 3–14.

Civil, M. 1983. An Early Dynastic School Exercise from Lagaš (Al-Hiba 29). *Bibliotheca Orientalis* 40: 559–66.

Civil, M. 1994. *The Farmer's Instructions. A Sumerian Agricultural Manual*. Aula Orientalis, Supplementa 5. Sabadell.

Civil, M. 2013. Remarks on AD-GI$_4$ (A.K.A. "Archaic Word List C" or "Tribute"). *Journal of Cuneiform Studies* 65: 13–67.

Cohen, M. E. 2015. *Festivals and Calendars of the Ancient Near East*. Bethesda, Md.

D'Agostino, F. 2012. Some considerations on u$_4$-da-tuš (bear tamer) and jugglery in Ur III. *Revue d'Assyriologie et d'archéologie orientale* 106: 89–99.

Damerow, P. 2012. Sumerian Beer: The Origins of Brewing Technology in Ancient Mesopotamia. *Cuneiform Digital Library Journal* 2012:2.

De Maaijer, R. and Jagersma, B. 1997–98. Review of PSD A^{I}. *Archiv für Orientforschung* 44–45: 277–88.

Edzard, D. O. 2003. *Sumerian Grammar*. Handbook of Oriental Studies, Section One: The Near and Middle East 71. Leiden–Boston.

Foster, B. R. 1982. *Administration and Use of Institutional Land in Sargonic Sumer*. Mesopotamia: Copenhagen Studies in Assyriology 9. Copenhagen.

Foster, B. R. 1989. A Sargonic Archive from the Lagash Region, in: H. Behrens, D. Loding, M. T. Roth (eds.), *DUMU-E$_2$-DUB-BA-A. Studies in Honor of Åke W. Sjöberg*. OPSKNF 11. Philadelphia: 155–65.

Foster, B. R. 2010. Clothing in Sargonic Mesopotamia: Visual and written evidence, in: C. Michel and M.-L. Nosch (eds.), *Textile Terminologies in the Ancient Near East and Mediterranean from the Third to the First Millennia BC*. Oxford: 110–45.

Friberg, J. 2007. *A Remarkable Collection of Babylonian Mathematical Texts*. Manuscripts in the Schøyen Collection, Cuneiform Texts 1. New York.

Gelb, I. J. 1972. The Arua Institution. *Revue d'Assyriologie et d'archéologie orientale* 66/1: 1–32.

Green, M. W. 1980. Animal Husbandry at Uruk in the Archaic Period. *Journal of Near Eastern Studies* 39/1: 1–35.

Hallo, W. W. 2001. Carcasses for the Capital, in: W. H. can Soldt (ed.), Veenhof Anniversary Volume. *Studies Presented to Klaas R. Veenhof on the Occasion of his Sixty-Fifth Birthday*. Leiden: 161–71.

Hasselbach, R. 2005. *Sargonic Akkadian. A Historical and Comparative Study of Syllabic Texts*. Wiesbaden.

Heimpel, W. 1990. Maus. *Reallexikon der Assyriologie und Vorderasiatischen Archäologie* 7: 605–9.

Heimpel, W. 1993. Zu den Bezeichnungen von Schafen und Ziegen in den Drehem- und Ummatexten. *Bulletin on Sumerian Agriculture* 7: 115–60.

Heimpel, W. 1995. Plow animal inspection records from Ur III Girsu and Umma. *Bulletin on Sumerian Agriculture* 8: 71–171.

Hruška, B. 1990. Das landwirtschaftliche Jahr im alten Sumer. *Bulletin on Sumerian Agriculture* 5: 105–14.

Jagersma, B. 2010. A Descriptive Grammar of Sumerian. Ph.D. dissertation, University of Leiden.

Krebernik, M. 1982. Zur Syllabar und Orthographie der lexikalischen Texte aus Ebla. Teil I. *Zeitschrift für Assyriologie und Vorderasiatische Archäologie* 72/2: 178–236.

Krebernik, M. 1998a. Die Texte aus Fara und Tell Abū Ṣalābīḫ, in: P. Attinger and M. Wäfler (eds.), *Mesopotamien. Späturuk-Zeit und Frühdynastische Zeit.* Orbis Biblicus et Orientalis 160/1. Fribourg–Göttingen: 237–427.

Krebernik, M. 1998b. ^{d}NAM$_2$.NUN. *Reallexikon der Assyriologie und Vorderasiatischen Archäologie* 9/1–2: 140–41.

Krebernik, M. 2000. Nin-girima. I. Beschwörungsgöttin. *Reallexikon der Assyriologie und Vorderasiatischen Archäologie* 9/5–6: 363–67.

Krebernik, M. 2002. Zur Struktur und Geschichte des älteren sumerischen Onomastikons, in: M. P. Streck and S. Weninger (eds.), *Altorientalische und semitische Onomastik.* Alter Orient und Altes Textament 296. Münster: 1–74.

Krebernik, M. 2014. ^{d}TU(-da). *Reallexikon der Assyriologie und Vorderasiatischen Archäologie* 14/1–2: 152–54.

Krebernik, M. 2016. Etymological and Historical Problems Concerning Akkadian *tamkāru* 'merchant', in: L. Kogan, N. Koslova, S. Loesov and S. Tishchenko (eds.), *Babel und Bibel 9: Proceedings of the 6th Biennial Meetings of the International Association for Comparative Semitics and Other Studies.* Winona Lake, Ind., 119–29.

Krebernik, M., Steible, H. and Yıldız, F. 2014. Prä-Fāra-zeitliche Texte aus Fāra, in: N. V. Koslova, E. Vizirova and G. Zolyomi (eds.), *Studies in Sumerian Language and Literature. Festschrift Joachim Krecher.* Babel und Bibel 8. Winona Lake, Ind.: 327–82.

Krecher, J. 1973. Neue sumerische Rechtsurkunden des 3. Jahrtausends. *Zeitschrift für Assyriologie und Vorderasiatische Archäologie* 63/2: 145–271.

Krecher, J. 1978. Das sumerische Phonem /ĝ, in: B. Hruška and G. Komoróczy, *Festschrift Lubor Matouš* 2. Budapest: 7–73.

Lipiński, E. 1997. *Semitic Languages. Outline of a Comparative Grammar.* Orientalia Lovaniensia Analecta 80. Leuven.

Maekawa, K. 1986, The Agricultural Texts of Ur III Lagash of the British Museum (III). *Acta Sumerologica* 8: 85–120.

Marchesi, G. 2015. Toward a Chronology of Early Dynastic Rulers in Mesopotamia, in: W. Sallaberger and I. Schrakamp (eds.), *Associated Regional Chronologies for the Ancient Near East and the Eastern Mediterranean. History and Philology.* ARCANE 3. Turnhout: 139–56.

Meyer-Laurin, V. 2010. Die *marû*-Basen der sumerischen Verben tum$_2$ "hin-, wegführen" und re$_6$/de$_6$ "bringen, liefern". *Zeitschrift für Assyriologie und Vorderasiatische Archäologie* 100: 1–14.

Middeke-Conlin, R. and Proust, C. 2014. Interest, Price, and Profit: An Overview of Mathematical Economics in YBC 4698. *Cuneiform Digital Library Journal* 2014:3.

Milano, L. 1993. Mehl. *Reallexikon der Assyriologie und Vorderasiatischen Archäologie* 8/1–2: 22–31.

Molina, M. 1989. Las piedras preciosas en los textos económicos de Ur de la tercera dinastia. *Aula Orientalis* 7/1: 81–93.

Molina, M. 1991. Tablillas sargónicas del Museo de Montserrat, Barcelona. *Aula Orientalis* 9: 137–53.

Molina, M. and Sanchiz, H. 2007. The Cuneiform Tablets of the Varela Collection. *Studi Epigrafici e Linguistici sul Vicino Oriente Antico* 24: 1–15.

Monaco, S. F. 2015. More on Pre-Sargonic Umma, in: A. Archi (ed.), *Tradition and Innovation in the Ancient Near East. Proceedings of the 57th Rencontre Assyriologique Internationale at Rome, 4–8 July 2011*. Winona Lake, Ind.: 161–66.

Neumann, H. 2001. Zu den Buchungseinträgen in den neusumerischen Handwerkerpräsenzlisten aus Ur, in: J. Høyrup and P. Damerow (eds.), *Changing Views on Ancient Near Eastern Mathematics*. Berlin: 37–51.

Paoletti, P. 2012. *Der König und sein Kreis. Das staatliche Schatzarchiv der. III. Dynastie von Ur*. Biblioteca del Próximo Oriente Antiguo 10. CSIC Madrid.

Pomponio, F. 1987. *La prosopografia dei testi presargonici di Fara*. Studi Semitici NS 3. Rome.

Powell, M. A. 1978. Texts from the Time of Lugalzagesi. Problems and Perspectives in Their Interpretation. *Hebrew Union College Annual* 49: 1–58.

Powell, M. A. 1980. Karkar, Dabrum, and Tall Gidr: An Unresolved Geographical Problem. *Journal of Near Eastern Studies* 39/1: 47–52.

Powell, M. A. 1990. Masse und Gewichte. *Reallexikon der Assyriologie und Vorderasiatischen Archäologie* 7: 457–517.

Powell, M. A. 1992. Timber Production in Presargonic Lagas. *Bulletin on Sumerian Agriculture* 6: 99–122.

Rubio, G. 2013. SANGA$_2$: A Graphic Story. *Revue d'Assyriologie et d'archéologie orientale* 107: 101–4.

Rudik, N. 2011. Die Entwicklung der keilschriftlichen sumerischen Beschwörungsliteratur von den Anfängen bis zur Ur III-Zeit. Ph.D. dissertation, Friedrich-Schiller-Universität Jena.

Sallaberger, W. 1993. *Der kultische Kalender der Ur III-Zeit*. Untersuchungen zur Assyriologie und Vorderasiatischen Archäologie 7/1–2. Berlin–New York.

Sallaberger, W. 1994. Review of MC 4. *Zeitschrift für Assyriologie und Vorderasiatische Archäologie* 84: 144–47.

Sallaberger, W. 1996. *Der babylonische Töpfer und seine Gefässe nach Urkunden altsumerischer bis altbabylonischer Zeit sowie lexikalischen und literarischen Zeugnissen*. MHEM III. Ghent.

Sallaberger, W. 1999. Ur III-Zeit, in: W. Sallaberger and A. Westenholz, *Mesopotamien. Akkade-Zeit und Ur III-Zeit*. Orbis Biblicus et Orientalis 160/3. Fribourg–Göttingen: 121–390.

Sallaberger, W. 2012. Bierbrauen in Versen: Eine neue Edition und Interpretation der Ninkasi-Hymne, in: C. Mittermayer and S. Ecklin (eds.), *Altorientalische Studien zu Ehren von Pascal Attinger: mu-ni u$_4$ ul-li$_2$-a-aš ĝa$_2$-ĝa$_2$-de$_3$*. Orbis Biblicus et Orientalis 256. Freiburg: 291–328.

Sallaberger, W. 2015. Special Cases and Legal Matters. Diction and Function of Letters in the State of the Third Dynasty of Ur (2110–2003 BC), in: S. Procházka, L. Reinfandt and S. Tost (eds.), *Official Epistolography and the Language(s) of Power. Proceedings of the First International Conference of the Research Network "Imperium & Officium", Comparative Studies in*

Ancient Bureaucracy and Officialdom, University of Vienna, 10-12 November 2010. Vienna: 15–30, pl. 1.

Sallaberger, W. 2016. Getreide messen, in: P. Corò, E. Devecchi, N. De Zorzi and M. Maiocchi (eds.), *Libiamo ne' lieti calici. Ancient Near Eastern Studies Presented to Lucio Milano on the Occasion of his 65th Birthday by Pupils, Colleagues and Friends.* Alter Orient und Altes Testament 436. Münster: 237–48.

Sallaberger, W. and Huber Vulliet, F. 2005. Priester. A. I. Mesopotamien. *Reallexikon der Assyriologie und Vorderasiatischen Archäologie* 10/7–8: 617–40.

Sallaberger, W. and Schrakamp, I. 2015. Philological Data for a Historical Chronology of Mesopotamia in the 3rd Millennium, in: W. Sallaberger and I. Schrakamp (eds.), *Associated Regional Chronologies for the Ancient Near East and the Eastern Mediterranean. History and Philology.* ARCANE 3. Turnhout: 1–136.

Schrakamp, I. 2010. Krieger und Waffen im frühen Mesopotamien. Organisation und Bewaffnung des Militärs in frühdynastischer und sargonischer Zeit. Ph.D. dissertation, Philipps-Universität Marburg.

Schrakamp, I. 2012a. Review of CUSAS 13. *Bibliotheca Orientalis* 69/3–4: 275–90.

Schrakamp, I. 2012b, Zu den vor-Ur III-zeitlichen Keilschrifttexten des World Museum, Liverpool. *Journal of Cuneiform Studies* 64: 145–62.

Schrakamp, I. 2013. Review of CUSAS 11. *Journal of Cuneiform Studies* 65: 201–28.

Schrakamp, I. 2015a. Geographical Horizons in Presargonic and Sargonic Archives, in: W. Sallaberger and I. Schrakamp (eds.), *Associated Regional Chronologies for the Ancient Near East and the Eastern Mediterranean. History and Philology.* ARCANE 3. Turnhout: 197–262.

Schrakamp, I. 2015b. The Value sig_x of SAR in Third Millennium Sources. *Altorientalische Forschungen* 42/2: 196–98.

Schrakamp, I., 2016: Akkadian Empire, in: J. M. MacKenzie (ed.), *The Encyclopedia of Empire.* Wiley: 1–10.

Selz, G. J. 1993. Frühjahrslämmer, Herbstlämmer. *Nouvelles Assyriologiques Brèves et Utilitaires* 1993: 41–42 no. 50.

Selz, G. J. 1995a. Den Fährmann bezahlen! Eine lexikalisch-kulturhistorische Skizze zu den Bedeutungen von addir. *Altorientalische Forschungen* 22/2: 197–209.

Selz, G. J. 1995b. Maš-da-ři-a und Verwandtes. Ein Versuch über da–ři "an der Seite führen": ein zusammengesetztes Verbum und einige nominale Ableitungen. *Acta Sumerologica* 17: 251–74.

Sommerfeld, W. 1987. Untersuchungen zum Altakkadischen. Habilitationsschrift, Westfälische Wilhelms-Universität.

Sommerfeld, W. 2010. Prä-Akkadisch. Die Vorläufer der "Sprache von Akkade" in der frühdynastischen Zeit. *Babel und Bibel* 4/1: 77–163.

Sommerfeld, W. 2011. Altakkadische Duelle, in: G. Barjamovic, J. L. Dahl, J. Goodnick Westenholz, U. S. Koch and W. Sommerfeld (eds.), *Akkade is King. A Collection of Papers by Friends and Colleagues Presented to Aage Westenholz on the Occasion of his 70th Birthday, 15th of May 2009*, PIHANS 118. Leiden: 287–99.

Sommerfeld, W. 2012. Hasselbach, Rebecca: *Sargonic Akkadian. A Historical and Comparative Study of the Syllabic Texts.* Ein Rezensionsartikel. *Wiener Zeitschrift für die Kunde des Morgenlandes* 102: 193–284.

Sommerfeld, W. Markina, K. and Roudik, N. 2005. Altakkadische Texte der St. Petersburger Eremitage, in: L. Kogan *et al.* (eds.), *Memoriae Igor M. Diakonoff, Babel und Bibel* 2. Winona Lake, Ind.: 185–231.

Steible, H. 2015. The Geographical Horizon of the Texts from Fara/Shuruppak, in: W. Sallaberger and I. Schrakamp (eds.), *Associated Regional Chronologies for the Ancient Near East and the Eastern Mediterranean. History and Philology*. ARCANE 3. Turnhout: 157–61.

Steinkeller, P. 1981a. Studies in Third Millennium Palaeography, 1: Signs TIL and BAD. *Zeitschrift für Assyriologie und Vorderasiatische Archäologie* 71: 19–28.

Steinkeller, P. 1981b. The Renting of Fields in Early Mesopotamia and the Development of the Concept of "Interest" in Sumerian. *Journal of the Economic and Social History of the Orient* 24: 113–45.

Steinkeller, P. 1987a. On the meaning of zabar-šu. *Acta Sumerologica* 9: 347–49.

Steinkeller, P. 1987b. The Name of Nergal. *Zeitschrift für Assyriologie und Vorderasiatische Archäologie* 77/2: 161–68.

Steinkeller, P. 1987c. Review of USP. *Wiener Zeitschrift für die Kunde des Morgenlandes* 77: 182–95.

Steinkeller, P. 1995. Review of ZATU. *Bibliotheca Orientalis* 52: 689–713.

Steinkeller, P. 1995–96. Review of R. K. Englund and H. J. Nissen, *Die lexikalischen Listen der archaischen Texte aus Uruk* (ATU 3). *Archiv für Orientforschung* 42–43: 211–14.

Steinkeller, P. 2004. Studies in Third Millennium Paleography, 4: Sign KIŠ. *Zeitschrift für Assyriologie und Vorderasiatische Archäologie* 94: 175–85.

Steinkeller, P. 2013a. An Archaic "Prisoner Plaque" from Kis. *Revue d'Assyriologie et d'archéologie orientale* 107: 131–57.

Steinkeller, P. 2013b. Corvée Labor in Ur III Times, in: S. J. Garfinkle and M. Molina (eds.), *From the 21st Century BC to the 21st Century AD. Proceedings of the International Conference on Neo-Sumerian Studies Held in Madrid, July 22–24, 2010*. Winona Lake, Ind.: 347–424.

Steinkeller, P. 2015. On the Reading of the Pre-Sargonic Personal Name DI-^{d}Utu and Related Matters. *Journal of Near Eastern Studies* 74/1: 39–44.

Stol, M. 1994. Milch(produkte). A. In Mesopotamien. *Reallexikon der Assyriologie und Vorderasiatischen Archäologie* 8/3–4: 189–201.

Stol, M. 2000. *Birth in Babylonia and the Bible*. Cuneiform Monographs 14. Groningen.

Stol, M. 2012. Bitumen in Ancient Mesopotamia. The textual evidence. *Bibliotheca Orientalis* 69/1–2: 48–60.

Studevent-Hickman, B. 2006. The Organization of Manual Labor in Ur III Babylonia. Ph.D. dissertation, Harvard University.

Such-Gutiérrez, M. 2005–6. Untersuchungen zum Pantheon von Adab im 3. Jt. *Archiv für Orientforschung* 51: 1–44.

Taylor, J. 2002. On the reading of SILA$_3$.ŠU.DU$_8$(.A) ("cup-bearer"). *Nouvelles Assyriologiques Brèves et Utilitaires* 2002/2: 28 no. 29.

Thomsen, M.-L. 1984. *The Sumerian Language. An Introduction to Its History and Grammatical Structure*. Mesopotamia: Copenhagen Studies in Assyriology 10. Copenhagen.

Van de Mieroop, M. 1987. *Crafts in the Early Isin Period. A Study of the Isin Craft Archive from the Reigns of Išbi-Erra and Šū-ilišu*. Orientalia Lovaniensia Analecta 24. Leuven.

Veenhof, K. R. 2004. Pfand. A. The 3rd millennium B.C. *Reallexikon der Assyriologie und Vorderasiatischen Archäologie* 10/5–6: 442–43.

Visicato, G. 1995. *The Bureaucracy of Šuruppak. Administrative Centres, Central Offices, Intermediate Structures and Hierarchies in the*

Economic Documentation of Fara. Abhandlungen zur Literatur Alt-Syrien-Palästinas und Mesopotamiens 10. Münster.

Visicato, G. 2012. Two Governors of Umma called Surus-kin in the Sargonic Period. *Annali dell'Università degli studi di Napoli "L'Orientale"* 72, 169–74.

Volk, K. 2004. Palme. *Reallexikon der Assyriologie und Vorderasiatischen Archäologie* 10/3–4: 283–92.

Waetzoldt, H. 1975. Hirt. A. Philologisch (neusumerisch). *Reallexikon der Assyriologie und Vorderasiatischen Archäologie* 4: 421–25.

Waetzoldt, H. 1980-1983. Leinen (Flachs). *Reallexikon der Assyriologie und Vorderasiatischen Archäologie* 6: 583–94.

Waetzoldt, H. 1990. Zu den Bewasserungseinrichtungen in der Provinz Umma. *Bulletin on Sumerian Agriculture* 5: 1–29.

Waetzoldt, H. 2006. Zu den Siegeln der Vorsteher der Opferschauer Nannazišag̃al und Enlilzišag̃al. *Zeitschrift für Assyriologie und Vorderasiatische Archäologie* 96: 178–84.

Waetzoldt, H. 2011. Spinnen. A. Philologisch. *Reallexikon der Assyriologie und Vorderasiatischen Archäologie* 13/1–2: 1–3.

Wilcke, C. 1976. Neue Rechtsurkunden der Altsumerischen Zeit. *Zeitschrift für Assyriologie und Vorderasiatische Archäologie* 86: 1–68.

Wilcke, C. 2007. *Early Near Eastern Law. A History of its Beginnings: The Early Dynastic and Sargonic Periods*. 2nd rev. edn., Winona Lake, Ind.

Indexes

Personal Names

Occupations, Social and Legal Statuses

Deities and Deified Objects

(Only rare divine names that appear in personal names are indexed here)

Geographical Names

Cities and Towns

Fields

Gardens and woods

Waterways

Other

TEMPLES, HOUSEHOLDS, ADMINISTRATIVE BUILDINGS

Year Names

Unidentified Signs, Numbers, and Terms Discussed

Unidentified Signs

Numbers Discussed

Terms Discussed

Cornell University Studies in Assyriology and Sumerology
(CUSAS)

David I. Owen, Editor-in-chief

CUSAS 1: *The Cornell University Archaic Tablets*
Salvatore Monaco. 2007. Pp. xiv + 370. ISBN 978-1934309-001

CUSAS 2: *Sumerian Proverbs in the Schøyen Collection*
Bendt Alster. 2007. Pp. xvi + 156. ISBN 978-1934309-018

CUSAS 3: *The Garšana Archives*
David I. Owen and Rudolf H. Mayr with the assistance of Alex Kleinerman. 2007. Pp. xii + 528. ISBN 978-1934309-025

CUSAS 4: *Analytical Concordance to the Garšana Archives*
Alexandra Kleinerman and David I. Owen. 2009. Pp. x + 795. ISBN 978-1934309-032

CUSAS 5: *Workers and Construction Work at Garšana*
Wolfgang Heimpel. 2009. Pp. xx + 394. ISBN 978-1934309-049

CUSAS 6: *Garšana Studies*
David I. Owen, ed. 2011. Pp. xii + 457. ISBN 978-1934309-056

CUSAS 8: *A Late Old Babylonian Temple Archive from Dūr-Abiešuḫ*
Karel van Lerberghe and Gabriella Voet. 2009. Pp.xviii + 276. Pl. 22. ISBN 978-1934309-079

CUSAS 9: *Babylonian Tablets from the First Sealand Dynasty in the Schøyen Collection*
Stephanie Dalley. 2009. Pp. xviii + 320. Pl. 182. ISBN 978-1934309-087

CUSAS 10: *Babylonian Literary Texts in the Schøyen Collection*
A. R. George. 2009. Pp. xx + 160. Pl. 62. ISBN 978-1934309-094

CUSAS 11: *Early Dynastic and Early Sargonic Tablets from Adab in the Cornell University Collections*
Giuseppe Visicato and Aage Westenholz. 2010. Pp. xxvi + 124. Pl. 94. ISBN 978-1934309-100

CUSAS 12: *The Lexical Texts in the Schøyen Collection*
Miguel Civil. 2010. Pp. xxii + 308. ISBN 978-1934309-117

CUSAS 13: *Classical Sargonic Tablets Chiefly from Adab in the Cornell University Collections*
Massimo Maiocchi. 2009. Pp. xxii + 334. Pl. 38. ISBN 978-1934309-124

CUSAS 14: *Early Dynastic Cereal Texts in the Cornell University Collections*
Salvatore Monaco. 2011. Pp. xii + 289. ISBN 978-1934309-391

CUSAS 15: *Cuneiform Texts in the Carl A. Kroch Library, Cornell University*
Alhena Gadotti and Marcel Sigrist with the assistance of Nicole M. Brisch and David I. Owen 2011. Pp. xx + 214. Pl. 29. ISBN 978-1934309-254

CUSAS 16: *Ur III Tablets from the Columbia University Libraries*
S. Garfinkle, H. Sauren, and M. Van De Mieroop. 2010. Pp. xxviii + 341. ISBN 978-1934309-285

CUSAS 17: *Cuneiform Royal Inscriptions and Related Texts in the Schøyen Collection*
A. R. George, ed. 2011. Pp. xxxii + 312. Pl. 101. ISBN 978-1934309-339

CUSAS 18: *Babylonian Divinatory Texts Chiefly in the Schøyen Collection*
A. R. George, 2013. Pp. xxviii + 441. Pl. 100. ISBN 978-1934309-476

CUSAS 19: *Classical Sargonic Tablets Chiefly from Adab in the Cornell University Collections, II*
Massimo Maiocchi and Giuseppe Visicato. 2012. Pp. xx + 208. ISBN 978-1934309-407

CUSAS 20: *Middle Sargonic Tablets Chiefly from Adab in the Cornell University Collections.* Francesco Pomponio and Giuseppe Visicato. 2015. Pp. xxxii + 250. ISBN 978-1934309-605

CUSAS 21: *Archaic Bullae and Tablets in the Cornell University Collections.* Salvatore Monaco. 2014. Pp. xii + 228. ISBN 978-1934309-551

CUSAS 22: *Entrepreneurs and Enterprise in Early Mesopotamia: A Study of Three Archives from the Third Dynasty of Ur.* Steven J. Garfinkle 2012. Pp. xii + 282. ISBN 978-1934309-414

CUSAS 23: *Miscellaneous Early Dynastic and Sargonic Texts in the Cornell University Collections.* Vitali Bartash 2013. Pp. xiv + 242. Pl. 23. ISBN 978-1934309-490

CUSAS 24: *The Domestication of Equidae in Third-Millennium BCE Mesopotamia.* Juris Zarins 2014. Pp. xi + 432. ISBN 978-1934309-513

CUSAS 25: *Hemerologies of Assyrian and Babylonian Scholars.* Alasdair Livingstone 2013. Pp. viii + 278. ISBN 978-1934309-520

CUSAS 26: *A Third-Millennium Miscellany of Cuneiform Texts.* Aage Westenholz 2014. Pp. xviii + 238. Pl. 6. ISBN 978-1934309-568

CUSAS 27: *The "Šu-ilisu Archive" and Other Sargonic Texts in Akkadian.* Lucio Milano and Aage Westenholz 2015. Pp. xii + 322. ISBN 978-1934309-612

CUSAS 28: *Documents of Judean Exiles and West Semites in Babylonia in the Collection of David Sofer.* Laurie Pearce and Cornelia Wunsch 2014. Pp. xlii + 334. Pl. 105. ISBN 978-1934309-575

CUSAS 30: *Middle Babylonian Texts in the Cornell University Collections I. The Later Kings,* Wilfred van Soldt 2015. Pp. xii + 585. Pl. 21. ISBN 978-1934309-629

CUSAS 31: *Archaic Cuneiform Tablets from Private Collections*
Salvatore F. Monaco, 2016. Pp. x + 310. ISBN 978-1934309-650

CUSAS 32: *Mesopotamian Incantations and Related Texts in the Schøyen Collection*
A. R. George, 2016. Pp. xiv + 196. Pl. 151. ISBN 978-1934309-667

CUSAS 33: *Early Dynastic and Early Sargonic Administrative Texts Mainly from the Umma Region in the Cornell Cuneiform Collections,* Palmiro Notizia and Giuseppe Visicato, 2016. Pp. xii + 312. ISBN 978-1934309-704

CUSAS 34: *Assyrian Archival Texts in the Schøyen Collection and Other Documents from North Mesopotamia and Syria,* A. R. George, Thomas Hertel, Jaume Llop-Raduà, Karen Radner, and Wilfred H. van Soldt, 2017. Pp. xxii + 136. Pl. 92. ISBN 978-1934309-711

CUSAS 35: *Sumerian Administrative and Legal Documents ca. 2900–2200 BC in the Schøyen Collection,* Vitali Bartash, 2017. Pp. xviii + 536. ISBN 978-1934309-735